THE
UNSEEN HAND

An Introduction to the
Conspiratorial View of History

By
A. Ralph Epperson

THE UNSEEN HAND

published by
PUBLIUS PRESS
3100 So. Philamena Place (ste. B)
Tucson, Arizona 85730
telephone (602) 886-4380

Library of Congress Card Number
84-06227

International Standard Book Number
0-9614135-0-6

Printed in the United States of America

printing history
First printing   August, 1985
Fifteenth printing   March, 1994

WRITE TO OR CALL
THE PUBLISHER
for a catalog of other books and videos
written and produced by
Ralph Epperson including his second
book entitled
THE NEW WORLD ORDER
published in 1990

THE UNSEEN HAND

An Introduction into the Conspiratorial View of History

TABLE OF CONTENTS

page

TABLE OF CONTENTS

DEDICATION

To my God, who gave me my freedom;

and

To my mother and father, who gave me life and thus my ability to enjoy my freedom;

and

To my nieces Kelley and Robyn, who are the reasons I fight for freedom;

and

To Congressman Larry McDonald (1935-1983), (murdered aboard the Korean Airlines flight 007 by those in the Soviet Union who obey instructions from these criminals), because he dared to expose the very conspiracy that killed him;

and

To all those who have been attempting to warn America of the peril to her freedoms;

I dedicate this book.

From Abraham Lincoln

When we see a lot of framed timbers, different portions of which we know have been gotten out at different times and places and by different workmen, and when we see these timbers joined together and see that they exactly make the frame of a house or a mill, all the lengths and proportions of the different pieces exactly adapted to their respective pieces, and not a piece too many or too few, not omitting even scaffolding, or if a single piece be lacking, we can see the place in the frame exactly fitted and prepared to yet bring such piece in; in such case, we find it impossible to not believe that they all understood one another from the beginning, and all worked upon a common plan or draft drawn up before the first lick was struck."

About the Cover

The reader of this book will discover, as he or she pages through it, that the Conspiracy unveiled by the author conceals many of its truths by the use of symbols.

The cover of this book is symbolic: each color represents a concealed truth.

The black represents evil; the white represents good; and the gold represents what little money or freedoms the good have left.

Good and evil are in conflict over the remaining freedoms and possessions the decent people of the world have remaining.

The reader is urged to notice which color is in the dominance.

About the Author

The most difficult thing I know to do is to write about myself, but I think that the reader of this book has the right to know something about me, the author, and what motivated me to write it.

I am a graduate of the University of Arizona, and like the typical graduate of an institution of higher education, I felt that what I had been taught was the truth. I thought that the only thing I needed to complete my education in the future was additional information to confirm the knowledge to which I had already been exposed.

So I faced the future with great anticipation.

But a close friend of mine, sensing that my knowledge was both incomplete and one-sided, suggested that I start reading material dealing with what was called "Revisionist History." This was the alternative explanation of history to what I had been taught was the truth.

There are over 300 books on both sides of this issue that I've read that are part of the research for this book. That figure, I am certain, is not an impressive number to those who are true "book addicts," but I mention it only to illustrate that the ideas in this book are not mine, but those of the individuals who have taken the time to record their perspective on the events in which they were personally involved or which they researched in depth.

But as I read, I noticed that there was no one volume that covered a complete history of the Conspiracy, and it is this void that I hope to fill. It is my intent to catalog as much of the history of this Conspiracy as is possible in a single volume.

I have made extensive use of quotations from the works of others as a means of convincing the skeptic that the evidence of the Conspiracy's existence comes from others than this author.

What the reader will see as he progresses through this book, I am convinced, is a picture of a giant conspiracy so immense that it poses the greatest threat to the freedoms and rights of all human beings, not only in the United States, but all over the world.

It is likely that, as the reader completes this book, despair will replace curiosity, especially if this explanation of the events being reviewed has never been explored before. That is an unfortunate consequence of my research, and the author is sorry that he must be the bearer of such bad tidings.

Despair, however, can reasonably be replaced with cautious optimism. The battle is not yet over, and there is reason to be encouraged.

But you are the final participant.

What happens will largely be dependent on your action once you've read this book.

Introduction

Wars start when one nation moves into the territory of another; depressions occur when markets take unexpected downturns; inflations occur when prices are driven up by shortages; revolutions start when the people, always spontaneously, rise up to overthrow the existing government.

These are the traditional explanations of historical events. Events happen by accident. There do not seem to be any causes.

But this explanation of history leaves gnawing questions in the minds of serious students. Is it possible that government leaders and others planned these events and then orchestrated them to their desired conclusions? Is it possible that even the great catastrophes of history were part of this plan?

There is an explanation of historical events that answers these questions in the affirmative. It is called the Conspiratorial View of History and it is the alternative to the Accidental View, the view that is commonly held today. It is possible, therefore, to summarize the major events of history into two alternative schools of thought:

The Accidental View of History: historical events occur by accident, for no apparent reason. Rulers are powerless to intervene.

The Conspiratorial View of History: historical events occur by design for reasons that are not generally made known to the people.

James Warburg in his book, *The West In Crisis*, explains the Accidental

6

View thus: "History is written more by accident than design, often by the wholly irrational acts of madmen."[1]

Another who has offered the Accidental View as the explanation of the major events of the world is Zbigniew Brzezinski, President Jimmy Carter's National Security Advisor. He has written: "History is much more the product of chaos than of conspiracy. ... increasingly, policy makers are overwhelmed by events and information."[2]

But there are those who disagree with the positions of Warburg and Brzezinski. One, for instance, was Franklin D. Roosevelt who certainly saw many monumental events occur during his consecutive administrations. President Roosevelt has been quoted as saying: "In politics, nothing happens by accident. If it happens, it was planned that way."

If harmful events are planned, it follows that the people who were about to suffer through the scheduled event would act to prevent the event from occurring if they knew about it in advance. The people expect government to protect them from harmful events.

But if the events still occur after the government officials had been expected to prevent them, the government officials have failed in their assigned duties. There are only two explanations as to why they failed:

1. The events overwhelmed them, and could not have been prevented; or
2. The events were allowed to occur because the officials wanted them to occur.

It is difficult for the casual observer to believe that these incredible events could not have been prevented, as humane people of conscience do not allow harmful events to occur.

If a planned and unwanted event is allowed to happen, those who planned the event would have to have acted in secret so as to prevent discovery of their plans by those who would be adversely affected.

Planners working in secret to plan an event that the people do not wish to occur are, by definition, members of a conspiracy. Webster's defines conspiracy as a "combination of people, working in secret, for an evil or unlawful purpose."

Not only must the Conspirators work in secret, they must make every effort to insure that their plans are not made public. The first task of a conspiracy, then, becomes that of convincing the people that the conspiracy itself does not exist.

This makes the task of uncovering the machinations of the conspiracy all the more difficult.

There are three ways of exposing a Conspiracy:

One is for any of the participants in the conspiracy to break with it and to expose his or her involvement. This takes an extremely courageous individual, and that type of exposure is indeed rare.

The second group of exposers are those who have unknowingly participated in a conspiratorial planning of an event but who didn't realize it until later. These individuals, and there aren't many in the history of the world, have also exposed the inner workings of the conspiracy at great peril to themselves.

The third method of exposing a conspiracy is for researchers to uncover conspiratorial designs in the events of the past. Your author is one of these researchers.

It will be the position of this book that a conspiracy does indeed exist, and that it is extremely large, deeply entrenched, and therefore extremely powerful. It is working to achieve absolute and brutal rule over the entire human race by using wars, depressions, inflations and revolutions to further its aims. The Conspiracy's one unchanging purpose has been to destroy all religion, all existing governments, and all traditional human institutions, and to build a *new world order* (this phrase will be defined later) upon the wreckage they have created.

Notice that if the Conspiracy does exist, it will do everything it can to deny the charges of both those who seek to expose it and those who claim to have been a part of it.

There are those, perhaps not knowing the importance of their contributions to the study of the conspiracy, who have added estimates of the size of this ruling group.

One was Walter Rathenau, who in 1909 controlled German General Electric. He said: "Three hundred men, all of whom know one another, direct the economic destiny of Europe and choose their successors from among themselves."[3]

Another informed observer, Joseph Kennedy, the father of the late president John Kennedy, identified the number of individuals who run America. He said: "Fifty men have run America and that's a high figure."[4]

Dr. Carroll Quigley, a professor of History at Georgetown University's Foreign Service School, and who formerly taught at Princeton and Harvard, has written a thirteen hundred page book entitled *Tragedy and Hope*. This book, published in 1966, was, according to the author, the result of twenty years of research into the Conspiracy. Dr. Quigley concludes:

> There does exist, and has existed for a generation, an international Anglophile network which operates, to some extent, in the way the radical Right believes the Communists act. In fact, this network, which we may identify as the Round Table Groups, has no aversion to

cooperating with the Communists, or any group, and frequently does so.

I know of the operations of this network because I have studied it for twenty years and was permitted for two years, in the early 1960's, to examine its papers and secret records.

But Quigley took a step none of the exposers have publicly taken. He admits that he is a supporter of the Conspiracy he has written about:

I have no aversion to it or most of its aims, and have, for much of my life, been close to it and many of its instruments.

I have objected, both in the past and recently, to a few of its policies . . . , but in general my chief difference of opinion is that it wishes to remain unknown, and I believe its role in history is significant enough to be known.[5]

The ultimate purpose of this Conspiracy is power. There are some who desire this more than even material goods, although the two frequently go together. One such individual was the previously mentioned Joseph Kennedy. Family admirer and author Pearl Buck wrote the following in her book, *The Kennedy Women*: "Rose Kennedy (the wife of Joseph Kennedy) knew that the man she loved loved a power beyond the power of money. He wanted the power of government, and he would have it."[6]

The Conspiracy that Dr. Quigley and others saw, then, needs conspirators, and it is logical to ask why illustrious men of wealth and fortune would join such an enterprise. One who answered this question was author Blair Coan who wrote in his book, *The Red Web*: "The answer is quite the reverse of the question: These men (involved with the Conspiracy) became illustrious primarily because they were part of the Conspiracy."[7]

So those involved do not become rich and/or illustrious and then join the Conspiracy; they become rich and illustrious because they are members of the Conspiracy.

But what is their motive? What prompts men to seek wealth and position? Former Congressman John Schmitz explains that there is an additional goal: Power! Men join the Conspiracy to gain money and then power. Schmitz wrote: "When a person has all the money he needs, his goal becomes power."[8]

Benjamin Franklin explained this connection between money and power when he said: "There are two passions which have a powerful influence on the affairs of men. These are . . . love of power and love of money. . . . When united . . . they have the most violent effects."[9]

However, power itself has a corrupting influence on those who seek it. In an oft-quoted truth, Lord Acton explained power thus: "Power corrupts; absolute power corrupts absolutely."

Those who seek power will be corrupted by it. They will be willing to intentionally cause depressions, revolutions, and wars in order to further their desire for more power. This corrupting nature of the very pursuit of power explains why the moral mind of the individual who neither desires power over others nor understands the desire for such power cannot fathom why power-seekers would want to create human misery through wars, depressions, and revolutions.

In other words, the conspirators are successful because the moral citizen cannot accept the conclusion that other individuals would actually wish to create incredibly destructive acts against their fellow citizens.

Another power seeker, the Russian anarchist Bakunin, explained that this process of corruption even affected those dedicated to freedom who were given power to protect the powerless. He wrote that "... the possession of power transformed into a tyrant even the most devoted friend of liberty."[10]

The delight in the possession of power over others was explained by another observer of the power-seeking Joseph Kennedy: "I like Joe Kennedy. He understands power. Power is the end. What other delight is there but to enjoy the sheer sense of control? He would say: 'Let me see any other motive in the people who command.' "[11]

So the motive of the Conspirators has been identified:
It is Power!

Chapter 1
God or Government?

The Conspiracy that will be examined in this volume has been in existence for many years. Comprehending how it could survive for such a long period of time has been difficult.

One explanation of its lengthy existence was offered by George Orwell, the British Socialist, who wrote *Animal Farm* and *1984*, two books on the subject of absolute power in the hands of a few. He wrote: "The Party is not concerned with perpetuating its blood but with perpetuating itself. Who wields power is not important provided the hierarchical structure remains always the same."[1]

The method by which the Conspiracy recruits new members to replace those who retire or die is explained by Norman Dodd, an investigator and researcher into the existence of the Conspiracy. Mr. Dodd explained: "The careers of men are watched. The men who indicate that they would be especially capable in terms of the aims of this group are approached quietly and invited into the inner circles. They are watched as they carry out assignments and eventually they are drawn into it under circumstances which make it virtually impossible for them to ever get out of it."[2]

What is the ultimate goal of the Conspiracy? If total power is the final object, then, any system which maximizes power into the hands of a few is the system to be desired. In terms of government, then, the ultimate form of power is Communism. This is the seat of the maximum power over the economy and of the individual. The Conspirators: "want big government because they understand that Socialism (and Communism as well) is not a humanitarian system for redistributing wealth, but for concentrating and controlling it. They also recognize it as a system for concentrating and controlling people."[3]

It is common for detractors of this position to claim that the last thing that the wealthy of the world want is government control over or ownership of the factors of production. But, as we shall see, Socialism or Communism offers the Conspiracy the greatest vehicle for concentrating and controlling the wealth. This is the ultimate goal of these planners: power over not only the wealth of the world, but also the producers of that wealth, the people themselves. So the Conspiracy uses government to get control of the government, and total government control is their goal.

If government is being used by the Conspiracy to consolidate power into its hands, it behooves those who wish to preserve their freedoms to understand the very nature and function of government. Once the character of government is understood, efforts can be directed against the increase in governmental powers over both the national economy and the lives of its citizens.

A good place to begin such a study is to examine the two sources claimed to be the source of human rights. There are only two, presuming that it is admitted that humans do indeed have rights: either man himself, or someone or something external to man himself, a Creator.

Many of America's founding fathers were aware of the difference between these two alternatives. Thomas Jefferson, for instance, stated his concern and understanding thus: "The God who gave us life gave us liberty. Can the liberties of a nation be secure when we have removed a conviction that these liberties are the gift of God?"

However, the corresponding alternative explanation argues that our rights come from government, the creature of man himself. This contention holds that man creates government to give man his rights.

A stern warning for those who do not distinguish between these two alternatives came from William Penn. He wrote: "If men will not be governed by God, they then must be governed by tyrants."

There are four references to a Creator in the Declaration of Independence, but certain of America's leaders are now asking that God must be separated from the affairs of the government. If this separation is made, as Mr. Penn indicated, the people will be governed by tyrants, and future tyrants will do all that they can to separate a belief in God from the existence of government.

A good example of the philosophy that governments grant human rights to their citizens is found in the *International Covenants on Human Rights*, passed in 1966 by the United Nations. It reads, in part: "The States parties to the present Covenant recognize that, in the enjoyment of those rights provided by the State, in conformity with the present Covenant, the State may subject such rights only to such limitations as are determined by law...."[4]

This document, passed unanimously by all of the parties voting, including the United States, concluded that man's rights are granted by the government. It further concluded that these rights could be limited by law; in other words, that which the government grants can be controlled by the granting body, the government. That which the government gives can also be taken away.

Man's rights under this thought are not very secure. Governments can change, and with the change, man's rights can disappear. Knowledge of this fact did not escape America's founding fathers, who wrote in the Declaration of Independence: "We hold these truths to be self evident, that all men are created equal, that they are endowed by their Creator with certain inalienable rights...."

Here, then, is the other theory of the source of man's rights: they are given to man by his Creator. Man's rights are inalienable (defined as incapable of being transferred) which means that they can not be taken away by anyone except the entity that gave the rights in the first place: in this case, the Creator.

So here are the two competing and contradictory theories about the rights of man: one holds that they are given by the Creator, and therefore can only be removed by the entity that created them in the first place; the other holds that man's rights come from man himself and therefore can be limited or removed by man or by other men, as "determined by law."

Therefore, the man who wishes to protect his rights from those who wish to limit them must protect himself and his human rights by creating an agency that has the power to exceed that exerted by those who violate human rights. The agency created is called government. But granting power to government to protect human rights also grants power to those who can abuse it as a vehicle to destroy or limit the rights of the people who created the government.

Those who wrote the Constitution realized that this tendency existed when they wrote the Bill of Rights, the first ten Amendments to the Constitution. The purpose of these amendments is to restrict the power of the government to violate the rights of the citizens of the nation. The founding fathers wrote these restrictions with phrases like:

"Congress shall pass no law . . . ."
"The right of the people . . . shall not be infringed."
"No person shall be . . . deprived."
"The accused shall enjoy the right."

Notice that these are not restrictions on human rights, but are restrictions on the activities of governments.

If rights are granted by the Creator of those rights, what are rights granted by government? It becomes important to distinguish between a Right and a Privilege by defining these two terms.

A Right is a freedom to act morally without asking permission;

A Privilege is a freedom to act morally but only after permission has been granted by some governmental entity.

Perhaps a good illustration of the misuse of human rights occurred during World War II when the German government, acting through its leader, Adolf Hitler, decided that certain of the people did not have the right to life, and decrees were issued to exterminate those who the government felt had no human rights.

The right to life, then, granted to each individual by his Creator, no longer was a right in Germany, it had become a privilege. Man lived by permission of the government, which had the power to limit and even curtail the human right to life.

The human rights that the individual wishes to protect are simple in nature, and include the right to Life, Liberty and Property.

These three rights are in essence only one right: the right to Life.

These rights are in accord with man's basic nature. Man (the author will use the generic term "man" to mean all of humanity, both male and female) is created hungry and needs to produce food to sustain his life. Without the right to keep what he has produced (his property) man will surely starve to death. Not only must man be allowed to keep the products of his labors, he must be free to produce the property he needs for his sustenance (the right known as Liberty.)

Governments do not need to take man's life to kill him. Governments can remove man's right to property or the freedom to produce the property needed to maintain his life. A government that restricts man's ability to keep what he produces (his property) has an equal ability to kill a man as surely as a government that takes his life wantonly (such as in the case of Germany.) As will be shown in subsequent chapters, there are government entities that restrict man's right to property or his right to liberty without terminating his life directly. But the effect is still the same.

One of the objections of "pro-life" supporters, those opposed to the government legalizing abortion, is that government is now justifying the termination of life because the life has been termed "unwanted" by its mother. This was the reason offered by Hitler for his decision to terminate the lives of countless millions of individuals in Germany. The Jews and others were "unwanted" and therefore the government could take away their right to live.

As will be illustrated later, the Communists wish to abolish "private property," or the individual's right to keep what he produces.

One who spoke in favor of the concept of private property was Abraham Lincoln, who said: "Property is the fruit of labor; property is desirable; it is a positive good in the world. That some should be rich shows that others may become rich, and hence is just encouragement to industry and enterprise. Let not him who is houseless pull down the house of another, but let him work diligently and build one for himself, thus by example assuring that his own shall be safe from violence when built."[5]

Chapter 2
Freedom

Liberty is the only thing you cannot have unless you are willing to give it to others.

Liberty is defined as rights with responsibilities. Its opposite, License, is defined as rights with no responsibilities. Another word for License would be Anarchy, or a situation where there are no rules, rights, or privileges. The strong devour the weak; the powerful destroy the powerless. In the animal world, License is defined as "the Law of the jungle."

Those who love freedom must recognize that others have equal rights to their freedom as well, and that only by recognizing this fact will all be totally free. That means that all individuals must restrict their freedom to harm others, or none will be free to enjoy their rights to life, liberty, and property.

The Creator of man laid down some guidelines about the rights of others. These guidelines are written in the negative in at least six of the Ten Commandments. The guideline is written "Thou shall not ...," which means that all will be free if all men confine their activities to those which do not harm others.

America's founding fathers, when they wrote the Constitution and the Bill of Rights, also wrote their guidelines in the negative: "Congress shall pass no laws...." But these restrictions enable man to be freer because man's life would be free of governmental restraints.

Those who wrote the Constitution were concerned about the concept of equal rights. They were attempting to separate themselves from a monarchy as a form of government where certain individuals, the king and his court, had more rights than the common citizens. These individuals had superior rights because of their positions. Conversely, the common people had little if any rights. America's founding fathers were convinced that they would not allow this inequality to occur in this country as they wrote the founding documents.

They wrote it into the Constitution that all men were created equal, that the lowest had the same rights to Life, Liberty, and Property as did the highest. Modern man, through the misuse of government, passes laws to make men equal in all areas of their lives. This obvious misunderstanding of man's nature has caused much grief as long as man has been attempting to create government.

The solitary man, alone in his environment, need not concern himself with rights and the need to create government to protect those rights. No one exists to plunder his goods or take his life. There is no need to protect his rights, They are secure.

It is only when another individual or groups of individuals join him in his solitary existence that concerns about rights become important.

Each of the inhabitants has an equal right to life, liberty and property. That right is protected as long as each inhabitant recognizes the equal right of the others. No individual nor any group of individuals has the right to take the life, liberty or property of another individual or group of individuals.

There is no question that any individual, or group of individuals, has the *ability* to violate the rights of any individual. The question being discussed here is whether or not the violator has the right to do so.

If each individual has the right to his life, liberty and property, and no one has the right to take these rights, then it follows that man must have the right to protect his rights. This right is called the Right to Self Defense. Each individual has this right in equal proportion to any other individual.

If each individual has the right to self-defense and each has it equally, then each individual has the right to pool his individual right with others so that all can protect their rights from those who come to violate all of their rights at the same time.

In other words, if each has the right individually, then all have the right collectively. Such collective poolings of individual rights to self defense are called governments.

Men create governments when they pool their individual rights to self defense to create an agency that has the collective right to protect both the individual and the collective body of individuals.

Men can only grant to government those rights they themselves have. If an individual does not have a right, it is not possible for that individual to grant that right to government. Government can only have those rights that each individual has.

These truths about human rights can best be illustrated by a brief and simple economic model based upon two assumptions about human nature:

1.   All people consume equally; and
1.   All people produce unequally.

Assumption #1 is not an absolute, obviously, since not all people *consume* exactly the same, but basically this statement is correct. Notice that the participants at a banquet are all given an equal portion, whether they are large or small, and each serving at a drive-in restaurant is the same size. So, for the sake of this discussion, it will be assumed that all people pretty well consume equally.

Such is not the case with Assumption #2. Each person, if given equal opportunity to produce his sustenance, would produce unequally. Some would produce more than others. Generally, the young, the energetic and the skilled would produce more than the old, the lazy, and the unskilled. The well would produce more than the infirm. But each would consume about the same. This means that some individuals produce more than they consume, while others consume more than they produce.

The author has constructed an economic model that will illustrate the validity of the concept of private property based upon these two assumptions.

There will be seven individuals in this economic model who have grouped themselves together on an island. These individuals will have no outside interference from other individuals.

Each individual, herein identified by a letter, produces at an unequal rate, and consumes at an equal rate. Hence:

Individual	Production	Consumption
A.	1,200	500
B.	750	500
C.	600	500
D.	400	500
E.	300	500
F.	250	500
G.	-0-	500
TOTALS:	3,500	3,500

In this economic model, individuals A, B, and C produce more than they consume; D, E, and F consume more than they produce; and G is completely dependent on the rest of the individuals present on the island.

18

Individual G is willing but totally unable to produce. For the sake of this model, all individuals will be presumed to be functioning at their utmost capacity. There are no slackers. All are producing to their fullest extent possible. Also, there is no waste in this model. All goods produced are consumed.

That means that some individuals produce a Surplus, defined as an excess of production over consumption. (This is also defined as Wealth.) And some individuals produce a Deficit, defined as a shortage of production over consumption. This can be illustrated thus:

Individual	Production	Surplus	Deficit	Consumption
A.	1,200	700		500
B.	750	250		500
C.	600	100		500
D.	400		100	500
E.	300		200	500
F.	250		250	500
G.	-0-		500	500
TOTALS	3,500	1,050	1,050	3,500

The important thing to recognize is that certain individuals, in this case, D, E, F and G, are dependent, in varying degrees, upon the rest of the individuals in this model. In fact, individual G is completely dependent upon the rest of the individuals, because if the others didn't exist, individual G would surely die.

A logical question to ask at this point would be whether individual G would have the right to prevent the others from leaving the island should they choose to do so. A similar question that could be asked is whether G would have the right to force the others to produce what individual G requires to maintain his existence.

These are real questions for all governments and individuals to ponder, and, as will be shown later, there are governments that have taken the position that individual G would have both the right to keep others within the environment and the right to force the others to produce for G's individual needs.

The next question that needs to be answered is whether the less productive individuals D, E, F, and G have a right to the surplus of individuals A, B, and C. There are governments and individuals that believe that this is indeed a right, and that governments are created to make certain that their individual needs are met, by distributing the surplus of the productive. These forms of government will be identified later.

There are, obviously, two positions on the question of to whom the

19

surplus belongs. Those who hold that private property rights grant them the right to keep that surplus are obviously in disagreement with those who hold that the surplus goods belong to those who do not produce them.

There are only two methods by which the surplus of individuals A, B, and C can be divided: either with their consent or without it. Either the property belongs to those who produce it or it doesn't.

Presume that the four individuals, D, E, F, and G, ask A, B, and C to divide their surplus voluntarily, and the latter refuse. Does that refusal grant the right to D, E, F and G to take the goods from them?

If property rights have any meaning, the answer must surely be in the negative. Does the right to property include the right to protect it from the plundering acts of those who come to take it by force? Does an individual have the right to protect his property against the acts of another individual? Does the individual have the right to protect his property against the acts of a group of individuals? Does the group have the right to protect their property against the acts of another group?

Realizing that the property of the productive A, B, and C cannot be taken from them by force, it behooves the less productive to find another way to acquire the surplus. Presume that they develop a new strategy. They call a meeting to discuss the question of the surplus, and all seven individuals attend. The question of how to handle the surplus is discussed and then acted upon, allowing the majority to decide how to divide the property. In this case, D, E, F, and G vote to divide the property equally, and A, B and C vote against it.

Do D, E, F and G have the right to vote away the property rights of the minority. Does it make it right because all were given an equal opportunity to express their opinion?

Does it make it right if they call the meeting a government? Does it make it right if the *majority* says that whatever the majority decides will be what the entirety will do? Does the minority have any rights?

If the majority votes to take the minority's property, what is it called?

It is called a Democracy!

Next, presume that the majority is able to create a government to take the surplus from the producers, and that the producers decide among themselves to only produce what they consume the next year, in this case 500 units apiece. Would the minority have that right?

That means that A, B, and C will only produce what they consumed the previous year, or 500 units apiece. The remainder of the people continue to produce what they did the year before. The figures for the second year will be as follows:

2nd Year:

Individual	Production	Consumption
A.	500	350
B.	500	350
C.	500	350
D.	400	350
E.	300	350
F.	250	350
G.	-0-	350
TOTALS:	2,450	2,450

The surpluses and deficits become:

Individual	Production	Surplus	Deficit	Consumption
A.	500	150		350
B.	500	150		350
C.	500	150		350
D.	400	50		350
E.	300		50	350
F.	250		100	350
G.	-0-		350	350
TOTALS:	2,450	500	500	2,450

Notice that the total production dropped from 3,500 units to 2,450 units, a drop of 1,050 units. Each individual's share also decreased as well, from 500 units per person to 350.

Now does the majority have the right to force the minority to produce up to last year's productivity? Even if the majority tried, would the minority produce up to the standard that the majority expected of them? Will the use of force make them produce?

Last, would the majority have the right to keep A, B, and C in the workplace should they choose to leave it? Would they have the right to build a wall around the environment to make certain that they did not leave?

Certain socialists in today's world have taken just that position. "Iron" and "Bamboo" Curtains are the results of the majority's realization (or at least of the realization of the ruling class claiming to act on behalf of the majority) that they need the productive talents of the minority, and because of this needed production, the majority builds walls to keep the minority inside.

What then, should the incentive be to encourage production? Should it be the incentive of the government (fear) or the incentive of the market place (profit)?

The key to production is the incentive of the marketplace, the right to keep what is produced, the Right to Private Property! The right of the individual to better his life by producing more than he consumes and to keep what he produces.

This economic model has many illustrations in the world today. One is occurring today in the Soviet Union, where the basic philosophy that motivates the government is the proposition that whatever is produced in the society belongs to all in that society. However, even in Russia, there is a small percentage of the country where the individual can keep what he produces:

> According to the government's own figures . . . , private plots with a mere three percent of the nation's own acreage accounted for 30 percent of the gross harvest, other than grains, 40 percent of all cattle-breeding, 60 percent of the country's potato crops, 40 percent of all vegetables and milk, 68 percent of all meat products.

> Their fruit yields . . . are double those of state orchards for equivalent areas, its potato harvest per hectare two-thirds higher than on collective farms.

> Even in grain, which is a very minor element in the private sector, it produces one-third more per sown unit than an average socialized farm.[1]

Why is just a small percentage of cultivated land area able to out-produce the remainder? It is because the producers can keep what they produce! The producer has the right to Private Property! Governments can not take what has been produced in this free market environment, for any reason.

People who are allowed to keep what they have produced will always out-produce those who have their production taken from them for the benefit of society. And no one can force the producer to equal his peak production in a free market.

Even Communist China has discovered the truth of this proposition, according to an article in *Time* magazine on the Jun Tan brigade. It is here that China allows the workers to keep for themselves all the produce over the government set quota.

The brigade's leader is quoted as saying: "All the peasants feel happy. They work twice as hard as they used to because they know that if they work harder, they can make more money."

The article cited the results of China's experiment with the right to Private Property: "Its per-person annual revenue of $201 is well above the national rural average of only $91."[2]

But even with these glaring examples of the wisdom of the right to

Private Property, there are still those who wish to challenge this premise. One, for instance, is Nicole Salinger, who was quoted as saying: "In France and some other countries it is being proposed that there be a specified differential between the lowest paid worker and the highest paid executive."[3]

Another, noted American economist John Kenneth Galbraith, also wanted to limit man's rewards for his productivity: "Sooner or later there will probably be some such rule. If a full-time assembly line worker in the United States got $12,000 a year, then a top executive would have a ceiling, say, five times as much, or $60,000. That is a living wage."[4]

If the top executives of the nation were earning more than Mr. Galbraith or some government bureaucrat felt they should be earning, their wages would be reduced by some governmental edict. One can only wonder what Mr. Galbraith would do if any individual having his wages cut wished to leave his position because he felt he wasn't being rewarded adequately, especially if he were in a specialized field where only he had the experience or ability to perform the job. Perhaps Mr. Galbraith would use the force of government to require that he stay.

Another question unanswered by Mr. Galbraith is the question of what he would do if no one wanted to perform the job because no one felt the salary was adequate.

But Salinger and Galbraith and this economic model have not adequately answered the question of just how the society provides for individual G who is unable to provide for himself.

Basically, there are only two ways for the society to satisfy this individual's basic needs. Either method takes the surplus produced by the more productive individuals in the society and divides it, either:

1.   Voluntarily, or
2.   Coercively.

In other words, the society can either steal the surplus or they can ask the producers to share it voluntarily with the less productive. Sharing a surplus voluntarily is called Charity; sharing it through the use of force is called Welfare.

Just imagine the public outcry should one of America's charitable institutions choose to collect their needed revenues through the use of coercion: "Our needs are more than what you wish to give voluntarily. We will take what we need."

Every person so wronged could expect that the force of government would be used to require the charitable institution to return the stolen property. That is one of the functions of government: to right a wrong such as the taking of property by force.

Returning to the seven individual Economic Model, what is it called when D, E, F, and G join together to violently take the property of A, B and C?

It is called Stealing!

If each group, A, B, and C, and D, E, F, and G, were separate nations, and the latter came to take the former's property by force, the action would be called a war! In either case, the individuals and the nations wronged have the right to defend themselves against the attack on their property.

Individuals have the right to self-defense, and they can combine these individual rights to self-defense by forming a government that has the right to collective self-defense. Once governments have been formed, individual nations can join together to protect themselves from other nations. These nations have the right to hire individuals, called soldiers, to assist in the defense of the nation, just as individuals have the right to protect their life and liberty by hiring a "bodyguard."

Should war as a means of acquiring property fail, those who wish to acquire the property of others must design other strategies. One method that was devised was the use of the majority vote, already discussed. The use of a democracy is another method of taking property away from the minority under the guise of whatever excuse the minority would accept as valid.

Notice that in such questions as are decided by majority vote, that whatever the majority decides is what the entirety gets. Notice that there is no question as to whether or not what the majority wants is right or wrong: the majority rules!

However, the question should never be *who* is right, but *what* is right. Just because a majority decides what the action to be taken is, it does not necessarily follow that the action to be taken is correct.

Notice that there are no minority rights in a true democracy: the majority rules. Notice that if the government (in the name of the majority) decides to grant privileges just to a minority, then the majority must give up its rights. "Majorities do not determine right and wrong. Right is right though everyone votes against it, and wrong is wrong though all but God favor it."[5]

Next, presume that the majority legitimizes its vote by declaring that they have created a government, and that all are bound to obey the decisions of the majority. It is proper to ask the inevitable question: where did the majority get this right?

People can only give to government those rights that they themselves have . Does an individual have the right to take from another? Do two individuals have the right to take from another group of individuals? Do three individuals have the right? Do a grouping of individuals, when acting in concert, have the right? Can a group of individuals get together, call themselves a government, and then grant that government a right that they themselves do not have? Even if that group is a majority?

Can man change the Commandment taken from the Ten Commandments, that reads: "Thou shall not steal" and convert it to: "Thou shall not steal, except by majority vote!" Or to: "Thou shall not steal, except that portion of thy neighbor's wealth which exceeds thine own!"

Taking the property of another, no matter what the motive, is called stealing, no matter whether an individual, or a group of individuals acting through an agency they call government, commits the crime.

Another word for stealing is Plunder, and when governments legitimize the taking of another's property, it is called Legal Plunder. What happens when a government legalizes stealing?

> I have long been convinced that institutions purely democratic must, sooner or later, destroy liberty or civilization, or both.

How does this happen?

> The adoption of democracy . . . is fatal to good government, to liberty, to law and order, to respect for authority, and to religion, and must produce chaos from which a new world tyranny will arise.[6]

> You can never have a revolution in order to establish a democracy. You must have a democracy in order to have a revolution.[7]

Is there any form of government that protects minority rights (or majority rights, for that matter) if Democracies are unable to do so?

Those who created the American government believed that there were indeed ways to accomplish this vital protection. They wrote in the Declaration of Independence:

> We hold these truths to be self-evident, that all men are created equal, that they are endowed by their Creator with certain inalienable rights, that among these are life, liberty and the pursuit of happiness, that to secure these rights, governments are instituted among men . . .

There are, indeed, some "self-evident truths" in that short paragraph, and America's founding fathers were quite aware of them. One of these was the proposition that men were *created* equal, but were *not* equal. This means that men have equal access to their rights to life, liberty, and property, no matter what their social status, their color, their nationality, their sex, or their religion. It did not mean that all men *were* equal in ability or personal merit and that property should be divided equally amongst them.

This particular position was extremely important as the founding fathers had come from a monarchy as a form of government where certain individuals, just because of their position or social status, had superior rights to those born of "common" stock. It is quite apparent that the founding fathers were attempting to limit this concept of the European nobility.

Another "self-evident truth" in that paragraph was the recognition that man's rights were inalienable, which meant that other men, or other governments, could not tamper with them.

The founding fathers attempted to define what these human rights were: the right to "life, liberty and the pursuit of happiness." (They recognized that these were not the only rights of man, but that these were "amongst others.")

And lastly, that man creates governments to protect these inalienable rights.

James Madison has been quoted as saying that: "Government is instituted to protect property of every sort. This being the end of government, that alone is a just government which impartially secures to every man, whatever is his own.... That is not a just government where...property...is violated by...seizures..is violated by...seizures of one class of citizens for the service of the rest."

Two other examples of the concern about the rights of man can be found in the Virginia Bill of Rights, adopted on June 12, 1776, and the Alabama Constitution.

Article I of the Virginia Bill of Rights states:

> That all men are by nature equally free and independent, and have certain inherent rights, of which, when they enter into a state of society, they cannot, by any compact, deprive or divest their posterity;
>
> Namely the enjoyment of life and liberty, with the means of acquiring and possessing property, and pursuing and obtaining happiness and safety.

Article 1 of the Alabama Constitution reads, in part:

> That the sole object and only legitimate end of government is to protect the citizen in the enjoyment of life, liberty and property, and when the government assumes other functions it is usurpation and oppression.

Since government is the accumulation of individual rights to use force in the protection of individual or collective rights to life, liberty and property, great care should be exercized in the granting of power to the government. The question is always just how much power can be granted to government before it, in itself, becomes an enemy of human rights.

George Washington addressed this problem when he stated: "Government is not reason, it is not eloquence. It is force, and like fire, it is a dangerous servant and a fearful master."[8]

President Washington likened the power of government to the power of fire: both were useful and necessary but both had the power to destroy. Both were dangerous to the individual.

The homeowner, anxious to warm his house, brings fire into the exterior walls, but builds a furnace wall around it so that it will not destroy his home. Obviously, the fire can be both beneficial and dangerous and man must learn its nature and protect himself against its consequences.

Those who create government must design some structure to keep the government within its proper confines for exactly the same reason: government also has the power to destroy not only the individual but the entire nation as well.

America's founding fathers attempted to contain the government's power to destroy the rights of the individual by use of the containing walls of the Constitution. This document was not intended to restrain the power of the people. It was intended to restrain the power of the government. Notice that government is restricted to the powers enumerated in the first three Articles of the Constitution: those that define the powers of the Legislative, the Executive, and the Judicial branches of the government. The purpose was to properly confine the power of government to those enumerated and those alone.

A parallel to the limitation of powers in the Constitution to those enumerated specifically can be found in the Property Insurance field.

There are two methods of insuring real and personal property:

1.   The "Named Peril" method; and
2.   The "All Risk" method.

The former covers the property for damage by certain perils enumerated by the policy. For instance, the property is insured when damaged by a Fire, a Windstorm, or a Vehicle, etc., because those were included as coverages under the terms of the policy. For there to be coverage under the policy, the property would have to be damaged by a specific peril exactly described by the coverage part of the policy. If the property was damaged by an avalanche, it would not be covered, because Avalanche damage is not an enumerated peril.

Under the "All Risk" method, all losses would be covered unless the specific peril causing the loss was excluded by the policy. To see if a certain loss is covered, the policy holder would have to read the exclusions. For instance, in the above example, the damage to the property caused by the avalanche would be covered unless it was specifically excluded by the terms of the policy.

Governments are like the two methods of insurance: governments can either have enumerated powers (those specifically granted by the people to the government) or governments can have all power unless specifically prohibited by some document.

The former type is the government of free men; the latter is the government of slaves. Kings, dictators, and tyrants want all power in their hands; free men attempt to limit government to specifically enumerated powers.

It would be difficult to limit the powers of the government in the "All Risk" method: every conceivable instance where government was not intended to operate would have to be enumerated. The task of detailing the exact conditions where government could not operate would be impossible, especially if the intent was to limit the powers of government.

America's founding fathers were aware of the difference between the two methods and attempted to limit government to a "Named Peril" form: they listed the exact powers they granted government. They spelled these out, specifying the powers exactly. Congress was granted the power "to declare war," "to coin money," to establish "post offices and post roads," and to "raise and support armies," amongst others.

As a further evidence that they were concerned about limiting the powers of government, they added the Bill of Rights to the Constitution. These were specific limitations on governmental authority. But the ultimate limitation on the power of the federal government was the 10th Amendment. This read: "The powers not delegated to the United States by the Constitution, nor prohibited by it to the States, are reserved to the States respectively, or to the people."

In other words, the founding fathers gave us a "Named Peril" form of government. They limited the powers of government to those specifically enumerated in the Constitution.

Confirmation of this fact comes frequently from our Congressmen, although less often than before. One supporter of this limited power position stood up in the House of Representatives in 1814 and addressed the nation. He said:

> The Government of the United States is a Government of limited powers. You take by grant; your powers are special and delegated — that must be construed strictly.
>
> All powers not delegated are reserved to the States or the people. Your authority is defined — you take nothing by inference or application, except what may be "necessary and proper for carrying into execution" the powers expressly granted.[9]

There are those, unfortunately, who believe that their power in the halls of Congress is nearly unlimited. Most cite the so-called "General Welfare" clause of the Constitution as the source of their supposed authority to legislate in all areas. This clause is contained in Article I, Section 8 and reads: *"The Congress shall have power to* lay and collect taxes, duties, imposts, and excises, to pay the debts and *provide for the* common defense and *general welfare* of the United States...." (emphasis added.)

James Madison, one of the three writers of the *Federalist Papers* which were written in an attempt to explain the new form of government to the American people, wrote this about the General Welfare Clause: "The powers delegated by the proposed Constitution to the federal government are few and defined. Those which are to remain in the State governments are numerous and indefinite." (Federalist Paper #45)

And in Federalist Paper #41, Madison attempted to reply to a supporter of the broad interpretation of the General Welfare Clause who wrote: "The power...to provide for the...general welfare...amounts to an unlimited commission to exercise every power which may be alleged to be necessary for the...general welfare."

Madison wrote that those who felt that the General Welfare Clause gave an enormous grant of power to Congress were in "error," and that the supporter's idea was an "absurdity."

Yet this claim continues to be heard around the nation.

Hugh Williamson of North Carolina, a member of the Constitutional Convention, also took a position on the General Welfare Clause, when he wrote the following in 1781:

> If Congress can apply money indefinitely to the general welfare and are the sole and supreme judges of the general welfare, they may take the care of religion into their hands; they may establish teachers in every state, county and parish, and pay them out of the public treasury; they may take into their hands the education of children, establishing in like manner schools throughout the Union; they may undertake the regulation of all roads other than post roads.
>
> In short, everything from the highest object of state legislation down to the most minute objects of police, would be thrown under the power of Congress.
>
> For every object I have mentioned would admit the application of money, and might be called, if Congress pleased, provisions for the General Welfare.

(Mr. Williamson was indeed a prophet before his time!)

So America's founding fathers had concerns about the amount of power that should reside in the federal government. They attempted to limit that power by constructing a Constitution in such a manner that government had specific, defined, and strictly limited powers.

Frederic Bastiat, a French economist, statesman, and author, wrote during the years of the second French Revolution of 1848. He saw that the taking of one man's property for the use of another was an improper activity, one that he called Plunder. When government performed the same activity, they had the power to make it legal, and Bastiat called this form of stealing Legal Plunder. Government in his day had taken the power to do what the individual members of his nation couldn't do: take property from one to give to another.

He wrote the following in his classic book *The Law:*

But how is this legal plunder to be identified?

Quite simply: See if the law takes from some persons what belongs to them, and gives it to persons to whom it does not belong.

See if the law benefits one citizen at the expense of another by doing what the citizen himself cannot do without committing a crime.

Then abolish the law without delay. If such a law, which is an isolated case — is not abolished immediately, it will spread, multiply and develop into a system.[10]

Bastiat mentioned that Legal Plunder could manifest itself in two forms:

1.   The taking of property by government from the individual it belongs to and the giving of it to someone it does not belong to; and

2.   The granting of a privilege to one group at the expense of another.

Bastiat further went on to predict what would happen under this system of government:

As long as it is admitted that the law may be diverted from its true purpose, that it may violate property instead of protecting it, then everyone will want to participate in making the law, either to protect himself against plunder or to use it for plunder[11]

A truism about Legal Plunder can be stated thus:

Government cannot give anything it first doesn't take from someone else.

So government cannot be the great giver, as it has nothing to give. Governments can only take. But for those who demand that government should provide the people with their food, their housing, their education, their clothing, their medical care, their livelihood, and their recreation, there is already a governmental agency providing these services to certain of their fellow citizens.

These services are provided by government in a prison. There are two classes of citizens in a prison: those who provide the services and those who receive them. The persons who receive the services are not free to provide these services for themselves. Those who provide the services are free to come and go as they choose. Those for whom the services are provided are called Prisoners; those who provide the services are called Wardens.

It is also important to examine whether or not government exists to protect man from himself. John Stuart Mill addressed this question when he wrote:

> That the only purpose for which power can be rightly exercised over any member of a civilized community, against his will, is to prevent harm to others.
>
> His own good, either physical or moral, is not a sufficient warrant.
>
> He cannot rightly be compelled to do or forbear because it will make him happier, because, in the opinion of others, to do so would be wise, or even right.
>
> These are good reasons for remonstrating with him, or entreating him, but not for compelling him, or visiting him with any evil in case he does otherwise.
>
> To justify that, the conduct from which it is desired to deter him must be calculated to produce evil to someone else.[12]

So government does not exist to protect man from himself. It does not exist to re-distribute wealth from one group of individuals to another. It does not exist to grant privileges to one group over another. And it does not exist to operate in every situation envisioned by the mind of man.

Government simply exists to protect individual rights to Life, Liberty, and Property. That is its sole function.

Andrew Jackson summarized these sentiments quite well when he wrote the following: "There are no necessary evils in government. Its evils exist only in its abuses. If it would confine itself to equal protection, and, as Heaven does its rains, shower its favors alike on the high and the low, the rich and the poor, it would be an unqualified blessing."[13]

Chapter 3
Forms of Government

If the democratic form of government (rule by a majority) does not protect the rights of the minority, is there a form of government that does? If Democracies protect only the strong, is there a form of government that protects both the strong and the weak?

Various forms of government exist, but basically there are only two:

Rule by God: a theocracy
Rule by man: various forms

Man has no control over whether or not God wishes to form a theocratic form of government. This is God's decision. God will create one, or not create one, depending on His plans. So this study of governmental forms will not consider this form of government as a viable alternative. There are various forms of government by man. Some of the more common types are briefly defined as:

Rule by no one: anarchy
Rule by one man: a dictatorship; or a monarchy
Rule by a few men: an oligarchy
Rule by the majority: a democracy

Anarchy is a form of government in transition between two other forms of government. Anarchy is created by those who wish to destroy one form of government so that it can be replaced with the form of government the anarchists wish. It too will be discarded as a viable alternative.

It is generally conceded that even a monarchy or a dictatorship is an oligarchy, or a government run by a small, ruling minority. Every monarchy has its small circle of advisors, who allow the king or dictator to rule as long as he does so in a manner pleasing to the oligarchy. It is doubtful that there has ever been a true dictatorship (rule by one person) anywhere in the world, except in some isolated instances, such as in a tribe or in a clan.

Such is also the case with a democracy, for this form of government is traditionally controlled at the top by a small ruling oligarchy. The people in a democracy are conditioned to believe that they are indeed the decision-making power in the government, but in truth there is almost always a small circle at the top making the decisions for the entirety. So the only true form of government throughout history has been the oligarchy, a rule by a minority.

As proof of these contentions, one has only to read the *1928 United States Army Training Manual*, which defined a democracy as:

> A government of the masses. Authority derived through mass meeting or any form of direct expression. Results in mobocracy, attitude toward property is communistic — negating property rights.
>
> Attitude toward law is that the will of the majority shall regulate, whether it be based upon deliberation or governed by passion, prejudice, and impulse, without restraint or regard to consequence.
>
> Results in demagogism, license, agitation, discontent, anarchy.[1]

A democracy, according to this definition, is actually controlled by a demagogue, defined as: "A speaker who seeks to make capital of social discontent and gain political influence."

So demagogues are usually hired by those supporting an oligarchy as a form of government to create the anarchy or social discontent that the oligarchs convert into a true oligarchy. Democracies are converted to anarchy, where no one rules, as the oligarchs seek to control the government themselves. And anarchy ends with a dictatorship or a tyrannical form of government when the oligarchy imposes total control over all of the people.

The 1928 definition of a democracy was later changed by those who write Army manuals, however.

In 1952, this became the definition of a democracy in the *Soldier's Guide*:

Because the United States is a democracy, the majority of the people decide how our government will be organized and run — and that includes the Army, Navy and Air Force. The people do this by electing representatives, and these men and women then carry out the wishes of the people.[2]

(This is a strange definition to offer the American fighting man: that democratic policies manage the Armed Services. It is doubtful that enlisted men elect their officers or make decisions as to how to conduct the war.)

So if democracies are in truth oligarchies, where the minority rules, is there a form of government that protects both minority and majority rights? There is, and it is called a republic, which is defined as:

Rule by law: a republic

In the republican form of government, the power rests in a written constitution, wherein the powers of the government are limited so that the people retain the maximum amount of power themselves. In addition to limiting the power of the government, care is also taken to limit the power of the people to restrict the rights of both the majority and the minority.

Perhaps the simplest method of illustrating the difference between an oligarchy, a democracy and a republic would be to discuss the basic plot of the classic grade B western movie.

In this plot, one that the moviegoer has probably seen a hundred times, the brutal villain rides into town and guns down the unobtrusive town merchant by provoking him into a gunfight. The sheriff hears the gunshot and enters the scene. He asks the assembled crowd what had happened, and they relate the story. The sheriff then takes the villain into custody and removes him to the city jail.

Back at the scene of the shooting, usually in a tavern, an individual stands up on a table (this individual by definition is a Demagogue) and exhorts the crowd to take the law into its own hands and lynch the villain. The group decides that this is the course of action that they should take (notice that the group now becomes a democracy where the majority rules) and down the street they (now called a mob) go. They reach the jail and demand that the villain be released to their custody. The mob has spoken by majority vote: the villain must hang.

The sheriff appears before the democracy and explains that the villain has the right to a trial by jury. The demagogue counters by explaining that the majority has spoken: the villain must hang. The sheriff explains that his function is to protect the rights of the individual, be he innocent or guilty, until that individual has the opportunity to defend himself in a court of law. The sheriff continues by explaining that the will of the majority cannot deny this individual that right. The demagogue continues to exhort the democracy to lynch the villain, but if the sheriff is persuasive and convinces the democracy that he exists to protect their rights as well, the scene should end as the people leave, convinced of the merits of the arguments of the sheriff.

The republican form of government has triumphed over the democratic form of mob action.

In summary, the sheriff represents the republic, the demagogue the control of the democracy, and the mob the democracy. The republic recognizes that man has certain inalienable rights and that government is created to protect those rights, even from the acts of a majority. Notice that the republic must be persuasive in front of the democracy and that the republic will only continue to exist as long as the people recognize the importance and validity of the concept. Should the people wish to overthrow the republic and the sheriff, they certainly have the power (but not the right) to do so.

But the persuasive nature of the republic's arguments should convince the mob that it is the preferable form of government.

There is another example of the truths of this assertion. It is reported in the Bible.

The republic, in the form of the Roman government, "washed its hands of the matter" after finding the accused Jesus innocent of all charges, and turned Him over to the democracy, which later crucified Him.

It is easy to see how a democracy can turn into anarchy when unscrupulous individuals wish to manipulate it. The popular beliefs of the majority can be turned into a position of committing some injustice against an individual or a group of individuals. This then becomes the excuse for the unscrupulous to grab total power, all in an effort to "remedy the situation."

Alexander Hamilton was aware of this tendency of a democratic form of government to be torn apart by itself, and he has been quoted as writing: "We are now forming a republican government. Real liberty is not found in the extremes of democracy, but in moderate governments. If we incline too much to democracy, we shall soon shoot into a monarchy (or some other form of dictatorship.)"

Others were led to comment on the perils of a democratic form of government. One was James Madison who wrote: "In all cases where a majority are united by a common interest or passion, the rights of the minority are in danger!"[3] Another was John Adams who wrote: "Unbridled passions produce the same effects, whether in a king, nobility, or a mob. The experience of all mankind has proved the prevalence of a disposition to use power wantonly. It is therefore as necessary to defend an individual against the majority (in a democracy) as against the king in a monarchy."[4]

In a democracy then, Might makes Right.
In a republic, Right makes Might.
In a democracy, the law restricts the people.
In a republic, the law restricts the government.

When Moses of the Bible carried the Ten Commandments down to the people, they were written on stone. The majority of the people did not vote to accept them. They were offered as the truth, and were in stone to teach the people that they couldn't change them by majority vote. But the people rejected the Commandments anyway, just as they can reject the principles of the republican form of government should they choose to do so.

America's founding fathers, while not writing the laws in stone, did attempt to restrict man's ability to tamper with them. The rules for revising or amending the Constitution are rigidly set out in the provisions of the Constitution itself.

George Washington, in his farewell address to the American people as he was leaving the presidency, spoke about the amending of the Constitution:

> If in the opinion of the people, the distribution or modification of the Constitutional power be in any particular wrong, let it be corrected by an amendment in the way in which the Constitution designates. But let there be no change by usurpation, for though this, in one instance, may be the instrument of good, it is the customary weapon by which free governments are destroyed.

It was about the same time that a British professor named Alexander Fraser Tyler wrote: "A democracy cannot exist as a permanent form of government. It can exist only until the voters discover they can vote themselves largess (defined as a liberal gift) out of the public treasury. From that moment on, the majority always votes for the candidate promising the most benefits from the public treasury, with the result that democracy always collapses over a loose fiscal policy, always to be followed by a dictatorship."

Here is outlined the procedure by which democratic, or even republican, forms of government can be turned into a dictatorship.

This technique of subverting a democracy into a dictatorship was spelled out in a book in 1957 by Jan Kozak, a member of the Secretariat of the Communist Party of Czechoslovakia. Mr. Kozak titled his book *How Parliament Took a Revolutionary Part in the Transition to Socialism and the Role of the Popular Masses.* The American version of his book is titled *And Not a Shot is Fired, the Communist Strategy for Subverting a Representative Government.* Mr. Kozak describes what has been called the "Pincers Movement," the method by which the conspirators can use the parliament, the "Pressure from Above," and the mob, the "Pressure from Below," to convert a democracy into a dictatorship. Mr. Kozak explained his strategy:

> A preliminary condition for carrying out fundamental social changes and for making it possible that parliament be made use of for the purpose of transforming a capitalistic society into a socialistic one, is:
>
> a. to fight for a firm parliamentary majority which would ensure and develop a strong 'pressure from above,' and
>
> b. to see to it that this firm parliamentary majority should rely on the revolutionary activity of the broad working masses exerting 'pressure from below.'[5]

What Mr. Kozak proposed was a five part program to seize control of a government.

The first step consisted of having the conspiracy's own people infiltrate the government (the "pressure from above.")

The second step was to create a real or alleged grievance, usually through either an action of government or through some situation where the government should have acted and didn't.

The third step consisted in having a mob created by the real or alleged grievance that the government or the conspiracy caused demand that the problem be solved by a governmental action (the "pressure from below.")

The fourth step consisted in having the conspirators in the government remedy the real or alleged sitiuation with some oppressive legislation.

The fifth step is a repeat of the last three. The legislation that the government passes does not solve the problem and the mob demands more and more legislation until the government becomes totalitarian in nature by possessing all of the power.

And total power was the goal of those causing the grievance. The plan is, as Nesta Webster wrote in her book *World Revolution*: "the systematic attempt to create grievances in order to exploit them."[6]

This technique was used, with a slight variation, by Adolf Hitler, who sent his own party loyalists into the streets (the "Pressure from Below") to create the terror that he blamed on the government (the "Pressure from Above.") The German people, told by Hitler that the government in power couldn't end the terror even though they passed oppressive legislation in an effort to stop it, listened to the one man who was offering relief: Adolf Hitler. He was in a position to stop the terror. He was the one causing it! And therefore he could end it! And he promised that he would end it when he was given the power of government!

The people believed Hitler and voted him into office. And once in office, he called in his party loyalists and the terror ended, just like he promised. Hitler appeared to be a hero: he did what he said he would.

There are some who saw this strategy at work in the passing of the Eighteenth Amendment ("Prohibition") to the Constitution. If the creation of an organized crime syndicate was the reason for the passage of this Amendment, then what happened makes sense.

Anyone who knew human nature realized that the Amendment would not cause the drinking of liquor to stop: it would only make drinking illegal. And the American people responded by purchasing their liquor from those willing to risk penalties and fines for selling illegal liquor. The more that the government clamped down on the illegal sale of liquor, the more they played into the hands of those who wished to create a crime syndicate. The more the pressure on those selling the liquor, the more the price went up. The more the price went up, the more unscrupulous became the seller of the liquor. The more unscrupulous the seller, the more crime in the streets. The more crime in the streets, the more pressure on the sellers of the liquor. Finally, only the most ruthless survived. And the price of liquor was raised even higher because of the risk involved in selling it.

The American people thought that the crime syndicate that survived the government's pressure would cease after Prohibition was repealed. But they stayed, much to the continued distress of the American people.

Some very well-known Americans benefited from Prohibition. In fact: "Frank Costello, the so-called 'Prime Minister of the Underworld' . . . informed Peter Maas, author of *The Valachi Papers* that he and Joseph Kennedy (the father of the late President, John Kennedy) were partners in the liquor business."[7]

This startling connection between organized crime and the father of the late President was confirmed in an article in *Parade* Magazine on November 16, 1980.

A more current example of this technique was used by those who wanted to prolong the Vietnamese War. This strategy was used throughout the war with extreme effectiveness.

One of the truths of the economic system under which America operates is that the name on the bottom line of the payroll check is the employer, and the name on the top line is the employee. As long as the employee continues to perform as requested by the employer, the employee continues getting payroll checks. When the employee ceases to perform as requested, the checks are no longer issued.

The same principle applies in the funding of the public universities during the Vietnamese War.

A good percentage of the anti-government, anti-Vietnamese War protestors came from the college campuses in the United States. These schools were heavily financed by the very government that the college students were protesting against.

Yet the funding from the federal government continued. In other words, the employee (the schools) were producing a product (the anti-war protestors) that was pleasing to the employer (the federal government.) And as long as the schools kept producing a product pleasing to the employer, the checks continued.

Is it possible that the government, acting as the "pressure from above," intentionally funded schools because it wanted these schools to produce anti-government dissidents, the "pressure from below?"

Is it possible that the government's purpose was to prolong the war? Is it possible that this was the method by which the American people were conditioned to support the "no-win" strategy of America's involvement in the war?

The American people, until at least the Korean War, believed that our government should first avoid wars, but once in one, they believed the government should win and then leave. But the government's strategy during the Vietnamese War was never to win but to find ways to prolong the war, and the anti-war protestors were created for that purpose.

The strategy was simple. The public was told by the major media that covered every meeting of three or more anti-war protestors, that to oppose the war was un-American. The protestors were to do everything to discredit the American flag, the nation, and the military. To do this they burned the flag, used obscenities, and carried the flag of the enemy, the Viet Cong. All of these activities were calculated to tell the American people that there were only two choices in the war:

1. Support your government in whatever action they might take in the war; or
2. Join the protestors in objecting to the war by burning the flag, using obscenities, and carrying the flag of the enemy.

Another slogan made popular during the war was: "Your country: love it or leave it."

There were only two options being offered: either support your government in its "no-win" strategy, or leave the country. The traditional goal of America's strategy in a war, victory, was not being offered as an alternative.

The most glaring, although not commonly understood, example of the "no-win" war strategy, was the use of the "peace" sign, made by extending the first two fingers into a "V." This gesture was first made popular during World War II by Winston Churchill who meant the symbol to mean "victory." (No one ever explained what the letter "V" had to do with the word "peace," but it didn't matter, as it was intended to cause the American people to think of "peace" and not "victory" in the Vietnamese war.)

The strategy worked. The American people allowed the various administrations involved to wage the war without the goal of a victory, and the war continued for about ten years.

It is a well known fact that the quickest and surest path to victory in any war is to deny the enemy the materials he needs to wage the war. In 1970, the world's largest petition drive focused on the fact that America was supplying Russia with strategic military items while Russia was supplying eighty percent of North Vietnam's war materials. This petition drive was supported by the signatures of around four million Americans, yet it hardly received any press coverage. As the petitions were assembled, they were sent to U.S. congressmen and senators, but nothing was done, and the aid and trade to Russia continued. There was no question in the minds of those who circulated the petitions that the war would have been over in a very short time if this aid and trade stopped.

The strategy worked. The American people, no longer offered a victory as an alternative, and turned off by the protestors who urged them to end the war, supported their government's "no-win" strategy, and the war kept grinding on, killing and injuring scores of American fighting men and women, as well as countless Vietnamese on both sides of the war.

Others have become aware of Kozak's strategy and have used it in a beneficial manner. One such individual explained the method in 1965:

1. Non-violent demonstrators go into the streets;
2. Racists unleash violence against them;
3. Americans demand federal legislation;
4. The administration initiates measures of immediate intervention and remedial legislation.

The author of those words was Martin Luther King, Jr., who wrote them in an article in *Saturday Review*.[8] It appears that Mr. King somehow had heard of Jan Kozak's book, as the methods are nearly identical. Those who have studied Mr. King's background before he became America's Civil Rights leader are certain that Mr. King was in a position to have read and studied Kozak's book itself. The Augusta, Georgia, *Courier* of July 8, 1963, printed a picture of Mr. King at the Highlander Folk School in Monteagle, Tennessee during the Labor Day weekend of 1957. This school had an interesting history. After King visited there, the school was closed by the Tennessee Legislature in 1960 after having conducted hearings into its true nature. The school was cited as being a "meeting place for known Communists and fellow travelers," and as a "Communist Training School."[9]

Mr. King's association with the Communists and the Communist Party was not restricted to just those he met during the weekend at the Folk School, as Communists virtually surrounded him as he planned his civil rights activities. The Reverend Uriah J. Fields, the Negro clergyman who was King's secretary during the early stages of the bus boycott that made King famous, wrote this about those associated with him: "King helps to advance communism. He is surrounded with Communists. This is the major reason I severed my relationship with him during the fifties. He is soft on communism."[10]

Another who supported the assertion that the Communists were involved in the activities of Mr. King was Karl Prussion, a former counterspy for the Federal Bureau of Investigation. Mr. Prussion testified in 1963 after attending Communist Party meetings in California for five years: "I further swear and attest that at each and every one of the aforementioned meetings, one Reverend Martin Luther King was always set forth as the individual to whom Communists should look and rally around in the Communist struggle on the many racial issues."[11]

So Mr. King certainly had the opportunity to read the book by Jan Kozak, and he was surrounded by those who certainly should have been familiar with the method of this Communist strategist. And King even put the strategy on paper for all to see.

The purpose of the Civil Rights movement was best summarized by a comment made by two of the past presidents of the American Bar Association, Loyd Wright and John C. Satterfield. They once wrote the following about the Civil Rights Bill, one of the major "accomplishments" of the Civil Rights movement: "It is ten percent civil rights and ninety percent extension of Federal executive power. The 'civil rights' aspect of this legislation is but a cloak; uncontrolled Federal Executive power is the body."[12]

So King's major purpose was to increase the role of the government in the everyday lives of the American people.

Chapter 4
Economic Terms

It will be helpful at this point for certain economic terms to be defined to assist the reader in understanding the Conspiratorial View of History.

Two of these terms are:

Consumption Good: goods acquired for consumption purposes (food, drink, etc.)
Capital Good: goods utilized for producing consumption goods

The distinction between these two economic terms can be illustrated by the use of a simple example, such as a primitive tribesman living in a remote jungle. His diet consists of the rabbit (a Consumption Good) which first must be caught before it can be consumed. The tribesman quickly learns that the rabbit is exceptionally quick and that catching it for a daily meal is rather difficult. But, by using his intelligence, the tribesman fashions a crude blow-gun to assist him in acquiring the Consumption Good. The moment that the tribesman builds the blow-gun, he becomes a Capitalist, because the blow-gun is a Capital Good: it is created to assist the tribesman in acquiring Consumption Goods.

Therefore, it is possible now to define Capitalism as:

Capitalism: any economic system that utlizes Capital Goods in acquiring or producing Consumption Goods

Notice that by this definition even the most primitive economic systems are Capitalist if they choose to utilize Capital Goods in meeting their Consumption Good needs.

It follows logically, then, that the blow-gun is only effective when the tribesman agrees to use it, and that without his efforts the blow-gun is a meaningless wooden tube. The tribesman gives utility to the blow-gun only by using it.

It follows then, that the acquisition of Consumption Goods is not dependent on Capital Goods alone, but by someone using the Capital Goods. Human effort is the key ingredient in any Capitalistic economy. Without human effort, there will be no Consumption Goods produced.

Should the tribesman not wish to secure the needed Consumption Goods by use of the Capital Goods, he and all those dependent on his efforts will go hungry. Increasing the number of Capital Goods, or blow-guns, will in no way alleviate the problem. The only way to produce Consumption Goods is for the individual to decide to utilize the Capital Goods for that purpose, and that without that human decision, there will be nothing produced.

The ultimate Capitalistic society is one, then, where all things become Capital Goods, including the individual efforts of all of the individual workers who comprise the society. The individual himself becomes the ultimate Capital Good, for without his efforts, there will be no Consumption Goods produced.

It follows logically for some, unfortunately, that the society has the right to make certain that efforts are made towards the production of Consumption Goods, even if the individual members of the society do not wish to produce any.

The Soviet Union, for instance, was cited in 1974 for forcing the ultimate Capital Good, man himself, to produce against his will. The article identifying Russia's use of forced labor stated:

> The Soviet Union has been officially cited under the rules of the International Labor Organization as having failed to meet its commitment to observe the organization's ban on forced labor. . . . the failure concerns the convention, a binding international obligation, outlawing "forced or compulsory labor in all of its forms" that Moscow ratified in 1956. The panel of experts noted in a report. . . that Soviet law permitted "idlers" to be given a one year jail or "corrective labor" sentence if they refused to take a job assigned to them.[1]

Since each society needs Consumption Goods to survive, it follows that the society needs the productive efforts of all members of that society, or it will fail.

There are only two ways by which these goods can be produced: either through the use of force against the producing individuals, or through the creation of an economic environment wherein the individual is encouraged to produce the maximum quantity of Consumption Goods.

All Capitalistic societies soon discover that all Capital Goods tend to deteriorate through time and usage and therefore lose their utility. The blow-gun in the primitive society breaks or bends and becomes worthless. When this occurs, the tribesman must discard the useless Capital Good and construct a replacement.

But other Capital Goods, humans themselves, also lose their utility. They grow tired, old or become injured. There are societies today that also discard tired, old and injured human Capital Goods as well as old, tired or broken Capital Goods such as a broken blow-gun. One such society is the nation of Russia. A Russian native, Igor Gouzenko in his book *The Iron Curtain*, confirmed this, by writing: "Lishnetzy is the Russian word for the aged and ailing who have become the superfluous ones. . . . as an ardent young Communist I never regarded the Lishnetzy as something monstrous. It seemed practical and just to me then. As Komsonols (young Communists) . . . we had actually reached the conclusion that when one became a lishnetz (an old Capital Good), that is one condemned to this form of civic extermination, one should be duty bound to free the country of a useless consumer by having the courage to commit suicide. That opinion was nationally encouraged to such an extent that, even today, the suicide rate in Russia is higher than in any other country in the world."[2]

If Capitalism, then, is an economic system that utilizes Capital Goods to produce Consumption Goods, what is the difference between the Communist system and the Capitalistic system in the United States? Both systems utilize the same type of Capital Goods: the factories, the railroads, and the other factors of production.

The difference is not in the existence of these Capital Goods, it is the ownership of the goods. In the Communist system, the state owns the Capital Goods, and in the Free Enterprise system, a better name for America's economic system, the individuals own the Capital Goods.

In brief, the difference between the two systems can be summarized thus:

Economic System	Capital Goods	
	Owned By:	Controlled By:
Free Enterprise	private owners	private owners
Communism	the state	the state

Control of the factors of production is equally as important as owner-ship: ownership of an automobile is meaningless if someone else drives (controls) it.

But there is an economic system not included in the above definitions: the system where the individual private owner owns the factors of produc-tion, but the state controls them. This system is called Fascism. It can be added to the above summary as follows:

Economic System	Capital Goods Owned By:	Controlled By:
Free Enterprise	private owners	private owners
Fascism	private owners	the state
Socialism	the state	the state

Perhaps the most well-known advocate of the Fascist economic system was the titular head of the Italian government just prior to and during World War II, Benito Mussolini. It has been said that Premier Mussolini, a dedicated Socialist, did not wish to oppose the Roman Catholic Church and the Pope, both housed inside the territory of Italy, and feared that the Church would officially oppose any economic system not favored by the hierarchy of the Church. It was well known that the Church had long opposed any form of Socialism (the ownership and control of property by the state) so Musso-lini, aware that control is equally as important as ownership, asked the Catholic population of Italy to support the compromise that he offered: Fascism, the economic system where the Catholic population could legally own their property, in accordance with the wishes of the Pope and the Church, but where the state would control it. The net effect, as Mussolini knew, was still the same as offered by the Socialists: the state would own the factors of production through control of the factors of production. ". . . Fas-cism recognizes the legal right to private ownership. . . . Such ownership still means little in practice, for the state can and does tell the owner what to produce, what prices to charge, and what to do with the profits."[3]

Those who advocate that the Capital Goods should be owned or controlled by the state frequently justify their position by declaring that they are doing so in the name of the poor, the workers, the aged, or any other minority deemed to be voiceless in the society and hence unable to be in a position to own any Capital Goods. However, those who lose sight of man's God-given right to own property also fail to see the connection between the right to private property and the right to one's own life. It is the Socialists/Communists who support the state's right to own all Capital Goods. In addition, they also support the right of the state to divide the property between those who have varying amounts of goods. Once this process starts, the state must decide who is to receive the society's surplus. It then logically follows that the state has the right to terminate the lives of those that the state feels are not worthy of receiving their share of the surplus.

One who took great care in pointing this position out in detail was George Bernard Shaw, a leading Socialist of his day. Mr. Shaw wrote a book entitled *The Intelligent Woman's Guide to Socialism* in which he detailed his concern about this problem:

> I also made it quite clear that Socialism means equality of income or nothing, and under Socialism you would not be allowed to be poor.
>
> You would be forcibly fed, clothed, lodged, taught, and employed whether you like it or not. If it were discovered that you had not the character and industry enough to be worth all this trouble, you might be executed in a kindly manner, but whilst you were permitted to live, you would have to live well.[4]

The Socialist government would permit all to live (their right to life becomes a privilege) only so long as the government felt each was worth "all the trouble." But should the government feel that the individual's value had decreased, the government would terminate that individual's life in an unspecified "kindly manner."

Mr. Shaw also connected the economic philosophy of Socialism with the truth that human labor is essential to the production of all Capital Goods, and that those who do not produce have no right to life, when he wrote: "Compulsory labour with death as the final victory is the keystone of Socialism."[5]

In the Socialist scheme of things, the individual is not to be free, and it is not intended that he be free. Karl Kautsky, to this day one of the leading theoreticians of the Socialist position, wrote: "Socialist production is not compatible with liberty of work, that is to say, with the worker's freedom to work when or how he likes. In a socialist society, all the means of production will be concentrated in the hands of the state, and the latter will be the only employer; there will be no choice."[6]

Proof that Kautsky's argument can become official government policy lies in what happened in the Socialist country of Germany, just prior to the beginning of World War II: "No German worker could change his job without obtaining permission, while if he absented himself from work without proper excuse, he was liable to imprisonment."[7]

Obviously, this type of government is not popular with the working class, the supposed benefactor of the economic philosophy of Socialism, so the strategy became one of deceiving the worker so that the Socialism that the worker is induced to support in theory is different from the Socialism that the worker would experience once the Socialists came to power. The problem exists in how to conceal this truth from the worker. Norman Thomas, the Socialist Party presidential candidate for about twenty years, and the leading Socialist in the United States prior to his death, said: "The American people will never knowingly adopt Socialism, but under the name of Liberalism they will adopt every fragment of the Socialist program until one day America will be a Socialist nation without knowing how it happened."[8]

Mr. Thomas was never successful in his quest for the Presidency as an identified Socialist, but he was extremely pleased with Socialist progress nevertheless. The American people were buying his Socialist ideas by electing others not publicly identified as Socialists, but who supported the economic and political ideas of the Socialist Party. Thomas wrote: ". . . Here in America more measures once praised or denounced as socialist have been adopted than once I should have thought possible short of a socialist victory at the polls."[9] "The United States is making greater strides towards Socialism under Eisenhower than even under Roosevelt."[10] Most people would agree that President Roosevelt gave the American government more control over and ownership of the factors of production than any other president, but few would feel that President Eisenhower did more than Roosevelt. Yet the Socialist candidate for President praised the "non-Socialist, pro free-enterprise" Dwight Eisenhower for his support of Socialist programs. This means that Socialism has been concealed from the American people. That the American people are being lied to by those who could be called "closet Socialists." Someone once described the deception as: "One way they look, another way they steer." The strategy is to promise the American people one thing and to deliver another. Never make it appear that you, the candidate, are supporting socialism or are a Socialist, even though the platforms you will support after your election are indeed socialist in nature. And you must never deliver so much socialism that the American people will discover the exact nature of the game and remove you from office.

Arthur Schlesinger Jr., a noted historian, outlined the program of giving the American people their socialism in gradual doses: "If socialism is to preserve democracy, it must be brought about step by step in a way which will not disrupt the fabric of custom, law and mutual confidence. . . . There seems no inherent obstacle in the gradual advance of socialism in the United States through a series of new deals . . . ."[11]

The reason the socialists must deceive the unsuspecting citizen was made clear by the London, England, *Sunday Times* which stated that Socialism was defined as: "competition without prizes, boredom without hope, war without victory, and statistics without end."[12]

In other words, most people don't want Socialism and they don't wish to live under the Socialist economy, so the Socialists must resort to trickery and deception, by a series of lies offered to the people by lying politicians.

For the sake of the purist, is there any difference between Socialism and Communism? The absence of any essential differences was explained thus: "There is no economic difference between socialism and communism. Both terms . . . denote the same system. . . . public control of the means of production as distinct from private control. The two terms, socialism and communism, are synonyms."

This position was confirmed by no less a Communist luminary than Marshal Tito, the now deceased dictator of the Yugoslavian Communist government, who said: "Communism is simply state capitalism in which the state has absolute ownership of everything including all the efforts of the people."[13]

Notice that Marshal Tito has confirmed that everything, including the efforts of the people, becomes a Capital Good under Communism. Perhaps this is the sole difference between these two economic systems: the Communists readily admit that the human itself is a Capital Good, and the Socialist conceals it. But in both systems, the individual and all he produces belongs to the state.

Most Communists have made this point abundantly clear in their writings. Karl Marx, the so-called "father of modern Communism," once wrote: "From each according to his ability, to each according to his needs."[14]

This basic tenet of Communism has become a principle of the Russian Constitution, which states: "Article 12: In the U.S.S.R. work is a duty and a matter of honor for every able bodied citizen in accordance with the principle: 'He who does not work shall not eat.' The principle applied in the U.S.S.R. is that of Socialism: 'From each according to his ability, to each according to his work.'[15]

It is interesting that the last word of Marx's dictum has been changed from "need" to "work." Notice that if one doesn't work, one doesn't eat. How does this system provide for those unable to work? This question has been answered by others, one of whom has stated that these individuals would be "executed in a kindly manner." Others have suggested that they should commit suicide (become a "lishnetzy.") In other words, to restate the principle, when a Capital Good becomes unable to produce, it is discarded, even if that Capital Good is a human being.

Once the Socialist/Communist decides that the state exists to divide Consumption Goods and Capital Goods, then it behooves him to involve himself with politics. Sam Brown, President Jimmy Carter's director of ACTION, the voluntary agency, is one who has discovered this truth. He said: "Politics is a struggle to redistribute power and wealth."[16]

Notice that Mr. Brown admitted that this political process of goods redistribution is a "struggle," which means that some will not want to give up their property. Since Mr. Brown didn't say, one can only wonder what Mr. Brown wished to do with those who resisted.

Another "closet communist" who agrees with those who feel government exists to divide surplus goods, wrote the following: "We are going to try to take all of the money that we think is unnecessarily being spent and take it from the 'haves' and give it to the 'have-nots' that need it so much."[17]

Notice that this statement is nearly identical with that of the Communist Karl Marx who wrote: "From each according to his ability, to each according to his need." Only the words have been changed. That means that the speaker, the "closet communist," supported the Marxist philosophy that government exists to take from one to give to another. Those who know President Lyndon Johnson, the speaker of the words above, and his "Great Society," know that this was indeed his goal: to redistribute wealth from the wealthy to the poor. Few, however, will dare to compare Johnson's governmental philosophy with the writings and teachings of Marx. But the comparison is inevitable: the action and its results are the same, no matter whether it is called the "Great Society," or Marxist Communism. Both seek to use government to divide wealth. But it is not fashionable to favorably compare the two by noticing the similarity between the "Great Society" and the teachings of Karl Marx.

Sometimes the support of this Marxist philosophy about the purpose of government comes from the "respectable right," from those the observer would never suspect of being a "closet communist."

Take, for instance, the thoughts on this subject from two respectable "right wing Conservatives." One has written: "Congress shall appropriate funds for social welfare only for the benefit of those states whose per capita income is below the national average."[18] This writer advocated a newer brand of Marxism: "From each *state* according to its ability, to each *state* according to its needs." (emphasis added.) This writer advocated that the national government divide the wealth, taking it from the wealthier states and giving it to the less productive. Pure Marxism, except the writer involved both the state and the federal governments rather than just the federal government as Marx envisioned. This is only expanding Marx one step: the result is the same. Property is distributed by the government just as before. The shock is that this new thought came from the pen of William F. Buckley, Jr., hardly a paragon of Marxism. But notice that Buckley's intent is the same as that of Marx: to use government to redistribute Consumption and Capital Goods.

Another method of income redistribution by government was proposed by another respected member of the "Conservative Right." His proposal is called the Negative Income Tax, which would use the Income Tax as a method of redistributing wealth. Under this proposal, the poverty level individual would have but to show his non-income on the Income Tax form, and the government would take some of the taxes paid by the more prosperous tax-payers, and give it to the poorer individual in the form of an income tax "refund." The utilization of the income tax as a vehicle to divide wealth apparently must satisfy the concern of those who wish to use government as an income distributor, but do not wish to become associated with the Marxist "Left" which openly advocates Marxist theories. In other words, if it bothers the listener to be recognized as a supporter of the preachings of an open Marxist, he might find relief by supporting the proposals of a member of the "Conservative Right," Professor Milton Friedman, the "Free Enterprise Economist," who proposed the Negative Income Tax.

Sometimes a member of the clergy becomes involved in the subject of income distribution. Here is the statement of a Pope, in this case Pope Paul VI, who wrote the following at Easter, 1967: "But nowadays, no country can keep its wealth just for itself alone. It should be normal, now, for the developed nations to help the under-developed with some agreed percentage of their additional income."[19] Here the Pope speaks in favor of a national income distribution program where one country taxes itself for the benefit of another nation in accordance with the principle: "From each *nation* according to its ability, to each *nation* according to its need." (emphasis added.)

But the American people must never fear or despair: the American government will save them from this creeping Socialism.

"Administration opens battle on socialism" reads the headline of an article written on January 26, 1975. The article explained: "Concerned about what it fears is a national drift toward socialism, the Ford (President Gerald Ford) administration is mounting a major campaign to restrain the growth in Social Security benefits and other income redistribution programs."[20]

The writer of the article informed the reader that the purpose of the Social Security program was "...income redistribution." One must honestly admire the cleverness of the administration in concealing this fact from those who have believed that it was intended to be a retirement plan for those of the working population who reached retirement age. The article went on to point out that the concern of the Ford administration was that the spending for Social Security would rise to where it would be one-half of the total Gross National Product. If this happened, the United States would be irreversibly on the road toward a controlled economy. (Fascism.)

The ultimate purpose of all income redistribution schemes is people control. This was graphically illustrated by Leon Trotsky, one of the founders of the Communist government in Russia in 1917, who wrote: "In a country where the sole employer is the State, opposition (to the State) means death by slow starvation. The old principle... 'who does not work shall not eat' has been replaced by a new one . . . 'who does not obey shall not eat.' "[21]

The ultimate Communism is total control over all mankind. All of the efforts of the people belong to the state and if the worker does not produce, he will be slowly starved unto submission, or unto death. Here the difference between Socialism and Communism shows itself in the attitude of what to do with the unwilling worker: the Socialist wishes to execute him in a "kindly manner," while the Communist wishes to slowly starve him to death. It is hardly a difference worth debating.

The socialist machine slowly climbs the ladder to total control of the market place. The next logical step in the climb is to have the state become the final employer of all workmen and for that state to issue a "worker's card" so that the government can say who shall have the privilege of working. Without the card, the worker cannot find work. Leon Trotsky didn't recommend a card, apparently, but he certainly would have supported the concept as being consistent with the principle: "who does not obey shall not eat."

The proposal for a work card issued to the American people was the idea of Benjamin Civiletti, former President Jimmy Carter's Attorney General, according to an Associated Press article of June 28, 1980. The article read "Civiletti urges 'card for all U.S. workers.' Attorney General Benjamin R. Civiletti yesterday said he favored requiring Americans and aliens in this country to carry a 'work card' in order to apply for a job."[22]

If the American citizen doesn't obtain a card, the American citizen doesn't work. And if the American citizen doesn't work, the American citizen starves.

Others have continued the thought that the national government should issue a worker identification card. *The Arizona Daily Star* of March 25, 1981 carried an article with the following headline: "(Senator Dennis) DeConcini (Democrat from Arizona) 'not averse' to national worker ID to curb alien influx."[23]

The article went on to detail that various senators were supporting legislation that would require an identification card for all Americans that would do away with the "tremendous benefits there are in coming over here illegally."

The bill would require the possessor of the card to show it when applying for a job. The illegal alien would presumably not have the card, and therefore would not be able to get a job, according to the reasoning of those who support the legislation. How they would handle the problem of those Americans who did not feel it was Constitutional for the American government to issue such a card was not answered by the article. What would happen to those dissenters is apparently not worthy of an explanation.

An article that appeared on March 21, 1982, should be of interest to those supporters of President Ronald Reagan who are certain that their "conservative" President would never allow such an unConstitutional abomination as the national ID card. The article was entitled: "Reagan 'open' to national ID card," and included this comment: "It was the first time the Reagan administration had indicated it is not opposed to plans for creating a nationwide identity card to deal with illegal immigration."[24]

So now the American people can begin to understand why the United States government is not doing more to prohibit the immigration of millions of illegal aliens. The problem of illegal immigration serves to justify the "solution" which is a national ID card. The American people must have an identification card and the borders must come down so that there will be a reason for the issuance of the card.

The Vietnamese Communists apparently do not have an illegal immigration problem so they avoided all of the formality of the issuance of cards to their workers. They just resorted to the use of the radio to broadcast the following work order: "All citizens who have the strength and the ability to work must absolutely carry out the state mobilization orders, and serve in any capacity or any mission assigned to them by the state. Those who do not want to work or do not carry out the state's orders will be forced to carry out work in order to be useful to our society."[25]

One of the North Vietnamese generals during the war made it clear that the Communists have nothing but disdain for human life. He is quoted as saying: "Every minute hundreds of thousands of people are dying all over the world. The life or death of a hundred or a thousand or tens of thousands of human beings even if they are our own compatriots really represents very little."[26]

Fortunately for those who love their freedoms eloquent spokesmen occasionally arise to oppose the intrusion of government into every aspect of human life, and their words are terse and to the point. One such spokesman was Thomas Jefferson, who wrote the following: "That government is best that governs least."

And for every such advocate there arises an equally eloquent spokesman for more and more government intrusion. Take for instance, the following statement of a former U.S. Senator, Joseph Clark:

> The size, range and complexity of government increases, and will likely continue to do so.... I would defend the proposition that this expansion is good not bad.
>
> Surely we have reached the point where we can say, for our time at least, that Jefferson was wrong: that government is not best which governs least....

The fallacy in Jefferson's argument is the assumption that the expansion of government leads to curtailment of individual freedoms.

That just is not true.[27]

This position was further expanded by the Ford Foundation, which in 1969 published a "think piece" entitled *Planning and Participation*, in which it declared: "The world is too complex for an abatement of government powers. If anything, the role of government must be strengthened...."[28]

And so we have those who wish to extend the government's control into all aspects of human activity and those who wish to reduce it.

The remaining chapters deal with this battle.

And with those who are winning.

Chapter 5
Inflation

Inflation:
- — allows you to carry money in a basket, and your goods in a wallet!
- — allows you to live in a more expensive neighborhood without moving!
- — is the price we pay for all the government benefits we thought were free!

These rather humorless phrases about inflation do not answer the only question worth asking about the subject: What causes it?

Everyone agrees that inflation is a drop in the value of money (any given amount of money buys less). But that understanding doesn't answer the question of what causes it.

The traditional definition of Inflation is as follows: "... a rise in the general level of prices." Its causes are three in number: 1. When consumers, businesses and governments spend too heavily on available goods and services, this high demand can force prices up. 2. If costs of production rise and producers try to maintain profit levels, prices must increase. 3. The lack of competition between producers can also contribute to inflation.[1]

It appears by this definition that everything causes inflation! But whatever it is that causes it, there is little one can do to prevent it. One who felt this way was Federal Reserve Chairman Arthur Burns who said the following in 1974: "Inflation cannot be halted this year."[2]

One of the reasons no one can supposedly prevent inflation is because Inflation is part of the Inflation-Deflation cycle. At least this is the opinion of one economist: "Nikolai Dimitriyevich Kondratyev, Soviet economist-... believes that capitalistic economies naturally follow long term cycles: first a few decades of prosperity, then a few decades of slump."[3] (An interesting contemporary example that brought Kondratyev's cyclical theory into question occurred recently in Chile, the South American country that voted Marxist Salvador Allende into office in 1970. Under Allende's Communist government inflation reached 652 percent a year, and the Wholesale Price Index rose by a staggering 1,147 percent a year. That meant that wholesale prices were doubling every month.[4] After a coup ousted Allende in 1973, and the Pinochet administration changed the government's direction, inflation dropped to less than 12 percent a year and the Wholesale Price Index actually fell. It is doubtful that Chile's successful reduction in the inflation rate can be attributed to a long-term cycle!)

Another economist believes that America's lifestyle is the major cause of inflation. Alfred E. Kahn "... the nation's new chief inflation fighter has named his foe: every American's desire for economic improvement.... The desire of each group with power or instruments to improve its economic situation... is after all what the problem of inflation is."[5] The solution, then, is a "Smaller piece of the pie." "The living standard of Americans must decline if inflation is to be controlled, says... Peter Emerson... a key aide to Alfred Kahn."[6]

No matter what the cause of inflation, one thing for certain is that it is never caused by government, at least according to President Jimmy Carter, who said: "It is a myth that government itself can stop inflation."[7]

Congress has a typical solution to the problem: impose wage and price controls on rising wages and prices. And it seems that these measures never work. Is it possible that the reason Congress can't control inflation is that Congress is not aware of its real cause? Is it possible that they are attacking the effect of inflation, and not the cause? The attempt to end inflation by the imposition of wage and price controls is not an new idea. (In fact, neither is inflation!) Free market Economist Murray N. Rothbard has gone on record as saying: "From the Roman Emperor Diocletian down to the American and French Revolutions and to Richard Nixon from 1971 to 1974, governments have tried to stop inflation by imposing wage and price controls. None of these schemes have worked."[8]

The reason wage and price controls do not work, and have never worked, lies in the simple fact that they attack the effect of inflation and not the cause. The proof that this statement is true can be found in a simple definition found in a dictionary. *Webster's 3rd Unabridged Dictionary* defines inflation thus: "An increase in the volume of money and credit relative to available goods resulting in a substantial and continuing rise in the general price level."

Inflation is *caused* by an increase in money (credit is a result of increases in the supply of money and for the sake of this discussion, money shall be the sole cause of inflation.)

The result of inflation is a price rise.

Another dictionary, this time the *Webster's Collegiate*, defines inflation thus: "Relatively sharp and sudden increase in the quantity of money, or credit, or both, relative to the amount of exchange business. Inflation always causes a rise in the price level." The cause of inflation, an increase in the money supply, *always* produces a price rise. Inflating the money supply always increases prices. This is an economic law: the effect of a money supply increase will always be the same.

In summary, then, inflation has both a cause and an effect:

Cause: an increase in money

Effect: a rise in prices

Now it is possible to see why wage and price controls do not work: they attack the effect (the price rise) and not the cause (the increase in the money supply.)

An example of how Inflation is caused could be offered by the use of a simple model.

Suppose that sea shells are used as money on Island A, and that the prices on the island are determined by the number of shells in circulation. As long as the quantity of shells remains relatively constant and there is no rapid increase, prices will remain relatively stable. Suppose that some of the more adventurous islanders row over to a nearby island and collect a large quantity of sea shells, identically the same as those in circulation as money on the main island. When these additional sea shells are brought back to Island A and put into circulation as money, they will cause an increase in the price level. More sea shells (money) will enable each islander to bid up the price of any given good. If the islander has more money, he can afford to pay a higher price for the product he wishes to purchase.

There are certain elements in society that wish to increase the money supply for their own benefit at the expense of the other members. These people are called "counterfeiters," and are punished for their crime when discovered. They are punished because their counterfeiting of extra supplies of money decreases the value of the legitimate money held by the members of that society. They have the illegal and immoral power to cause inflation by increasing the money supply, causing the value of the other money to drop. This activity, the counterfeiting, is actually a crime against property, the money of the society, and the citizens have the legal and moral right to seek an end to this destruction of their private property, their money.

How is it possible for inflations to persist if those who have the ability to counterfeit are punished by the public for their crime? The solution for the counterfeiters lies in making it legal to counterfeit money. Those who counterfeit can really reap the benefits for their crime if they can get control of the government and make their crime legal. The government has the ability to make even counterfeit money "legal tender" (requiring all citizens of the nation to accept the counterfeit money along with the legal money.) If government could make counterfeiting legal, there would be no crime for counterfeiting, and this became the goal of the criminals.

Those who sought to make government all powerful in the lives of their citizens soon learned that inflation could also increase the impact and scope of government as well. The marriage between the socialists and the counterfeiters was inevitable. Nobel Peace Prize winner and economist Friederich von Hayek detailed this relationship thus: Inflation is probably the most important single factor in the vicious circle wherein one kind of government action makes more and more government control necessary."

The government-and-inflation circle could be described also in terms of the "Pincers Movement" described by Kozak. The bottom of the pincer is the price rise, the result of the Inflation (the legal counterfeiting of the new money,) caused by the top of the pincer, the government. The people, sensitive to the rise in the prices, start demanding that the government take some remedial action to put a stop to the inflation, and government, informing the public that more government action is the solution to the inflation problem, passes the legislation. The distance between the two pincer arms shortens, until the result is total government. And all of this activity is in the name of stopping inflation.

One famous economist, John Maynard Keynes, detailed the procedure in his book, *The Economic Consequences of the Peace*:

> Lenin, (the Russian Communist) is said to have declared that the best way to destroy the Capitalist system was to debauch the currency.
>
> By a continuing process of inflation, governments can confiscate, secretly and unobserved, an important part of the wealth of their citizens. By this method they not only confiscate, but they

confiscate arbitrarily, and while the process impoverishes many, it actually enriches some.

There is no subtler, no surer means of overturning the existing basis of society than to debauch the currency.

The process engages all the hidden forces of economic law on the side of destruction, and does it in a manner not one man in a million is able to diagnose.

There are several important thoughts contained in this quote from Mr. Keynes' book. Notice that the purpose of inflation, at least according to the Communist Lenin, was to destroy Capitalism. Lenin realized that inflation had the power to destroy the free market. Lenin also realized that the only agency that could cause inflation legally was the government.

Inflation was also to serve as an income redistribution system. It could impoverish those who held their assets in money, and enrich others who held their wealth in items that increased in value during periods of inflation.

Inflation, to be successful, must be concealed from those who stand to lose the most: the money holders. Concealment becomes the goal of those who do the counterfeiting. Never must the true *cause* of inflation be properly identified. Inflation must be blamed on everything: the market place, the housewife, the greedy merchant, the wage earner, the unions, oil shortages, the balance of payments, the common housefly! Anything but inflation's true cause: the increase in the money supply.

Keynes (and Lenin) admitted that the results of inflation would constantly operate in a predictable manner. Inflation was an economic law. And "not one in a million" would be able to diagnose the correct cause.

In 1978, the United States Chamber of Commerce at its annual meeting, honored Dr. Arthur Burns, the past Chairman of the Federal Reserve System, for "his contributions to the nation and the enterprise system, during his government service." The interesting thing about this event was that Dr. Burns, as the head of the Federal Reserve, controlled the growth of the money supply. He had the power to increase the money in circulation. Therefore, he was the one who was creating inflation!

Yet the major American business organization commended Dr. Burns for his efforts in preserving the free enterprise system. The very man who was causing the increase in the money supply and therefore causing the inflation that was destroying the free enterprise system was being honored by those in the free enterprise system!

Keynes and Lenin were certainly right: not one in a million would be able to diagnose the true cause of Inflation! Including the American businessman!

On page 94 of the Chamber of Commerce's magazine, *Nation's Business*, an editorial informed the reader that Dr. Burns "... has authored a broad, well-reasoned plan to turn back the inflationary threat...." But a review of the editorial and Dr. Burns' proposals indicates that nowhere did Dr. Burns mention the money supply, nor stopping the rapid increase of it! The past Chairman of the Federal Reserve writes, instead, that the causes of inflation are other than an increase in the money supply. No wonder that Dr. Burns is smiling as he accepts the award from the Chamber of Commerce. He has fooled the American business community.

Keynes also went on to explain why he agreed with Lenin that inflation is intended to destroy the business community, when he wrote: "The decadent international but individualistic capitalism, in the hands of which we found ourselves after the War (World War I) is not a success. It is not intelligent; it is not beautiful; it is not just; it is not virtuous — and it does not deliver the goods. In short, we dislike it and are beginning to despise it."[9]

If you "despise capitalism," and wish to replace the system with another that you prefer, it becomes imperative to find a way to destroy it. One of the most effective methods of destruction is inflation, the "debauching of the currency." "Lenin was certainly right."

Who is the victim of inflation? James P. Warburg correctly answered that question, when he wrote the following in his book *The West in Crises*: "In recent times perhaps the greatest enemy of a middle class society...has been inflation."[10]

Why would the middle class be the target of inflation? John Kenneth Galbraith informed the reader that inflation is a method of income redistribution: "Inflation takes from the old, the unorganized, and the poor and gives it to those who are strongly in control of their own incomes. . . . Income is reallocated from the old to the people of middle years and from the poor to the rich."[11]

So inflation has a purpose. It is not an accident! It is the tool of those who have two objectives:

1. to destroy the free enterprise system, and

2. to to take wealth from the poor and the middle class and "redistribute" it to the rich.

So inflation can now be understood. The reader is now "one in a million" able to diagnose its true cause!

Chapter 6
Money and Gold

The Bible teaches that the love of money is the root of all evil. Money by itself is not the root. It is the love of money, defined as greed, that motivates certain members of society to acquire large quantities of money.

It becomes important, then, for the members of the middle class to understand what money is and how it works. Money is defined as: "anything that people will accept in exchange for goods or services in a belief that they may in turn exchange it for other goods and services."

Money becomes a Capital Good. It is used to acquire Consumption Goods (and other Capital Goods as well.) Money also becomes a method of work avoidance. Money can work for its possessor: "When money was put to work, it worked twenty-four hours a day, seven days a week, three hundred and sixty five days a year, and stopped for no holidays."[1]

So the desire to acquire money to reduce a need to work became the motive of many individuals in the society.

The first man was self-sufficient. He produced what he wanted and stored what he needed for those times when he was unable to produce. He had no need for money until other humans appeared and joined him in the acquisition of Consumption Goods. As populations grew, specialization grew, and certain individuals produced Capital Goods instead of Consumption Goods. Man soon discovered that he needed something as a store of value to enable him to purchase Capital Goods when he was not producing Consumption Goods.

Durable commodities, those that didn't spoil with the passage of time, slowly became that store of value, and in time the most durable, a metal, became the money of society. The ultimate metal, gold, became the final store of value for a variety of reasons:

1. Gold was universally accepted; 2. it was malleable, and had the capacity to be minted into small quantities; 3. it was in short supply and difficult to locate: the quantity of gold couldn't be increased rapidly, thereby reducing its ability to be inflated;, 4. because of its scarcity, it soon acquired a high value per unit; 5. it was easily portable; 6. gold also had other uses. It could be used in jewelry, in art, and in industry; 7. lastly, gold was extremely beautiful.

But as the producer of gold saw the need to set this money aside for future use, problems arose as to how and where it should be stored. Since gold had a high value in what it could purchase in both Capital Goods and Consumption Goods, it became a temptation to those who were willing to take it from the owner by force. This led the owner of gold to take means to safeguard his holdings. Certain individuals, already experienced in the storage of non-durable goods, wheat for instance, soon became the storage facility for gold as well.

These warehouses would take the gold and issue the gold owner a warehouse receipt, certifying that the owner had a given quantity of gold in storage at the warehouse. These gold receipts could be transferred from one person to another, usually by writing on the back of the receipt that the owner was transferring his claim on the gold in the warehouse to another person. These receipts soon became money themselves as men accepted the receipts rather than the gold they represented.

Since gold is scarce and the quantity is limited, it was impossible to make counterfeit money. It was only when the warehouseman realized that he could issue more gold receipts than there was gold in the warehouse that he could become a counterfeiter. He had the ability to inflate the money supply, and the warehouseman frequently did this. But this activity only acted temporarily because as the quantity of gold receipts in circulation increased, because of the economic law known as inflation, the prices would rise. The receipt holders would start to lose confidence in their receipts and return to the warehouseman to claim their gold. When more receipt holders showed up than there was gold in the warehouse, the warehouseman had to go bankrupt, and frequently he was prosecuted for fraud. When more receipt holders ask for their gold than there is gold in the warehouse, it is called a "run," and is caused because the people have lost faith in their paper money and have demanded that the society return to the gold standard where gold becomes the money supply.

The people's check on the warehouseman, i.e. their ability to keep the warehouseman honest by constantly being able to redeem their gold receipts, acted as a restraint to the inflation of the gold supply. This limited the greed of the counterfeiters and forced them into looking for alternative methods of increasing their wealth. The next step was for the counterfeiter to ask the government to make the gold receipts "Legal Tender" and also prohibit the receipt holder from redeeming the receipt into gold. This made the paper receipt the only money able to be circulated. Gold could no longer be used as money.

But this posed an additional problem for the counterfeiter. He now had to include the government in his scheme to increase his personal wealth. The greedy leader of the government, when approached by the counterfeiter with this scheme, often decided to eliminate the warehouseman altogether ("off with his head") and operate the scheme himself. This was the final problem for the counterfeiter. He had to replace the leader with someone he felt he could trust and who would not use government to remove the counterfeiter from the plot. This process was costly and extremely risky, but the enormity of the long-term wealth that could be accumulated by this method was worth all the extra hazards.

A classic example of this entire scheme occurred between the years of 1716 and 1721 in France. These events were set in motion with the death of King Louis XIV in 1715. France was bankrupt with a large national debt of over 3 billion livres. A seedy character by the name of John Law, a convicted murderer who had escaped from Scotland to the continent, saw the plight of the French government and arranged with the newly crowned King to save his country. His plan was simple. He wanted control of a central bank with an exclusive monopoly to print money. (France at the time was under the control of the private bankers who controlled the money supply. However, France was on the gold standard, and the private bankers were unable to inflate the money supply through the issuance of more gold receipts than there was gold.) John Law was granted his wish by the desperate king. He was granted the exclusive monopoly and the king decreed that it was illegal to own gold. John Law then could proceed with the inflation of the money supply and the people couldn't redeem their decreasingly worthless paper money for gold. There was a short term prosperity, and John Law was hailed as an economic hero. The French debt was being paid off, necessarily with paper money of decreasing value, but that was the cost of the short term prosperity. And the French people probably didn't understand that it was John Law who was causing the loss in the value of their money.

However, the king and John Law got greedy and the number of receipts increased too rapidly. The economy nearly collapsed with the increasing prices, and the desperate people demanded an economic reform. John Law fled for his life, and France stopped the printing of worthless paper money.

This printing of paper money, unbacked by gold, is not the only method utilized by the counterfeiters. Another method is more visible than the paper method and is therefore less popular with the counterfeiters. It is called Coin Clipping. Gold is monetized by the bank's minting of the gold into coins. This process involves the melting of the gold into small, uniform quantities of the metal. As long as the coins made are pure gold and all gold in circulation is minted into coins the only method of inflating the gold coinage is to either locate additional supplies of gold (that is, as discussed earlier, difficult, especially as the amount of gold available to the miner is decreasing) or by calling in all of the gold coins, melting them down, and then increasing their number by adding a less precious metal into each coin. This enables the counterfeiter to increase the number of coins by adding a less expensive metal to each coin. Each newly minted coin is then put back into circulation with the same markings as the previous coins. The public is expected to use the coin exactly as before, except that there are now more coins in circulation than before, and as surely as economic law, the increase in the money supply causes inflation, and prices rise.

The early Roman Empire practiced this coin clipping in what has become a classic example of the coin clipping method. Early Roman coins contained 66 grains of pure silver, but, due to the practice of coin clipping, in less than sixty years their coins contained only a trace of silver. Coins clipped of their value by the addition of less precious metals soon drove out the silver coins that remained, in keeping with another economic law, called Gresham's Law, which states: "Bad money drives out good."

As an illustration of this law, the clipped coins minted during the middle 1960's and placed in circulation by President Lyndon Johnson's administration have forced the silver coins out of circulation.

America's founding fathers were concerned with the practice of coin clipping and tried to keep this power out of the hands of the counterfeiters. Unfortunately, they did not completely restrict the government's ability to clip the coins when they wrote the following Congressional power into the Constitution:

> Article 1, Section 8: Congress shall have the power ... to coin money, regulate the value thereof, and fix the standards of weights and measures.

There are several interesting thoughts contained in that simple sentence.

First, the only power Congress has in creating money is in the coining of it. Congress has *no* power to *print money*, only to *coin* it. In addition, Congress was to set the value of money, and the power to coin money was placed together in the same sentence as the power to set the standard of weights and measures. It was their intent to set the value of money just as they set the length of a 12 inch foot, or the capacity of an ounce or a quart. The purpose of this power was to set constant values so that all citizens could rely on the fact that a foot in California was the same as a foot in New York.

A third way to inflate the gold standard consists in calling in all of the gold or silver coins and replacing them with coins made of a more plentiful metal, such as copper or aluminum. The most recent example of this activity, called "coin substitution," occurred during the administration of Lyndon Johnson when the government replaced silver coins with ones made of strange combinations of more plentiful, and therefore less expensive, metals.

For the counterfeiter who finds such methods less than perfect, the surest course to the acquisition of great wealth through inflation, is for him to get the government off the gold standard altogether. Under this method, the gold standard (the requirement that the government issue only gold coins, or paper directly issued on a one-for-one basis to gold as money) is eliminated, and money is printed without any backing, with the official sanction of the government making it legal.

By dictionary definition, such a money is called: Fiat Money: paper money of government issue which is legal tender by fiat or law, does not represent nor is it based upon gold and contains no promise of redemption.

One can see the transformation of America's gold standard into the fiat standard by reading the printing on a one dollar bill.

The early American money carried the simple promise that the government would redeem each gold certificate with gold simply by the surrender of the certificate at the treasury. The Series of 1928 dollar had changed this promise on the front of the bill to: "Redeemable in gold on demand at the U.S. Treasury or in good or lawful money at any Federal Reserve Bank." There are those who question the true nature of this dollar if its holder can redeem it for "lawful money" at a Reserve Bank. Does it mean that what the holder was trading in was "unlawful money?"

In any event, by 1934, the one-dollar bill read:

> This note is legal tender for all debts, public and private and is redeemed in lawful money at the Treasury or at any Federal Reserve Bank.

And in 1963, this wording had again changed to: "This note is legal tender for all debts, public and private." This bill was no longer redeemable in "lawful money" so the question of whether the previous money was "unlawful money" is now moot. But even more importantly, the bill was now a "note." This meant that this dollar had been borrowed from those who have an exclusive monopoly on printing paper money, and the ability to lend it to the U.S. government. The bill identifies the source of the borrowed money: The Federal Reserve System (the top line of the bill reads "Federal Reserve Note.")

America was on the gold standard until April, 1933, when President Franklin Roosevelt ordered all Americans to turn their gold bullion and gold coins into the banking system. For their gold, the American people were given irredeemable paper currency (Fiat Money) by the banks who turned the gold over to the Federal Reserve System. President Roosevelt called in America's gold without benefit of a law passed by Congress by using an unconstitutional Presidential Executive Order. In other words, he did not ask Congress to pass a law giving him the authority to call in America's privately owned gold; he took the law into his own hands and ordered the gold turned in. The President, as the Chief of the Executive Branch of the government, does not have the power to make laws, as this power constitutionally belongs to the Legislative Branch. But the American people were told by the President that this was a step to end the "national emergency" brought about by the Great Depression of 1929, and they voluntarily turned in the majority of the country's gold. The President included in his Executive Order the terms of the punishment if this order was not complied with. The American people were told to turn in their gold before the end of April, 1933, or suffer a penalty of a fine of $10,000 or imprisonment of not more than 10 years, or both.

Once the majority of the gold was turned in, President Roosevelt on October 22, 1933, announced his decision to devalue the dollar by announcing that government would buy gold at an increased price. This meant that the paper money that the Americans had just received for their gold was worth less per dollar. One dollar was now worth one thirty-fifth of an ounce of gold rather than approximately one twentieth as it had been prior to the devaluation.

Roosevelt, when he announced this move, made the following statement in an attempt to explain his action: "My aim in taking this step is to establish and maintain continuous control... We are thus continuing to move towards a managed currency." (It is rather ironic, and also extremely revealing, that Democratic candidate Roosevelt ran on a 1932 Democratic platform that supported the Gold Standard!)

However, not all of the American gold was turned in: "By February 19, gold withdrawals from banks increased from 5 to 15 million dollars a day. In two weeks, $114,000,000 of gold was taken from banks for export and another $150,000,000 was withdrawn to go into hiding."

The gold was being called in at $20.67 an ounce and anyone who could hold their gold in a foreign bank only had to wait until the price was raised by the government to $35.00 an ounce and then sell it to the government at a rather substantial profit of approximately 75%.

A similar profit was made by a Roosevelt supporter, Bernard Baruch, who invested heavily in silver. In a book entitled *FDR, My Exploited Father-In-Law*,[2] author Curtis Dall, Roosevelt's son-in-law, recalls a chance meeting with Mr. Baruch in which Baruch told Mr. Dall that he had options on 5/16ths of the world's known silver supply. A few months later, to "help the western miners," President Roosevelt doubled the price of silver. A tidy profit! (It pays to support the right people!)

There were some, however, who saw the sinister purposes behind these maneuvers. Congressman Louis McFadden, Chairman of the House Banking Committee, charged that the seizure of gold was "an operation run for the benefit of the international bankers." McFadden was powerful enough to ruin the whole deal "and was preparing to break the whole deal when he collapsed at a banquet and died. As two assassination attempts had already been made against him, many suspected poisoning."[3]

A giant step in the direction of remedying this dilemma, of returning to a gold standard, occurred in May of 1974, when legislation was signed by the President allowing the American people to once again legally own gold. This legislation did not put the United States back on the gold standard, but at least it afforded those concerned about inflation an opportunity to own gold should they choose to do so.

However, those who purchase gold have two generally unknown problems. One is the fact that the price of gold is not set by the free market, where two parties get together and arrive at a mutually satisfactory price. It is set: " . . . twice a day on the London gold market by five of Britain's leading dealers in bullion. They meet in the offices of N.M. Rothschild & Sons, the City Bank, and agree upon the price at which all are prepared to trade in the metal that day." So the price of gold is not set by the free activity of buyer and seller but by five bullion traders.

Even though the purchaser of gold still thinks that the gold he purchased belongs to him, the American government still may call it in. There is a little known provision of the Federal Reserve Act that reads: "Whenever in the judgment of the Secretary of the Treasury such action is necessary to protect the currency system of the United States, the Secretary . . . in his discretion, may require any or all individuals . . . to pay and deliver to the Treasurer of the United States any or all gold coins, gold bullion, and gold certificates owned by such individuals." So if the government wants to recall the gold of the American citizen, it has but to use this law and the force of government, and it will be called in. And the only options the gold owner has to surrender his gold or face the penalties of the judicial system.

But the government also has the power to call in paper money by destroying its value through a rapid increase in the money supply. This process is called "hyper-inflation."

Perhaps the classic example of this method of calling in the paper money occurred after World War I when Germany destroyed the value of the German mark by printing large quantities of nearly worthless new marks.

After the end of World War I, the peace treaty signed by the belligerents, called the Treaty of Versailles, required that the defeated German nation pay war reparations to the victors. The Treaty: "had fixed the amount that Germany must pay in reparations at two hundred and sixty nine billion gold marks, to be paid in forty-two annual installments . . . .[4]

The entire process was initially set into motion when the Reichsbank suspended the redeemability of its notes in gold with the outbreak of the war in 1914. This meant that the German government could pay for their involvement in the war by printing fiat money, and by 1918, the amount of money in circulation increased fourfold. The inflation continued through the end of 1923. By November of that year, the Reichsbank was issuing millions of marks each day.

In fact, by November 15, 1923, the bank had issued the incredible sum of 92,800,000,000,000,000,000 (quintillion) paper marks. This astronomical inflation of the money supply had a predictable effect upon prices: they rose in an equally predictable manner. For instance, prices of three representative household commodities rose as follows: (in marks):

Commodity	1918	Price in November, 1923
lb. potatoes	.12	50,000,000,000
one egg	.25	80,000,000,000
one pound of butter	3.00	6,000,000,000,000

The value of the German mark fell from a value of twenty to the English pound to 20,000,000,000 to the pound by December, 1923, nearly destroying trade between the two countries. It is apparent that Germany decided to print their way out of the war reparations rather than tax their people for the costs of the war for several reasons. Obviously, taxing the people is a very open and visible method of paying for the war debt, and certainly is not very popular. The result of the printing press is not visible in that the people can always be told that the price rises are the result of the shortages of goods caused by the war, rather than the increase in the money supply. Secondly, those candidates for high office in government who promise to end the inflation if and when elected are capable of doing so because the government controls the printing presses. So the middle class, who suffered the greatest during this inflation, looks for solutions and will frequently seek the nearest candidate who promises a solution. One such candidate was Adolf Hitler: "It is extremely doubtful whether Hitler could ever have come to power in Germany had not the inflation of the German currency first destroyed the middle class...."[5]

Hitler certainly was given an issue to attack the German government with. He could blame the current government for the hyper-inflation and all German citizens could know what he was saying, because the price rise affected nearly all of the German people.

Even more thought provoking is the possibility that there were those who actually wanted Hitler, or someone like him, to come to power, and who structured the Treaty of Versailles in such a manner as to force Germany to turn on the printing presses to pay for the costs of the reparations. Once these conditions were created and the printing of large quantities of paper money began, it was possible for a Hitler to promise that he'd never allow such a travesty to occur under his administration should he be given the power of government.

As John Maynard Keynes pointed out in his book *The Economic Consequences of the Peace,* there are those who benefit by hyper-inflation, and these individuals are the ones most likely to benefit by the rise to power of a Hitler who attacked the government for allowing such a thing to occur no matter what the cause. Those who controlled the money supply could purchase Capital Goods at a reduced price (measured in pre-inflation marks) because they had unlimited access to unlimited quantities of money. Once they had acquired as many Capital Goods as they desired, it would be to their advantage to have the economic situation return to normal. They could turn off the printing presses.

Those who sold property prior to the hyper-inflation were the greatest losers, for they were paid in marks worth far less than when they created the mortgage. A mortgagee could not go into the market place and buy a similar piece of property for the price of the mortgage just paid up. The only ones able to continue buying property were those who controlled the printing presses.

Is it possible that the German hyper-inflation was intentionally caused to eliminate the middle class? That certainly was the result of the printing press money, according to Dr. Carroll Quigley, the noted historian, who wrote: "... by 1924, the middle classes were largely destroyed."[6]

Some economists understand this damaging process and have taken pains to point it out. Professor Ludwig von Mises, for one, lived in Germany during the hyper-inflation and wrote:

Inflationism is not a variety of economic policy. It is an

instrument of destruction; if not stopped very soon, it destroys the market entirely.

Inflationism cannot last; if not radically stopped in time, it destroys the market entirely.

It is an instrument of destruction; if not stopped very soon, it destroys the market entirely.

It is an expedient of people who do not care a whit for the future of their nation and its civilization.[7]

Chapter 7
Additional Economic Terms

It will be instructive at this point to present the definitions which will assist the reader in further understanding the methods and motives of those involved in the Conspiracy.

The first definition is:

Monopoly: One seller of a particular good in a market place

There are two types:

Natural Monopoly: One that exists at the pleasure of the market place; entry to the market is not restricted except by the wishes of the consumer.

For instance, the owner of a pet store in a small town where it isn't profitable for another similar store to compete, would have a Natural Monopoly.

Coercive Monopoly: Government either creates or allows the monopoly to exist and then uses force to restrict the access of others into the market place to compete.

An example would be a cab company in a city where it alone is allowed to transport passengers for a fee, by the edict of the governmental agency that created it. No one else is allowed to compete. The price charged is set by the government.

The advantage of a monopoly is obvious: the seller sets the price of a good. It is not set by the interaction of a buyer and a seller, each with the option of dealing with others. The seller can make exorbitant profits if there is no competition, especially if the government insures that the seller will receive no competition from other sellers.

Natural monopolies enable the greedy profit seeker only a short term to make an exorbitant profit. Competition tends to reduce the price of the goods sold, thereby reducing the profit made. It is when the monopolist realizes that the secret to long-term wealth is through the utilization of governmental power to limit access of other sellers into the market place that extreme fortunes are made.

Another definition is:

Monopsony: One buyer in a market place.

Once again, as in the case of a monopoly, there are two types: a natural monopsony and a coercive monopsony.

As an example, the creation of a coercive monopsony was the intent of legislation introduced in 1977 that would have made the United States government rather than the privately owned oil companies the "sole buyer of foreign oil." The advantages are obvious. If the seller of foreign oil wishes to sell his product in the United States, he must sell it at a price set by the government, and that price might not have any relationship to the price set by a free market.

The third definition is:

Cartel: A few sellers in a market place combine to set the price of a good sold.

There is one major disadvantage to the cartel: the monopolist has to divide both the market place and the profits with the other sellers.

A simple example should suffice to explain how this system works.

The first producer of any product has the option of setting the price of the good where the profits are maximum. A product that costs $1 to produce can easily be sold for, say, $15 to enable the seller to make a profit of $14 on each item sold.

However, in the free-enterprise system, where access to the market place is not restricted, this type of profit encourages others to enter in an effort to acquire all or at least part of the profits being made. The second seller must reduce the price to induce the buyer to purchase his product. The buyer, to save a dollar on the purchase price, now shifts his purchases to the second seller. This price reduction forces the first seller to reduce his price to match the new price of $14 or to a new price of $13 to re-capture the market place. This see-sawing of the price will continue until the price reaches a level where one of the sellers will no longer sell his product.

It is conceivable that one of the sellers will reduce his price to one below the cost of production (his selling price will become $.50 even though it costs $1 to produce) in an attempt to bankrupt his competitor. This price has two obvious disadvantages, though:

1. The seller who sells his product at $.50 must return the profits previously made at the higher price to the market place because he must continue to pay all of his costs. This is not popular with aspiring monopolists for obvious reasons.

2. With the reduced price, more product can be purchased, (a buyer can now buy 30 units at $.50 apiece as compared to one product at $15. This means that the seller will be forced to return large quantities of his previously acquired profits back to the market place and the consumer.

A natural monopoly can be broken by competition without the force of government nor the threat of governmental action.

There is one other option that the monopolist has in his quest of exorbitant profits. He can join with the another seller and set the price together by dividing the market place. As stated previously, this forms a cartel, and under this agreement, the two sellers can set the price at $15 and avoid the head-to-head competition that tended to reduce profits for both. But as pointed out earlier, this form of agreement is not popular because each now must divide the market place and share the profits. The only advantage is that it curtails the cut-throat competition between the two.

So the cartel raises the price back up to $15 but this higher price invites competition from a third seller, and the competitive process starts all over again. No cartel, in a free market place where access is open to all sellers, can survive the price-cutting tendencies of competition. The way to break any cartel is to allow competitors to compete.

This encourages the two cartel members to invite the third seller into the cartel to avoid the price-cutting war which will break the strength of the original two member cartel. But once again, the market is now divided between three sellers instead of two, or even one. This market sharing is also not popular with the monopolists.

The key to monopoly control of the market place lies, then, in fixing it so that no one can compete with the monopolist. This arrangement can be made with the only agency with the force to restrict competition in the market place: the government. This agency has the power to curtail competition if the monopolist can gain control of government. This inescapable conclusion soon became apparent to those who wished to control the market place, and the monopolist quickly moved to get control of governments by influencing the outcome of elections.

This connection between the monopolists and government was correctly discerned by Frederick Clemson Howe, PhD., an economist, lawyer, and a special assistant to Henry Wallace, the Secretary of Agriculture and Vice-President to Franklin Roosevelt. He wrote: "These are the rules of big business: Get a monopoly! Let society work for you, and remember that the best business is politics, for a legislative grant, franchise, subsidy, or tax exemption is worth more than a Kimberly or Comstock Lode, since it does not require any labor either mental or physical, for its exploitation."[1]

John D. Rockefeller, one who correctly assessed the situation as well, expressed the opinion that "Competition is a sin."[2]

Another who wrote of this connection was Dr. Antony Sutton, who wrote in his book *Wall Street and FDR*:

> Old John Rockefeller and his 19th century fellow capitalists were convinced of an absolute truth: that no great monetary wealth could be accumulated under the impartial rules of competitive laissez-faire society (the free-enterprise system) society.
>
> The only sure road to the acquisition of massive wealth was monopoly: drive out your competitors, reduce competition, eliminate laissez-faire and above all get state protection for your industry through compliant politicians and government regulation.
>
> The last avenue yields a huge monopoly and a legal monopoly always leads to wealth.[3]

And in his book, *Wall Street and the Bolshevik Revolution*, Dr. Sutton further amplified his point:

> The financiers...could by government control...more easily avoid the rigors of competition.
>
> Through political influence they could manipulate the police power of the state to achieve what they had been unable, or what was too costly, to achieve under the private enterprise system.
>
> In other words, the police power of the state was a means of maintaining a private monopoly.[4]

The best known cartel in the world is OPEC, the Organization of

Petroleum Exporting Countries, which has recently become extremely influential in the oil markets of the world. This cartel is thought to be foreign, primarily Arabian, in ownership. However, there is ample reason to believe that the principle ownership of OPEC is not primarily Arabian but international, including American.

Dr. Carroll Quigley, in his massive book entitled *Tragedy and Hope*, discussed an oil cartel formed in 1928:

> This world cartel had developed from a tripartite agreement signed on September 17, 1920 by Royal Dutch Shell, Anglo-Iranian, and Standard Oil.
>
> These agreed to manage oil prices on the world market by charging an agreed fixed price plus freight costs, and to store surplus oil which might weaken the fixed price level.
>
> By 1949 the cartel had as members the seven greatest oil companies in the world: Anglo-Iranian, Socony-Vacuum, Royal Dutch Shell, Gulf, Esso, Texaco, and Calso.
>
> Excluding the United States domestic market, the Soviet Union and Mexico, it controlled 92% of the world's reserves of oil....[5]

James P. Warburg, who should know, further discussed the cartel in his book *The West in Crisis*. Apparently the cartel had grown to include an additional member:

> Eight giant oil companies — five of them American — control the non-Communist world's supply of oil, maintaining administered prices which... yield exorbitant profits.
>
> The oil companies extract oil from the Middle East, which contains 90% of the known reserves of the non-communist world, at a cost of 20 to 30 cents a barrel and sell it at a collusive price, varying over a period of recent years from $1.75 to $2.16 per barrel, f.o.b., the Persian Gulf.
>
> The resulting profit has, as a rule, been split on a fifty-fifty basis with the government of the country in which the oil is produced.[6]

Using the following figures, it is easy to extrapolate price increases to today's oil market prices.

Years	Cost	Price	Profit	% of Profit
1950	$ .30	$ 2.16	$ 1.86	620
1979 **	$3.25	$20.00	$16.75	515

**   presuming a 10% per year increase in costs and using the OPEC price of $20.00 in 1979, the profit of $16.75 is approximately the same as that pointed out in Warburg's book.

In other words, the OPEC countries are increasing oil prices today in order to maintain their profit percentages of 30 years ago.

It is interesting to note that both Dr. Quigley and Mr. Warburg wrote about the years 1949 and 1950. OPEC was formed in 1951, right after both authors pointed out that the Arabian oil reserves were owned by non-Arabian oil companies.

It is doubtful that these non-Arabian oil companies gave up the ability to make a 620 percent profit to the OPEC nations when OPEC was formed.

In summary, then, these agreements that artificially set prices, (the cartels, monopolies, and monopsonies,) lead to the accumulation of large quantities of amassed wealth. These marketplace aberrations exist solely because the monopolists have formed a partnership with the government, and the result is higher prices for the consumer.

Chapter 8
The Secret Societies

Author Arthur Edward Waite wrote:

> Beneath the broad tide of human history there flow the stealthy undercurrents of the secret societies, which frequently determine in the depths the changes that take place upon the surface.[1]

British Prime Minister Benjamin Disraeli, 1874-1880, confirmed the above assertion about the control by the secret societies in the affairs of men when he wrote:

> There is in Italy a power which we seldom mention in this House (the House of Parliament)....
> I mean the secret societies....
> It is useless to deny, because it is impossible to conceal, that a great part of Europe...to say nothing of other countries...is covered with a network of these secret societies.... What are their objects?
> They do not want constitutional government.... They want to change the tenure of the land, to drive out the present owners of

the soil and to put an end to ecclesiastical establishments.[2]

Notice that the two goals of the secret societies, according to Disraeli, are the same as those of what is called organized Communism: the abolition of private property and the ending of the "ecclesiastical establishments," the religions of the world.

Is it possible that so-called Communism is in reality the tool of the secret societies? Is it realistic to believe that Communism is controlled by forces above it in an organized hierarchy?

Today's version of history teaches that Communism is the intended result of public demands for a change in the organization of their society, usually through revolutionary action that overthrows the old system. Is it possible that these revolutions are in reality the machinations of the secret societies, seeking to communize the world after the revolution?

There are those who believe so:

> Communism is never a spontaneous or even willing rising of downtrodden masses against the bosses who exploit them — but exactly the opposite.
>
> It is always imposed on a people from the top down by bosses who are seeking to increase their power.
>
> All of the agitation at the bottom is stirred up, built up, financed, and controlled by the Insiders, at the top, to give them-selves the means and the excuse for seizing more power — always under the guise of stopping or preventing these revolutionary activities among the masses at the bottom.[3]

> Communism is a front for something deeper. Communism is not a revolt of the "poor" but a conspiratorial plot of the "rich."
>
> The international conspiracy does not originate in Moscow — but probably in New York. It is not an idealistic crusade for the poor and the humble but a disguised power grab of the rich and the arrogant.

The story of modern-day Communism begins with a secret society called the Order of the Illuminati.

It was about this organization that the 1953 *Report of the California Senate Investigating Committee on Education,* stated: "So called modern Communism is apparently the same hypocritical world conspiracy to destroy civilization that was founded by the Illuminati, and that raised its head in our colonies here at the critical period before the adoption of our Constitution."[4]

Another historian, Oswald Spengler, has taken the investigating committee one step further. He has linked Communism with the moneyed interests of the world. He has written: "There is no proletarian, not even Communist, movement that has not operated in the interests of money, in the directions indicated by money, and for the time being permitted by money—and that without the idealists among its leaders having the slightest suspicion of the fact."[5]

According to Mr. Spengler, even the leaders of Communism are not aware of the secret workings of their own movement. Is it possible that Gus Hall and Angela Davis, the 1980 Communist Party candidates for President and Vice-President of the United States, who ran on a platform opposing "the big banks and monopoly corporations that control the economy" are really being used by the very organizations they ostensibly oppose? Is it possible that the wealthy banks and monopoly corporations want and support the Communist Party because they want the Party to oppose them?

One Communist Party member, Dr. Bella Dodd, a member of the National Committee of the Communist Party of the United States, apparantly decided that there was indeed a connection between wealthy "capitalists" and the Party. She noticed that every time the National Committee couldn't reach a decision, one of their members would leave, go to the Waldorf Towers in New York City, and meet with a particular individual, later identified as Arthur Goldsmith. Dr. Dodd observed that every time Mr. Goldsmith made a decision, it was later confirmed by the Communist Party in Moscow. But what truly amazed Dr. Dodd was that Mr. Goldsmith was not only a member of the Communist Party, but an extremely wealthy American "capitalist."

So if the preceding commentators are correct in their charges that Communism is a front for secret societies, including the Illuminati, it behooves the student of the conspiratorial view to examine the origins and history of this organization.

The Illuminati was founded on May 1, 1776, by Adam Weishaupt, a Jesuit priest and a professor of Canon Law at Ingolstadt University in Bavaria, today part of Germany. There is some evidence that Professor Weishaupt had become affiliated with secret societies before he founded the Illuminati.

The founding date of May 1 is still celebrated by Communists around the world as May Day, although the purists claim that May Day is celebrated because that was the beginning date for the Russian Revolution of 1905. But this doesn't change the date of May 1, 1905 as an anniversary of the founding of the Illuminati on May 1, 1776.

Weishaupt's organization spread quickly, especially among fellow "intellectuals" at his university. In fact, all but two of its professors had become members of this organization in the first few years of its existence.

The basic philosophy that was being offered to the prosective member of the Illuminati was a reversal of the traditional philosophy taught by the church and the educational system. It has been summarized by Weishaupt himself as follows: "Man is not bad except as he is made so by arbitrary morality. He is bad because religion, the state, and bad examples pervert him. When at last reason becomes the religion of men, then will the problem be solved."[6]

There is reason to believe that Weishaupt's contempt of religion started on July 21, 1773, when Pope Clement XIV "forever annulled and extinguished the Jesuit order."

The Pope's action was in response to pressure from France, Spain, and Portugal, which independently had come to the conclusion that the Jesuits were meddling in the affairs of the state and were therefore enemies of the government.

The response of one ruler, King Joseph of Portugal, was typical. He "hastened to sign a decree by which the Jesuits were denounced as 'traitors, rebels and enemies to the realm...'"[7]

So the three nations presented "the categorical request that he (the Pope) should suppress the Jesuit order throughout the world."[8]

The Pope agreed and banned the order.

Weishaupt, a Jesuit priest, certainly must have been concerned by the Pope's action, possibly to the point where he wished to organize an institution strong enough to ultimately destroy the Catholic Church itself.

Pope Clement's action was short-lived, though, as Pope Pius VII in August, 1814 reinstated the Jesuits to all of their former rights and privileges.[9]

Pope Pius' reinstatement did not go without notice in the United States, as ex-President John Adams wrote to his successor, Thomas Jefferson: "I do not like the re-appearance of the Jesuits. If ever there was a body of men who merited eternal damnation on earth... it is this Society...."[10]

Jefferson replied: "Like you, I disapprove of the restoration of the Jesuits, for it means a step backwards from light into darkness."[11]

The Jesuits are still in trouble with the Church just as they were during the early 1700's. On February 28, 1982, Pope Paul II told the Jesuits "to keep clear of politics, and honor Roman Catholic tradition."[12]

An article on the Pope's action in the *U.S. News and World Report* stated that the Jesuits had indeed meddled in the affairs of certain nations. The article said: "Jesuits have played leading roles in Nicaragua's Sandinista revolution. Some Jesuits have joined Communist parties. One priest in El Salvador has claimed that his order is working for the advancement of Marxism and revolution, not for God."[13]

The article continued by stating that Jesuits have "joined left-wing rebel movements in Central America and the Philippines, and have advocated a molding of Marxism and Roman Catholicism in what is called 'liberation theology.' "[14]

Weishaupt's contempt for religion manifested itself with his thought that man's ability to reason would set the moral tone of the society rather than the teachings of the Bible.

This thought was not new.

The Bible teaches that the first man and woman, Adam and Eve, were instructed by God not to eat the fruit of the Tree of the Knowledge of Good and Evil. Man was not to set his own moral precepts; he was to listen to the laws of God. Man was tempted by Satan with the ability to "be as Gods, knowing good and evil," capable of using his own mind to decide what was right and wrong.

So Weishaupt's call to man's reason to determine man's morality was not new; it was the continuing battle between man's mind and the teachings of God.

One well-known example of man's rebellion to the laws of God occurred when Moses of the Old Testament of the Bible brought God's laws in the form of the Ten Commandments to the people. While Moses was absent, the people had constructed their own god, a mouthless golden calf incapable of offering any instructions or moral teachings. It is easy to worship something that does not require any obedience nor has the ability to issue laws by which to live.

So man continued his rebellion against God. Weishaupt furthered the trend by teaching that man could free himself by emancipating himself from religion. Even the name of his organization, the Illuminati, revealed his concern about man's mind. The "Illuminated Ones" of the Illuminati would be those possessing the greatest ability to discern the truths of the universe gleaned from the workings of the human mind. Once unhindered by religion, pure reason would lead man out of the spiritual wilderness.

Those who believe in the teachings of God as revealed to man through the Holy Bible do not believe that God's laws are restrictions on man's freedoms, but are exactly the opposite. They enable man to enjoy his freedom by not fearing the plundering of his life, liberty and property by others.

The commandment "Thou shalt not kill" restricts man's ability to kill his neighbor, thereby increasing man's ability to live. "Thou shalt not steal" encourages man to allow his neighbor to accumulate the property he needs to sustain his own life. "Thou shalt not covet thy neighbor's wife" discourages adultery and encourages fidelity, thus strengthening the sacredness of God's institution of marriage.

God's laws allow maximum freedom to those who will abide by them. Man becomes less free when his wife, his property, and his very life belong to those who feel they have the right to take them from him.

Weishaupt even admitted that he was founding a new religion when he founded the Illuminati. He wrote: "I never thought that I should become the founder of a new religion."[15]

So the goal of the new religion became the substitution of the religious man with the illuminated man: man solving man's problems through the use of his mind. Weishaupt declared: "Reason will be the only code of man."[16] "When at last reason becomes the religion of man, so will the problem be solved."[17]

Weishaupt believed that man was a product of his environment and that man would be happy if he could re-structure the environment completely.

Today that teaching is the foundation of the philosophy in the courts that frees criminals even before the victim can file the charges against the criminal. The rational, illuminated mind sees that the society, the environment, and not the criminal, is at fault for the actions of the individual. This thinking holds that the society must be punished for the acts of the criminal, and that the criminal must be released back into the society so that it can be punished for the failure to meet the criminal's needs.

So Weishaupt saw religion as the problem because religion taught that only moral means may be utilized to achieve a moral end. Weishaupt saw this as an obstacle to his achieving his desired result: the complete alteration of man's society. He wrote: "Behold our secret. Remember that the end justifies the means, and that the wise ought to take all the means to do good which the wicked take to do evil."[18]

Any activity, either moral or immoral, becomes moral or acceptable to the member of the Illuminati as long as that activity promotes the goals of the organization. Murder, looting, wars, whatever, becomes acceptable behavior to the real believer of the new religion.

Another major obstacle to man's progress, according to Weishaupt, was nationalism. He wrote: "With the origin of nations and peoples the world ceased to be a great family.... Nationalism took the place of human love...."[19]

Weishaupt was not an anarchist (one who believes in the absence of government) but believed that there was a need for world government to replace what used to be the national governments. This entity was in turn to be ruled by the members of the Illuminati: "The pupils (of the Illuminati) are convinced that the order will rule the world. Every member therefore becomes a ruler."[20]

So the ultimate goal of the Illuminati, and hence all of its successors, becomes power: worldwide power. The power of government over all the people of the world.

If Weishaupt wished to so alter man's life in a manner only his supporters wanted, than it becomes imperative that his goals be kept secret from his intended victims. He wrote: "The great strength of our order lies in its concealment: let it never appear in any place in its own name, but always covered by another name and another occupation."[21]

Under the protection of its concealment, the order quickly grew. However, as has been the case with all of the secret organizations that controlled the so-called Communist organizations, it did not attract, nor was it intended to attract, the "downtrodden masses," the "lowly" peasant-worker it was supposedly created to assist. It drew from the near powerful, the representatives of that layer of society just underneath the power holders. For instance, a partial listing of the occupations of some of the members of the Illuminati revealed this statement was true: marquis, baron, lawyer, abbe, count, magistrate, prince, major, professor, colonel, priest, and duke.

These were the occupations of the individuals who, without fear of discovery, could meet secretly and conspire against the government, the army, the church and the establishment. These were the people who did not possess the ultimate power of control over their respective fields of endeavor, but they saw the Illuminati as the means of achieving their goals of individual power.

The members of the Illuminati whenever together or in correspondence with fellow members assumed aliases to conceal their real identities. Weishaupt assumed the name of Spartacus, a Roman slave who led an uprising against the Roman government centuries before.

What was the goal of these conspirators?

Nesta Webster, one of the major researchers into the Illuminati, has summarized their goals as follows:

1. Abolition of monarchy and all ordered government.
2. Abolition of private property.
3. Abolition of inheritance.
4. Abolition of patriotism (nationalism).
5. Abolition of the family (i.e. of marriage and all morality, and the institution of communal education of children).
6. Abolition of all religion.[22]

In 1777, Weishaupt was initiated into the Masonic Order, the Lodge Theodore of Good Council, in Munich, Germany. His purpose in joining was not to become part of this benevolent order, but to infiltrate it and then to control it altogether.

In fact, the Masons held an International Congress at Wilhemsbad in July, 1782, and "Illuminism was injected into Freemasonry by indoctrinating the Masonic leaders...."[23]

However, the secrecy of the Illuminati was soon broken in 1783 when "four professors of the Marianen Academy...were summoned before the

Court of Enquiry and questioned on . . . the Illuminati."[24]

The Bavarian government had discovered the philosophies and purposes of the Illuminati and, more importantly, its desire to overthrow the Bavarian government. Hearings were held and the government abolished the order. But discovery of the organization was perhaps a blessing in disguise: the members fled the persecution of the Bavarian government and they took the Illuminati with them, establishing new societies all over Europe and America.

The Bavarian government countered this expansion by warning other European governments about the exact purposes of the Illuminati, but the rulers of Europe refused to listen. Those decisions would later come back to haunt these governments. As Nesta Webster observed: "The extravagence of the scheme therein propounded rendered it unbelievable, and the rulers of Europe, refusing to take Illuminism seriously, put it aside as a chimera (a foolish fancy)."[25]

The fact that the rulers of Europe wouldn't believe the goals of the Illuminati is a problem that is recurring all over the world today. It is difficult for the observer to believe that such a giant, well organized conspiracy does exist, and that the goals they envision for the world are real. This disbelief by the public is what fuels their success and it behooves the Conspiracy to plan their events in such a way that the truth becomes so incredible and so preposterous that no one would believe that they were intentionally created.

A Frenchman named Danton said this in French, and loosely translated, what he said means: "Audacity, audacity, always audacity!"

One of the countries to which the Illuminati fled was America, and they formed their first chapter in Virginia in 1786, followed by fourteen others in different cities.[26] They organized the Callo-Italian Society, and with the onset of the American Revolution, disciples in America began to call themselves the Jacobins.[27]

Much of what is known about the Illuminati today comes from a book written in 1798 by Professor John Robison, a professor of Natural Philosophy at Edinburgh University in Scotland. He entitled his book *Proofs of a Conspiracy Against all the Religions and Governments of Europe Carried On In the Secret Meetings of the Free Masons, Illuminati, and Reading Societies.* Professor Robison, himself a Mason, had been asked to join the Illminati but felt he should investigate the order before he joined. Robison concluded that the association had been formed "for the express purpose of rooting out all the religious establishments and overturning all the existing governments of Europe."[28]

These charges, even today, have fallen on deaf ears among many of Robison's fellow Masons. One of the more scholarly works supporting the

Freemasons is a book entitled *An Encyclopaedia of Freemasonry* by Albert Mackey, M.D., himself a 33rd degree Mason, the highest level attainable in the Masonic Order.

Dr. Mackey makes these statements about Professor Robison's book: Many of his statements are untrue and his arguments illogical, exaggerated, and some of them altogether false. (His) theory is based on false premises and his reasonings (are) fallacious and illogical.

He wrote that the founder of the Illuminati, Professor Weishaupt, was "a Masonic reformer. Weishaupt could not have been the monster that he has been painted by his adversaries."[30]

In fact, Dr. Mackey praised the Illuminati: "The original design of Illuminism was undoubtedly the elevation of the human race."[31]

Dr. Mackey dismissed the Illuminati as being no threat to civilization because he apparently felt that the organization had disappeared: " . . . by the end of the last century (by 1900) it had ceased to exist."[32]

This might be true, as far as the name Illuminati is concerned, but there is strong evidence, mainly through the perpetuation of the philosophy through like-minded organizations, that the Order perpetuated self by frequently changing its name and surfacing again.

In 1798, shortly after the publication of Professor Robison's work on the Illuminati, American minister Reverend G.W. Snyder sent a copy of the book to President George Washington, who was a very visible member of the Masonic Order. On September 25, 1798, President Washington wrote a letter to Rev. Snyder: "I have heard much of the nefarious and dangerous plan and doctrines of the Illuminati, but never saw the book until you were pleased to send it to me. It was not my intention to doubt that the doctrine of the Illuminati had not spread in the United States. On the contrary, no one is more satisfied of this fact than I am . . . ."[33]

But not all of America's founding fathers agreed with President Washington. Thomas Jefferson, after reading part three of the writings of another exposer of the Illuminati, the Abbe Barruel, wrote: "Barruel's own parts of the book are perfectly the ravings of a Bedlamite."[34] (Webster's dictionary defines a Bedlamite as an inhabitant of the Bedlam hospital for lunatics in London, England.)

Jefferson also wrote the following about the founder of the Illuminati: "Weishaupt seems to be an enthusiastic philanthropist. Weishaupt believes that to promote the perfection of the human character was the object of Jesus Christ. His (Weishaupt's) precepts are the love of God and love of our neighbor."[35]

(It is truly amazing that two people could read the works of Weishaupt, or the writings of those who were out to expose him for what he was, and come away with two such divergent opinions about his purposes. Yet there are still defenders of the Illuminati even today.)

Some of the more vocal critics of the Illuminati believe that they were instrumental in fomenting the American Revolution itself. But a simple review of the nature of this revolution will show the difference between a revolution created by the Illuminati and the American Revolution. *Life* magazine summarized it quite well in its series on Revolutions: "The American revolution was strictly a war of independence. It gave later revolutions a noble ideal and gave America itself the freedom to pursue its own destiny, but it left the structure of American society in all essentials unchanged."[36]

In other words, the American Revolution did not dissolve the family, abolish religion, nor eliminate the national borders, the three targets of the Illuminati. The American Revolution was fought to disengage the United States from the government of England. This fact is confirmed by the Declaration of Independence. The founding fathers wrote: "When in the course of human events, it becomes necessary for one people to dissolve the political bands which have connected them with another . . . ."

But the Illuminati *has* had its hands directly in other revolutions, the most notable being the French Revolution of 1789.

The facts of their involvement in this uprising are not well known. The traditional explanation of the French Revolution is that the French people, tired of being oppressed by King Louis XVI and Marie Antoinette, rose up in opposition to the monarchy and started the revolution by storming the Bastille prison. This activity, according to the official historical record, started the revolution that was to culminate in the replacing of the monarchy with the so-called "French Republic."

The French people commemorate the start of their "revolution" by making Bastille Day, July 14, an annual holiday. This further supports the contention that the people of France truly revolted and overthrew the King of France.

However, those who have studied the revolution in depth have discovered the real reason for the storming of the Bastille prison. As Nesta Webster explained it, "A plan of attack on the Bastille had already been drawn up, it only remained now to set the people in motion."[37]

The plan of attack was to storm the Bastille, not to release the hundreds of "oppressed political prisoners" supposedly imprisoned there, but to capture the needed weapons to start the revolution. This was confirmed by the fact that, when the mob reached the Bastille, so-called "torturous" prison of the "oppressive" King Louis XVI, there were only seven prisoners incarcerated there: four forgers, two lunatics, and the Comte de Solages, incarcerated for "monstrous crimes against humanity" at the request of his family. In fact, "The damp, dark dungeons had fallen into complete disuse;

since the first ministry of Necker in 1776, no one had been imprisoned there."[38]

The second erroneous presumption about the causes of the French Revolution is that the revolution was the action of the masses of the French people. This concept of large numbers of Frenchmen supporting the revolution is erroneous, because, in truth "Out of the 800,000 inhabitants of Paris only approximately 1,000 took any part in the siege of the Bastille..."[39]

Those who were directly involved in the storming of the prison were in fact paid by those who directed the entire affair.

> That brigands from the South (of France) were deliberately enticed to Paris in 1789, employed and paid by the revolutionary leaders, is a fact confirmed by authorities too numerous to quote at length; and the further fact that the conspirators felt that such a measure to be necessary is of immense significance, for it shows that in their eyes the people of Paris were not to be depended on to carry out a revolution. In other words, the importation of the contingent of hired brigands conclusively refutes the theory that the Revolution was an irrepressable rising of the people.[40]

In addition, not only Frenchmen were employed by those directing the revolution: "...the motley crew of 'brigands,'...thirsting for violence, consisting not only of the aforesaid Marsailles (those Frenchmen from the 'South,' cited above) and Italians, but also...of large numbers of Germans...."[41]

One who was in a position to witness the actual siege of the Bastille in Paris was a Dr. Rigby, who was in Paris as a tourist during the French Revolution. His letters to his wife during these days offer an interesting insight into what actually happened. Nesta Webster, in her book *The French Revolution*, commented on Dr. Rigby's correspondence: "So little commotion did the siege of the Bastille cause in Paris that Dr. Rigby, unaware that anything unusual was going on, went off early in the afternoon to visit the gardens of Monceaux."[42]

Another of the observers of the French Revolution was Lord Acton, who confirmed that there was a hidden hand at work at fomenting the French Revolution: "The appalling thing in the French Revolution is not the tumult but the design. Through all the fire and smoke, we perceive the evidence of calculating organization. The managers remain studiously concealed and masked; but there is no doubt about their presence from the first."[43]

The plan of the conspirators was simple: to create "popular" grievances in order to exploit them to their benefit. They created five particular grievances to create the impression that the King himself was responsible. It was hoped that the difficult conditions would be sufficient to arouse enough people to join those already hired so that it would appear that the revolution was indeed one with popular support. The conspirators could then control the events and bring about their desired results.

The first of these contrived grievances was the shortage of grain. Webster says: "Montjoie asserts that agents employed by the Duc d' Orleans deliberately bought up the grain, and either sent it out of the country or concealed it in order to drive the people to revolt."[44]

So the Duc d' Orleans, a member of the Illuminati, purchased large quantities of grain to cause the people to take their grievances to the King whom they were led to believe had caused the shortage. It was, of course, the Illuminati that spread the story that the King had intentionally caused the grain shortage. This tactic is similar to the one detailed by Jan Kozak in his book *Not A Shot Is Fired*, written about 160 years later.

The second of these contrived grievances was the enormous debt that caused the government to tax the people to pay for it. The national debt was estimated to be 4 1/2 billion livre, worth about $800 million in the dollar of the day. The money had been borrowed by the French government to assist the United States in the American Revolution of 1776. (The connection between the Illuminati of France and the founding fathers of the American Revolution, will be discussed in a later chapter of this book.) It has been estimated that two-thirds of the French debt had been created by those loans.

The third contrived grievance was the false impression that the French people were starving. Dr. Rigby, previously mentioned, stated that: ". . . we have seen few of the lower classes in rage, idleness and misery."[45]

Nesta Webster explained further: ". . . Dr. Rigby continues in the same strain of admiration — an admiration that we might attribute to lack of discernment were it not that it ceases abruptly on his entry into Germany. Here he finds a 'country to which Nature has been equally kind as to France, for it has fertile soil, but as yet the inhabitants live under an oppressive government.' At Cologne, (Germany) he finds that 'tyranny and oppression have taken up their abode.' "[46]

The fourth major grievance caused by the Illuminati and its fellow conspirators in the government was massive inflation which was bankrupting the working classes. 35 million assignats were printed in a short time and this was partially the cause of the shortages. The government's response was to impose food rationing, and this further continued to anger the people. This tactic is, once again, similar to the strategy detailed by Jan Kozak.

The fifth distortion of the truth was the alleged "oppressive" reign of King Louis XVI. The truth is that France was the most prosperous of all the European states prior to the Revolution. France held one-half of the money in circulation in all of Europe, and in the period of 1720 to 1780, foreign trade was multiplied by four. One half of the wealth in France was in the hands of the middle class, and the "serfs" owned more land than anyone else. The King had abolished forced labor on public works in France and had outlawed the use of torture in interrogation. In addition, the king had founded hospitals, established schools, reformed the laws, built canals, drained the marshes to increase the quantity of arable land, and had constructed numerous bridges to ease the flow of goods inside the country.

So in this, the first of several "revolutions" to be reviewed in this book, we see the classic example of the Conspiracy at work. The benevolent King was fostering a rise of the middle class by encouraging a better and healthier society. This situation was intolerable to those who were in the layer just underneath the ruling class, as the rising middle class began to assume power themselves. The conspirators intended to eliminate not only the King and the present ruling class but the middle class as well.

The enemy of the Conspiracy is always the middle class, and in the other revolutions to be reviewed elsewhere in this book, it shall be shown that the Conspiracy foments these contrived "revolutions" for just that purpose.

So the French Revolution was a fraud and hoax. The people were being manipulated for reasons not made known to them.[47]

The invisible hand that guided the entire French Revolution was the Illuminati, only thirteen years in existence, yet powerful enough to cause a revolution in one of the major countries of the world.

But the members of the Illuminati had laid down the plans for the Revolution years before, and had infiltrated another secret group, the Masons: "France's galloping revolution was assisted in the decades previous to 1789 by the growth of the Masonic Brotherhood."[48]

Freemasonry had come to France in 1725, but by 1772, the organization had split into two groups, one of which became known as the Grand Orient Lodge of Freemasonry. The first Grand Master, the equivalent of president, of the Lodge was the Duc d' Orleans, also a member of the Illuminati.

The Grand Orient Lodge spread quickly throughout the entirety of France so that by 1789 there were a total of 600 lodges all over France as compared to only 104 in 1772. Members of the Grand Orient were also active in government, as 447 of the 605 members of the Estates General, France's parliament, were members.

The plan of the Illuminati was to infiltrate the Masonic Order, convert it into a branch of the Illuminati, and then use its secrecy as the vehicle to overthrow the monarchy. The new head of the government would be the Duc d' Orleans. The strategy worked for awhile, but later the Duc suffered the ultimate penalty for his treason against the French government: he died on the guillotine.

What, then, was offered to the French people instead of their old society? What was to be the guiding force behind the new society offered by the Illuminati?

That question was answered by an author who has studied the Revolution: "The French Revolution represented the first attempt to use the religion of reason...as the foundation of a new order of society."[49]

In fact, in November, 1793: "...the multitude assembled in the Cathedral of Notre Dame to worship the Goddess of Reason, personified by an actress...placed naked by government decree upon the altar...."[50]

So the French Revolution was created to replace God with the "Goddess of Reason." The conspirators offered the French people the essential program of the the Illuminati: man's mind would solve man's problems.

In spite of all of the evidence of the planning, however, there are still those who believe the French Revolution was the spontaneous activity of an oppressed population rising up against a tyrannical king. *Life* magazine, in a series of articles on the subject of Revolution, wrote: "The French Revolution was not planned and instigated by conspirators. It was the result of a spontaneous uprising by the masses of the French people...."[51]

There are reasons other than historical ignorance that *Life* magazine takes this position, and these will be examined later in a subsequent chapter.

Chapter 9
Communism

It has been fairly well established by traditional historians that Karl Marx was the founding father of Communism. This is, in addition, the official position offered by the Communists themselves. Their position is that this previously unknown young man suddenly rose out of obscurity to write the *Communist Manifesto* and thereby launched the Communist movement.

However, the truth is that this explanation is only partially correct. And the truth is far more interesting than the partially correct story.

To understand why this is so, it becomes important to first examine Karl Marx, the individual.

Marx, born in 1818, went to Paris, France, in 1843 to study economics, and while at a university met Frederick Engels, the son of a wealthy Lancashire, England, cotton spinner. Marx soon learned the joys of possessing unearned wealth, for Engels constantly assisted Marx, and later Marx and his family, with an income from his father's cotton mills in England. Marx didn't care for the traditional forms of labor to earn the necessities of life, relying instead on the largess of his friend Engels to keep himself alive for nearly all of his adult life.

Marx frequently made appeals to Engels for more money because he said his daughters "must have a bourgeois education so they can make contacts in life."[1]

Traditional historians have not dwelt much upon this relationship between Marx and Engels. Those that do find it strange that Marx, the "champion of the oppressed and the downtrodden workers" would spend nearly all of his adult life living off the profits acquired from a "capitalistic" cotton mill in England. Engels' father, if consistent with the charges against the "propertied class" of the day, was "exploiting the working class, those who produce all of the capital of the world." Yet Marx continued living off the income provided by Engels' share of the cotton mill.

If Marx had been true and consistent to his principles, he would have rejected this money and lived by the earnings of his own labors. Yet the only official job Marx ever had was as a correspondent for a newspaper for a short time.

In his early youth Marx was a believer in God. But while at the university Marx changed his views. He once wrote that he wished to avenge himself "against the One who rules above."[2]

It was no coincidence that his change in his basic belief came after he joined the highly secret Satanist Church. As evidence of his membership in this sect, Marx grew a heavy beard and let his hair grow long. These outward manifestations were ". . . characteristic of the disciples of Joana Southcott, a Satanic priestess who considered herself in contact with the demon Shiloh."[3]

By 1841 his conversion was nearly complete as a friend of his had observed: "Marx calls the Christian religion one of the most immoral of religions."[4]

Not only did Marx attack the Christian religion, but the Jewish religion as well. In 1856 Marx wrote in the *New York Tribune*: "Thus do these loans...become a blessing to the House of Judah. This Jew organization of loanmongers is as dangerous to the people as the aristocratic organization of landowners."[5]

But generally Marx took out his anger against religion itself: "The abolition of religion as the illusory happiness of man is a demand for their real happiness."[6]

The reasons for Marx's bitterness against religion are numerous: Marx saw religion:

1.   as the mechanism of the wealthy to keep the poor, downtrodden worker in his state of poverty;
2.   as the teaching that one man's property did not belong to another;
3.   as the teaching that man should not covet another man's property; and
4.   as the teaching that each man should be self-sufficient and earn his own sustenance.

Marx saw this unequal distribution of wealth as the cause of man's unhappiness. If only property could be equally divided, man would be happy. And the vehicle that kept man from acquiring his fair share of the property was organized religion that taught that one man could not take the property of another by force: "Thou shalt not steal." Religious teaching also included the commandment that it was wrong to desire more property than you were able to acquire by your own efforts: "Thou shalt not covet thy neighbor's goods."

Marx reasoned, therefore, it was the religious system that kept man in poverty, as if the ownership of property was the only requirement for human happiness. It then followed, according to Marxist logic, that the capitalist system had to be destroyed because it encouraged every individual to produce his own necessities through his individual labor.

Therefore, the happiness of man was contingent upon abolishing not only the religious system but the "Capitalistic" system as well.

One of Marx's friends, Mikhail Bakunin, once wrote this about Marx: "Since Marx rejected the idea of God, he could not explain the 'human condition' as the result of sin. He blamed all evil, both moral and psychological, on the economic system which he said had to be overthrown by revolution so that the society of man could be restructured."[7]

But even the abolishment of religion and the Capitalistic System was not enough for the Marxists. Marx himself wished to abolish "all social conditions," not just the church and the free enterprise system. Marx wrote: "The Communists . . . openly declare that their ends can be attained only by the forcible overthrow of all existing social conditions."[8]

Marx wrote frequently on these subjects. He wrote the following about the subject of the family: "The bourgeois clap trap about family and education, about the co-relation of parent and child, becomes all the more disgusting . . . .[9]

And on nationality: "The working men have no country. We cannot take away from them what they have not got."[10]

Marx realized that the main vehicle to be utilized in the destruction of these values was the government, and he was correct. Take, for instance, the following newspaper article that appeared in 1980:

FAMILY LIFE HARMED BY GOVERNMENT, POLL SAYS

Pollster George Gallup said Friday nearly half of those who responded to his organization's 1980 survey on the American family believe that the federal government has an unfavorable influence on family life.[11]

Ideas on how the family unit can be further damaged are now being offered by a variety of people. One, an assistant professor at a college, offered this thought on the subject: "... the fact that children are raised in families means there is no equality. In order to raise children with equality, we must take them away from families and communally raise them."[12]

To show their individual contempt for the traditional view of family life, both Frederick Engels and Marx had affairs: Engels with the wife of a friend, and Marx with his maid. (When Marx married Jenny von Westphalen, the daughter of a rich and respected Prussian official, her mother gave the couple a maid as a wedding present. Marx showed his appreciation by getting his gift pregnant.) Marx further showed his contempt for his family by allowing two of his six children to starve to death, because Marx's contempt for industrious labor frequently failed to provide for his family's sustenance. In addition, two of his other children later committed suicide, perhaps because of their wretched existence as children.[13]

Marx's views on marriage and the family were consistent with the way he lived his life, but in other areas his hypocrisy was very evident.

For instance, in June, 1864, "in a letter to his uncle, Lion Phillips, Marx announced that he had made 400 pounds on the stock exchange."[14]

Here Marx, the great champion of the working man against the "exploiting capitalists" (those who make their money on the stock exchange,) admits that he himself had made a profit on the stock exchange (in effect admitting that he considered himself a member of this class.) Notice that this was eighteen years after he urged the proletariat (the working class) to overthrow the bourgeois (the wealthy class), those who make profits on the stock exchange.

On one occasion, he wrote to Engels asking for the final settlement of the Wolff legacy. He said: "If I had had the money during the last ten days, I would have been able to make a good deal on the stock exchange. The time has now come when with wit and very little money, one can really make a killing in London."[15]

The Wolff legacy referred to in Marx's letter was the remains of an inheritance left to Marx by Wilhelm Wolff, an obscure German admirer. The total legacy inherited by Marx was 824 pounds, when the annual income of the "exploited working class" was approximately 4.5 pounds. In rough equivalents today, that would mean that Marx inherited approximately $365,000 assuming that the average wage of an American workman in 1980 was $20,000.

It was not as if Marx could not have earned an adequate living by his own efforts. Mr. Marx was indeed Dr. Marx, as he had earned a doctorate in philosophy from the University of Jena. With this degree, he could have been employed by a European university and made a comfortable living. (Marx never actually attended the university. He purchased his doctorate through the mail.)

In about 1846, both Marx and Engels joined a group calling itself The Communist League which "sprang from what was known as the League of the Just. The latter, in turn, was an offshoot of the Parisian Outlaws League, founded by German refugees in that city. After a turbulent ten-year period, the League of the Just found its 'center of gravity' as Engels put it, in London where, he added, a new feature came to the fore: 'from being German' the League became international."[16]

After the Illuminati was discovered in Bavaria, Germany, its members scattered throughout Europe. The League was an "off-shoot of the Parisian Outlaws League, founded by German refugees." One can only wonder if those refugees were the scattering Illuminati.

In any event, at the Second Congress of the Communist League (the official title of the Manifesto, in German, is *Manifest der Kommunistichen Partei*. (History has translated "Partei" variously as "Party" or "League.") Marx and Engels were selected to write a party platform. Apparently both encountered delays in achieving this result, and the two writers "caused the Central Committee of the League to serve notice sharply that if the manifesto was not ready by February 1, 1848, measures would be taken against Marx and Engels. Results followed."[17]

So Marx and Engels were given the task of writing a party platform for an already existing international group. The *Manifesto* was not the work of an inspired nobody by the name of Karl Marx (or Frederick Engels, for that matter,) who suddenly sprang up from obscurity. Both were hired by an already existing group that now felt its power was strong enough for them to come out from the "smoke-filled" rooms and make their organization, and its platform, known to the people of Europe.

But why was it so important for the manifesto to be completed by the first of February? Because the "spontaneous revolutions" that had already been planned all over Europe could "spontaneously" erupt on schedule. In fact, these "spontaneously planned" revolutions started on March 1, 1848 in Baden followed by others in Vienna on March 12; Parma, March 13; Venice, March 22; London, April 10; Spain, May 7; and Naples, May 15. Sixty-four revolutions "spontaneously erupted" all over Russia during the year as well.

So the *Manifesto of the Communist Party* was issued in London, England, on February 1, 1848, as an explanation of the cause of the revolutions already planned. Fortunately for the people of Europe, nearly all of these revolutions failed.

Because of these failures, the name of the manifesto was changed to the *Communist Manifesto* and the name of Karl Marx was added as its author. This event occurred in 1868, twenty years after its original publication.

What, then, did the Communist Party want Marx and Engels to write?

Marx saw the proletariat (the working class) wresting " . . . by degrees, all capital from the bourgeoisie (the propertied class)...by means of despotic inroads on the rights of property."[18]

This meant that Marx and his contemporaries had to develop a program that would slowly destroy the rights to private property in the society until one day the working class would own all of the property. This would not require the use of force, just the action of an increasingly powerful government which would steadily expand its role in the affairs of the society.

Marx and Engels wrote the following for the Communist Party: [19] "These measures will of course be different in different countries. Nevertheless, in the most advanced countries the following will be pretty generally applicable:

1.   Abolition of property in land and application of all rents of land to public purposes."

Marx had written elsewhere in the manifesto: "You are horrified at our intending to do away with your private property. Precisely so, that is just what we intend."[20]

So the first plank of the Manifesto was in keeping with the rest of the philosophy of Marx, although this plank only dealt with property in the form of land.

"2.   A heavy progressive or graduated income tax."

Here Marx adds the income tax as a method of taking property from the "propertied class" to give it to the "working class." This plank is in accord with Marx's statement about the obligation the wealthy have to the poor: "From each according to his ability, to each according to his need."

Government was to become the great income distributor. It was to take from the producers (the "haves,") and give it to the non-producers, (the "have-nots.")

"3.   Abolition of all right of inheritance."

Not only was the producer of capital goods going to find out that, as his efforts increased his rewards would decrease, but, whatever was left after the government took what it felt was needed for the poor, could not be left to his heirs. Property was to become only the temporary possession of the producer.

"4.   Confiscation of the property of all emigrants and rebels."

Those who wished to leave the Communist state would have to forfeit their property to those who remained, and those who opposed the government would have their property confiscated.

"5.   Centralization of credit in the hands of the State by means of a national bank with State capital and an exclusive monopoly."

The Communists told Marx to make certain that only the Communists would have the sole power to create inflation. This power would grant them the ability to destroy the private property rights of those citizens who kept their property in the form of cash.

"6.   Centralization of the means of communication and transport in the hands of the state."

The state would restrict the citizen's right to speak out against the state by controlling his access to a mass audience, as well as control the society's right to freely disburse the goods they produced.

"7.   Extension of factories and instruments of production owned by the State, the bringing into cultivation of waste lands, and the improvement of the soil generally in accordance with a common plan."

The government would own all of the capital goods and the state would determine what was to be grown on the land.

"8.   Equal liability of all to labor. Establishment of industrial armies, especially for agriculture."

All capital goods, including the labor force itself, were to belong to the state. An industrial army would be formed, capable of being moved by its commander to whatever area the state felt needed workers, especially in the agricultural area.

"9.   Combination of agriculture with manufacturing industries; gradual abolition of the distinction between town and country by a more equable distribution of population over the country."

The ultimate capital good, man himself, would lose his ultimate freedom: the right to live where he chose. Possibly Marx envisioned the growth of the labor union as a vehicle to combine "agricultural and manufacturing industries."

"10.   Free education for all children in public schools. Abolition of children's factory labor in its present form. Combination of education with industrial production etc., etc."

The State would assume the responsibility for the education of all of the children in the society. It is presumed that Marx would not have tolerated a private school where parents could teach their own children what they felt was appropriate. If the state were the only educator, it could teach the children whatever it wanted.

The ultimate goal of the state would be to set the values of the society through the public school system. It is also presumed that Marx envisioned the ultimate abolition of the family itself, as the state assumed not only the role of the teacher in the life of the child but the role of the parent as well.

The ten planks of the *Communist Manifesto* were written in 1848. It is interesting to see just how far these programs have advanced in the American society since that date.

1.   Abolition of private property in land:

The United States government now owns 33.5 percent of the land of the U.S., completely in violation of the U.S. Constitution.

Article I grants powers to the Legislative Branch of the Federal Government. Section 8 of Article I grants the power: "To exercise exclusive legislation in all cases whatsoever over such district (not exceeding ten miles square) as may, by cession of particular States and the acceptance of Congress, became the seat of government of the United States, and to exercise like authority over all places purchased by the consent of the Legislature of the State in which the same shall be, for the erection of forts, magazines, arsenals, dockyards, and other useful buildings."

That means that any land owned by the government in excess of Washington D.C. and the necessary military bases is owned in violation of the U.S. Constitution.

And the government owns over one-third of the land in the United States.

In addition, that land which the government does not own is controlled through such controls as land use regulations, governmental bureaucratic edicts, zoning laws, etc. Rent controls are not normally imposed by the federal government, but by local governments, but the effects upon private property are the same. The government controls the land and property of its citizens by controlling the prices the property owners may charge for the rental of their property. (Fascism was defined as control, but not ownership of the factors of production.)

2.   Progressive or graduated income tax:

The United States government passed the Graduated Income Tax in 1913, after several previous attempts had failed.

3.   The Inheritance Tax:

The United States government imposed the Inheritance Tax upon the American people in 1916.

4.   The confiscation of the property of emigrants and rebels:

In 1980, Congress took a giant step towards confiscation of property of emigrants when it passed H.R. 5691, which makes it a crime to transport or even to attempt to transport "monetary instruments" totalling five thousand dollars or more into or out of the country without filing the required reports with the government.

5.   Centralization of credit; a national bank:

The United States set up its national bank, the Federal Reserve, in 1913.

6.   Centralization of communication and transport:

The United States created the Federal Trade Commission in 1916, and the Federal Communications Commission in 1934.

7.   Factors of production owned by the state:

Amtrak, the federal government's railway system, is a recent example of the intrusion of the government into those areas traditionally operated by the free-enterprise system. However, other governmental intrusions into the affairs of the American businessman take the form of governmental controls of the factors of production (Fascism) rather than direct ownership. (The 1980 loan to the Chrysler Corporation was a good example.) In addition, government bureaus of every form and shape issue edicts for the privately owned business to follow.

8.   Equal liability to labor:

The American government has not moved into this area as yet, but has moved into the position of being the employer of last resort through such programs as the Comprehensive Employment and Training Act, the Civilian Conservation Corps, the draft, and a proposal known as the Universal Military Service, where all of military age are obligated to serve their country in some capacity.

9.   Forced distribution of the population:

Very little has been done in this area of Marxist thought except in rather isolated instances, such as the call for "Urban Renewal." Under this proposal, the government forces people out of low rent areas in the name of renewing urban decay. Few of these people return to the renewal area after completion of the housing projects.

10.   Free education in public schools:

The United States government took a giant step, albeit without constitutional authority, towards controlling America's system of education, by funding colleges and universities after Russia orbited the artificial satellite called Sputnik in 1957.

Another step towards this goal occurred in 1980 when the Department of Education was established as a separate governmental department.

Students of Marx have noticed that he wanted the Communists to use both the Graduated Income Tax and the Central Bank as a means of making "inroads into the property of the bourgeoisie." An understanding of how these two instruments of destruction work together will follow in subsequent chapters of this book.

To show how close some of the Marxists are in everyday life to abolishing the right to private property, the communists in the Democratic Party in Oregon passed a rather revealing platform plank at their annual statewide convention in 1972. It read: "Land is a common resource and should be held in public ownership."[21]

The Communists are getting closer.

Chapter 10
The Russian Revolution

The Russian Revolution of 1917 was started by starving Russian workers who were being oppressed by the tyrannical leader of Russia, Czar Nicholas II.

This is a one-sentence summary of the official explanation of the cause of the Communist Revolution. But is there another explanation? Is it possible that the Russian workers were being used by someone else for another reason, just as in the French Revolution of 1789?

Perhaps the true cause of the Russian Revolution can be traced to a war of competition in the oil industry that started after the American Edward L. Drake drilled the first oil well in 1859. Drake was not the one, however, who saw the enormous potential in the oil business for exorbitant profits.

John D. Rockefeller was one of the early refiners of oil, as he started in 1863 with two partners. Rockefeller's interest was not satisfied with just one refinery, however. As author William Hoffman observed: "What he wanted was to be the largest refiner in the world, the only refiner in the world."[1]

By 1872, Rockefeller controlled twenty-five percent of America's refining capacity and by 1879 he controlled ninety-five percent.[2] His goal shifted now from national control to international control. His company, Standard Oil, was supplying ninety percent of America's foreign oil sales and America was the sole source of an exportable surplus. But something was happening to his international market. "The wall of Standard's international oil monopoly had been breached with the opening of Russia's great Baku field on the Caspian Sea. By 1883, a railroad had been built to the Black Sea, and the Czar had invited the Nobel brothers and the Rothschild family to help develop these great oil riches."[3]

Standard Oil now had an international competitor in the oil business!

The Rothschild family was now in a position to compete favorably with Standard Oil in the sale of oil in the world market. By 1888, this new oil source had overtaken Standard Oil as the international seller of crude oil.

The development of Russia's oil supply to the point where it could overtake the United States can be illustrated by the following table:

Petroleum Production:

Year	USA	Russia
1860	70,000 tons	1,300 tons
1885	3,120,000 tons	2,000,000 tons
1901	9,920,000 tons	12,170,000 tons

The rapid growth of the oil industry led Russia into the industrialized world. The traditional explanation of Russia's economy at this time was that the nation was an agrarian economy, far behind the other European economies. However, during the period of 1907 to 1913, Russia's increase in its industrial production rate exceeded that of the United States, England, and Germany, long believed to be the industrialized giants of the day.

The following is typical of the conclusion of many researchers who have examined this period in history: "The Russian revolution of 1917 came not at the end of period of stagnation and decay, but rather after more than a half-century of the most rapid and comprehensive economic progess." And with this progress came the development of a middle class, the enemy of the conspiracy.

There are historians who now believe that the Russian Revolution of 1917 was in truth a revolution instigated by the American and European oil interests to wrest control of the Russian oil fields from the Rothschild-Nobel combination.

But other forces were at work as well in the Russian Revolution. After the defeat of Napoleon and the occupation of Paris in 1814 by Russian troops, many Russian aristocrats visited France. The liberal ideas of the French Revolution appealed to many of them and resulted in the formation of two secret Masonic lodges (in Russia), the Northern Star and the Southern Star. Both lodges enlisted as members many influential and wealthy Russian nobles.[4]

The secret society had been brought to Russia. In a book entitled *Russia 1917*, author George Katkov cited the enormous influence the secret societies had in the Communist Revolution: "There is no doubt . . . that a widespread net of conspiratorial organizations modeled on freemasons' lodges worked for revolution in Russia and played a decisive role in the formation of the first Provisional Government."[5]

With the arrival of the secret society, the near powerful could conspire to replace the monarchy as a form of government through control over the Provisional Government that replaced the Czar after he abdicated. The conspirators now had two of the three essential parts of the "pincers movement" written about by Jan Kozak.

The third part, the "mob," was organized in 1895, when Vladimir Ilyich Lenin and nine others, including Leon Trotsky, formed the Social Democratic Labor Party, the forerunner of the Communist Party.

Perhaps the incident that provoked Lenin's hatred of the Russian monarchy and the Czar occurred in 1881, when his older brother was executed for having taken part in the assassination of Czar Alexander II, the grandfather of Nicholas II, the Czar at the time of Lenin's revolution.

Lenin's revolutionary career began while he was a student at the University of Kazan, where he became a devotee of Karl Marx. Lenin learned that Marx had anticipated two revolutionary methods for total control of a society: the violent and the non-violent.

Marx's ten-plank program discussed in an earlier chapter constituted Marx's non-violent method of communizing a society.

The Russian Communist Party was torn between the advocates of both methods. Lenin preferred a violent revolution to gain control of Russia, and Trotsky preferred the non-violent. The supporters of Lenin became the majority on the debates on the issue and became known as the Bolsheviks (translated as "the majority" in Russian), and the supporters of Trotsky became the minority and were known as the Mensheviks ("the minority)."

Perhaps the most crucial event in the Russian Revolution occurred in the spring of 1905, when the British Fabian Society, a non-violent revolutionary group, met the Bolsheviks, a violent revolutionary group, in London, England. It was at this meeting that loans were arranged between the two groups so that the Bolsheviks could start their revolution. Joseph Fels, a member of the Fabian Society and a wealthy American soap manufacturer, loaned the Bolsheviks large sums of money, as did other members of the Fabians.[6]

Arrangements also were made to finance the Japanese government in a war with the Russian government in an attempt to weaken the monarchy so that it would make the task of the Bolsheviks much easier. From New York, Jacob Schiff, J.P. Morgan, the First National Bank, and the National City Bank loaned Japan approximately $30,000,000 to attack the Russian government from the east.[7]

In 1905, with financing from members of the Fabian Society and with the knowledge that American bankers had loaned Japan money to move against Russia's eastern front, Lenin started his revolution on May 1, the anniversary of the founding of the Illuminati.

But Lenin and his Bolsheviks were not initially successful in their revolution in spite of all of the assistance of the wealthy banking interests and members of the Fabian Society. The Czar exiled Lenin to Switzerland, Trotsky to the United States, and Joseph Stalin to Siberia.

The Bolsheviks were at least partially successful in weakening the monarchy, as the Czar responded to the charges of the Revolution and instituted a series of reforms. For instance, he recognized the principle of limited government, proclaimed a set of fundamental laws, and established a national parliament (called the Duma) with a share in the law-making process for the people. In other words, the monarchy was changing into a democratic republic.

In an extremely puzzling move, the Czar, possibly the richest man in the world, deposited $400,000,000 in the Chase Bank (the Rockefeller interests,) the National City Bank, Guaranty Bank (the Morgan interests,) the Hanover Trust Bank, and the Manufacturers Trust Bank, and $80,000,000 in the Rothschild Bank in Paris. It is possible that he realized that his government was in trouble and he was hoping that his deposits would buy toleration from these interests after their attempt to remove him failed in 1905.

The revolution led inexorably on, and on March 15, 1917, the Czar abdicated in favor of a provisional government led ultimately by the Socialist Alexander Kerensky. One of the first acts of this government was to issue amnesty to the exiled Bolsheviks and back to the Russian Revolution came Lenin, Trotsky, and Stalin.

Many historians feel that the Kerensky government was a temporary front for the Bolsheviks, for three important reasons:

1. Kerensky was allowed to live after Lenin assumed control of the government while virtually all the other members of the Provisional Government were butchered in the revolution that followed.

2. Kerensky issued a general amnesty not only for the Bolshevik leaders, but all others exiled since the aborted revolution of 1905. It is estimated that this act freed over 250,000 dedicated revolutionaries.

3. Kerensky himself admitted that the Kerensky government had "received some support privately from industry in America," possibly from

the same individuals who financed Lenin in 1905.[8]

So back came the major Communist revolutionaries to the revolution. Trotsky left New York City on March 27, 1917, on the S.S. *Christiana* with 275 other followers on his way to Canada. He and his followers were detained in Halifax, Nova Scotia, by the Canadian government, which found $10,000 on his person. This large quantity of money held by Trotsky was indeed a strange amount, as he himself had admitted that the only money he had received during the years of 1916 and 1917 while in New York was $310 that he later admitted he had distributed among 5 emigrants who were returning to Russia.

The subject of Trotsky's $10,000 came up in 1919 during a Senate investigating committee's hearings into the subject of Bolshevik propaganda and German money. "It is quite remarkable that the (Overman) Committee adjourned abruptly before the source of Trotsky's funds could be placed into the record. When questioning resumed the next day, Trotsky and his $10,000 were no longer of interest."[9]

Some did know where the money had come from, however, even if officially the United States government did not want to know. Congressman Louis McFadden, the Chairman of the House Banking Committee, went on record as saying: "They (the private banking monopolies) financed Trotsky's mass meetings of discontent and rebellion in New York. They paid Trotsky's passage from New York to Russia so that he might assist in the destruction of the Russian empire. They fomented and instigated the Russian Revolution and they placed a large fund of American dollars at Trotsky's disposal in one of their branch banks in Sweden."[10]

The Canadian government, discovering that Trotsky carried an American passport, questioned the American government as to why they would allow Trotsky to return to Russia when not only were Canadian troops fighting the Germans in World War I, but American troops as well. It followed, according to the Canadian reasoning, that if the Russian goverment, led by Trotsky and Lenin, signed a peace treaty with Germany, because Russia was also at war with Germany at the time, it would free German troops at war with Russia to kill American troops as well as Canadian. It certainly appeared to the Canadians that it was in America's best interest to keep Russia in the war against Germany and not assist Trotsky in his desire to overthrow the Czar.

Canada's efforts failed, as the Wilson administration pressured the Canadian government into releasing Trotsky. Trotsky and his followers sailed as they had intended.

Perhaps one of the reasons that the Democratic President Woodrow Wilson permitted Trotsky to leave Nova Scotia was that Charles Crane, of the Westinghouse Company and Chairman of the Democratic Finance Committee, was accompanying Trotsky.[11]

Lenin also started his return to Russia along with thirty-two other Russian revolutionaries. These activists left Switzerland in an armored train protected by German troops and they journeyed across war-torn Germany. This was strange as Germany was at war with Russia, and it was unusual for Lenin and his followers not to be prisoners of war. Their destination was Sweden, where Lenin received something like 22 million marks held for him in a Swedish bank.

There are some historians who believe the reason that Lenin and his fellow Russian revolutionaries received such preferential treatment was because the German government and Lenin had reached an agreement to end their war when the Bolsheviks took control of the government.

Stalin returned from Siberia, and now the key individuals were in place for the continuation of the revolution. The Bolsheviks replaced the Kerensky government on November 7, 1917. The provisional government had set November 25th as the first general election ever held in Russia. For the first time in their history, the Russian people would hold free elections and they could choose Bolshevism should they choose to do so.

There was some dissension amongst the Bolsheviks as to whether they should allow the elections to be held as scheduled. Trotsky took the position that they should and his view ultimately prevailed. The people would get the opportunity to choose the form of government they wanted.

There were nearly 42 million votes cast, and the Bolshevik Communists only received thirty percent of the vote. The Bolsheviks, when the Russian people had a chance to accept or reject Communist leadership of their government, were rejected by the people by a seventy to thirty margin.

Yet the claim is continuously made that the Russian people rose up and overthrew the Czar because they wished to replace the monarchy with a Communist government.

Another of the interesting charges made by the Bolshevik government is that they had captured the seven members of the Imperial family: the Czar, the Czarina (the Czar's wife,) the Czarevitch (the Czar' only son,) and their four daughters. The claim was made that all seven had been murdered in the basement of the Ipatiev House in Ekaterinburg, Russia.

The claim continued that the bodies of the Imperial family had been dumped into an abandoned mine near the small town. Yet when various investigators attempted to check this story out, "no bodies, bones, skulls, or dental work of members of the Imperial family were ever found."[12]

Rumors that the family had survived their captivity at Ekaterinburg and had not been murdered started to make the rounds of Europe shortly after the story was told that they had been murdered, but the Bolsheviks continued to deny them, holding to their official position that they were all dead.

These rumors were just rumors until a colonel (the Polish equivalent of general) in the Polish Army Intelligence defected to the United States in 1961. He had supplied the Western countries with the names of hundreds of Soviet spies safely hidden in Western governments prior to his leaving the Polish government.

The charges the colonel made while in Poland had been tested by the courts of the Western countries, and in each case, the spies he had named were found guilty. The American government tested his information as well, and "... former FBI agent John Norpel testified before the Senate Internal Security Subcommittee that, to his knowledge, no information (the defector) gave our government ever turned out to be wrong."[13]

The defector, named Michael Goloniewski, brought additional names of Soviet spies with him when he defected. But there was one individual that the colonel named that was never brought to trial. The colonel contended that "... Secretary of State Henry Kissinger has been a Soviet agent and that his involvement with Soviet Intelligence was made to agencies of our government even before his rise to prominence."[14]

This charge was detailed in a book by Frank Capell, entitled *Henry Kissinger, Soviet Agent*, that was published in 1974. Capell reported: "that under the name of 'Bor,' and described as an agent of ODRA, (a spy group under the command of a Soviet intelligence general,) was Sergeant Henry Kissinger, a U.S. Army counter-intelligence interrogator and instructor at the Military Intelligence School...."[17]

This is the charge that Goloniewski made that never got a hearing in an American court. Those charged in Europe with being Soviet spies, in each case, had been tried and convicted, but for some unexplained reason, his charges against Kissinger never made it to court.

But the story about Goloniewski is even more interesting.

He also claimed that the Imperial family, the Czar of Russia and the rest of his family, had survived the ordeal at Ekaterinburg and had lived in Europe since 1918. He claimed that they had been taken out of Russia in the back of trucks, and then taken by ship to friendly ports where they could live in anonymity.

Goloniewski's charge was partially substantiated by an article that appeared in the Detroit Free Press in 1970 that claimed: "British government documents recently made public in London indicate that President Woodrow Wilson backed a secret mission to Russia in 1917 which may have resulted in the rescue of Czar Nicholas and his family the following year. The documents... state that the U.S. government placed $75,000 at the disposal of Sir William Wiseman, a partner in the New York banking house of Kuhn, Loeb & Co."[16]

The article went on to explain why the Russian Communists had agreed to let the Czar and his family escape: "There is also mounting evidence that the unpublished complete text of the Treaty of Brest-Litovsk, signed March 3, 1918, contains a guarantee from the Lenin government that 'no harm' will come to the Romanovs, according to researchers."[17]

The treaty, named after the city where it was signed, was a peace treaty signed between the German and Russian governments to end their involvement against each other in World War I. Many historians now believe that the charge in the newspaper article about there being such a secret codicil in this Treaty is correct.

But Goloniewski makes one more astonishing charge: he claims to be the Czarevitch, the son of the Czar of Russia. The Colonel's claim was investigated by the American government: "A number of skull measurements and comparison of facial features, ears, relative distances between mouth, nose, eyebrow, forehead, etc., have been made of Goloniewski and compared with photographs and paintings of the young Czarevitch Alexis. In general, they have turned out to be more affirmitive than not."[18]

One fact that would certainly improve the Colonel's case that he was the son of the Czar would be some sort of evidence that he had a blood condition similar to the one that the young Czarevitch exhibited as a boy. This condition, which reduces the ability of the blood to coagulate, was called hemophilia by those who knew the young Czarevitch as a boy, as that was the state of the medical profession at the time.

Goloniewski "has been tested by Dr. Alexander S. Wiener, a co-discoverer of the Rh factor in blood, who found that the Colonel does indeed suffer from a blood disease, the main feature of which is slow blood coagulation."[19]

Other tests, on his fingerprints and sole (foot) prints, blood tests, dental X-rays, and handwriting tests, also suggest that his claim could be true.

In fact, the individual who had the colonel tested was Herman Kimsey, the Chief of Research and Analysis of the Central Intelligence Agency, who, according to sworn testimony, claimed that: "Michael Goloniewski (was) in reality the Tsarevich Aleksei, a fact Kimsey and his staff personally confirmed...."[20]

The colonel's charges that the Imperial family had survived their capture and reported assassination were in part confirmed in 1977 by another source, when a woman claiming to be Anastasia, the Czarevitch's sister, had her charges certified by a French ear expert. This expert made ear comparisons between her ears and the known pictures of the young Anastasia. These comparisons, made by one of France's best known forensic experts, would be admissible in French courts as proof of Anastasia's claims.

But the Colonel has had difficulty in proving his claims in an American court, and few, if any, in government will listen any more. Perhaps the reason the Colonel is having difficulty lies in the fact that the Czar left millions of dollars in American and European banks, and that this wealth is today worth billions of dollars. If the Colonel is certified to be the heir to the Czar, he would have a good claim on these deposits, money that he has no aversion about saying would be used to destroy Communism around the world. The Colonel is no friend of the international bankers who were the recipients of these deposits.

(It is interesting that the colonel charges that Herman Kimsey, the C.I.A. official who conducted the tests that certified that he was who he claimed to be, was murdered in January, 1971, by means of a "wrong blood transfusion.")

The Russian people were being conditioned to the fact that the Czar was dead and that the revolution had succeeded in replacing the monarchy with a Communist form of government. The United States, during the revolution, took little or no direct action against the Bolsheviks, although it appeared to other nations, especially in Europe, that the American government was supporting the Communists. At least that is the gist of a correspondence the American government received from the U.S. legation in Bern, Switzerland, which read: ". . . people are asking why the President expresses support of Bolsheviki, in view of rapine, murder and anarchy of these bands."[21]

(Rapine is defined as the seizing and carrying away of things by force and plunder.)

Just what was the American government supporting?

Lenin had answered that question by writing: "Our power does not know liberty or justice. It is entirely established on the destruction of the individual will. We are the masters. Complete indifference to suffering is our duty. In the fulfillment of our calling, the greatest cruelty is a merit."[22]

And: "Though a systematic terror, during which every breach of contract, every treason, every lie will be lawful, we will find the way to abase humanity down to the lowest level of existence. That is indispensible to the establishment of our dominance."[23]

Lenin also declared his philosophical kinship with Karl Marx when he declared on November 8, 1917, just after the Communists took over the Russian government: "The right of private property in land is forever abolished. All land owned by the Church, private persons, by peasants, is taken away without compensation."[24]

It is interesting that the peasants of Russia, the supposedly landless class that the Russian Communists were causing a revolution to assist, lost their land as well.

Lenin had lied to the people. He had promised them that the land would be taken away from the landed gentry and given to them, the "poor, downtrodden working class." Some of the peasants already owned land that was taken away by Lenin's decree.

The Revolution, with American help, was now complete: the Bolsheviks had seized control of the once prosperous Russian government.

One of the first acts of the Bolshevik government in 1917 was to dissolve the lodges of the Freemasons.

But the most insidious activity of the new Communist government occurred when they signed a peace treaty with Germany to end their involvement in World War I, just as the Canadian government had feared. As a result of this peace treaty, the Germans were able to move their troops to the western front to kill American and Canadian soldiers.[25]

With the war in eastern Europe now over, the secret Communist organizations could start Communist revolutions all over Europe. For instance, the German Communists, calling themselves the German "Spartacists" after the Roman slave Spartacus who led an uprising against the Roman empire, (or was it because Adam Weishaupt, the founder of the Illuminati, had called himself Spartacus in his dealings with his fellow Illuminati members) revolted against the German government.

Revolutions were also instigated in Austria and Hungary, but all of these failed and the traditional method of governmental rule prevailed.

Life magazine, in its article on revolution, correctly identified the enemy of these revolutions: "Their nemesis was Europe's solid middle class . . . a class once weakly represented in Russia. Chiefly because of it, no Communist Party has been able to seize power in Western Europe to this day."[26]

As is the case in every major Communist revolution, the enemy is the middle class, and their elimination becomes the reason for the revolution.

But the American support of the Bolshevik government did not end with the ending of the fighting between the Germans and the Russians. President Woodrow Wilson refused Japan's request to enter the revolution against the Bolsheviks in 1919.[27] This effort would have put enormous pressure on the Bolsheviks who would have had trouble raising an army against the Japanese, just like the Czar had in 1905.

The Fabian Society, non-violent Marxists, also assisted the Bolshevik government later when they pressured the labor unions in England: "The sweeping threat by British trade unions to 'down tools' in 1920 was instigated by an arch-Fabian Arthur Henderson. This threat effectively ended British military intervention in Russia and enabled the Bolsheviks to capture large stores of British-made munitions — a decisive factor in the survival of Bolshevik armed rule . . . ."[28]

The "non-violent" branch of the Conspiracy was now assisting the "violent," even though Lenin himself was warning the world that his intent was to destroy the free-enterprise system: "As long as Capitalism (the free-enterprise system) and Communism remain, We cannot live in peace. In the end, one or the other will perish."[29]

Lenin also received assistance from those who supposedly had the most to lose in a Communist Russia: the wealthy American "capitalists" themselves.

The director of the Federal Reserve Bank of New York, William B. Thompson, gave a personal contribution of $1,000,000 to the Bolsheviks. Mr. Thompson was also a heavy stockholder in the Chase National Bank, owned by the Rockefeller interests.[30]

The Morgan and Rockefeller interests also contributed cash to the cause, as did Jacob Schiff, the senior partner of Kuhn, Loeb and Co., who gave Lenin $20,000,000. Schiff was a partner of Paul Warburg, the Chairman of the Federal Reserve, and a participant at the Jekyll Island, Georgia, meetings that wrote the Federal Reserve bill that created America's central banking system.

In addition to assistance from the Americans, primarily the banking interests, Lenin also received, according to Alexander Kerensky, the sum of forty million gold marks (about $5,000,000) from the German banking interests.[31]

While the banking fraternity was financing the Russian Revolution, they were also bringing World War I to a close by causing the Treaty of Versailles to be signed. President Woodrow Wilson led the American delegation to the signing of the treaty, taking along with him, as delegates or assistants to the delegation, his trusted assistant Colonel Edward Mandell House; Thomas Lamont, a partner of J.P. Morgan; Paul Warburg; and four young visionaries: Allen Dulles, later the head of the Central Intelligence Agency; John Foster Dulles, later the Secretary of State in President Eisenhower's cabinet; Walter Lippmann, later a nationally syndicated columnist; and Christian Herter, later the Secretary of State who replaced John Foster Dulles.

The German delegation to the signing included Paul Warburg's brother, Max, who was the president of the M.N. Warburg and Co., international bankers, and the individual who assisted Lenin in crossing war-torn Germany during his return to Russia from exile in Switzerland.

But even with all of the financial assistance given to Lenin by the wealthy "capitalists," the Bolsheviks only controlled a small percentage of Russia. The Communists now had to consolidate their power and expand it through the remainder of Russia. The strategy utilized to achieve this goal was forced starvation of the Russian people.

The Bolsheviks, in keeping with Lenin's dictum to utilize terror in their quest for political power, would move into an area, grab all of the food supplies and the livestock, and then inform the peasants who previously owned these items that they were to be placed on a "collective farm" where the property would be owned by the state in the name of the people. Those who resisted the imposition of the collective were either starved or murdered, or placed into concentration camps so that they could learn about the merits of collectivism through the teachings of the Bolsheviks.

One of the Bolsheviks committing these heinous crimes against the people was Nikita Khrushchev, later to become the leader of the Russian government. His crimes were documented in a seven part study conducted by the House Committee on Un-American Activities, in a report entitled *The Crimes of Khrushchev.* This report concluded that "Khrushchev . . . as the No. 1 Communist official in the Moscow area . . . sent thousands to their death, (and) scores of thousands to hideous slave-labor camps."[32]

Obviously, food production dropped when the government took producers off the fields. So the starvation perpetuated itself to the point where millions of Russian peasants starved all across the nation.

It was now important that the Bolshevik government have outside assistance if it was to survive.

The American government again filled a very important void in the Russian economy.

This time it was Herbert Hoover who "saved Lenin's dictatorship from popular revolt in the early 1920's. There is further proof that Hoover, then President Harding's Secretary of Commerce, knew U.S. shipments of food, which the American people were told were to save starving Russians, actually were used to strengthen Bolshevik power. In his book *Herbert Hoover and Famine Relief to Soviet Russia,* professor Benjamin Weissman of Rutgers University revealed that Hoover continued to send public foodstuffs to Russia long after it was obvious the Bolsheviks were shipping their own food abroad in order to purchase machinery."[33]

Because of this American assistance, Lenin and the Bolsheviks were able to take power in the remainder of Russia. They began to build "the Socialist Order." This program included the following:

1. Private ownership of land was abolished.
2. Banks were nationalized.
3. Most industrial enterprises were nationalized.
4. The merchant marine was nationalized.
5. The stock market was slowly abolished.
6. The right of inheritance was abolished.
7. Gold was declared a state monopoly.
8. All government debts were declared null and void.
9. The old criminal courts were replaced by revolutionary tribunals in which any citizen could act as judge or lawyer.
10. The old strict marriage and divorce laws were replaced by very lenient civil codes.

11. The church was not abolished, but its lands were seized and religious teaching was forbidden in the schools.[34]

Lenin, in keeping with Marx's teachings that the state should create a central bank and have an exclusive monopoly on the issuance of money took control of the Russian banking system. His first priority in this move was to create massive inflation. He "...used the printing press to destroy the people's savings and redistribute the wealth by sharing the poverty. In 1921, Communist economist Eugene Preobrazhensky had even dedicated a book to the 'printing press of the People's Commissariat of Finance,' which he described as that 'machine-gun which attacked the bourgeois regime in its rear — its monetary system — by converting the bourgeois economic law of money circulation into a means of destruction of that same regime and into a force of financing the revolution.' "[35]

Lenin used the printing press to increase the number of rubles in circulation "nearly 20,000 times from 1921 to 1923."[36] In fact the quantity of rubles issued each month was so staggering, the Communists weren't even capable of remembering the exact quantity issued. "In March, 1922, the Commissar of Finance...announced that the issues of that month alone amounted to either twenty-three of twenty-four trillions, he wasn't sure which."[37]

The resulting inflation raised the general index of prices to 16,000 times what it was in 1913. It had its desired effect. The middle class was eliminated as a class in Russia.

Now that the local banks had been nationalized, the next step was to create an international bank, which was formed in the fall of 1922. It was based on a "syndicate that involved the former Russian private bankers and some new investment from German, Swedish, American and British bankers."[38]

So Lenin now rewarded those who had helped him finance the Russian Revolution by allowing them to become part of the international bank he was creating. In fact, the Rockefellers were included in his plans as well. "In the 1930's the Chase National was one of four American banks and financial houses to institute relations with the Soviets (in addition to Equitable Trust, Guaranty Trust, and Kuhn Loeb.)"[39]

It was in 1929 that the final piece fell into place. The Russian government made it a crime for the Russian people to own gold in any form. The people had lost their right to check government's intrusions into the money supply by their ability to print increasingly worthless paper money.

Now that the middle class had been destroyed as a class of people through inflation, the Soviets focused their attention on the poor. The starvation continued, even after Lenin died and Stalin replaced him. In 1930 Stalin began his campaign to confiscate the lands of the peasant farmers and herd these men and their families into 'collective' or state farms. To crush their spirit, the regime created a man-made famine. Armed squads stripped vast areas of all grain, cattle, and food. More than 3.5 million more peasants died in concentration camps. Prominent Bolshevik Nikolai Bukharin admitted 'we are conducting a mass annihilation of defenseless men together with their wives and children.' "[40]

In 1970, the Senate Internal Security Subcommittee released a study entitled *The Human Cost of Soviet Communism* which asserted that at least 21.5 million persons have been executed or have died in prison camps in the Soviet Union during the past fifty-one years. The author of the report stated that his estimate was conservative and that the real figure may have been as high as 45 million.

But even this cost in human misery is not considered too high by certain Americans. President Harry Truman was quoted by author Eldorous L. Dayton in his book *Give 'em Hell, Harry* as saying: "Moscow emerged from the dark ages only in 1917."[41]

So, in summary, Communism was imposed down on the people: the people did not rise up and demand Communism. But, even with the ample evidence supporting this statement, others still do not choose to believe that this is true. *Life* magazine, for one, in its series on Revolutions, concluded this about the Russian Revolution of 1917: "The Russian Revolution began spontaneously in an urban insurrection against a feudal regime...."[42]

Another author, Robert Goldston, in his book *The Russian Revolution*, stated his opinion thus: "Revolutions are not conspiracies — they are vast social upheavals as inevitable and self-justifying as earthquakes."[43]

In fact, four American presidents felt that the price the Russian people paid for Bolshevik "progress" was too high and they showed their contempt for the Bolshevik government by refusing to recognize them as Russia's government. This American policy lasted until 1933 when President Franklin Roosevelt granted diplomatic recognition to the Communist government, legitimizing the brutal regime, and in essence approving their methods in achieving control of the Russian government.

Chapter 11
The Cuban Revolution

Other countries have shared Russia's "emergence from the dark ages" by changing their governmental configuration to Communism as well. Cuba is one of these "fortunate" countries.

The typical explanation of the reasons for Cuba's Communist experiment is that Cuba was a poverty-stricken country beset with internal problems so intense that the people were forced to seek a change in their government. "There was a general misconception that the events in Cuba were brought about by low standards of living and social inequalities. The facts belie this."[1]

In fact, Cuba of all of the countries in Latin America, had a rising standard of living, and the people were moderately prosperous. Cuba was, amongst the Latin American countries:

third in percentage of literacy;
first in percentage of education;
lowest in mortality-rate;
second in number of doctors per 1,000 people;
third in the number of dentists per 1,000 people;
first in the number of cars per person;

first in the number of TV sets;

third in the number of telephones;

fourth in wages per employee; and

second in per capita income.

Cuba in 1958, prior to the government of the Communist Fidel Castro, paid its employees an average of $3.00 per hour, which was higher that year than Belgium ($2.70); Denmark ($2.86); France ($1.74); West Germany ($2.73); and comparable to the United States ($4.06).

After the Cuban revolution, the standard of living dropped, as evidenced by these comments gleaned from four recent American magazine articles on Cuba:

Anyone can observe the streets recalling that once they were filled with autos and now there are few.[2]

Although food items are limited, they are available. Other products are simply not to be had. Such a system of shortages makes a ripe condition for black marketing.[3]

No matter how much money a family has, it finds itself equal before the Cuban rationing system, which includes practically all food and consumer goods.

Every Cuban has a packet of ration books, one for each category.[4]

The work hours are long, shortages are real, and the many activities, freedoms, and possessions that Americans consider necessary to happiness are either limited or unavailable.[5]

Since the Revolution, organized religion has markedly lost power. The greatest change was the takeover of the schools, always a large part of the Catholic Church's activities.[6]

An article in the *U.S. News and World Report,* June 26, 1978, further confirmed the scarcities and shortages in the Cuban "paradise:"

Food shortages are a way of life in Castro's Cuba. Havana's best restaurants consistently run short of meat and other staples.

Because almost everything is owned by the state, Cubans are enmeshed in endless red tape....

Most workers lack motivation because of low pay. Often, four or five persons work on a job that requires only one. Nobody does a good job. Here in Cuba, you do only what you have to do, and care little about the quality of your work.[7]

The author of the book *Inside Cuba Today*, Fred Ward, was concerned about the dismal record of Cuba, especially after Cuba had once been one of the most prosperous countries in Latin America. He interviewed many Cubans and they had difficulty with his simple question: "No one asked by the author in Cuba could answer the basic concern of any student of Communism: If the system is so successful and desirable, why won't it work without the massive restrictions on individual liberty?"[8]

The life is so undesirable in Cuba that many have voted against it with their feet: "About 800,000 Cubans have emigrated to America since Fidel Castro seized power in Cuba in 1959."[9]

If the Cuban people knew what they know about the dismal record of Communism in Cuba, they certainly would not have allowed their country to go Communist. But the Cubans had the information necessary to determine if Communism had worked anywhere in the world prior to 1959, but the country went Communist anyway. The question should be asked, then, just why the country is Communist.

The American Ambassador to Cuba during the Communist Revolution, Earl E. T. Smith, has this to say about the answer to that question: "To the contrary, Castro could not have seized power in Cuba without the aid of the United States. American government agencies and the United States press played a major role in bringing Castro to power. As the U.S. Ambassador to Cuba during the Castro-Communist revolution of 1957-59, I had first-hand knowledge of the facts which brought about the rise of Fidel Castro. The State Department consistently intervened — positively, negatively, and by innuendo — to bring about the downfall of President Fulgencio Batista, thereby making it possible for Fidel Castro to take over the government of Cuba. On January 1, 1959, the government of Cuba fell. The United States continued to aid the Castro regime by maintaining the long-standing subsidy for Cuban sugar exports."[10]

The question that has long plagued those who supported the guerilla activities of Fidel Castro has been whether or not Castro was a Communist prior to his becoming the leader of the Cuban Communist government.

The evidence was that Castro was indeed a long-term Communist prior to the commencement of his guerilla activities against the Batista government and this fact was known to those in the American government who supported his revolution. This conclusion is now a matter of fact, as the evidence of history confirms the fact that Castro had been a Communist since his early college days. In 1948 there was an attempted Communist takeover in Colombia, South America. Fidel Castro led a student group into a radio station where he grabbed a microphone to announce: "This is Fidel Castro from Cuba. This is a Communist revolution. The president has been killed. All of the military establishments are now in our hands. The Navy has capitulated to us, the revolution has been a success."[11]

This statement was heard by William D. Pawley, former American Ambassador to Brazil and Peru, who heard Castro on his car radio while he was in Bogota, Columbia, during the attempted revolution.

Castro fled Colombia and went to the Cuban mountains, where he started his revolution against the Batista government. This was in December, 1956, and Castro had a total of eighty-two followers. This number soon dwindled to eleven, and by June of 1957 Castro had only thirty guerillas. The claim is constantly made that Castro's revolution was a popular one, and that the workers of Cuba flocked to assist him. The numbers just aren't there to support this conclusion.

One of the early supporters of Fidel Castro was Herbert Matthews, a reporter for the *New York Times*, and a member of the Council on Foreign Relations.[12] On February 25, 1957, Mr. Matthews reported to his readers: "There is no communism to speak of in Fidel Castro's movement."[13]

It was about this time, however, that the U.S. government learned that Mr. Matthews was incorrect: "A complete dossier on Castro...and the Communists surrounding Castro, prepared by the G-2 (Intelligence) of the Cuban Army, was hand carried to Washington in 1957 and delivered to Allen Dulles, head of the C.I.A."[14]

Unfortunately for the Cuban people and ultimately for the world as well, Allen Dulles, also a member of the Council on Foreign Relations, did nothing with this information.

Once again, in 1958, official reports of Castro's Communist connections were delivered to William Wieland, Latin American Specialist in the State Department. As a response to these reports, Mr. Wieland requested that the U.S. government cancel all arms shipments to the Cuban government of Fulgencio Batista.

About this time, Castro gave a written interview to Jules DuBois in which he declared: "I have never been nor am I a Communist...."[15]

Further support for the "non-Communist" Castro came from the American Ambassador to Cuba who declared that Batista no longer had the support of the U.S. government and that he should leave Cuba.[16]

To show that this statement was true, and that the U.S. government was supporting Castro, Roy Rubottom, the Assistant Secretary for Latin American Affairs, declared in December, 1958: "There was no evidence of any organized Communist elements within the Castro movement or that Senor Castro himself was under Communist influence."[17]

One who disagreed was Major Pedro Diaz Lanz, head of Fidel Castro's Air Force. He visited the United States in July of 1959 to proclaim that he had first-hand knowledge that Castro was a Communist. He went on a nation-wide speaking tour proclaiming this fact, but few who could do anything about it were listening.

Ambassador Smith gave credibility to the charges of Major Lanz when he reported: "From the time Castro landed in the province of Oriente in December, 1956, the State Department received reports of probable Communist infiltration...of the 26th of July movement (the name of Castro's guerilla army.)"[18]

Smith placed the blame for Castro's assumption of power in Cuba where he felt it should be placed: "The U.S. government agencies and the U.S. press played a major role in bringing Castro to power."[23]

The debate as to whether or not Castro was a Communist ended when Castro himself proclaimed the following on December 2, 1961: "I have been a Communist since my teens."[24]

Those who had been stating that Castro was not a Communist had been wrong, but the damage had already been done. Castro assumed power in Cuba, and the United States government quickly granted diplomatic recognition to his government. The State Department added its assurance of its "good will" towards the new government.

Castro now had the opportunity to put his Communist ideas to work in Cuba. One of the first steps he took was in May, 1959, when he passed the Agrarian Reform Law. This Communist program instructed the farmers in what products they could grow and what price they could charge for them. In addition, Castro passed the Urban Reform Law which cancelled all leases and mortgages, thereby dealing a staggering blow to the middle and upper classes in Cuba.

But the position of the United States government was changing, at least in the secret confines of the various departments in charge of such things. President Eisenhower gave the C.I.A. permission to organize a group of Cuban exiles in the United States into an armed force trained to return to Cuba and attempt to overthrow the Castro government. Eisenhower placed the head of the C.I.A., Allen Dulles, in charge of the program. Both Dulles and Eisenhower were members of the Council on Foreign Relations.

The C.I.A. developed the plans for the armed invasion of Cuba, and selected two preliminary invasion sites in 1961: the Bay of Pigs, and the town of Trinidad, Cuba. The latter had several distinct advantages over the Bay of Pigs: it was 100 miles farther from Havana, the seat of Castro's power; it had a basically anti-Castro population; it had an airfield located nearby, suitable as a site for unloading the troops, ammunition and supplies so vital to the success of the invasion; and the town had one ingredient necessary should the invasion fail: there was a range of mountains nearby into which the anti-Castro Cubans could flee. These mountains could hide the force, enabling them to rally support of other anti-Castro soldiers in a guerilla war against the Castro government.

The plans for the invasion were discussed and approved by a committee of various officials in the Kennedy administration, even though Mr. Dulles was the official designee as the chief of the operation. The members of this committee were:

Secretary of State Dean Rusk, member of the C.F.R.;

Secretary of Defense Robert McNamara, member of the C.F.R.;

General Lyman Lemnitzer, Chairman of the Joint Chiefs of Staff, member of the C.F.R.;

Admiral Arleigh Burke, Chief of Naval Operations;

Adolf A. Berle, Jr., Head of the Latin American Task Force, member of the C.F.R.; and

McGeorge Bundy, Special Assistant to the President for National Security Affairs, member of the C.F.R.[21]

It is revealing that five of the six members of this committee were members of the Council on Foreign Relations, described by one author as "The Invisible Government" of the United States.

In addition, President Kennedy, now the President after replacing Eisenhower, called a meeting on April 4, 1961, of the National Security Council in order to have a full-dress debate on the plan. Those attending included:

Allen Dulles, member of the C.F.R.;

Richard Bissell, member of the C.F.R.;

General Lemnitzer, member of the C.F.R.;

Mr. Rusk, member of the C.F.R.;

Mr. McNamara, member of the C.F.R.;

Adolf Berle, member of the C.F.R.;

Arthur Schlesinger, member of the C.F.R.;

McGeorge Bundy, member of the C.F.R.;

Thomas Mann;

Paul Nitze, member of the C.F.R.;

Douglas Dillon, member of the C.F.R.; and

Senator William Fulbright.

The invasion force entered Cuba at the Bay of Pigs, the second choice of the two locations, and even though there were some early successes, the invasion failed. In the first few moments, the invaders held control of approximately 800 square miles, but when Castro's air force suddenly appeared to control the skies over the invasion site, the invasion was doomed.

There has been much written on both sides about the question of whether the invading Cubans were promised American air cover.

The anti-Castro Cubans were aware of how essential air cover was to the success of the mission and they have taken the position since the invasion that the American government had indeed promised this protection. The American government's position has basically been that no such air cover was promised.

In any event, there was no American air cover and the invasion failed.

One of the early signs that the invasion was planned to fail was the appearance of an article in the *New York Times* on January 10, 1961, that carried this headline about three months prior to the invasion: "U.S. Helps Train Anti-Castro Force at Secret Guatemalan Air-Ground Base"[27]

The article included a map showing the location of the training base on Guatemalan soil. It went on to report that the Guatemalan government was training a force to protect Guatemala against a Cuban invasion, but indicated that other Guatemalans were not accepting that explanation: "Opponents of the Ydigoran Administration (the current Guatemalan president) have insisted that the preparations are for an offensive against the Cuban regime of Premier Fidel Castro and that they are being planned and directed and to a great extent being paid for, by the United States."[28]

So all Castro had to do to know about the invasion that was yet to come was to read the *New York Times*!

So the invasion was held on April 16, 1961, and Castro's armed forces and air force were victorious. There are several things about the invasion that are extremely revealing about how poorly it had been planned:

1. The Cuban invasion force was told that there were no reefs in the landing area, yet the bottoms of three landing craft were ripped open by the reefs, hidden by the tide.

2. Without any air support, Castro's air force was able to sink two supply ships. Without the needed supplies being brought ashore, many of the soldiers on the beaches ran out of ammunition within the first twenty-four hours.

3. The C.I.A. armed the 1,443 man invasion force with weapons requiring over thirty different types of ammunition. The guns were purchased in second-hand stores to "avoid identifying the invading force with the U.S. (government)."

4. Planned coordination of an underground uprising of anti-Castro Cubans on Cuba were mismanaged and word to over one hundred underground organizations was never given. They were not told when the invasion was planned.

5. Radio SWAN, the C.I.A.'s short wave broadcast station gave one conflicting and false report after another about uprisings all over Cuba, none of which were true.

After the Bay of Pigs invasion failed, the Castro government could claim that tiny Communist Cuba had defeated the mighty United States, and U.S. prestige as a result of this failure sunk to a new low in Latin America. The lesson was clear. The powerful United States could not train a force capable of putting an end to Communism in Cuba but, by inference, anywhere else in Latin America. And any country needing American assistance in solving their internal battles with Communism had best not ask the United States government to assist.

One of the American journalists who reported on this turn in popular support was Dr. Steuart McBirnie, who toured the area shortly after the Bay of Pigs. He reported that many leaders of the Latin American countries he visited reported that they felt that they couldn't trust the American government any longer as a protector of their government against Communism. Dr. McBirnie reported these attitudes in America through his extensive radio broadcasts and writings, but nothing changed.

Cuba returned to the international spotlight once again a year later during what has been called "The Cuban Missile Crisis."

On October 16, 1962, President John Kennedy called a meeting at the White House because his intelligence sources were advising him that the Russian government was placing missiles and atomic weapons in Cuba. Present at that meeting were nineteen others, all key members of the Kennedy administration, including his brother, Attorney General Robert Kennedy.

The Central Intelligence Agency made a formal presentation to those in attendance by showing them photographs taken at various missile sites in Cuba. Robert Kennedy later wrote a book entitled *Thirteen Days*, in which he commented on those pictures. He wrote: "I, for one, had to take their word for it. I examined the pictures carefully, and what I saw appeared to be no more than the clearing of a field for a farm or the basement of a house. I was relieved to hear later that this was the same reaction of virtually everyone at the meeting including President Kennedy."[25]

Of the twenty people at the meeting, fifteen were members of the Council on Foreign Relations.

President Kennedy, apparently after being convinced that he should see missiles in pictures where there were no missiles, decided to take stern measures against the Russian government. He went on television and told the American people that several of the Cuban bases included "ballistic missiles" capable of reaching a portion of the United States. He then called on Premier Khrushchev of Russia to withdraw the "missiles" from Cuba. When *The New York Times* carried the story of Kennedy's speech the next day, their article carried no pictures of either a missile or a missile base. However, the next day, October 24, 1962, they published a picture of a supposed "missile site" with what they identified as "missiles on launchers." The supposed "missiles" in the picture were no larger than an actual pencil dot, but the *Times* was certain that those dots were "missiles."

Whatever the objects were that the Russians had in Cuba, they agreed to remove them on October 28, subject to "United Nations verification."[26] The American Navy was actually prepared to board the departing Russian ships to verify that actual missiles were being removed. But no one actually boarded any Russian ship supposedly carrying missiles. American photographers took pictures of the Russian ships as they flew over them while the ships were in the ocean, but all these photos showed were tarpaulin covered objects of unknown contents. The media quickly labelled these objects as "Soviet missiles."[27]

The myth that Russia was actually removing missiles has been perpetuated for many years. As recently as March 29, 1982, *U.S. News and World Report* carried a picture of the stern end of a ship moving through the water with a tarpaulin covered object on the deck. The caption under the picture read "Soviet ship removes nuclear missiles from Cuba in 1962 showdown."[28]

It is not known, because it has never been revealed, just how the American government or the American press knew that there were actual missiles under those tarpaulins, especially since the government had stated that one of the conditions of their removal was that someone other than the Cubans was to actually inspect the Russian ships for verification purposes.

So only the Russians and the Cubans know for certain. And they have made no known statement to the effect that the objects under the tarpaulins and the little dots on large photographs were actually missiles. What they were saying, in essence, was that if the American government wanted to believe that those objects were missiles, they had every right to do so. (It would certainly be foolish for the Cubans and the Russian to admit that they had actually lied to the people of the world and had shipped out wooden crates containing nothing but humid air.)

It was later revealed that President Kennedy, as part of the agreement for the Russians to remove the alleged missiles, agreed to remove actual missiles from American bases in Turkey and Italy.

In addition to the removal of American missiles, President Kennedy agreed to another condition. The American government would give assurances to the Russian and Cubans governments that they would intercede in any invasion of Cuba by anti-Castro forces.

Anti-Castro Cubans, unaware of this agreement between the Russians and the Americans, were purchasing weapons and ships in the United States at the time and were making preparations for a counter-revolution in Cuba. As they moved towards the Cuban shore, they were stopped by the U.S. Coast Guard and their ships and weapons were taken away. The Castro regime was now being protected from an anti-Castro invasion by the U.S. Coast Guard.

There are many who believe that this was indeed the purpose of the "Cuban missile crisis;" wooden crates were removed in exchange for an agreement on the part of the American government to do two things:

1.   Remove actual strategic missiles from the borders of Russia, and
2.   guarantee that Castro's government would not be subject to an anti-Castro invasion.

One of the Americans who felt that the American government had actually created the Castro movement and later imposed the Castro government down on the Cuban people was President John Kennedy. According to the *New York Times* of December 11, 1963, President Kennedy gave an interview in which he was quoted as saying: "I think we have spawned, constructed, entirely fabricated without knowing it, the Castro movement."[29]

For his part in assisting Castro's rise to power, Herbert Matthews of the *New York Times* was elevated to the Editorial Board of that newspaper. And for his efforts, William Wieland was given the important post as Consul General for Australia.[30]

Castro was now guaranteed the opportunity to literally destroy the Cuban economy with his mistaken ideas of the efficiency of Cuban Communism, and to have the U.S. Coast Guard protect his government from offshore invasion.

And President Kennedy, who apparently figured it all out, was dead about three weeks before the *Times* carried the interview.

Chapter 12

The American Revolution

Someone once wrote: "God cannot alter the past, only historians can!"

It is certainly not possible for historians to know about the "smoke-filled" rooms where the future is planned unless they are made privy to the future history being planned there. Therefore, most historians report the historical events without really knowing how the events were created.

In addition, those who plan the wars, depressions and other human calamities do not want the truth about their planning activities known. So the Revisionist Historians (those who seek the true causes of the historical events) must pursue the truth through the concealed accesses to the events of the past as seen by those who were there and have recorded their knowledge of the event as they remember it. These sources are generally hidden from the general public, but they do exist.

The version of history contained in the following chapters is not the traditionally accepted one, but it is nevertheless true. It has taken detailed research to ferret out this version of history, sifting through the smoke of the "smoke filled" rooms.

Reginald McKenna, past Chairman of the Board of the Midlands Bank of England, has written this about the power of the banking establishment:

"I am afraid the ordinary citizen will not like to be told that banks can and do create money . . . . And they who control the credit of the nation direct the policy of Governments and hold in the hollow of their hands the destiny of the people."[1]

Abraham Lincoln also warned about a banking establishment, although he chose to call it the "money power." He wrote: "The money power preys upon the nation in times of peace and conspires against it in times of adversity. I see in the near future a crisis approaching that . . . causes me to tremble for the safety of my country. The money power of the country will endeavor to . . . work . . . upon the people, until the wealth is aggregated in a few hands, and the republic destroyed."[2]

Another who warned about the powers of a banking establishment was Sir Josiah Stamp, a past President of the Bank of England: "If you want to remain the slaves of the bankers, and pay the costs of your own slavery, let them continue to create money and control the nation's credit."[3]

President James Garfield also voiced a similar opinion: "Whoever controls the volume of money in any country is absolute master of all industry and commerce."[4]

The goals of these banking establishments was detailed by Dr. Carroll Quigley in his book *Tragedy and Hope*: ". . . the powers of financial capitalism had another far-reaching aim, nothing less than to create a world system of financial control in private hands able to dominate the political system of each country and the economy of the world as a whole. The system was to be controlled in a feudalist fashion by the central banks of the world acting in concert, by secret agreements arrived at in frequent private meetings and conferences."[5]

Thomas Jefferson was also aware of the power of the banking establishment, and he attempted to warn the American people of the money-debt cycle: "It is incumbent on every generation to pay its own debts as it goes — a principle which, if acted on, would save one half of the wars of the world."

And: "The principle of spending money to be paid by posterity, under the name of funding, is but swindling futurity on a large scale."[6]

Another of our founding fathers who feared the banking establishment and its ability to create money and debt was Benjamin Franklin, who wrote: "The Borrower is a Slave to the Lender, and the Debtor to the Creditor . . . . Preserve your freedom, and maintain your independence. Be industrious and free; be frugal and free."[7]

These warnings are very explicit. Banking establishments create national debt. National debt makes slaves of those who owe the debt. It becomes important, then, to understand the nature of banking establishments if they have the ability to create such human misery as has been described by the above cited authors.

Bankers who loan to governments all over the world are called "international bankers." And like all bankers, their success in business depends on their ability to have their loans repaid by the borrower. Just like the local banker, who must secure his loan with some form of collateral, the international banker is concerned with the debtor pledging something of value, something that could be sold to satisfy any outstanding balance owed by the defaulting borrower.

A local bank loans money on a house by having the debtor pledge the home as collateral. The banker can "foreclose" on the mortgage and become the sole owner should the payments not be made as promised.

The international banker faced a more complex problem than the local banker, though. What could he secure his loan with when he loaned money to the leader of a government? The head of the government had one power not shared by the homeowner: the right to "repudiate" the loan.

Repudiation is defined as: "The refusal of a national or state government to pay real or alleged pecuniary obligations."

The bankers had to develop a strategy by which they could make certain that the government they loaned to did not repudiate the loan that the bankers made to the governments.

The international bankers slowly developed their plan. It was called "Balance of Power Politics." This meant that the bankers loaned to two governments at the same time, affording them the opportunity to play one against the other as a means of forcing one to pay his debts to the banker. The most successful tool of insuring compliance with the terms of payment was the threat of war: the banker could always threaten the defaulting government with a war as a means of forcing it to make their payments. This act of repossessing the nation would almost always work as the head of government, anxious to keep his seat of power, would agree to the terms of the original loan, and continue making his payments.

The key to using this tool, however, was making certain that both kingdoms were nearly the same size, so that one nation would not become so powerful that the threat of a war with a weaker neighboring nation would not be sufficient to force it into making its payments.

In other words, both nations had to be approximately the same size and to have nearly the same potential to wage war with the other; if one nation had a larger potential than another, the larger nation would act as a threat against the smaller, but the smaller would not act as a threat against the larger. Both had to have the same potential or one would no longer be a threat to the other.

With the basic understanding of how international bankers operate, it is now possible to truly understand the nature of the recent past.

In his book, *The Real History of the Rosicrucians*, the author Arthur

Edward Waite makes this statement: "Beneath the broad tide of human history, there flow the stealthy undercurrents of the secret societies, which frequently determine in the depths the changes that take place upon the surface."[8]

With this explanation in mind, a study of the recent past should start with the American Revolution of 1776. The traditional historians of the past have explained that the cause of the Revolution was America's resistance to "taxation without representation." But this supposed cause doesn't hold up when measured against the taxation the English government was imposing upon the Colonists. The tax was less than one percent of the nation's Gross National Product. And it would seem that it would take more than that to inflame the American people into a full-scale revolution against the British government, since the American taxpayers in 1980 were paying approximately forty percent of their income to the American government with little direct representation (for instance, when did the American people directly vote for foreign aid, the space race, welfare, etc.) without a revolution against the American government.

Perhaps Mr. Waite is correct. Possibly the "secret societies" he mentions were at work in the American colonies prior to the founding of this nation, and the revolution against the English government.

Perhaps the beginning of the American Revolution can be traced back to June 24, 1717, when four masonic lodges united in London, England, to form the Grand Lodge of London. The basic tenet of the new Freemasonry, which up to that time was generally that of a guild of stone masons and other builders, changed during this uniting of these four lodges. From a guild, Freemasonry became a church, a new religion. It changed from a professional Masonry, to a philosophical Masonry: "The inherent philosophy of Freemasonry implied a belief that mystic thought and feeling were bound to disappear and to be replaced by a strictly logical and rational era."[9]

Freemasonry: ". . . tried to cooperate with the Church so as to be able to work from the inside, rationalize the doctrine of Jesus and empty it gradually of its mystic content. Freemasonry hoped to become a friendly and legal heir to Christianity. They considered logic and the rules of scientific thinking as being the only absolute and permanent element of the human mind."[10]

The new Masonry ". . . did not defend revelation, dogmas, or faith. Its conviction was scientific and its morality purely social. The new Masonry did not aim to destroy churches, but, with the aid of the progress in ideas, it prepared to replace them."[11]

This new morality spread to France in 1725, and a few years later, in the early 1730's, to the United States, where Lodges of the Freemasons were formed in Philadelphia in 1731, and in Boston in 1733.[12] One of the well known members of the Philadelphia Lodge was Benjamin Franklin, who joined in 1732. Mr. Franklin later became Grand Master (the equivalent of President) of his lodge in 1734.

It was this Philadelphia Lodge that started the move to confederate the various colonies in America into a union of states. In 1731, this St. John Lodge in Philadelphia "got in touch with the Grand Lodge of London, and the Duke of Norfolk, then Grand Master of English Freemasonry, appointed a Grand Master for the Central Colonies. His name was Daniel Coxe. Coxe was the first public man to advise a federation of the colonies...."[13]

Other early members of the Masons in America were George Washington, Thomas Jefferson, John Hancock, Paul Revere, Alexander Hamilton, John Marshall, James Madison and Ethan Allen, all well known American patriots heavily involved with the American Revolution.

More recently, at least twelve other American Presidents have been members of the Masons: Andrew Jackson, James K. Polk, James Buchanan, Andrew Johnson, James Garfield, William McKinley, Theodore Roosevelt, William Howard Taft, Warren G. Harding, Franklin Roosevelt, Harry Truman and Gerald Ford.

In addition to the direct influence of the Masons in the American Revolution, other Masons were also influencing America in indirect ways. One of these influences started on July 4, 1776, when the Continental Congress appointed Benjamin Franklin, Thomas Jefferson, and John Adams to a committee of three to design the Seal of the United States. Two if not all three were members of the Freemasons, and the seal they designed, especially the reverse side, conceals Masonic symbols and secrets. According to the Masons: "Being on the reverse of the Seal, this design reveals the 'Hidden Work,' the 'Lost Word' of Ancient Freemasonry. The motif used is the pyramid, for in ancient eras, where Freemasonry originated, the mission was the same as it is today: to do God's will on Earth. This labor is unfinished; therefore the pyramid on the Seal is not completed. Each Brother must contribute his portion, knowing that his work is watched over and guided by the All-seeing Eye of God."[14]

Whatever the Freemasons are, they have stirred a constant controversy amongst the various levels of society, ever since their founding in 1717. The first formal declaration against this organization came just twenty-one years later, in 1738, when: "the Roman Catholic Church officially condemned Freemasonry... in the form of a Bull issued by Pope Clement XII...."[15]

The condemnations of the Masons have continued since 1738 as: "No fewer than eight Popes have condemned Freemasonry on 400 occasions since it was founded in Britain in 1717. The first publicly pronounced ban by Clement XII called the movement 'unprincipled.'"

One of his successors, Pope Leo XXIII, charged the Masons with aiming at the "overthrow of the whole religious, political and social order based on Christian institutions and the establishment of a state of things based on pure naturalism."[16]

One of the more recent stands against the Freemasons came on March 21, 1981, when the Roman Catholic Church again warned that "all Roman Catholics who belong to Masonic lodges risk excommunication."[16]

According to the book *A New Encyclopaedia of Freemasonry* "the Latin Church... has agreed to regard Freemasonry as... those forces which are at work in the world against the work of the Church in that world."[17]

In any event, "In the tense times before the American Revolution the secrecy of the Masonic lodges offered the Colonial patriots the opportunity to meet and plan their strategy."[18]

One of the pre-American Revolutionary events obviously planned in secret was the Boston Tea Party where a group of individuals, disguised as Indians, dumped boxes of tea into the Boston harbor. The identity of these patriots has not been generally made known, until the Freemasons themselves offered this explanation of the event: "The Boston Tea Party was entirely Masonic, carried out by members of the St. John's Lodge (in Boston) during an adjourned meeting."[19]

This revolutionary act had an almost immediate effect in the English Parliament, which passed laws closing the Boston port to all trade by sea and allowing the quartering of British troops in Massachusetts. These laws brought a deluge of protests from all of the colonies in America.

There is reason to believe that those who caused the event were intending to use the English retaliatory activities as the incidents to unify the American colonies against the English government. And the strategy worked.

The call to unify the states into a federal government was strong and the Masons were the key to that call. They were the ones who had a nationwide membership, many of whom were well known enough to expect the colonists to listen to their message. In fact, fifty-three of the fifty-six signers of the Declaration of Independence were members of the Masons,[20] as were the majority of the members of the Continental Congress.

Benjamin Franklin, partly because of his visibility as a member of the Masons, became a key to opening the doors of some of the European nations, often led by fellow Masons. His membership could gain him critical audiences with other Masons all over Europe and these contacts were to be used to gain support for the American Revolution.

Franklin also understood the true cause of the American Revolution. He was asked in London once: "How do you account for the prosperity in the American colonies?"

Mr. Franklin replied: "That is simple. It is only because in the colonies we issue our own money. It is called Colonial Script and we issue it in the proper proportion to accommodate trade and commerce."[21]

In other words, the colonies didn't use their power to create money to create inflation, and as a result the American nation was becoming prosperous.

This situation was to change, however, during the 1760's when the Bank of England introduced a bill in Parliament that no colony could issue its own script. The colonies, according to this legislation, would have to issue bonds and sell them to the Bank, who would then loan them the money they were to use in their colonies. America's money was to be based upon borrowed debt. The colonies would have to pay interest for the privilege of carrying their own money.

This action caused great unemployment when put into effect as the Bank of England only allowed the colonies to borrow one-half of the quantity of money previously in circulation.[22] Franklin and others realized this, and Franklin is on record as saying: "The colonies would gladly have borne the little tax on tea and other matters had it not been that England took away from the colonies their money, which created unemployment and dissatisfaction."[23]

And in a quote attributed to him, he said: "The refusal of King George III to allow the colonies to operate an honest colonial money system, which freed the ordinary man from the clutches of the money manipulators, was probably the prime cause of the revolution."

Franklin acknowledged that the cause of the Revolution was the resistance of the colonies to the idea of borrowed money, resulting in debt and inflation as well as interest payments, and not "taxation without representation," as is commonly believed.

One of the countries visited by the Mason Benjamin Franklin was France. In January of 1774, Franklin was dealing with certain Masonic leaders to buy guns for the American colonies. This transaction was made with the knowledge and support of the French Foreign Minister Vergennes, a fellow Mason.

In addition, the French government, again with the support of Vergennes, was loaning the American colonies a total of three million livres.

Another nation was also involving itself, although indirectly, in the American Revolution: "At the birth of the American nation, during the Revolutionary War, Empress Catherine the Great of Russia, refused the plea of King George III of England to send 20,000 Russian Cossacks to crush the rebellion of the colonies...which...helped the colonies to survive."[24]

Russia, without a central bank controlling its decisions, had assisted the United States by refusing to send troops against the struggling colonies. Russia was exhibiting her friendship for the United States for the first time and would assist the United States once again in the Civil War, as will be shown in a later chapter.

It is interesting to discover why the two major leaders in the American Revolution of England were fellow Masons Benjamin Franklin and George Washington. "When America needed a national army and a national diplomat, it turned to Brother George Washington as the only officer who not only had national fame but who, due to his Masonic application, had friends in all parts of the Continent. At the crucial moment when America, on the verge of defeat, needed foreign alliances, it turned to Brother Franklin — the only American who had world-wide fame and who, due to Masonry, had friends all over the world."[25]

Washington in turn surrounded himself with fellow Masons: "All the staff officers Washington trusted were Masons, and all the leading generals of the Army were Masons."[26]

These decisions by Washington paid an additional bonus, as it is likely that Washington himself had decided to staff his armies with fellow Masons for this reason: "It seems even likely that the unforgettable and mysterious laxness of certain English military campaigns in America, particularly those of the Howe brothers, (one an admiral and the other a general) was deliberate and due to the Masonic desire of the English General to reach a peaceful settlement and shed as little blood as possible."[27]

In other words, Washington selected fellow Masons as his general staff because he knew that the commanding general of the English troops was also a Mason. The fact that a Mason is duty bound not to kill a fellow Mason if he knows that his opponent is also a Mason, has made it extremely difficult for many non-Mason generals to get their troops to perform well in battle.

To show his public support for the Masons, after the American army retook the city of Philadelphia from the British army on December 27, 1778, General George Washington "his sword at his side, in full Masonic attire, and insignia of the Brotherhood, marched at the head of a solemn procession of three hundred brethren through the streets of Philadelphia....This was the greatest Masonic parade that had ever been seen in the New World."[28]

But even with the popular support of the Masons, Washington and the American people had to pay for the costs of the War against the British. In 1775, the Continental Congress voted to issue paper currency (Fiat Money) to finance the war. This money was not borrowed from any banking establishment. It was simply printed as a means of paying the government's expenses in the war. Therefore, it contained no provision for the paying of interest to a group of bankers who had created it out of nothing.

Most of the independent state legislatures, as a sign of good faith and as a recognition that the central government had saved the American people countless millions of dollars in interest payments, passed laws requiring citizens to accept the Continental currency as legal tender.

But by the end of 1776 the "Continental," as it was called, commanded only forty cents on the dollar when exchanged for silver coin. The federal printing presses continued printing these dollars, however, so that by 1776, there were $241.6 million of "Continentals" in circulation.

The merchants of America were accepting these dollars at a rate of 2.5 cents on the dollar, and for less than half a penny just two years later. Inflation had taken its toll in the value of the currency. It had become nearly worthless when measured against real money, a hard metal. The lowest trading price of the "Continental" occurred at the end of the war, when it took 500 paper dollars in exchange for one silver dollar.

It is now apparent why the American people coined the phrase "not worth a Continental." Inflation had occurred once again, in accordance with the economic law that works in every case where the quantity of money, unbacked by gold or silver, is increased rapidly.

It was during this time that a vital disagreement amongst the leading American patriots was coming to the surface.

The issue was whether or not the American government should establish a central bank. Thomas Jefferson was opposed to the establishment of any such bank and Alexander Hamilton was in favor. Jefferson supported his position by stating: "If the American people ever allow private banks to control the issue of currency, first by inflation, then by deflation, the banks and corporations that will grow up around them will deprive the people of their property until their children will wake up homeless on the continent their fathers conquered."[29]

It was Hamilton's proposal that the United States create the Bank of the United States, a profit making institution to be privately owned and to enjoy special access to the public funds. The bank would have the legal power to create money out of nothing, and loan it, at interest, to the government.

Hamilton felt that the majority of the people couldn't handle their own money. He proposed that these matters would be best left up to the wealthy. He wrote: "No society could succeed which did not unite the interest and credit of rich individuals with those of the state. All communities divide themselves into the few and the many. The first are rich and well-born, the other the mass of the people. The people are turbulent and changing; they seldom judge or determine right."[30]

Jefferson responded with his charge that banking establishments, when given the ability to inflate and deflate the quantity of money at will, lend themselves to a continuing series of oppressions of the people. He wrote: "Single acts of tyranny may be ascribed to the accidental opinion of a day; but a series of oppressions, begun at a distinguished period, and pursued unalterably through every change of ministry, too plainly prove a deliberate, systematical plan of reducing us to slavery."[31]

The conspiracy that Jefferson saw forming in the United States was a group called the Jacobins, created by the French Branch of the Illuminati.[32]

Today's dictionary defines the Jacobins as "one of a society of radical democrats in France during the revolution of 1789; hence a plotter against an existing government."

John Robison in his classic work on the Illuminati, titled *Proofs of a Conspiracy*, said this about the Jacobins: "The intelligent saw in the open system of the Jacobins the hidden system of the Illuminati."[33]

(This group will play an important part in the Civil War of 1861-65 as will be covered in a later chapter.)

Unfortunately for the United States, President George Washington appointed Alexander Hamilton as the Secretary of the Treasury in 1788. Three years later, in 1791, the United States government granted a twenty-year charter to its first national bank, called the First Bank of the United States. This charter was to expire in 1811, and then the American citizens were to have a chance to discuss the Bank and its merits before it could be re-chartered.

Jefferson quietly joined in the discussion about the First Bank, stating that Congress did not have any Constitutional authority to charter such an institution and that the Bank was therefore a non-entity. He based his arguments on Article I, Section 8, of the Constitution. This section reads: "The Congress shall have the power to coin money, regulate the value thereof...."

Jefferson argued that Congress had no authority to delegate the money power to another agency, certainly not to an agency that was privately owned and had not only the power to coin money but to print it and then loan it back to the government. However, such questions about the constitutionality of the Bank were, unfortunately, just questions, and the Bank survived until 1811, when President James Monroe let the charter lapse.

Even with the pressure on the government from the Bank to borrow to pay off the debts of the American revolution, Presidents Jefferson and Monroe paid off all of the debts of the United States Government without their assistance.

But the pressure to re-charter the Bank started the next year when England started the War of 1812 against the United States. This war was intended to force the United States into a position of needing a central bank to pay for the costs of the war, thus creating interest payments and debt. It was hoped by the English bankers that the Americans would re-charter the First National Bank, or create another under a different name.

Two Americans, Henry Clay and John C. Calhoun, were early supporters of the American government's entry into the War of 1812. They were also the main supporters of creating another bank under another name: The Second Bank of the United States.

The war with England proved expensive, and raised the debt of the United States from $45 million to $127 million.

Some Americans saw the war as the workings of a conspiracy. One, for instance, was the president of Harvard, Joseph Willard, who made what is now a famous speech declaring the involvement of the secret Illuminati in the events of the day. He said, on July 4, 1812: "There is sufficient evidence that a number of societies of the Illuminati have been established in this land. They are doubtless striving to secretly undermine all our ancient institutions, civil and sacred. These societies are clearly leagued with those of the same order in Europe. The enemies of all order are seeking our ruin. Should infidelity generally prevail, our independence would fall of course. Our republican government would be annihialated...."

Unfortunately, the American people did not heed his warnings and the conspiracy continued its deadly work in the United States.

The pressure to find a way to pay the costs of the War of 1812 through the re-chartering of a national bank continued, and in 1816, the Second Bank of the United States was chartered with a twenty-year charter. This bank was given the ability to loan the government $60 million The money was created out of nothing, evidenced by bonds, and loaned to the federal government.

The Second Bank now had the ability, as one writer put it, "to control the entire fiscal structure of the country...."[34]

In 1816, Thomas Jefferson once again tried to warn the American people, this time in a letter to John Taylor:

> I believe that banking institutions are more dangerous to our liberties than standing armies.
>
> Already they have raised up a money aristocracy that has set the Government at defiance.
>
> The issuing power should be taken from the banks and restored to the Government, to whom it properly belongs.[35]

It didn't take long for the Bank to exercise its powers. "The inflationary policies of the Second United States Bank in the first few years after 1812 caused banks to spread fairly discriminately through Kentucky, Tennessee, and other Western States. Then, with the depression of 1819, the big Bank, reversing its policy, began a peremptory contraction. Specie flowed out of the West, leaving in its wake a trail of bankruptcies and a large debtor population unable to meet its obligations."[36]

The Bank was using its powers to increase and decrease the money supply to cause, first inflation, and then deflation. This cycle was of benefit to the bankers who were able to repossess large quantities of property at a fraction of its real value.

But the debt of the War of 1812 was paid up by the end of 1834, an action that was not certain to please the owners of the Second Bank.

But one thing that happened was pleasing to the bankers. The Bank was declared constitutional in 1819 by Supreme Court Justice John Marshall, a member of the Masons, in the case of McCulloch vs. Maryland.[37]

He decreed that Congress had the implied power to create the Bank of the United States.

There was no specific power granted to Congress to create the Bank, so the Constitution was stretched to fit the circumstances by declaring that the Constitution had some mysterious "implied power" that enabled it to do whatever the "stretchers" wanted. The arguments of Jefferson had not been heeded. Hamilton had won.

The next relevant step in America's history occurred in 1826 when a member of the Freemasons, Captain William Morgan, published a book entitled: *Illustrations of Masonry By One of the Fraternity Who Has Devoted Thirty Years to the Subject; Captain W. Morgan's Exposition of Freemasony.*

This rather thin book of only 110 pages contained the "secrets" of the Freemasons, or as Captain Morgan put it: ". . . the Lodge — room Signs, Grips, and Masonic Emblems."

Less than a month after the book appeared, Captain Morgan was: "carried away . . . by a number of Freemasons . . . "[38] and murdered.

It was alleged, according to a book entitled *The Revolutionary Age of Andrew Jackson,* by Robert Remini, that: ". . . the Masonic Order had arranged his abduction and probable murder."[39]

The charge that Morgan was killed because he had broken his pledge of secrecy in all Masonic affairs by publishing a book detailing all of the secrets of the Order was certainly in keeping with an understanding of the Masonic ritual. Captain Morgan detailed the procedures of the ritual of becoming a Mason wherein the prospective Mason is caused a slight pain and then warned: "As this is a torture to your flesh, so may it ever be to your mind and conscience if ever you should attempt to reveal the secrets of Masonry unlawfully."[40]

This single act by Captain Morgan was to have major ramifications in the years to come, especially in the Presidential election of 1832. This election was the second one for Andrew Jackson who had been elected first in 1828, primarily because he was in opposition to the Second Bank of the United States. Jackson was on record as saying: "I was one of those who do not believe that a national bank is a national blessing, but rather a curse to a republic; inasmuch as it is calculated to raise around the administration a moneyed aristocracy dangerous to the liberties of the country."[41]

The election of 1832 was a crucial one to the Bank, because the charter was to be renewed during the term of the president elected that year.

Jackson promised the American people: "The Federal Constitution must be obeyed, state rights preserved, our national debt must be paid, direct taxes and loans avoided, and the Federal Union preserved."

(Is is revealing that even then, in 1832, Jackson was concerned about the preservation of the Union, the issue that would supposedly cause the Civil War several years away.)

He continued: "These are the objects I have in view, and regardless of all consequences, will carry into effect."[42]

It was prior to this election, in 1830, that a new political party was formed, called the Anti-Mason party, primarily as a warning to the American people about the menace of the Masons in the country and as a response to the murdering of Captain Morgan.[43] According to Mackey's *Encyclopaedia*, the new party was organized: "... to put down the Masonic Institution as subversive of good government...."[46]

The Anti-Masons met on September 11 in Philadelphia, where delegates from eleven states met to "denounce the Freemasonic Order and to call upon their countrymen to join a political crusade to save the nation from subversion and tyranny at the hands of the Masons."[45]

(One of the delegates to that convention was William Seward from New York, who later became Secretary of State under President Abraham Lincoln.)

Another of those who became concerned about the Masons was John Quincy Adams, president from 1825 to 1829. He published a series of letters "abusive of Freemasonry, directed to leading politicians, and published in the public journals from 1831 to 1833."[46]

But the main issue of the 1832 election was the renewal of the charter of the Second Bank of the United States. The President of this organization, Nicholas Biddle, "decided to ask Congress for a renewal of the Bank's charter in 1832, four years before its current charter expired."[47]

The strategy behind Biddle's move was simple: "... since Jackson was seeking re-election, he might see it to his advantage not to allow the matter to become an issue and thus permit the Bank to have its recharter."[48]

Henry Clay, later to become the Republican candidate for the presidency against Jackson, and his colleague Daniel Webster took the lead in guiding the re-chartering bill through the Congress. They were not to be disappointed as the bill passed the Senate by a vote of 28 to 20 and the House by a vote of 107 to 85. But President Jackson had the last opportunity to act on the Bill and he vetoed it on July 10, 1832. In his veto, Jackson again warned the American people by saying:

It is regretted that the rich and powerful too often bend the acts of governments to their selfish purposes. Distinctions in society will always exist under every just government.

Equality of talents, of education, of wealth, cannot be produced by human institutions.

In the full enjoyment of the gifts of heaven, and the fruits of superior industry, economy and virtue, every man is equally entitled to protection by law, but when the law undertakes to these natural and just advantages artificial distinctions, to grant titles, gratuities and exclusive privileges, to make the rich richer, and the potent more powerful, the humble members of society — the farmers, mechanics, and laborers — who have neither the time nor the means of securing like favors to themselves, have a right to complain of their injustice to their government.[50]

He continued by stating that he held "the belief that some of the powers and privileges possessed by the existing bank are unauthorized by the Constitution, subversive of the rights of the States, and dangerous to the liberties of the people...."[51]

However, even though he had vetoed the re-chartering bill, thereby risking the wrath of the American people had they decided they had wanted the Bank, Jackson decided to let the 1832 election decide its fate. Jackson, who ran on the basic platform of "Bank and no Jackson or No Bank and Jackson," faced great opposition, especially in the press of the United States, "largely because of advertising pressure."[52]

This meant that there were elements inside the business community which had something to gain by the re-chartering of the Bank.

The only ones, apparently, who did not favor the re-chartering were the American people, who responded by re-electing Andrew Jackson by the following vote:

Candidate	Percentage of total votes cast
Jackson	55 percent
Clay	37 percent
the Anti-Masons	8 percent

That meant that approximately 2 out of every 3 voters, those who voted for either Jackson or the Anti-Masons, voted against the rechartering of the Second Bank of the United States. (An interesting footnote to history is the fact that the Anti-Masons actually carried the state of Vermont and thereby received its votes in the Electoral College.)

After the election, President Jackson ordered Biddle to withdraw government funds on deposit in the Bank, and Biddle refused. And to show his displeasure at Jackson's directive, Biddle called for a "general curtailment of loans throughout his entire banking system. Biddle's order was so sudden and its financial effect so devasting, that it pitched the country into an economic panic. Which was precisely what Biddle wanted."[53]

The awesome power of the Bank to destroy in the market place was now being utilized against the American people, even though they voted against it in the 1832 election. The people were right. They wanted no part of a banking establishment and they were being punished for their votes against it.

Biddle reduced the amount of loans outstanding between August 1, 1833, and November 1, 1834, by $18,000,000 and for the next five months, they were reduced by almost $14,500,000. Then Biddle reversed himself and forced the banks to increase the quantity of money from $52,000,000 on January 1, 1833, to $108,000,000 a year later, and to $120,000,000 a year after that.

Biddle was "in fact embarked on the campaign the radicals above all feared: the deliberate creation of a panic in order to blackmail the government into re-chartering the Bank." He was quoted as saying "Nothing but the evidence of suffering abroad will produce any effect in Congress.... My own course is decided — all other Banks and all the merchants may break, but the Bank of the United States shall not break."[54]

And of course, the contraction and expansion cycle caused the types of economic problems that Biddle had anticipated. "Businesses failed, men were thrown out of work, money was unobtainable."[54]

President Jackson saw through Biddle's activities and once again warned the American people: "The bold effort the present bank had made to control the Government, the distress it had wantonly produced ... are but premonitions of the fate that awaits the American people should they be deluded into a perpetuation of this institution, or the establishment of another like it."[55]

Jackson not only saw that Biddle's efforts would destroy the economy of the United States, he also felt that Europe would suffer as well. But his real fears were that the Bank constituted a threat to his very existence. He told his Vice President, Martin Van Buren, "The Bank, Mr. Van Buren, is trying to kill me. But I will kill it."[56]

It is not certain whether Jackson meant that the Bank was trying to destroy his political career or to murder him, but on January 30, 1835, a would-be assassin named Richard Lawrence stepped into his path and fired two pistols at close range at him. Both pistols misfired, and President Jackson was not hurt. Lawrence later claimed that he had been "in touch with the powers in Europe, which had promised to intervene if any attempt was made to punish him."[57]

In addition to being the subject of the first presidential assassination attempt in the United States, President Jackson was made the subject of the first censure of a President. The Senate, in March, 1834, "agreed by a vote of 26 to 20 to officially censure Andrew Jackson for removing the government's deposits from the Bank of the United States without the express authorization of the United States Congress."[58]

Jackson apparently blamed the Bank. He said: "So glaring were the abuses and corruptions of the Bank . . . so palpable its design by its money and power to control the government and change its character. . . ."[59] Someone had attempted to control the government by removing him from the presidency.

The Senate of 1837 later reversed this action by voting to expunge the censure by a vote of 24 to 19.

Even with all of the toils and tribulations of the period, Jackson was able to completely liquidate the national debt during his eight years in office.

As Jackson was leaving the presidency, he once again warned the American people in his Farewell Address: "The Constitution of the United States unquestionably intended to secure to the people a circulating medium of gold and silver. But the establishment of a national bank by Congress, with the privilege of issuing paper money receivable in the payment of public dues . . . drove from general circulation the constitutional currency and substituted one of paper in its place."[60]

But all of these defeats at the hands of Jackson and the American people didn't deter the bankers from attempting to re-charter the Bank. President John Tyler vetoed two bills in 1841 to revive the Second Bank of the United States.

So the Bank's charter expired in 1836 and, for the next 24 years, until the Civil War started in 1861, the United States had no central bank. So for the years up until 1841, at least, the bankers had been foiled in their attempts to completely enmesh the United States in the web of a permanent banking establishment.

Chapter 13
The Rothschild Family

In his book *The History of the Great American Fortunes*, author Gustavus Myers had identified the major power behind the Second Bank of the United States as being the Rothschild family.[1]

This European banking family was started by the father, Amschel Moses Bauer (they were later to change their last name to Rothschild) who started in the banking business in a meager way. After some early success in the loaning of money to local governments, Amschel decided to expand his banking establishment by loaning to national governments. He set up his five sons in banking houses, each in a different country.

Meyer Rothschild was sent to Frankfort, Germany; Solomon to Vienna, Austria; Nathan to London, England; Carl to Naples, Italy; and James to Paris, France.

With the Rothschild sons scattered all over Europe, each operating a banking house, the family could easily convince any government that it should continue to pay its debts, or the force of the "balance of power" politics would be used against the debtor's nation. In other words, the Rothschild family would play one government against another by the threat of war. Each government would feel cornered into paying its debts by the threat of a war which would take away its kingdom. The brothers could finance both sides of the conflict thereby insuring not only that the debtor would pay its debts but that enormous fortunes would be made in the financing of the war.

This power was visualized by Meyer Rothschild when he summarized the strategy thus: "Permit me to control the money of a nation, and I care not who makes its laws."[2]

One of the early events that solidified the Rothschild control of the English government was the battle of Waterloo in June, 1815.

The Rothschilds had created a system of Rothschild couriers in Europe so that important information could be exchanged amongst the five brothers. The sign that identified the messengers as being couriers for the Rothschild family was a red pouch that they carried. This pouch enabled them to cross national borders with impunity, as most European nations had instructed their guards that the pouch carrier was not to be detained, even if that nation was at war with the nation represented by the pouch carrier.

This method ensured that the Rothschild family had immediate information about the major events in Europe, even before the rulers of the countries involved. This device was also known to the other banking families in Europe and the Rothschild access to quick information often gave them an early advantage in the market place.

England was at war with France, and the battle of Waterloo was to be the deciding battle in this war. If Napoleon, the commanding general of the French forces, defeated Wellington, the commanding general of the English forces, there was little left to deter him from controlling all of Europe. The other bankers around London knew of the significance of this battle and looked to Nathan Rothschild for advance information as to the outcome, because the bankers knew of the promptness of Rothschild's courier system.

Nathan was seen in the corner of the London bond market looking exceedingly glum, and this was interpreted by the bankers as meaning that Nathan knew who had won the Battle of Waterloo: France and Napoleon had defeated Wellington and England. At least that was what the English bankers thought, and because they felt that their nation had lost, they started selling the government bonds that they owned.

And as always, when large quantities of bonds are sold at the same time, their price drops. And the more that the price fell, the more gloomy Nathan looked.

But unknownst to the English bond holders, Nathan's agents were buying English bonds, and he was able by this method to acquire large quantities of these bonds at a small percentage of their true value.

Nathan Rothschild had purchased the English government.

When the official English courier finally appeared at the bond market and announced that the English had defeated the French and that all had not been lost, Nathan was nowhere to be found.

The exact profit made on this ruse might never be known, as the Rothschild banks are always partnerships and never corporations. Because there are no stockholders, the brothers and their successive heirs have only to share the knowledge of the size of all profits made by the bank with the other brothers and whatever partners they might take in, and not the stockholders of the corporation.

Chapter 14
The Monroe Doctrine

On December 2, 1823, President James Monroe issued what has been called The Monroe Doctrine. His statement was blunt and to the point, declaring "that the American continents, by the free and independent condition which they have assumed and maintain, are henceforth not to be considered as subjects for future colonization by any European powers."[1]

President Monroe added an explanation, declaring that the political systems in European countries were different from those in the Americas: "We owe it, therefore, to candor and to the amicable relations existing between the United States and those powers to declare that we should consider any attempt on their part to extend their system to any portion of this hemisphere as dangerous to our peace and safety."[2]

Monroe's action came as the result of a treaty, called the Treaty of Verona, signed by the government leaders of Austria, France, Prussia, and Russia who, according to a then current observer, American Senator Robert Owen, had:

> well-laid plans also to destroy popular government in the American colonies which had revolted from Spain and Portugal in Central and South America under the influence of the successful example of the United States.

It was because of this conspiracy against the American republics by the European monarchies that the great English statesman, Canning, called the attention of our government to it, and our statesmen then, including Thomas Jefferson, took an active part to bring about the declaration by President Monroe in his next annual message to the Congress of the United States that the United States would regard it as an act of hostility to the Government of the United States and an unfriendly act if this coalition or if any power of Europe ever undertook to establish upon the American Continent any control of any American republic or to acquire any territorial rights.[3]

Senator Owen entered the Treaty in the *Congressional Record* in 1916. It reads, in part:

The undersigned... have agreed as follows:

Article 1: The high contracting powers being convinced that the system of representative government is equally as incompatible with the monarchial principles as the maxim of the sovereignty of the people with the divine right, engage mutually... to sue all their efforts to put an end to the system of representative governments, in whatever country it may exist in Europe, and to prevent its being introduced in those countries where it is not yet known.

Article 2: As it can not be doubted that the liberty of the press is the most powerful means used by the pretended supporters of the rights of nations to the detriment of those of the princes, the high contracting parties promise reciprocally to adopt all proper measures to suppress it, not only in their own states but also in the rest of Europe.

Article 3: Convinced that the principles of religion contribute most powerfully to keep nations in the state of passive obedience they owe to their princes, the high contracting parties declare it to be their intention to sustain in their respective states those measures which the clergy may adopt... so intimately connected with the preservation of the authority of the princes....[4]

Monroe's bold declaration struck the European governments a rather severe blow. Many European diplomats spoke out against it, but it was popular with the citizens of the South American nations it protected.

Monroe's Secretary of State was John Quincy Adams, and he was largely responsible for writing the Doctrine. The American people, pleased with what he had written, responded by electing him President of the United States in 1824.

But more importantly, another move by the European powers into the affairs of the American people had been repulsed.

Karl Marx (left), the Communist, wrote "From each according to his ability, to each according to his need."

Lyndon Johnson (below), not a Communist, wrote "We (in government) are going to try to take all of the money that we (in government) think is unnecessarily being spent and take it from the 'haves' and give it to the 'have nots' that need it so much."

ADAM WEISHAVPT.

Oswald Spengler, right, (1880-1936), a German historian and author, came to the realization that "Communist" movements were controlled by wealthy interests, supposedly the "enemy" of the Communists. He wrote "There is no proletarian, not even Communist, movement that has not operated in the interests of money . . .and without the idealists among its leaders having the slightest suspicion of the fact."

Adam Weishaupt, left, a former Jesuit priest, founded the Illuminati on May 1, 1776. His organization was dedicated to the destruction of Christianity and all religion. There is evidence that the Iluminati is still in existence, but under other names.

Dr. Bella Dodd, a former member of the Communist Party felt that "the Communist Conspiracy (was) merely a branch of a much bigger conspiracy." She discovered that any one of three wealthy American "capitalists" could make decisions for the Party. These decisions were always ratified later by the Communist Party in Russia.

This cartoon by Robert Minor in the St. Louis *Post-Dispatch* appeared in 1911. It depicted the acceptance of Marxist Communism by the "wealthy capitalists," supposedly the enemies of Marx and his followers. The financiers depicted are: John D. Rockefeller, J. P. Morgan, John D. Ryan of National City Bank, and Morgan partner George W. Perkins. Immediately behind Karl Marx is Teddy Roosevelt.

Alexis, the son of Nicholas II, Czar of Russia, in 1914, and Colonel Michal Goloniewski, who claims to be the adult Alexis, in 1964. The Communist government supposedly murdered the entire family of the Czar in 1918, but the Colonel charges that they were spirited out of Russia to safety in Europe. The colonel's claim to be the son of the Czar was confirmed by the American government, yet few outside of those who investigated this claim will agree that the family survived the alleged massacre. Perhaps the reason this is so is that any legally certified heir to the Romanov fortune would inherit several billions of dollars deposited in American and European banks by the Czar prior to the revolution.

Thomas Jefferson, left, warned the American people about
creating a national debt. He wrote: "To preserve our
independence, we must not let our leaders load us with perpetual
debt. We must make our election between economy and liberty, or
profusion and servitude. It is incumbent on every generation to
pay its own debts as it goes—a principle which, if acted on,
would save one half of the wars of the world." In 1984, America's
national debt was approximately $1,600,000,000,000 ($1.6
trillion).
Andrew Jackson, right, as President of the United States, fought a
battle with the federally chartered Second Bank of the United
States. He later claimed that it was responsible for the
assassination attempt made against him in 1835.

Civil War General William Tecumseh Sherman wrote in his book *Memoirs I*: "The truth is not always palatable, and should not always be told." Historians are still uncovering evidences of the European and American conspiracy that split the United States into a North and a South so that they could finance both sides in the ensuing conflict.

President Abraham Lincoln wrote that a "money power" was at work in the Civil War and that it assisted in the passage of the National Banking Act of 1863. This bill created a national bank with the ability to create money and loan it, at interest, to the United States government. It was this same "power" that was involved in his assassination in 1865.

Chapter 15
The Civil War

General William Tecumseh Sherman, one of the participants in the Civil War, made this rather cryptic comment in his book *Memoirs I*: "... the truth is not always palatable and should not always be told."[1]

A similar comment was made by the author of the biography of Senator Zachariah Chandler of Michigan, a Senator during the Civil War: "The secret history of these days... concealing many startling revelations, has yet been sparingly written; it is doubtful if the veil will ever be more than slightly lifted."[2]

Those who have attempted to lift the veil have discovered that there are indeed many hidden truths about this fateful period in American history. One who only hinted at the truth about the real causes of the War was Colonel Edward Mandell House, who wrote his book entitled *Philip Dru, Administrator*, in 1912. In it, he has one of his characters make this statement: "Cynical Europe said that the North would have it appear that a war had been fought for human freedom, whereas it was fought for money."[3]

Is it possible that the Civil War was fought for reasons other than those traditionally offered? Is it possible that the real reasons for the war are among the secrets that some wish not to be revealed? Is it possible that slavery and states rights were not the real causes of the War?

After the demise of the Second Bank of the United States, the state banks, those chartered by the various states in the Union, operated the banking system of the United States and issued all of the money. Almost exclusively, this money was backed by gold, not by debt and paper money.

However, the financial position of the federal government had been slowly deteriorating: "At the outbreak of the war the United States Treasury was in greater shambles than Fort Sumter. Southern banks had been quietly withdrawing large amounts of funds on deposit in the North. When Lincoln took office, he found his Treasury almost empty."[4]

The Civil War started in 1837, the year after the charter of the Second Bank had expired, when the Rothschild family sent one of their representatives to the United States. His name was August Belmont, and he arrived during the panic of 1837. He quickly made his presence felt by buying government bonds. His success and prosperity soon led him to the White House, where he became the "financial advisor to the President of the United States."[5]

Another of the pieces of this enormous puzzle fell into place in 1854 when a secret organization known as the Knights of the Golden Circle was formed by George W. L. Bickley,[6] who "declared that he had created the fateful war of 1861 with an organization that had engineered and spread secession."[7]

Another of the leading characters in the story of the Civil War was J.P. Morgan, later to become one of America's most wealthy and influential industrialists and bankers. Mr. Morgan went to Europe in 1856 to study at the University of Gottingen in Germany. It is not inconceivable that one of the people he met while in college was Karl Marx, who was active during this time writing and publicizing his ideas about Communism, since Marx was in and out of Germany on a regular basis.

In any event, it was during this time that the European bankers began plotting the Civil War. "According to John Reeves, in an authorized biography entitled *The Rothschilds, the Financial Rulers of Nations*, a pivotal meeting took place in London, in 1857. It was at this meeting that the International Banking Syndicate decided that (in America) the North was to be pitted against the South under the old principle of 'divide and conquer.' This amazing agreement was corroborated by MacKenzie in his historical research entitled The Nineteenth Century."[8]

The plotters realized that once again the American people would not accept a national bank without a reason for having one, and once again the plotters decided upon a war. Wars are costly, and they force governments into a position where they must borrow money to pay for them, and the decision was made once again to force the United States into a war so that it would have to deal with the issue of how to pay for its costs.

But the plotters had a difficult problem: what nation could they induce to fight against the United States government? The United States was too powerful, and no country, or combinations of countries, could match them in a "balance of power" showdown. Canada to the north and Mexico to the south were not strong enough and couldn't raise an army adequate for the anticipated conflict, so they were discounted. England and France were 3,000 miles away and across a huge ocean that made the supplying of an invading army nearly impossible. And Russia had no central bank so the bankers had no control over that nation.

So the bankers made the decision to divide the United States into two parts, thereby creating an enemy for the government of the United States to war against.

The bankers first had to locate an issue to use in causing the southern states to secede from the United States.

The issue of slavery was ideal.

Next the bankers had to create an organization that could promote secession amongst the southern states so that they would divide themselves away from the federal government.

The Knights of the Golden Circle was created for that purpose. Abraham Lincoln began to see the drama unfold as he was campaigning for the Presidency in 1860. He saw the war as an attempt to split the Union, not over the issue of slavery, but just for the pure sake of splitting the Union. He wrote: "I have never had a feeling politically that did not spring from the sentiments embodied in the Declaration of Independence. If it (the Union) cannot be saved without giving up that principle, I was about to say I would rather be assassinated on this spot than surrender it."[9]

So many of his fellow Americans also saw the war as an attempt to split the Union that "it was not uncommon for men to declare that they would resign their officer's commission if the war for the Union was perverted into an attack on slavery."[10]

Curiously, Mr. Lincoln started having thoughts about his own assassination during the 1860 convention.

> He went upstairs and, exhausted by repressed excitement, he lay down on the couch in Mrs. Lincoln's sitting room.
>
> While lying there he was disturbed to see in the mirror two images of himself which were alike, except that one was not so clear as the other. The double reflection awakened the primitive vein in the superstition always present in him. He rose and lay down again to see if the paler shadow would vanish, but he saw it once more....
>
> The next morning ... he went home and reclined on the couch

to see if there was not something wrong with the mirror itself. He was reassured to find it played the same trick. When he tried to show it to Mrs. Lincoln, however, the second reflection failed to appear.

Mrs. Lincoln took it as a sign that he was to have two terms in the Presidency, but she feared the paleness of one of the figures signified that he would not live through the second term.

'I am sure,' he said to his partner once, 'I shall meet with some terrible end....'[11]

The Knights of the Golden Circle were successful in spreading the message of secession amongst the various Southern states. As each state withdrew from the United States, it left independently of the others. The withdrawing states then formed a Confederation of States, as separate and independent entities. The independence of each state was written into the Southern Constitution: "We, the people of the Confederate States, each state acting for itself, and in its sovereign and independent character...."[12]

This action was significant because, should the South win the war, each state could withdraw from the confederation, re-establish its sovereign nature and set up its own central bank. The southern states could then have a series of European-controlled banks, the Bank of Georgia, the Bank of South Carolina, etc., and then any two could have a series of wars, such as in Europe for centuries, in a perpetual game of Balance of Power politics. It would be a successful method of insuring that large profits could be made on the loaning of money to the states involved.

President Lincoln saw the problem developing, and was fortunate that the government of Russia was willing to assist his government in the event of a war with England and France. "While still President-elect, he (Lincoln) had been informed by the Russian minister to the United States that his country was willing to aid the Washington government should it be menaced by England and France."[13]

Eleven southern states seceded from the Union to form the Confederacy. But in a rather enigmatic move, the flag adopted by the Confederacy had thirteen stars on it. As mentioned before, the number thirteen has significance to the Freemasons.

The South started the Civil War on April 12, 1861, when they fired upon Fort Sumter, a Northern fort in South Carolina.

One of the members of the Knights of the Golden Circle was the well known bandit Jesse James, and it was Jesse's father, George James, a Captain in the Southern Army, who fired the first shot at the fort.

Abraham Lincoln, now President of the Northern States, once again reported to the American people that the war was a result of conspiratorial forces at work in the South. He told the North that: "combinations too powerful to be suppressed by the ordinary machinery of peacetime government had assumed control of various Southern states."[14]

Lincoln, and later the Russian government, saw that England and France were aligning themselves against the North on the side of the South, and immediately issued orders for a sea blockade of the Southern states to prevent these two nations from using the seas to send supplies to the South.

The Russian minister to the United States also saw this alignment and he advised his government in April, 1861, that: "England will take advantage of the first opportunity to recognize the seceded states and that France will follow her."[15] (It is interesting that two of the Rothschild brothers had banks in England and France.)

The Russian foreign minister instructed his American minister in Washington in July, 1861,, "to assure the American nation that it could assume 'the most cordial sympathy on the part of our August Master (the Czar of Russia) during the serious crisis which it is passing through at the present.' "[16]

Lincoln was receiving great pressure from certain of the banking establishment to float interest-bearing loans to pay the costs of the war.

Salmon P. Chase, after whom the Chase Manhatten Bank, owned by the Rockefeller interests, is named, and Lincoln's Secretary of the Treasury during the Civil War, "threatened the (rest of the) bankers that, if they did not accept the bonds he was issuing, he would flood the country with circulating notes, even if it should take a thousand dollars of such currency to buy a breakfast."[17]

So Abraham Lincoln decided not to borrow money from the bankers nor to create interest bearing money by creating a national bank that would loan the government the needed money by printing large quantities of paper money. Lincoln issued the "Greenback" in February, 1862. This money was not only unbacked by gold, but was debt free.

Lincoln was playing a deadly game. He had crossed the international bankers. The war was being fought to force the United States into a position of having to create a national bank, run independently by the European bankers, and Lincoln had turned his back on them by issuing his own Fiat Money.

The international bankers also out-manuevered Lincoln, at least to a degree, when on August 5, 1861, they induced Congress, mostly at the urging of Secretary of the Treasury Chase, to pass an income tax. They imposed "a three-percent federal income tax. This was superseded almost at once by an act of March, 1862, signed in July, while maintaining a three-percent tax on income below $10,000, increased the rate to five percent above that level."[18]

It was a graduated income tax, just as proposed by Karl Marx just thirteen years before.

England and France now moved to increase the pressure on Lincoln's government. On November 8, 1861, England "dispatched 8,000 troops to Canada as tangible proof that she meant business"[19] in supporting the South. France marched troops into Mexico after landing them on the coast and imposing their choice of rulers, the emperor Maximillian, as the head of Mexico. Lincoln could see that he was being flanked by the European governments.

In 1938, Jerry Voorhis, a Congressman from California, wrote a pamphlet entitled *Dollars and Sense*, in which he shared a little bit of history with the American people about the events of the Civil War:

> In July 1862, an agent of the London bankers sent the following letter to leading financiers and bankers in the United States soon after Lincoln's first issue of greenbacks: "The great debt that capitalists will see to it is made out of the war must be used to control the volume of money. To accomplish this the bonds must be used as a banking basis.
>
> We are not waiting for the Secretary of the Treasury (Salmon P. Chase) to make this recommendation to Congress.
>
> It will not do to allow the greenback, as it is called, to circulate as money any length of time, for we cannot control them. But we can control the bonds and through them the bank issues."[20]

In order to curtail the flow of the military equipment the largely rural South needed to wage the war, Lincoln, on April 19, 1861, imposed the naval blockade previously mentioned. The Confederacy needed "to go abroad and replace privateers with powerful warships which (they were) to buy or have built to order. The first of these vessels, the *Sumter*, was commissioned in the spring of 1861, and was followed in 1862 by the *Florida* and the *Alabama*."[21]

The South was purchasing these ships from England and France to break the blockade, and Secretary of State William Seward saw the importance of keeping these two nations out of the war. He "warned the British government: 'If any European power provokes war, we shall not shrink from it.' Similarly Seward advised Mercier that French recognition of the Confederacy would result in war with the United States."[22]

Lincoln continued to see the danger from the European bankers and the two European countries of France and England. He saw the main issue of the war as being the preservation of the union. He repeated his statement that preserving the Union was his main task: "My paramount object in this struggle is to save the Union. If I could save the Union without freeing any slaves, I would do it."[23]

But even though Lincoln was not conducting the war over the issue of slavery, he issued the Emancipation Proclamation freeing the slaves on September 22, 1862, claiming the right to do so as the Commander-in-Chief of the Army and Navy. There was no act of Congress, just the solitary act of the President of the United States. But his act had the force of law, and the American people accepted it as such.

In addition to the external threat from England and France, Lincoln also had an internal threat to contend with: the central bank. On February 25, 1863, Congress passed the National Banking Act. This act created a federally chartered national bank that had the power to issue U.S. Bank Notes, money created to be loaned to the government supported not by gold but by debt. The money was loaned to the government at interest, and became Legal Tender. This bill was supported and urged by the Secretary of the Treasury, Salmon P. Chase.

Lincoln, after the passage of this act, once again warned the American people. He said: "The money power preys upon the nation in times of peace and conspires against it in times of adversity. It is more despotic than monarchy, more insolent than autocracy, more selfish than bureaucracy. I see in the near future a crisis approaching that unnerves me, and causes me to tremble for the safety of my country. Corporations have been enthroned, an era of corruption will follow, and the money power of the country will endeavor to prolong its reign by working upon the prejudices of the people, until the wealth is aggregated in a few hands, and the republic is destroyed."[24]

A few months after the passage of the act, the Rothschild bank in England wrote a letter to a New York firm of bankers:

> The few who understand the system (interest-bearing money) will either be so interested in its profits, or so dependent on its favors that there will be no opposition from that class, while on the other hand, the great body of people, mentally incapable of comprehending the tremendous advantages that capital derives from the system, will bear its burdens without complaint, and perhaps without even suspecting the system is inimical to their interests.[25]

Lincoln was betting on the blockade he had imposed around the South as a means of keeping England and France out of the war. The blockade was effectively doing this, at least on the surface, but others were using it as a means of making enormous profits. Private individuals were "running" the blockade by equipping several ships with essential provisions for the South, and then hoping that a percentage of these ships would make it through the blockade, so that the blockade runner could charge exorbitant prices for the goods in Southern cities. One of these individuals was Thomas W. House, reportedly a Rothschild agent, who amassed a fortune during the Civil War. House was the father of Colonel Edward Mandell House, the key to the election of President Woodrow Wilson and the passage of the Federal Reserve bill in 1913.

Lincoln realized that the North needed an ally to keep the European countries out of the war directly, as both nations were building ships capable of running the blockade, and the entry of England and France directly into the war could spell the end of the North. He looked to other European countries for assistance and found none willing to provide the support for his government. There was one country, however, that had no central bank and therefore no internal force preventing its support of the United States government.

That country was Russia.

Russia had a large navy and had already pledged its support to Lincoln prior to the beginning of the war. It could now involve itself and keep England and France out of the war because these two nations feared a war with the Russian government.

Lincoln needed something that he could use as a means of encouraging the Russian people to send their navy to the defense of the United States government. Lincoln issued the Emancipation Proclamation to free the slaves as a gesture to the Russian people who had their Czar free the serfs with a similar proclamation in 1861. Lincoln anticipated that this one act would encourage the Russian people to support their government when it lent support to Lincoln's government.

The Czar of Russia, Alexander II, issued orders to his imperial navy to sail for the American ports of New York City and San Francisco as a sign of support for Lincoln and his government. It also served as a dramatic means of indicating to France and England they would have to contend with the Russian government as well should they enter the war on the side of the South. These ships began arriving in the United States in September, 1863.

It was commonly understood why these ships were entering the American waters. "The average Northerner (understood)... that the Russian Czar was taking this means of warning England and France that if they made war in support of the South, he would help the North ....[26]

In October, 1863, the city of Baltimore issued a proclamation inviting the:

> officers of the Russian ships of war now in or shortly to arrive
> at that Port (New York) to visit the city of Baltimore...and to
> accept of its hospitalities, as a testimonial of the high respect of the
> authorities and citizens of Baltimore for the Sovereign and people
> of Russia, who, when other powers and people strongly bound to
> us by ties of interest or common descent (England and France?)
> have lent material and support to the Rebels of the South, have
> honorably abstained from all attempts to assist the rebellion, and

have given our government reliable assurances of their sympathy and good will.[27]

The Czar issued orders to his Admirals that they were to be ready to fight any power 'and to take their orders only from Abraham Lincoln.

And in the event of war, the Russian Navy was ordered to "attack the enemy's commercial shipping and their colonies, so as to cause them the greatest possible damage."[28]

In addition to all of these problems, Lincoln faced one more: the machinations of an internal conspiracy. Lincoln had anticipated such a conspiracy in 1837 when he stated: "At what point then is the approach of danger to be expected? I answer, if it ever reaches us it must spring up amongst us; it cannot come from abroad. If destruction be our lot, we must ourselves be its author and finisher. As a nation of free men, we must live through all time, or die by suicide."[29]

So Lincoln feared that the ultimate death of his nation would be caused by her own sons, his fellow Americans.

Early in 1863, Lincoln wrote a letter to Major General Joseph Hooker, in which he said: "I have placed you at the head of the Army of the Potomac. I have heard, in such a way as to believe it, of your recently saying that both the army and the government needed a dictator."[30]

Apparently what Lincoln had heard about General Hooker was true, as Hooker had "once been feared as the potential leader of a Radical coup d'etat."[31]

The Radicals referred to in Lincoln's letter to General Hooker were a group of Republicans, amongst others, who saw that the North would ultimately win the war with the South, and they wanted Lincoln to make the South pay for its rebellion after the victory. Lincoln favored the softer approach of allowing the Southern states to return to the Union after the war ended, without reprisals against them or their fighting men. The Radicals were frequently called the "Jacobins" after the group that fomented the French Revolution of 1789. As mentioned earlier, they were an offshoot of the Illuminati.

But Lincoln's biggest battle was yet to be fought: the battle for his life. The visions of Lincoln's earlier years about not serving two complete terms, and his fears about internal conspiracies, were about to come true.

On April 14, 1865, the conspiracy that Lincoln both feared and had knowledge of assassinated him. Eight people were tried for the crime, and four were later hung. In addition to the conspiracy's successful attempt on Lincoln's life, the plan was to also assassinate Andrew Johnson, Lincoln's Vice President, and Secretary of State Seward. Both of these other attempts failed, but if they had been successful, there is little doubt who would have been the one to reap all of the benefits: Secretary of War Edwin Stanton.

In fact, after the successful assassination of Lincoln, Stanton "became in that moment the functioning government of the United States, when he assumed control of the city of Washington D.C. in an attempt to capture Lincoln's killer."

The man who killed Lincoln, John Wilkes Booth, had several links with societies of the day, one of which was the Carbonari of Italy, an Illuminati-like secret organization active in Italian intrigue.

One of the many evidences of Stanton's complicity in the assassination attempts is the fact that he failed to block off the road that Booth took as he left Washington D.C. after the assassination, even though Stanton had ordered military blockades on all of the other roads.

It is now believed that Stanton also arranged for another man, similar in build and appearance to Booth, to be captured and then murdered by troops under the command of Stanton. It is further believed that Stanton certified that the murdered man was Booth, thereby allowing Booth to escape.

But perhaps the most incriminating evidence that Stanton was involved in the assassination of Lincoln lies in the missing pages of the diary kept by Mr. Booth. Stanton testified before Congressional investigating committees "that the pages were missing when the diary was given to him in April of 1865. The missing pages contain the names of some seventy high government officials and prominent businessmen who were involved in a conspiracy to eliminate Lincoln. The purported eighteen missing pages were recently discovered in the attic of Stanton's descendants."[32] And Booth was even linked to those involved with the conspiracy in the South: "A coded message was found in the trunk of Booth, the key to which was discovered in Judah P. Benjamin's possession. Benjamin . . . was the Civil War campaign strategist of the House of Rothschild."[33] (Mr. Benjamin held many key positions in the Confederacy during the Civil War.)

So it appears that Lincoln was the subject of a major conspiracy to assassinate him, a conspiracy so important that even the European bankers were involved. Lincoln had to be eliminated because he dared to oppose the attempt to force a central bank onto the American people, and as an example to those who would later oppose such machinations in high places.

(One of the early books on the subject of this conspiracy was published just months after the assassination of President Lincoln. It was entitled *The Assassination and History of the Conspiracy*, and it clearly identified the Knights of the Golden Circle as the fountainhead of the assassination plot. The back cover of the book carried an advertisement for another book that offered the reader "an inside view of the modus of the infamous organization, its connection with the rebellion and the Copperhead movement at the North." The second book was written by Edmund Wright, who claimed to be a member of the Knights.) After the attempt on his life failed, and after Lincoln's death, Vice-President Johnson became the President of the United

States. He continued Lincoln's policy of amnesty to the defeated South after the war was over. He issued an Amnesty Proclamation on May 29, 1865, welcoming the South back into the Union with only a few requirements:

1. The South must repudiate the debt of the war;
2. Repeal all secession ordinances and laws; and
3. Abolish slavery forever.

The first requirement did not endear President Johnson to those who wished the South to redeem its contractual obligations to those who loaned it the money it needed to fight the war. One of these debtors was the Rothschild family, who had heavily funded the South's efforts in the war.

Johnson also had to face another problem.

The Czar of Russia, for his part in saving the United States government during the war by sending his fleet to American waters, and apparently because of an agreement he made with Lincoln, asked to be paid for the use of his fleet. Johnson had no constitutional authority to give American dollars to the head of a foreign government. And the cost of the fleet was rather high: $7.2 million.

So Johnson had Secretary of State William Seward arrange for the purchase of Alaska from the Russians in April, 1867.

This act has unfairly been called "Seward's folly" by those historians unfamiliar with the actual reasons for Alaska's purchase, and to this day, Secretary of State Seward has been criticized for the purchase of what was then a piece of worthless land. But Seward was only purchasing the land as a method by which he could pay the Czar of Russia for the use of his fleet, an action that probably saved this nation from a more serious war with England and France.

But the real problem Johnson was to have during his tenure as President of the United States was still to occur.

He asked for the resignation of Secretary of War Edwin Stanton, and Stanton refused.

The Radical Republicans, also called the Jacobins, in the Senate started impeachment proceedings against President Johnson. These efforts failed by the slim margin of only one vote, and Johnson continued in office. In an interesting quirk of fate, the Chief Justice of the Supreme Court at the time was Salmon P. Chase, and it was his task to preside over the impeachment trial of President Johnson. Chase had resigned as Secretary of the Treasury to become the Chief Justice. It was almost as if the conspiracy had anticipated the impeachment proceedings and had wanted a man they felt they could trust in that key position.

Senator Benjamin F. Wade, President Pro-Tempore of the Senate, and next in line of succession to the Chief Executive's position, had been so confident that Johnson would be found guilty of the charges against him and removed from office that he had already informally named his new cabinet. Ironically, Stanton was to become the Secretary of the Treasury.[34]

Chief Justice Chase's role in these events would be recognized years later by John Thompson, founder of the Chase National Bank (later to be called the Chase Manhattan Bank, after its merger with the Manhattan Bank owned by the Warburgs,) who named his bank after him. In addition, other honors came to the Chief Justice. His picture now is found on the $10,000 bill printed by the U.S. Treasury. This bill is the highest existing denomination currency in the United States.

After the Civil War ended, President Johnson "had no doubt there was a conspiracy afoot among the Radicals (the Jacobins) to incite another revolution."[35]

It was the intent of the Jacobins to stir up the newly freed slaves and then use this dissatisfaction as the reason for starting another Civil War. And in fact there was a large riot in Memphis, Tennessee, in April, 1866, where a group of whites attacked negroes and forty-six of the Negroes were killed. Later, in July, 1866, there was a riot in New Orleans where a group of marching negroes were fired upon and many of them were killed.

The Radicals blamed Johnson for these killings, but some knew that the rioting was the work of others. Gideon Wells, the Secretary of the Navy, was one and he wrote in his diary: "There is little doubt that the New Orleans riots had their origin with the Radical members of Congress in Washington. It is part of a deliberate conspiracy and was to be the commencement of a series of bloody affrays through the States lately in the rebellion (the South.) There is a determination to involve the country in civil war, if necessary, to secure negro suffrage in the States and Radical ascendancy in the general government."[36]

Even President Johnson was aware of the attempts to incite another Civil War as he once . . .

> told Orville Browning that "he had no doubt that there was a conspiracy afoot among the Radicals to incite another revolution, and especially to arm and exasperate the negroes."
>
> The President himself was coming to believe that Stevens and Sumner (the leaders of the Radicals, also known as the Jacobins) and their followers intended to take the government into their own hands.
>
> It was an "unmistakable design," he once told Welles. They would declare Tennessee out of the Union and so get rid of him, and then set up a Directory based on the French Revolution's model.[37]

One of the groups acting to incite the riots was the Knights of the Golden Circle, whose war-time members included John Wilkes Booth and Jefferson Davis, the head of the Confederacy. Another member, Jesse James, was secretly hoarding large quantities of gold stolen from banks and mining companies in an attempt to buy a second Civil War. It has been estimated that Jesse and the other members of the Knights had buried over $7 billion in gold all over the western states.

Jesse James, a 33rd degree Mason, lived to be 107 years old. He claimed that his secret to his long life was that he changed his name frequently after first locating a cowboy with approximately his same physical characteristics. He then would kill or have him killed by shooting him in the face. He would then plant some items known to be his on the body, such as jewelry or clothing. His next step would be to have a known relative or a close friend identify the body as being that of Jesse James. Since there were no other means of identifying the body such as pictures or fingerprints, the public assumed that the relative or friend knew what they were saying when they identified the body. Grateful townspeople were happy to think that the notorious bankrobber, or any or his dangerous aliases, was dead, so they tended to believe that the identification was correct. Jesse claimed that it was by this method that he assumed the identities or aliases of some seventy-three individuals. In fact, he claimed that one of his aliases he used in later years was that of William A. Clark, the copper king and later a U.S. Senator from the Las Vegas area of Nevada. It is after Senator Clark that Clark County, Nevada is named.

Another group that was formed in 1867 to spread terror amongst the Negroes was a group known as the Ku Klux Klan, named after the Greek word Kuklos, which meant "band" or "circle."

Someone suggested that the name should be changed to Ku Klux, and this is the name that has existed to this very day. This organization was "brother to those secret organizations made up of other victims of despotism: the Confrereries of medieval France, the Carbonari of Italy, the Vehmgerict of Germany, (and) the Nihilists of Russia."[38]

It was the Nihilists who were credited with the assassination of the Czar of Russia, Alexander II, in 1881. This was the same Czar who sent the fleet to America during the Civil War. So he, like Lincoln, had to pay the price for outwitting the international bankers who had caused the Civil War. The connection between the Ku Klux Klan and the Knights of the Golden Circle has now become known. One author has written that "the Ku Klux Klan was the military arm of the Knights of the Golden Circle."[39]

The final important act of the Civil War came in 1875, when Congress passed the Specie Redemption Act, declaring it the policy of the government to redeem President Lincoln's "greenbacks" at par in gold on January 1, 1879.

Lincoln had outwitted the international bankers.

The United States still did not have a central bank.

It was time for the conspiracy to change the strategy.

Chapter 16
The Federal Reserve

After their successive failures at convincing the American people that they needed a Central Bank by forcing them into a series of wars, the international bankers connected with the conspiracy decided to change their methods. Instead of utilizing wars for this purpose, they would convince the unsuspecting American citizen that they needed a central bank through the use of artificially created depressions, recessions, and panics.

It was easy for the international bankers to create a banking panic.

Because of the nature of the banking business, the bankers knew that only a small percentage of the deposits stored in a bank by the depositors is ever called for on any given day. Because of this, only a small percentage, say twenty percent, is kept at the bank at any one time. The other eighty is loaned out, at interest, to borrowers who in turn reinvest it in Capital Goods or Consumption Goods.

Therefore, it would be easy for the bankers to cause a bank panic, called a "run," by convincing the depositors of any particular bank that the bank was insolvent and didn't have the money to pay the depositors should they withdraw their cash. This was of course a true statement, and if all of the depositors went to the bank at the same time to withdraw their deposits, the individual who had made the statement would prove to be rather prophetic in his analysis of the situation.

The news that a particular bank didn't have the deposits belonging to the depositors would cause other depositors at other banks to withdraw their funds as well to make certain that their deposits were safe. What would start as a "bank run" on a particular bank would end in a full-fledged national panic.

And the individual who made the assessment of the bank's insolvency would be recognized as a prophet of the first order.

The banks who would experience a run on their deposits would ask those to whom they loaned the money to return it and there would be a rush to sell properties to pay off the mortgages. When this happened all at once, property values would drop, allowing those with extra cash to buy properties at a reduced price. The pre-planned panic could work two ways: the bankers who knew it was coming could withdraw their cash prior to the beginning of the panic, and then go back into the market to buy Capital Goods at a reduced price.

This became, then, a powerful tool in the hands of those who wished to change our banking system from one where individual bankers functioned to one where a small group of bankers operated a national bank. The bankers would then blame the current banking system for the troubles in the economy.

But more importantly, the international bankers who caused the problem could offer their desired solution: a central bank.

So the tactic changed from one of creating wars to one of creating bank panics to influence the American people into the creation of a permanent central bank.

One of the prime movers in this movement was J.P. Morgan, whose father was one of the Rothschild agents who made a huge fortune in running President Lincoln's blockade during the Civil War.

(It is interesting to note that the J.P. Morgan, the supporter of America's need for a central bank, is related to Alexander Hamilton, the supporter of America's need for a central bank in the days of America's revolutionary war against the English Government. This connection was revealed in 1982, when *Time* magazine announced that Pierpont Morgan Hamilton, the great-great grandson of Alexander Hamilton and nephew of J.P. Morgan, had passed away.)[1]

In 1869, J.P. Morgan went to London and reached an agreement to form a company known as Northern Securities that was intended to act as an agent for the N.M. Rothschild Company in the United States.

The first major panic created by the international bankers occurred in 1893 when local bankers around the nation were told to call in their loans.

Senator Robert Owen "... testified before a Congressional Committee that the bank he owned received from the National Bankers' Association what came to be known as the 'Panic Circular of 1893.' It stated: 'You will at once retire one-third of your circulation and call in one-half of your loans....'"[2]

Congressman Charles A. Lindbergh, the father of the famous aviator, saw the circular that Senator Owen reported on, and said that it was intended to cause a "stringency" (a tightness) to cause "business men to appeal to Congress for legislation that would favor the bankers."[3]

(The bankers didn't create the panic by advising the American people that the banks were insolvent. They issued a circular to have the bankers cause it themselves. They would hold the former strategy for later panics.)

This tactic, of course, is exactly the same as that explained by Jan Kozak in his book *Not a Shot is Fired*: create the problem, and then encourage the people affected to ask Congress for laws favorable to those who created the problem.

Congress also took this opportunity to pass an income tax, including it in what was called the Tariff Act of 1894. So the two planks of *The Manifesto* created to destroy the middle class were being offered to the American people at the same time: the central bank and the income tax.

One courageous Congressman, Robert Adams, went on record as opposing the income tax. He is quoted as saying: "The imposition of the tax will corrupt the people. It will bring... the spy and the informer. It will be a step toward centralization.... It is expensive in its collection and cannot be fairly imposed."[4]

But in spite of the actions of the conspirators, the income tax as a law passed by Congress was declared to be unconstitutional by the Supreme Court. So the decision was made to add the income tax to the Constitution as a Constitutional Amendment.

It was now 1900, and the administration of President William McKinley was prosecuting the Northern Securities Company under the anti-trust laws. McKinley changed his vice-presidents for his second term, and less than a year later he was assassinated. His second vice-president, Theodore Roosevelt, became president, and the prosecution of Northern Securities stopped.

Roosevelt was later elected in his own right in 1904.

Another agent of the British Rothschild banking interests, Colonel Edward Mandell House, wrote an extremely important book in 1912. It was entitled *Philip Dru, Administrator*, and contained the personal beliefs of the author in the form of a novel. Even though the book was written in 1912, it contained predictions about future events the author hoped would come true.

The plot of the novel concerns a meeting in 1925 between John Thor, described as the "high priest of finance," and Senator Selwyn, a very important Senator.

Selwyn had discovered "that the government was run by a few men, that outside of this little circle, no one was of much importance. It was (Selwyn's) intention to break into it if possible and (his) ambition now leaned so far as to want, not only to be of it, but later, to be IT."[5]

Senator Selwyn was not content with just electing the President of the United States, he also "planned to bring under his control both the Senate and the Supreme Court."[6] "It was a fascinating game to Selwyn. He wanted to govern the Nation with an absolute hand, and yet not be known as the directing power."[7]

The nation came to know of this conspiracy between these two important individuals by a fluke, when Mr. Thor's secretary played back a tape recording made on a dictagraph that had been inadvertently turned on during the meeting. The secretary gave the recording to the Associated Press which spread the story of the conspiracy across the nation. America read the story and knew that "revolution was imminent."

The hero of the story, Philip Dru, who is not directly involved in the plot, organizes an army of 500,000 men and leads them on a march to Washington. He actually clashes with government troops prior to his arrival in Washington, and he scores a decisive victory over the Army. The President, named Rockland in the novel, flees the country, and Selwyn is appointed acting President in his absence. One of his first acts as President is to surrender to Philip Dru.

Dru moves in, keeps Selwyn as the President, but assumes "the power of a dictator" as he allows Selwyn to continue functioning as President, although Dru himself would make all of the decisions. He is now in a position to give the United States a new form of government, Dru describes it as ". . . Socialism as dreamed of by Karl Marx.")

He arranges for several key Marxist programs, such as a graduated income tax, and a graduated inheritance tax. He also prohibits the "selling of . . . anything of value," abolishing, at least in part, the right of private property, just as spelled out by Marx in his writings.

Dru starts making the laws of the nation, as ". . . there were no legislative bodies sitting, and the function of law-making was confined to one individual, the administration (Philip Dru) himself."[8]

Dru also re-wrote the "obsolete . . . and grotesque" Constitution of the United States.

Dru also meddled in the internal affairs of other nations, including England, and concerned himself with the nation of Russia as he: ". . . wondered when her deliverance would come. There was, he knew, great work for someone to do in that despotic land."[9]

(In other words, Colonel House, the author of *Philip Dru*, was hoping that there would be a revolution in Russia. He was urging the Russian

Revolution upon the Russian people, an event that was still five years away, as the so-called "despotic" Czar of Russia was replaced by "Socialism as dreamed of by Karl Marx.")

After the publication of the novel, it became known that Colonel House admitted that the book formulated "his ethical and political faith." House saw himself "in his hero. Philip Dru is what he himself would like to have been. Every act in his career, every letter, every word of advice that passed from him to (President) Woodrow Wilson was consistent with the ideas enunciated by Philip Dru."[10]

Colonel House had arranged to elect the next president of the United States, Woodrow Wilson, in the election of 1912. Wilson became the student of Colonel House, and as he began to learn the thoughts of his mentor, he became so close that Wilson later said that House's "thoughts and mine are one."

Wilson is confusing, a sort of enigma in the events of that day. He admitted that there was a giant conspiracy, yet he became involved with it. He wrote: "There is a power somewhere so organized, so subtle, so watchful, so interlocked, so complete, so pervasive that they better not speak above their breath when they speak in condemnation of it."[11]

Mr. Wilson didn't identify the power he had become aware of as being that of the Masons, but he was, in fact, a member.[12]

One of the many people that House gave a copy of his book to was another member of the Masons, Franklin Delano Roosevelt, who is reported to have read the book with great interest. One evidence that Roosevelt enjoyed the book was that he called his meetings with the American public over the radio his "fireside chats," possibly because of the fact that in House's book, Dru, the hero, "sat contentedly smoking by a great log fire in the library...."

House was an extremely important person during the Wilson years, as he once told biographer Charles Seymour: "During the last fifteen years I have been close to the center of things, although few people suspect it. No important foreigner has come to America without talking to me. I was close to the move ent that nominated Roosevelt."[13]

So not only did House create Woodrow Wilson, he also was involved in making Franklin Roosevelt the President of the United States.

So House became the "secret power" behind both Wilson and Roosevelt, exactly like his fictional character Senator Selwyn had hoped to become.

Another representative of the Rothschild interests, J.P. Morgan, was preparing for the next scheduled event in the creation of America's central bank. Morgan during the early months of 1907 was in Europe for five months, shuttling back and forth between London and Paris, homes of two branches of the Rothschild banking family.

Apparently the reason Morgan was in Europe was because the decision was being made to have Morgan precipitate a bank panic in America. When he returned, he started rumors that the Knickerbocker Bank in New York was insolvent. The bank's depositors became frightened because they thought that Morgan, being the best known banker of the day, might very well be right. Their panic started a run on the bank. Morgan was right, and the panic at the Knickerbocker also caused runs on other banks, and the Panic of 1907 was complete.

The propaganda started almost immediately that the state-chartered bankers couldn't be trusted anymore with the banking affairs of the nation. The need for a central bank had become apparent by the Panic of 1907, or at least this is how the conspiracy argued.

Historian Frederick Lewis Allen, writing in *Life* magazine, became aware of the plot. He wrote: "...certain chroniclers have arrived at the ingenious conclusion that the Morgan interests took advantage of the un-settled conditions during the autumn of 1907 to precipitate the Panic, guiding it shrewdly as it progressed, so that it would kill off rival banks, and consolidate the pre-eminence of the banks within the Morgan orbit."[14]

Woodrow Wilson, who was president of Princeton University in 1907, spoke to the American people, attempting to remove whatever blame might be placed upon the Morgan shoulders. He said: "All this trouble could be averted if we appointed a committee of six or seven public-spirited men like J.P. Morgan to handle the affairs of our country."[15]

So Wilson wanted to hand over the affairs of the nation to the very person who had caused all of the concern: J.P. Morgan!

But the main thrust of the explanations about the causes of the 1907 Panic was that the American people needed a strong central bank to prevent the abuses of the "Wall Street" bankers: "What finally convinced Congress of the need for better control over the nation's banking was one stark event: the Panic of 1907. The panic subsided. Agitation grew for an effective national banking system."[16]

So the American people, who had suffered through the American Revolution, the War of 1812, the battles between Andrew Jackson and the Second Bank of the United States, the Civil War, the previous panics of 1873 and 1893, and now the Panic of 1907, were finally conditioned to the point of accepting the solution offered by those who had caused all of these events: the international bankers.

That solution was a central bank.

The invididual the bankers used to introduce the legislation that created the central bank was a Senator from Rhode Island, a Mason, and the maternal grandfather of the Rockefeller brothers, David, Nelson, et al., by the name of Nelson Aldrich. He was appointed to a National Monetary Commission and charged "to make a thorough study of financial practices before formulating banking and currency reform legislation."

So for two years, this Commission toured the banking houses of Europe, learning (supposedly) the secrets of the central banking systems of Europe, (there are those who believe that they already knew the secrets of the central banking systems of Europe!)

Upon Senator Aldrich's return, in November, 1910, he boarded a train in Hoboken, New Jersey, for a ride to Jekyll Island, Georgia. His destination was the Jekyll Island Hunt Club, owned by Mr. Morgan. It was here that the legislation that would give America its central bank was written.

Aboard the train, and with Senator Aldrich later in Georgia, were the following individuals:

A. Piatt Andrew, Assistant Secretary of the Treasury;

Senator Nelson Aldrich, National Monetary Commission;

Frank Vanderlip, President of Kuhn-Loeb's National City Bank of New York;

Henry Davidson, Senior Partner of J.P. Morgan;

Charles Norton, President of Morgan's First National Bank of New York;

Paul Warburg, Partner in the banking house of Kuhn-Loeb & Company; and

Benjamin Strong, President of Morgan's Banker's Trust Company.

The railroad car that these gentlemen travelled in belonged to Senator Aldrich, and while they were aboard, they were sworn to secrecy and asked to refer to each other by first names only.

One of those, Mr. Vanderlip, later went on to reveal his role in the writing of the bill that created the Federal Reserve System. He wrote in the *Saturday Evening Post*:

> ... in 1910, when I was as secretive, indeed as furtive, as any conspirator. I do not feel it is any exaggeration to speak of our secret expedition to Jekyll Island as the occasion of the actual conception of what eventually became the Federal Reserve System.
>
> We were told to leave our last names behind us. We were told further that we should avoid dining together on the night of our departure. We were instructed to come one at a time and as unobtrusively as possible to the terminal of the New Jersey littoral of the Hudson, where Senator Aldrich's private car would be in readiness, attached to the rear end of the train for the South.
>
> Once aboard the private car, we began to observe the taboo that had been fixed on last names.
>
> Discovery, we knew, simply must not happen, or else all our time and effort would be wasted.[17]

Notice that the conspirators did not want the American people to know what they had in store for them: a central bank. The legislation was to be written not by a group of legislators, but by a group of bankers, mostly connected with the man responsible for the Panic of 1907: J.P. Morgan.

The conspiracy also had one additional problem. They had "to avoid the name Central Bank, and for that reason (they) had come upon the designation of Federal Reserve System. It would be owned by private individuals who would draw profit from ownership of shares and who would control the nation's issue of money; it would have at its command the nation's entire financial resources; and it would be able to mobilize and mortgage the United States by involving (the United States) in major foreign wars."[18]

The method the conspirators used to defraud the American people was to divide the Federal Reserve System into twelve districts so that the American people could not call the bank a "central bank." The fact that the twelve districts had one director, called the Federal Reserve Chairman, apparently was not to be considered relevant.

The one non-banker at Jekyll Island was Senator Nelson Aldrich, but he certainly could have qualified as a wealthy man, capable of starting his own bank. When he entered the Senate in 1881, he was worth $50,000. When he left the Senate in 1911, he was worth $30,000,000.

Now that the legislation creating the central bank was written, it would need a president who would not veto the bill after it passed the House and the Senate. The President in 1910 and 1911 was William Howard Taft, elected in 1908, and he was on record as saying that he would veto the bill should it come to his desk for him to sign. He was a Republican and was surely to be re-elected to a second term in 1912.

The conspiracy needed to defeat him, so it supported first the campaign of ex-President Teddy Roosevelt, a fellow Republican, to defeat Taft in the Republican primaries. This activity failed as Taft was re-nominated, so the conspiracy planned on defeating him with the Democratic candidate, Woodrow Wilson.

However, the supporters of Wilson soon found that their candidate would not draw enough votes to defeat Taft in the general election. It was discovered that Taft would defeat Wilson by a 55 to 45 margin.

This obviously caused a problem for the supporters of the Federal Reserve Bill, which would be defeated if Taft were to be re-elected. What they had fought wars for and had caused depressions for, was now within their grasp, and it all could be prevented by one man: President William Howard Taft.

The supporters needed someone to draw votes away from Taft in the general election, so they urged Teddy Roosevelt to run against both Wilson and Taft. It was theorized that Roosevelt, a fellow Republican, would draw votes from the other Republican in the race, Taft, and enable Wilson to win without a majority of the votes cast. (Wilson, of course, had agreed to sign the Federal Reserve Bill should it get to his desk for him as President to sign.)

This strategy was confirmed in a book by Ferdinand Lundberg, entitled *America's 60 Families*. Lundberg wrote:

> In view of the vast sums subsequently spent by him (Frank Munsey) and Perkins, (two Roosevelt supporters, both of whom were closely allied with the J.P. Morgan interests) to forward the Progressive campaign (of Roosevelt) and insure Taft's defeat, the suspicion seems justified that the two were not over-anxious to have Roosevelt win.
>
> The notion that Perkins and Munsey may have wanted Wilson to win, or any Democratic candidate other than (William Jennings) Bryan, is partly substantiated by the fact that Perkins put a good deal of cash behind the Wilson campaign.
>
> In short, most of Roosevelt's campaign fund was supplied by the two Morgan hatchet men who were seeking Taft's scalp.[19]

The tactic of dividing the votes of the apparent winner so that a candidate with a minority of the votes could be elected has been used frequently in the United States, most notably in the nomination of George McGovern in 1972, and also in the election of 1980 which will be discussed in another chapter.

In the case of the McGovern election, it was established prior to the Democratic primaries that he apparently would not be able to garner more than thirty to thirty-five percent of the primary election votes against Hubert Humphrey, the party's favorite, and their nominee in 1968. Yet it was important for McGovern to get the nomination (for reasons that will be covered later in another context.) To implement this decision, the Democrats offered the Democratic voters a candidate of every political stripe and persuasion in the primaries. These candidates were to divide Humphrey's vote so that McGovern would win the primaries with thirty to thirty-five percent of the vote. This would enable McGovern, with his hard-core following, to win the Democratic nomination with but a small percentage of the vote.

The strategy worked.

McGovern won the nomination against the party favorite, Hubert Humphrey.

So the election of 1912 became history. The three candidates, Taft, Wilson and Roosevelt, waited for the results.

When the votes were counted, Wilson won the election with but forty-five percent of the vote, Roosevelt received more votes than did Taft, and Taft ran third. But the interesting thing is that the total of the votes cast for Taft and Roosevelt, when added together, would have been enough to defeat Wilson, fifty-five percent to forty-five percent. It was extremely likely that in a two-man race, Taft would have defeated Wilson rather handily.

The plot worked. Wilson was elected and then inaugurated in January, 1913. Wilson could now sign the Federal Reserve Bill in December, 1913, after it had passed the House and the Senate. And he did.

What did the American people get from the Federal Reserve System?

The System itself publishes a paperback textbook entitled *The Federal Reserve System, Purposes and Functions,* that is used in colleges to explain the activities of the System to college students, especially in a class entitled Money and Banking.

This booklet explains the functions of the Federal Reserve: "An efficient monetary mechanism is indispensible to . . . the nation. . . . The function of the Federal Reserve is to foster a flow of money and credit that will facilitate orderly economic growth, a stable dollar, and long-run balance in our international payments."[20]

(It is a fair question to ask the Federal Reserve System, if the Americans haven't had an "orderly economic growth, a stable dollar and a long-run balance in our international payments" which has been America's history since the creation of the System, why is it allowed to continue?

It would seem that such a system with such a dismal record for about seventy years would be abolished without delay.

Could it be that the system was created to ensure that America didn't have an "orderly economic growth, a stable dollar, and a long-run balance in our international payments?"

In other words, the System was created to do exactly the opposite of what it tells the American people! The System is working!)

There were those who opposed the creation of the System at the time and made that opposition public. One such individual was Congressman Charles Lindbergh, Sr.

Congressman Lindbergh warned the American people that the Federal Reserve Act ". . . established the most gigantic trust on earth. When the President signs this act, the invisible government by the money power- . . . will be legitimized. The new law will create inflation whenever the trusts want inflation. From now on, depressions will be scientifically created."[21]

The Congressman had put his finger on the pulse of the problem: the Federal Reserve System was created to foster economic emergencies.

This instrument of economic destruction was now in place. The staffing of the System's key positions with those who created and supported it followed.

The first governor of the New York Federal Reserve branch was Benjamin Strong of Morgan's Bankers Trust Company, a participant in the Jekyll Island writing of the bill. The first Governor of the Board of Directors was Paul Warburg, a partner in the banking house of Kuhn, Loeb and Company, also a participant at the Jekyll Island Meeting.

What had those who called the system "Federal" created? Was it really a "Federal" Reserve System?

It is "a private organization, since the member banks own all of the stock, on which they receive tax-free dividends; it must pay postage, like any other private corporation; its employees are not on civil service; it may spend whatever it wishes; . . . and its physical property, held under private deeds, is subject to local taxation."[22]

In fact, America's elected officials know that the "Federal" Reserve System isn't federal. In speeches to the American people, recent Presidents Richard Nixon, Gerald Ford, and Jimmy Carter have joined Dr. Arthur Burns, former head of the System, the Associated Press, the House of Representatives in a primer on the System, and others, in stating that the System is "independent," (or words to that effect.)

In other words, these individuals and entities know that the system is not "Federal." It is privately owned and operated.

Other Congressmen, more recent than Congressman Lindbergh, have also warned the American people about the dangers of the non-federal Federal Reserve System. Congressman Wright Patman, the Chairman of the House Banking and Currency Committee, said: "In the United States today, we have in effect two governments. We have the duly constituted government. Then we have an independent, uncontrolled and un-coordinated government in the Federal Reserve System, operating the money powers which are reserved to Congress by the Constitution."[23]

Ludwig von Mises, a free-market economist, has spoken somewhat humorously on the subject of the governments that create national banking systems like the Federal Reserve: "Government is the only agency that can take a perfectly useful commodity like paper, smear it with ink, and render it absolutely useless."

The privately owned Federal Reserve System is in control of the money supply and therefore has the ability to create inflation and deflation at will.

The money supply per capita in 1913, when the Reserve System was created was around $148. By 1978, it stood at $3,691.

The value of the 1913 dollar, taken as a base of 1.00, had shrunk to approximately 12 cents by 1978.

(This must be what the Federal Reserve System calls a "stable dollar.")

The quantity of money in January, 1968, stood at $351 billion, and in February, 1980, it was $976 billion, a 278 percent increase. In fact, the quantity of money doubles approximately every ten years. But strangely, this increase in the money supply, or so the American people are told, does not cause inflation. Even though the dictionary definition of inflation states that an increase in the money supply *always* causes inflation.

The Federal Reserve System admits that the ability to create inflation rests with their agency: "Thus, the ultimate capability for expanding or reducing the economy's supply of money rests with the Federal Reserve."[24]

Not all of the banks in America, however, were interested in the creation of inflation. Some were concerned about their membership in the System and were withdrawing. In fact, William Miller, then the Chairman of the Federal Reserve, in 1978 warned that the flight of the member banks out of the System was "weakening the financial system of the United States."

A total of 430 members banks had left the Federal Reserve in an eight-year span, including 15 major banks in 1977, with deposits of more than $100 billion, and another 39 banks left in 1978. As a result of this attrition, twenty-five percent of all commercial bank deposits and sixty percent of all banks were now outside of the system.

Miller continued: "The ability of the system to influence the nation's money and credit (became) weaker."[25]

The trend away from the Federal Reserve System continued, and in December, 1979, Federal Reserve Chairman Paul Volcker informed the House Banking Committee that "... some 300 banks with deposits of $18.4 billion have quit the Fed (the Federal Reserve System) within the past 4½ years.' He said another 575 of the remaining 5,480 member banks, with deposits of more than $70 billion, 'have given us some indication of their intent to withdraw.' "[26]

And in February, 1980, it was reported that: "In the last four months, 69 banks (had) withdrawn from the Federal Reserve System, taking with them seven billion dollars in deposits. Another 670 banks, holding $71 billion in deposits, have expressed a desire to leave the system."[27]

This exodus from the System could not be allowed to continue, so in 1980, Congress passed the Monetary Control Act which gave the Federal Reserve System control of *all* depository institutions, whether or not the banks were previously members of the System itself.

But in any event, the System after its creation in 1913 was in a position to loan the federal government large sums of money. Their first real opportunity to do this occurred just a few years later during World War I.

The following table illustrates just how much money the System loaned the United States government during the War: (in millions of dollars, rounded).

Year	Rounded Receipts	Rounded Outlays	Surplus or Deficit
1916	$ 761	731	$- 48
1917	1,101	1,954	- 853
1918	3,645	12,677	- 9,032
1919	5,139	18,493	-13,363
1920	6,649	6,358	291

The table shows how the size of the government grew from 1916 to 1920, and how enormous quantities of debt were accumulated. This money, in large part, was borrowed from the Federal Reserve System, America's central bank, which ". . . hath benefit of interest on all moneys which it creates out of nothing."[28]

In addition to the ability to create interest-bearing debt, the Federal Reserve System also has the ability to create economic cycles through the expansion and contraction of the quantity of money and credit. Their first major opportunity to create a depression by this method occurred in 1920, when the Federal Reserve created what has become known as the Panic of 1920.

One of those who saw how this was the result of prior economic planning was Congressman Lindbergh, who in 1921 wrote in his book *Economic Pinch*, the following: "Under the Federal Reserve Act, panics are scientifically created; the present panic is the first scientifically created one, worked out as we figure a mathematical problem."[29]

The process works in the following manner: the System increases the money supply (from 1914 to 1919, the quantity of money in the United States nearly doubled.) The media then encourages the American people to borrow large quantities of money on credit.

Once the money is out on loan, the bankers contract the money supply by calling in their outstanding loans. The entire process was laid out by Senator Robert L. Owen, Chairman of the Senate Banking and Currency Committee, and a banker himself. He wrote:

> In the early part of 1920, the farmers were exceedingly prosperous.
>
> They were paying off their mortgages and buying a lot of land, at the insistence of the government—had borrowed money to do it—and then they were bankrupted by a sudden contraction of credit which took place in 1920.
>
> What took place in 1920 was just the reverse of what should have been taking place.
>
> Instead of liquidating the excess of credits created by the war

176

through a period of years, the Federal Reserve Board met in a
meeting which was not disclosed to the public.

They met on the 16th of May, 1920, and it was a secret meeting.

Only the big bankers were there, and the work of that day
resulted in a contraction of credit (by ordering banks to call in
outstanding loans) which had the effect the next year of reducing
the national income fifteen billion dollars, throwing millions of
people out of employment, and reducing the value of lands and
ranches by twenty-billion dollars.[30]

Not only did the bankers transfer large quantities of land from the
farmers to the bankers by this contraction, but the process also transferred
large numbers of banks from the hands of those bankers who could not meet
the demands of the Federal Reserve and had to sell their banking assets for a
reduced price to those who had the money to buy bankrupt banks (the Panic
of 1920 bankrupted 5,400 banks.)

One of the major non-banking targets of this panic was Henry Ford, the
automobile manufacturer.

Despite inflation, Ford ordered a price cut for his automobiles,
but demand was still insufficient and a number of Ford plants had
to be shut down.

Rumor had it that a huge loan was being negotiated. But Ford,
who thought New York bankers were nothing short of vultures,
was determined not to fall into their hands. . . .

Bankers . . . lined up to offer their "help" in return for his
surrender of independence.

The game was clear to Mr. Ford.

One representative of a Morgan-controlled bank in New York
came forward with a plan to "save" Ford. . . .

Ford saved his company by turning to his dealers, to whom he
now shipped his cars collect in spite of the slowness of the
market. . . .

Demand grew . . . and the plants were re-opened."[31]

Ford, had out-smarted the bankers who had planned the Panic, in part,
to destroy him. He did not need to borrow large quantities of money and
surrender control of his company to the bankers who would certainly wish
to control that which they subsidized.

The Panic of 1920 was a success, and this success led the bankers to plan
another: the Crash of 1929.

The first step was, once again, to increase the money supply, and this
was done from 1921 to 1929, as is illustrated by the following table:

Years	Quantity of money (in billions)
June 1920	$ 34.2
June, 1921 (low)	31.7
June, 1922	33.0
June, 1923	36.1
June, 1924	37.6
June, 1925	42.6
June, 1926	43.1
June, 1927	45.4
June, 1928 (high)	45.7
June, 1929	45.7

The figures reveal that the Federal Reserve expanded the money supply from a low of $31.7 billion in 1921, to a high of $45.7 billion in 1929, an increase of approximately 144 percent.

To move this increase in the money supply into the economy, individual banks could borrow money from the Federal Reserve and re-loan it to the buying public. The money was borrowed at 5 percent interest, and was re-loaned at 12 percent.

Contributing to the increase in the money supply, or the money being made available by the Federal Reserve, was the money being made available by the large corporations, which were loaning their surplus funds to buyers on Wall Street. These loans from these non-banking sources were approximately equal to those from the banking system. For instance, call loans to brokers in 1929 made by some leading corporations were as follows:

Lender	Peak amounts
American and Foreign Power (J.P. Morgan)	$ 30,321,000
Electric Bond and Share (J.P. Morgan)	157,579,000
Standard Oil of New Jersey (the Rockefellers)	97,824,000

In addition, J.P. Morgan and Company had nearly $110,000,000 in the call-loan market.[32]

This expansion in the money supply brought prosperity to the country, and the American people were encouraged by the media to buy into the stock market. They were told that those who did were making large quantities of money.

The stock brokers who were handling the new influx of buyers coming to make a fortune in the stock market were using a new tool to induce them into buying more shares of stock than they had anticipated. This new tool was called "buying on margin," and it enabled the stock buyer to borrow money and to use it to buy stock.

The buyer was encouraged to buy stock with only ten percent down, borrowing the remaining ninety percent from the stock broker, who had arranged for the buyer to borrow from either a bank or a large corporation. The following example will illustrate how this method worked:

A share of stock sells for $100, but because of the ability of the purchaser to buy on margin, with only ten percent down, ten shares could be bought, with the same $100 instead of only one:

	One share	*Ten shares*
Buyer's cash:	$100	$ 100
Borrowed cash:	-0-	900
Total:	− $100	$1,000

Therefore for the same investment, $100, a purchaser could borrow $900, using the stock as collateral for the loan, and therefore buy ten shares for the same investment of $100.

Now, for this example, presume that one share of stock went up ten percent in the stock market, or to $110. This would increase the profits made by the stock buyer:

Value of one share:	$110	Ten shares:	$1,100
Buyers investment:	$100		$ 100
Profit:	$ 10		$ 100
Profit on investment	10%		100%

The investor could now sell the shares of stock, and make a one-hundred percent profit with only a ten-percent increase in the stock's value (the buyer could double his investment) after paying off the loan to the lender.

There was one catch, however, as the money was loaned to the buyer on what was called a "24 hour broker call loan." This meant that the broker could exercise his option and require that the borrower sell his stock and return the loan amount 24 hours after the lender had asked for it. The buyer had 24 hours to repay the loan and had to either sell the stock or come up with the loan amount to pay off the lender of the money.

This meant that, whenever the brokers wanted to, they could require all of the stock buyers to sell at the same time by calling all of the loans at the same time. This activity would precipitate a panic on the stock market, when all of the stock owners went to sell their stock. And when all the sellers offer stock at the same time, the price drops rapidly. The whole process was detailed by one author who wrote:

> When everything was ready, the New York financiers started calling 24-hour broker call-loans.
>
> This meant that the stock brokers and the customers had to dump their stock on the market in order to pay the loans.
>
> This naturally collapsed the stock market and brought a banking collapse all over the country, because the banks not owned by the oligarchy were heavily involved in broker call-loans at this time, and bank runs soon exhausted their coin and currency, and they had to close.
>
> The Federal Reserve System would not come to their aid, although they were instructed under the law to maintain an elastic currency.[33]

The Federal Reserve "would not come to their aid," even though they were required by law to do so, and many banks (and individuals) went bankrupt. Notice that those banks owned by the oligarchy had already gotten out of the broker call-loan business, without any damage, and those who didn't went bankrupt.

Is it possible that the Federal Reserve planned it exactly as it happened? Is it possible that those banks that knew the game plan had gotten out while the prices were high and then came back into the market when they were low? Is it possible that some banks knew when the crash was coming and all that they had to do to buy bankrupt banks was to wait until after the crash, and then buy up the troubled banks at only a percentage of the true value?

After the Stock Market Crash of 1929, even a casual observer had to notice that the ownership of the banking system had changed. In fact, today "100 out of 14,100 banks (less than 1%) control 50% of the nation's banking assets. Fourteen big banks have 25% of the deposits."[34]

In any event, the stock market crashed. The stock market index shows the effects of this manipulation:

1919	$138.12
1921	66.24
1922	469.49
1932	57.62

One of the spectators of the stock market crash was Winston Churchill who was brought to the stock market exchange on October 24, 1929, by Bernard Baruch. Some rare historians are convinced that Churchill was brought to witness the crash firsthand because it was desired that he see the power of the banking system at work.[35]

Even though many stockholders had to sell their stock, it is not commonly questioned as to who bought all of the stock that was being sold. The history books generally discuss all of the selling that went on during the crash, but fail to discuss all of the buying.

John Kenneth Galbraith in his book *The Great Crash 1929*, wrote this about the buyers:

Nothing could have been more ingeniously designed to maximize the suffering, and also to insure that as few as possible escaped the common misfortune.

The fortunate speculator who had funds to answer the first margin call presently got another and equally urgent one, and if he met that there would still be another.

In the end, all the money he had was extracted from him and lost.

The man with the smart money, who was safely out of the market when the first crash came, naturally went back in to pick up bargains.[36]

Naturally!

One of those "fortunate speculators" who got out early was Bernard Baruch, the individual who brought Winston Churchill to witness the crash. He has said: "I had begun to liquidate my stock holdings and to put my money into bonds and into a cash reserve. I also bought gold."[37]

Another who got out early was Joseph P. Kennedy, the father of President John Kennedy, who in the winter of 1928-29 got out of the market. "The profits he took from the sale of his . . . holdings were not reinvested, but kept in cash."[38]

Others who sold their stock before the crash included international bankers and financiers Henry Morgenthau and Douglas Dillon.[39]

The selling on credit during the crash had another effect already mentioned. About sixteen-thousand banks, or fifty-two percent of the total, went out of business.

Some of the stockholders went to their banks to withdraw whatever cash they had in the bank to pay whatever they could of their stock call in cash. This caused a nearly nation-wide bank run. To end this panic, President

Franklin D. Roosevelt, two days after his inauguration in March of 1933, shut down all the banks for a "holiday."[40]

There weren't many who saw what was happening to the American people by these machinations of the bankers, but one who did was Congressman Louis McFadden, who was quoted as saying:

> When the Federal Reserve Act was passed, the people of these United States did not perceive that a world banking system was being set up here.
>
> A super-state controlled by international bankers and international industrialists acting together to enslave the world for their own pleasure.
>
> Every effort has been made by the Fed to conceal its powers but the truth is — the Fed has usurped the Government.
>
> It controls everything here and it controls all our foreign relations.
>
> It makes and breaks governments at will.[41]

After the stock market crash had run its course, Congressman McFadden charged that: "The money and credit resources of the United States were now in the complete control of the banker's alliance between J.P. Morgan's First National Bank group, and Kuhn, Loeb's National City Bank."

On May 23, 1933, McFadden brought impeachment charges against the Federal Reserve Board, the agency he thought had caused the Stock Market Crash of 1929, with these charges, amongst others:

> I charge them . . . with having . . . taken over $80,000,000,000 (eighty billion dollars) from the United States Government in the year 1928. . . .
>
> I charge them . . . with having arbitrarily and unlawfully raised and lowered the rates on money, . . . increased and diminished the volume of currency in circulation for the benefit of private interests . . . ."

And then McFadden expanded his understanding of those who benefitted in the crash to include the international bankers: "I charge them . . . with . . . . . having conspired to transfer to foreigners and international money lenders title to and control of the financial resources of the United States . . . ."

He then ended with this statement that the cause of the depression was not accidental: "It was a carefully contrived occurrence. . . . The international bankers sought to bring about a condition of despair here so that they might emerge as the rulers of us all."[42]

McFadden had a price to pay for his attempts to explain the causes of the depression and the stock market crash: "On two occassions assassins attempted to kill McFadden with gunfire; later he died, a few hours after attending a banquet, and there is little doubt that he was poisoned."[43]

Now that the stock market had crashed, the Federal Reserve took steps to reduce the nation's quantity of money:

Dates	Quantity of money (in billions)
June, 1929 (high)	$45.7
December, 1929	45.6
December, 1930	43.6
December, 1931	37.7
December, 1932	34.0
June, 1933 (low)	30.0

The quantity of money went from a high of nearly $46 billion to a low of $30 billion in just four years. This action of the Federal Reserve rippled throughout the entire business world to the point where "production at the country's factories, mines, and utilities fell by more than one-half. The total output of goods and services dropped by one-third."[44]

In spite of all of the evidence to the contrary, there are still those who don't know who, or what, caused the Stock Market Crash of 1929. One of these is economist John Kenneth Galbraith, who, in his book *The Great Crash, 1929*, wrote that: "The causes of the Great Depression are still far from certain."

In fact, Galbraith knows that people did not cause the crash and the resulting depression:

No one was responsible for the great Wall Street Crash. No one engineered the speculation that preceded it. . . .

Hundreds of thousands of individuals . . . were not led to the slaughter. They were impelled . . . by the . . . lunacy which has always seized people who are seized in turn with the notion that they can become very rich.

There were many Wall Streeters who helped to foster this insanity. . . .

There was none who caused it.[45]

The media now entered the fray, by proclaiming that the free-enterprise system had failed, and that government was needed to solve the economic problems caused by the lack of wisdom inherent in the system. The solution was ". . . new government measures and controls. The powers of the Federal

Reserve Board—have been strengthened."[46]

More recently, it has been illustrated just how much power the Federal Reserve has. Take, for instance, the two articles in the Portland *Oregonian* of Saturday, February 24, 1972. The two articles are on top of one another on the same page.

The top article is captioned: "Reserve Board Raises Lending Rate for Banks" and the bottom article is entitled: "Wall Street Values Plunge."

Anyone could protect a fortune in the stock market by knowing in advance when the Board was going to take an action that would force the market down. Conversely, a fortune could be made if the advance information foretold a rise in the market.

In fact, the Federal Reserve System doesn't even have to do anything as even a rumored action will cause the stock market to operate in a downward direction. For instance, a rumor spread on December 16, 1978, that the Federal Reserve System was anticipating a certain action, and the market went down!

Later another Congressman attempted to investigate the Federal Reserve. Congressman Wright Patman introduced a bill which would have authorized a full and independent audit of the System by the General Accounting Office. Patman claimed that the audit was essential to give the public's elected representatives complete and accurate information on the internal operations of the System, since they had not been audited since their inception in 1913.

Patman was frankly astonished by the opposition to his bill. He wrote: "Although I had anticipated that officials of the Federal Reserve System would vigorously oppose my bill, I am frankly amazed by the massive lobbying campaign now underway, to prevent enactment of this measure. This itself is further proof, if any is needed, that a thorough and independent audit . . . is an absolute necessity in the public interest."[41]

Congressman Patman did score a "small victory," however. The Congress passed his bill but attached an amendment that will limit the audit to administrative expenditures only, presumably the expense accounts of the executives of the System, the numbers of pencils purchased per employee, etc., hardly what Patman had in mind.

Later Congressman Patman, Chairman of the House Banking Committee, was removed from his Chairmanship after the elections of 1974, because, as one Congressman voting to remove him told one of his constituents, Patman was "too old."

Or maybe "too smart!"

Chapter 17
Graduated Income Taxes

Author and economist Henry Hazlitt observed in his book *Man vs. the Welfare State*:

> In the Communist Manifesto of 1848, Marx and Engels frankly proposed a "heavy progressive or graduated income tax" as an instrument by which the proletariat will use its political supremacy to wrest, by degrees, all capital from the bourgeois, to centralize all instruments of production in the hands of the State, and to make despotic inroads on the right of property....[1]

How does the graduated income tax wrest property from the "bourgeois" (the propertied class?)

The graduated income tax increases the percentage of tax withdrawn from the taxpayer's income as his income increases. (A cartoon recently appeared in a newspaper that showed a husband explaining to his wife: "The 8 percent raise we got raises us even with inflation, but in a higher tax bracket. We lose $10. a week!")

Karl Marx was the visible author of the plan of using the graduated income tax and the central bank together to destroy the wage earning middle class. And Senator Nelson Aldrich was the individual who introduced the legislation in the Congress of the United States that gave America both the graduated income tax and the central bank!

An example verifying the simple cartoon can be taken from the income tax tables prepared by the Internal Revenue Service:

Income:	Tax:	Percent of income:
$ 5,000	$ 810	16%
10,000	1,820	18%
20,000	4,380	22%

Notice that as the income doubles, taxes go up as a percentage of that income because of the graduated features of the Personal Income Tax. In other words, those who belong to unions that claim that they have assisted their member-workers by obtaining a "cost of living increase," pegged to inflation rate increases, have in truth been hurt by their unions who did not include an increase to provide for the graduated income tax. What the unions should insist upon is a "cost of living increase, plus a graduated income tax increase" for their members. Notice that this generally doesn't happen. In fact, the unions are frequently blamed as being the cause of inflation, a charge not often refuted by the unions.

When the Graduated Income Tax was finally passed as the 16th Amendment to the Constitution, there were those who were in support of the Amendment that claimed that the tax imposed was not significant. They argued:

No one who had taxable income under five thousand dollars had to pay any income tax at all.

When (the wage earner) reached that sum all he had to pay was four-tenths of one percent — a tax of twenty dollars per year.

If he had an income of ten thousand dollars, his tax was only seventy dollars per year.

On an income of one hundred thousand dollars, the tax was two and one-half percent, or twenty-five hundred dollars.

And on incomes of half a million dollars the tax was twenty-five thousand dollars or five percent.[2]

But even this minimal tax could not fool those who felt that the tax would become an oppressive burden on the American taxpayer in the near future. During discussion of the Amendment in the Virginia House of Delegates, in 1910, Speaker Richard R. Byrd expressed his opposition to the income tax, by warning:

It will extend the federal power so as to reach the citizen in the

186

ordinary business of life.

A hand from Washington will be stretched out and placed upon every man's business; the eye of a federal inspector will be in every man's counting house.

The law will of necessity have inquisitorial features; it will provide penalties.

It will create a complicated machinery. Under it business will be hauled into court distant from their business.

Heavy fines imposed by... unfamiliar tribunals will constantly menace the taxpayer.

They will compel men of business to show their books and disclose the secrets of their affairs....

They will require statements and affidavits...[3]

During the debate on the Amendment in the Senate, several Senators expressed the fear that the low tax rate would only be a beginning of higher taxes. One Senator suggested that the rate would increase to perhaps a rate as high as twenty percent of a taxpayer's income.

Senator William Borah of Idaho felt that such speculation was outrageous, declaring: "Who could ever impose such a confiscatory rate?"[4]

But even with opposition and concern such as this, the Graduated Income Tax became the 16th Amendment to the Constitution on February 25, 1913.

What has happened to the taxpayer since the 16th Amendment has passed can be illustrated by the following table:

Year	Income tax per capita
1913	approximately: $ 4
1980	approximately: $ 2,275

(That 1980 per capita tax amounts to about 40 percent of total personal income.)

A monitor of the impact on these income taxes upon the average wage earner is a group called the Tax Foundation, and they have coined a name for the day on which the taxpayer actually begins earning for himself. They call this day Tax Freedom Day, and that day has been occurring later each year in the following way:

Year	Tax freedom day	Percent of year completed
1930	February 13	11.8
1940	March 8	18.1
1950	April 4	25.5
1960	April 18	29.3
1970	April 30	32.6
1980	May 11	35.6

That means that, in 1980, the average wage earner worked 35.6 percent of the year, until May 11, for the government. From that day on, what the wage-earner earned belonged to the individual.

Even though the tax was sold to the American people as a "soak the rich" scheme (making the rich pay the most taxes as a percentage of their income) it is the middle class income wage-earners who pay the majority of the taxes. This point was made clear by an Associated Press article on September 13, 1980, headlined: "Middle-incomers may be a minority, but they pay 60.1% of all taxes."[5]

The article went on to report that tax returns with incomes:

a. under $10,000 accounting for 43.9 percent of nearly 91 million returns paid only 4.4 percent of the total.
b. incomes of from $15,000 to $50,000 were 38.2 percent of the returns processed and this group paid 60.1 percent of the tax; and
c. incomes of more than $50,000 made 2.4 percent of the tax returns but paid 27.5 percent of the tax.

Now that the income tax and the central bank were in place, the planners could more rapidly increase the size of government. For instance, Franklin Roosevelt was President in 1945 when the Federal Government spent a total of $95 billion. 1945 was obviously during World War II and the people expected a government to increase spending to pay the costs of the war. But since that time, government spending has truly escalated, as is illustrated by the following:

Year	President	Proposed the first
1962	John Kennedy	$100 billion budget
1970	Richard Nixon	$200 billion budget
1974	Nixon-Gerald Ford	$300 billion budget
1978	Jimmy Carter	$400 billion budget
1979	Jimmy Carter	$500 billion budget
1981	Carter/Ronald Reagan	$700 billion budget
1984	Reagan	$800 billion budget
1986	projected	$900 billion budget
1988	projected	$1,000 billion budget

It is certainly a truism that the larger the budget, the more possibilities there are for waste to creep into the spending by the government. In fact, as will be discussed in a later chapter of this book, government is intentionally wasting money by finding wasteful ways to spend it. If government spending is a goal, then government waste is one easy method to increase government spending.

This would, at least partially, explain why such articles as these appear in America's newspapers and magazines, often without further action by the government:

"Welfare overpayments pass $1 billion mark."[6]

"Billions down the Pentagon drain."[7]

One other indication that the federal government was intentionally wasting money came from an article authored by Dr. Susan L.M. Huck who discovered that for the eighteen years since its inception in 1954 (until 1972) the budget for the Department of Health, Education and Welfare, (the HEW) had grown from $5.4 billion to $80 billion. But the most startling discovery of all was that "the Establishment Insiders set a 27.5 percent annual increase as their goal for the budget...."[8]

In other words, the budget increases were set according to a pre-determined percentage: the budgets were not set on need, but on spending money. HEW was obligated to spend a certain amount of money each year, whether or not there was a need to spend it! The HEW had to find ways to spend money! Spend, even if you must waste!

The spending continued after Dr. Huck's article. For instance, HEW spent over $200 billion in the 1979-80 fiscal year.

But this agency is not alone in increasing the spending of government. In fact, seminars are now being promoted which instruct the attendee on "How to get More Grants" from the federal government.

Such spending proposals have been borne by the tax-paying American citizen as per capita spending by the Federal Government has grown from

189

$6.90 per-capita in 1900 to over $3,000 in 1980.

This increase in spending enables the government to increase the deficits each year, thereby causing the national debt to increase. The increase in this national debt enables those who loan the money to the government, the central bank, in the United States the Federal Reserve, to charge interest payments to be paid for by the taxpayer.

The connection between government spending and the national debt and its annual interest payments can be illustrated in the following table:

Year	National debt	Per capita	Annual interest
1845	15 million	$ .74	$ 1 million
1917	3 billion	28.77	24 million
1920	24 billion	228.23	1 billion
1945	258 billion	1,853.00	4 billion
1973	493 billion	2,345.00	23 billion
1979	830 billion	3,600.00	45 billion
1980	1,000 billion	4,500.00	95 billion

These unbalanced budgets since 1978 become all the more ludicrous when it is realized that it is against the law to not balance the budget. Public Law 95-435, adopted in 1978, states unequivocally: "Beginning with the fiscal year 1981, the total budget outlays of the Federal government shall not exceed its receipts."[9]

An even more dramatic set of statistics is the figure of how much the various Presidents of the United States spent each day while they were in office. For instance, George Washington spent, on the average, $14,000 each day while in office. That daily figure is compared to $1,325,000,000 spent by Jimmy Carter.[10] But President Ronald Reagan will become the unquestioned champion in daily spending. It is anticipated by his projected 1988 budget, if he is re-elected in 1984, that he will be spending $3,087,000,000 each day in 1988 (that is over $3 billion dollars every day.)

Just what is the end of all of this debt creation?

Perhaps the answer appeared in an Associated Press article that appeared in the Portland *Oregonian* on May 22, 1973. It was entitled: "Talks begin on changing money setup." The article included the following comments: "With the dollar under pressure in Europe, a panel of international financial officials opened debate Monday on a draft of a new world monetary system. According to IMF sources (the IMF is the International Monetary Fund, the agency which met to draft the new outline) the draft outline... would provide more leeway in determining when a country with surpluses in its balance of payments would be forced to change the value of its currency."[11]

Notice that the country with problems in their monetary system would have no choice in handling their own problems, but would have to submit to the orders of the new international agency which would force the nation to change the value of its currency.

The American people would truly lose control over their own money.

Chapter 18
Non-Violent Organizations

Karl Marx, the mis-named "Father of Communism," formulated two methods of achieving the Communist state he wrote about:

The Violent Method, and

The Non-Violent Method.

The Violent Method was tried in the French Revolution of 1789, the Communist Revolutions in Europe in 1848, and in the Russian Revolutions of 1905 and 1917.

The Non-Violent Method has succeeded in socializing the English nation, and is the method being utilized in socializing the United States.

Both of these methods frequently work together to achieve the goal of both: a Communist state. And on other occasions, they are placed in opposition to each other. But the end result is always the same: an increase in the number of Communist nations in the world.

Perhaps the Non-Violent Method could be better understood if the various organizations promoting the Marxist ploy were to be exposed to the observer.

The secret ingredient for the success of this method is the ability to induce non-Communists into supporting Communist objectives and goals, by having them join organizations set up by the Communists under innocuous sounding names. Frequently those who join do not truly understand the nature and purpose of the organizations they associate with.

This strategy was laid down in 1938 by Georgi Dimitrov, a leader of the Comintern, in Russia, who said: "Let our friends do the work. We must always remember that one sympathizer is generally worth more than a dozen militant communists. Our friends must confuse the adversary for us, carry out our main directives, mobilize in favor of our campaigns people who do not think as we do, and whom we could never reach."[1]

THE RHODES SCHOLARSHIPS

Cecil Rhodes, who amassed a fortune in the gold and diamond mines in South Africa in the late 1800's with the financial support of the Rothschilds, had a vision (other than making large sums of money) which motivated him during his lifetime. His purpose "... centered on his desire to federate the English-speaking peoples and to bring all the habitable portions of the world under their control."[2]

Mr. Rhodes' biographer explained who Rhodes thought might be the leader of this world government rather succinctly: "The government of the world was Rhodes' simple desire."[3]

After the death of Mr. Rhodes, his will set up a scholarship program where certain very intelligent young men would be allowed to study in England. Between two and three thousand men in the prime of life from all over the world would be the recipients of his scholarships so that each one would have "impressed upon his mind in the most susceptible period of his life the dream of the Founder...."[4]

The "dream of the Founder" was, of course, a one world government.

Some well known American Rhodes Scholars in public life are: Dean Rusk, former Secretary of State; Walt Whitman Rostow, government official; J. William Fulbright, former Senator; Nicholas Katzenbach, former Attorney General; Frank Church, former Senator; Howard K. Smith, newscaster; Supreme Court Justice Byron White; and Senator Bill Bradley. Those who have studied the voting records and public proclamations of these individuals agree that not one is a so-called "conservative."

THE FABIAN SOCIETY

The Fabian Society is an English organization founded in 1884. It is named after a third-century Roman General, Quintus Fabius Maximus who successfully defeated Hannibal.

The Fabians discovered the secret of the general's strategy: never confront the enemy directly in the open battlefield, but defeat him gradually through a series of small battles, running after each successful foray. Fabius was a successful guerrilla fighter using the simple strategy of patient gradualism. He knew that he couldn't defeat the mighty armies of Hannibal with an open confrontation because his armies were outnumbered. He never confronted his enemy directly.

This is the strategy adopted by the Fabian Society. They decided that the forces of the free-enterprise system have a superior philosophy and that their strategy must never be to confront the free-enterprise system head on. They must be content with a series of small victories, the lump sum of which will be a rather stunning victory and the ultimate triumph of Socialism.

Their original symbol was a tortoise, symbolizing the slow, gradual progress of that animal, but this symbol was later changed to that of a wolf in sheep's clothing "... which George Bernard Shaw (a member of the Fabian Society) long ago suggested was more appropriate than the tortoise as a heraldic device for the Fabian Society."[5]

The philosophy of the Society was simply written in 1887 and each member is obliged to support it. It reads:

> It (The Fabian Society) therefore aims at the reorganization of society by the emancipation of land and Industrial Capital from individual and class ownership....
>
> The Society accordingly works for the extinction of private property in land....[6]

The Fabian Society acknowledges the principal tenet of Marxism: the abolition of private property, in this case the right to own land. They then align themselves with the non-violent arm of the Marxist Conspiracy by accepting the non-violent road of patient gradualism to total government.

The entire strategy was detailed by H.G. Wells, the noted science fiction writer, also a member of the Fabian Society, who wrote:

> It (will be) left chiefly to the little group of English people who founded Fabian Socialism to supply a third system of ideas to the amplifying conception of Socialism, to convert revolutionary Socialism to Administrative Socialism.
>
> Socialism (will cease) to be an open revolution and will become a plot.

George Orwell, also a member of the Fabian Society, in his novel entitled *1984*, had his character O'Brien say: "We know that no one seizes power with the intention of relinquishing it. Power is not a means; it is an end. One does not establish a dictatorship in order to safeguard a revolution; one makes a revolution in order to establish a dictatorship."

All of these efforts of all of these Fabian Socialists were brought to a head when, in 1905, the Fabian Society hosted a branch of the Violent Method of Marxist ascendancy to power, the Bolshevik Communists. The main purpose of this meeting in London was for members of the Fabian Society to loan money to the Bolsheviks for the 1905 revolution in Russia. John Maynard Keynes, also a member of the Fabian Society, was present at these meetings and later confided to his mother in a letter after meeting the Bolsheviks, that "The only course open to me is to be buoyantly Bolshevik."[7]

Keynes was later to boast that he shared the Bolsheviks' desire to destroy the free-enterprise system by stating that his economic ideas were going to be "the euthanasia (a merciful killing) of capitalism."

Benito Mussolini, the Italian Fascist, read some of the works of Keynes and personally set his approval on one of the books he read. He said: "Fascism entirely agrees with Mr. Maynard Keynes, despite the latter's prominent position as a Liberal. In fact, Mr. Keynes' excellent little book, *The End of Laissez-Faire* (1926) might, so far as it goes, serve as a useful introduction to fascist economics. There is scarcely anything to object to in it and there is much to applaud."[8]

Keynes' ideas have made him "by wide agreement the most influential economist of this century,"[9] according to John Kenneth Galbraith, another economist.

But there are other economists who are familiar with the ideas of Keynes who do not agree. One is Dr. Friederich A. Hayek who advised the world that: "The responsibility for current world-wide inflation, I am sorry to say, rests wholly and squarely with the economists who have embraced the teachings of Lord Keynes. It was on the advice and even urging of his pupils that governments everywhere have financed increasing parts of their expenditure by creating money on a scale which every reputable economist before Keynes would have predicted would cause precisely the sort of inflation we have got."

Unfortunately for the world, they do not listen to Dr. Hayek, even though he was a co-recipient of the 1974 Nobel Memorial Prize in Economic Science, and the world gets inflation whenever they listen to the economists who have listened to Keynes.

THE LONDON SCHOOL OF ECONOMICS

Sidney Webb, a founder of the Fabian Society, created an economic school intended to teach the ideas of the Socialists to the sons of the very wealthy. It was called The London School of Economics.

Its early funding came from the very wealthy: from the Rockefeller Foundation, the Carnegie United Kingdom Trust Fund, and from Mrs. Ernest Elmhirst, the widow of J.P. Morgan partner Williard Straight, amongst others.

Some of the illustrous students who attended the School were: Joseph

Kennedy Jr., the son his father Joseph Kennedy Sr. wanted to become the first Catholic President of the United States; John Kennedy, who later became President; David Rockefeller; Robert Kennedy, Jr., the son of Robert Kennedy; Senator Daniel Moynihan; Jomo Kenyatta, who was later to form the African terrorist group known as the Mau-Maus who would butcher thousands of their fellow Africans; and Eric Sevareied, CBS broadcaster.

THE COUNCIL ON FOREIGN RELATIONS

Thomas Jefferson attempted to warn the American people about internal conspiracies when he stated: "Single acts of tyranny may be ascribed to the accidental opinion of a day; but a series of oppressions, begun at a distinguished period and pursued unalterably through every change of ministers, too plainly prove a deliberate, systematical plan of reducing us to slavery."[10]

Jefferson attempted to answer the question of those who wonder why nothing changes when they vote in a change in the American government by voting for the opposition party. He says, in essence, that if nothing changes, it is fair to presume that there is a conspiracy.

There are many who believe that the major reason nothing changes during changes in administrations is the Council on Foreign Relations, (the CFR) formed on July 29, 1921, in New York City.

Although the organization today has about 2,000 members representing the most elite in government, labor, business, finance, communications and the academy, it is not well known to the American people.

The major reason it is basically unknown is because of Article II of the CFR by-laws. This article requires that the meetings of the membership remain secret, and anyone releasing the contents of these meetings is subject to instant dismissal.

The CFR was founded by a group of "intellectuals" who felt that there was a need for world government and that the people of America were not ready for it. After the League of Nations treaty failed to pass the Senate, the founders of the CFR organized this association for the specific purpose of conditioning the people to accept a world government as being a desirable solution to the problems of the world.

The founders included many of those who had been at the signing of the Treaty of Versailles after the end of World War I and included: Colonel Edward Mandell House, the author of the book *Philip Dru, Administrator*; Walter Lippmann, later to become one of the Liberal Establishment's favorite syndicated columnist; John Foster Dulles, later to become President Eisenhower's Secretary of State; Allen Dulles, later to become the director of the Central Intelligence Agency; and Christian Herter, later to become Dulles' successor as Secretary of State.

Money for the founding of the CFR came from J.P. Morgan; John D.

Rockefeller; Bernard Baruch; Paul Warburg; Otto Kahn; and Jacob Schiff, amongst others.

The CFR has repeatedly told the American people what their goals are through their publications, one of which is a magazine called *Foreign Affairs*. In addition, they frequently print position papers, one of which was called *Study No. 7*, published on November 25, 1959. This document detailed the exact purpose of the CFR as advocating the "building (of) a new international order (which) may be responsible to world aspirations for peace (and) for social and economic change. . . . An international order- . . . including states labelling themselves as Socialist (Communist)."[11]

The words "a new international order" are the catch words for a world government.

A former member of the CFR, Rear Admiral Chester Ward (USN, ret.), told the American people the following about the intentions of the organization. He wrote:

> The most powerful clique in these elitist groups have one objective in common — they want to bring about the surrender of the sovereignty and the national independence of the United States.
>
> A second clique of international members in the CFR . . . comprises the Wall Street international bankers and their key agents.
>
> Primarily, they want the world banking monopoly from whatever power ends up in the control of global government.
>
> They would probably prefer that this be an all-powerful United Nations organization; but they are also prepared to deal with and for a one-world government controlled by the Soviet Communists if U.S. sovereignty is ever surrendered to them.[12]

The Reece Committee of Congress, while studying foundations, chided the CFR for not being "objective." It said the CFR's "productions are not objective but are directed overwhelmingly at promoting the globalism concept."[13]

Dan Smoot, one of the earliest researchers into the CFR, summarized the CFR's purpose as follows: "The ultimate aim of the Council on Foreign Relations . . . is . . . to create a one-world socialist system and make the United States an official part of it."[14]

Rear Admiral Ward told the American people that their overall influence is used for the purpose of "promoting disarmament and submergence of U.S. sovereignty and national independence into an all- powerful one-world government."[15]

It is now clear that many of the founders of the CFR, for instance, Walter Lippmann, Allen Dulles, and Christian Herter, also wrote the League of Nations charter, which, it was hoped, would become the world government that the war was fought for (see a later chapter for the discussion of the connection between World War I and the one-world government.)

In fact, Point Fourteen of President Woodrow Wilson's famous "Fourteen Point" speech, given on January 8, 1918, stated that: "a general association of nations must be formed...."

The CFR was well represented at the founding of the second prospective world government, the United Nations, in 1945, after the League failed to establish a one-world government. In fact, forty-seven members of the CFR were members of the United States delegation, including Edward Stettinius, the Secretary of State; John Foster Dulles; Nelson Rockefeller; Adlai Stevenson; and the first Chairman of the UN, Alger Hiss.

The CFR has made its presence known in Washington D.C., as well: "Its roster of members has, for a generation under Republican and Democratic administrations alike, been the chief recruiting ground for cabinet-level officials in Washington."[16]

A typical comment about how the CFR is utilized came from John McCloy, a member of the CFR, who became Secretary of War Henry Stimson's Assistant Secretary in charge of personnel. McCloy has recalled: "Whenever we needed a man we thumbed through the roll of the Council members and put through a call to New York (the headquarters of the CFR.)"[17]

Mr. McCloy's recollections about how the CFR has filled important governmental positions is indeed correct. Of the eighteen Secretaries of the Treasury since 1921, twelve have been members of the CFR.

Another twelve of the sixteen Secretaries of State have been members. The Department of Defense, created in 1947, has had fifteen Secretaries, including nine CFR members. And the Central Intelligence Agency, also created in 1947, has had eleven directors, seven of whom belonged to the CFR.

Six of the seven Superintendents of West Point, every Supreme Allied Commander in Europe, and every U.S. Ambassador to N.A.T.O. have been members of the CFR.

Other positions in the executive branch of government have not gone without notice by the CFR as well. There are four key positions in every administration, both Democratic and Republican, that have almost always been filled by members of the CFR. They are: National Security Advisor, Secretary of State, Secretary of Defense, and Secretary of the Treasury.

As a recent confirmation of this fact, President Ronald Reagan appointed three members of the CFR to these four positions: Alexander Haig, Secretary of State; Casper Weinberger, Secretary of Defense; and Donald Regan, Secretary of the Treasury.

The fourth position, that of National Security Advisor, was given to

Richard Allen, not a member of the CFR. Mr. Allen was fired by President Reagan shortly after his appointment.

Even the Legislative Branch of the government has its share of CFR members. In fact, in 1978 there were fifteen Senators who were members, and, in the crucial voting to give the Panama Canal away to the nation of Panama, fourteen voted in favor of the bill. It would be fair to presume that the CFR was in favor of giving the Canal to the Panamanian government.

But the major impact of the CFR has come in the election of the President and Vice President of the United States. The CFR has been very active in both parties, exactly as Dr. Carroll Quigley indicated in his book, *Tragedy and Hope*. Dr. Quigley wrote "... the business interests, some of them intended to contribute to both and allow an alternation of the two parties in public office in order to conceal their own influence, inhibit any exhibition of independence by politicians and allow the electorate to believe that they were exercising their own free choice."[18]

The CFR controlled some of the past elections by giving the voting public the following members of the CFR to choose from:

Year	Democratic Candidate	Republican Candidate
1952	Adlai Stevenson	Dwight Eisenhower
1956	Adlai Stevenson	Dwight Eisenhower
1960	John Kennedy	Richard Nixon
1964	none	none
1968	Hubert Humphrey	Richard Nixon
1972	George McGovern *	Richard Nixon
1976	Jimmy Carter **	Gerald Ford ***
1980	Jimmy Carter **	Ronald Reagan ****
1984	Walter Mondale *****	Ronald Reagan ****

*	George McGovern later joined the CFR but was not a member when he ran.
**	Jimmy Carter was not a member of the CFR when he ran, but did become a member in 1983. He was a member of the Trilateral Commission, the CFR's sister organization.
***	Gerald Ford was not a member of the CFR, but has attended meetings of the Bilderberg organization, closely related to the CFR.
****	Ronald Reagan is not a member of the CFR, but George Bush, his Vice President, was a member of the Trilateral Commission and the CFR.

***** Walter Mondale is a former member of the Trilateral Commission and a current CFR member

(A little pamphlet published by the Advertising Council entitled "The American Economic System," defined Communism as: ". . . a socialist economy ruled by a single political party."[19] There are those who believe that America is "ruled by a single political party:" the Council on Foreign Relations.)

Pogo, the cartoon character, once mused: "How's I s'posed to know what to say less'n you tells me how to think."

It is one of the purposes of the major media today to tell the American people how to think and what to say, exactly as noted by Pogo. The CFR has played a major role in this indoctrination by having owners, writers, columnists and broadcasters join the CFR.

This control over America's media started in 1915, according to a Congressman in office at the time, Oscar Callaway, who placed these comments in the Congressional Record:

> In March, 1915, the J.P. Morgan interests . . . got together 12 men high up in the newspaper world and employed them to select the most influential newspapers in the United States and sufficient number of them to control generally the policy of the daily press of the United States.
>
> These 12 men worked the problem out by selecting 179 newspapers, and then began by an elimination process to retain only those necessary for the purpose of controlling.
>
> They found it was necessary to purchase control of 25 of the greatest papers.
>
> An editor was furnished for each paper to properly supervise and edit information regarding the questions of preparedness, militarism, financial policies, and other things of national and international nature considered vital to the interests of the purchasers.[20]

Morgan's early control of the newspapers has been continued through the fact that most of all of the various forms of the media are either owned by members of the CFR, or employ members. For instance, the following major news media had the following number of CFR members, on their payroll in key positions as of October, 1980:

Television Networks:

CBS:	12
NBC:	8
RCA Corp.:	7

ABC:	5
Wire Services:	
Associated Press:	5
United Press:	1
Newspapers:	
New York Times:	8
The Washington Post:	3
Dow Jones & Co.:	5
(includes the *Wall Street Journal*)	
Times Mirror:	2
(includes the *Los Angeles Times*)	
Field Enterprises:	3
(includes the *Chicago Sun-Times*)	
New York *Daily News*:	1
Magazines:	
Time, Inc.:	8
(includes *Fortune, Life, Money,*	
People, Sports Illustrated,	
and *Time*	
Newsweek:	3
Reader's Digest:	2
Atlantic Monthly:	1
Harper's Magazine:	1
National Review:	1
Columnists:	
Marquis Childs	
Joseph Kraft	
Bill Moyers	

(Is it possible that *Life* magazine, in their articles on Revolution already cited in the chapters on the revolutions of the past, intentionally fabricated their conclusions that there were no conspiracies at work in the various revolutions already studied elsewhere in this book? Is there really a conspiracy that *Life* magazine is aware of but is attempting to conceal from the public? These questions will have to be answered by the reader.)

Many of America's magazine editors and newspaper publishers and editors have attended the two most prestigious journalism schools in the United States, Columbia and Harvard. Presidents of these institutions have been members of the CFR. Their function is to make certain that the students attending classes learn what the CFR wants them to learn, so that they can in turn teach the American public through their particular form of media what the CFR wants.

One who has testified that one of the CFR-controlled media has indeed slanted its news intentionally was Herman Dinsmore, editor of the foreign edition of the *New York Times* from 1951 to 1960. Mr. Dinsmore has charged that the: *"New York Times . . .* is deliberately pitched to the so-called liberal point of view." And: "Positively and negatively, the weight of the *Times* has generally been on the side of the Communists since the end of World War II."[21]

The *New York Times* has a motto that is used as its philosophy for determining what it will print: "All the news that's fit to print."

Mr. Dinsmore titled his book: *All the News that Fits.*

The fact that Mr. Dinsmore discovered that the *New York Times* has been supporting the Communist point of view was no new revelation, as there were other voices saying nearly the same thing. In his book, *Witness,* Whittaker Chambers, an ex-member of the Communist Party of the United States, wrote that: "There is probably no important magazine or newspaper in the country that is not Communist-penetrated to some degree."[22]

The important thing to realize is that most of the important magazines and newspapers in the United States are owned by or controlled by CFR members. The question as to why the CFR controlled media allows the Communist Party to infiltrate its newspapers and magazines is generally not answered by those in the media.

Another major way that the people of America, especially the young people, are indoctrinated towards a particular point of view is through the music of the nation.

Someone once wrote: "I know a very wise man who believes that, if a man were permitted to make all the ballads, he need not care who should make the laws of a nation."

Ann Landers, nationally syndicated adviser, apparently was reluctant to admit that the music the young people were listening to was dangerous to their minds, but in October, 1979, she concluded: "I've been hearing about the filthy rock and roll lyrics for a long time and decided to tune in and listen. Twenty-three years of this column have made me virtually shock-proof, but some of the lyrics were incredibly crude." The filth of the lyrics was not unintentional. The young people were being used by the recording industry for some very important reasons. One who attempted to make some sense of the reasons for the crudity of the music was the author Gary Allen, who wrote:

> Youth believes it is rebelling against the Establishment. Yet the Establishment owns and operates the radio and TV stations, the mass magazines, and the record companies that have made rock music and its performing artists into a powerful force in American life.
>
> Does it not seem strange that the same Establishment which

has used the mass media to ridicule and denigrate the anti-Communist movement should open its door to those who think they are the Establishment's enemy?[23]

The connection between the music and the purpose of the music was discussed by Dr. Timothy Leary, the self-proclaimed king of the drug LSD: The person who says "... rock 'n roll music encourages kids to take drugs is absolutely right. It's part of our plot.... Drugs are the most efficient way to revolution...."[24]

A musician, Frank Zappa, the leader of the rock group called Mothers of Invention, added this incredible statement: "The loud sounds and bright lights of today are tremendous indoctrination tools. Is it possible to modify the human chemical structure with the right combination of frequencies? If the right kind of beat makes you tap your foot, what kind of beat makes you curl your fist and strike?"[25]

The thought that music was created for the express purpose of controlling young people is an alien idea to the parents of those who listen to the music, so the message in the music had to be concealed in a special language so that only the young people would understand it. It takes very gifted musicians and song writers to write the music in such a way that the parents interpret it one way and the young people in another, but this has been the case in the modern music of today.

This concealed message was accomplished by many groups, but one of the most successful was a rock 'n roll group known as the Beatles. Their particular message was intended to teach young people the merits of drug use through such songs as:

"Yellow Submarine"	A "submarine" is a "downer" drug, one that slows the user down.
"Lucy in the Sky with Diamonds"	The first initials of the main words in the title, "L," "S" and "D" represent the drug LSD.
"Hey Jude"	The term is widely interpreted as being a song about the drug known as methadrine.
"Strawberry Fields"	Opium poppies are often planted in strawberry fields to avoid detection.
"Norwegian Wood"	A Britisher's term for marijuana

A more recent phenomenon in the music industry is the preparation of the young people for a Satanic experience through a group of musicians named KISS. The name conceals their true purpose:

*K*nights *I*n *S*ervice to *S*atan (KISS)

There are even groups who are using their recordings to subliminally place thoughts in the minds of the listener through the use of certain phrases placed backwards on the record. The Tucson *Citizen* of April 30, 1982, carried an article that asked and then answered the question:

> Records Tuning Subconscious in to Satan?
>
> Members of the (California) state Assembly's Consumer Protection . . . Committee listened intently to a Led Zeppelin rock music tape — played backward.
>
> Perceptible in the cacaphony of the backward tape of (the song) "Stairway to Heaven" were mumbled words such as "Here's to my sweet Satan," and "I live for Satan."
>
> William Yarroll of Aurora, Colorado, who said he studies the brain, told members the subconscious mind can decipher the messages even when the record is played forward.
>
> Yarroll contended that the messages, placed there by rock stars in league with the Church of Satan, are accepted by the brain as fact.[26]

The connection between the rock 'n roll music and Marxism was illustrated by a song entitled "Imagine" written by John Lennon, a member of the Beatles. A careful reading of the lyrics to the song reveals that Lennon was aware of the teachings of Karl Marx:

Song	Marx's teachings
Imagine there's no heaven It's easy if you try No hell below us Above us only sky	The attack on religion
Imagine all the people Living for today	The "do your own thing" today philosophy; do not worry about tomorrow
Imagine there's no countries	The attack on nationalism

It isn't hard to do Nothing to kill or die for and no religion too	The attack on religion
Imagine all the people Living life in peace	
Imagine no possessions	The abolition of private property
I wonder if you can No need for greed or hunger A brotherhood of man Imagine all the people Sharing all the world	The "new international order"
You may say I'm a dreamer But I'm not the only one I hope someday you'll join us And the world will be as one.	A one world government

The establishment either owns the major record companies outright, or controls them through the ability to make or refuse loans to those record companies that request them. Those record companies that do not promote the songs the establishment considers important to their goals do not get the loans and thereby do not operate at all. For those who question why the banks make the loans in the first place, the banks can always claim that they are only making loans to those companies that have given the indication that they will meet the needs of the music-buying public. It is the old question of which came first: the chicken or the egg?

And the young people continue to listen to music their parents don't understand.

THE SKULL AND BONES

In the September 1977 issue of *Esquire* magazine, author Ron Rosenbaum wrote an article entitled "The Last Secret of Skull and Bones," in which Mr. Rosenbaum discussed a secret society at Yale.

He reported that an organization had existed for nearly a century and a half (since the 1820's or 1830's) that he called "the most influential secret society in the nation."

There are some who might disagree with this evaluation, but it is hard to disagree with some of his other conclusions. One, for instance, is rather startling. He wrote: "I do seem to have come across definite, if skeletal, links between the origins of Bones rituals and those of the notorious Bavarian Illuminists, (the Illuminati.)[27]

Mr. Rosenbaum also mentions the names of some of this group's more illustrious members. Included in this list are two names of particular interest to those who study conspiracies today: William F. Buckley, Jr., the "conservative" who frequently states that there is "no conspiracy," and George Bush, Ronald Reagan's Vice President and a member of the Trilateral Commission and the Council on Foreign Relations.

THE BILDERBERGERS

This group has no known formal name but has been called the Bilderbergers by the conspiratorialists who first discovered them at their 1954 meeting at the Bilderberg Hotel in Oosterbeek, Holland.

The first Chairman of this group was Prince Bernhard, the husband of ex-Queen Juliana of the Netherlands (Queen Juliana recently abdicated in favor of her daughter.) This family, known as the House of Orange, is extremely wealthy. Dutch journalist Wim Klingenberg estimated that Queen Juliana owned 5 percent of the stock of Royal Dutch Shell, which was worth approximately $425,000,000 in 1978.

It has been reported that she also holds stock in Exxon, the world's largest oil company.

Her total wealth has been estimated to be around $2 billion.[28]

Her husband, Prince Bernhard, carefully explained his philosophy a few years ago when he wrote: "Here comes our greatest difficulty. For the governments of the free nations are elected by the people, and if they do something the people don't like they are thrown out. It is difficult to re-educate the people who have been brought up on nationalism to the idea of relinquishing part of their sovereignty to a supernational body.... This is the tragedy."[29]

The Bilderberg organization has been described as being: "like the CFR, another of the formal conspiracies dedicated to creating a 'new world order.' The Bilderbergers meet once or twice a year at some obscure but plush resort around the world. Their secret conferences are attended by leading internationalists in finance, academics, government, business, labor from Western Europe and the United States."[30]

The meetings are secret, and very little information is available to the public about the exact nature of their discussions. However, they frequently make known at least the broad subject matter prior to their meetings. It is always interesting to see just how long it takes for the various nations represented at the meetings to change their government's direction after a meeting on a particular subject.

One researcher into this organization reported: "But even the fragmentary reports available indicate that decisions made at these affairs soon become the official policies of governments around the world."

The importance of this organization can be at least partially exhibited by studying the 1966 meeting when a group of relatively unknown individuals were among the participants. These individuals were: Henry Kissinger of the United States; Palme of Sweden; Bieusheuval of The Netherlands; Gerald Ford of the United States; Helmut Schmidt of West Germany; Rumor of Italy; and Giscard d'Estaing of France; (Mr. d'Estaing did not attend the 1966 meeting but was present at the 1968 meeting.)

These men were then comparatively unknown, but eight years later each was the chief executive of his respective country or involved in top-level government positions.[31]

Gerald Ford not only attended the 1966 meetings, he also attended the 1962, 1964, 1965 and 1970 meetings. And in fact, Prince Bernhard came to the United States in 1952 to campaign for Mr. Ford when he first ran for Congress.

A review of the membership lists of other meetings is very revealing, and shows the connection between the very wealthy of America and those of other countries:

1971:   Henry Kissinger; George Ball; Cyrus Vance; David Rockefeller; Robert Anderson, president of ARCO; and Baron Edmond de Rothschild, from France.

1975:   Garrett Fitzgerald, Irish Foreign Minister; Denis Healey, British Chancellor of the Exchequer; Robert McNamara, World Bank; David Rockefeller; Edmond de Rothschild; Margaret Thatcher, then the leader of the British Conservative Party, and later the Prime Minister of England; Father Theodore Hesburgh, President of Notre Dame University; and William F. Buckley, Jr.

The researchers into this organization have found that certain of the tax-free foundations have been funding these meetings. For instance, at the 1971 meeting at Woodstock, Vermont: "... all expenses ... (were) picked up by the two tax-exempt (Ford and Rockefeller) Foundations."[32]

THE TAX-FREE FOUNDATIONS

When the Sixteenth Amendment, the Graduated Income Tax, was added to the Constitution, one of the provisions it contained under the legislation that created it was the ability to create tax-free foundations. By this method, certain wealthy individuals could avoid the graduated features of the income tax.

Certain Americans had already set up foundations that would become tax-free under the acts of Congress after the imposition of the Graduated Income Tax. Andrew Carnegie, the steel magnate, and John D. Rockefeller, for instance, set up their tax-free foundations prior to the income tax laws of 1913.

Other foundations have been created by the government under these laws to the point where it is estimated that there are over 100,000 of these organizations now operating in the United States.

Dr. Martin Larson, a researcher into the income tax laws and the tax-free foundations, tells the reader of his books that there are advantages in establishing a foundation:

1. The property conveyed to the foundation is a deductible contribution to charity;
2. Upon the death of the donor, it is immune to inheritance and estate taxes;
3. The fortune or business remains intact;
4. If the donor is a parent-company, this continues in business exactly as before;
5. The foundation is exempt from all taxation in perpetuity;
6. The individuals who comprise the interlocking directorate or management are in a strategic position to enrich themselves by transactions which, though neither charitable nor ethical, are nevertheless quite legal; and even if not, may be practiced with virtual immunity.[33]

In 1952, the 82nd Congress passed House Resolution 561 to set up a "Select Committee to Investigate Foundations and Comparable Organizations."

This Committee was instructed to determine whether or not any of the foundations had been: "using their resources for un-American and subversive activities or for purposes not in the interests of the United States."[34]

Congressman B. Carrol Reece, a member of that Committee, has stated: "The evidence that has been gathered by the staff pointed to one simple underlying situation, namely that the major foundations by subsidizing collectivistic-minded educators, had financed a socialist trend in American government."[35]

The reason that the foundations are operated in this manner is in part explained by former Communist official Maurice Malkin who testified that, in 1919, a Soviet agent named Ludwig Martens ordered us "... to try to penetrate these organizations, if necessary take control of them and their treasuries; ... that they should be able to finance the Communist Party propaganda in the United States...."[36]

The importance of the collectivistic-minded foundations is measured by the endowment funding that they provide for universities around the country, as together they stimulate about two-thirds of the total. Is this the reason that the large universities usually do not have a "free market" economist on the staff teaching economics, or a "conspiratorialist" teaching history?

The purpose of at least one of these foundations was illustrated in a conversation that Norman Dodd, the chief investigator and director of research for the committee, had with H. Rowan Gaither, the then President of the Ford Foundation. Mr. Gaither had asked Mr. Dodd to come to the foundation to ask him about the investigation. During the conversation, Mr. Gaither told Mr. Dodd: "all of us here at the policy-making level have had experience, either in the OSS, or the European Economic Administration, with directives from the White House. We operate under those directives here. Would you like to know what those directives are?"

Mr. Dodd indicated that he would, so Mr. Gaither told him: "The substance of them is that we shall use our grant-making power so as to alter our life in the United States that we can be comfortably merged with the Soviet Union."[37]

What Mr. Gaither presumably meant was that the American economy, its military power, its maritime power, etc., all had to be lowered so that America could be merged with the Soviet Union in a one-world government.

Economically, the then expressed desires of the Ford Foundation are coming true.

An Associated Press article of August 11, 1981, headlined: "Faltering U.S. now no. 8 in income per person."

One of the methods the foundations are promoting to reduce America's standard of living is socialism. One researcher, Gary Allen, has been studying the several Rockefeller foundations for some time and has concluded that he has been: "unable to find a single project in the history of the Rockefeller foundations which promotes free-enterprise."[38]

That is quite a revelation for a foundation that derives its funds from the free-enterprise system.

As a demonstration that this statement is correct in the case of another foundation, in this case the Ford Foundation, Henry Ford II, a member of its Board of Directors, resigned his position because he felt that "the foundation is a creature of Capitalism. It is hard to discern recognition of this fact in anything the foundation does. It is even more difficult to find an understanding of this in many of the institutions, particularly the universities, that are the beneficiaries of the foundation's grant programs. (He was) suggesting to the trustees and the staff that the system that makes the foundation possible very probably is worth preserving."[39]

One of the universities that has been funded by both the many Rockefeller foundations and the Rockefeller family is the University of Chicago. One of the instructors at this school is Dr. Milton Friedman, the supposed "conservative" free-market economist. Dr. Friedman is on record as saying: "Over 40 percent of the income of the American people is now spent on their behalf by civil servants.... We talk about how we avoid Socialism. Yet 48 percent of every corporation is owned by the U.S. government. We are 48 percent Socialist. ... What produced the shift... to our present 48 percent Socialist society? It was not produced by evil people for evil purposes. There was no conspiracy."[40]

One of the more famous graduates of the University of Chicago is David Rockefeller who received his doctorate in economics there.[41] Dr. Rockefeller shares the view of Dr. Friedman that there is no conspiracy.

THE INSTITUTE OF PACIFIC RELATIONS

"In 1925, the Institute of Pacific Relations (the IPR) was established as an association of national councils.... The United States council was called the American Institute of Pacific Relations (the AIPR.) From 1925 until 1950, the IPR received 77 percent of its finances from American foundations and the AIPR. In turn, the AIPR received 50 percent of its financial support from the Rockefeller Foundation, the Carnegie Corporation and the Carnegie Endowment. ... The major institutional contributions to the AIPR included: Standard-Vacuum Oil (Rockefeller controlled); International General Electric; National City Bank; Chase National Bank (now called the Chase Manhattan Bank, and controlled by the Rockefellers); International Business Machines; International Telephone and Telegraph; Time, Inc.; J.P. Morgan and Company; Bank of America; and Shell Oil."[42]

What did the very wealthy get for their investments in the AIPR and the IPR?

In 1951 and 1952, the Senate Internal Security Subcommittee held hearings on the AIPR and the IPR and concluded that:

> The IPR has been considered by the American Communist Party and by Soviet officials as an instrument of Communist policy, propaganda, and military intelligence.
>
> The IPR disseminated and sought to popularize false information including information originating from Soviet and Communist sources.

Members of the small core of officials and staff members who controlled the IPR were either Communist or pro-Communist.

The IPR was a vehicle used by the Communists to orientate American far eastern policies toward Communist objectives . . . .[43]

Witnesses before the McCarren Committee (have) identified forty-seven persons connected with the Institute of Pacific Relations as having been Communists or Soviet agents.[44]

The IPR sought to change the minds of the American people about the American goverment's Pacific relations, namely its interest in the Chinese government. One of the ways they accomplished this was to change the thoughts of the American student. For this purpose: "American schools bought a million copies of IPR-prepared textbooks. The U.S. Government distributed some 750,000 copies of IPR pamphlets to American G.I.'s in the Pacific theater."[45]

Some of the IPR's members, however, did not completely support what the IPR was doing, and attempted to let others know of the particular slant of the IPR. Mr. Alfred Kohlberg, an American businessman and a member of the IPR, testified before the Cox Committee that was discussing the Foundations, that he:

> . . . had never paid much attention to what it was producing until 1943 when he saw some material which he found questionable.
>
> He then studied an accumulation of IPR material and made a lengthy report which he sent in 1944 to Mr. Carter, the Secretary of the IPR, and to the trustees and others.
>
> As a result he came into communication with Mr. Willets, a Vice-President of the Rockefeller Foundation. In the summer of 1945, an arrangement was made, apparently through Mr. Willets, for a committee of three persons to hear Mr. Kohlberg's charges and his evidence of Communist infiltration and propaganda, and to make a report to IPR and to the Rockefeller Foundation.
>
> Later, apparently at the insistence of Mr. Carter, Mr. Willets withdrew as mediator. Mr. Carter had indicated that he would take the matter up himself.
>
> No investigation was held. The Rockefeller Foundation nevertheless went right on supporting the Institute.
>
> According to Mr. Willet's statement, great reliance was placed upon a special committee of IPR trustees who "reported that the Executive Committee had investigated Mr. Kohlberg's charges and found them inaccurate and irresponsible."[46]

The overall purpose of the Institute of Pacific Relations did not surface until after the Chinese Revolution which ended when the Chinese Communists grabbed control of the government after a very bloody and lengthy revolution.

The story of the IPR's role in these events started in 1923, when Dr. Sun-Yat-Sen, China's ruler, became enchanted with the idea of Communism for the whole of China. He began relations with the Russian Communists and accepted their advice, "... since he was a friend and admirer of Lenin, a devotee of the economic philosophies of Karl Marx....[47]

Sun-Yat-Sen sent his heir apparent, Chiang Kai Shek, to Moscow to learn the merits of the Communist philosophy. But someone else had other advice for him, and sent him a copy of a book "... called *The Social Interpretation of History* by a New York dentist named Maurice William... a charter member of the Socialist Party. But intimate association with the Socialist hierarchy led him (William) to the conclusion that such radicals are escapists and frauds. He broke with the Socialist Party and set down his reasons in this book..."[48]

The book had an enormous impact on Dr. Sun-Yat-Sen, who: "read and re-read William's book. Within months he had repudiated the Communists and was working to establish a Republic like that outlined by our own Founding Fathers in the Constitution of the United States."[49]

Sun-Yat-Sun ruled for two more years before his death in 1925 made Chiang the ruler of China. It was about this time that Chiang was undergoing a religious experience after meeting May Lin Soong, the daughter of a Christian missionary. After Chiang went to her family asking for her hand in marriage, he became a Christian himself. This occurred in 1927, after Chiang expressed a liking for the quality and dedication of those who he knew were Christians. One who knew Chiang during this period was Dr. Walter Judd, a Christian missionary and later an American Congressman, who testified that this was the main reason Chiang had forsaken his religion to become a Christian.

It was no coincidence, then, that the Chinese Communist Revolution began in 1927 as well, started by Chou En Lai and Mao Tse Tung, amongst others.

Chiang began a change in the basic direction of the Chinese government when on May 5, 1931, he convened a People's Convention of 447 delegates, elected by the farmers' associations, labor unions, Chambers of Commerce and other businessmen's associations, educational and professional associations, and the Kuomintang, Sun-Yat-Sen's political party. These delegates were not directly elected by the people, but were elected by the members of the various associations and organizations.

Chiang was attempting to do two things with this convention:

1. He wanted the delegates to adopt a Provisional Constitution, the first ever for China, and

2.   He was hoping that he could turn over some of the authority he possessed to the people themselves, through their elected representatives.

The Convention did indeed adopt a Provisional Contitution, and it was hoped and anticipated that the people could elect their own convention directly by popular vote four years later, in 1935.

In addition to the Constitution, the convention promised the Chinese people that the government would:

1.   develop all natural resources along modern lines;
2.   modernize agricultural methods;
3.   increase the production of raw materials;
4.   establish new industries to manufacture and process the nation's raw materials;
5.   extend the nation's communications, including railways, highways, and airlines;
6.   undertake vigorously forestation and river control;
7.   guarantee protection to all who invest their money in productive enterprises;
8.   provide measures for the harmonious cooperation of capital and labor;
9.   simplify the currency;
10.   encourage investment of hoarded capital; and
11.   place taxation on a scientific basis.[50]

Chiang's government was called the Nationalist government of China and many have praised it for the dramatic changes it was making in the method of governing the Chinese people, and for the important benefits it was offering them.

One such supporter was Dr. Arthur Young, the financial advisor to the Chinese government from 1929 to 1946. He wrote: "When the Nationalist government took over, they set out on a program of financial rehabilitation. During the period from 1928 to 1937, they succeeded in unifying and stabilizing the currency. They developed quite promptly very large revenues from the customs and internal revenue with the result that the Government had a large degree of financial stability by 1937."[51]

In other words, Chaing's government was benefiting the Chinese people by protecting the value of their money by ending the destructive influences of inflation. Also, when government functions to protect the rights of the people, and their money is stable, a middle class develops.

Professor John Fairbank, certainly no supporter of Chiang, had to admit in his book *The United States and China* that: "The National government of China at Nanking in the decade from 1927 to 1937 was the most modern and effective that China had known."[52]

However, China's experiment with democracy started to experience exterior problems when Japan attacked Shanghai, China, on August 13, 1937. Suddenly Chiang had a two-front war: on one front he was repelling the Japanese invaders, and on the other his troops were fighting the Chinese Communists.

The attack by Japan caused the most problems, however, as ". . . the Japanese rapidly overran the principal cities and destroyed the sources of revenue. The Chinese government, therefore, was forced to rely on paper money as their main financial resource available for the purpose of fighting the war."[53]

The Chinese government was in need of allies, and they turned to America after Japan attacked at Pearl Harbor. Chiang sent the following telegram to President Roosevelt on December 8, 1941: "To our new common battle, we offer all we are and all we have to stand with you until the Pacific and the world are freed from the curse of brute force and endless perfidy."[54]

America, in addition to fighting Japan after Pearl Harbor, was also at war with Italy and Germany and became the ally of Russia, also fighting the Germans in Europe.

America's solution to the war, especially during the early stages, was what it called Lend Lease: the equipping of the military forces of its allies. However, America's priorities seemed a bit out of order, as in some cases it chose to equip its soldiers after its allies.

America decided to equip its soldiers in the European theater first; its ally Russia second; General Douglas MacArthur's military forces in the Pacific theater third, and China last. Aid to Russia's military forces had higher priority than America's fighting forces in the Pacific. And Chiang never received more than five percent of America's war material during the course of the war.

Chiang, desperate for assistance ". . . arranged for a loan of $250 million in gold from the United States to stabilize his money. The man in charge of delivering the gold to China was Assistant Secretary of the Treasury Harry Dexter White (a) Soviet agent (and a member of the CFR.) Over a period of three and a half years, White shipped only $27 million of the $250 million that had been promised Chiang."[55]

Notice that Mr. White broke the law by not delivering the aid that Congress had voted. But the story does not end there, as: "In 1945, Congress voted a second loan, this one of $500 million — but not one cent of this ever reached China. Again, Soviet agent Harry Dexter White was the culprit. China's currency collapsed."[56]

Even with all of these problems, Chiang continued the fight against both the Communists and the armies of Japan. After the war ended in 1945, Chiang called a National Assembly on November 15, 1946, to approve a permanent constitution, which was approved on December 25, 1946. The plan was for this constitution to go into effect one year later, in 1947.

The new constitution provided for a social insurance system and for government management of the public utilities, but also contained a "Bill of Rights" to guarantee personal liberty and rights for the citizens of China. It also provided for the first nationwide election held in China (there had never been an election in China) on November 21 through 23, 1947.

The constitution also planned the convening of a National Assembly on March 29, 1948, where 1,744 delegates were to select the president and vice president of China.

Chiang repeatedly refused to run for the presidency of China, but the delegates to the Convention elected him for a six-year term by a vote of about seven to one.

But the Communists would not accept the popular mandate of the Convention and they continued their aggressive attack against Chiang's newly elected government.

But Chiang's enemy was not the Japanese government, nor even the Communists under the leadership of Chou En Lai and Mao Tse Tung. It was the American government and Secretary of State George Marshall, a member of the CFR.

Secretary Marshall took measures in 1946 to impose "an embargo on the sale and shipment of arms from the United States...."[57]

Using Marshall's own boastful language: "As Chief of Staff I armed 39 anti-Communist divisions, now with a stroke of the pen I disarm them."[58]

Chiang's elected government was doomed to failure and the Communists under Mao and Chou finally succeeded in forcing Chiang and his government to leave the mainland of China and to move his armies onto the offshore Chinese islands of Formosa.

The pressure mounted on the American government to recognize the Communists as the legitimate government of China. This pressure was in part assisted by the appearance of twenty-nine books published during the period of 1943 to 1949. John T. Flynn, in his book *While You Slept*, reviewed these books and classified twenty-two of them as being "pro-Communist" and the other seven as being "anti-Communist." The twenty-two books were reviewed with what Flynn called "glowing approval" in literary reviews appearing in the *New York Times*, the *Herald Tribune, The Nation, The New Republic,* and the *Saturday Review of Literature.*

Nine authors wrote twelve of these books and these same nine authors submitted forty-three reviews. In other words, the same pro-Communist authors were reviewing the pro-Communist books, either neglecting the anti-Communist books or ridiculing them.

The general line of the pro-Communist books was that Chou and Mao were "agrarian reformers" seeking to change the tenure of the land from the large landowners to the poor peasants. For instance, even George Marshall in 1946 said this about the Communism of Mao and his followers: "Don't be ridiculous. These fellows are just old-fashioed agrarian reformers."[59]

Chiang and his supporters were now safely ensconced on the islands of Formosa, and it is now possible, with hindsight, to see what type of government Chiang gave the Taiwanese, the people who were on the islands before Chiang and his followers appeared.

Taiwan developed a true agrarian reform where today seventy-five percent of the farm land is owner-cultivated. This reform was achieved without a bloody revolution.

In addition, Chiang Kai Shek and his successors, have been elected by the people of Formosa, and Mao and his successors on mainland China have never allowed the Chinese the opportunity to freely elect their rulers.

Congressman Eldon Rudd in 1979 issued a message further detailing the differences between the mainland Chinese government of the Communists and the Taiwanese government of Chiang and his successors: "With 270 times the land area and 53 times the population, the Gross National Product of Mainland China is only 10 times the G.N.P. of Taiwan.... The figures I have cited illustrate beyond contradiction the material abundance created by freedom's climate. In my view, this is the smallest and least important of the remarkable differences between the People's Republic of China and the free government of Taiwan. The true difference is spirit — the human condition, the absence of compulsion and regimentation, the presence of individual opportunity."[60]

What was the cost of the Chinese Revolution spawned by Secretary of State George Marshall, Harry Dexter White, and the Communists Mao Tse Tung and Chou En Lai?

In 1971, the Senate Committee on the Judiciary issued a twenty-eight page document entitled "The Human Cost of Communism in China" that concluded that Chou and Mao, were "responsible for the deaths of as many as 64 million people."[61]

In addition to the deaths of as many as 64 million Chinese, the Communist government has other areas of progress to be proud of. Valentin Chu is a professional journalist who was born and raised in China but who escaped from the Communist regime. He wrote a book in 1963 called *Ta Ta, Tan Tan, the Inside Story of Communist China*. Mr. Chu devotes a chapter to Communist efforts to destroy the family, from which the following was taken:

The family everywhere is man's source of strength and courage as well as his emotional harbor at times of natural disaster and personal misfortune.

In China it was even more so. It was society itself.

The Chinese Communists were acutely aware that their control of the people could never be effective unless the monolithic family system was destroyed, along with religion and conventional morals.

This they set out to do as soon as they came to power.[62]

Another move of the Chinese Communists to destroy the family was to move the Chinese mothers away from the home and into the fields as farm workers. As the *Boston Globe* put it on January 31, 1973: "Ninety percent of the women work in factories and on farms and then attend school,"[63] which obviously leaves little time to function as wives, mothers and homemakers.

A related move, according to Chu, was the commune system, which summarily put men, women, children and the aged in segregated labor camps, destroyed ancestral graves, and reduced marital relations to brief, Party-rationed sex-breaks.[64]

But there are some who feel that all of these costs, the sixty-four million dead, the destruction of the family, and the establishment of the commune, was worth the price.

David Rockefeller said this about the cost of the Revolution after his return from a visit to China in 1973:

Whatever the price of the Chinese Revolution, it has obviously succeeded not only in producing a more efficient and dedicated administration but also in fostering high morale and community of interest....

The social experiment of China under Chairman Mao's leadership is one of the most important and successful in human history.[65]

This statement by Rockefeller was a little more than three years after Chairman Mao urged the "World to defeat U.S." by appealing to the peoples of the world to: "Unite and defeat the U.S. aggressors and all their running dogs."[66]

The American policy towards Communist China was now due for a change. It was now time for the American government to recognize the Communists as the legitimate government of the Chinese people and to break all diplomatic relations with the Taiwanese government of Chiang and his successors. On July 15, 1971, Premier Chou En Lai, on behalf of the People's Republic of China, according to a press release issued by President Richard Nixon's staff: "extended an invitation to President Nixon to visit

China at an appropriate date before May, 1972. Nixon accepted the invitation with pleasure."[67]

It was no coincidence that President Nixon accepted that invitation on July 15, 1971, the very day that Radio Peking, China's official radio station, issued the following statement: "People of the World, unite and defeat the U.S. aggressors and all their running dogs."[68]

The American press and President Nixon refused to acknowledge the hypocrisy of the Chinese government and accepted the invitation the same day they were calling for a world wide revolution against the United States.

Nixon's support of Red China was strange, indeed. As a Presidential candidate in 1968, Nixon said: "I would not recognize Red China now, and I would not agree to admitting it to the United Nations...."[69] And in his book, *Six Crises*, he wrote: "admitting Red China to the United Nations would be a mockery of the provision of the Charter which limits its membership to 'peace-loving nations.' And what was most disturbing was that it would give respectability to the Communist regime which would immensely increase its power and prestige in Asia, and probably irreparably weaken the non-Communist governments in that area."[70]

So President Nixon went to China and opened the doors to the Chinese Communist government of Mao and Chou.

The next step in America's betrayal of the Chinese people came in 1976 when first Chou En Lai and later Mao Tse Tung passed away. The tributes that flowed from the mouths of the world's leaders about these two bloody butchers was amazing.

These comments were made about Chou En Lai by the following individuals:

> Gerald Ford: "Chou will be long remembered as a remarkable leader."
>
> Secretary of State Henry Kissinger: "I admired Chou En Lai very much."
>
> Former President Richard Nixon: "Chou's legacy will be that he helped end the darkness. Only a handful of men in the 20th century will match Premier Chou's impact on world history."

These comments were made about Mao Tse Tung:

> Premier Pierre Trudeau of Canada: "The People's Republic of China stands as a monument to the spirit and political philosophy of Chairman Mao. Canadians recognize the path-breaking spirit of community that, under Chairman Mao's guidance, had contributed to the modernization of China."
>
> President Gerald Ford: "Mao was a very remarkable and a very great man."

Secretary of State Henry Kissinger: Mao was "one of the titans of the age."

Former President Richard Nixon: "A visionary poet, deeply steeped in the history of the Chinese people."

The *New York Times*: "a moralist who deeply believed- . . . that man's goodness must come ahead of his mere economic progress."

Boston Globe: "the symbol of millions of human beings around the world for the possibility of social change, of economic and political progress, of dignity for the exploited."

These efforts came to a head in December, 1978, when the American government recognized the Chinese Communists as the official and legitimate government of China, after fifty-five years of accepting the governments of Sun-Yat-Sen and Chiang Kai Shek as the representatives of the Chinese people.

Others did not approve of the move of the American government. One, a former Chinese citizen, Dr. Chiu-Yuan Hu, told a Congressional Committee in Washington: "To recognize the Chinese Red Regime is to discourage the people in the whole world. . . . It will make the world know that the great nation of the United States is unworthy to be a friend, that it sometimes betrays its most loyal allies."[72]

Senator Barry Goldwater was one who felt that the move was improper. He told a news conference: "I have no idea what motivated him other than (that) the Trilateral Commission, composed of bankers in this country and others, want to expand big business. This is a dangerous thing because it puts fear in our allies, especially our small allies, as to how the U.S. will keep its word." *Arizona Daily Star* (Tucson), Dec. 17, 1978, p. A-11.

But the final betrayal to the Chinese people occurred on January 1, 1979, when President Jimmy Carter severed diplomatic relations with the only elected government China has ever had, the government on Taiwan, and went so far as to state that the United States position was that: "there is but one China, and Taiwan is part of China." *Arizona Daily Star* (Tucson), Dec. 16, 1978, p. A-1.

The Nationalist government on Taiwan took the betrayal rather bitterly but stated that they would "neither negotiate with the Chinese Communist regime nor compromise with Communism."

Both moves caused Senator Barry Goldwater to charge that President Carter's motives were economic, saying that "he did it for the big banks of the world — Chase Manhattan and the French bankers — and for companies like Coca-Cola."[72]

Ronald Reagan called the break with Taiwan a "betrayal."

The hypocrisy of the entire China scenario was dramatically illustrated in May, 1979, when the *New York Times* ran a picture showing Commerce

Secretary Juanita Kreps in China touring the Great Wall of China, and she was smiling and apparently enjoying herself. This picture was attached to and just underneath the main article on the same page that headlined: "(Chinese) Poster says political prisoners tortured, starved in Chinese 'Eden.' "[73]

The article doesn't say whether the smiling Secretary visited any of the "tortured" and "starving" Chinese prisoners, but it is doubted.

The question as to why the visiting American journalists and dignitaries who toured China in the '70's failed to mention the tortured existence of many of the Chinese people was partially answered by Edward N. Luttwak, associate director of the Washington Center of Foreign Policy Research at John Hopkins University, who also visited Mainland China.

Mr. Luttwak wrote an article for the April, 1977, *Reader's Digest* in which he asked a series of questions:

> Why have Amirican journalists failed to convey to us such fundamental Chinese realities? After all, the miserable poverty of the country is everywhere in evidence.
>
> Why, moreover, have previous visitors not been revolted by the schoolrooms where children are taught from booklets replete with the brutal images of harsh class-war propaganda?
>
> Why have our "Asia scholars" failed to denounce the militarism of a system where the cheapest suit of clothing for little boys is a mini-uniform complete with rifle?
>
> And above all, how could they have missed the central phenomenon of (Red) Chinese life: its unique, almost pure totalitarianism?

But it was too late. Secretary of State George Marshall, the Institute of Pacific Relations, and modern politicians had betrayed the only elected government of China and replaced it with the most brutal and bloody government on the face of the earth.

China was now truly Communist.

THE NATIONAL COUNCIL OF CHURCHES

In 1831, Alexis de Tocqueville, a young Frenchman, was sent to the United States by the French government to study America's prisons and penetentiaries.

Upon his return to France, he wrote a book titled *Democracy in America*, an examination into the reasons why America had been successful in its experiment with a republican form of government.

He summarized his findings thus:

> I sought for the greatness and genius of America in her fertile fields and boundless forests; it was not there.

I sought for it in her free schools and her institutions of learning; it was not there.

I sought for it in her matchless constitution and democratic Congress; it was not there.

Not until I went to the churches of America and found them aflame for righteousness did I understand the greatness and genius of America.

America is great because America is good.

When America ceases to be good, America will cease to be great.

On December 2, 1908, Walter Rauschenbusch and Harry Ward formed the Federal Council of Churches of Christ in America, commonly called the Federal Council of Churches, (the FCC.)

Dr. Rauschenbusch was a theologian who wrote: "If ever Socialism is to succeed, it cannot succeed in an irreligious country."[74]

Dr. Harry Ward, a teacher at the Union Theological Seminary, was identified under oath as a member of the Communist Party by Manning Johnson, also a member. Mr. Johnson referred to Dr. Ward as "the chief architect for Communist infiltration and subversion in the religious field."[75]

The organization that these two created received a percentage of their income from a rather unusual, but not unexpected, source: ". . . John D. Rockefeller Jr. (who) had, from 1926 to 1929, contributed over $137,000 to the Federal Council of Churches — a sum equal to about ten percent of its total annual income from all sources."[76]

Others became aware of the FCC as well. In 1927, Congressman Arthur M. Free introduced a resolution in the House of Representatives describing the Federal Council of Churches as a "Communist organization aimed at the establishment of a state-church. . . ."[77]

The FCC partially repaid the support of the wealthy when, in 1942, it issued a platform calling for "a world government, international control of all armies and navies, a universal system of money, and a democratically controlled international bank."[78]

The pressure against the FCC became too intense as the knowledge of its activities grew. So, the FCC decided to change its name but not its direction. On November 29, 1950, the FCC became the National Council of the Churches of the Church of Christ, (the NCC.)

The direction of the NCC was no different from that of the FCC. This was revealed in an interview with Gus Hall, the General Secretary of the Communist Party, USA, that appeared in the July 15, 1968, *Approach* magazine. Mr. Hall declared that Communism and the Church (apparently the NCC) share so many goals that "they ought to exist for one another." Hall continued by citing "current Red goals for America as being 'almost identical to those espoused by the Liberal Church. We can and we should work together for the same things.' "[79]

Whatever the NCC was offering, many found it attractive. One "church," the Church of Satan, led by "high priest" Anton LaVey of San Francisco, recently became a member of the NCC.[80]

THE WORLD COUNCIL OF CHURCHES

This world-wide organization was formed on August 23, 1948, and follows much the same course as the National Council of Churches.

One example of this similarity is the fact that the secretary-General of the World Council (the WCC) in 1975, Philip Potter, said he "may sometimes be more radical than most Marxists."[81]

Another official in the WCC has echoed Mr. Potter's sentiments. In 1982, Emilio Castro, the head of the Council's Commission on World Mission and Evangelism, said: "The philosophical basis of capitalism is evil, totally contrary to the Gospel."[82]

These expressions of support for Marxism and against the free enterprise system are shared by those who attended their global conferences. In the meeting in November, 1975, the Jamaican Prime Minister, Michael Manley, told the assemblage of delegates: "that Christendom must help destroy the capitalist system and create a new world economic order. His speech . . . received prolonged applause . . . ."[83]

The WCC puts its money where its convictions are. The organization has created a Program to Combat Racism, (the PCR.) Since 1970, this organization has given over $5,000,000 to more than 130 organizations that are ostensibly fighting racism in thirty countries.

But nearly half of that money has gone to guerillas seeking the violent overthrow of white regimes in Southern Africa.[84]

But the WCC is rather selective in that "not a cent of PCR money goes to dissident groups in the Soviet Union . . . ."[85]

This is curious since it is estimated that there are nearly 5,000,000 Russians in 3,000 forced labor concentration camps in Russia. One who should know is Avraham Shifrin, a Russian who was exiled by the Russian government in 1970 and who is executive director of the Research Center for Prisons, Psychprisons and Forced Labor Concentration Camps of the U.S.S.R. He has stated that "the largest group of individuals in the concentration camps is made up of faithful Christians" who are there strictly and solely because they are Christians.[86]

FREEMASONRY

In 1871, a Freemason named Albert Pike copyrighted an 861 page book titled *Morals and Dogma of the Ancient and Accepted Scottish Rite of Freemasonry prepared for the Supreme Council of the Thirty-Third Degree for the outhern Jurisdiction of the United States and Published by its Authority.* Many historians believe that Mr. Pike wrote the book himself.

He had an interesting background. Many historians claim that he was selected by Guiseppe Mazzini to head the Illuminati in the United States. In addition, he became a brigadier general in the Confederate Army during the Civil War.

Mazzini wrote Pike in January, 1870, about the need to create a "super-rite" inside the traditional Masonic order:

> We must allow all of the federations (the Masons) to continue just as they are....
>
> We must create a super-rite, which will remain unknown to which we will call those Masons of high degree whom we shall select....
>
> These men must be pledged to the strictest secrecy.
>
> Through this supreme rite, we will govern all Freemasonry which will become the one international center, the more powerful because its direction will be unknown.[87]

Mazzini's letter was written before Pike wrote his study of the thirty-two degrees of Masonry titled *Morals and Dogma* so it is conceivable that his book, which Pike states is not "intended for the world at large," is intended for this "super-rite" inside the Masons. In any event, its contents are extremely revealing as can be illustrated from the following gleaning of some of its more salient points.

The book makes the statement that Masonry is a religion: "Every Masonic Lodge is a temple of religion, and its teachings are instructions in religion." "Masonry is a worship...." He later identified what it was that Masonry worshiped: "Behold the object, the end, the ultimate annihilation of evil and restoration of Man to his first estate by Reason...." "In the beginning was... the word... the Reason that speaks." "The Ancient and Accepted Scottish Rite of Masonry has become... a teacher of great truths, inspired by an upright and enlightened reason." "Reason is the absolute, for it is in it we must believe."

Pike stated what the greatest delight of his "religion of reason" would be when "Human reason leaps into the throne of God and waves her torch over the ruins of the universe."

He ridiculed Christianity: "The teachers, even of Christianity, are in general the most ignorant of the true meaning of that which they teach." "... Jesus of Nazareth was but a man like us...." (Masonry) ... sees in Jesus (a) great teacher of morality."

And a belief in God: "Self,... the true ruler of the Universe." "The conception of an Absolute Deity outside of or independent of Reason is the idol of Black Magic."

Pike's religion has many of the objects and beliefs of traditional Christianity: an altar ("Masonry, around whose altars...."); a "born again experience: (Initiation [into the Mysteries] was considered to be a mystical death...and the [initiate] was then said to be regenerated, new born....") and a baptism: (...baptism...[is a symbol] of purification necessary to make us perfect Masons.")

Pike identifies the subject of Masonic worship: "Lucifer, the Light-Bearer! Lucifer, the Son of the Morning! It is he who bears the Light...."

He limits the individual's God-given right to life: "It is not true to say that 'one man, however little, must not be sacrificed to another, to a majority or to all men.' That is not only a fallacy, but a most dangerous one. Often, one man and many men must be sacrificed, in the ordinary sense of the word, to the interests of the many."

And finally, Mr. Pike states what the ultimate goal of the Masons was: "...the world will soon come to us for its sovereigns (political leaders) and pontiffs (religious leaders.) We shall constitute the equilibrium of the universe and be rulers over the masters of the world."

The goal of the Masons, according to Mr. Pike, is to become the "rulers over the masters of the world."

The secret power behind the power!

Chapter 19

Population Control

Dr. Paul Ehrlich wrote a book entitled *The Population Bomb* in which he prophesied: "It is already too late to avoid famines that will kill millions, possibly by 1975."

Ehrlich also predicted: "the total pollution and death of the world's oceans by 1979."[1]

Harper's magazine for January, 1970, carried a full-page advertisement titled: "Whatever your cause, it's a lost cause unless we control population."

The article urged the American government to: "Control the flood of humanity that threatens to engulf the earth."

Kenneth Boulding, a University of Colorado economist, warned the world in February, 1973, that the human population must stop growing: "or in several hundred years there will be standing room only."[2]

The belief that the world was suffering from a "population explosion" and was in danger of having only enough room on the earth for people to stand on each other's heads in a few centuries can be quickly illustrated as a giant fraud by the use of simple mathematics.

Oregon, a rather small state by comparison to others in the United States, has a total of 95,607 square miles inside its borders. The world has approximately 4,000,000,000 (four billion) inhabitants. If the entire population of the world moved to Oregon, all four billion, and left the remainder of the world completely devoid of human life, a family of four would have a piece of Oregon approximately 50' by 53'. This is about half the size of a typical residential lot in a subdivision.

The people of the world have been told that the reason there is starvation in India is because their population is too large for their food production. But a thoughtful review of that nation's history will reveal that India has been starving for many centuries, even though their population was much smaller in the past and the size of their country has remained constant.

Could there be another explanation for India's starving population other than that there are just too many people?

Could the reason be that India has a Socialist government that believes that whatever an individual produces belongs to the state? Could it be that this Socialist government has destroyed the incentive to produce? And has done so for centuries?

India has approximately 500 people per square mile living within its borders, Japan has approximately 700, and Holland approximately 800. But notice that Japan and Holland have far more prosperous economies than does India, because Holland and Japan basically allow their producers to keep what they produce.

The "population explosion" was, then, a giant fraud. But it is interesting to see what solutions were being offered to this imaginary problem.

One came from a Washington psychologist and sex therapist who suggested: "that the world's nations remove 'the right to reproduce' from their people as the only solution to the global population explosion... by such means as placing temporary sterilizing chemicals in food and water supplies... whether or not it was with the individual's approval and consent."[3]

Another individual said that the United States had too many people. He saw the problem and offered a solution: "It is necessary that the United States cut its population by two-thirds within the next 50 years, according to Howard Odum, a marine biologist at the University of Florida. Odum said that the nation will be unable to support the present population of 225 million. Once the population is cut to 75 million... it could be stably employed in subsistence agriculture."[4]

How Odum intended to cut the population was not mentioned by the article. Perhaps he planned on "executing them in a kindly manner."

John Maynard Keynes, the Fabian Socialist-Communist, also had some comments to make about the population explosion: "The time has already come when each country needs a considered national policy about what size of population, whether larger or smaller than at present or the same, is most expedient. And having settled this policy, we must take steps to carry it into operation. The time may arrive a little later when the community as a whole must pay attention to the innate quality as well as the mere number of its future members."[5]

As far as the article reported, Mr. Keynes did not explain just how he planned on limiting the size of the population. It must be frustrating for people like Keynes to see a problem and not be able to explain to the people that their solution is the mass killing of those they consider to be excess population. It must be difficult for Keynes and the others to explain to those they wish to see murdered that it is important that they die so that others might live.

India has taken steps to control its population growth by the use of forced sterilization of its citizens. In the Indian states of Maharashtra, for instance, where Bombay is located, all men up to age 55 and women to age 45 must be sterilized within six months after the birth of their third child. Couples with 3 children who have no child under the age of 5 are exempt — but they must have an abortion if pregnancy occurs.[6] In fact, during one period of a "special emergency," the Indian government performed some 10 million forced sterilizations.[7]

China is still the leading nation in population control, however. They are currently limiting each family to one child. "Those who have more will not get rations for them."[8]

The decision about birth, as well as death, has become a "collective decision," according to a Chinese physician, wherein: "the residents in each street get together and decide how many babies will be born during the year.... Those who are obliged by collective decision to forego pregnancy are not permitted the excuse that they forgot to take the pill. A volunteer-...distributes pills each morning when the women arrive at their place of work."[8]

One of the lingering Chinese customs, even with all of the Communist attacks on the family structure, is the tradition that male children must provide for their parents in their old age. Now that China is limiting the family to only one child, many Chinese couples are concerned that, if their first child is a female, they will not be provided for in their older years, and they are *murdering* their female offspring. In fact, many of the parents are leaving their dead female child at the doorstep of the local Communist Party headquarters.[10]

But not only is China controlling the birth of its citizens as a means of controlling its population size, but it is also controlling the death of its elderly. In a government report entitled *Communist Persecution of the Church in Red China and North Korea*, dated March 26, 1959, it is reported that: "All the elderly people 60 years of age and above who cannot work are put in the old people's 'Happy Home.' After they are placed in the home they are given shots. They are told these shots are for their health. But after the shots are taken, they die within two weeks."[11]

In addition, the solutions to the imaginary population explosion are affecting those of the middle age as well. In an essay entitled "An International Mortality Lottery," students in America read about a lottery: ". . . that would solve the world over-population crisis. Each year, 5 percent of the earth's inhabitants between the ages of 30 and 40 would be exterminated. . . ."[12]

But, in summary, there is another purpose for the myth of over-population. It was summed up in a *Reader's Digest* article, written by Laurence Rockefeller, the brother of David Rockefeller, entitled "The Case for a Simple Life-Style." The article read, in part,: "In total, this all adds up to a new pattern of living. . . . If we do not follow it voluntarily and democratically, it may be forced upon us. Some economists and analysts argue that, if we continue consuming resources as we are now, the only way to bring about a balance between demand and supply will be through authoritarian controls. Robert Heilbroner, the distinguished economist, is particularly pessimistic about the capacity of a democratic and capitalist state to impose the discipline necessary to survive in a world of scarcity."[13]

So the reason for the "population explosion" is total government control of not only the citizen but his environment as well. This transfer of authority from the individual to the state is further supported by another individual, Zbigniew Brzezinski, who wrote: "I think we accept the idea of a vast expansion in social regulation. It may take such forms as legislation for the number of children, perhaps even legislation determining the sex of children once we have choice, the regulation of the weather, the regulation of leisure, and so forth."[14]

Once again, as in the case of the organizations discussed in the previous chapter, it becomes important to ask just who has been paying for the "population explosion" campaign. Once again, the inquisitive find the money of the tax-free foundation: "the first large foundations to make grants in the population field were the Rockefeller Foundation and the Carnegie Foundation. These foundations were joined by the Ford Foundation. . . ."[15]

And the "Rockefellers put money into the population-control movement by financing the Population Council, Planned Parenthood and The Population Reference Bureau."[16]

But those in China who murder female babies because they are the wrong sex, are not alone. Others emulate their behavior in America: "Doctors around the country (the United States) have begun helping some pregnant women kill their unborn babies because the parents wanted a child of the opposite sex, according to an article in the Washington Post."[17]

But are such extreme measures necessary? Must we control the population of the world, no matter how many people there are, because they are starving in a world soon to be so crowded that there will be no room for food production? Are the people of the world starving?

One who believed that food supplies are increasing was Bob Berglund, Secretary of Agriculture in President Jimmy Carter's administration, who is quoted as saying: "In fact, the four billion people who inhabited the earth in 1978 had available about one-fifth more food per person to eat than the world's 2.7 billion had twenty five years ago."

And American farmers are taking fertile land out of production. Agriculture Secrerary John Block in 1983 reported that these farmers had agreed to idle about one-third of their land, a total of eighty-two million acres, in exchange for certain subsidy programs.

And in the United States, there is concern that our population growth rate is declining too rapidly: "By the year 2000, the federal government may have to subsidize childbearing if the birthrate continues to plummet, according to a Temple University sociologist."[18]

Someone who believes that there are sinister forces at work behind the "population explosion" is researcher Gary Allen, who has written that "... by playing upon forces of impending social and environmental chaos, the Left is hoping to convert sincere and legitimate concern over our environment (and the number of people in it) into acceptance of government control of that environment. The object is federal control of the environment in which we all must live."[19]

The federal control Mr. Allen is discussing must manifest itself in every aspect of the lives of every citizen. The new phrases to describe the all-encompassing changes are: "The New Economic Order," or "The New International Economic Order," or "The New World Order."

These phrases all mean the same thing and are used interchangeably. The United Nations' World Population Conference at Bucharest called for a "new economic order by eradicating the cause of world poverty, by ensuring the equitable distribution of the world resources ...."

This is simple Marxism carried only one step further: "From each (nation) according to its ability, to each (nation) according to its needs."

If governments are going to create a New Economic Order, and they are going to divide the wealth between the wealthy nations and the poor nations, they will need a method by which to accomplish this. One method proposed by the United Nations in 1969 and 1970. "The General Assembly adopted without dissension Thursday a declaration calling for: (the use of) the world fiscal system and government spending for a more equitable distribution of income."[20]

The United Nations later considered a proposal where: "everybody in the world would pay a sales tax on certain home appliances and some luxury items to help poor nations."[21]

(It is readily apparent just which nations have "home appliances and some luxury items:" the wealthier nations, those which protect the right to private property.)

Further discussions about this problem of providing for the poor, overpopulated nations of the world continued in 1979 when the representatives of 156 nations met "... to debate the best way to divide the world's dwindling resources. A bloc of 80 poor nations will call for $25 billion in new aid from (the) rich nations."

The caption over the article read: "Haves, have-nots meet," and pictured then UN Secretary-General Kurt Waldheim and Phillippine President Ferdinand E. Marcos.[22]

A similar caption was on top of another article discussing the Cancun, Mexico, meetings held in October, 1981. It read: "Haves, Have-nots gathering to debate new economic order."[23]

If there is going to be a world-wide tax collected to provide for the poor nations, there will have to be a world-wide tax collector, and this is coming in the near future. For instance, James Warburg told a Senate Subcommittee on February 17, 1950: "We shall have world government (a world tax collector) whether or not you like it, by conquest or by consent."[24]

Even one of the Popes of the Catholic Church, in this case Pope Paul VI, in his Encyclical entitled, *This is Progress*, also went on record of supporting a world government. He wrote "The need is clear to have in course of time world government by a world authority."[25]

The world tax collector is very nearly in place.

Chapter 20

The Trilateral Commission

On December 13, 1973, a little known governor of a small Southern state appeared on a television panel program called "What's My Line" and stumped the panel who attempted to guess who he was. No one knew him.

Yet in November, 1976, less than three years later, that same gentleman was elected President of the United States.

His name was Jimmy Carter.

The story of how Mr. Carter rose from the governorship of one of the smaller states to the highest elected office in America so quickly is the story of an organization that was created around him known as the Trilateral Commission.

In his book entitled *I'll Never Lie to You*, candidate Jimmy Carter told the American people: "The people of this country know from bitter experience that we are not going to get these changes merely by shifting around the same group of insiders. The insiders have had their chance and they have not delivered. And their time has run out. The time has come for the great majority of Americans... to have a president who will turn the government of this country inside out."[1]

Candidate Carter was telling the American people that he would not allow the Council on Foreign Relations and the Bilderbergers to continue to run this country, or so one could presume by his statement. If he was elected, he would select those who were not identified as insiders, men and women who have never had the chance to run this country.

And true to his word, he selected members of a new group not previously known called the Trilateral Commission to fill important positions.

Apparently some of the minions beneath him had not read the script. Before Carter's election, his advisor Hamilton Jordan said: "If, after the inauguration (of Jimmy Carter) you find Cy Vance as Secretary of State, and Zbigniew Brzezinski as head of National Security, then I would say that we failed, and I'd quit."[2]

But strangely enough, after the inauguration, we found these two gentlemen in exactly the positions Mr. Jordan predicted. But Mr. Jordan did not quit. It appears that Mr. Jordan was told to read the script after he made his statement. Apparently, Mr. Carter did not consider these two gentlemen to have been "insiders" who had been running the previous government, even though both were members of the Council on Foreign Relations, heavily involved in American government since its creation in 1921.

The organizational meetings of the Trilateral Commission were held on July 23 and 24, 1972, at the estate of David Rockefeller, chairman of the CFR. In fact, all eight American representatives to the founding meeting of the Commission were members of the CFR.[3]

The other individuals present were citizens of either Japan or western European countries, (the three areas represented the "Tri-" in the Trilateral.)

The Trilateral Commission tells the curious what their purpose is. They explain: "Close Trilateral cooperation in keeping the peace, in managing the world economy, in fostering economic re-development and alleviating world poverty will improve the chances of a smooth and peaceful evolution of the global system."[4]

But there are others who disagree with this stated purpose and have tried to detail what they think their exact purpose is. One of these is Senator Barry Goldwater who wrote the following in his book *With No Apologies*: "What the Trilaterals truly intend is the creation of a worldwide economic power superior to the political government of the nation-states involved. As managers and creators of the system they will rule the world."[5]

Shortly after the founding of the Commission, in the fall of 1973, the little-known Governor of Georgia was in London, England, having dinner with David Rockefeller. Exactly what the Governor of Georgia was doing in London with Rockefeller has never been told, at least satisfactorily, but there are only two alternatives. Either:

1.   Jimmy Carter asked David Rockefeller to have dinner with him; or
2.   David Rockefeller asked Jimmy Carter.

(It will be presumed that the third alternative, of these men meeting by chance, should not be considered seriously.)

A careful examination of the first alternative will reveal that it is possible, but not very probable.

It is possible that Mr. Carter, desiring to become president of the United States, discovered that Mr. Rockefeller, because of his closeness with the Council on Foreign Relations and their ancillary organizations, had the power to make any one of their choosing President, and he arranged the meeting.

This is quite possible, as Mr. Rockefeller is an extremely important individual. In fact, during 1973: "David Rockefeller met with 27 heads of state, including the rulers of Russia and Red China."[6]

This is truly incredible because David Rockefeller has neither been elected or appointed to any governmental position where he could officially represent the United States government.

Author Ferdinand Lundberg, author of the book *The Rockefeller Syndrome*, wrote this about the Rockefeller power:

> One of the little-noticed features of the (Rockefeller) brothers is the ready entree they have to all high-level quarters, foreign and domestic.
>
> A telephone call from David at Chase (Manhattan Bank) can unlock practically as many tightly shut top-level doors all over the world as a call from the President of the United States, perhaps more.
>
> This is power.[7]

Three examples of the power that Rockefeller has might illustrate the power that Jimmy Carter might have seen prior to their London meeting.

It is known that in January, 1974, David Rockefeller, who is not a Catholic, had an audience with Pope Paul VI, the same Pope who wrote the Encyclical urging the nations of the world to form a world government. This has long been a goal of David Rockefeller and the Council on Foreign Relations, the organization of which Mr. Rockefeller was then Chairman.

Less than a month later, in February, 1974, Pope Paul recalled Josef Cardinal Mindszenty, the Catholic Primate of Hungary and a long time enemy of the Communist regime in Hungary. When the Cardinal reached Rome, the Pope asked him to remain silent and no longer speak out against Communism.

Were the two events connected?

Possibly the reason for these strange actions of the Pope occurred in

November, 1977, when the State Department of the United States returned the Crown of St. Stephen to the Communist government of Hungary.

The Crown has an interesting history. It was given to King Stephen, the King of Hungary, in the year 1,000 by Pope Sylvester II, after the King had converted to Catholicism. It has become a national treasure of immense historic and symbolic significance to the Hungarian people.

The Hungarian people believe that the authority to rule Hungary is inherent in the crown itself ("he who holds the Crown rules Hungary.")

The Crown was kept in Hungary until the Russians overran the country near the end of World War II. Before the Soviets could seize the Crown, Hungarian patriots delivered it to General George Patton, the commander of the American army near Hungary.

The Crown, along with other items of value to the Hungarian people, was brought to the United States and safeguarded by the State Department.

It was understood that this symbol of freedom would remain in the United States until Hungary could once again function as a constitutional government established by the Hungarian people through choice.

The Hungarian people's desire to keep the Crown out of the hands of the Communist government was betrayed by President Carter when he announced that the Crown would be returned to the Communist government in Hungary, ruled by the Communist dictator Janos Kadar, in December, 1977.

(It was Janos Kadar who, as Minister of the Interior, gave the orders for Cardinal Mindszenty's arrest and subsequent torture many years before.)

And it was Cardinal Mindszenty who fervently pleaded with the American government not to release the Crown to the Kadar government.

It is not a coincidence that it was on the twenty-first anniversary of the anti-Communist revolt in Hungary in 1956 that President Carter announced that the Crown would be returned to Hungary and given to the Kadar government. It certainly appeared as a way of expressing to the world that the United States was now giving its official blessing to the Communist government in Hungary. In addition, the timing of the announcement was intended to broadcast to the world that the American government was no longer supporting the aspirations of oppressed people around the world to be free from tyrannical Communist governments.

This action, of course, came as no shock to Cardinal Mindszenty who once charged that "the late President Eisenhower was responsible for the defeat of the Hungarian Freedom Fighters revolution in 1956."[8]

So the Cardinal was used to America's betrayal of just causes.

The second example of an unusual door opening up to David Rockefeller occurred in July, 1964, when David visited the Soviet Union and met with Russian Premier Nikita Khrushchev for two and a half hours.[9]

The meeting of these two individuals, when one is not the elected or appointed representative of his government, is indeed odd. Especially when the communists teach that any wealthy Capitalist is to be hated.

In any event, less than four months later, in October, 1964, Premier Khrushchev lost his job for no apparent reason (or at least to those who are not aware of the Conspiratorial View of History). Did the "Chairman of the Board" fire a "Branch Manager?" This is the unanswered question that certainly leads to speculation about why Khrushchev resigned.

The third example of Rockefeller's enormous power was reflected in August, 1976, when visiting Australian Prime Minister Malcolm Fraser met with Mr. Rockefeller before he met with President of the United States Gerald Ford.[10]

The second alternative about the London meeting of Rockefeller and Carter, that Rockefeller discovered Carter, is more plausible and much more consistent with the facts.

The Trilateral Commission was the idea of Zbigniew Brzezinski, or so the public is told, who went to David Rockefeller for his assistance in creating the organization. There is some indication that Brzezinski liked Carter even before the forming of the Commission.

According to the *New York Times* of March 21, 1978, Brzezinski "enjoys his public role. The key to his confidence is his close relationship with Mr. Carter. The two men met for the first time four years ago [in 1974, which appears to be incorrect] when Mr. Brzezinski was executive director of the Trilateral Commission, an organization favoring closer cooperation among Western Europe, Japan and the United States, and had the foresight to ask the then obscure former Governor to join its distinguished ranks. Their initial teacher-student relationship blossomed during the campaign and appears to have grown closer still."[11]

And again, in the *New York Times Magazine* of May 23, 1976, the reader is informed that "Zbig was the first guy in the Community to pay attention to Carter, talked to him, sent him his books and articles. For the better part of three years (from 1973, not 1974 as was reported above in the other *New York Times* article) Brzezinski (along) with Professor Richard N. Gardner of Columbia had Carter virtually to himself . . . "[12]

Mr. Carter himself commented on this learning experience as a member of the Trilateral Commission when he wrote the following in his election-year book entitled *Why Not the Best?*: "Membership on the commission has provided me with a splendid learning opportunity, and many of the other members have helped me in my study of foreign affairs."[13]

It is interesting that Mr. Carter admitted that he was being taught by members of the Trilateral Commission, and that he received his greatest understanding from Mr. Brzezinski, especially from his "books."

It appears that one of the things that Zbigniew taught Mr. Carter was his desire to increase the scope of government in the lives of the American people. Brzezinski had once written: "I should like to address myself to the problem of political change. I think we accept the idea of a vast expansion in social regulation. It may take such forms as legislation for the number of children, perhaps even legislation determining the sex of children once we have choice, the regulation of weather, the regulation of leisure, and so forth."[14]

One of the "books" written by Mr. Brzezinski that Mr. Carter might have read was a book entitled *Between Two Ages*, written in 1970.

A careful reading of this book reveals that Mr. Brzezinski has some rather shocking things to say about America and the rest of the world.

On page 300, for instance, Zbigniew reveals that the American people will be introduced to two new concepts in their economic life:

1.   A new monetary system replacing the American dollar; and
2.   A reduced standard of living in order to achieve it.

He wrote: "In the economic-technological field some international cooperation has already been achieved, but further progress will require greater American sacrifices. More intensive efforts to shape a new world monetary structure will have to be undertaken, with some consequent risk to the present relatively favorable American position."[15]

Brzezinski also revealed his views about the economic philosophies of Karl Marx:

> *page 72*: Marxism represents a further vital and creative stage in the maturing of man's universal vision. Marxism is simultaneously a victory of the external man over the inner, passive man, and a victory of reason over belief.
>
> *page 73*: Marxism has served as a mechanism of human progress even if its practice has often fallen short of its ideals. Teilhard de Chardin notes at one point that 'monstrous as it is, is not modern totalitarianism really the distortion of something magnificent, and thus quite near to the truth?'
>
> *page 83*: Marxism, disseminated on the popular level in the form of communism, represented a major advance in man's ability to conceptualize his relationship to his world.
>
> page 123: Marxism provided a unique intellectual tool for understanding and harnessing the fundamental forces of our time. It supplied the best avaliable insight into contemporary reality.

Brzezinski theorizes that the liberal, democratic societies would support an authoritarian form of government if they were given a choice between a dictatorship and social and intellectual disorder:

page 118: In the absence of social consensus, society's emotional and rational needs may be fused — mass media makes this easier to achieve — in the person of an individual who is seen as both preserving and making the necessary innovations in the social order.

Given the choice between social and intellectual disorder — and by this is not meant anything that even approaches a revolutionary situation — and authoritarian personal leadership [a dictator] it is very probable that even some present constitutional and liberal democratic societies would opt for the latter.

He also sees a threat to liberal democracy involving:

page 252: the gradual appearance of a more controlled and directed society.

Such a society would be dominated by an elite whose claim to political power would rest on allegedly superior scientific know-how.

Unhindered by the restraints of traditional liberal values, this elite would not hesitate to achieve its political ends by the latest modern techniques for influencing public behavior and keeping society under close surveillance and control.

And then Brzezinski details his desires to move towards a world government:

page 296: Movement toward a larger community of the developed nations . . . cannot be achieved by fusing existing states into one larger entity.

It makes much more sense to attempt to associate existing states through a variety of indirect ties and already developing limitations on national sovereignty.

Then he detailed the reasons for founding the Trilateral Commission:

page 296: Movement toward such a community will in all probability require two broad and overlapping phrases.

The first of these would involve the forging of community links among the United States, Western Europe and Japan.

Such a loose-knit community would need a taxation power and Brzezinski has already predicted this:

page 304: . . . it might also eventually lead to the possibility of something along the lines of a global taxation system.

And then he sums it all up by declaring:

page 308: Though the objective of shaping a community of
the developed nations is less ambitious than the goal of world
government, it is more attainable.

Brzezinski doesn't completely discount the possibility of a world
government; he just theorizes that it would be easier to achieve control of the
developed nations through an association of these nations.

But Brzezinski just doesn't stop with getting the United States strangled
with ties to other nations, he has also suggested that the American government should become dependent on the Soviet Union and Red China for our
oil needs.

While Mr. Brzezinski was director of the Trilateral Commission, they
published a report in 1977 entitled "Collaboration With Communist
Countries in Managing Global Problems: An Examination of the Options."
It read: "Both the U.S.S.R. and [Communist] China are exporters of energy
and apparently possess substantial oil reserves. The Trilateral countries
import energy, of which very little now comes from the U.S.S.R. or China.
The global situation appears likely to tighten in the coming years. There are
immediate advantages for the Trilateral countries in diversifying their
sources of supply. Trilateral-Communist cooperation in energy may thus be
feasible and desirable. This cooperation might take the form of investment
by Trilateral countries in Soviet or Chinese energy production to secure
energy exports from these countries."[16]

And lastly, Brzezinski, the teacher of President Carter, does not believe in
the Conspiratorial View of History: "History is much more the product of
chaos than of conspiracy. . . . increasingly, policy makers are overwhelmed
by events and information."[17]

But the support of the presidential campaign of Jimmy Carter did not
come just from members of the Trilateral Commission. He received financial
support from the following, amongst others: Dean Rusk, CFR member; C.
Douglas Dillon, CFR member; and Henry Luce, *Time* magazine's Vice
President and CFR member.

In addition, Carter surrounded himself with the following members of
the CFR before his election: Theodore Sorenson, W. Averill Harriman,
Cyrus Vance, Richard Gardner, Paul Nitze, and Paul Warnke.

And candidate Jimmy Carter even spoke before the Chicago branch of
the CFR in May, 1976, wherein he called for "a just and stable international
order," the phrase of those who understand the nature of the future. It was
almost as if Mr. Carter was paraded before the CFR to reveal that he was
indeed one of them.

But the major support after the election came from the Trilateral
Commission. As the *Washington Post* revealed after the election of President
Jimmy Carter: "If you like Conspiracy theories about secret plots to take over

the world, you are going to love the administration of President-elect Jimmy Carter. At last count 13 Trilateralists had gone into top positions in the administration. This is extraordinary when you consider that the Trilateral Commission only has about 65 American members."[18]

We have been told that, at the Democratic convention, after Carter received the Presidential nomination, he had not as yet made up his mind on whom he was going to select as his vice-president. The American people were told that he had narrowed his list of possible candidates down to seven men.

He selected a fellow member of the Trilateral Commission: Walter Mondale.

But even with the support of the wealthy establishment members of the CFR and some support of the media from CFR members, Jimmy Carter still spoke out against the liberal establishment: "Accepting the Democratic presidential nomination in New York, Carter denounced those 'unholy alliances that have formed between money and politics.'"

One of the interesting connections in the Trilateral Commission is the fact that the: "Majority of the important Frenchmen [who are members of the Commission], perhaps all of them, belong to the Grand Orient Lodge of Free Masonry."[19]

But the Commission needs financial support, and it gets it from "the Ford Foundation, [which] has been its largest contributor."[20]

But are those who are concerned about the influence and direction of the Trilateral Commission just exaggerating the danger? Should we agree with those who say that "There's certainly nothing sinister about the group."?

One who is concerned is Senator Barry Goldwater who on national television at the 1980 Republican Convention warned the nation that "This might be the last Republican convention and, in two weeks, the last Democratic convention. There are forces working against our country. There are selfish forces working for their own interest in our country."[21]

(Was it just an inadvertent omission that CFR member Dan Rather failed to ask Senator Goldwater on nationwide television, shortly after Goldwater made his charges, just what he meant by his statement?)

Goldwater went on to describe just who he thought, at least in part, these forces were. In his chapter entitled "The Non-Elected Rulers," in his book *With No Apologies*, the Senator wrote: "In my view, the Trilateral Commission represents a skillful, coordinated effort to seize control and consolidate the four centers of power: political, monetary, intellectual and ecclesiastical."[22]

There are even critics residing outside the United States. Take this comment by England's *Weekly Review*, about the Trilateral Commission for instance. They wrote: "International Communism of the Moscow order has many features in common with David Rockefeller's Trilateral Commission — such as undermining the national sovereignty of the United States. It is for this reason, plus others, that one finds known Marxists supporting the goals of the new world economic order sought by the Trilateral Commission...."[23]

The economic intent of the Trilateral Commission was pointed out by Jeremiah Novak in 1977: "The Trilateral Commission's most immediate concern is the creation of a new world monetary system to replace gold and the dollar as the international exchange with a new currency called Special Drawing Rights (SDR's.)"[24]

The purpose of a common money was spelled out by John Foster Dulles, a CFR founder, years before. He wrote: "... the establishment of a common money might be vested in a body created by and responsible to the principal trading and investing peoples. This would deprive our government of exclusive control over a national money...."[25]

A precursor of this common money revealed itself when six Common Market nations in Europe agreed to join in a monetary system.[26]

So the process marches on.

Now that the Trilateral Commission was in place, and their selected candidate was installed as the President of the United States, they could have the American government act in a manner that was important to the Commission. A brief review of some of the major accomplishments of the Carter administration informs the student of just what the Commission wanted from President Carter:

1.   The Betrayal and Expulsion of the Shah of Iran:

A senior Iranian diplomat in Washington stated: "President Carter betrayed the Shah and helped create the vacuum that will soon be filled by Soviet-trained agents and religious fanatics who hate America."[27]

A possible motive as to why Carter did this is answered by a review of the record of the Shah in the years prior to his leaving Iran. His record as head of the Iranian government was summarized in an article that stated that:

> Under the direction of its able monarch, Iran had been transferred in a single generation from a near-feudal agricultural society to an urbanized, burgeoning, industrial, and modern country.
>
> His plan was to make Iran a technologically advanced, economically diversified, and self-sustaining nation so that, in the next century when the oil ran low, Iran would not go into an economic decline and return to the dark ages.[28]

The Shah "had written into law in Iran... the principles of religious toleration, separation of church and state,... and an advisory parliament was set up to which, over the years, additional powers were granted."[29]

In other words, the Shah had intended to structure the government in such a way that a middle class would develop in his country. And once again, just as in the economies of China, Russia and Cuba, this was not acceptable to the master planners of the world.

He had to be replaced.

One clue that this statement is correct is this comment, made in the book entitled *Trilaterals Over Washington, Volume II*, written by Antony Sutton and Patrick M. Wood. They have written "The Shah was induced to invest his funds (estimates range from $½ billion to $25 billion,) with Chase Manhattan."[30]

The method Carter used has been partially revealed in various newspaper articles. He sent General Robert E. Huyser, Deputy Commander of U.S. Forces in Europe, to Iran. His purpose was to tell the Iranian Generals not to stage a "coup" against the impending government of the Khomeini. The Generals, loyal to the Shah, did nothing. A few hours after Khomeini took over, the Generals were shot.

These charges against President Carter were confirmed by the memoirs of the deposed Shah of Iran who wrote that "the Americans wanted me out. Certainly this is what the human rights champions in the State Department wanted."

The Shah then revealed why, in his opinion, the Carter administration truly wanted to replace him. The Shah "repeatedly argued in the memoirs that for years the great multinational oil companies, possibly in league with the U.S. government, had been subverting his rule because of his insistence that Iran get a greater share of oil revenues."[31]

(That is a strange comment in view of the fact that the American people were told that OPEC member Iran's oil prices were set by the government of Iran, not by the multinational oil companies.)

According to a book entitled *The Energy Cartel*, by Norman Medvin,[32] written in 1974, Iran has three major oil companies, the Iranian Offshore Petroleum Co., the Iranian Oil Consortium, and the Lavaan Petroleum Co.

Each company is a joint venture involving the following companies:

Name	Companies involved
Iranian Offshore Petroleum Co.	CFP, Atlantic Richfield, Cities Service, Superior, Kerr-McGee, Sun, National Iranian Oil Co.

Iranian Oil Consortium	BP, Shell, Gulf, Mobil, Exxon, Texaco, Standard of California, CFP, Am. Independent
Lavaan Petroleum Co.	Atlantic Richfield, Murphy Oil, Union Oil, National Iranian Oil Company

So now it is possible, if the Shah was right, to see which oil companies wanted to replace the Shah of Iran with the Ayatollah Khomeini.

Carter's strategy worked. The Shah of Iran left and was replaced by the Ayatollah.

Another interesting revelation about the whole Khomeini affair is the charge that the Khomeini in Iran today is not the same Khomeini that was exiled by the Shah in 1965, even though he is supposed to be. A memorandum written by an individual considered to be one of the world's best-informed international intelligence sources states:

> In its edition of June 11, 1979, on page A-2, the Los Angeles *Herald Examiner* carried a story which questioned the authenticity of the Ayatollah Khomeini. The article quoted a column by William Hickey in the *London Express* which included photographs of the Ayatollah Khomeini, which were taken while he was in France, showing that he had only 9 fingers. The middle digit of his right hand was missing.
>
> Recent photographs show that the present "Ayatollah Khomeini" has 10 fingers.

In addition, Iranian Premier Amir Hoveida testified: "I know him and I can assure you he had only nine fingers. This Khomeini is an imposter."

Shortly after making that statement, Hoveida was shouted down in the court he was testifying in and pulled out of the building and shot.[33]

Just who the new Khomeini is and why the previous one had to be replaced, was not explained. One clue to the mystery was offered by the Polish Army Intelligence Colonel, Michael Goloniewski, an expert on Soviet intelligence. He charged that the Soviets had penetrated the Shiite Moslem sect of which the Ayatollah is a member, and that the Ayatollah was a Soviet agent.

2. Support of Communist Terrorists in Southern Africa:

When Senator Barry Goldwater returned to the United States from a trip to Southern Africa, he charged the Carter Administration with basing its African policies on a " 'deliberate scheme with pro-Soviet overtones.' Goldwater said that 'everything the Carter Administration has done in Africa has played directly into the hands of the Soviet Union. These actions are so obviously subverting the strategic interests of the United States that it almost seems that someone must be following a deliberate scheme with pro-Soviet overtones.' He says that the Administration is 'meddling in a dangerous way in many African situations which are beyond its control. The effect is the creation of the kind of fear and confusion upon which Communism thrives and Soviet objectives are advanced.' "³⁴

3.   Delivery of the Panama Canal to a Marxist Dictator:

During the televised debates in 1976 between President Gerald Ford and candidate Jimmy Carter, Mr. Carter explained: "I would never give up complete or practical control of the Panama Canal Zone. But I would continue to negotiate with the Panamanians . . . . I would not relinquish the practical control of the Panama Canal Zone anytime in the forseeable future."³⁷

Perhaps the reason that Carter decided that "never" was 1977 was the growing inability of the government of Marxist Omar Torrijos to pay the interest on their growing government debt. It is very revealing that, when Torrijos seized power over Panama in 1968, its national debt was only $160 million. When it was time to acquire the Panama Canal in 1977, it was $1.4 billion.

Columnist Charles Bartlett agreed that the dictatorial Torrijos regime "has put the small nation so deeply in the red that the canal treaty has no supporters more fervent than the American bankers whose hopes for payment rest on a revival of faith in the Panamanian economy."³⁶

The Panamanian debt to the United States banks was so large that Panama had to "allocate some $47 million—which is 39 percent of its national Budget—to debt service [interest] on the massive loans. Undoubtedly the directors of the creditor U.S. banks, which include Chase Manhattan Bank, First National City Bank, Bank of America, Banker's Trust, First National Bank of Chicago, Republic National Bank of Dallas, and Treaty negotiator Sol Linowitz's Marine Midland Bank, see that the only way of getting back their money with interest is to get control of the Canal and Canal Zone from Torrijos so he can extort the money owed to the international banks from shipping fees."³⁷

It is very revealing that, under the terms of the treaty that gave the Canal to Panama, the United States paid the Panamanian government millions of dollars so that the Panamanian government would take the canal.

It is important to remember that "of the 30 or so banks that had made rather shaky loans, one-half of them had at least one Trilateral on their boards of directors. Had Panama defaulted on these loans, some major international banks would have faced financial ruin."³⁸

It is also revealing that fifteen of the sixteen senators in the U.S. Senate who had either been a member of the CFR or were currently a member, voted for the Treaty.[39]

The American people, who according to the polls taken just before the Treaty was signed, were opposed to it by a 70 to 30 margin, remembered those Senators who had voted for the Treaty and were up for re-election in 1978 and 1980.

Twenty of these Senators were defeated.[40]

4.   Betrayal of the government of Nicaragua:

Perhaps the most glaring example of Carter's misuse of his presidential power occurred in the overthrow of the government of Nicaragua in 1979 and 1980. Congressman Larry McDonald, on September 17, 1980, laid the blame for the fall of the Nicaraguan government on President Carter (and thus onto the Trilateral Commission): "The policies of the United States of America, the policies of this Administration, were deliberately and calculatingly designed to destroy the elected government of the people of Nicaragua and to bring the Cuban-dominated Sandinistas to power."[41]

The elected president of Nicaragua, a West Point-trained officer, Anastasio Somoza, also came to the same conclusion as Congressman McDonald. After he left office, President Somoza wrote a book entitled *Nicaragua Betrayed,* in which he made the following observation: ". . . I come to one startling conclusion: There is a planned and deliberate conspiracy in the United States of America to destroy that republican form of government."[42]

Somoza saw that this conspiracy was also responsible for the overthrow of his government, and he specifically zeroed in on President Carter: "His put Nicaragua in the hands of the Communists."[43]

And again: ". . . the betrayal of steadfast anti-Communist allies places Mr. Carter in the company of evil worldwide conspiratorial forces. I repeat, the treacherous course charted by Mr. Carter was not through ignorance, but by design."[44]

President Somoza again laid the blame on the American government: ". . . when the United States assumes leadership in a conspiratorial fashion to annihilate anti-Communist nations, I believe it is my duty to speak out. When I have factual evidence that the United States of America has actually aided and abetted the evil forces of Communism, I believe the people of the United States should share in such facts and incontrovertible manifestations."[45]

For all of President Somoza's efforts to warn the American people and the remainder of the world about a truth that other nations had learned before him, that the United States government could not be trusted in preventing a Communist takeover of a friendly government, he met a violent death in an assassination in September, 1980. This murder took place just a few weeks after his book was published.

The Soviet-trained Sandinistas were now fully in command of the Nicaraguan government, and their opposition leader had been eliminated.

Have they offered the Nicaraguan people a better government than the supposedly "tyrannical despot" Somoza?

One former Sandinista leader doesn't believe so. He reported:

Nicaragua's Communist rulers have done more damage in nine months than Somoza did in ten years.

Something like 12,000 opponents of the regime are still in jail. Hundreds of others have simply disappeared.

Every aspect of life in Nicaragua today is being dictated by the Communists.

Every day, the junta seizes more property. More than one million acres of farmland have already been taken over, but less than one-fifth of the land is now in use. In two months, hundreds will be starving for lack of food.[46]

A former Major in the Nicaraguan National Guard is another who agrees. He told a congressional committee that the Sandinistas are working to encourage revolutions in El Salvador, Honduras, Guatemala and Costa Rica. He said: "The consolidation of Central America, the allegiance of the parties in power in Mexico and Venezuela, will give access to the rich oil fields of the continent. If you do not take action to neutralize this error in policy immediately, you will be fighting a war in your territory in no more than five years."[47]

After the betrayal of Niciragua to the Sandinistas, President Carter's administration released $75 million in aid, after the President "certified that Nicaragua's Marxist regime was not aiding Communist guerillas in El Salvador and Guatemala."[48]

There were those in the United States who agreed with the above charges. The American Legion passed the following resolution at its 1980 national convention. The resolution demanded "in the best interests of our country that the Congress of the United States launch a comprehensive investigation into the Trilateral Commission and its parent organization, the Council on Foreign Relations, to determine what influence has been and is being exerted over the foreign and domestic policies of the United States."

But the real message in the actions of the United States government lies in the following statement of the former Prime Minister of England, Edward Heath, who was quoted as saying: "We in Europe will no longer be able to expect the United States to take action in any part of the world to put right something we don't like."[49]

In other words, America is no longer an ally of those who seek freedom for their nation against any Communist tyrant.

5.   The Election of 1980:

But the final drama in the current run of the Trilateral Commission came in the presidential election of 1980, when Jimmy Carter and Walter Mondale ran for re-election. They were opposed by non-member Ronald Reagan and member George Bush.

An interesting dimension to this election was added by Trilateral Commission member John Anderson, running as an independent. An article dated August 1, 1980, stated that "Anderson might quit if Carter is dumped"[50] by the Democratic convention. In other words, the "independent candidate" was running against Jimmy Carter. It seems strange that the Trilateral Commission would allow two of their members to run against each other unless they wanted President Carter out of office. This was further illustrated when Anderson supported Mondale for the Presidency in 1984.

That possibility raises the interesting question as to why they wanted the other candidate, Ronald Reagan, in office in 1980.

Reagan didn't appear to be the early choice of the Trilateral Commission. For instance, the *U.S. News and World Report* magazine began mentioning the candidacy of two other members of the Trilateral Commission early in 1978.

On February 27, 1978, the magazine wrote: "In the view of the President's top political advisers, a Republican ticket of Texan George Bush [a Commission member] and Illinois Governor James Thompson [a Commission member] would provide the most formidable opposition for Carter in 1980".[51]

And again on July 3, 1978: "Ronald Regan's backers are pinpointing Governor James Thompson [a Commission member] of Illinois as the candidate in the race for the 1980 Republican presidential nomination."[52]

And the magazine continued the call for Commission members again in 1980, first on February 11, 1980: "George Bush's [a Commission member] sudden emergence in the Republican presidential race . . . calls for a moderate vice-presidential nominee from the west—possibily John Anderson [a Commission member] or Governor James Thompson [a Commission member], both from Illinois."[53]

And then again on October 6, 1980: "Top Republicans already are talking about who would lead the party if Ronald Reagan loses his presidential bid. Early consensus: Representative Jack Kemp of New York [not a Commission member] for conservatives, Illinois Governor James Thompson [a Commission member] for moderates—with George Bush [a Commission member] appealing to yet others."[54]

Candidate Ronald Reagan was asked whether he would allow any Trilateral Commission members in his Cabinet during the Florida primary, on March 17, 1980, and this is how he replied: "No, I don't believe that the Trilateral Commission is a conspiratorial group, but I do think its interests are devoted to international banking, multi-national corporations, and so forth. I don't think that any administration of the U.S. government should have the top 19 positions filled by people from any one group or organization representing one viewpoint. No. I would go in a different direction."[55]

Just prior to the election, candidate Ronald Reagan was asked about who truly ran this country. He replied: "I think there is an elite in this country and they are the ones who run an elitist government. They want a government by a handful of people because they don't believe the people themselves can run their lives. . . . Are we going to have an elitist government that makes decisions for people's lives or are we going to believe as we have for so many decades, that the people can make these decisions for themselves?"

After the election, Reagan: "assembled a 'transition team' which would later select, screen and recommend appointees for major administration posts. Of the fifty-nine people Reagan named to that team, twenty-eight were members of the CFR, ten belonged to the secret and elite Bilderberg group, and no less than ten were Trilaterals."[56]

There was concern during the Republican convention that Reagan would appoint George Bush as his Vice-Presidential nominee. The day before he made that decision, a group of conservative activists visited Reagan to present the case for him to appoint a conservative running mate, one not connected to the elitist groups Reagan had publicly spoken out against.

Reagan didn't listen and appointed George Bush, not only a member of the Trilateral Commission, but a member of the Council of Foreign Relations as well.

Even before Reagan had officially made his decision about George Bush at the convention, and as an early indication of what was to come, Reagan lieutenants "shot down a proposed plank [to the Republican Party platform] that would have denouced the Trilateral Commission and the Council on Foreign Relations. Among the things Reagan's subsequent selection of Bush has accomplished is the elimination of the Trilateral Commission and the Council on Foreign Relations as issues the Republican Party can use in the campaign."[57]

In other words, Reagan knew that he was going to nominate George Bush as his vice-president even before the time he officially selected him, and he and his supporters didn't want the Trilateral Commission to be denounced at the convention. It was extremely important that that particular platform plank be defeated.

And it was, and Trilateral Commission member George Bush became Reagan's nominee. And the Trilateral Commission and the Council on Foreign Relations did not become campaign issues.

After the election, President Ronand Reagan continued his support of both the Trilateral Commission and the Council on Foreign Relations by appointing:

> 64 CFR members;
> 6 Trilateral Commission (TC) members;
> 6 TC and CFR members; and
> 5 former members of the TC

to positions in his administration.

Chapter 21

The Purpose

What is the overall purpose of these secret and semi-secret organizations? Why do some of these organizations select and then support the candidates for major political office?

Perhaps the best answer to these questions was given by Norman Thomas, the Socialist Party's presidential candidate in every national election between the years of 1928 to 1948. Mr. Thomas said: "We have learned that it is possible, to a degree not anticipated by most earlier Socialists, to impose desirable social controls on privately owned enterprises by the development of social planning, by proper taxation and labor legislation and by the growth of powerful labor organizations."[1]

Mr. Thomas was revealing the game plan for the ultimate success of Socialism: the utilization of non-Socialist hands to gradually achieve the goals of Socialism. The question was how could the Socialists get the American people to accept Socialism when the American people had made it clear through the years they didn't want the economic philosophy known as Socialism.

Mr. Thomas answered this question on another occasion: "The American people will never knowingly adopt Socialism, but under the name of Liberalism, they will adopt every fragment of the Socialist program until one day America will be a Socialist nation without knowing how it happened."2

The key to success for the Socialists was to get the American people to support candidates that they perceived were "anti-Socialist" but were in truth secretly supporting the cause of the Socialist Party in increasing the size and scope of government in the lives of the American people.

Mr. Thomas later identified one of these "Liberal" "closet" "Socialists" when he wrote: "The United States is making greater strides toward Socialism under [President Dwight] Eisenhower than under [President Franklin] Roosevelt . . . ."3

There are many who considered Roosevelt to be a semi-Socialist, but Eisenhower has been perceived as a "conservative" by the American people. Yet Thomas told the American people that Eisenhower as President was doing more to promote Socialism than had Roosevelt as President.

Another individual hiding his Socialism, according to Norman Thomas, was President Lyndon Johnson. Thomas was pleased with Johnson's Great Society: "I ought to rejoice and I do. I rub my eyes in amazement and surprise. His war on poverty is a Socialistic approach . . . ."4

Thomas also heaped praise upon another "closet" socialist, Hubert Humphrey, who "is the type of Democrat I like and one who would be a Socialist if he got to England."5

Another so-called "conservative, anti-Socialist" President was President Richard Nixon. But John Kenneth Galbraith, the Paul Warburg Professor of Economics at Harvard University, identified him as a "closet" socialist, one doing the work of the Socialist Party.

First, Professor Galbraith presented his credentials that enabled him to determine if anyone else was a Socialist. He made a statement that indicated that he personally was a Socialist. He advocated that " . . . a certain number of industries should be publicly owned. For moving and housing people at moderate cost, private enterprise does not serve."

Then he makes the connection between Socialism and President Nixon: "But I had come reluctantly to the conclusion that Socialism, even in this modest design, was something I would never see. Now I am being rescued by this new Socialist upsurge, promoted, of all things, by socialists, not on the Left, but on the Right, and they have the blessing and conceivably much more, of a Republican Administration. Certainly, the least predicted development under the Nixon administration was the great new thrust to Socialism. As an opponent of Socialism, Mr. Nixon seemed steadfast."6

What these people were saying was that it didn't make any difference whether the American people voted Republican and "anti-Socialist," or Democratic and "Liberal," they get the same thing: more Socialism.

This statement becomes graphically clear when the following issues are examined in light of what the two major political parties have done in support of them. Both parties have at one time or another supported:

1. Ratification of the Genocide Convention;
2. A guaranteed annual income;
3. Federal Minimum Wage Legislation;
4. Federal Food Stamp Program;
5. Abolition of the death penalty;
6. Peaceful Coexistence;
7. Socialized medicine;
8. Disarmament;
9. Repeal of the Internal Security Legislation aimed at Communism;
10. Federal Civil Rights Legislation;
11. Reapportionment of Electoral Districts on the basis of Population;
12. Federal aid to education;
13. Federal child-care centers;
14. Ratification of the 1963 Nuclear Test Ban Treaty;
15. Termination of American sovereignty in the Panama Canal Zone; and
16. Increased agricultural and commercial trade with the Communist nations.

Not only have either or both of our major parties supported these programs, but another party has as well.

In fact, these are some of the planks in the official party platforms of:

The Communist Party, U.S.A.[7]

Chapter 22
Iron Mountain

Wars are fought because one nation wants something another nation has.

Protecting a nation from outside attack is another reason for war.

These two reasons for war are called the Visible Reasons for War. Research now has concluded that there are what are called Invisible Reasons for War, as well.

One such report that has done research into the Invisible Reasons for War is a report called the *Report From Iron Mountain on the Possibility and Desirability of Peace*.[1] Written in 1963 and released in March 1966, this report examines the visible and invisible functions or reasons of not only war but peace as well.

The report claims to have been written at an underground nuclear hideout near the town of Hudson, New York, that has been provided as a "substitute corporate headquarters... where essential personnel could presumably survive and continue to work after [a nuclear] attack. . . . ."

The corporations that have created Iron Mountain include Standard Oil of New Jersey (the Rockefeller interests); Manufacturers Hanover Trust (the Morgan interests); and the Shell Oil (the House of Orange,) amongst others.

The report dates back to at least 1961, when Robert McNamara, McGeorge Bundy, and Dean Rusk, all members of the CFR, noticed that no serious study had been made about planning for a long-term peace. Not only were they concerned about the lasting effects of a long-term peace, they also wished to examine the functions, both visible and invisible, of war.

The report states that: "War has provided . . . society with a debatable system for stabilizing and controlling national economies. No alternate method of control has yet been tested in a complex modern economy that has shown it is remotely comparable in scope or effectiveness."

War, therefore, was not fought for the usual reasons outlined above. It was fought to "control economies." These individuals apparently were concerned that there had been no efforts made to detail how they were to control economies during a time of peace: "War fills certain functions essential to the stability of our society; until other ways of filling them are developed, the war system must be maintained, and improved in effectiveness."

So, in a manner not detailed in the report itself, these three somehow arranged for a study of these problems. The report states that fifteen members of the investigating team got together to write the report, and that it was unanimously agreed to. Furthermore, no minutes of the meetings were maintained, as it was thought they would be "too inhibiting." The team which wrote the report recommended that the report not be made public after it was completed.

One of those who read the report attempted to locate the authors. It was his theory that it had been written by the Hudson Institute. He wrote: "There is considerable evidence that the Report is the work of the Hudson Institute and Herman Kahn. . . . There is an Iron Mountain just a stone's throw [literally] from the Hudson Institute near Croton-on-Hudson, [New York.]"[2]

The Hudson Institute is not well known among the American public, but it is known to government officials who have used it as a "think-tank" by hiring it to report on the issues of national concern.

The Hudson Institute was started in 1961 when Mr. Kahn, the owner, decided "to help determine the entire future of the U.S. — and, time permitting, much of the world beyond."[3]

The Institute primarily receives its income from the government. Hudson listed five sources for its $1.36 million of income in 1968: The Office of Civil Defense, The Office of Secretary of Defense, the Military Services, Other Government and Non-U.S. Government.[4]

Kahn and his "think tankers" have become so important to the American government that they are frequently accused of setting older administrations on a path that new adminstrations cannot alter. "This is a process of invisible power. At its extreme this influence can commit a nation to special programs and military actions which have neither been fully explained nor publicly debated. One day, as that power pervades and grows more sophisticated, it may so affect the course of government that any nation's policies may be locked in, as if by automatic pilot, years before the men who are elected to govern ever take office."[5]

The Hudson Institute has a published list of what it calls "Public Members" and "Fellows." Ten of the twenty-one listed Public Members are members of the Council on Foreign Relations, as are fifteen of the thirty-four Fellows.

Two of the Fellows are known to the public: Henry Kissinger (CFR member) and Dr. Milton Friedman.

The report starts by defining the traditional view of the functions of war. It claims that there are three:

1.　to defend a nation from military attack by another or to deter such an attack;
2.　to defend or advance a national interest; and
3.　to maintain or increase a nation's military power for its own sake.

It continues by stating that these are the "visible" functions, and that there are "invisible, or implied, functions" as well. These are spelled out in the report, but all functions have one common purpose: "War has provided both ancient and modern society with a debatable system for stabilizing and controlling national economies. No alternate method of control has yet been tested in a complex modern economy that has shown it is remotely comparable in scope or effectiveness. War fills certain functions essential to the stability of our society; until other ways of filling them are developed, the war system must be maintained — and improved in effectiveness."

The report then goes on to detail what the "invisible functions" of war are:

War...is the principal organizing force in most societies. ...The possibility of war provided the sense of external necessity without which no government can long remain in power.

The historical record reveals one instance after another where the failure...of a regime to maintain the credibility of a war threat led to its dissolution.

War...provides anti-social elements with an acceptable role in the social structure.

The younger, and more dangerous, of these hostile social groupings have been kept under control by the Selective Service System.

As a control device...the draft can again be defended....

The level of the draft calls tends to follow the major fluctuations in the unemployment rate....

Man destroys surplus members of his own species by organized warfare.

War is the principal motivational force for the development of science....

War is a...general social release...for the dissipation of general boredom.

War...enables the physically deteriorating older generation to maintain its control of the younger, destroying it if necessary.

An excellent summation of the report is contained in a novel by Taylor Caldwell, entitled *Ceremony of the Innocent*. She wrote: "...there will be no peace in the tormented world, only a programmed and systematic series of wars and calamities—until the plotters have gained their objective: an exhausted world willing to submit to a planned Marxist economy and total and meek enslavement—in the name of peace."[6]

Apparently the individual who wrote that "War was Peace" knew what he was talking about.

Chapter 23
World War I

World War I was started when the nations went to war to avenge the assassination of the Archduke Francis Ferdinand, the heir to the Habsburg throne, on June 28, 1914.

This is the typical explanation. But the "revisionist historian" knows just what caused and what the purpose was of the conflagration of World War I.

Up until America's entry into this war, the American people had followed the wise advice of President George Washington given in his farewell address, delivered to the nation on September 17, 1796. President Washington said: "It is our true policy to steer clear of permanent alliance with any portion of the foreign world.... Why, by interweaving our destiny with that of any part of Europe, entangle our peace and prosperity in the toils of European ambition, rivalship, interest, humour or caprice?"

President Washington attempted to warn the American people about getting embroiled in the affairs of Europe. But in 1914, it was not to be. There were those who were secretly planning America's involvement in World War I whether the American people wanted it or not.

The pressure to involve the American government started in 1909, long before the actual assassination of the Archduke.

Norman Dodd, former director of the Committee to Investigate Tax Exempt Foundations of the U.S. House of Representatives, testified that the Committee was invited to study the minutes of the Carnegie Endowment for International Peace as part of the Committee's investigation. The Committee stated: "The trustees of the Foundation brought up a single question. If it is desirable to alter the life of an entire people, is there any means more efficient than war.... They discussed this question...for a year and came up with an answer: There are no known means more efficient than war, assuming the objective is altering the life of an entire people. That leads them to a question: How do we involve the United States in a war. This is in 1909."[1]

So the decision was made to involve the United States in a war so that the "life of the entire people could be altered." This was the conclusion of a foundation supposedly committed to "peace."

The method by which the United States was drawn into the war started on October 25, 1911, when Winston Churchill was appointed the First Lord of the Admiralty in England.

Winston Churchill is an interesting individual, as he later came to the conclusion that there was indeed a master conspiracy at work in the major events of the world, when he wrote the following in 1920: "From the days of Spartacus—Weishaupt to those of Karl Marx, to those of Trotsky (Russia-)...this world-wide conspiracy for the overthrow of civilization...has been steadily growing."[2]

The second key appointment made during the pre-war period was the appointment of Franklin Delano Roosevelt as Assistant Secretary of the Navy by President Woodrow Wilson.

Roosevelt is also on record as concluding that there was a conspiracy, at least in the United States. He once wrote to Colonel Edward Mandell House: "The real truth of the matter is, as you and I know, that a financial element in the larger centers has owned the government ever since the days of Andrew Jackson, and I am not wholly excepting the administration of W.W. (Woodrow Wilson.) The country is going through a repetition of Jackson's fight with the Bank of the United States—only on a far bigger and broader basis."[3]

The next step in the maneuvering of the United States into the war came when the Cunard Lines, owner of the ocean liner, the *Lusitania*, turned the ship over to the First Lord of the Admiralty, Winston Churchill. It now became a ship of the English Navy and was under the control of the English government.

The ship was sent to New York City where it was loaded with six million rounds of ammunition, owned by J.P. Morgan & Co., to be sold to

England and France to aid in their war against Germany.

It was known that the very wealthy were interested in involving the American government in that war, and Secretary of State William Jennings Bryan was one who made note of this. "As Secretary [Bryan] had anticipated, the large banking interests were deeply interested in the World War because of wide opportunities for large profits. On August 3, 1914, even before the actual clash of arms, the French firm of Rothschild Freres cabled to Morgan and Company in New York suggesting the flotation of a loan of $100,000,000, a substantial part of which was to be left in the United States, to pay for French purchases of American goods."[4]

England broke the German war code on December 14, 1914, so that "By the end of January, 1915, [British Intelligence was] able to advise the Admiralty of the departure of each U-boat as it left for patrol . . . ."[5]

This meant that the First Lord of the Admiralty, Winston Churchill, knew where every U-boat was in the vicinity of the English Channel that separated England and France.

The ocean liner was set to sail to England already at war with Germany. The German government had placed advertisements in the New York newspapers warning the American people considering whether or not to sail with the ship to England that they would be sailing into a war zone, and that the liner could be sunk.

Secretary Bryan promised that "he would endeavor to persuade the President (Woodrow Wilson) publicly to warn the Americans not to travel [aboard the *Lusitania*]. No such warning was issued by the President, but there can be no doubt that President Wilson was told of the character of the cargo destined for the *Lusitania*. He did nothing . . . ."[6]

Even though Wilson proclaimed America's neutrality in the European War, in accordance with the prior admonitions of George Washington, his government was secretly plotting to involve the American people by having the *Lusitania* sunk. This was made public in the book *The Intimate Papers of Colonel House*, written by a supporter of the Colonel, who recorded a conversation between Colonel House and Sir Edward Grey of England, the Foreign Secretary of England:

Grey: What will America do if the Germans sink an ocean liner
            with American passengers on board?
House: I believe that a flame of indignation would sweep the
            United States and that by itself would be sufficient to
            carry us into the war.[7]

On May 7, 1915, the *Lusitania* was sunk in the English Channel by a U-boat after it had slowed to await the arrival of the English escort vessel, the *Juno*, which was intended to escort it into the English port. The First Lord of the Admiralty, Winston Churchill, issued orders that the *Juno* was to return to port, and the *Lusitania* sat alone in the channel. Because Churchill knew of the presence of three U-boats in the vicinity, it is reasonable to presume that he had planned for the *Lusitania* to be sunk, and it was. 1201 people lost their lives in the sinking.

This sinking has been described by Colin Simpson, the author of a book entitled *The Lusitania,* as "the foulest act of wilful murder ever committed on the seas."[8]

But the event was not enough to enable President Wilson to declare war against the German government, and the conspirators changed tactics. They would use other means to get the American people involved in the war, as the "flame of indignation" did not sweep the United States as had been planned.

Robert Lansing, the Assistant Secretary of State, is on record as stating: "We must educate the public gradually — draw it along to the point where it will be willing to go into the war."[9]

After the sinking of the *Lusitania,* two inquiries were held, one by the English government, in June, 1915, and one by the American government in 1918. Mr. Simpson has written that "Both sets of archives . . . contain meager information. There are substantial differences of fact in the two sets of papers and in many cases it is difficult to accept that the files relate to the same vessel."[10]

But in both inquiries, the conclusions were the same: torpedoes and not exploding ammunition sank the *Lusitania,* because there was no ammunition aboard. The cover-up was now official.

But there have been critics of these inquiries. One was, of course, the book written by Colin Simpson, who did the research necessary to write his book in the original minutes of the two inquiries.

The *Los Angeles Times* reviewed Mr. Simpson's book and concluded: "The *Lusitania* proves beyond a reasonable doubt that the British government connived at the sinking of the passenger ship in order to lure America into World War I. The Germans, whose torpedo struck the liner, were the unwitting accomplices or victims of a plot probably concocted by Winston Churchill."[11]

President Wilson was seeking re-election in 1916. He campaigned on his record of "keeping us out of the War" during his first term of office from 1912 to 1916.

But behind the scenes, Wilson was secretly plotting America's entry into the War, mainly through the machinations of Wilson's major advisor, Colonel Edward Mandell House. House had already committed America to a participation in the war: "The House-Grey memorandum . . . pledged American intervention on the side of the Allies if Germany would not come promptly to the peace table. This agreement was approved by Wilson eight months before the 1916 election."[12]

But the real reason the War was being fought was slowly emerging. One of the first revelations occurred on May 27, 1916, when President Wilson proposed a the League of Nations in a speech before the League to Enforce Peace. Wilson argued that what the world needed to prevent the recurrence of a similar war was a world government.

Some were not happy with the slowness of America's entry into the war. One of these was Franklin Roosevelt, who:

> In the early months of 1917 [before the official declaration of war by the United States government] he had been in constant conflict with his chief, Secretary of the Navy, Joseph Daniels, over the same issues.
>
> For Daniels, who resisted every move that might carry the United States into the war, those four months (January through April) of 1917 were the "agony of Gethsemane."
>
> He opposed convoying [the intentional sending of American ships into the war zone in the hope that one would be sunk by the German Navy]. He opposed the arming of merchant ships [intentionally provoking the German Navy into believing that the ship was a ship of war].
>
> Roosevelt favored both.
>
> And when a filibuster prevented congressional authorization of the arming of merchantmen, Roosevelt was impatient with Wilson for not immediately using his executive power to arm [the ships]. He dined at the Metropolitan Club with a group of Republican "warhawks" [Roosevelt was a Democrat]. It included Theodore Roosevelt, General Wood, J.P. Morgan, and Elihu Root [one of the founders of the CFR].
>
> The primary topic of discussion was, according to Roosevelt's diary, "how to make Administration steer a clear course to uphold rights."
>
> This was an euphemism for an aggressive policy on the highseas that would result in incidents and involve the United States in the war.[13]

Roosevelt's badgering apparently paid off, for on April 2, 1917, President Wilson asked Congress for a Declaration of War, and it was granted on April 6. The United States was now in the war "to end all wars," and "to make the world safe for democracy."

The war wound its horrible course through the destruction of human lives and ended on November 11, 1918.

Historian Walter Mills wrote the following about the purpose of the war and about House's basic intent: "The Colonel's sole justification for preparing such a batch of blood for his countrymen was his hope of establishing a new world order [a world government] of peace and security...."[14]

The official treaty that ended the war was the Treaty of Versailles, where representatives of all sides sat down at a conference table and wrote the treaty.

Several interesting personalities attended these meetings. In the British delegation was the British economist John Maynard Keynes, and representing the American banking interests was Paul Warburg, the Chairman of the Federal Reserve. His brother, Max, the head of the German banking firm of M.M. Warburg and Company, of Hamburg, Germany, and who "was not only in charge of Germany's finances but was a leader of the German espionage system"[15] was there as a representative of the German government.

The Treaty was written to end the war, but another delegate to the conference, Lord Curzon of England, the British Foreign Secretary, saw through what the actual intent was and declared: "This is no peace; this is only a truce for twenty years." Lord Curzon felt that the terms of the Treaty were setting the stage for a second world war, and he correctly predicted the year it would start: 1939.

Lord Curzon was indeed a prophet: he picked the actual year that World War II would start!

One of the planks of the Treaty called for large amounts of war reparations to be paid to the victorious nations by the German government. This plank of the Treaty alone caused more grief in the German nation than any other and precipitated three events:

1. The "hyperinflation" of the German mark between 1920 and 1923;
2. The destruction of the middle class in Germany; and
3. The bringing to power of someone who could end the inflation: a dictator like Adolf Hitler.

This plank was written by John Foster Dulles, one of the founders of the Council on Foreign Relations, and later the Secretary of State to President Dwight Eisenhower.

Even John Maynard Keynes became concerned about the Treaty. He wrote: "The peace is outrageous and impossible and can bring nothing but misfortune behind it."[16]

In addition to writing the Treaty of Versailles, the nations who were victorious in the war also wrote the Charter of the League of Nations, which was ratified on January 10, 1920, and signed by President Wilson for the American government. Wilson brought the treaty back to the United States and asked the Senate to ratify it. The Senate, remembering George Washington's advice to avoid foreign entanglements and reflecting the views of the American people who did not wish to enter the League, refused to ratify the treaty. President Wilson was not pleased, possibly because he saw himself, as Senator Henry Cabot Lodge was quick to point out, as: "...a future President of the world."[17]

It is now apparent that Wilson intended to head up the world government the war was fought to give the world, and he became depressed when the Treaty was not ratified. Imagine the disappointment of one who had come so close to becoming the very first President of the World, only to have it taken away by the actions of the Senate of the United States. Imagine the sense of incredible power that Wilson must have felt, thinking he would become the very first individual in the history of mankind to rule the world. Others had tried and failed, but Wilson was confident that he would succeed.

But the American people, expressing their displeasure through the Senate, would not let him.

Others were not so disappointed, however. "The war, in brief, provided an unparalled opportunity for the richest families to grab [exorbitant profits] at the expense of the public and, without exception, they made the most of this opportunity. The rich families, to be sure, wanted the war to be won, but they took care that the victory was expensive to the common taxpayers. They uttered no cries for government economy ... so long as the public treasury was at their disposal."[18]

One of the families who reaped the exorbitant profits were "the Rockefellers, who were very eager for the United States to enter World War I, [and who] made far more than $200,000,000 from that conflict."[19]

But support for the League of Nations continued. The Grand Orient Lodge of Freemasonry of France was one which advised all of its members: "It is the duty of universal Freemasonry to give its full support to the League of Nations...."[20]

As could have been anticipated, the League of Nations became a major issue during the Presidential election of 1920.

The Republican candidate Warren G. Harding was on record as opposing the League and further attempts to ratify the charter: "It will avail nothing to discuss in detail the League covenant, which was conceived for world super-government. In the existing League of Nations, world governing with its super-powers, this Republic will have no part."

He was opposed in the Republican primaries by General Leonard Wood, one of the Republican "warhawks," who was "...backed by a powerful group of rich men who wish(ed) a military man in the White House."

The American people, once again manifesting their disapproval of the League, voted for Harding as an evidence of that distrust and concern. Harding outpolled his opposition by a greater margin than did President Wilson who had "kept us out of the war" during the election of 1916. Wilson got only fifty-two percent of the vote, and Harding got sixty-four percent.

Harding was a supporter of William Howard Taft, the President who opposed the bankers and their Federal Reserve Bill. After his election, he named Harry M. Daugherty, Taft's campaign manager, as his Attorney General.

His other Cabinet appointments were not as wise, however, as he unexplainedly surrounded himself with men representing the oil industry. For instance:

> his Secretary of State was Charles Evans Hughes, an attorney of Standard Oil;

> his Secretary of the Treasury was Andrew Mellon, owner of Gulf Oil;

> his Postmaster General was Will Hays, an attorney for Sinclair Oil; and

> his Secretary of the Interior was Albert Fall, a protege of the oil men.

It was Mr. Fall who was to be President Harding's downfall, as he later accepted a bribe from Harry Sinclair in exchange for a lease of the Navy's oil reserves in Teapot Dome, Wyoming.

There are many who believe that the scandal was intended to discredit the Harding administration in an attempt to remove him from office for two very important reasons:

1. Harding was consistently vocal against the League of Nations, and there was still a chance that its supporters could get the United States to join as the League had survived the Senate's prior refusal to ratify the treaty, and

2. Attorney General Daugherty had been prosecuting the oil trusts under the Sherman anti-trust laws.

These activities did not please the oil interests who had created the Teapot Dome scandal. But Harding unfortunately did not live to see the full repercussions of the artificial scandal, as he died on August 2, 1923, before the story completely surfaced. (There are those who believe that there were some who couldn't wait for the Teapot Dome Scandal to remove President Harding, and that he was poisoned.)

But the oil interests allowed it to completely play its course as a warning to future Presidents of the United States not to oppose the oil interests.

The warning has been generally heeded. Not many have chosen to contend with the true rulers of the United States.

Chapter 24
World War II

It is in the Thule Society that one has to look for the real inspiration of Naziism.

The Second World War started when Adolf Hitler joined a secret society called the Thule Society in 1919. It was in this group that he found the perverted beliefs that were later to lead him in his control of the German government.

In the Thule Society: "...the sun played a prime role...as a sacred symbol of the Aryans, in contrast to...the moon, revered by the Semitic peoples. The Fuhrer saw in the Jewish people, with their black hair and swarthy complexions, the dark side of the human species, whilst the blond and blue-eyed Aryans constituted the light side of humanity. ...Hitler undertook to extirpate from the material world its impure elements."[1]

In addition to sun (or light) worship, the Thule Society also practiced Satan worship: "The inner core within the Thule Society were all Satanists who practiced Black Magic."[2]

The Society was not a working-man's group as it included amongst its members: "judges, police-chiefs, barristers, lawyers, university professors and lecturers, aristocratic families, leading industrialists, surgeons, physicians, scientists, as well as a host of rich and influential bourgeois . . . ."[3]

The membership of the Thule Society also became the foundation of the Nazi Party: ". . . the Committee and the forty original members of the New German Workers' Party were all drawn from the most powerful occult society in Germany—the Thule Society."[4]

One of the founders of both groups, the Nazi Party and the Thule Society, was Dietrich Eckart: "a dedicated Satanist, the supreme adept of the arts and rituals of Black Magic and the central figure in a powerful and wide-spread circle of occultists—the Thule Group. [He was] one of the seven founder members of the Nazi Party . . . ."

Eckart claimed to be the initiator of Hitler into the secrets of Satan worship. He is quoted as saying on his deathbed: "Follow Hitler. He will dance, but it is I who have called the tune! I have initiated him into the 'Secret Doctrine;' opened his centres in vision and given him the means to communicate with the Powers. Do not mourn for me: I shall have influenced history more than any German."

But it was not just the Thule Society that gave Hitler the support he needed to become the leader of the German government. There were additional sources of Hitler's strength. One who offered an explanation of Hitler's easy rise to power was Walter Langer, a noted psychoanalyst. Langer wrote in his book *The Mind of Adolf Hitler* that it was his theory that Hitler was himself one-quarter Jewish and the grandson of a Rothschild. He wrote:

> There is a great deal of confusion in studying Hitler's family tree.
>
> Adolf's father, Alois Hitler, was the illegitimate son of Maria Anna Schicklgruber. It was generally supposed that the father of Alois Hitler was Johann Georg Hiedler . . . .
>
> Alois, however, was not legitimized, and he bore his mother's name until he was forty years of age when he changed it to Hitler.
>
> A peculiar series of events, prior to Hitler's birth, furnishes plenty of food for speculation.
>
> There are some people who seriously doubt that Johann Georg Hiedler was the father of Alois. Thyssen and Koehler, for example, claim that Chancellor Dolfuss (the Chancellor of Austria) had ordered the Austrian police to conduct a thorough investigation into the Hitler family. As a result of this investigation a secret document was prepared that proved Maria Anna Shicklgruber was living in Vienna at the time she conceived.
>
> At that time she was employed as a servant in the home of Baron Rothschild. As soon as the family discovered her pregnancy she was sent back to her home in Spital where Alois was born.[5]

In a postscript in Langer's book, Robert G.L. Waite adds this comment:

> But even when Langer is mistaken and his guesses prove incorrect, he is often on the right track.
>
> Consider his hint that Hitler's grandfather might have been a Jew. There is no reason to believe the unlikely story told by Langer's informant that Hitler's grandmother Maria Anna Schickelgruber, a peasant woman in her forties from the Waldvietral of rural Austria, had had an intimate liason with a Baron Rothschild in Vienna.
>
> But Hitler had worried that he might be blackmailed over a Jewish grandfather and ordered his private lawyer, Hans Frank, to investigate his paternal lineage.
>
> Frank did so and told the Fuehrer that his grandmother had become pregnant while working as a domestic servant in a Jewish household in Graz.
>
> The facts of this matter are in dispute — and a very lengthy dispute it has been.
>
> The point of overriding psychological and historical importance is not whether it is true that Hitler had a Jewish grandfather, but whether he believed that it might be true.
>
> He did so believe and the fact shaped both his personality and his public policy.[6]

It is possible that Hitler discovered his Jewish background and his relation to the Rothschilds, and aware of their enormous power to make or break European governments, re-established contact with the family. This would partially explain the enormous support he received from the international banking fraternity, closely entwined with the Rothschild family, as he rose to power.

One thing is certain, however. Hitler started World War II by moving into Austria first. It has been theorized that he moved into this country for two reasons. First, he wanted to silence Dolfuss who Hitler believed knew that he was a descendant of the Rothschilds, and secondly, he wished to remove all traces of his ancestry from the Austrian records.

But the major source of Hitler's power came from a chemical cartel called I.G. Farben, (the name is an abbreviation of the complete name: Interssen Gemeinschaft Farben.) The importance of I.G. Farben's support for the Socialist movement was pointed out in a book about the cartel, in which it is stated: "without I.G.'s immense production facilities, its far reaching research, varied technical experience and overall concentration of economic power, Germany would not have been in a position to start its aggressive war in September, 1939."[7]

But I.G. Farben had a little-known source of its enormous economic power: Wall Street, U.S.A. "Without the capital supplied by Wall Street, there would have been no I.G. Farben in the first place, and almost certainly no Adolf Hitler and World War II."[8]

I.G. Farben had its beginning in 1924 when American banker Charles Dawes arranged a series of foreign loans totalling $800 million to consolidate gigantic chemical and steel combinations into cartels, one of which was I.G. Farben. Professor Carroll Quigley terms the Dawes Plan: "largely a J.P. Morgan production."[9]

Three Wall Street houses, Dillon, Read & Co.; Harris, Forbes & Co.; and National City handled three-quarters of the loans used to create these cartels.[10]

The importance of I.G. Farben to the plans of the German Nazi Party can be illustrated by a product that an I.G. dominated company manufactured. It was called Zyklon B, the lethal gas utilized by the exterminators at Auschwitz, Bitterfeld, Walfen, Hoechst, Agfa, Ludwigshafen, and Buchenwald. (I.G. Farben, being a chemical company even before it was merged with other chemical companies to form the cartel, was also the producer of the chlorine gas used during World War I.) American support for I.G. Farben continued as Henry Ford merged his German assets with those of I.G. in 1928.[11]

But the real importance of I.G. to the war efforts of Adolf Hitler came in the utilization of the process known as hydrogenation, the production of gasoline from coal, created by the I.G. Farben chemical cartel. Germany had no native gasoline production capabilities, and this was one of the main reasons it lost World War I. A German scientist discovered the process of converting coal (Germany was the possessor of large quantities of coal) into gasoline in 1909, but the technology was not completely developed during the war. In August, 1927, Standard Oil agreed to embark on a cooperative program of research and development of the hydrogenation process to refine the oil necessary for Germany to prepare for World War II.[12]

And finally, on November 9, 1929, these two giant companies signed a cartel agreement that had two objectives:

> First, the cartel agreement granted Standard Oil one-half of all rights to the hydrogenation process in all countries of the world except Germany; and
>
> Secondly, the two agreed: "... never to compete with each other in the fields of chemistry and petroleum products. In the future, if Standard Oil wished to enter the broad field of industrial chemicals or drugs, it would do so only as a partner of Farben.
>
> Farben, in turn, agreed never to enter the field of petroleum except as a joint venture with Standard."[13]

In the words of a Standard Oil official: "The I.G. are going to stay out of the oil business — and we are going to stay out of the chemical business."[14]

This cartel agreement was extremely important to the war effort, because, by the end of the war, Germany was producing about seventy-five percent of its fuel synthetically.[15]

But even more significant was the fact that these plants were not the subject of Allied bombing raids, so that, by the war's end, twenty-five to thirty of its refineries were still operating with only about fifteen percent damage.[16]

Standard Oil got into the refining business as well. In fact, William Dodd, the U.S. Ambassador in Germany, wrote the following in his diary about the pre-war years around 1936: "The Standard Oil Company of New York, the parent company of the Vacuum (Oil Company,) has spent 10,000,000 marks in Germany trying to find oil resources and (in) building a great refinery near the Hamburg harbor."[17]

Meanwhile, back in the United States, preparations were being made to elect a President. In 1932, President Herbert Hoover, a member of the CFR, was seeking re-election, He was approached by "Henry Harriman, President of that body (the United States Chamber of Commerce who) urged that I agree to support these proposals (the National Industry Recovery Act, the NRA, amongst others,) informing me that Mr. Roosevelt had agreed to do so. I tried to show him that this stuff was pure fascism; that it was merely a remaking of Mussolini's 'corporate state' and refused to agree to any of it. He informed me that in view of my attitude, the business world would support Roosevelt with money and influence."[18]

Hoover, later in 1940, indirectly explained why he refused the support of the American business community. He saw inherent problems with government control of the business world:

> In every single case before the rise of totalitarian governments there had been a period dominated by economic planners.
>
> Each of these nations had an era under starry-eyed men who believed that they could plan and force the economic life of the people.
>
> They believed that was the way to correct abuse or to meet emergencies in systems of free enterprise.
>
> They exalted the state as the solver of all economic problems. These men thought they were liberals. But they also thought they could have economic dictatorship by bureaucracy and at the same time preserve free speech, orderly justice, and free government.
>
> They might be called the totalitarian liberals.
>
> Directly or indirectly they politically controlled credit, prices, production of industry, farmer and laborer.
>
> They devalued, pump-primed, and deflated. They controlled

private business by government competition, by regulation and by taxes. They met every failure with demands for more and more power and control....

Then came chronic unemployment and frantic government spending in an effort to support the unemployed.

Government debts mounted and finally government credit was undermined.

And then came the complete takeover, whether it was called Fascism, Socialism, or Communism.

Yet, even with Hoover's refusal to support the goals of "big business," Roosevelt's presidential campaign of 1932 consistently attacked President Hoover for his alleged association with the international bankers and for pandering to the demands of big business. The pervasive historical image of FDR is one of a president fighting on behalf of "the little guy," the man in the street, in the midst of unemployment and financial depression brought about by "big business" speculators allied with Wall Street. "Roosevelt was a creation of Wall Street [and] an integral part of the New York banking fraternity...."[19]

The 1932 presidential campaign strategy was very simple: "big business" wanted Roosevelt, but ran him as an "anti-big business" candidate.

Hoover was "anti-big business," but the media convinced the American people that he was "pro-big business."

The result was predictable. Roosevelt defeated the incumbent Hoover. He could now start his move, what he called the "New Deal," towards a Fascist state. One observer, Whitaker Chambers, the American Communist Party member who defected, commented thus about the "New Deal:" "(It) was a genuine revolution, whose deepest purpose was not simply reform within existing traditions but a basic change in the social, and above all, the power relationship within the nation."[20]

It was about this time that an incredible scheme concerning the presidency of the United States started taking shape. From July, 1932 through November, 1933, a well known and popular military general, Major General Smedley Butler of the U.S. Marine Corps "...was sought by wealthy plotters in the United States to lead a putsch (revolution) to overthrow the government and establish an American Fascist dictatorship."[21]

Butler was tempted into the plot by "...the biggest bribe ever offered to any American — the opportunity to become the first dictator of the United States." He was approached by three gentlemen: Grayson Mallet-Provost Murphy, a director of Guaranty Trust, a J.P. Morgan Bank; Robert S. Clark, a banker who had inherited a large fortune from a founder of the Singer Sewing Machine Company; and John W. Davis, the 1924 Democratic candidate for President and the chief attorney for J.P. Morgan and Company. Their plan was to ". . . seize the White House with a private army [of 500,000 veterans], hold Franklin Roosevelt prisoner, and get rid of him if he refused to serve as their puppet in a dictatorship they planned to impose and control."[22]

The plotters revealed to Butler that they had "$3 million in working funds and could get $300 million if it were needed."[23]

Why the plotters selected General Butler is a mystery, as Butler truly understood his role as a general in the Marine Corps. He was on record as saying: "War was largely a matter of money. Bankers lend money to foreign countries and when they cannot repay, the President sends Marines to get it."

Butler didn't say it, but his role in the military was exactly in accordance with the "Balance of Power" political game described in a previous chapter. He continued: "I know — I've been in eleven of these expeditions."[24]

Butler's assertions that the military actually acted as a collection agency for the big bankers was confirmed in 1934 by the Senate Munitions Investigating Committee which "confirmed his (Butler's) suspicions that big business — Standard Oil, United Fruit, the sugar trust, the big banks — had been behind most of the military interventions he had been ordered to lead."[25]

In addition, Congress created the McCormack-Dickstein Committee to investigate Butler's charges. The conclusions of this group confirmed General Butler's charges: "(it) found five significant facts that lent validity to Butler's testimony."[26]

Jules Archer, the author of the book on Butler's charges, entitled *The Plot to Seize the White House*, interviewed John J. McCormack, the co-chairman of the Committee and asked for his views on the plot:

> Archer: Then in your opinion, America could definitely have been a Fascist power had it not been for General Butler's patriotism in exploding the plot?
>
> McCormack: It certainly could have. The people were in a very confused state of mind, making the nation weak and ripe for some drastic kind of extremist reaction. Mass frustration could bring about anything.[27]

There are those, however, who believe that the intent of the plotters was not the imposition of Butler as the leader of the government, but was actually to use the incident as a means by which Roosevelt could impose a dictatorship down upon the American people after Butler led his army upon the White House. This action, after Roosevelt termed it to be a "national emergency," could have enabled him to take complete control of the government in the emergency, and the American people would probably have cheered the action. So Butler was, according to this theory, only the excuse to take complete control of the machinery of the government, and was never intended to be the new dictator.

The plan failed, after Butler revealed the existence of the plot, and Roosevelt had to be content, if the theory is correct, with just being the President and not the dictator of the United States. Roosevelt had other plans for a fascist United States, however. Frances Perkins, Roosevelt's Labor Secretary, reports that "At the first meeting of the cabinet after the President took office in 1933, the financier and advisor to Roosevelt, Bernard Baruch, and Baruch's friend, General Hugh Johnson, who was to become the head of the National Recovery Administration, came in with a copy of a book by Gentile, the Italian Fascist theoretician, for each member of the Cabinet, and we all read it with care."[28]

So the plan was to move the American government into the area of Fascism or government control of the factors of production without a Butler-led revolution. It was decided that one of the main methods of achieving this goal was through a war, and the plans for a war involving the United States were being laid.

One of the sources for confirming the fact that these plans were underway is Jim Farley, Roosevelt's Postmaster General and a member of Roosevelt's Cabinet. Mr. Farley wrote that at the second cabinet meeting in 1933: "The new President again turned to the possibility of war with Japan."[29]

It is possible that President Roosevelt knew that war with Japan had been planned even before 1933. According to one historian, Charles C. Tansill, professor of diplomatic history at Georgetown University, war with Japan was planned as early as 1915.

In a book entitled *Pearl Harbor, Roosevelt and the Coming of the War*, published by D.C. Heath and Company, Professor Tansill makes this interesting observation:

> The policy of pressure upon Japan antedated [President Roosevelt's Secretary of War Henry] Stimson some two decades... .
>
> Under Woodrow Wilson, a three-pronged offensive was launched against Nippon [Japan]. . . .
>
> In January, 1915, the American minister at Peking... sent to the Department of State a series of dispatches so critical in tone that they helped to create in American minds a fixation of Japanese wickedness that made eventual war with Japan a probability.

It will be recalled that Franklin Roosevelt had been appointed Wilson's Assistant Secretary of the Navy, so it is both conceivable and probable that he knew about these dispatches and the plans to involve us in a future war with

Japan as early as 1915.

If the professor is correct, it was not Roosevelt's purpose to bring President Wilson's plans into fruition. All that was needed was an act that could be utilized as the reason for a declaration of war against Japan.

That reason was an attack at Pearl Harbor.

In fact, the American government knew that they were vulnerable at Pearl Harbor, the site of Japan's "surprise" attack to start World War II. It was at Pearl Harbor in 1932 that the United States Navy conducted maneuvers to test the chances of success of an attack from the sea. They discovered that Pearl Harbor was vulnerable from as close as sixty miles off the shore. That meant that Japan could attack from sixty miles away from Pearl Harbor and be undetected. The American Navy had proved it.[30]

Not only was the government concerning itself with a possible war with Japan, but it was also aware that American capitalists were creating a war machine in Germany in the early 1930's, years before Germany started their involvement in World War II.

William Dodd, the U.S. Ambassador in Germany, wrote Roosevelt from Berlin:

> At the present moment, more than a hundred American corporations have subsidiaries here or cooperative understandings.
>
> The DuPonts have their allies in Germany that are aiding in the armament business. Their chief ally is the I.G. Farben Company, a part of the government which gives 200,000 marks a year to one propaganda organization operating on American opinion.
>
> Standard Oil Company . . . sent $2,000,000 here in December, 1933 and has made $500,000 a year helping Germans make ersatz [a substitute] gas [the hydrogenation process of converting coal to gasoline] for war purposes; but Standard Oil cannot take any of its earnings out of the country except in goods.
>
> The International Harvester Company president told me their business here rose 33% year [arms manufacture, I believe], but they could take nothing out.
>
> Even our airplanes people have secret arrangements with Krupps.
>
> General Motors Company and Ford do enormous business here through their subsidiaries and take no profits out.[31]

In addition to these American companies, others were assisting the Germans in creating the materials they needed to wage war. For instance, International Telephone and Telegraph (I.T.T.) purchased a substantial interest in Focke-Wolfe, an airplane manufacturer which meant "that I.T.T. was producing German planes [fighter aircraft] used to kill Americans."[32]

I.G. Farben's assets in America were controlled by a holding company called American I.G. Farben. The following individuals, among others, were members of the Board of Directors of this corporation: Edsel Ford, President of the Ford Motor Co.; Charles E. Mitchell, President of Rockefeller's National City Bank of New York; Walter Teagle, President of Standard Oil of New York; Paul Warburg, Chairman of the Federal Reserve, and the brother of Max Warburg, the financier of Germany's war effort, and Herman Metz, a director of the Bank of Manhattan, controlled by the Warburgs.

It is an interesting and revealing fact of history that three other members of the Board of Governors of the American I.G. were tried and convicted as German "war criminals" for their crimes "against humanity," during World War II, while serving on the Board of Governors of I.G. Farben. None of the Americans who sat on the same board with those convicted were ever tried as "war criminals" even though they participated in the same decisions as the Germans.[33] It appears that it is important whether your nation wins or loses the war as to whether or not you are tried as a "war criminal."

It was in 1939, during the year that Germany started the war with its invasions of Austria and Poland, that Standard Oil of New Jersey loaned I.G. Farben $20,000,000 of high-grade aviation gasoline.

The two largest German tank manufacturers were Opel, a wholly owned subsidiary of General Motors and controlled by the J.P. Morgan firm, and the the Ford subsidiary of the Ford Motor Company.[34]

In addition, Alcoa and Dow Chemical transferred technology to the Germans, as did Bendix Aviation, in which the J.P. Morgan-controlled General Motors had a major stock interest, which supplied data on automatic pilots, aircraft instruments and aircraft and diesel engine starters. (35)

In addition to direct material support, other "capitalistic" companies supplied support: "In 1939 the German electrical equipment industry was concentrated into a few major corporations linked in an international cartel and by stock ownership to two major U.S. corporations (International General Electric and International Telephone and Telegraph.)"[36]

Further support for the American owned or controlled corporations came during the war itself, when their industrial complexes, their buildings and related structures, were not subject to Allied bombing raids: "This industrial complex (International General Electric and International Telephone and Telegraph) was never a prime target for bombing in World War II. The electrical equipment plants bombed as targets were not affiliated with U.S. firms."[37]

Another example of a German General Electric plant not bombed was the plant at Koppelsdorf, Germany, producing radar sets and bombing antennae.[38]

Perhaps the reason certain plants were bombed and others weren't lies in the fact that, under the U.S. Constitution, the President is the Commander-in-Chief of all armed forces, and therefore the determiner of what targets are bombed.

The significance of America's material support to the German government's war efforts comes when the question as to what the probable outcome of Germany's efforts would be: "... not only was an influential sector of American business aware of the nature of Nazism, but for its own purposes aided Nazism wherever possible (and profitable) with full knowledge that the probable outcome would be war involving Europe and the United States."[39]

Even Hitler's ideas about exterminating the Jews were known to any observer who cared to do a little research. Hitler himself had written: "I have the right to exterminate millions of individuals of inferior races, which multiply like vermin."

In addition, Hitler made his desires known as early as 1923 when he detailed his plans for the Jews in his book *Mein Kampf*. Even the SS Newspaper, the *Black Corps* called for: "The extermination with fire and sword, the actual and final end of Jewry."[40]

This material support continued even after the war officially started. For instance, even after Germany invaded Austria in March, 1938, the Ethyl Gasoline Corporation, fifty percent owned by General Motors and fifty percent by Standard Oil, was asked by I.G. Farben to build tetra-ethyl plants in Germany, with the full support of the U.S. Department of War which expressed no objection to the transactions.[41]

And in August, 1938, I.G. Farben "borrowed" 500 tons of tetra-ethyl lead, the gas additive, from Standard Oil.

Later, after the invasion of Austria, and prior to the German invasion of Poland in 1939, Germany and Russia signed a pact on August 23, 1939, with a secret clause for the division of Poland by these two war-time allies.

All of the material support and all of the secret agreements came to a head on September 1, 1939, when Germany invaded Poland in accordance with the terms of the pact signed with Russia.

The Second World War had begun.

The date of September 1, 1939, when Germany invaded Poland, is remembered as the date the war started. But little is remembered about the date Russia also moved into Poland, on September 16, 1939. The nation of Poland was now divided between these two war-time allies.

It is interesting to notice what the responses of the major allied nations were to these two dates. When Germany entered the western portion of Poland, Britain and France declared war on Germany. But when Russia moved into eastern Poland, there was no war declaration by either nation.

The Soviets caused one of the tragic events of history after they occupied their portion of Poland. They captured approximately 10,000 Polish officers and brutally murdered them, most of them meeting their death in Katyn Forest near the Russian town of Smolensk. The traditional story about their deaths was that the officers had been killed by the German army, but now the evidence is clear that the Russians committed this crime. The other victims were taken aboard a barge which was towed out to sea and then sunk.

Even with all of these efforts of the American businessman to construct the German war machine with the full knowledge and approval of President Roosevelt, he kept repeating that the nation would continue its "neutral" position: it would remain out of the war. On September 1, 1939, when the war started, he was asked by a reporter whether America would stay our of the war and Roosevelt replied: ". . . I believe we can, and every effort will be made by the Administration to do so."[42]

Roosevelt responded by appointing George Marshall, a CFR member, as Chief of Staff of the Army over General Douglas MacArthur, not a member of the CFR, and other senior officers.

Others did not believe Roosevelt's claim that America would remain neutral. On September 12, 1939, Hans Thomsen, the German charge d' affaires in Washington, cabled the German government: ". . . if defeat should threaten the Allies (England and France), Roosevelt is determined to go to war against Germany, even in the face of the resistance of his own country."[43]

But Germany's war efforts were still dependent on oil resources, and it came from a variety of sources, some external to the German border. Before Rumania was invaded by the Germans, it was selling oil to Germany. *Life* magazine of February 19, 1940, has a picture of Rumanian oil being loaded into oil tank cars. The picture has a caption under it which reads, in part: "Oil for Germany moves in these tank cars of American Essolube and British Shell out of Creditul Minier yards near Ploesti (Rumanina.) Notice that cars are marked for German-American Oil Co. and German Railways, consigned to Hamburg and Wuppertal in Germany. They were sent from Germany to speed up Rumanian oil shipments."[44] This picture was taken after Germany had invaded Austria and Poland, yet American and British oil companies are transporting oil for the German government, (the tank cars in the picture are clearly marked "Essolube," and "Shell").

And other sources supplied oil as well: ". . . when the German air force ran short of fuel, this was generously supplied from the great refinery belonging to the Standard Oil Company situated on the island of Aruba via Spanish tankers."[45] This occurred during the war itself, yet these tankers were not sunk by American submarines.[46]

Even with the purchases of oil from non-German sources, the major supplier of oil was still the cartel: "The I.G. Farben-Standard Oil cooperation for production of synthetic oil from coal gave the I.G. Farben cartel a monopoly of German gasoline production during World War II. Just under one half of German high octane gasoline in 1945 was produced directly by I.G. Farben, and most of the balance by its affiliated companies."[47]

But as the war in Europe continued, America's leaders were attempting to get America involved, even though the American people didn't want to become part of it. Roosevelt, the presidential candidate, was promising the American people that the Roosevelt administration would remain neutral should he be re-elected. Others knew better. One, for instance, was General Hugh Johnson, who said: "I know of no well informed Washington observer who isn't convinced that, if Mr. Roosevelt is elected (in 1940), he will drag us into war at the first opportunity, and that, if none presents itself, he will make one."[48]

Roosevelt had two opportunities to involve America in World War II: Japan was at war with China, and Germany was at war with England, France and other countries. Both war zones presented plenty of opportunities to involve the American government in the war, and Roosevelt was quick to seize upon the opportunities presented.

His first opportunity came from the war in the Pacific. It was in August, 1940, that the United States broke the Japanese "purple" war-time code. This gave the American government the ability to read and understand all of their recoverable war-time messages. Machines were manufactured to de-code Japan's messages, and they were sent all over the world, but none was sent to Pearl Harbor.

Roosevelt's public efforts to involve America, while ostensibly remaining neutral, started in August, 1940, when the National Guard was voted into Federal service for one year. This was followed in September by the Selective Service Act, also for one year's duration.

But the key to America's early involvement occurred on September 28, 1940, when Japan, Germany and Italy signed the Tripartite Treaty. This treaty required that any of the three nations had to respond by declaring war should any one of the other three be attacked by any of the Allied nations. This meant that should Japan attack the United States, and the United States responded by declaring war against Japan, it would automatically be at war with the other two nations, Germany and Italy.

Roosevelt now knew that war with Japan meant war with Germany. His problem was solved.

He had made secret commitments to Winston Churchill and the English government to become involved in the war against Germany and he knew ". . . that the only way he could fulfill his secret commitments to Churchill to get us into the war, without openly dishonoring his pledges to the American people to keep us out, was by provoking Germany or Japan to attack."[49]

Roosevelt moved towards the Pacific theater first, knowing that, if he could provoke Japan to attack America first, America would automatically be at war with Germany as well. He also knew that, should Germany attack America, Japan would have to declare war on America. So Roosevelt attempted to get either nation to attack the United States first. Japan was to get the first opportunity.

In October, 1940, Secretary of the Navy Frank Knox sent for Admiral J.O. Richardson, Commander-in-Chief of the American fleet in the Pacific. Knox advised him that "the President wanted him to establish a patrol of the Pacific—a wall of American naval vessels stretched across the western Pacific in such a way as to make it impossible for Japan to reach any of her sources of supply; a blockade of Japan to prevent by force her use of any part of the Pacific Ocean. Richardson protested vigorously. He said that would be an act of war, and besides, we would lose our navy. Of course Roosevelt had to abandon it."[50]

This scene in history poses two rather interesting questions:

1.   Why did Roosevelt, the Commander-in-Chief of all armed forces, including the Navy, not directly order Admiral Richardson to do as he wished? Why did he choose to use his Secretary of the Navy to almost politely ask him to create the naval patrol?

Is it possible that Roosevelt did not choose to use his supreme power because he knew that this was indeed an act of war and that he did not want to be identified as the originator of the plan. If Richardson had agreed to Knox's proposal, and Japan had attacked an American naval vessel, Roosevelt could have directly blamed the admiral for allowing the vessel to get into the position of being fired upon by the Japanese Navy in the first place.

Roosevelt wanted a scape-goat and Richardson refused.

2.   Why did Roosevelt not replace the admiral with someone who would do exactly as he wished?

It is possible that Roosevelt realized that Richardson now knew about the plan, and since he did not approve, he would be in a position to clearly identify Roosevelt as the source of the idea should the second admiral agree to it.

Roosevelt did not want to jeopardize his carefully constructed image as a "dove" in the question of whether or not America should become involved in the war.

It is important to remember that, in November, 1940, just after this incident, candidate Roosevelt told the American people: "I say to you fathers and mothers, and I will say it again and again and again, your boys will not be sent into foreign wars."

Richardson later appraised his situation at Pearl Harbor and felt that his position was extremely precarious. He visited Roosevelt twice during 1940 to recommend that the fleet be withdrawn to the west coast of America, because:

1.   His ships were inadequately manned for war;
2.   The Hawaiian area was too exposed for Fleet training; and
3.   The Fleet defenses against both air and submarine attacks were far below the required standards of strength.[51]

That meant that the American government had done nothing to shore up the defenses of Pearl Harbor against an offshore attack since the naval manuevers of 1932 discovered just how vulnerable the island was.

Richardson's reluctance to provide Roosevelt's incident for the United States to enter the war, and his concern about the status of the Fleet, led to his being unexpectedly relieved of the Fleet command in January, 1941.

The American Ambassador to Tokyo, Joseph C. Grew, was one of the first to officially discover that Pearl Harbor was the intended target of the Japanese attack, as he corresponded with President Roosevelt's State Department on January 27, 1941: "The Peruvian minister has informed a member of my staff that he had heard from many sources, including a Japanese source, that, in the event of trouble breaking out between the United States and Japan, the Japanese intended to make a surprise attack against Pearl Harbor . . . ."[52]

In March 1941, President Roosevelt was still hoping for an incident involving the United States and Germany, according to Harold Ickes, Roosevelt's Secretary of the Interior. He reported: "At dinner on March 24, he [Roosevelt] remarked that 'things are coming to a head; Germany will be making a blunder soon.' There could be no doubt of the President's scarcely concealed desire that there might be an incident which would justify our declaring a state of war against Germany . . . ."[53]

Roosevelt and Churchill had conspired together to incite an incident to allow America's entry into the war. According to Churchill:

> The President had said that he would wage war but not declare it, and that he would become more and more provocative. If the Germans did not like it, they could attack American forces.
>
> The United States Navy was taking over the convoy route to Iceland.
>
> The President's orders to these escorts were to attack any U-boat which showed itself, even if it were two or three hundred miles away from the convoy . . . .
>
> Everything was to be done to force "an incident."
>
> Hitler would be faced with the dilemma of either attacking the convoys and clashing with the United States Navy or holding off,

thus "giving us victory in the Battle of the Atlantic. It might suit us in six or eight weeks to provoke Hitler by taunting him with this difficult choice."[54]

But Hitler was attempting to avoid a confrontation with the United States. "He had told his naval commanders at the end of July [1941] to avoid incidents with the United States while the Eastern compaign [the war against Russia] is still in progress . . . . A month later these orders were still in force."[55]

Churchill even wrote to Roosevelt after the German ship the *Bismarck* sank the British ship the *Hood*, recommending in April, 1941: ". . . that an American warship should find the *Prinz Eugen* (the escort to the *Bismarck*) then draw her fire, 'thus providing the incident for which the United States would be so thankful,' i.e., bring her into the war."[56]

Hitler was not as wise in other matters. He attacked his "ally" Russia on June 22, 1941, even though Germany and Russia had signed a treaty not to declare war on each other.

With this action, the pressure to get the United States involved in the war really accelerated. Roosevelt, on June 24, 1941, told the American people: "Of course we are going to give all the aid that we possibly can to Russia."[57]

And an American program of Lend-Lease began, supplying Russia enormous quantities of war materials, all on credit.

So with Hitler pre-occupied with the war against Russia and refusing to involve himself with the Americans on the open sea, Roosevelt had to turn his attentions back to Japan for the incident he needed.

The next step was to assist other countries, the English and the Dutch, to embargo oil shipments to Japan in an attempt to force them into an incident that would enable the United States to enter the war.

Japan, as a relatively small island, and with no oil industry to speak of, had to look elsewhere for its oil, and this was the reason for the proposed embargo. It was thought that this action would provoke Japan into an incident. Ex-President Herbert Hoover also saw the manipulations leading to war and he warned the United States in August, 1941: "The American people should insistently demand that Congress put a stop to step-by-step projection of the United States into undeclared war . . . ."[58]

But the Congress wasn't listening.

President Roosevelt wasn't listening either to the charges of Congressman Martin Dies, Chairman of the House Committee on Un-American Activities. By August of 1941, "The Dies committee had assembled a large amount of evidence which more than confirmed the suspicions which we had entertained on the basis of surface appearances: It was clear that the Japanese were preparing to invade Pearl Harbor and that they were in possession of vital military information."[59]

This information was made available to the Roosevelt administration by Congressman Dies personally. But this was the second time that Dies had appealed to Roosevelt about his knowledge of Japan's intention to attack Pearl Harbor: "Early in 1941 the Dies Committee came into possession of a strategic map which gave clear proof of the intentions of the Japanese to make an assualt on Pearl Harbor. The strategic map was prepared by the Japanese Imperial Military Intelligence Department."

Dies telephoned Secretary of State Cordell Hull who talked to President Roosevelt.[60]

Congressman Dies was told not to release the document to the public, and the Roosevelt administration did nothing.

(In April, 1964, when Dies told the American public of these revelations, he added this comment: "If anyone questions the veracity and accuracy of these statements, I will be glad to furnish him with conclusive proof.")[61]

It was also in August, 1941, when the new product of the I.G. Farben cartel was tested on humans for the first time. The product was called Zyklon B and it was to be used on the Jews and others at the concentration camps.

In the Pacific Theater, Japan's war messages, being read in Washington, started asking their spy in Pearl Harbor to report ship movements, and, later, the exact nature and location of the ships in the harbor.

Japan's request for more information on what was happening at Pearl Harbor was followed on October 16, 1941, by the resignation of the Prince's cabinet in Japan. These resignations were followed by the military administration of General Tojo and his cabinet. All of this activity was recognized by the American government as a decided step toward war, but still nothing was done to alert Pearl Harbor.

It was on this day that Henry Stimson, Roosevelt's Secretary of War, wrote the following in his diary: ". . . and so we face the delicate question of the diplomatic fencing to be done so as to be sure that Japan be put into the wrong and to make the first bad move — overt move."[62]

Stimson was to repeat this concern that faced the Roosevelt administration when he testified before one of the Committees investigating Pearl Harbor. There he was quoted as saying: "The question was how we should maneuver them [the Japanese] into the position of firing the first shot without allowing too much danger to ourselves."[63]

The Japanese would still not respond with the incident to provoke the United States into retaliating, but America was convinced that it would happen ultimately. For instance, Secretary of State Cordell Hull told Roosevelt on Novbember 7, 1941, that he foresaw "every possibility of an early war with Japan."

Japan continued its efforts towards staying out of a war with the United States and had its Ambassador in Washington continue his efforts towards securing a no-war treaty with the Secretary of State. On November 22, 1941, they wired their Ambassador: "Do your best, spare no efforts and try to bring about the solution we desire."

But even though Japan was attempting to avoid war with the United States, the Japanese were being encouraged by an unlikely source to strike out at the United States. "On May 17, 1951, the New York *Daily News* featured an article by its Washington correspondent, John O'Donnell, concerning various old Far Eastern intelligence reports which were being closely guarded in Washington. Among those documents were the 32,000 word confession of Soviet spy Richard Sorge."

Mr. Sorge was a Russian spy who had infiltrated the German embassy in Japan and worked hard to convince Japanese officials that Japan should not attack Russia, but move south, at the risk of war with the United States. "When [Sorge] informed the Kremlin [in Russia] in October, 1941, that the Japanese intended to attack Pearl Harbor within 60 days, . . . he . . . received thanks for his report and the notice that Washington — Roosevelt, Marshall, Admiral Stark, et al. — had been advised of the Japanese intentions."[64]

On November 25, 1941, the day that the Japanese fleet sailed for Pearl Harbor, President Roosevelt convened a meeting of the various Cabinet officers: Secretaries Stimson, Knox, Marshall and Admiral Harold R. Stark, Chief of Naval Operations. According to Stimson's testimony: "The President brought up the event that we were likely to be attacked perhaps [as soon as] next Monday, for the Japanese are notorious for making an attack without warning."[65] "In spite of the risk involved, however, in letting the Japanese fire the first shot, we realized that in order to have the full support of the American people, it was desirable to make sure that the Japanese be the ones to do this so that there should remain no doubt in anyone's mind as to who were the aggressors."[66]

On November 26, 1941, the Japanese Embassy in Washington sent the following message to Tokyo: "Hull said . . . I am sorry to tell you that we cannot agree to it [Japan's treaty Proposal]."[67]

The British Intelligence Service, which had men inside the Japanese diplomatic agencies in the United States, took the November 26th telegram to Tokyo as meaning that the "Japanese negotiations off. Services expect action within two weeks."[68]

And Roosevelt and the Department of the Army also knew this, as " . . . a very important American Army Intelligence officer, in service in the Far East during 1941 . . . had gained knowledge of the Yamamoto plan to send a task force to attack Pearl Harbor and sent three separate messages to Washington revealing this information, and at least two of these reached the Army files well before the attack on Pearl Harbor."[69]

Finally, in desperation, the Japanese government sent a message to their

Washington embassy on December 6, 1941, in essence breaking off all negotiations with the American government. After the message was intercepted by the American government, de-coded and given to Roosevelt, he is quoted as saying: "This means war."[70]

Roosevelt now knew that Japan planned on attacking the United States, but still he did nothing about warning the American forces at Pearl Harbor.

And on December 7, 1941, Japan launched a "surprise attack."

The American forces were not prepared for the attack. And the attacking Japanese forces had orders from Japan to return to Japan should they detect any evidence that the Americans had been alerted.

As their air force attacked Pearl Harbor, they reported that the American planes were having difficulty in getting off the ground.

This was because the American planes had been grouped in circles, with their propellors all facing inward as the result of an order by President Roosevelt. It was reported that Roosevelt had ordered the planes grouped in this fashion because he feared "acts of sabotage" against the planes and he was acting to protect them.

Since airplanes do not have a "reverse gear" the grouping of the planes in this manner made it extremely difficult for them to rapidly get out of the circle and into the air. One critic of the circling of these airplanes, Harry Elmer Barnes, has written: "Bunching the planes in a circle, wing to wing, would [make them] helpless in the event of a surprise air attack."[71]

Another strange circumstance was the make-up of the fleet anchored at Pearl Harbor at the time of the attack. The Pacific Fleet consisted of nine battleships and three aircraft carriers along with a host of smaller ships. During the attack, the Japanese sank or seriously damaged eight battleships but no aircraft carriers.

The American government had reasoned that the aircraft carriers would have an extremely important role to play in the type of war they felt would be waged in the Pacific theater. So all of the aircraft carriers were moved out of Pearl Harbor and all of the less valuable battleships were left behind. The battleships were expendable because most of them had been constructed prior to or during World War I, which meant that they were old and obsolete.

Along with the aircraft carriers, Roosevelt's government also withdrew the smaller, more mobile ships that they knew could be more efficiently utilized in a sea war. "On November 28th, Admiral William F. Halsey was sent to Wake [Island] with the carrier Enterprise, three heavy destroyers and nine destroyers. On December 5th, Admiral John E. Newton was sent to Midway with the carrier Lexington, three heavy cruisers and five destroyers. The carrier Saratoga had been sent to the Pacific Coast. . . ."[72]

Admiral Husband Kimmel, the commander of the naval forces at Pearl Harbor, clearly places the blame for Pearl Harbor's unpreparedness on

President Roosevelt. He has written: "We were unready at Pearl Harbor because President Roosevelt's plans required that no word be sent to alert the fleet in Hawaii."[73]

The Rt. Hon. Oliver Lyttleton, a member of Churchill's war cabinet, declared in an address to the American Chamber of Commerce in London on June 24, 1944: "America provoked [the Japanese] to such an extent that the Japanese were forced to attack Pearl Harbor. It is a travesty of history to say that America was forced into the war."[74]

The Council on Foreign Relations published an article in its publication called *Foreign Affairs* in January, 1974, that agreed with Lyttleton. The article stated that "Japan's attack on Pearl Harbor actually thrust the United States into World War II, but the Roosevelt administration decided a year and a half earlier to risk war in order to prevent the totalitarian domination of all Europe."[75]

So on December 8, 1941, President Roosevelt asked the Congress to declare war on Japan, stating that December 7, 1941 would go down in history as a "day of infamy."

So when Roosevelt addressed the nation through his speech inCongress, he lied when he said: "We don't like it — and we didn't want to get in it — but we are in it and we're going to fight it with everything we've got."[76]

So Roosevelt asked for, and received, a Declaration of War against Japan. Germany followed on December 11th with a Declaration of War against the United States. This action was in accordance with the terms of the Tripartite Treaty signed earlier by Germany, Italy and Japan.

Roosevelt's activities in the planning of Pearl Harbor had a costly price. The final toll was 2,341 U.S. servicemen dead and 1,143 wounded; eighteen ships including the eight battleships were sunk or heavily damaged; more than two hundred Army Air Corps and Navy planes were destroyed or unusable; and sixty-eight civilians were killed.[77]

For his supposed unpreparedness at Pearl Harbor, Admiral Kimmel was relieved of his command, and he retired on January 7, 1942.

After the war was over, Congress looked into the reasons for the lack of preparation at Pearl Harbor. Their conclusions are most revealing:

1. The attack was unprovoked by America;
2. There was no evidence that the President, Secretary of State, Secretary of War, Secretary of Navy, provoked the attack;
3. The American government made every effort to avoid the war with Japan;
4. The attack was caused by the Army's and Navy's failure to detect hostile forces; and
5. The errors made were errors of judgment and not derelictions of duty.[78]

The last conclusion was apparently intended to relieve the commanders of the armed forces from responsibility so that they could not be court-martialed. Admiral Kimmel and General Walter C. Short, the commander of the armed forces at Pearl Harbor, continuously pleaded for a court martial to clear their reputations, but they were never granted.

Admiral Robert Theobold, the Commander of all destroyers at Pearl Harbor, wrote a book entitled *The Final Secret of Pearl Harbor*, in which he detailed his conclusions about the "surprise attack." He wrote:

1. President Roosevelt forced Japan to war and enticed them to initiate hostilities by holding the Pacific fleet in Hawaiian waters as an invitation to that attack;
2. The plans to use Pearl Harbor as the bait started in June, 1940;
3. War with Japan meant war with Germany; and
4. Roosevelt, Marshall and Stark knew about Pearl Harbor 21 hours before the attack.[79]

But in spite of all of this evidence that the Japanese attack on Pearl Harbor was known by Roosevelt and his top advisors well in advance of that actual event, there are those who still hold to the position that the government, and Roosevelt specifically, knew nothing about it.

One of these skeptics is Walter Scott, who writes the question-and-answer series called "Personality Parade" in the *Parade* magazine. In answer to the question: "Is it true that Franklin D. Roosevelt knew that Japan was going to attack Pearl Harbor in World War II?" Mr. Scott answered: "Not true."[80]

So America now had a two-front war against Japan in the Pacific and against Germany in Europe.

Just as planned!

Chapter 25
Communist Betrayal

The entry of the United States into the war was now complete. After years of planning and plotting on the part of the American government, the fighting men of the American armed forces were now committed to a life and death struggle in two widely separated theaters of war.

On January 1, 1942, the twenty-five nations at war against Germany and Japan signed a "Declaration by the *United Nations*," (emphasis added) which pledged that any one nation involved would not sign a separate armistice or peace.[1]

When General Douglas MacArthur was appointed as the commander-in-chief of the armed forces in the Pacific theater, he was appointed as the "*United Nations* Commander of the South Pacific."[2] (emphasis added.)

So it was becoming apparent just what the purpose of the war was: to give the world a one-world government: a *United Nations*.

The second reason the war was being fought was for Russia to expand its imperialism into the countries of Eastern Europe. This secondary motive was made clear in June, 1942, when Churchill and Roosevelt postponed a planned 1943 invasion of Europe by the Allied armed forces for one more year until 1944. This delay had the effect of allowing Russia more time to advance from the east, thereby assuring it control of the many Eastern European countries it occupied with its armed forces as it moved westward.

In addition, this move had to be couched by the activities of the war; in other words, the Russians would be allowed to communize Eastern European countries under the disguise of the war. Because Russia was advancing easterly at a slower rate than was anticipated, the Allies had to give her more time; hence the delay in the invasion of Western Europe.

Senator Joseph McCarthy attributed this decision to Secretary of State George Marshall: "We now come to what was without question the most significant decision of the war in Europe: the decision by Marshall . . . to concentrate on France and leave the whole of Eastern Europe to the Red Armies."[3]

Another event that occurred during the war seems to indicate that this interpretation of these decisions is correct.

In the spring of 1943, Admiral Wilhelm Canaris, head of the German Secret Service, met with George Earle, the American Naval Attache in Istanbul, Turkey. Admiral Canaris came to discuss the surrender of the German armed forces. He reported that he had joined with other German leaders in an assassination plot to remove Hitler from power. After this was accomplished, they would take over the German government, and surrender to the Allies, with only one condition:

There must be no Soviet advance into Central Europe.

Mr. Earle sent President Roosevelt a note informing him of Canaris' proposal.

He received no reply.

Earle tried again, and this time he received what has been termed a "brush-off" from President Roosevelt.

So Earle flew to Washington. Roosevelt told him that his concerns were overly anxious, that Germany would soon surrender after the planned attack commenced through Western Europe.

Earle was very disappointed, and returned to Istanbul. He advised Canaris of what he had learned, and he returned to Germany, where he and the other plotters against Hitler's life were found out and either hung or shot for their efforts to shorten the war and prevent the expansion of the Russians into Eastern Europe.[4]

If Roosevelt had accepted Canaris' offer: ". . . the war might have ended in 1943. Countless lives would in all probability have been saved, and, of greatest importance, the Allies wouldn't have supplanted one dangerous ideology with another. The Soviet hordes would have been stopped at the Polish border. The entire map of Europe would have been different."[5]

Earle returned to the United States. He wrote "I decided to make known some of my views and observations about the so-called allies, the Soviets, so as to wake up the American people about what was really going on. I contacted the President about it, but he reacted strongly and specifically forbade me to make my views known to the public. Then upon my requesting active duty in the Navy, I was ordered to Samoa, in the far-distant South Pacific."[6]

In fact, Earle was warned by Roosevelt's daughter in a letter to him "... that if he carried out his outlined program of publicly criticizing and commenting on some of the Soviet moves, he could be adjudged guilty of treason."[7]

It is indeed unfortunate that the Roosevelts took this position on the "Soviet moves," the movement of Russian troops into the Eastern European countries as the war was ending, as evidenced by President Roosevelt's inaction in the Canaris case, and the letter of his daughter in the Earle case, because the citizens in these countries did not want the Russians to occupy their nations. This fact was made brutally apparent as millions of these patriots actually joined with the German armed forces in an attempt to keep the Russians from advancing into their respective countries.

So Roosevelt could have truly assisted these patriots in keeping their countries free of Communism by assisting the Canaris group, and Earle could have been of immense assistance in bringing these matters to the attention of the American people.

But it was not to be, and the Eastern European countries were occupied by the Russian Communists much to the chagrin of millions of patriots. Roosevelt continued his support of the Russian government as the war ended by guaranteeing their occupation of these nations by the agreements made at the wartime conferences with the major leaders of the Allied governments.

In February, 1945, Roosevelt met with Joseph Stalin at Yalta, one of the wartime conferences, even though he was showing signs of severe illness. There are many now who insist that Roosevelt was dying of cancer, one being his personal physician. A magazine article stated: "As early as April 1944, the White House physician, Vice Admiral Ross McIntire, began systematically lying to everyone about the President's condition, and perhaps because the war was going well the press did not seriously challenge him."[8]

In 1979, Dr. Harry S. Goldsmith, a Dartmouth Medical Surgeon and a student of Roosevelt's health history, announced that he felt Roosevelt had been secretly suffering from cancer when he died of a stroke in 1945, even though there were reports of his being well.

One author, Frazier Hunt, in his book entitled *Douglas MacArthur*, has stated that the reason Roosevelt's physicians were lying to the American people about his health was that Roosevelt had a strong reason to survive until after the war ended. That reason was that Roosevelt had been offered the presidency of the world government, the United Nations that was to be created after the war was over: "The sick and undependable Roosevelt, his already handicapped mind inflamed with grandiose ideas of a World State that he would head...."9

So when Roosevelt met Stalin at Yalta, he was providing Stalin with whatever he wanted as a gesture to the Communists that he was truly assisting their plans for the occupying of these countries. For instance, at Yalta he gave the Russians, in addition to the European countries: Port Arthur in the Yellow Sea, the port of Dairen, the Kurile Islands, Outer Mongolia, and the lower half of Sakhalin Island.

Most of these lands were previously occupied by America's other World War II ally, China.

American Ambassador William C. Bullitt, after discovering what had happened at Yalta, said this: "No more unnecessary, disgraceful and potentially disgraceful document has ever been signed by a president of the United States."10

In addition, Roosevelt also gave Russia three votes in the yet to be created General Assembly of the United Nations (one vote each for ByloRussia, the Soviet Union, and the Ukraine) even though every other nation, including the United States, has only one vote.

Roosevelt, when asked about the three votes for Russia issue, said: "I know I shouldn't have done it. But I was so tired when they got hold of me."11

But Roosevelt was not the only one providing European countries to the Russians. Winston Churchill, according to papers made public in 1973, agreed "... in 1944 to Soviet domination of Poland in exchange for Joseph Stalin's support of British interests in the Far East and the Mediterrean."12

It is strange, indeed, that Churchill, the originator of the term "Iron Curtain" to describe the wall built around Eastern Europe by the Communists, also had his share in the building of that wall. In his book *Triumph and Tragedy*, Churchill himself confirmed that he was involved with the building of that same Iron Curtain. He wrote: "I said to Stalin: "Let us settle our affairs: How will it do to have 90% predominance in Rumania, for you, for us to have 90% of the same in Greece, and 50%, about, in Yugoslavia? I wrote on a half-sheet of paper:

> Rumania: Russia 90%, others 10%
> Greece: Great Britain: 90 %, Russia 10%
> Yugoslavia: 50-50
> Hungary: 50-50
> Bulgaria: Russia 75%, others 25%

Stalin took a pencil and made a large tick upon it, and passed it to me. It was settled in no more time than it takes to set it down."

But the giving of Eastern Europe to the Russian Communists was not just the work of these two individuals. Others were involved as well. For instance, the decision to allow the Russians to reach Berlin before the Americans, thereby guaranteeing Communist control of part of this major city, was the responsibility of the Supreme Allied Commander, General Dwight David Eisenhower, according to military documents released in 1970.[13]

But the overall responsibility for the Communization of Eastern Europe rests squarely with the administration of President Roosevelt, who desired to assist them at any cost. He is quoted as saying on March 8, 1944: "I think the Russians are perfectly friendly. They aren't trying to gobble up the rest of Europe. These fears that have been expressed by a lot of people here that the Russians are going to try and dominate Europe, I personally don't think there is anything to it."[14]

And according to Ambassador Bullitt, Roosevelt told him: "I have just a hunch that Stalin...doesn't want anything but security for his country, and I think that if I give him everything I possibly can, and ask nothing in return, he won't try to annex anything and will work for a world of democracy and peace."[15]

It is not known why Roosevelt placed such misguided trust in the Russian Communist Stalin, but it is known that Roosevelt and Eisenhower approved of the forced repatriation of some six million people back to Russia, many of whom were tortured or killed after they reached their destination.

Two Russians who have written about this abominable decision of these American leaders are Nikolai Tolstoy and Alexandr Solzhenitsyn. The Americans called this repatriation "Operation Keelhaul," after the naval form of punishment or torture where the prisoner is hauled under the keel of a ship by a rope tied to the prisoner's body.

These six million individuals were not only soldiers who had fought on the side of the Germans against the Russians, but they were women and children as well.

700,000 of this total were soldiers under the command of Lt. Gen. Andrei Vlasov, a brilliant Soviet officer and one of the heroes of the battle of Moscow in 1942. In April of 1945, General Vlasov led his troops to the American lines so that they could surrender and then volunteer to return to Communist Russia and attempt to oust the Bolshevik government. They laid down their arms and considered themselves to be American Prisoners of War.

Vlasov was informed that permission to pass through the American lines had been refused, so he had to order his unarmed men to save themselves as best they could. Most of them were forcibly repatriated back to Russia and executed. General Vlasov himself was taken from an American escort by Soviet troops and spirited to Moscow where he was later executed.

The British government behaved no more honorably. Despite guarantees to the contrary, more than 30,000 Cossacks, including women and children, led by General P.N. Krasnov, were disarmed and forcibly turned over to the Russian Army. Many committed suicide rather than be repatriated back to the Communist government in Russia.

Even though it was Churchill and Roosevelt who made these incredible decisions to repatriate millions of anti-Communist Russians back to certain death, it was General Dwight Eisenhower who enforced "Operation Keelhaul," with no apparent pangs of conscience.

The morality of these decisions on the part of the leaders of the victorious Allied governments to send millions of people to certain death in Russia was brought back into the public limelight during the trial of Adolf Eichmann, a German "war criminal" who was tried for his involvements with the extermination of millions of Europeans in the concentration camps of the Nazi regime.

The Israeli court that tried Eichmann observed that: "The legal and moral responsibility of he who delivers the victim to his death is, in our opinion, no smaller, and may be greater, than the liability of he who does the victim to death."[17]

Another example of Russia's perfidy occurred during the war in July, 1944, when Polish General Bor-Komorowski had rallied an army of 250,000 Polish patriots who were waiting for the Russians to reach Warsaw so that together they could defeat the Germans. The Germans had been retreating as Russia moved west after the Battle of Stalingrad, and Russia had reached the bank of the Vistula River, the river flowing through Warsaw.

The general's army, described as the best and most effective underground resistance army in Europe, waited for word from the Russians before they started the battle against the German army.

The General's radio picked up a broadcast in Polish from Moscow signed by Molotov, a representative of the Russian government. It said: "Poles, the time of liberation is at hand. Poles, to arms! Make every Polish home a stronghold against the invader [the Germans]. There is not a moment to lose!"

The General, believing that the Russians planned on moving into Warsaw, gave the order to revolt against the Germans. "The whole affair was, of course, a typically ruthless Stalin trap. The Russians stopped advancing. Stalin refused to allow airplanes to drop supplies which the insurgents so desperately needed. . . . At the end of two months the whole Polish Home Army [under the command of the General] was completely annihilated. This of course had been the purpose of the ruse."[18]

But this was not the only example of the barbaric actions of the Russian government that was certain to reach the ear of Roosevelt.

Alexander Solshenitsyn, the Russian who defected to the West in the 1960's, was a Captain in the Russian Army during the war. He testified that, as the Russians moved into Germany: "... all of us knew very well that if the girls were German they could be raped and then shot."[19]

This raping of the German women was the result of a Russian propaganda leaflet given to the Russian soldiers during the war which read: "Kill! Nothing in Germany is guiltless, neither the living nor the yet unborn. Follow the words of Comrade Stalin and crush forever the fascist beast in its den. Break the racial pride of the German woman. Take her as your legitimate booty. Kill, you brave soldiers of the victorious Soviet Army."[20]

But the raping of the German women was not the only crime of the Russian Army. The Russians also looted and plundered: "The Russians... swept the native population clean in a manner that had no parallel since the days of the Asiatic hordes."[21]

These soldiers were under the command of President Roosevelt's "perfectly friendly" ally, Premier Joseph Stalin of Russia.

Colonel Edward Mandell House, left, was directly involved in making Woodrow Wilson and Franklin Roosevelt president of the United States. He wrote the book *Philip Dru, Administrator,* in 1912 wherein his hero, Philip Dru, gives America "Socialism as dreamed of by Karl Marx." According to author G. S. Vierek, "every word of advice that passed from him to Wilson was consistent with the ideas enumerated by Dru."

Congressman Louis T. McFadden, right, Chairman of the Banking and Currency Committee charged that the stock market crash of 1929 was the work of a grouping of international bankers. He wrote: "When the Federal Reserve Act was passed, the people of these United States did not perceive that a world system was being set up here. The depression was not accidental. It was a carefully contrived occurrence." Many believed he was assassinated by poisoning.

H. Rowan Gaither, right, President of the tax-free Ford Foundation, told the chief investigator of a Congressional Committee studying such foundations that he was using their "grant-making power so as to alter our life in the United States that we can be comfortable merged with the Soviet Union."

Zbigniew Brzezinski, President Jimmy Carter's teacher and later his National Security Advisor, wrote a book entitled *Between Two Ages*. Mr. Brzezinski wrote: " . . . Marxism represents a further vital and creative stage in the maturing of man's universal vision. Marxism is simultaneously a victory of the external, active man over the inner passive man and a victory of reason over belief."

The British liner *Lusitania* was loaded with tons of ammunition by the wealthy banker J. P. Morgan and intentionally sent into a war zone. The British and American governments were hoping that the ship would be sunk and that the American people would demand that their government enter World War I.

Norman Thomas, left, the Socialist Party's presidential candidate in every national election from 1928 through 1948, understood that "Socialism" under that name would never be accepted by the American people. He wrote: "The American people will never knowingly adopt Socialism, but under the name of Liberalism, they will adopt every fragment of the Socialist program until one day America would be a Socialist nation without knowing how it happened."

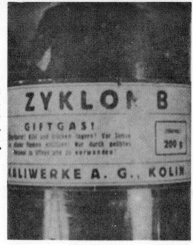

ZYKLON B, the lethal gas used in the German concentration camps during World War II. It was manufactured by I. G. Farben, a company created by American bankers prior to the war.

General Albert C. Wedemeyer felt that Russia and not America won World War II. He wrote: "Stalin emerged as the only victor of the war. The Allies insured the emergence of a more hostile, menacing predatory power than Nazi Germany, one which has enslaved more people than we liberated."

These two individuals, the Russian "Communist" **NIKITA KHRUSHCHEV**, and the American "Capitalist" **CYRUS EATON**, are supposedly mortal enemies. Yet they are smiling, because American and European "Capitalists" have been selling Russia strategic goods since about 1920. One researcher has written: "There is no such thing as Soviet technology. Almost all, perhaps 90 to 95 percent came directly or indirectly from the United States and its Allies."

James Roosevelt, right, son of the former President Franklin Roosevelt, and George Racey Jordan, below, an expediting officer for Lend-Lease supplies to Russia during World War II, have both written books alleging that President Roosevelt sent Russia the plans and materials to build an atomic bomb in 1943-1944.

Jerry Rubin, left, one of the leading revolutionaries during the
turbulent 1960's, admitted that some wealthy Americans were
controlling the anti-government movement of which he was a
part. He wrote: "The hip capitalists have some allies within the
revolutionary community; longhairs who work as intermediaries
between the kids on the street and the millionaire businessmen."
John Dewey, right, the "father of Progressive Education" and
about whom it has been said: "no individual has influenced the
thinking of American educators more," was a leading American
aetheist. He wrote, "There is no God and no soul. Hence, there
are no needs for the props of traditional religion. With dogma
and creed excluded, then immutable (unchangeable) truth is also
dead and buried. There is no room for fixed, natural law or
permanent moral absolutes."

Chapter 26
The Atomic Bomb

It was in 1945 that the war started to unwind. But the war was not to end as quickly as it could have.

The Japanese attempted to end the war on February 14, 1945, when the American government learned of their efforts to surrender through a decoded message between their government and the Russian government.[1] But the American government was not ready to accept Japan's efforts to end the war. "Marshall [George Marshall, the Army Chief of Staff] made it clear that he had little faith in the Japanese overtures for peace."[2]

These peace overtures were repeated again in June, 1945, when Russia received word that Japan was ready to end the war. These messages were once again intercepted by the American government, but nothing was done.

The reason for America's reluctance to end the war became clear on August 6, 1945, when the United States dropped the first atomic bomb on Hiroshima, Japan. The American Air Force tried to warn the people of the city that it was certain to be destroyed, as they dropped 720,000 leaflets onto the city stating that Hiroshima would be "...obliterated unless Japan surrendered at once."[3] A good many people left the city, but it was estimated that around 250,000 people remainded.

The decision to drop a second bomb was made: "No top level meeting had been convened to discuss the necessity of a second bomb, no attempt made to determine if the first bomb or Russian entry (Russia had declared war on Japan on August 8, 1945) into the conflict had quickened Japan's intent to surrender."[4]

Harry Truman, who had assumed the presidency after President Roosevelt's death on April 12, 1945, is quoted as saying, after the first bomb was dropped on Hiroshima, that: ". . . this is the greatest thing in history."[5]

There are those in high places in the American government who felt that it was not necessary to drop either bomb on Japan. One, Admiral William Leahy, was on record as saying: "I was of the firm opinion that our war against Japan had progressed to the point where her defeat was only a matter of time and attrition."[6]

There is still speculation as to why the two cities of Hiroshima and Nagasaki were selected as the targets for the two atomic bombs, since neither were military targets, in the main. One author offers an explanation: "Hiroshima and Nagasaki . . . were the chief centers in Japan of a native Christian population."[7]

There is some evidence that before the bombs were dropped on Japan, President Roosevelt had some second thoughts about the use of these enormously powerful and destructive weapons on innocent people: "The President . . . prepared a speech for delivery on Jefferson Day. Roosevelt had intended to expose openly to the world 'the danger that politicians will accept as inevitable the destruction of innocent people to achieve their goals and that scientists will concentrate on the means and ignore the ends of their research.' "[8]

In any event, before he could deliver the address, Roosevelt passed away, so the world will never know for certain just what he intended by this speech.

It is interesting to note that Japan never attacked Russia during the war. Russia was America's World War II ally and therefore a presumed enemy of Japan. Neither had Russia attacked Japan prior to the dropping of the first atomic bomb. This is strange as Russia was at war with Japan's ally Germany, and according to the terms of the Tripartite Treaty already referred to, both nations should have been at war with each other. Japan's attacking of Russia would have had dramatic results in assisting the nation of Germany, for two reasons.

1. It would have opened up a second front for Russia, which would have been forced to move troops needed in its war against Germany to the war against Japan, thereby relieving some of the pressure on Japan's ally, Germany; and

2. It possibly could have closed the Russian port of Vladivostok, where much of America's Lend-Lease war material was being

unloaded. This action would have aided Germany as it would have eliminated much of the war supplies Russia needed to conduct the war against Germany.

August 8, 1945, was the day that Russia finally decided to enter the war against Japan, and this was but six days prior to that nation's surrender. It has been theorized that the reason this occurred in this sequence was to rationalize the giving of Japanese property or interests to the Russians after the war, since they were then an official enemy of Japan.

One of the Americans who observed the strange behavior of the American government was General George S. Patton. He had seen enough to cause him to want to resign from the military so that he could "say what I want to" about America's "soft on Communism" stance during the war. Patton knew enough about the military that he couldn't merely retire and speak out, because military men of high rank, even though retired, are still under the control of the government. This subjection to government authority includes their ability to speak out on the main issues of the day. Should Patton resign, he would be free to speak as he saw fit.

Patton had a strong dislike for what happened as the Russians acquired much of Eastern Europe, and it is said by many that he was going to speak about this betrayal to the American people after the war was over.

But, before he had a chance to resign, he was killed after an automobile accident caused him to be hospitalized.

In 1979, a former undercover agent for the Office of Strategic Services, the OSS, gave an interview in which he claimed that he had been asked to kill Patton. This agent was ". . . Douglas Bazata, a veteran intelligence agent, who said he received a contract on Patton's life in 1944. According to Bazata, the order for the 'hit' came down to him from none other than the legendary Office of Strategic Services direct from [its administrator] 'Wild Bill' Donovan."[9]

When Bazata was asked why he was finally going public with this admission after so many years, he said he ". . . was in poor health and wanted the American people to know the truth."

The newspaper that carried the interview claimed that it had "a professional analyst subject Bazata's interview to the rigors of a content analysis using a Psychological Stress Evaluator (P.S.E.) His report: Bazata gives no evidence of lying."

It was Bazata's contention that, although he collected more than $10,000 for the death of Patton, he was not responsible for Patten's actual death. He claimed that he knows, however, who did kill him, and that Patton was killed by a dose of cyanide in the hospital where he was taken after the automobile accident, and that it was the cyanide rather than the accident that took his life.

About the same time as Patton's death, the Second World War wound down to a halt. But the tragic events of the war were not to come to a close as yet.

The victorious Allies had to move over sixteen million Germans from their homes in Central and Eastern Europe. The reasons for this expulsion are not presently clear, although the removal was agreed to by the Allied governments.

In October, 1944, the Soviet Army was advancing westward through the eastern nations of Europe. This westward movement "... triggered a massive flight of German civilians to the West. Four to five million persons fled.... Millions of Germans also remained.... Large German enclaves- ... remained in other areas of pre-war Poland, in Hungary, Romania, and Yugoslavia. In the last two years of the war, however, a far-reaching Allied policy had been taking form ... aimed at ... the radical removal of Germans from Eastern and Central Europe. At the conclusion of the Potsdam Conference (17 July — 2 August, 1945) a protocol was announced, Article XIII of which authorized the transfer of the Eastern Germans to what was left of the Reich (Germany)."[10]

As the Germans were being forcibly removed from their homes, "acts of incredible cruelty and sadism were committed. Helpless civilians were evicted from their homes with clubs, women were raped, men were con- scripted into slave labor, thousands were interned in camps awaiting expulsion...."[11]

After the war ended, the victorious Allies conducted War Crime trials at Nuremburg. One of those convicted of the forced deportation of Germans and others into forced labor was Albert Speer, Germany's Minister of Arms and Munitions. In his book *Inside the Third Reich,* Speer wrote: "Deporta- tion of labor is unquestionably an international crime. I do not regret my sentence, even though other nations are now doing the same thing we did."[12]

Others also saw the depravity of the deportations and attempted to bring it to the attention of the U.S. government. One of these was Robert Murphy, U.S. Political Adviser for Germany, who wrote to the U.S. State Department: "In viewing the distress, ... the mind reverts instantly to Dachau and Buchenwald. Here is retribution on a large scale ... practiced ... on women and children, the poor, the infirm."[13]

No one listened, especially the United States, and the deportations continued. The tragedy is that "over 2 million Germans did not survive their involuntary migration."[14]

The war was now over, the Germans had been removed from their new homes, and Europe could begin to rebuild from the enormous destruction. The costs of the war could now be totalled:

More than 50 million persons, 23 million of them in uniform,
the rest civilians, were killed, most of them by horrible deaths.[15]

There were no victors in World War II except the nations who now controlled the lands under dispute during the war. One American general, Albert C. Wedemeyer, correctly concluded that Russia was the only victor: "Stalin was intent on creating favorable conditions for the realization of Communist aims throughout the Balkans and Western Europe. He emerged as the only victor of the war. We [the Allies] insured the emergence of a more hostile, menacing predatory power than Nazi Germany, one which has enslaved more people than we liberated."[16]

A European who agreed with General Wedemeyer was Prince Michel Sturdza, former Foreign Minister of Rumania, who wrote the following about World War II in his book *The Suicide of Europe*: "World War II . . . was to leave only one victor . . . : International Communism as embodied in Soviet Russia."[17]

So the Second World War was over.

But, as was pointed out by General Wedemeyer, America had created a far more menacing power: Soviet Russia.

Chapter 27

The Exposers

The strange events of World War II had predictable effects among certain of the American people. Some saw them as being the machinations of those who actually wanted Russia to win the world war.

There were at least three individuals who, in positions of power and hence in a position to expose the true reasons behind these events, attempted to do so.

The first of these was Frank Murphy, a Supreme Court Justice at the time of his discovery. He had been appointed by President Roosevelt as Attorney General in 1938, and later to a vacancy on the Supreme Court.

He once had an occasion to meet with Congressman Martin Dies, the Chairman of the House Committee on Un-American Activities. Murphy told Dies: "We're doomed! The United States is doomed! The Communists have control completely. They've got control of Roosevelt and his wife as well."[1]

A few years later, in 1949, Murphy went into a Detroit hospital and died from a heart attack, just before he was scheduled to be released as recovered.

Congressman Dies was convinced that he had been murdered.

The second individual who apparently figured it out was James

Forrestal, America's first Secretary of Defense. Forrestal's credentials for this position were impressive. He became a partner and President of Dillon, Read and Company, an international banking firm, and in April, 1944, he was appointed Secretary of the Navy. This was followed on September 17, 1947, by his appointment as Secretary of Defense. He was later asked to resign by President Harry Truman, and he did so on March 2, 1949.

Forrestal had viewed the events at the ending of the World War with much dismay, as he saw the American government consistently yield to the Russians in important matters. His explanation for these events was simple: "These men are not incompetent or stupid. They are crafty and brilliant. Consistency has never been a mark of stupidity. If they were merely stupid, they would occasionally make a mistake in our favor."[2]

Such thoughts on the part of the Secretary of Defense were certain to make enemies of those who were subverting America. An author has summarized the situation:

> The Communists, both American and European, had good reason to hate Jim Forrestal: he hated them. He emerged from the Second War dedicated to the destruction of Communism.
>
> He had opposed every concession to bring Russia into the war against Japan. He fought General Marshall's effort to force Chiang Kai-shek to coalesce with the Chinese Communists. He battled those men in the State Department who tried to give the Mediterranean to Russia.[3]
>
> [He] . . . was alarmed by what he took to be Roosevelt's trust in Stalin. . . . Forrestal's nightmare was that capitalism itself was under seige all over the world.
>
> During the war his personal files fattened alarmingly — filled with the names of journals and organizations and individuals who were "under Communist influence."[4]

After Truman asked him to resign, Forrestal went to Florida. Sensing that he was under emotional strain, the White House sent the chief of neuropsychiatry at the U.S. Naval Hospital at Bethesda, Maryland to see Forrestal. Forrestal did not request that this doctor, Doctor George N. Raines, visit him. In fact, there was no reason for even the White House to send him as Forrestal was no longer in the employ of the government and, therefore, no longer the direct concern of the federal government.

But it was decided that Forrestal should go to the Bethesda Naval Hospital. Even before Forrestal left Florida for the hospital, his personal diaries: ". . . consisting of fifteen loose-leaf binders totalling three thousand pages, were hastily removed from his former office in the Pentagon and locked up in the White House where they remained for a year."[5]

Before Forrestal left for Bethesda, he told a friend that he had been followed and that his telephone had been tapped. He further discussed the impending war in Korea, a war still fifteen months from beginning. Forrestal said: "They're going to catch us unprepared. American soldiers will be dying in a year."[6]

Forrestal apparently saw the same forces at work planning the war in Korea a full fifteen months before it started. He must have felt that these were the same planners who had arranged the debacle of post-war Europe, where, in Forrestal's mind, the Eastern European countries had been given over to Communism.

After Forrestal went to Bethesda, his brother asked Dr. Raines whether his brother was fundamentally okay. Dr. Raines answered in the affirmative.

But Dr. Raines' behavior in regards to not allowing Forrestal to see both his own brother and his family priest, Monsignor Maurice S. Sheehy, was unusual, to say the least. He utterly refused to allow them to see Forrestal. (Sheehy had attempted to see Forrestal six times, and each time he was refused.)

Finally, Henry Forrestal, his brother, decided to take his brother into the country on May 22, 1949. He then phoned the hospital and told them he was arriving to take his brother. But only hours before Henry was due to board his train to go to Bethesda, he received the news that his brother was dead.

It is strange that James Forrestal died the very day his brother had planned to take him from the hospital.[7]

The ex-Secretary of Defense is said to have jumped to his death from a sixteenth floor window of the hospital on May 22, 1949. His body was found sprawled grotesquely on a third floor projection of the building. The cord of his bathrobe was wound tightly around his neck and tied in a knot.

The hospital issued a prepared statement that Forrestal had committed suicide. This was followed almost immediately by an almost identical coroner's verdict.

It was theorized that, on the night of May 22, Forrestal had left his bed and walked across the hall to an unlocked window. It was here that he tied one end of his bathrobe cord around a radiator and the other end around his neck. He then, according to this theory, opened the window and jumped out "in an attempt to hang himself."

Several things about his purported suicide do not ring true. For instance:

Forrestal left no suicide note.

He was not critically ill, so he had no medical reason to terminate his life. In fact, Dr. Raines had admitted that he had progressed to the point that his discharge from the hospital was imminent.

Not one shred of the bathrobe cord or mark on the radiator

existed to indicate that the cord had ever been there.

The cord hadn't broken during the purported hanging. The cord was tightly wrapped around Forrestal's neck, but ex-Navy man Forrestal apparently had not tied the other end tightly around the radiator.

In summary, then:

Contrary to the impression given the public at the time, Forrestal had none of the usual reasons for killing himself.

He had no financial worries. He had no personal worries. He was basically in good health.

The only possible motive he could have had for taking his life, everyone agreed, was depression over losing his job as Secretary of Defense and/or over the smears of newspaper columnists and radio commentators.

However, Forrestal could hardly have killed himself for these reasons either. All his life he had been a fighter. He was actively planning, as soon as he left the hospital, to start a career as a newspaperman and write a book. These projects, he had told friends, would allow him to take the offensive against his attackers and expose their real motives.

As far as "depression over losing his job" as a possible suicide motive, he had intended leaving his government post soon in any event.[8]

Monsignor Sheehy placed the blame on Forrestal's death on those who kept him from seeing his long-time friend: "Had I been allowed to see my friend, Jim Forrestal . . . and put his mind at ease with the oldest and most reliable medicine known to mankind [religion], he would be alive today. His blood is on the heads of those who kept me from seeing him."[9]

There was a semi-official investigation into Forrestal's death. It was conducted by the medical officer in command of the Bethesda Naval Hospital and it "did not find that Forrestal had committed suicide. The word 'suicide' was not once used: the board found only that Forrestal had died 'as a result of injuries, multiple, extreme, received incident to a fall . . . '[10]

Perhaps the key to Forrestal's death is in his diaries. These papers were: "subjected to censorship . . . from three different sources . . . the White House; . . . the Pentagon; and, finally, they were condensed and gutted by Walter Millis under the guise of editing [for serialization in the *New York Tribune*]."[11]

Millis was also responsible for the publishing of the diaries by the Viking Press in 1951. So what Forrestal had written in his diaries will probably never be known to the American public. The three acts of censorship have probably eliminated the meat of Forrestal's concerns.

One possible clue of what they contained comes from Monsignor Sheehy, who is on record as saying: "Many, many times in his letters to me, Jim Forrestal wrote anxiously and fearfully and bitterly of the enormous harm that had been, and was unceasingly being done, by men in high office in the United States government, who he was convinced were Communists or under the influence of Communists, and who he said were shaping the policies of the United States government to aid Soviet Russia and harm the United States."[12]

It is interesting to see that the opinion that Forrestal was insane at the time of his death is still the version being offered to the American public. Take, for instance, the answer Walter Scott in his *Parade* magazine column called "Personality Parade" offered to the following question on May 24, 1981:

> Question: Did President Harry Truman ever conspire with the American press to hide the truth about the insanity of James Forrestal, our first Secretary of Defense?
> Answer:... the press declined to reveal to the public that Forrestal suffered from a severe psychosis in the late 1940's. He was obviously insane at the time....[13]

Dr, Carroll Quigley voiced the same opinion in his book entitled *Tragedy and Hope* by informing the reader that: "His mind collapsed under the strain and he resigned in 1949, committing suicide shortly afterward."[14]

The American people will probably never know what happened to James Forrestal. Only the clues to his tragic death remain.

The third individual who came to realize that there was something wrong with America's policies was Senator Joseph McCarthy who was to pay for this knowledge with both his reputation and later with his life.

The campaign to vilify Senator McCarthy was long in duration and in fact has continued to the present. An examination of the facts will reveal why his name is so sullied even to this day.

Appropriately, it was: "Forrestal who personally alerted the freshman Senator to the Communist menace and 'named names' to him of key persons in our federal government who were consistently shaping our policies and programs to benefit Soviet Russia."[15]

The story of McCarthy begins, perhaps, on March 22, 1947, when President Harry Truman issued Executive Order #9835, establishing a federal loyalty program that forbade the employment of loyalty risks.[16] This action was followed on June 10, 1947, by a memorandum sent to Secretary of State George C. Marshall by the Senate Committee on Appropriations. The memo read, in part, as follows:

> On file in the Department is a copy of a preliminary report of
> the FBI on Soviet espionage activities in the United States which
> involves a large number of State Department employees, some in
> high official positions....
>
> There is a deliberate, calculated program carried out, not only
> to protect Communist personnel in high places, but to reduce
> security and intelligence protection to a nullity.
>
> Should this case break before the State Department acts, it will
> be a national disgrace.[17] [18]

This report was completely ignored by Secretary Marshall.

This inaction caused Senator McCarthy to write the following about
George Marshall in his book, *America's Retreat From Victory*: "If he was
wholeheartedly serving the cause of the United States, these decisions were
great blunders. If they followed a secret pattern to which we do not as yet have
the key, they may very well have been successful in the highest degree."[19]

Later, on March 13, 1948, President Truman softened his position on
security risks when he: "issued an order instructing all federal employees to
withhold personnel loyalty and security information from members of
Congress...."[20]

This order obviously would make it extremely difficult to pursue any
security or loyalty risks through government channels, and certainly
hampered the investigations by those agencies responsible for ferreting out
those who jeopardized the security of the American government.

Later, just after Thanksgiving, 1949, three men came to Senator
McCarthy's office and:

> ... showed the Senator a one-hundred page summary of Commu-
> nist subversion in the United States, including serious penetration
> of the State Department. The report, which had been prepared
> under the direction of J. Edgar Hoover [the head of the F.B.I.], had
> already been supplied to the White House, the Secretary of State,
> and heads of other federal departments concerned.
>
> It detailed the operations of spy networks operating in the U.S.
> government and involving a large number of State Department
> employees, some in very high positions.
>
> Senator McCarthy read the report and was so shocked by what
> it revealed that he committed himself to do something about it.[21]

And so began the McCarthy saga.

It was but a few months later, on February 9, 1950, that Senator
McCarthy "did something about it." He gave a speech to the Ohio County

Women's Republican Club of Wheeling, West Virginia, in which he said: "I have in my hand fifty-seven cases of individuals who would appear to be either card-carrying members or certainly loyal to the Communist Party, but who nevertheless are still helping to shape our foreign policy."[22]

McCarthy's sensational charges began appearing in newspapers across the country.

> In Salt Lake City, he withdrew the offer to give [Secretary of State Dean] Acheson the names. A presidential order was then in effect prohibiting the government from turning over loyalty records of U.S. employees to anyone outside the Executive Department, including, of course, congressional investigating committees.
>
> What would be the use of giving Acheson the names of Communists and their sympathizers, McCarthy argued, unless their actual records could be obtained and proof shown to the people.
>
> What would prevent the Secretary of State from simply accepting the list, announcing that nobody on it was either a Communist or a security risk, and thus end the matter.[23]

On February 11, 1950, Senator McCarthy sent a wire to President Truman: "calling upon him to furnish Congress with a list of all State Department employees considered bad security risks and asking him to revoke the presidential order."

Senator McCarthy was certain that the State Department loyalty files would prove his case, but he never got a chance to receive them, as: "The State Department's press officer...issued a heated denial. 'We know of no Communist members in this Department and if we find any they will be summarily dismissed.' "[24]

Those who felt McCarthy was libelling and slandering innocent people now know that he was very concerned about not releasing the names of the individuals he had on his lists, and: "on February 20, 1950, without naming names, he gave his colleagues [in the Senate] a resume of the facts from the files of eighty-one individuals — the fifty-seven referred to at Wheeling and twenty-four additional cases of less importance and where the evidence was less conclusive."[25]

Two days later: "...a Special Subcommittee of the Senate Foreign Relations Committee was appointed and charged with conducting 'a full and complete study and investigation as to whether persons who are disloyal to the United States are or have been employed by the Department of State.' Instead of investigating McCarthy's accusations, however, the Committee investigated McCarthy. Millard Tydings, the Committee Chairman, set the tone for the inquiry when he boasted: 'Give me three days of public hearings and McCarthy will never show his face in the Senate again.' "[26]

The anti-McCarthy feelings in the United States started rising. Even the Communist Party newspaper, the *Daily Worker*, of April 15, 1950, added its concerns: "Communists are keenly aware of the damage the McCarthy crowd is doing."[27]

Gus Hall, the head of the American Communist Party urged: "Communist Party members and all anti-fascists to yield second place to none in the fight to rid our country of the fascist poison of McCarthyism."[28]

So McCarthy had to face both the Communist Party and the government investigating committee in an effort to force the government to rid itself of the subversives already known to exist within its ranks.

McCarthy appeared to have won a victory when, on May 4, 1950, President Truman changed his mind and announced that the loyalty files on McCarthy's cases would be made available to the Committee.[29] But when they were delivered to the Committee, McCarthy charged that they had been "raped," "skeletonized," and "tampered with."[30] Later, on July 12, 1950, McCarthy released the documents on which he based his charges that the files had been stripped. "These documents are affidavits from four persons who had been employed by the [State] Department on a temporary basis in the Fall of 1946 and assigned to a 'file project,' the purpose of which, they said, was to remove from the personnel files of Department employees all derogatory information."[31]

So McCarthy was taking on the State Department and it was countering with a concealment of the truth.

McCarthy also told the American public that it was at the Yalta conference in 1945 that Roosevelt and Stalin planned, not only the Korean War that the United States was then involved in, but also the Vietnamese war that was to follow some 10 to 12 years later. It was on September 23, 1950, that McCarthy charged: "Here was signed the death warrant of the young men who were dying today in the hills and valleys of Korea. Here was signed the death warrant of the young men who will die tomorrow in the jungles of Indochina [Vietnam]."

He also saw that all of these machinations were the work of a giant conspiracy and he said so. He wrote: "How can we account for our present situation unless we believe that men high in Government are concerting to deliver us to disaster? This must be the product of a great conspiracy, a conspiracy on a scale so immense as to dwarf any previous such venture in the history of man. A conspiracy of infamy so black that, when it is finally exposed, its principals shall be forever deserving of the maledictions of all honest men...."[32] "What can be made of this unbroken series of decisions and acts contributing to the strategy of defeat? They cannot be attributed to incompetence.... The laws of probability would dictate that part of ... [the] decisions would serve this country's interest."[33]

(Notice the similarity of this statement and the one made by James Forrestal about "consistency never being the mark of stupidity.")

McCarthy was becoming too dangerous to the conspiracy that he had begun to discover. So the smear job began that it hoped would destroy him, the smear job that went something like: "I like what he is doing, but I object to his methods." Or: "He is smearing individuals with guilt by association."

McCarthy knew that these smear jobs against him were inaccurate, and he wrote about them in his book, published in 1952: "Whenever I ask those who object to my methods to name the 'objectionable methods;' again I hear parroted back to me the Communist *Daily Worker* stock phrase: 'irresponsible charges' and 'smearing innocent people.' But as often as I have asked for the name of a single innocent person who has been 'smeared' or 'irresponsibly charged,' nothing but silence answers."[34]

The government later substantiated McCarthy's charges in 1953 when it published a report, on July 30, entitled *Interlocking Subversion in Government Departments*, which was written by the Senate Internal Security Subcommittee. It read, in part: "The Soviet international organization has carried on a successful and important penetration of the United States Government, and this penetration has not been fully exposed. This penetration has extended from the lower ranks to top-level policy and operating positions in our government. Despite the fact that the Federal Bureau of Investigation and other security agencies had reported extensive information about this Communist penetration, little was done by the Executive branch to interrupt the Soviet operatives in their ascent in Government...."[35]

So the decision was made to "get McCarthy," as there were those who felt that he was getting too close to the truth. So on January 21, 1954: "...an anti-McCarthy strategy meeting [was] held ... in the office of the Attorney General."[36]

Present at this meeting were: Henry Cabot Lodge, U.S. Ambassador to the United Nations; Attorney General Herbert Brownell; Deputy Attorney General William Rogers (later President Nixon's Secretary of State); White House aides Sherman Adams and Gerald Morgan; and John G. Adams, counselor, Department of the Army.

At this meeting: "It was decided that John Adams would start compiling notes to be used as the basis for filing charges against Senator McCarthy...."[37]

(One of the efforts to expose McCarthy was a book written by Richard H. Rovere entitled *Senator Joe McCarthy*.[38])

It has been pretty well established by America's major media that the most serious charge against McCarthy is that he maliciously "smeared" innocent people, by calling them names.

Mr. Rovere, certainly no supporter of the Senator, called him the following names in his book: a bully, a seditionist, a species of nihilist, a screamer, a political thug, a master of the mob, a black arts practitioner, a champion liar, a prince of hatred, possibly a homosexual, a true hypocrite, morally indecent, perhaps crazy, an outrageous fourflusher, a fraud, a heavy drinker, and a demon.

It is comforting to know that it was the Senator who smeared people by calling them names!

Mr. Rovere did like certain people, however. He called the Socialist Norman Thomas a "devoted champion of liberty and decency."

The famous Army-McCarthy hearings started a few months later on April 22, 1954, after McCarthy questioned the Army's decision to promote a suspected Communist.

The next step in the destruction of Senator McCarthy occurred on May 17, 1954, when President Eisenhower, who had replaced Harry Truman, "issued an Executive order prohibiting testimony at the hearings from any member of the Executive without prior permission — which of course was not given."[39]

Eisenhower himself admitted to some strong negative feelings about McCarthy. He wrote about these feelings in the April, 1969, *Reader's Digest*: "From the beginning, I was urged by a great many people ... to 'smash' McCarthy by a public denunciation. When I refused, I was criticized bitterly in many quarters. Actually, I yearned in every fiber of my being to do precisely what my critics were urging — but I felt sure this was the wrong tactic."[40]

The charges against McCarthy came to a head on July 30, 1954, when Senator Ralph Flanders introduced a resolution condemning Senator McCarthy for "conduct unbecoming a member." It contained forty-six different counts, and a committee was appointed to investigate the charges. After hearings, it recommended that McCarthy be censured, not on the forty-six counts, but on only two.[41]

The charges introduced by Flanders, however, were not written by him nor members of his staff: "What is generally not known is that the speech made by Senator Flanders in introducing the resolution, as well as the resolution itself, were written for him by the National Committee for an Effective Congress, [which was] created by . . . Arthur Goldsmith . . . ."[42]

(It is very revealing that the Arthur Goldsmith who created the organization which wrote the charges against McCarthy was the same Arthur Goldsmith who had the ability to make decisions for the Communist Party of the United States. It will be recalled that it was Dr. Dodd, a member of the Communist Party, who revealed that it was the wealthy Goldsmith who had this incredible power.)

The Senate later voted on the charges when they voted to "condemn" and not "censure" the Senator. ("Condemning" is milder than "censuring.")

After all of the allegations against McCarthy about his "smearing innocent people," was he personally able to substantiate his charges?

Now, in retrospect, it is possible to look at the record. Was McCarthy able to substantiate his allegations that there were at least eighty-one security risks in the State Department?

1. Fifty-seven of these cases were later summoned by a Loyalty Board, and fifty-four of the accused confirmed McCarthy's charges by resigning under fire.
2. By November of 1954, all of the eighty-one persons on McCarthy's list had left government employ by dismissal or resignation.
3. The Senate Internal Security Subcommittee revealed that, on June 27, 1956, the State Department's own security chief, Scott McLeod, drew up a list of 847 security risks in the State Department.

> It would seem that Joe McCarthy's major sin was that he underestimated the extent to which the Communists had penetrated the State Department.[43]

It is also revealing that an organization named The Constitutional Educational League of New York "offered a $10,000 reward for any person who could prove that Senator McCarthy ever called anyone a Communist or a Communist Fronter who, in fact, was not. Although this offer was widely publicized from coast to coast, no one ever claimed that reward."[44]

How did Senator McCarthy account for, first, the smear and, then, the vote to condemn him? It will be recalled that he wrote the following in his book, *America's Retreat From Victory*: "How can we account for our present situation unless we believe that men high in this government are concerting to deliver us to disaster? This must be the product of a great conspiracy, a conspiracy on a scale so immense as to dwarf any previous such venture in the history of man."[45]

He also went on to explain what he felt was the purpose of this conspiracy: "to diminish the United States in world affairs, to weaken us militarily, to confuse our spirit with talk of surrender in the Far East, and to impair our will to resist evil. To what end? To the end that we shall be contained and frustrated and finally fall victim to Soviet intrigue from within and Russian military might from without."[46]

McCarthy's life came to an end on May 2, 1957, when he died at Bethesda Naval Hospital, the same hospital where Secretary of Defense James Forrestal "committed suicide." It was stated that McCarthy died of "acute hepatic failure." And it is now known that McCarthy did have infectious hepatitis. In his book, *The Assassination of Joe McCarthy*, the author, Dr. Medford Evans, examines McCarthy's death:

> A man with a history of *infectious hepatitis* could indeed succumb abruptly to *toxic hepatitis*, a deadly affair in any case.

Toxic hepatitis is caused, as the name indicates, by any of several poisons, including chloroform, mercury, and snake venom, but most conveniently, perhaps, by carbon tetrachloride, the common dry-cleaning solvent.

A scarely noticeable or quickly dissipated concentration might be fatal to a man already suffering from a liver complaint hepatitis].[47]

When McCarthy went into the hospital, he was "immediately placed in an oxygen tent," and Evans asked this question: "Do you suppose anybody could have got any carbon tetrachloride into that thing?"[48]

It is his theory that carbon tetrachloride easily could have been placed under the oxygen tent and then dissipated quickly as McCarthy was sleeping. The breathing of a poison by a man suffering from infectious hepatitis would have been fatal.

Dr. Evans comments on McCarthy's overall health: "... Joe McCarthy's health was such in the Spring of 1957 as to make it incredible that he should die so swiftly of natural causes."[49]

In any event, no autopsy was performed on McCarthy's body,[50] so the truth about what caused his death may never be revealed.

At Senator McCarthy's funeral, the eulogy was delivered by the Right Reverend Monsignor John K. Cartwright, who observed: ". . . Communism is the greatest enemy of our society. . . . Not everybody saw from the beginning, and many still do not see, that the threat of Communism is domestic as well as foreign, civil as well as military. But this man saw it clearly and knew that it is an evil with which there can be no compromise . . . "[51]

Louis Budenz, a former member of the Communist Party, said this about the Senator: "The destruction of Joe McCarthy leaves the way open to intimidate any person of consequence who moves against the Conspiracy. The Communists made him their chief target because they wanted to make him a symbol to remind political leaders in America not to harm the Conspiracy or its world conquest designs."[52]

But Dr. Evans notes that it was not the Communist Party that ultimately secured the destruction of Senator McCarthy. He wrote: "A note is necessary on the relationship of the [Communist] Party — McCarthy's declared enemy, as he was theirs — to the American 'establishment,' which is presumably anti-Communist, and which McCarthy never attacked, but which attacked him, and was, indeed, more immediately the instrument of the destruction than was the Communist Party."[53]

It was the very "establishment" that should have joined the Senator in his attack against the Communist Party that finally brought him down.

It was indeed a strange partnership.

But it succeeded.

Chapter 28
The Korean War

In 1944, the Council on Foreign Relations prepared a confidential memorandum for the State Department that began the process of involving us in a war in Korea. It read, in part: "The sovereignty fetish is still so strong in the public mind that there would appear to be little chance of winning popular assent to American membership in anything approaching a super-state organization. Much will depend on the kind of approach which is used in further popular education...."

A review of the memorandum stated that: "a further difficulty was cited, namely that [difficulty] arising from the Constitutional provision that only Congress may declare war. This argument was countered with the contention that a treaty would override this barrier, let alone the fact that our participation in such police action as might be recommended by the international security organization need not necessarily be construed as war."[1]

That treaty was the United Nations Treaty, created in 1945, essentially by the Council on Foreign Relations (there were forty-seven members in the American delegation to the U.N. Conference at San Francisco.)

The Korean War had a unique place in history: "... for the first time, a world organization voted to use collective force to stop armed aggression."[2]

The Korean War was made possible at the Potsdam and Yalta conferences, as World War II was ending, when the Allied governments, represented by Churchill, Stalin, and Roosevelt, divided Korea into a North and South. North Korea quickly created an army of 187,000 men, with Russia supplying the military equipment (the artillery, tanks and planes, etc,) necessary to wage the war. The South only raised an army of 96,000 men, with sparse military equipment.

One of the reasons for this inadequacy of their military equipment was the fact that, even though the United States had voted $10 million in military assistance for South Korea, only a small percentage of it reached that country.[3]

General Douglas MacArthur, who was later to command these forces, wrote in his book *Reminiscences*:

> The South Koreans had four divisions along the 38th Parallel [the dividing line between North and South Korea].
>
> They had been well trained, and the personnel were brave and patriotic, but they were equipped and organized as a constabulary force, not as troops of the line.
>
> They had only light weapons, no air or naval forces, and were lacking in tanks, artillery, and many other essentials.
>
> The decision to equip and organize them in this way had been made by the State Department. The argument advanced by the State Department for its decision was that it was a necessary measure to prevent the South Koreans from attacking North Korea, a curious myopic reasoning that, of course, opened the way for a North Korean attack.[4]

But North Korea's attack should not have come as a surprise as General Albert Wedemeyer had warned President Harry Truman that the North Koreans were preparing for an invasion. And on June 25, 1950, they crossed the 38th Parallel and started the war.

The Russians could have prevented the United Nations from getting involved had they wanted to by vetoing the U.N. efforts: "The Soviets, using the non-membership of Red China in the U.N. as an excuse, walked out of the Security Council. The Council, with Russia absent, then voted U.N. intervention in Korea—a decision which the Soviet Union could have blocked with its veto if it had been present. After the vote, and with Red China still not seated in the United Nations, the Soviets returned to the Security Council."[5]

Some have seen Russia's absence during this crucial vote as an intentional maneuver on the part of the Russians: "... the Soviets started the war themselves. This means that they knew when it would start. If they wanted to keep us out, Stalin would have told his U.N. delegate, Jacob Malik, to forget the boycott, to take his seat at the Security Council, and vote nyet [no]. The fact that the Soviets didn't do this is proof, not just that they didn't want to keep us out of the Korean War, but that they wanted to trick us in."[6]

Two days after the invasion of South Korea, the Chinese on Taiwan, sensing that the time was ripe for them to move against the Communist government on mainland China, got severely reprimanded by President Truman: "... I am calling upon the Chinese government on Formosa [Taiwan] to cease all air and sea operations against the mainland."[7]

Not only did Truman declare it was against American policy for the free Chinese to reclaim Communist China, but he also ordered the American Fleet into the Straits of Formosa to insure this.[8]

General Douglas MacArthur later revealed that he saw this action as an intentional act on the part of the American government to insure the entry of Red China into the war. He wrote:

> The possibility of Red China's entry into the Korean War had existed ever since the order from Washington, issued to the Seventh Fleet in June, to neutralize Formosa, which in effect protected the Red China mainland from attack by Chiang-Kai-shek's forces of half a million men.
>
> This released the two great Red Chinese armies assigned the coastal defense of central China and made them available for transfer elsewhere.[9]
>
> This meant that the Communist China leaders need have little worry about a possible Nationalist landing on the mainland opposite Formosa, and that they could move Red troops northward to the Manchurian country above the Yalu River with perfect safety.
>
> It gave their Korean war plans a tremendous impetus, because Red China could now enter the Korean War at any time she chose without fear of being attacked on her flank and rear by the National-ist troops on Formosa.[10]

But this action by the American government did not deter the Taiwa-nese government of Chaing-Kai-Shek, who, less than a week after the North Koreans had crossed the 38th parallel, offered "the State Department an advance force of 33,000 troops that could be embarked for Korea within five days after the offer was accepted. The suggestion was politely refused."[11]

Formosa was, at the time, a member of the United Nations and therefore could have been represented in the United Nations Force, but the American government would not tolerate such a move.

It was a few months later that the results of the State Department's tactics began to show up. In October, 1950, General MacArthur began sensing that the Red Chinese were building up their troops in Manchuria, just north of the Yalu River. This intelligence report went unheeded by the State Department which advised MacArthur that there was no possibility of their intervening in the war. But the State Department was incorrect, as the Red Chinese crossed the Yalu River, the river separating North Korea and Red China, on October 15, 1950.

As the war against Red China and the North Koreans continued, General MacArthur continued to feel that there had been a leak in his intelligence and that his strategy was known in advance to the enemy. One of MacArthur's senior field commanders, General Walton Walker: ". . . continually complained . . . that his operations were known to the enemy in advance through sources in Washington."[12]

The truth is that MacArthur's strategies were indeed falling into the hands of the North Koreans who were being commanded by Russian officers.

The chain of command under the United States Constitution for any military officer leads upward through the Executive Branch of the government and ends with the President who is the ultimate authority for military decisions. MacArthur was, of course, constitutionally required to obey the orders of his ultimate commander, but under the treaty binding the United States to the United Nations, the command chain went past the President into an office in the United Nations known as the Undersecretary for Political and Security Council Affairs who reported directly to the Secretary General.

Because of a secret agreement made by Secretary of State Edward Stettinius in 1945, this key position, the official who controlled such things as United Nations "police actions," was to be filled by a Communist from some Eastern European Communist country. At the time of the Korean War, this post was filled by Constantine Zinchenko, of Russia.

The North Koreans had Russian military advisors during the war, and it later became known just who was in charge of the North Korean war efforts. According to a Department of Defense press release dated May 15, 1964, high-ranking Russian military officers were actually on the scene in North Korea directing military operations. The release stated: "A North Korean Major identified two of these Russian 'advisors' as General Vasilev and Colonel Dolgin. Vasilev, he said, was in charge of all movements across the 38th parallel. Another prisoner . . . said he actually heard General Vasilev give the order to attack on June 25th."[13]

General Vasilev's chain of command went through the United Nations as well. He "had been the chairman of the United Nations Military Staff Committee which, along with the office of the Undersecretary General for Political and Security Council Affairs, is responsible for United Nations military action under the Security Council."[14]

That meant that two Russians shared authority in planning the North Korean war efforts, and one of them planned the efforts of the United Nations. "In effect, the Communists were directing both sides of the war!"[15]

The Russians were not only controlling both sides of the war and supplying technical advisors for the North Korean war effort, they were actually supplying Russian pilots for flights against the Americans: "Lt. Gen. Samuel E. Anderson, commander of the Fifth Air Force, revealed that entire Soviet Air Force units fought in the Korean War for over two and a half years...."[16]

General MacArthur, aware that the Red Chinese were about to enter the war, realized that one way to prevent their massive entry was to bomb the bridges crossing the Yalu River. He: "ordered General Stratemeyer, [Chief of the Air Force] to employ B-29's on the following morning to destroy the Yalu bridges and cut this easy line of communication between Manchuria and North Korea. An immediate dispatch came from Secretary [of State George] Marshall countermanding my order and directing me to 'postpone all bombing of targets within five miles of the Manchurian border.'"[17]

In addition, MacArthur was ordered not to pursue aircraft fleeing North Korea into Manchuria, nor could he bomb the supply base in the town of Racin.

MacArthur felt that of these decisions the "most incomprehensible of all was the refusal to let me bomb the important supply center at Racin. which was not in Manchuria or Siberia [Russia] but many miles from the borders, in northeast Korea. Racin was a depot to which the Soviet Union forwarded supplies from Vladivostok for the North Korean Army."[18]

On November 25, 1950, the Red Chinese Army commander, General Lin Piao, launched his full forces across the Yalu River and into North Korea. MacArthur felt that: "... information must have been relayed to them, assuring that the Yalu bridges would continue to enjoy sanctuary and that their bases would be left intact."[19]

This was, unfortunately, the truth, as even General Lin Piao later admitted that he "would never have made the attack and risked my men ... if I had not been assured that Washington would restrain General MacArthur from taking adequate retaliatory measures against my lines of supply and communication."[20]

General MacArthur would later write that the order not to bomb the Yalu bridges: "was the most indefensible and ill-conceived decision ever forced on a field commander in our nation's history."[21] One of General MacArthur's generals in the Air Force, George Stratemeyer, said that: "We had sufficient air, bombardment, fighters, reconnaissance so that I could have taken out all of those supplies, those airdromes on the other side of the

Yalu; I could have bombed the devils between there and Mukden, stopped the railroad operating and the people of China that were fighting could not have been supplied.... But we weren't permitted to do it. As a result, a lot of American blood was spilled over there in Korea."[22]

House Minority Leader Joseph Martin also expressed his dismay at the administration's apparent desire not to win the war in Korea by such tactics as not allowing the bombing of strategic military targets: "If we are not in Korea to win, this Administration should be indicted for the murder of thousands of American boys."[23]

Congressman Martin was involved in the last chapter of General MacArthur's story in the War in Korea. On March 8, 1951, he wrote to MacArthur asking for his views on foreign policy and overall strategy in the Far East, suggesting in addition that the Free Chinese government on Formosa should be employed in the war in Korea to take the pressure off the American forces.

General MacArthur replied to the letter on March 20, 1951, agreeing that the Nationalist Chinese should be allowed to enter the war. In addition he wrote: "It seems strangely difficult for some to realize that here in Asia is where the Communist conspirators have elected to make their play for global conquest, and that we have joined the issue thus raised on the battlefield; that here we fight Europe's war with arms while the diplomats there still fight it with words; that if we lose the war to communism in Asia, the fall of Europe is inevitable, win it and Europe most probably would avoid war and yet preserve freedom.... We must win. There is no substitute for victory."[24]

President Harry Truman apparently read General MacArthur's letter and concluded that generals should not set foreign policy. He decided to relieve him of his command. On April 10, 1951, he announced to the American people: "With deep regret, I have concluded that General of the Army Douglas MacArthur is unable to give his wholehearted support to the policies of the U.S. Government and of the United Nations in matters pertaining to his official duties."[25]

General MacArthur replied: "... never in the history was there a more drastic method employed than in my relief — without a hearing, without an opportunity for defense, with no consideration of the past."[26]

Truman replaced MacArthur with a general who he felt could be trusted to support the administration policies, General Matthew B. Ridgeway, a member of the Council on Foreign Relations.[27]

Under Ridgeway, the war was allowed to run down until an armistice was signed on July 27, 1953. American General Mark Clark, who signed the armistice for the United States, stated that he had gained: "... the unenviable distinction of being the first United States Army commander in history to sign an armistice without victory."[28]

One of the last public utterances General MacArthur made on the subject of the Korean War was a speech he gave on December 5, 1952: "Never before has this nation been engaged in mortal combat with a hostile power without military objective, without policy other than restrictions governing operations, or indeed without even formally recognizing a state of war."[29]

The significant results of the Korean War can be summarized as follows:

1.   The war helped Red China solidify control of its people who were becoming ripe for revolt because of famine and harsh living conditions;,

2.   The United States lost considerable prestige by becoming the paper tiger that could not even defeat tiny North Korea.

3.   The United States sacrificed tens of thousands of American lives and billions of dollars because other nations in the United Nations did not want America to fight back in earnest.

4.   The United States further conditioned the people to the idea of having future control of America's military forces under the control of the United Nations; and

5.   For the first time in American military history, the United States was not victorious.[30]

Chapter 29
Aid and Trade

In his monumental study entitled *The Decline and Fall of the Roman Empire,* historian Edward Gibbon listed five reasons that the enormous empire collapsed:

1. The increase in divorce, undermining the institution of the family;
2. The imposition of higher taxes for bread and circuses;
3. The drive for pleasure, sports becoming more exciting and brutal; and
4. The people lost their faith.

But the most important was the fifth reason:

5. The existence of an internal conspiracy, working to undermine the government from within, all the time that the government was proclaiming that Rome's enemy was external.

Gibbon reported that the conspiracy was building huge armaments for protection against both real and imaginary external enemies, all the while they were literally destroying the empire from within.

These causes have parallels in today's world as well. In fact, the creation of an external enemy is consistent with the lessons contained inside the book entitled *Report From Iron Mountain,* which teaches that: "The existence of an accepted external menace, then, is essential to social cohesiveness as well as to the acceptance of political authority. The menace must be believable, it must be of a magnitude consistent with the complexity of the society threatened, and it must appear, at least, to affect the entire society."[1]

An enemy must be created, and the Western powers, collectively called the "Free World," have created theirs: The Union of Soviet Socialist Republics, (Russia.)

Dr. Antony Sutton is probably the greatest writer on this subject, having written numerous books and articles on America's involvement in the building of the Soviet Union. His conclusions can be summarized in one sentence: "The United States and her NATO [North Atlantic Treaty Organization] allies [some of the major countries of the free world] have constructed their own enemy: Communism!"

In his book, *National Suicide, Military Aid to the Soviet Union,* Dr. Sutton has written: "The blunt truth is that trade with the Soviet Union from [the Russian Revolution of] 1917 to the present has built the Free World an enemy of the first order. Moreover, the technological component of this continuing trade enables the Soviet Union to pursue its programs of world conquest...."[2]

This position, of course, is in direct opposition to the traditional position taken by the historians of the day who claim that the "Capitalists" of the "Free World" are detested by the "Communists" of the "Communist" world.

In another of his books, in this case a book entitled *Wall Street and the Bolshevik Revolution,* Dr. Sutton continued his thoughts on this trade: "... one barrier to mature understanding of recent history is the notion that all capitalists are the bitter and un-swerving enemies of all Marxists and socialists. The idea is nonsense. There has been a continuous, albeit concealed, alliance between international political capitalists and international revolutionary socialists — to their mutual benefit."[3]

This mutual relationship was illustrated by an article in the December 5, 1971 issue of *Parade* magazine, that was captioned "Cyrus Eaton: The Communists' Best Capitalist Friend." It showed a series of pictures of Mr. Eaton, first with Premier Kosygin of Russia, then with Fidel Castro of Cuba, and then with Nikita Khrushchev of Russia, Eaton's host on a trip to Moscow, Russia. In all of the pictures, each individual is smiling warmly, showing that each was warmly greeting the other.

The role of the Western Capitalists in the construction of the Russian economy is extremely significant, so important that it becomes the very source of Russia's military power: "There is no such thing as Soviet technology. Almost all, perhaps 90 to 95% came directly or indirectly from the United States and its allies. In effect, the United States and the NATO countries have built the Soviet Union, its industrial and military capabilities."[4]

This transfer of technology is not a recent phenomenon: it was begun shortly after the Russian Revolution of 1917. "Bridge building to the Soviets began in 1918, under President Wilson, before the Bolsheviks had physically gained control of more than a fraction of Russia. As a result of this trade, the Bolsheviks were able to consolidate their totalitarian regime."[5]

Lenin himself wrote frequently of the need for this aid and trade. It is presumed that the reason he did so was to pacify his fellow Communists who couldn't understand Lenin's visible friendship with the "Capitalists" who other Communists considered to be the enemy. Lenin had to have some way of explaining why the "hated Capitalists" were now appearing in Russia to assist the Bolsheviks in Communizing Russia. He wrote the following in 1922: "First of all, we have to stabilize the economy. Without equipment and machinery from the capitalist countries, we could not hope to finish this task in the short time available to us. The most significant circumstance in ensuring our continued existence . . . was the commencement of economic relations with the capitalist countries."[6]

And once again: "When the time comes for us to hang the capitalists, they will compete with each other for the profits of selling us the rope. The capitalists will furnish credits and, by supplying us with materials and techniques which are not available to us, they will rebuild our war industry which is essential to our future attacks on our own suppliers. In other words, they will be laboring to prepare their own suicide."

Later, Lenin's replacement, Russian dictator Joseph Stalin, would tell the Russian people just what the real purpose of the aid was: ". . . it is essential that the proletariat of the advanced countries should render real and prolonged aid to the backward nationalities in their cultural and economic development. Unless such aid is forthcoming, it will be impossible to bring the various nations and peoples within a single world economic system that is so essential to the final triumph of socialism."[7]

The Communist strategy was to use the western technology as a means of creating a world-wide threat of military annihilation so that the Russians and the "Free World" could be merged into a one-world government.

To achieve this end, it was not essential for the Russians to buy large quantities of imported technology. One item would do; the Russians could duplicate whatever they purchased. Lenin, in 1921, established the Soviet trade policy of: ". . . acquaintance with European and American technology. . . . Moscow must have one specimen of all the most important machines from among the latest in order to learn and to instruct."[8]

A former Polish intelligence officer, Michael Cheeinski, who defected to the West, said: "Every machine, device or instrument imported from the West is sent to a special analytic group. Their job is not only to copy technical solutions but to adapt them to the specifications of Soviet military production."[9]

It was America's early plan to conceal the true intent of their sale of technology to Russia: to build a superior Russian military power. To accomplish this subterfuge, it became their task to convince the skeptical that the technology was being sold to Russia to assist them in reconstructing their war-ravaged economy, and that such trade was civilian and not military.

For instance, some of the first factories constructed in Russia in the 1920's and 1930's were "tractor" factories, constructed in the Russian cities of Volgograd, Kharkov, and Chelyabinsk. All three were constructed by American companies, the one at Volgograd being constructed by eighty American firms.

These "tractor" factories, ostensibly constructed to supply farm tractors to the Russian farmer, today produce tanks, armored cars, self-propelled guns, rocket launchers, missile carriers, anti-aircraft guns, and trucks.

In addition, military tanks, so essential to any military structure, are constructed in two key production plants: "... the Gorki plant and the Zil plant...." The Gorki plant was built from scratch by Henry Ford in the 1930's...."[10]

One of the early workers at the Gorki plant in Russia was Walter Reuther, later to become head of the United Auto Workers labor union. He visited Russia in 1933 for about eighteen months.[11] Walter and his brother Victor, both employees in this plant, later wrote a now famous letter:

> The daily inspiration that is ours as we work side by side with our Russian comrades in our factory, the thought that we are actually helping to build a society that will forever end the exploitation of man by man, the thought that what we are building will be for the benefit and enjoyment of the working class, not only for Russia, but the entire world, is the compensation we receive for our temporary absence from the struggle in the United States.
>
> Mel, you know Wal and I were always strong for the Soviet Union.
>
> You know we were always ready to defend it against the lies of the reactionaries....
>
> In all my life, Mel, I have never seen anything so inspiring.
>
> Mel, once a fellow has seen what is possible where workers gain power, he no longer fights just for an ideal, he fights for something which is real, something tangible.
>
> Carry on the fight for a Soviet America.
>
> Vic and Wal."[12]

The American government was aware that the Russians were quickly converting these plants to military uses:

> Official Washington also knows that Soviet industrialization has been preeminently Soviet militarization. The first priority in Soviet industrial plants was given to the military departments.
> Indeed, the original drive behind Russia's industrialization was military.
> This objective was clearly stated in 1929 by Unaschlicht, vice president of the Revolutionary Military Soviet, before American firms went into Russia to carry out the Five-Year Plans:
> "We must try to ensure that industry can as quickly as possible be adapted to serving military needs . . . ."[13]

In addition to building the plants that produce the military hardware essential to Russia's armed forces, the Americans constructed essential industries to assist the actual construction processes. For instance, there are two major steel plants in Russia, one in Magnitogorsk, and another in Kuznetsk. Both of these plants were constructed by American companies, the one in Magnitogorsk by the Arthur G. McKee & Co., the builder of the U.S. Steel plant in Gary, Indiana, and the other by the Freyn Engineering Company of Chicago.[14]

The oil industry also received American attention. After the Nobel family fled Russia following the Russian Revolution, Lenin gave three oil boring concessions to three major oil companies: Standard Oil Company; the Comparre Oil Company of New Jersey, formed by W. Averill Harriman; and Royal Dutch Shell.

In addition to the oil concessions, Standard Oil received a concession to build a 150,000 ton kerosene plant, capable of producing 100 octane gasoline. Standard Oil also concluded a deal with the Communists to market Russian oil in European markets.

These efforts in the oil industry have paid off, as today Russia is the world's largest petroleum producer. (A newspaper article in June, 1977, said one of the reasons Russia is selling oil outside of her borders is to pay for the import of Western technology. About one-tenth of their oil is sold to Eastern Europe, at OPEC prices.)

Dr. Antony Sutton has concluded that this Standard Oil concession to sell Russian oil has continued after 1935,[15] and Gary Allen, another researcher of merit into this subject, has stated: "It is possible the Rockefellers still own oil production facilities behind the Iron Curtain, drawing the profits out through Switzerland. By doing this, they would not have to share the loot with either their stockholders or the tax collector."[16]

The Americanization of the Russian oil industry was so immense that in August, 1960 " . . . an American petroleum industry delegation [visiting in Russia] was shown four refineries in August, 1960—three of them . . . Lend Lease refineries [lent to Russia during World War II] and the fourth, either a Lend Lease refinery or a Soviet copy of a U.S. installation."[17]

The tragic cost to the Russian people of this aid and trade was made known in 1934 when Henry Morgenthau, Roosevelt's Secretary of the Treasury: "removed restrictions on trade with Russia . . . although the U.S. Government had evidence concerning forced-labor camps in the Soviet Union. If forced labor was used, then production costs would be artificially lowered."[18]

(It goes without saying that the greatest profits are made when labor costs are the lowest. That would tend to please the "monopolistic capitalists" who enjoy making large profits.)

In addition to pursuing the military equipment needed for their Army, the Russians have utilized western technology and construction ability to produce a high percentage of both the Russian merchant marine, (Russia's sea-going merchant fleet) and their Navy. For instance, during the Vietnamese War, Dr. Sutton was able to identify eighty-four ocean going cargo ships being utilized by Russia in transporting military goods from Russian ports into the Vietnamese port of Haiphong. Sutton concluded from his research that: "None of the main engines in those ships were designed and manufactured inside the USSR. All the larger and faster vessels on the Haiphong run were built outside the USSR. All shipbuilding technology in the USSR comes directly or indirectly from the U.S. or its N.A.T.O. allies."[19]

Western shipbuilding efforts for Russia are illustrated in the following statistics collected by Professor Sutton: "68% of all Russian ships were constructed in the West; 80% of all Russian diesel engines were built in the West; and 20% of all Russian engines were built in the USSR but under Western licensing."[20]

Sutton went on to identify Japan and Western Germany as the largest suppliers of these ships.[21] But others are busy as well, as: " . . . no less than 95 percent of all ships manufactured in Finland since World War II have been on Soviet account.[22] "All of the 11,000 horsepower marine diesel engines made in Russia are constructed according to technology supplied by Burmeister and Wain of Denmark.[23]

Japan and West Germany and Finland and Denmark are supposed to be America's allies.

Western assistance to the Russian Navy is not recent, however. For instance, in March 1939, the American State Department approved a proposal by the English Boat Company of Groton, Connecticut, to send plans, specifications and construction services for the construction of a Russian submarine.

But the greatest military and technological assistance to the Russian government came during World War II, when the United States developed a program known as Lend Lease. This agreement obligated the Americans to supply the Russians with over $11 billion worth of a variety of war-making goods. Included in this list were the following items for the Russian Navy:

> 90 dry cargo vessels,
> 10 ocean going tankers,
> 46 110' submarine chasers,
> 57 65' submarine chasers,
> 3,320 marine diesel engines,
> 4,297 marine gasoline engines, and
> $2,700,000 naval guns.

In addition to the military equipment cited above, Lend Lease also supplied Russia with:

> A $29 million petroleum refinery,
> Patents for bombsights, military tanks, airplanes-helicopters, and bullet-resisting armor
> Five factories for synthetic rubber
> Locomotives
> TNT, dynamite, and smokeless powder
> Bombers and fighters
> Tanks, trucks and trailers.[24]

Lend Lease was also the excuse for sharing some of America's other military technology as well. For instance, General John R. Deane, who was secretary to the combined Chiefs of Staff in Washington during part of the war, reported: "Our policy was to make any of our new inventions in electronics and other fields available to Russia. Each month I would receive a revised list of secret American equipment about which Russia could be informed. . . . We never lost an opportunity to give the Russians equipment, weapons or information."[25]

In addition to Lend Lease during the war, America also permitted the Russian government to dismantle Germany's war making facilities, such as factories, dry-docks, cranes, etc., after the war as a form of war reparations. "There is no question that there were sizable Soviet equipment removals from occupied areas after World War II: a minimum figure in excess of $10 billion in 1938 prices can be set for equipment thus removed."[26]

The Russians literally dismantled factories down to the very foundation and removed them to Russia. These reparations were agreed to by the American and British governments at the meetings in Yalta and Potsdam.

The Russians also stripped Mongolia after World War II of: " . . . at least

$800,000,000 of movable assets under the specious claim that it was 'war booty.' "[27]

But the most important transfer to the Russians was the technology and material for the building of the atomic bomb.

It is customarily explained by the majority of current historians that the Russians received the secrets to the atomic bomb from convicted American spies Ethel and Julius Rosenberg who were charged with the giving of these plans to the Russians in 1950.

When Judge Irving Kaufman sentenced the Rosenbergs to death, he said: "I consider your crime worse than murder. . . . Your conduct in putting into the hands of the Russians the A-bomb years before our best scientists predicted Russia would perfect the bomb has already caused, in my opinion, the Communist aggression in Korea. . . . Indeed, by your betrayal you undoubtedly have altered the course of history to the disadvantage of our country."[28]

But the story of the atomic bomb occurred prior to the sentencing of the Rosenbergs. The American government had given Russia the bomb in 1943, during the Lend Lease program.

Major George Racey Jordan, an officer in the United States Army during the Second World War, was the officer in charge of the transfer of the Lend Lease supplies through the Great Falls, Montana, air base. It was here that the planes were loaded with the transferable goods prior to their being flown to Fairbanks, Alaska, where the planes were flown into Russia by Russian pilots.

Major Jordan, curious by nature, opened various briefcases and cartons, and saw various words he was not familiar with on various papers: uranium, cyclotron, proton, neutron, cobalt, and plutonium. In addition, Jordan discovered various reports from "Oak Ridge, Manhattan District" (it was the "Manhattan Project" in Oak Ridge, Tennessee, where the American scientists were developing the plans for the atomic bomb) containing phrases like "energy produced by fission."

Jordan also discovered ". . . at least three consignments of uranium chemicals. . . nearly three quarters of a ton. Confirmed also was the shipment of one kilogram, or 2.2 pounds, of uranium metal at a time when the total American stock was 4.5 pounds."[30]

These findings meant little to Major Jordan until 1949, when Russia exploded their first atomic bomb. It was then that he realized that he had been witness to the transfer of the materials and plans for construction of Russia's atomic bomb. And this occurred in 1943.

Major Jordan's charges were corroborated by a novel written by James Roosevelt, the son of Franklin Roosevelt, in 1980. The dust cover of the book describes the contents of the novel, entitled *A Family Matter*.[31] "[President]

Roosevelt... makes a bold secret decision — to share the results of the Manhattan Project with the Soviet Union."

The dust cover continues by informing the reader that Roosevelt has "written a novel of spine-chilling drama and *authenticity*." (emphasis added.)

The novel details how President Roosevelt gave Russia the plans for the atomic bomb in 1943 and 1944.

Not only did the United States government give Russia the plans for the atomic bomb, plus all of the ingredients to manufacture one, they also arranged for the Russians to secure a cyclotron at the end of the war. *Life* magazine detailed the circumstances in their October 3, 1949 article: "In May, 1945 — three months before the first bomb was dropped — Russians beat Americans to the punch and carried off the cyclotron in the Kaiser Wilhelm Institute in Berlin." It will be recalled that it was the plan of the Roosevelt administration to allow Russia to get to Berlin first.

But even with this technology supplied by the American government, there is still doubt that Russia exploded the atomic bomb in 1949, as it is claimed.

Life magazine of October 3, 1949, carried an article about the supposed explosion: "U.S. Detects Atomic Blast in Russia." President Harry Truman announced that "We have evidence that within recent weeks an atomic explosion occurred in the U.S.S.R."

The article reported: "It seems probable that the blast was caused by a bomb." It appeared that no one was certain that the Russians had exploded the bomb, including even the Russians: "Vishinsky, the Russian Foreign Minister, pretended ignorance, refused comment."

It would seem probable that, if Russia had exploded an atomic bomb, it would have proudly announced it to the world, complete with pictures documenting the fact.

Life attempted to prove their case with a: "Picture of possible A-bomb structure [that] appeared in a Russian-zone German paper."

The evidence that Russia had exploded an atomic bomb was a picture of a "possible" A-bomb, from an unspecified newspaper with no apparent reported connection with the Russian government.

Life then clinched the argument: "It is even remotely possible that the Russians have developed a superior bomb. No one knows. Most information on Russian accomplishments is purely conjectural."

But they continued the myth in a later article, in their October 10, 1949 issue entitled "Can Russia Deliver the Bomb?" "Now that Russia has the bomb — and perhaps a supply of them — ."

One would have to fairly conclude that the evidence confirming the supposed explosion was not very convincing.

But America has not ended its assistance of Russia's nuclear industry. An article in the *Wall Street Journal* of April 25, 1975, headlined: "U.S. Quietly Allows Uranium Shipments to Soviet Union for Processing Into Fuel" The article detailed that the State Department had approved the sale of 1.4 million pounds of uranium oxide mined in Wyoming and New Mexico to the Soviet government. It would in turn be processed into pellets rich in uranium 235. "This isotype provides the power for nuclear electric plants and for the *atomic bomb*." (emphasis added)[32]

The answer to the question as to why the State Department and the American government first gave Russia the plans for constructing the atomic bomb, and then later the materials to put into it, quite possibly was given by the authoress Rose Martin, in her book *Fabian Freeway*: "Until such time as international control of atomic energy has been achieved, the threat of nuclear destruction could always be raised to generate that atmosphere of perpetual crisis needed to justify Keynesian spending politics."[33]

How all of this aid and trade comes together was made abundantly clear on September 1, 1983, when the Russain government shot down an unarmed Korean Air Lines 747 jet over Russian waters. There were 269 passengers aboard the plane and they were all killed.

The media quickly reported that it was a Russian made airplane that had shot at least two Russian made aircraft-to-aircraft missiles into the plane.

The tragic truth was that even though the Russian missiles and the jet were built in Russia, they were built from American technology.

For instance, during the Lend Lease program of World War II, America "lent" Russia: 3,000 pursuit planes, communication equipment, radio direction finders, altimeters, radio compasses, radio locators, aircraft construction equipment, aircraft manufacturing factories; the Corps of Engineers built airports in Russia; radar, aircraft lubricating oils, gasoline, nitric acid (used in making explosives,) gyroscopes, and aluminum sheet factories.

Later, in 1946, America turned over two-thirds of Germany's aircraft manufacturing capacity to Russia. These factories and installations were crated off to Russia to form the nucleus of their jet aircraft industry. One of the engineers turned over to Russia later developed their MIG-15, the aircraft that was flown in Korea against American pilots. The MIG-15 was powered by a jet engine purchased from Rolls Royce of Great Britain, America's supposed ally. During that year, America sold Russia boring machines, balancing machines used in balancing jet engine shafts, and grinding machines.

Between 1960 and 1973, America sold Russia: aluminum oxide, rubber compound chemicals, airborne navigation equipment and parts, electronic computers, information on the distillation of petroleum, flexible printed circuits, technical data for the engineering and planning for aircraft production, and technical data for aircraft landing system instruments. In 1974, General Dynamics sent Russia technical data for aircraft construction. And America trained Yugoslavian jet pilots (Yugoslavia is Russia's Communist ally.)

In what can only be termed a strange arrangement, America sent its latest technology in jet aircraft, the F-16, on Russian ships to NATO countries in Europe in 1978. Technicians at Wright-Patterson Air Force Base, where the United States tests its latest aircraft technology, report that Russian generals are among its frequent visitors.

Czechoslovakia is the largest supplier of jet aircraft to Russia outside of its borders. Their largest plant, producing not only jet aircraft but other materials for war purposes, has an agreement with an American machine tool company to supply them with the latest in machine tools.

Russia's missiles also have an American background. The United States government has sold Russia accelerometers used to measure gravitational pull on missiles, ball bearings used in missile guidance systems, miniature ball bearings that gave Russia the ability to place multiple warheads on their missiles, technology on high explosives, and entire chemical plants capable of making explosives.

But there is something even more incredible in the story of the Korean Airlines flight 007. Diagrams in various American news magazines show the airplane "wandering off course" over the Kurile Islands and the Sakhalin peninsula, all within Russian territory. It will be remembered that these former Japanese territories were among the lands given to the Russian government at the end of World War II by President Roosevelt.

If President Roosevelt had not given these areas to the Russian government, flight 007 could not have "wandered off course."

There are some who are wondering whether the airplane was shot down, not because it strayed over Russian waters, but because one of the passengers on board was the most vocal opponent of such Russian aid and trade. Was it a coincidence that the most vocal anti-trade member of Congress, Congressman Larry McDonald, was aboard the plane shot down by American technology sent to Russia in the name of "peaceful trade?"

Chapter 30
Treason

The "space race" began on October 4, 1957, when the Russians announced that they had orbited the first man-made satellite in history, called Sputnik.

But Russia's ability to orbit an earth satellite was given to the Russian government by the American government at the end of World War II.

General George Patton, as he moved eastward into and through western Europe and Germany, captured the two German towns of Peenemunde and Nordhausen, where the German scientists were developing the V-1 and V-2 rockets. Patton was ordered by his commanding officer, the Supreme Allied Commander, General Dwight Eisenhower, to turn over these two cities in their entirety to the Russians. Included in this turn-over were thousands of German scientists who were transported to Russia with the factories of the two towns, removed down to the last office desk.

Fortunately, one of these scientists saw what was about to befall him and others involved with Germany's space efforts, and he led 129 of them from Germany where he surrendered to the American forces rather than to the Russians. This space scientist, Dr. Werner von Braun, became the head of America's space program, when he and the other scientists reached America.

Dr. von Braun was later unsuccessful in convincing the Eisenhower administration to orbit America's first satellite: "Long before the Soviet Union launched the first satellite...von Braun said his team had the capability to orbit a payload by putting an upper stage on the Redstone [rocket]. But President Dwight D. Eisenhower turned him down . . ."[1]

The same gentlemen who arranged for Russia to orbit the first satellite by turning over to the Russians nearly the entire German rocket capacity, now was in a position to insure that the Russians were able to orbit the first satellite before the Americans.

The Russians were now able to use the successful orbiting of this satellite to boast that Communism was obviously superior to Capitalism. "The old jesting about socialist inefficiency came to an end when the first Soviet Sputnik circled the earth."[2]

President Eisenhower turned this Russian "victory" into two major defeats for the United States:

1. It was now apparent, according to the Administration, that America lagged behind the Russians in the field of education or in the ability to engineer such a scientific feat.

It was imperative that the American government enter the field of education to narrow the gap between the two competing economic systems. So the Eisenhower Administration quickly pushed the federal government into the funding of education on a nationwide basis, completely in violation of the Constitution of the United States, which gave no such authority to the federal government.

2. Since the American government was now behind in the "space race," it was imperative that the American government compete with the Russians, first by orbiting a satellite, and then by reaching out into distant space.

In other words, the American government was taken out of the space race by President Eisenhower, and then put back in, at great cost to the American taxpayers. And the only way the planners felt that they could get the taxpayer to support the tax increase, was to convince them that there was a "space race" with the Communists.

A Russian writer on the subject of space research, Leonid Vladimirov, who defected to the West, has written in his book *The Russian Space Bluff*: "It is possible that, without having the fear of Soviet competition, the Americans would not have been in such a hurry to land on the Moon and would thus have saved themselves thousands of millions of dollars."[3]

Vladimirov discussed the state of the Russian missile industry after the orbiting of Sputnik. He informed his readers that the Russians, as late as

1959, had "... proposed making a 'cluster of clusters' — combining together five four-chamber engines to make one giant engine."[4]

The combining of a series of individual rockets, each no larger than a captured German V-2, indicated that the Russian missile industry had not matured much since the days when Eisenhower provided them with the V-2 rocket. It also meant that these rockets were cumbersome and extremely inaccurate, because of the difficulty in getting so many rockets to fire at the same time.

The state of the Russian missile industry was known to the American government, according to an article in 1980 in *Time* magazine: "Three years later [1959], the overhead view (from the U-2 spyplane overflights) of the Tyuratam site [where all Soviet missiles were then tested] gave the U.S. some needed reassurance. Determining that the rocket booster aperture at the base of the launch pad was 15 meters [50 ft.] in diameter, photo interpreters concluded that the Soviets were still using missiles boosted by auxiliary rockets strapped around the circumference of the main rocket. Because they were so cumbersome that they could not be practically deployed, the U.S. strategic planners concluded that the missile gap did not exist either."[5]

This statement of fact is extremely revealing, looking backwards from this 1980 article, because the "missile gap" that became one of the main debating issues on the Kennedy-Nixon debates during the 1960 Presidential election campaign, was not a "missile gap" at all. It will be recalled that John Kennedy contended that the Eisenhower Administration, which Richard Nixon had to defend because he was Eisenhower's Vice-President, had allowed the Russians to far exceed the then meager American rocket efforts, to the point where there was an enormous "missile gap," threatening the very safety of the American people. Nixon, it will be remembered, did not defend the position very well, and Kennedy was elected.

And all the time, Nixon knew (or should have known) that the "missile gap" did not exist. Russia did not have the technology it claimed it had.

America knew that the Russians had not perfected the single stage rocket but were, in essence, "gluing" a series of V-2 rockets to a central cluster. This clustering together of a series of rockets can be seen in the August 14, 1978 *Time* Magazine, on page 48, and in the Santa Ana *Register* of September 17, 1976. These pictures reveal a tall, slender, central rocket, with a series of four clusters along side the main engine, each with four internal rocket engines.

This means that, as recently as 1978, the Russians were not advanced enough to have developed the technology to construct a single-stage rocket capable of placing large payloads into space.

In fact, the Russians had been experimenting with such technology before, without success, according to Vladimirov: "Friends of mine among the rocket engineers used to tell me how copies of all the American rocket engines then known were built in Soviet factories on an experimental basis. The engines... all burnt out while they were being tested."[6]

Other rocketry-related efforts of the Russians have come under question. The "Lunik" moon landing in 1959, for instance, has been called a "hoax" by an American writer, Lloyd Mallan, who has written: "The Lunik, in short, was a cooly insolent, magnificent, international hoax. I found no hint... of any tracking station in the Free World having heard with scientific certainty the radio signals from Russia's moon-or-sun rocket."[7]

In another book on the same subject, Mr. Mallan reported that Cosmonaut Alexie Leonov's "walk in space" on March 18, 1965 "... was faked. Four months of solid research interviewing top experts in the fields of photo-optics, photo-chemistry and electro-optics, all of whom carefully studied the motion picture film and still photographs officially released by the Soviet government, convinced me...."

Mallan's conclusions were that the film showing Leonov in space:

> ... was double-printed.... The foreground (Leonov) was superimposed on the background (the Earth below.) The Russian film showed reflections from the glass plate under which a double print is made.
>
> Leonov was suspended from wire or cables.... In several episodes of the Russian film, light was reflected from a small portion of the wire (or cable) attached to Leonov's space suit.
>
> One camera angle was impossible of achievement. This showed Leonov crawling out of his hatch into space. It was a head-on shot, so the camera would have had to have been located out in space beyond the space ship.
>
> One still photo (the clearest one) shows Leonov emerging from his hatch standing straight up, his body still half-way inside the space ship. This contradicts the motion picture film which shows him squirming out of the hatch on his belly.
>
> If one very carefully observes the motions of Leonov as he laboriously wiggles through the extraordinarily long tunnel, it is obvious that he is under one 'g' (the force of normal, earth gravity) and exerts most of his muscular force against only one side of the duct, rather than bumping from side to side and moving forward with the ease one would expect in the absence of gravity.[8]

The question of who tracked Russian space efforts in the early stages of the "space race," is still a mystery.

It was thought that the U.S. North American Air Defense Command (NORAD) did, but since 1961, they have "had a Presidential order never to divulge *any* information about the tracking of foreign space vehicles."

And a spokesman for the Smithsonian Institute's world-wide network of tracking cameras commented: "We don't track Russian satellites."[9]

What that meant was that the American government, in the early stages of Russia's space efforts, had to believe whatever the Russians said.

Additional examples of the phoniness of Russia's space efforts are ample to illustrate the charge that the truth is less than what has passed as the evidence.

The February, 1962, *Scientific American* magazine carried an advertisement on page 91 placed there by the Sperry Gyroscope Company. This ad showed a drawing of a space station in orbit and individuals working on it in space suits.

This same drawing, with the addition of certain descriptive phrases attached to identify certain parts of the space station, appeared in the October 13, 1969 *New York Times,* on page 32, over seven years later.

But the *New York Times* used the drawing to illustrate: "One concept of a future Soviet space station in which the crewmen in a mother ship transfer through a transit chute to help assemble another ship is depicted here."

One would wonder why the *New York Times* had to resort to the use of a 1962 Sperry advertisement to illustrate a Russian space effort. The only conclusion one can draw from these facts is that the Russians did not have a space effort. It seems logical that, if they did, they would make it known to the world in large, easily identifiable pictures or drawings.

But that hasn't happened.

Whatever space successes the Russians have achieved have been made all the easier by American technology. It is commonly known that ball-bearings are absolutely essential to rocket and missile guidance systems. Dr. Antony Sutton's research into this vital industry has discovered that: "The entire ball-bearing production capability of the Soviet Union is of Western origin.... All Soviet missiles and related systems including guidance systems have bearings manufactured on western equipment or Soviet duplicates of this equipment."[10]

Part of this technology came from a Chicago-based company, which helped the Russians build a complete automotive bearing factory in March of 1975. This factory was capable of producing 60 million engine bearings a year.[11]

And the ability to produce miniature ball-bearings, vital to the missile and rocketry industries, came from an order filled by the Bryant Grinder Company of Springfield, Vermont.

The machines, capable of producing ball-bearings accurate to twenty-five millionths of an inch, were sold to Russia in 1972, and were approved as "non-strategic trade" by President Richard Nixon. Their immediate use is in guidance systems for missiles, but one Congressman, William L. Dickinson, reported that these machines have another important function: "These machines sold for $20 million. They were capable of producing high quality precision, miniature ball bearings of the type used in Intercontinental Ballistic Missile multiple warheads. As a consequence, Soviet missile accuracy improved dramatically to the point where 90 percent of our land-based ICBM force can now be destroyed in a first strike. This was a technology the Soviets did not have, which they bought for a cheap price and which endangers the lives of millions of Americans."[12]

How the Russians acquired these machines is an illustration of how such sales are made.

In 1960, the Soviets ordered 45 of these machines, but the export license needed for their sale to Russia was denied by President John Kennedy. Twelve years later, the Soviets ordered 164 of these same machines, and this time, the export license was appproved by President Nixon. The Soviet Minister of Machine Tool Industry was quoted at the time as saying: "We had waited twelve years to get these machines."[13]

Whatever the Soviets have achieved in their space program has been with the assistance of the American government. Whatever programs they faked or didn't have, the American government or media has certified as valid.

Another area that the United States has assisted the Russians is in the field of military hardware. During the Korean war, the Soviets were supplying the North Koreans and the Red Chinese with jet aircraft, including the MIG-15. This airplane was similar in configuration to the F-86, being flown by the South Korean and American pilots, and supplied by the American government.

Both of these planes were designed by the same man, a German who was captured at Nordhausen at the end of World War II. As discussed before, the scientist went to one nation, and his plans went to the other. But there is more to this story than this.

The MIG-15 was powered by reproductions of fifty-five Rolls-Royce jet engines sold to Russia by this English company in 1947. These engines were immediately reproduced and supplied to the manufacturers of the MIG-15 in Russia.[14]

Rolls-Royce later tried to sell larger jet engines to Russia in 1977. These engines, the largest produced at that time, provided 50,000 pounds of thrust to the jumbo jets envisioned by the master planners in the aircraft industry in Russia. These engines were not sold to the Russians, apparently because of the pressure from the American government which wanted General Electric to sell its CF6 nearly identical engine to the Soviets.

The CF6 engine is currently being used in the American airplane industry in the 747, the DC-10 and the world's largest cargo plane, the Air Force's C-5A.

Rolls-Royce was successful, however, in 1977, in selling the Red Chinese the necessary jet engines to power their newly developed F-12 jet airplane.

Perhaps the most extraordinary example of America's military assistance to the Russian government occurred during the Vietnamese war.

Dr. Sutton has concluded that "... the guns, the ammunition, the weapons, the transportation systems, that killed Americans in Vietnam came from the American subsidized economy of the Soviet Union."[15]

America's assistance to the cause of the North Vietnamese government had an early beginning.

In an article entitled "When Ho Chi Minh was an Intelligence Agent for the U.S.," author Lloyd Shearer details how the American government assisted the early efforts of the founder of the revolution against the South Vietnamese government. Ho Chi Minh was recruited into the American intelligence apparatus. The article states: "We had a trusted agent whom we regularly supplied with weapons, radio equipment, operators and medicine. All of it served to reinforce his position and status."[16]

So even before the Vietnamese war started, the Americans were supplying the guerilla army of the man who would ultimately lead the Viet Cong in a war against the Americans.

The American people, who were beginning to sense that something was wrong with the conduct of America's efforts in the war, started showing that concern at the polls. The aid and trade being sent to Russia during the war became a campaign issue in the 1968 Presidential campaign.

The Republicans at their convention that year included the following plank in their party platform: "Nations hostile to this country will receive no assistance from the U.S. We will not provide aid of any kind to countries which aid and abet the war efforts of North Vietnam."[17]

Republican Presidential candidate Richard Nixon also addressed himself to this plank when he told the American Legion Convention in September, 1968: "There should be no aid or credits of any kind with any country, including the Soviet Union, that aids the enemy in Viet Nam."[18]

Candidate Nixon's campaign literature repeated the Republican Party's concern in this matter. One of his campaign flyers covered this issue: "The United States should not provide anything that could be treated as, or classified as, aid to those [Communist bloc] nations if they persist in trading or aiding the enemy in North Vietnam."[19]

The reason that the Republican Party and their Presidential candidate Richard Nixon could make these statements is that the President of the

United States has the power to control exports of commodities behind the Iron Curtain.

The 1917 U.S. Trading With the Enemies Act forbids U.S. firms or their foreign subsidiaries from trading with enemies of the United States except under license. The ability to grant the necessary licenses has been given by the Congress of the United States to the President with the option to delegate this authority to such departments as he deems appropriate. In the past, Presidents have delegated this authority to the Department of Commerce. This means that the President has the authority to assume the direct responsibility should he (or she) choose to do so. This means that President Nixon, after his election, had the authority to prevent the sale of any commodity he deemed to be against the nation's security interests. President Nixon could have honored both his party's platform and his campaign promises should he have chosen to do so after his election.

The Department of Commerce publishes a listing of the commodities licensed for export to Eastern European destinations each quarter, and this report is made available to the public. A quick review of these reports will enable the skeptic to see if President Nixon delivered as he promised.

For instance, the Third Quarter report for 1971 is typical of the reports and reveals that our government, in that quarter alone, shipped a series of commodities to the Russian government while Russia was supplying eighty percent of the goods and war materials to North Vietnam.

Some of the commodities listed in that report are: Synthetic rubber; lubricating grease and oil; parts for automotive vehicles; electronic computers; foundry and metalworking equipment; parts for rolling mills; ball and roller bearings; oil and gas field production equipment; airborne navigation equipment and parts; and nearly $11 million of trucks and parts.[20]

In addition to the actual commodity sold to the Russians, the American government authorized the export of "technical data relating to the commodities and the processes indicated: Iron and steel foundry; foundry for producing engine components; lube oil additives; and distillation of petroleum.[21]

It becomes obvious that President Nixon did not deliver on the promises Candidate Nixon made. But the President is not the only one assisting the Communist governments. Others are involved as well.

For instance, in 1969, during the middle of the Vietnamese war when Americans were being killed by the Russian-supplied North Vietnamese, Congressman Earl Landgrebe of Indiana introduced an amendment to the Export Control Act, the act authorizing the licensing of exports to the Communist Bloc nations. The amendment read in part: "No commodities, military or otherwise, shall be authorized for shipment to any foreign nation which sells or furnishes to North Vietnam or which permits ships or aircraft under its registry to transport to or from [North Vietnam], any equipment. materials or commodities or gives any form of assistance to North Vietnam."[22]

It would be expected that the Congress of the United States, the agency responsible for protecting the American fighting man that they had sent there, would have overwhelmingly supported the amendment.

The Landgrebe amendment was defeated.

One of the reasons that the Landgrebe amendment failed, it appears, is because our government was actively encouraging American businessmen to sell to Russia during the Vietnamese war.

In August of 1966, the State Department issued a pamphlet entitled *Private Boycotts Vs. The National Interest*, which stated: "All American citizens should know that any American businessman who chooses to engage in peaceful trade with the Soviet Union or Eastern European countries and to sell the goods he buys is acting within his rights and is following the policy of his government. But any organization, however patriotic in intention, that undertakes to boycott, blacklist, or otherwise penalize or attack any American business for engaging in peaceful trade with Eastern European countries or the Soviet Union, is acting against the interests of the United States."[23]

This is incredible when it is assumed that government should protect the American fighting man by supporting such restrictions on those who were trading with those nations supplying the enemy.

In addition to the support of this trade by the American Congress, the Republican administration, led by the Commander-in-Chief of all armed forces, assisted by failing to block shipments of Russian commodities and equipment into the main North Vietnamese port of Haiphong.

This neglect was pointed out by Admiral U.S. Grant Sharp, Commander-in-Chief of Naval Operations in the Pacific during most of the Vietnamese War. He spoke about this issue: "From the beginning, we should have closed the harbor of Haiphong and prevented all of the vital imports from reaching that area. Instead, we permitted them to import all of the necessities of war without any difficulty whatsoever, despite the fact that we controlled the seas. This was a great mistake, of course, and immeasurably increased the casualties that our side incurred."[24]

This oversight was finally corrected by President Nixon when, on May 8, 1972, he announced to the nation: "There is only one way to stop the killing, and that is to keep the weapons of war out of... North Vietnam. I have ordered the following.... All entrances to North Vietnamese ports will be mined.... Countries with ships presently in North Vietnamese ports have been notified that ships will have... to leave...."[25]

These directives were, in many instances, to nations supposedly friendly to the United States. The ships of Great Britain, Japan, Greece, Norway, Lebanon, Italy, West Germany, and Panama were among those delivering Russian goods to North Vietnamese ports.

(Dr. Sutton, in his research, discovered one strange anomaly. Four of the Russian ships being used to haul goods to North Vietnamese ports still legally belonged to the United States. These four were "Liberty Ships" sent to Russia during the Lend Lease program of World War II. President Nixon should have notified President Nixon to remove American ships from the North Vietnamese harbors!)

One of the more tragic sales to the Russian government occurred in 1966 when the U.S. government: ". . . sent the Soviet Union the entire technical specifications which they needed to build a glycerol plant. Glycerol is used in the manufacture of explosives. Specifically, in Vietnam, glycerol is used as a detonator in booby traps. Over 50% of all American casualties suffered in Vietnam have come from booby traps."26

One of those who suffered from such a booby trap was Sgt. Peter Stark, a young and courageous Vietnam veteran who went on a nationwide speaking tour attempting to alert the American people to the dangers of such aid and trade. . . from his wheelchair. Sgt. Stark had had his legs blown off because of a booby trap.

One of the most recent examples of American technology coming back to haunt the American people has come from their experience in building the Kama River truck factory in Russia in 1969. This plant, capable of producing 100,000 heavy-duty trucks and 150,000 diesel engines per year, more than all U.S. manufacturers put together, cost the Russians over $1.4 billion. Nearly $1 billion of that total came from the United States in the form of computers, heavy equipment, and foundry equipment.

These efforts to assist the Russian government paid off in 1979 when the American government was notified that these trucks, in addition to engines being installed in armored personnel carriers and assualt vehicles constructed in the plant, began showing up in Russian military units in Eastern Europe. But even more incredible was the fact that these engines and trucks were being utilized by the Russians in their military assaults in Afghanistan.27

In addition to the direct assistance in the building of the vehicles used in Russia's attempt to conquer the freedom fighters in Afghanistan, the American government constructed the highways, or at least a portion of them, that the Russians used to travel to that country. Congressman Ron Paul in 1980 released a reproduction of a photograph of the invasion route over which the Russian Army travelled. He further reported that the American government constructed three hundred miles of double-lane highway through Afghanistan, being careful to: "connect our road to the one that [the] Soviet Army engineers were building."[28]

(The June 4, 1968 *New York Times,* on page seventeen printed a picture of one of these highways in Afghanistan with this caption: "New highways thread through Afghanistan, some, like this one, built with Soviet aid, and others with United States aid.") But some of the trade has even far more damaging importance to America's future security: "According to Dr. William Perry, Under-Secretary of Defense for Research and Engineering, the U.S.S.R. will be able to detect and monitor the location of all U.S. submarines by the year 2000. The reason? We export as 'oil exploration equipment' the most advanced American seismological and related high technology."[29]

The purchase of American (and Western) technology is expensive, and the American government has provided assistance to the Communist bloc nations in an effort to increase their purchases.

President Franklin D. Roosevelt, on February 2, 1934, created the Export-Import Bank by an executive order (critics point out, quite correctly, that the President does not have any such authority, according to the Constitution) for the purpose of guaranteeing commercial loans made to foreign, including Communist, nations to increase international trade. Not only does the Bank guarantee loans made, but actually makes loans itself.

But American banking interests also participate in the making of loans to assist Communist nations in purchasing American goods. One of the first banks involved was the Chase Manhattan Bank, controlled by the Rockefeller interests, which opened a banking office in Moscow, Russia, in 1972, at #1 Karl Marx Square. They later opened an office in Communist China in 1973.

Chase's interest in trade with Russia goes back to at least 1933, when Congressman Louis McFadden, then the Chairman of the House Banking Committee, posed the problem: "Find out what business has been transacted for the State Bank of Soviet Russia by its correspondent, the Chase Bank of New York."[30]

(Individuals also align themselves in support of this foreign trade. In 1977, former Secretary of State Henry Kissinger joined the international advisory committee of Chase Manhattan Bank.)

Other Banks are active as well. The Bank of America in 1975 offered the Soviet Government $500 million to finance imports from the United States.[31]

And on October 20, 1969, Rodman Rockefeller, the son of Nelson Rockefeller, and the London firm of N.M. Rothschild entered into a partnership to form a company known as the International Basic Economy Corporation, (IBEC,) to further Soviet-American trade.[32]

One of the most startling examples of this trade occurred in 1977 when the American government sold Russia the world's largest electro-magnet, capable of generating a magnetic field 250,000 times greater than that of the Earth itself. It was being utilized to: "continue the study of electromagnetic radiation and its application in the spheres of weather modification."[33]

Russia began research into the modification of the Earth's weather in 1974, and by 1976, they had four ground-based transmitters in Russia. That winter there was snow in Miami, Florida, for the first time in recorded history.[34]

One can hasten to remember the comment about weather modification made by Zbigniew Brzezinski: "I think we accept the idea of a vast expansion in social regulation. It may take such forms as legislation for the number of children, perhaps even legislation determining the sex of children, once we have choice, *the regulation of weather*, [emphasis added], the regulation of leisure, and so forth."[35]

Brzezinski went on to amplify his thoughts about the "regulation of weather" in his book *Between Two Ages*:

> Not only have new weapons been developed but some of the basic concepts of geography and strategy have been fundamentally altered: space and weather control have replaced Suez or Gibraltar as key elements of strategy.
>
> In addition to improved rocketry, multi-missiles, and more powerful and more accurate bombs, future developments may well include automated or manned space warships, deep-sea installations, chemical and biological weapons, death rays, and still other forms of warfare — even the weather may be tampered with....
>
> Techniques of weather modification could be employed to produce prolonged periods of drought or storm, thereby weakening a nation's capacity and forcing it to accept the demands of the competitor.[36]

(It is interesting to speculate as to which industries might be interested in the ability to produce severely cold, or prolonged periods of winter. The first one that comes to mind is the oil industry, which would sell more heating oil than in a normal winter.)

But Russia and the other eastern European Communist nations are not the only Communist countries to receive technological assistance from the American government. China is quickly being added to the list of countries.

For instance, in 1974, David Rockefeller formed the National Council for U.S.-(Red) China Trade. This was prior to the recognition of Red China as a most favored nation by the government on May 15, 1977, meaning that China would be eligible for U.S. Export-Import Bank credits. These agreements were made in spite of the fact that the American government recognized that at least ten percent of the Chinese people live in forced labor camps. Once again, the cheapest laborers are those who are not paid anything for their efforts.

But such aid and trade to China continues. On May 29, 1980, Secretary of Defense Harold Brown announced that the Carter Administration would allow Red China to purchase air defense radar, helicopters, and transport planes, and that they would authorize American companies to build electronics and helicopter factories in Red China.

But perhaps the true purpose for the recognition of Red China's need for America's latest technology came in an article that reported why America was interested in opening up the China door. A *New York Times* release on July 20, 1978, reported: "Four American oil companies are negotiating with China over the establishment of off shore drilling operations."[37]

The article identified the four companies: Pennzoil, Exxon Corp., Union Oil of California, and Phillips Petroleum.

But once again, the question must be asked as to how the Red Chinese plan on paying for these imports of American technology. China had an additional supply of goods to sell the Americans that other countries, especially Russia, do not have. Senator Barry Goldwater identified this commodity in 1977, when he stated: "reports from [Chinese] refugees- . . . prove beyond any doubt that Red China is the major source of the world's hard drugs. These reports indicate that, at a minimum, Communist China's annual income from drug smuggling is $500 million annually."[38]

The American dollars received in exchange for Chinese drugs are being used to purchase American technology. This is in accordance with a plan set in motion by Chou-En-Lai, the Chinese premier, who described his plan to an Egyptian publisher, Mohammed Heikal, in an interview. Chou said: "We are planting the best kinds of opium especially for Americans."[39]

This activity was confirmed by Ed Reid, a Pulitzer Prize winning author and crime researcher, who said: "There is no question but that the youth of this country are the victims of a conspiracy. The object is to get the kids on drugs and effectively destroy the next generation of adults."[40]

Congressman John Schmitz became aware of the program and intended to expose the evil intent of China's drug traffic: ". . . I intend to cry foul when an American President . . . protects the massive drug trade of an enemy nation in order to assure it the dollars necessary to buy products from a few favored U.S. corporations."[41]

The drug traffic also had another side-effect. It was preparing young people to quietly acquiesce when the government destroyed their rights and freedoms. This conclusion was graphically illustrated in an article that appeared in 1972. It quoted a young student, called a "hippie" in the article, who was a university graduate and who explained what the drug culture had done to him: "No, drugs are not the answer, but I've at least blown my mind so I don't have to ask any questions."[42]

The Chinese also have a purpose in expanding their trade with the United States. This was illustrated by Huang Hua, Foreign Minister of the Red Chinese government, in 1978. He said: "We are discussing trade with the U.S. with a view to expanding it and opening the door wider to take full advantage of the opportunities it presents to build socialism at home and abroad. By opening the door of China-U.S. relations, we are opening wide the door which leads to revolution in the U.S."[43]

The significance of selling equipment and technology to both the Red Chinese and the Russian governments who have both indicated that it is their intention to destroy the American capitalistic system, has not gone unnoticed.

The founding fathers of the United States were concerned about such trade, as they wrote the following into the Constitution of the United States, as Article III, Section 3:

> Treason against the United States shall consist only in levying war against them,
>
> or
>
> in adhering to their enemies, giving them aid and comfort.

The definition of treason includes two separate and distinct actions. Not only was treason an act of war against the United States, but it was also giving aid and comfort to the enemy. Notice that it was not imperative that the United States be at war with the "enemy" in the formal sense, at the time the act of treason was committed.

This is why businessmen and members of the armed forces face prison sentences when they sell military secrets to the Russians. For instance, four people in September, 1981, were indicted for selling microwave tuners and receivers used for electronic surveillance, computer systems and components to Communist East Germany.

Another seller of strategic goods or knowledge to the Russian government, in this case some "missile secrets," received a life sentence and was called a "traitor" by the judge who sentenced him.

Observers notice that the employees of the Department of Commerce approve the sale of similar items to the Russian government and it is not treason.

It is interesting to ask those who justify such programs as selling materials to the Communist countries for their reasons. One Congressman wrote a letter in 1977 to one who asked about why he had supported American trade with Russia. The Congressman replied: "As you probably know, this has always been the case since the United States leads the way in such technology. This is because democracy encourages innovative thinking which others emulate. However, I'm not sure this is bad. The more the Soviet Union adopts to western technology, the more their society opens up and thus the more susceptible to change they become."

The Congressman does not completely support his theory that governments become more open when they trade with the United States. When, in 1975, Congress was asked to vote to prohibit the importation of chrome from Rhodesia, the Congressman voted in favor of the bill.

It is a fair question to ask whether or not the American government knows whether the products that this nation sells to Russia are used in ways that kill people. Commerce Department official Lawrence J. Brady explained: "It is virtually impossible to insure that the advanced technology equipment shipped to the Soviet Union is not diverted to military uses."[44]

The reason that the American government sells strategic technology to the Communist nations around the world was made clear in a 1964 Senate Internal Security Subcommittee report entitled *The Many Crises of the Soviet Economy*. The report said: "On the Communist side, however, east-west trade, despite its apparently limited dollar volume, is not merely of critical importance: it may well be a matter of survival. The Communist bloc must have Western assistance . . . to cope with the chronic deficiencies of its industries."[45]

This position has been confirmed by various Soviet dissidents who have defected to the West and have brought out the truth about the importance of this strategic aid and trade to the Russian government.

One, Alexander Solzhenitsyn, informed the American people on July 5, 1975: "Our whole slave system depends on your economic assistance. When they bury us alive, please do not send them shovels and the most up to date earth-moving equipment."[46] He reiterated this view in another speech to the American people when he said: "Why do we hand over to Communist totalitarianism more and more technology — complex, delicate, developed technology which it needs for armaments and for crushing its own citizens."[47]

But in spite of his warnings, the aid and trade continues.

And the Russian government keeps "crushing its own citizens."

With America's help.

Chapter 31
Science Versus Reason

The world of science has not escaped the attention of the conspiracy, and its interest has been spurred of late by the sudden increase in the research into a competing theory.

The basic foundation block of current scientific thought is the theory of evolution. So important is this theory that there are those who say that anyone finding fault with it is ignorant: "No informed persons doubt any more that the many animal types that inhabit the earth today are the results of a process of evolution."[1]

This position is further strengthened by those who claim that evolution is no longer a theory: "... evolution is not a guess, it is an established theory that is fully proved by known facts."[2]

The purpose of evolution, according to the Socialists, at least in a book entitled *Evolution of Man*, published by the Socialist Worker's Party, is clear: "Modern Socialism is closely allied to the modern scientific theory of evolution. If laborers understand science, they become socialists."[3]

But the theory of evolution has another purpose, more pervasive than the desire to convert the reader to the theories of Socialism. Julian Huxley, a scientist, has explained that: "Darwin pointed out that no supernatural designer was needed since natural selection could account for any known form of life. There was no room for a supernatural agency in its evolution."[4]

So evolution has two direct, non-competing purposes: to convince the student that Socialism is the partner to evolution, and secondly that there is no creative force in the universe.

Huxley further went on to point out that: "The supernatural is being swept out of the universe.... God can no longer be considered as the controller of the universe.... "Operationally, God is beginning to resemble, not a ruler, but the last fading smile of a cosmic Cheshire cat."[5]

The Masonic Order also places a strong emphasis on the theory of evolution, according to W.L. Wilmhurst's book entitled *The Meaning of Masonry*, which adds "This — the evolution of man into superman — was always the purpose of ancient mysteries. Man, who has sprung from the earth and developed through the lower kingdoms of nature, to his present rational state, has yet to complete his evolution by becoming a god-like being and unifying his conscience with the Omniscient...."[6]

So one of the purposes of Masonry is to assist man in the fulfillment of his evolutionary progess on the road to perfection.

But recently, especially in the latter half of the 20th century, a competing theory to evolution was being developed. It is important to understand this new theory and its effect on evolution and science.

The two competing theories may be defined as follows:

1.   Organic Evolution: the theory that all living things have arisen by a materialistic, naturalistic evolutionary process from a single source which itself arose from a dead, inanimate world.

The Smithsonian Institute in Washington D.C. has defined evolution in this manner:

> Evolution is the concept that species change through time. Over millions of years small changes accumulate to become large differences, new species arise, others die out. Rates of change vary greatly, and directions of change are unpredictable.[7]

The competing theory is defined as:

2.   Creationism: the theory that all basic animal and plant types were brought into existence by acts of a Creator using special processes which are not operative today.

Notice that both theories are just that: theories. Neither can be proved today in the scientific laboratory. Both attempt to explain the Earth and its inhabitants from the various facts existent in the world.

The creationists claim that there are two scientific laws that disprove evolution. These laws are called the Laws of Thermodynamics (Thermodynamics is defined as the science of heat exchange or heat transfer.)

These Laws are as follows:

1. The First Law of Thermodynamics: The total amount of energy remains constant. Energy is not being created anywhere in the universe, it is only being changed.

2. The Second Law of Thermodynamics: Energy is changing through decay. Energy becomes less available for further work.

One of the world's leading creationists, Dr. Henry Morris, has stated that: "The Second Law demonstrates that there must have been a beginning or otherwise the universe would already be dead. The First Law demonstrates that the universe could not have begun itself, since none of the processes creates anything."[8]

Dr. Morris continued: "The real law of change, however, is one of decay, not of growth, a change 'down' instead of a change 'up.' Thus the laws of thermodynamics sharply conflict with the philosophy of evolution."[9]

Both of these theories look at the universe and then attempt to explain its origin. These two theories are contrary to each other. Evolution theorizes that the earth created life through a gradual process when first lower forms of life were created and then the higher forms evolved from the earlier.

The second theory, Creationism, contends that all animal as well as human life was created at nearly the same moment. Neither theory can be reproduced in the laboratory, and neither is taking place now.

The evolutionists explain that the first cause of life was chance. The creationist explain it as the act of a Creator.

Perhaps a review of the creationist's arguments will assist those who have never examined these two theories side by side. There are at least nine strong arguments against the theories of the evolutionists.

1. CHANCE: The evolutionists theorize that simple life originated from the creation of amino acids, which later combined in chains to form protein, all by the randomness of chance.

A simple protein would consist of a chain of about 100 simple amino acids. But not just any combination of these amino acids will give life. There is only one: all other combinations will not give life.

The chance of 100 amino acids aligning in exactly the right order is one chance in one followed by 158 zeroes, or

one in

100,000,000,000,000,000,000,000,000,000,000,000,000,000,000,000,
000,000,000,000,000,000,000,000,000,000,000,000,000,000,000,000,
000,000,000,000,000,000,000,000,000,000,000,000,000,000,000,000
chances.

"Astro-physicists estimate that there are no more than 10^{80} infinitesimal "particles" in the universe (one followed by 80 zeros), and that the age of the universe in its present form is no greater than 10^{18} seconds (30 billion years.)

"Assuming each particle can participate in a thousand billion 10^{12} different events every second, (this is impossibly high, of course) then the greatest number of events that could ever happen (or trials that could ever be made) in all the universe throughout its entire history is only 10^{80} x 10^{18} x 10^{12} or 10^{110} (one followed by 110 zeroes.)

Any event with a probability of less than one change in 10^{110} therefore cannot occur.

"Its probability becomes zero, at least in our known universe."

Thus, the above-suggested ordered arrangement of 100 components (100 amino acids forming in a chain to give simple life) has a zero probability. It could *never* happen by chance." (emphasis added)[10]

That enormous figure of 1 followed by 158 zeroes can be compared in its size with the estimate of today's scientists that there are only 1 followed by 22 zeroes stars in the universe.

If chaos cannot produce order of such miniscule proportions, how can it be expected to blindly generate all of the order that scientists find in the universe?

Edward Conklin, a biologist, has said that: "The probability of life originating from accident [or chance] is comparable to the probability of the unabridged dictionary resulting from an explosion in a print shop."

This question of whether chaos could produce order was faced by two of England's most eminent scientists. They studied the probability of life occurring by chance. The two scientists, Professor Sir Fred Hoyle and Professor Chandra Wickramasinghe, independently concluded that "the probability of life originating at random is so utterly miniscule as to make it absurd." Each found that the odds against the spark of life originating accidentally on earth was staggering -- in mathematical jargon 10 to the power of 40,000. (The number 1 followed by 40,000 zeroes. That would be approximately 12 pages of typewritten zeroes of 55 lines of 60 spaces per page.)

They concluded that it became sensible that "the favourable properties of physics, on which life depends, are in every respect deliberate. There is no other way in which we can understand . . . life except to invoke the creations on a cosmic scale. We realize that the only logical answer to life is creation— and not accidental shuffling."

The article that reported on their conclusions, the August 14, 1981, London *Daily Express,* carried this headline: "There *must* be a God."

In other words, life starting by chance doesn't have a chance!

2. THE FOSSIL EVIDENCE: *The Arizona Daily Star* of August 17. 1981, carried a picture of a recently deceased cow decaying on the desert. The picture revealed that there was nothing of the animal but some very bleached bones. There was no skin, hair, or internal organs left of the animal. These had been ravaged by the elements, by other animals, and by bacteria.

This decaying animal, soon to be little more than some badly decayed bones, raises an interesting question: how is a fossil made?

The longer the animal lies in the elements, the less there is to fossilize. Yet the scientists tell the world that it takes millions of years for the required amount of dust, mud or debris to cover the animal. Yet fossils have been found nearly intact, down to the skin and wrinkles (fossilized worms, for instance).

A fossilized worm, down to the little convolutions of its body, implies a sudden deposition of mud to cover it and then chemical exchange to make the animal hard enough to withstand the enormous pressure of the huge amounts of dirt above the fossil.

Clams have been found with their muscles intact, which implies a sudden deposition of debris over them, and then rapid chemical exchange, making the muscles inside the clam shell a hard fossil. It would be presumed that, if these clams had slowly decayed during the time it would take to slowly cover them up, the muscle would decay.

The problem of how the slow accumulation of dust covering up a carcass can account for the fossilization of a land animal is not the only problem for the evolutionists, however.

The same problem exists in the fossilization of animals in the water. One scientist indicated that: "when fish decay their bones disconnect in less than one week. [The scientist] said that means the presence of fish fossils in complete form is evidence of a catastrophe that covered the fish suddenly and locked their bones in place."[11]

This problem of fossil creation is a problem for the evolutionists but not for the creationists who believe in a worldwide flood that had the ability to suddenly and quickly deposit huge amounts of mud and dirt on dead animals, both on the land and in the sea.

But this is not the only problem for the evolutionists. The theory demands numerous intermediate living things which can be hooked together in an attempt to show an evolutionary sequence.

"However, the fossil record reveals a *profound change* from reptilian host to mammals — and without any proven intermediaries" (Emphasis in original.)[12]

The evolutionists theorize that the fossil record will show a step-by-step development of higher to lower forms of life, the deeper the scientist digs into the earth.

The creationists theorize that the fossil record will reveal the sudden appearance of life of high and low forms at the lowest strata with no evidence of lower forms changing to higher forms as the scientist moves upward through other strata of rock. This is because the creationist believes that all life arose spontaneously at roughly the same time.

The first identifiable life is found as fossil evidence in the Cambrian layer of rock, supposedly 500,000,000 (five hundred million) years old. There are no known fossil evidences in the two layers underneath. There have been billions of fossils found in this one layer alone and all have been of a highly complex nature. No one has found any fossil evidence of a development of life from a single cell, just as the creationists theorized.

One textbook agrees. Stansfield's *Science of Evolution*, published by Macmillan in 1977, says this about the Cambrian layer: "During the Cambrian Period, there suddenly appeared representatives of nearly all the major groups of animals now recognized. It was as if a giant curtain had been lifted to reveal a world teeming with life in fantastic diversity."[13]

Creationists have also pointed out another problem with the reasonings of the evolutionists. They question their conclusions that the oldest fossils are always found in the oldest rocks. One creationist has written:

> The fossil evidence that life has evolved from simple to complex forms over the geological ages depends on the geological ages of the specific rocks in which these fossils are found.
>
> The rocks are assigned geological ages based on the fossil assemblages which they contain.
>
> The fossils, in turn, are arranged on the basis of their assumed evolutionary relationships.
>
> Thus, the main evidence for evolution is based on the assumption of evolution.[14]

In other words, the reason the rocks are old is because the fossils in them are old. The reason the fossils are old is because the rocks they are contained in are old. This is called circular reasoning.

Another problem for the evolutionist in the fossil record is that "anything approaching the complete geological column is never found at any one place on the Earth's surface...." In fact, "... it is not at all unusual for strata to be found completely out of the approved order, with 'old' strata resting comfortably on top of 'young' strata."[15] (The geological column is a column that shows the various layers, one on top of another. The older layers are supposed to be on the bottom, the newer layers on the top. Each layer was supposedly laid down on top of the layer just underneath. This process assumedly took billions of years.)

In addition to this insurmountable problem for the evolutionists, there is another. "It is now known that complex plants existed in the Cambrian Period, which, on the evolutionary time scale, is 200 million years or so before even simple land plants are supposed to have evolved."[16]

And in Glacier Park, for example, "There are numerous localities around the world where supposedly older and simple fossils have been deposited in layers vertically above layers containing 'younger,' more complex, fossils."[17]

But one of the most startling discrepancies in the fossil record came to light when a tuatara lizard was found alive on some islands off of New Zealand after the animal was supposedly extinct. Because the scientists have not found any fossil remains of the lizard in any rock supposedly younger than 135 million years old, they presumed that the lizard was extinct. In other words, the animal once lived 135 million years ago, but not between then and the present, as there have been no fossil remains of the lizard found in those layers of rock above those supposedly 135 million years old. Finding some living tuaturas on the surface of the earth really puzzled them. Where are the fossil remains of the lizard for the last 135 million years?

Don't ask the evolutionist. Only the creationist has the answer: the assumptions made in dating fossils is wrong.[18]

Such anomalies are very common all over the world. For instance, one scientist became troubled when he was checking fossil remains in the Grand Canyon. He found a layer of rock containing a certain fossil. Above that layer was a thick barren layer, indicating that the fossil had become extinct. But the layer directly above the barren layer was a layer containing the fossil evidences again. "The evolutionary theory allows no backtracking, no renewal of a species, once it has become extinct."[19]

The fossil record's inability to explain the basic tenet of evolution, that simple life evolved into complex life, has been noted by some prestigious scientists. One, David Raup of Chicago's famous Field Museum, has said this about the fossil record: "We are now about 120 years after Darwin and the knowledge of the fossil record has been greatly expanded. Ironically, we have even fewer examples of evolutionary transition than we had in Darwin's time. By this I mean that some of the classic cases of darwinian change in the fossil record, such as the evolution of the horse in North America, has had to be discarded or modified as a result of more detailed information."[20]

In spite of all of these problems, the evolutionists still continue to hold up the fossil record as the evidence proving their case. Perhaps the reason this is so lies in the rather interesting fact that "more than half of the geologists in the world work directly for oil companies, and the support for many geologists in academic [pursuits] and [in] government comes from petroleum."[21]

3. MUTATIONS: The *Arizona Daily Star* of April 4, 1981, carried a picture

of a two-headed snake. The caption underneath the picture said that the associate professor of zoology at Arizona State University said that the snake "wouldn't last in the wild."[22] The snake was a mutation and it would have difficulty surviving in nature.

Evolutionists claim that mutations are the changes that account for the changes in species, yet scientists know that about ninety-nine out of one hundred mutations produce inferior creatures, such as the two headed snake, that "wouldn't last in the wild." If this is true, then the fossilized remains of these ninety-nine unsuccessful mutations should be in the fossil record, as well as the successful ones found so abundantly. The fossil record reveals no fossil remains of known mutations.

4.   TIME: The evolutionists theorize that there have been millions, if not billions, of years in which man and the various animals have been able to evolve into higher forms of life. Certain species have died out and become extinct before other species, including man, evolved.

At a debate between an evolutionist and a creationist in Tucson, the evolutionist, a professor at the University of Arizona, claimed that, if ever fossil records of man could be found alongside fossil records of the dinosaur, this find would seriously weaken, but not destroy, the evolutionary theory.

He explained that this was because the dinosaurs had become extinct, according to the evolutionary theory, around sixty million years before the appearance of man on the earth.

One of the spectators at the debate hastened to point out to the scientist that such fossil evidence did indeed exist at the Paluxy River near Glen Rose, Texas, south of Fort Worth. Apparently a flood in 1900 eroded away the top layer of the mud and exposed a limestone layer underneath it. This limestone layer, supposedly 120 million years old, contained a rather startling discovery. The stone contained human footprints! Since it is theorized that man appeared on Earth about 1 million years ago, approximately 119 million years of time had disappeared, at least if the rock was supposedly 120 million years old.

But there was even something more startling in the stone. The human footprints were side by side dinosaur footprints!

The theory is that the dinosaur died out about 60 million years ago. That means, according to the evolutionary theory, that it is impossible for man and the dinosaur to have been on the Earth at the same time.

The spectator asked the professor if he had an explanation. Did man and the dinosaur co-habitate the Earth at the same time? How could the rock be 120 million years old, the dinosaur footprints 60 million years old, and the man's footprints 1 million years old?

The scientist was quick to offer an explanation.

His position was that the rock was once soft, about 60 million years ago.

The dinosaur moved through the mud, leaving behind the evidence of his presence, his footprints. The mud became hard and then some 59 million years later, became soft once again. Man moved through the soft mud, leaving behind his footprints. Then, for some unexplained reason, the rock became hard again, leaving both the dinosaur and human footprints side by side.

When questioned as to why the dinosaur footprints didn't erode when the limestone became soft again, unless man's footprints were placed down in the soft mud precisely the same day the mud got soft and then hard again, the scientist had to admit that he had no answer.

Also, what mechanism did the professor know about that could cause rock to become hard, then soft, then hard, then soft, and then hard again? Once again, he had no answer. The scientist was unwilling to admit that the fossilized footprints "weakened, but didn't destroy" his evolutionary theory, even though that conclusion was his opening statement. He was bending the facts to explain his theory, rather than adjusting the theory to explain the facts. His evolutionary theory postulated that man and dinosaur couldn't have co-existed at the same time; therefore, the fossilized evidence must be incorrect or explained away. When confronted with the evidence, he approached the dilemma the only way he could: he had to deny the facts.

One scientist, when asked about some of the human footprints in the stone, while he was an observer to their uncovering at the site in about 1955, said that if the human footprints were alone in the rock, he would have to conclude that they were human. But since they were beside the dinosaur footprints, he wasn't sure.

To further complicate the problem for the professor at the debate, other scientists have carbon dated some plants in the limestone layer. They were found to be 38,000 to 39,000 years old, quite a bit earlier than the supposed age of the rock which is theorized to be 120,000,000 years old.

In addition, other scientists have found another problem for the evolution theory at this same site. They have found human footprints in rock layers below strata containing the footprints of the dinosaur.

All of these facts fit the creationist's theory that holds that man and the dinosaur lived at the same time, not millions of years apart, but thousands of years ago. This explains the footprints of both at the same site, in the same layer of limestone.

5.   SEQUENCE: The age-old question of "which came first, the chicken or the egg?" is an appropriate question to ask in the evolution versus creation debate. The world is full of examples of animals and plants that had to appear on the scene at precisely the same moment in the past.

For instance, the bee and the flower both had to appear at precisely the same time or the earlier would not be able to survive.

Another problem for the evolutionist is the question of when certain predators for certain animals evolved.

There is a naturally occurring balance of nature whereby the population of one species is kept in balance by another species, its natural predator. If the population of the hunted animal suddenly increases, the population of the second animal, the hunter, increases as well. As the population of the hunted animal decreases, so does the population of the second animal.

It is only when man artifically intervenes in the environment that this system gets out of balance.

Take, for example, the case of the rabbit in Australia. This animal is not native to this country and was reportedly brought there as a game animal to be hunted for sport. But since the rabbit has no natural predator in Australia and is a rapid breeder, the animal is increasing in numbers so quickly that it is starving other animals native to the land because it is consuming their share of the available food.

A similar problem is occurring in Oregon with the opposum. This animal is also not native to the area, having been brought to the Northwest by Southerners who came to build ships during World War II. After the war was over, the Southerners returned to the South and they released whatever animals they had on hand at the time. These animals breed rather rapidly and have spread all over the Northwest to the point where they are eating vital food needed by other animals. The opposum has no natural predators, and it is prospering to the detriment of other animals native to the area. (Some local wags have claimed that the only predator of the opposum is the '55 Chevy! It seems that the automobile is the major predator of this little animal because it strikes so many of them at night as they cross the roads looking for food.) It has become a real problem for those living in the Northwest.

But these examples ask the question that the evolutionists have trouble answering: the hunted animal and its predator, the hunter, had to "evolve" at precisely the same time, or either the world would be over-populated by the hunted animal, if it "evolved" first, or with large quantities of fossils of the hunter if it "evolved" before its food supply "evolved."

Man's attempts to artifically induce an animal into the environment where there is no natural predator proves that both the hunted animal and its predator had to "evolve" precisely at the same time.

The existence of such a balance of nature strongly implies a designer.

6.   MISSING LINKS: One of the areas most open to question by the creationists is the area of the "missing links," the humans and near humans who supposedly link man and his ancestors.

A quick look at some of these "missing links," or early men, shows how weak this evidence is for the case of the evolutionists.

a. The Zinjanthropus Man: The fossil evidence of this early "man" was discovered in strata supposedly 1 and 3/4 million years old. Yet when the scientists carbon dated other material in the same layer, that material was found to be approximately 10,000 years old.

b. The Nebraska Man: This connecting link was cited at the famous Scopes trial in Tennessee by leading scientists to prove than man had evolved from earlier forms of existence.

The fossil evidence of the Nebraska Man consisted of a tooth that was said to have come from a prehistoric man who supposedly lived one million years ago. Scientists used this tooth to reconstruct the Nebraska man's flesh, hair and family.[23] Yet when more fossils were unearthed at the same site, it was discovered that the Nebraska man was only a pig.

c. Piltdown Man: This man was supposed to be half a million years old and was constructed from a piece of jaw discovered in 1912. The fossilized jaw was considered to be authentic until 1953 when it was discovered that the jaw had turned out to be the jawbone of a modern ape. In addition, the jawbone had been filed down and stained to look older.

In other words, it was a deliberate hoax.[24]

d. Neandethal Man: This connecting link was once pictured as a link between apes and man, but was later found out to be strictly human, just another man.

One can only speculate as to why the evolutionary scientist is so quick to grasp at anything that appears to be a link connecting man with the ape. Perhaps the question has been answered by the following statement:

> The real reason why—after multitudes of fossil fragments have been examined and sorted by evolutionary anthropologists for over a hundred years—there is still no agreement as to man's evolutionary ancestry, is because he had no evolutionary ancestry!
>
> All of the real evidence indicates that man was true man right from the start.[25]

Maybe this is why some evolutionists are now shifting away from the theory that man evolved from apes or monkeys. Unfortunately, their predetermined prejudices stay with them when they develop new theories. Take, for instance, the new theory postulated by Dr. Geoffrey Bourne, Director of Yerkes Regional Primate Research Center of Emory University. Dr. Bourne is an Australian born, Oxford educated American cell biologist, anatomist, and now considered to be one of the world's leading primatologists.

He has declared his belief that "apes and monkeys are the evolutionary descendants of man!"[26]

This scientist wants man to believe that the ape and monkey are man's grandchildren!

7.   MALE AND FEMALE: The obvious fact that so many animal species have evolved into male and female types is another thorny problem for the evolutionists.

Both sexes are absolutely essential to the continued propagation of the animal species, and it is absolutely imperative that both evolved at precisely the same time. That means that, if one species of animal evolved a male into a higher form of life in the process of evolution, that animal had to have a female of exactly the same type evolve at precisely the same time, or the new male wouldn't have been able to reproduce itself.

8.   THE AGE OF THE UNIVERSE: It is claimed by the evolutionists that the Earth was created about 4.5 billion years ago. The creationists are now developing a very effective scientific argument that the Earth cannot be older than 10,000 years old.

Some of the arguments for a young Earth are as follows:

a. **Decay of the Magnetic Field:** National Aeronautical and Space Administration orbiting satellites have been measuring the Earth's magnetic field and have found that it is slowly decaying, or wearing down.

One scientist has interpreted these scientific data and has drawn this conclusion: "Since the Earth's magnetic field is decaying, extrapolation back into the past more than 10,000 years predicts a current flow so vast that the earth's structure could not survive the heat produced. Thus the Earth cannot be much older than 10,000 years."[27]

b. **Oil Seepage:** It is estimated that the amount of oil that seeps into the oceans is 5 million tons per year. It is also estimated that the total amount of offshore oil is 100 billion tons, which means that the total amount of oil would have been lost to the oceans 2500 times, if oil is estimated to be 50 million years old, or that it would only take about 20,000 years to deplete the entire quantity of offshore oil.[28]

c. **Helium Decay:** As plant and animal life dies and then decays, a certain amount of helium is released into the atmosphere. Estimating by the rate of addition of helium to the atmosphere from radioactive decay, the age of the Earth appears to be about 10,000 years old, even allowing for moderate helium escape to the space above the atmosphere.[29]

d. **Population Growth:** Evolutionists generally theorize that man evolved about 1 million years ago. These early humans have multiplied, so the theory goes, to the point where there are now about 4 billion people on the Earth. "The same population statistics which supposedly presage a serious population problem in the future also indicate a very recent origin of man in the past....

"An initial population of only two people, increasing at 2% a year, would become 3.5 billion in only 1,075 years....

"An average population growth of only ½ of one percent would generate the present world population in only 4,000 years."[30]

e. **Meteoritic Dust on the Earth:** "There is no measurable accumulation of meteoritic dust on the Earth's surface, but present rates of influx of such dust from space would produce a layer ⅛th of an inch thick all over the Earth in a million years, and a layer 54 feet thick in 5 billion years."[31]

f. Decay of the Sun: In 1980, two scientists discovered the ". . . sun has been contracting 0.1% per century . . . . "

They believed that this shrinkage was continuous and has occurred at the same rate as in the past.

If this is correct, only 100,000 years ago the sun would be twice as big as it is today; 20 million years ago, the surface of the sun would touch the Earth and the Earth would have been a cinder.[32]

g. Meteoritic Dust on the Moon: The scientists who planned America's lunar landing probe theorized that the moon was approximately 4.5 billion years old. They knew that, as the moon orbited through space, meteoritic dust fell on its surface. They were somewhat able to scientifically estimate the exact quantity of dust that had fallen during its supposed 4.5 billion year life.

The scientists theorized that the moon had large quantities of dust on its surface because it was so old. They then concluded that the lunar landing device would sink in this dust when it landed. So they devised the disc-shaped feet on the landing device so that the feet would support its weight when it landed.

Their theories were in part supported by the theory of R.A. Lyttleton of Cambridge University. He theorized that:

> Since there is no atmosphere on the moon, the moon's surface is exposed to direct radiation.
>
> Thus, the strong ultra-violet light and x-rays can destroy the surface layers of exposed rocks and reduce them to dust at a rate of a few thousandths of an inch per year.
>
> If a layer, say 0.0004 inch thick in pulverized matter, is formed per year, then, in 10,000 years a layer of about four inches in depth would be produced; in 100,000 years a layer of 40 inches; in 1,000,000 years a layer of 3.3 feet; in 1,000,000,000 years a layer of 6.3 miles; and in 4,500,000,000 years (4.5 billion years, the supposed age of the moon) a layer of about 28 miles in depth would be formed.

Yet when the lunar landing device landed on the moon, they measured the dust layer to be "⅛th inch to 3 inches in thickness."[33]

So if Professor Lyttleton's theories are correct, the moon is no older than about 10,000 years, or less, and certainly not 4,500,000,000 years in age.

9. Symbiosis: Symbiosis is defined as: "the intimate living together of two dissimilar organisms in a mutually beneficial relationship."

And the existence of several symbiotic relationships presents real problems for the evolutionists.

For instance, the Nile crocodile allows a small bird, called the Egyptian plover, to enter its mouth to clean its teeth of harmful bacteria. If the plover does not remove these intruders, the crocodile can be seriously harmed. The parasites are the Plover bird's sole source of nutrition.

In other words, the two animals need each other and had to occur at precisely the same time or one would not have been able to survive to wait for the other.

But symbiosis is not confined to the animal kingdom alone.

Frequently the plant and animal kingdoms join together in a symbiotic relationship, mutually beneficial to both parties. Such is the case of the yucca moth and the yucca plant. The moth collects a ball of pollen, stuffs it into a seed chamber of the yucca plant, and then lays a few eggs inside the seed. Since the larvae that hatch can feed only on developing yucca seeds, their growth is provided for; and since some seeds are left and this yucca cannot otherwise pollinate itself, the plant also benefits.

Neither the plant nor the animal would have been able to survive if both didn't occur at precisely the same time.

The occurrence of such design demands a designer!

But even in view of such problems in the field of evolutionary science, the evolutionists persist in their theories. Why is it so important that the theory of evolution be defended in view of the enormous evidence against it? Does it have a purpose that demands its defense?

Several have attempted to answer that question.

One, the scientist Julian Huxley, already quoted on this subject, informs the student: "It is clear that the doctrine of evolution is directly antagonistic to that of creation.... Evolution, if consistently accepted, makes it impossible to believe in the Bible."[34]

The author of a book on the subject of Humanism, Claire Chambers, has stated the following in answer to this question: "Before man can be enslaved, his state of mind must be reduced from spirituality to carnality. He must learn to think of himself as basically an animal with no spiritual purpose. Once man is freed from his obligations to God, the way is cleared for his ultimate obedience to the Communist State as his master."[35]

Another, writer H.L. Mencken, an observer at the famous Scopes evolution trial that tested the right of the state to limit school curriculums, said this:

> There is, it appears, a conspiracy of scientists afoot.
> Their purpose is to break down religion, propagate immorality, and so reduce mankind to the level of the brutes.
> They are the sworn and sinister agents of Beelzebub (the devil) who "yearns to conquer the world...."[36]

Chapter 32
Abortion and Laetrile

When a woman takes the life of her unborn child on the theory that she may do what she wishes with her own body, she receives the sanction of the Federal Supreme Court.

But if she purchases Laetrile in an attempt to save a life — either her child's or her own — she has participated in a criminal act.[1]

On October 21, 1980, the Supreme Court turned away arguments brought before it that would have allowed a terminal cancer patient the right to use Laetrile as an aid to eliminating the cancer. In essence, the Court stated that the individual's body did not belong to the individual but to the state, and that the state had the right to tell the individual what he or she may do with his or her own body.

On Monday 22, 1973, the Supreme Court struck down all restrictive laws against abortion, in essence saying that the individual had the right to do with her own body whatever she wanted; the individual's body did not belong to the state.

So the question of whom the individual's body belongs to, the state or the individual, has not been officially determined by the Supreme Court.

This hypocritical contradiction in the thinking of the Supreme Court is intentional, as can be illustrated by the examination of the circumstances behind these contradictory decisions.

The first industry to be examined in the search for the rationale of the Supreme Court's thinking is the food industry.

It is obvious from a reading of the list of ingredients on the label of a food product that more and more chemical substitutes or synthetic foods are appearing in the food consumed by the American people.

Perhaps the major reason for this shift from natural to synthetic or chemical foods is because of the cartel agreements signed between the giant chemical cartel, I.G. Farben, and the following American companies: Borden, Carnation, General Mills, M.W. Kellogg Co., Nestle's, and Pet Milk.[2]

And I.G. Farben either owns outright or has had a substantial financial interest in, or has had other cartel agreements with the following: Owl Drug, Parke Davis & Co., Bayer Co., Whitehall Laboratories, Chef-Boy-Ar-Dee Foods, Bristol Myers, and Squibb and Sons.[3]

The importance of these cartel agreements between I.G. Farben and some of America's largest food and drug suppliers becomes all the more evident when the claims of those supporting the use of Laetrile as a cancer cure or suppressant are studied.

Laetrile has an interesting history: "Dr Ernst T. Krebs Jr., a bio-chemist . . . had advanced the theory that cancer . . . is merely a deficiency disease aggravated by lack of an essential food compound abundantly in nature in over twelve hundred edible plants and [was] found virtually in every part of the world."[4]

Laetrile is found in such nuts, berries and foods as: bitter almonds, buckwheat, apricot seeds, alfalfa, cherry seeds, peas, grasses, berries, maize, macadamia nuts, sorghum, lentils, millet, linseed, and apple seeds.[5]

Some nutritionists have felt that the American public was not eating those grains, berries and foods high in Laetrile, and was therefore experiencing an increasing rate of cancer. They noticed that most of the grains consumed by the food consumer were hybridized and that Laetrile had been removed by genetic engineering. This meant that the grains high in Laetrile, such as millet and buckwheat, those that were the grain staples consumed by America's early pioneers, had either been eliminated or replaced by those hybridized grains containing little or no Laetrile.

In addition, some nutritionists have discovered entire societies where there is little or no cancer. One group, living in the remote recesses of the Himalaya Mountains between West Pakistan, India and China, known as the Hunzas, has never had a case of cancer in their society. These people consume the apricot and its Laetrile-bearing seed as the main staple of their diet.

(The eating of seeds for nutrition is a Biblical concept. Genesis 1:29 reads: "And God said: 'Behold I have given you every herb bearing seed upon the earth, and all trees that have in themselves seed of their own kind, to be your meat.'")

Other societies, also cancer free, consume large quantities of Laetrile-bearing grains and grasses as main staples of their diet.

Laetrile is a natural, non-toxic, water-soluble substance entirely normal to and compatible with human metabolism. The proper name for a food factor that contains these properties is a vitamin.

But every time the proponents of the use of Laetrile in cancer cases attempt to secure permission to conduct official tests in U.S. hospitals, they are turned down.

When famed chemist Linus Pauling, twice a Nobel Prize winner, tried to secure research funds from the National Cancer Institute for medical research on Vitamin C as a possible cancer cure, he was told that "The road to a vitamin answer to cancer is of no medical interest."[6]

Other researchers, especially those testing for chemical solutions to cancer, are far more successful. For instance, the Sloan-Kettering Institute for Cancer Research, in New York, is financed in part by: "... the federal government and the Rockefeller Foundation."[7]

But in 1981, according to the *U.S. News and World Report*, the government relented to pressure from those suggesting that Laetrile be tested as a possible cure to cancer, and agreed to a series of tests in four major medical centers. After running their tests, they concluded that it was not effective.[8]

The results brought charges from the Laetrile proponents.

For instance, Robert Henderson, a spokesman for the pro-Laetrile Committee for Freedom of Choice in Cancer Therapy, charged that the tests were neither honest nor fair and were "probably designed to fail." Mr. Henderson said: "... the researchers did not continue the intravenous injections of amygdalin, another name for Laetrile, long enough, and they used an 'impure form' of the compound."[9]

A few months later, in July, 1981, Robert Bradford and Michael Culbert of the Committee issued a joint statement charging the National Cancer Institute with: "gross fraud and deceit on the American public and of murder (negligent homicide) in the matter of cancer patients enrolled in the so-called 'Laetrile clinical trials'...."[10]

One author, G. Edward Griffin, in his book *World Without Cancer, Part I*, informed the reader why he felt that the medical establishment wanted the tests to fail: "There are far more people making a living from cancer than are dying from it. If the riddle were to be solved by a simple vitamin, this gigantic commercial and political industry could be wiped out overnight."[11]

But Laetrile has proven its effectiveness in country after country (as of 1973, there were 22 nations that had legalized its use in cancer therapy.) One nation, Mexico, after years of testing in Army hospitals, legalized its use, and in fact Dr. Ernesto Contreras at his Good Samaritan Cancer Clinic, in Tijuana, Mexico, has been effectively treating cancer with Laetrile for over 17 years.

But, in the U.S., those who want to take Laetrile as a treatment for their cancer can't, because the individual's body does not belong to the individual.

It does only if you wish to take the life of an unborn child!

The Supreme Court has so ruled!

Chapter 33
World Government

One of the most glaring differences between the so-called "conservative" and the so-called "liberal" is how each views the issues of man's relationship to the world.

Basically, this difference can be described as follows:

The conservative position: The conservative appeals to the spiritual nature of man, believing that man's problems arise because of the nature of man himself. The solution to the problems of the world lies in the changing of man himself.

The liberal position: The liberal appeals to the materialistic nature of man, believing that man's problems arise because of the environment. The liberal's solution is to change the environment so that man will be happy.

The ultimate device to completely control man's environment is a one-world government, and the current organization of the world into nations becomes the obvious obstacle to such a change.

This has been the program and the goal of each of the various individuals and organizations discussed in this study since the early formation of the Illuminati.

Various indicators have presented themselves to indicate that the goal of these planners, world government, is about to reach fruition.

On May 18, 1972, Roy M. Ash, from the Office of Management and Budget during the Nixon administration, laid down the time frame, as far as he could see it, for the world government: "Within two decades [sometime before 1992] the institutional framework for a World Economic Community will be in place . . . " when "aspects of individual sovereignty will be given over to supernational authority.[1]

James P. Warburg in his book *The West in Crisis*, also went on record of supporting the need for a world government:

"A world order without world law is an anachronism; and that, since war now means the extinction of civilization, a world which fails to establish the rule of law over the nation-states cannot long continue to exist. We are living in a perilous period of transition from the era of the fully sovereign nation-state to the era of world government."[2]

Warburg once told a Senate Committee, on February 17, 1950, how the peoples of the world would receive this world-government: "We shall have world government whether you like it or not, if not by consent by conquest."[3]

The world government envisioned by these seers includes plans for a world police force. One who has described the need for such a constabulary is historian Arnold Toynbee: "We are approaching the point at which the only effective scale for operations of any importance will be the global scale. The local states ought to be deprived of their sovereignty and subordinated to the sovereignty of a global world government. I think the world state will still need an armed police [and the] world government will have to command sufficient force to be able to impose peace."[4]

To convince the people of the world to give up their national sovereignty and turn it over to a world government is a monumental task. However, the planners do not feel it is insurmountable. One of those who foresaw the problem has also offered the solution. Dr. Brock Chisolm, director of the World Health Organization, is on record as stating:

> To achieve world government, it is necessary to remove from the minds of men their individualism, loyalty to family tradition, national patriotism and religious dogmas . . . .
>
> We have swallowed all manner of poisonous certainties fed us by our parents, our Sunday and day school teachers, our politicians, our priests, our newspapers and others with vested interests in controlling us.
>
> The reinterpretation and eventual eradication of the concept of right and wrong which has been the basis of child training, the substitution of intelligent and rational thinking for faith in the certainties of the old people, these are the belated objectives . . . for

charting the changes in human behavior.[5]

In addition to destroying man's basic loyalties to family, nation and religion, the nation must be conditioned to the belief that less is better than more. The standard of living of those in the affluent nations must be reduced. This will be done by a slow, gradual process of conditioning the citizens of the rich nations to survive on less than they produce.

This position was made clear by John Knowles, the President of the Rockefeller Foundation, in its annual report for 1975: "I am sure of only one thing—more is not necessarily better. The web of interdependence is tightening. We are one world and there will be one future—for better or for worse—for us all. Central to a new ethic of making less more is controlled economic growth which conserves scarce resources, provides more equitable distribution of income and wealth...."

In addition to controlling the supply of goods, Mr. Knowles also urges the control of the demand for goods: "It is also necessary to control fertility rates at the replacement level and to achieve zero population growth as rapidly as possible...."[6]

Once the people in the more productive nations have been conditioned to live with less, they can be conditioned to share their excess wealth with the less productive nations. This sharing of the wealth is called the New International Economic Order, a phrase that was defined by Senator Charles Percy, a member of the Council on Foreign Relations:

> The philosophy behind the new international economic order is based on the fact that the developed wealthier nations use a substantially greater share of the earth's resources... than do the less developed poor nations.
>
> The new order calls for a more equitable distribution of the earth's resources among the earth's people and redistribution of wealth among rich and poor nations.[7]

In keeping with this program, on March 30, 1979, Secretary of State Cyrus Vance, (also a member of the CFR), promised that the United States would step up its economic aid to the developing nations of the world in order to hasten "progress toward a more equitable and healthy new international economic order."[8]

The progress towards this world government has been steady, not because the people of the richer countries have freely chosen it after hearing the arguments on both sides, but because they have been lied to. A good case in point is the article written by Richard Gardner, a top advisor to President Jimmy Carter, who was also Ambassador to Italy, in the April, 1974, issue of *Foreign Affairs*, the monthly journal of the Council on Foreign Relations. He wrote that "the 'house of world order' will have to be built from the bottom up rather than from the top down.... An end run around national sovereignty, eroding it piece by piece, will accomplish more than the old fashioned frontal assault."⁹

The United States government has presented its blueprint for the transfer of America's military forces to the one-world government, in this case, the fledgling world government, the United Nations, in a document published in 1961.

This document, entitled *Freedom From War—State Department Publication 7277*, was strangely removed from publication a couple of years after the American people had had a chance to read it for themselves. It proposed the gradual surrender of all of the American forces to a world police force in a three-phase program:

> The first stage would significantly reduce the capabilities of nations to wage war by reducing the armed forces of the nations; 2: the nuclear capabilities would be reduced by treaties; and 3: U.N. "peace-keeping" powers would be strengthened.
>
> The second stage would provide further substantial reductions in the armed forces; and the establishment of a permanent international peace force within the United Nations.
>
> The third stage would have the nations retaining only those forces required for maintaining internal order, but the United States would provide manpower for the United Nations Peace Force.

This transfer would mean that the Secretary General of the United Nations would become the Commander-In-Chief of the armed forces of the United States, completely in violation of the Constitution of the United States. The Secretary General would, in turn, place the command of this new peace-keeping force over to the Under-Secretary in charge of all military affairs, the Under-Secretary in charge of the Department of Political and Security Council Affairs. This key position has been held by a Communist from either the Soviet Union or a Soviet controlled Communist state since the inception of the United Nations. (This position is the same one that General MacArthur had to report to during the Korean War.)

Since the American people were not completely ready to surrender to the United Nations, this report, as indicated above, was pulled out of circulation and declared to be out of print. But those in charge of having the United States become part of a one-world government have not rested. The next step in this program occurred on January 30, 1976, when the World Affairs Council announced the Declaration of Interdependence. This document was signed by 126 American Senators and Representatives, eight of whom later announced that they had either renounced their participation or admitted that their names had been used without their knowledge.

Former Senator Joseph P. Clark, a member of the sponsoring World Affairs Council, attempted to explain why this new Declaration of Interdependence was necessary:

> The size, range and complexity of government increases — and will continue to do so.
>
> I would defend the proposition that this expansion is good — not bad. Surely, we have reached the point where we can say- ... that Jefferson was wrong: that government is not best which governs least [Jefferson had written: that government is best which governs least].
>
> The fallacy in Jefferson's argument is the assumption that the expansion of government leads to the curtailment of individual freedoms.
>
> That just is not true.[10]

The Declaration supported by Senator Clark read, in part:

> Two centuries ago, our forefathers brought forth a new nation; now we must join with others to bring forth a new world order.
>
> To establish a new world order ... it is essential that mankind free itself from limitations of national prejudice....
>
> We affirm that the economy of all nations is a seamless web, and that no one nation can any longer effectively maintain its processes of production and monetary systems without recognizing the necessity of collaborative regulation by international authorities.
>
> We call upon all nations to strengthen the United Nations ... and other institutions of world order ....[11]

One of those Representatives who chose not to sign the Declaration was Congresswoman Marjorie Holt, who said this: "It calls for the surrender of our national sovereignty to international organizations. It declares that our economy should be regulated by international authorities. It proposes that we enter a 'new world order' that would redistribute the wealth created by the American people."[12]

World government is getting closer.

The New International Order is at hand.

Chapter 34
Peace

It is the ultimate objective of the Conspiracy to force the world to live in peace under a world government. But the planners have a problem: they had used war as a means of controlling the people. They now had to face the problem of how they could control the people during a time of peace.

This question was discussed in great detail by those who wrote the *Report From Iron Mountain.* These individuals foresaw the day when they would have to intentionally design special programs as a means of controlling people during the period of peace. This was an alien thought to them, since they reasoned that man had always operated to control other men by causing wars for that purpose.

They identified the problem: "A viable substitute for war as a social system cannot be a mere symbolic charade. It must involve real risk of real personal destruction and on a scale consistent with the size and complexity of modern social systems. Unless it provided a believable life-and-death threat it will not serve the socially organizing function of war."[1]

After the problem was identified, the next step was to develop solutions to the problem. These solutions were to become the substitutes for the real functions of war, those functions that served to control men during wartime.

First, these "surrogates," or substitutes for the real purpose of war, must meet two principal criteria:

1. They must be wasteful, and
2. They must operate outside the normal supply-demand system.

The second criterion means that the "surrogates" must not be accessible to the whims of the people. In other words, the people must not be able to demand that the government stop spending their tax money in a wasteful manner.

These are the substitutes that the writers of the *Report From Iron Mountain* came up with:

1. Complete government guaranteed health care for all;
2. Making available for all a professional degree through education;
3. Providing spacious living space for all;
4. Mass public transportation;
5. A guaranteed annual income;
6. A series of giant space research programs aimed at unreachable targets;
7. The threat of gross pollution as the principal threat to the survival of the species;
8. The reintroduction of slavery through some form of military service;
9. A universal requirement that procreation be limited to the products of artificial insemination, via the water supplies, to be offset by antidote provided by the government; and
10. A social welfare program.

It was a corollary of the study's position that the "magnitude of the waste . . . [in America's economy must not be less] than 10 percent of the gross national product . . . ."[2]

(In the May 11, 1981, *U.S. News & World Report*, there is a graph showing that the Federal government is spending, as of 1980, 22.9 percent of the gross national product now. This means, according to the *Report From Iron Mountain*, that the Federal Government could easily be spending nearly half of its income in an intentionally wasteful manner.)

The report concluded that: "no serious quantified studies have ever been conducted to determine . . . the minimum levels of population destruction necessary to maintain war-threat credibility under varying political conditions," and "optimum cyclical frequency of 'shooting' wars under varying circumstances of historical relationship" (varying alliances of "balance of power" policies).

This means that they hadn't detemined, as yet, just how often they should plan a war, and just how many people they should have killed, by means of that war, to control the populations of the various nations affected.

It seems incredible to the moral observer that the human mind could conceive such mind-boggling thoughts as the intentional creation of cycles of war and peace as a means of controlling people. Or the use of waste in government as a means of controlling the tax-payers.

Now the observer has the reason that the American government spends tax money to

> Study the mating calls of Central American frogs;
> Research the blood groups of Polish Zlotnika pigs;
> Study German cockroaches;
> Analyze the finish used on musical instruments; and
> Study the diving habits of seals.[3]

This thinking also explains why nothing is done by the government when the United Press wire service publishes a study that the

> U.S. throws away $10 billion through wasteful government spending.[4]

Government is *intended* to waste money!

Chapter 35
Humanism

It is commonly believed that education is aimed at teaching children the 3 R's: "reading, 'riting and 'rithmetic." Those who believe that this is the basic function of education are badly mistaken.

Education has far more important functions.

In 1979, the mother of a San Francisco high school graduate sued the district because her son, after twelve years of public "education," was barely able to read and write. An appeals court ruled that the district was not negligent, however, because: "The science of pedagogy [teaching] itself is fraught with differences and conflicting theories."[1]

Therefore, since no one knows what education is or what it is supposed to do, the district couldn't be held responsible for not teaching a child to read and write or anything else, for that matter.

One of the reasons for the sad state of the "science" known as education has been the gradual introduction into the school system of the religious philosophy known as Secular Humanism.

One of the conclusions of the Reece Committee Investigating Tax Free Foundations, according to the Committee's chief counsel, Rene Wormser, was that the evidence compiled during the investigation: "leads one to the conclusion that there was, indeed, something in the nature of an actual conspiracy among certain leading educators in the United States to bring about Socialism through the use of our school systems. The movement-... was heavily financed by leading foundations...."[2]

Mr. Norman Dodd, former director of the Congressional Committee, identified the source of some of these trends when he testified before the Illinois Joint Legislative Committee on Regional Government, in 1978. He testified about the trustees of the Carnegie Endowment for International Peace who realized that "... they must control education in this country. So they approach[ed] the Rockefeller Foundation with the suggestion that the task be divided between the two of them. The Carnegie Endowment takes on that aspect of education that has a tinge of international significance and the Rockefeller Foundation takes on that portion of education which is domestic in this relationship."[3]

Congressman Eugene Cox confirmed Mr. Dodd's conclusions when he testified: "The Rockefeller Foundation's funds have been used to finance individuals and organizations whose business it has been to get communism into the private and public schools of this country...."[4]

But the planners faced an immense problem. The American public was not ready to accept the introduction of communism into the school systems of the nation. The plan was to change the name, but not the basic philosophy, so that the American people would allow it to be taught in their schools.

The new name of the communist philospophy became Secular Humanism.

Secular is defined by the dictionary as being: "of or relating to worldly things as distinguished from things relating to church and religion; worldly."

Humanism has been defined by the American Humanist Association as: "the belief that man shapes his own destiny. It is a constructive philospohy, a non-theistic religion, a way of life."

Notice that Humanism, according to its own publications, is also a religion, a new way of living in and looking at the world.

Karl Marx was one of the first to link the philosophy of Communism with the philosophy of Humanism, when he said: "Communism as a fully developed naturalism is Humanism...."[5] And again: "Humanism is the denial of God, and the total affirmation of man.... Humanism is nothing else but Marxism."[6]

And in 1970, the New Program of the Communist Party, U.S.A., stated that: "Marxism is not only rational, it is humanist in the best and most profound meaning of the term."[7]

Sir Julian Huxley, a leading scientist, wrote: "I use the word humanist

to mean someone who believes that man is just as much a natural phenomenon as an animal or plant; that his body, mind, and soul were not super-
naturally created but were products of evolution and that he is not under the
control or guidance of any supernatural being or beings but has to rely on
himself and his own powers."[8]

The Humanist philosophy and religion is not new, but it took a
formalized step in 1933 when a group of scientists, educators, ministers,
authors, and others published *The Humanist Manifesto*. This document
contained three introductory paragraphs and then a series of 15 planks
detailing the position of their new philosophy and religion.

A partial reading of this manifesto reveals just what the Humanists
believe in:

> The time has come for widespread recognition of the radical
> change in religious beliefs through the modern world.
>
> Science and economic change has disrupted the old beliefs.
>
> Religions the world over are under the necessity of coming to
> terms with the new conditions created by a vastly increased knowl-
> edge and experience.
>
> In every field of human activity, the vital movement is now in
> the direction of a candid and explicit Humanism.
>
> We therefore affirm the following:
>
> First: Religious humanists regard the universe as self-existing
> and not created.
>
> Second: Humanism believes that man is part of nature and
> that he has emerged as a result of a continuous process.
>
> Sixth: We are convinced that the time has passed for theism (a
> belief in a Creator.)
>
> Fourteenth: The humanists are firmly convinced that the
> existing acquisitive and profit motivated society has shown itself to
> be inadequate. A socialized and cooperative economic order must
> be established to the end that the acquisitive distribution of the
> means of life be possible.[9]

A brief review of each of these statements reveals the nature of the
Humanist philosophy and religion.

The first plank details the position that the universe has always existed
and was not created. Therefore there is no need for a Creator.

The second plank states the belief in evolution as the history of man;
that man has arisen from nothing as the result of his constant battle with his
environment.

The sixth plank states that the Humanists believe that the time for
theism [a belief in a God or Gods], has passed. Therefore, the Humanists

believe, since there is no Creator, that there is no need to believe in one. The Humanists are atheists.

And the fourteenth plank states their belief that the free-enterprise system is inadequate and that it must be replaced with the communist system of forced sharing of all goods produced by the society.

Therefore, the Humanists in 1933 who signed this Manifesto placed their philosophy and religion squarely on a three-legged platform. The Humanists were Evolutionists, Atheists, and Communists.

Their beliefs are in complete agreement with the philosophies of Weishaupt, Marx and Lenin.

But the most significant impact of this Manifesto is the fact that one of the thirty-four signers in 1933 was John Dewey, the so-called "father of Progressive Education." Mr. Dewey's place in the field of education was made clear in 1974 when *Saturday Review* celebrated its 50th anniversary. The magazine polled the leading individuals in the various fields of endeavor, including education, and asked them to identify the most important individual in their respective field.

The leading educator during those 50 years, 1924 to 1974, according to those educators polled by *Saturday Review*, was John Dewey, the Humanist.

One of those polled by the magazine said this about Professor Dewey: "No individual has influenced the thinking of American educators more."

John Dewey made his views known to the observer in a series of books and publications during his days in education. One of his proclamations contained his basic philosophy about God and religion. He wrote: "There is no God and no soul. Hence, there are no needs for the props of traditional religion. With dogma and creed excluded then immutable truth is also dead and buried. There is no room for fixed, natural law or permanent absolutes."[10]

Here is Dewey expressing his views on two subjects of interest:

1. The question of truth, and
2. The question of moral absolutes.

Dewey's position that "immutable truth is dead" defies human logic. The word "immutable" means, according to the dictionary, "unchangeable," and the word "truth" means an "established fact." Just how an "unchangeable," "established fact" can be "dead" is apparently not considered relevant to Dewey.

When Dewey took this second position, on the absence of fixed, moral absolutes, he aligned himself further with Communist thought. Lenin himself also spoke similarly on the issue of morality when he stated: "We, of course, say that we do not believe in God. We do not believe in eternal morality. That is moral that serves the destruction of the old society." And further: "Everything is moral which is necessary for the annihilation of the old exploiting social order and for uniting the proletariat."[11]

Lenin identified the source of man's concepts of morality as religion. He wrote: "We must combat religion. Down with religion. Long live atheism. The spread of atheism is our chief task. Communism abolishes eternal truths. It abolishes all religion and morality."[12]

The question of how something that is fixed, absolute, or eternal can be abolished escaped Lenin, as it apparently did Dewey. The only thing possible is for these two to abolish those human agencies that teach morality: the family and the church. Once that is done, it is then possible to offer mankind an alternative: the "new morality."

This thinking slowly emerged and evolved into what today is called "Situation Ethics" which teaches that what is moral is determined by the individual and the situation in which the individual is involved. It is expressed as follows: "What is good for me may be evil for you; what is right to do at one moment may be wrong the next."[13]

And "... whatever is the most loving in the situation is the right and good thing. It is not excusably evil, it is positively good."[14]

Professor Joseph Fletcher, an Episcopalian theologian, wrote a book on the subject of situation ethics which includes the following statement: "For me, there are no rules, none at all. Anything and everything is right and wrong according to the situation. What is wrong in some cases would be right in others. And this candid approach is indeed a revolution in morals."[15]

It was indeed a revolution in morals. It was the new morality that was consistent with the economic theories of Communism, the scientific theories of evolution, and the religious theories of atheism.

A little twist to the morality of Situation Ethics was expressed by by Ernest Hemingway, the noted author. He has been quoted as saying: "I know only what is moral is what you feel good after and what is immoral is what you feel bad after."[16]

(It was not explained by Hemingway how he would attempt to rationalize the actions of a mad killer who killed because it gave him "pleasure." It would also be interesting to see what Hemingway would do if one of these "pleasure" seekers attempted to take his life.)

The morality known as Situation Ethics has also pervaded the teaching of sex education in the schools of the United States. One of the many lawsuits challenging what was taught in those courses was the one brought in San Francisco by an ad hoc committee of parents and teachers suing the State of California Board of Education to bar the teaching of sex education when it teaches that there are no right and wrong values.

The attorney for the plaintiff told the court: "This kind of teaching is summed up by the comment in a teachers' guide that says: "We hope you have learned that there are no right and wrong answers. Each person has a viewpoint that is right for them."[17]

There are some who blame the high suicide rate among the young with the teaching of "no-values" sex education. The young student is taught that whatever he desires and believes will give him pleasure is proper to take, and when he does, the same society that he thought had taught him these values comes to punish him. This poses a frequently insurmountable dilemma for the student who can see no other way out but suicide.

But such sexual freedom is not inconsistent with the plans of the great planners. Aldous Huxley in his 1948 book entitled *Brave New World* explained the plan: "As political and economic freedom diminishes, sexual freedom tends... to increase. And the dictator... will do well to encourage that freedom. In conjunction with the freedom to daydream under the influence of dope, the movies, and the radio, it will help to reconcile his subjects to the servitude which is their fate."[18]

So Humanism has become the new religion to replace the traditional Judaic-Christian religions. In fact, the president of the American Humanist Association, Lloyd Morain, has stated that Humanism is "... a religion without God, divine revelation or sacred scriptures."[19]

The position that Humanism is a religion was confirmed by the U.S. Supreme Court in 1965, when it ruled in the case of U.S. vs. Seeger: "A humanistic... belief that is sincerely professed as a religion shall be entitled to recognition as religious under the Selective Service Law."[20]

And again, in the case of Torcase vs. Watkins, the Court ruled that: "Among religions in the country which do not teach what would generally be considered a belief in the existence of God are Buddhism, Taoism, Ethical Culture, Secular Humanism and others."[21]

So when Madlyn Murray O'Hair got the Supreme Court to remove the right of the children to open their school day with a simple prayer because she wished to separate "Church and State," what she was doing was substituting one religion for another: a belief in God with a belief in Humanism. Mrs. O'Hair knew this because she had been the editor of the magazine, *The Free Humanist*, and was elected to the Board of the American Humanist Association in 1965, and was elected in 1973 for a second four-year term.[22]

Other humanists, or others who have expressed a faith in the Humanist religion, include Walter Mondale, President Jimmy Carter's Vice President and the 1984 Democratic nominee for President. He is on record as saying this about his religious beliefs: "Although I have never formally joined a humanist society, I think I am a member by inheritance. My preacher father was a humanist, and I grew up on a very rich diet of humanism from him. All of our family has been deeply influenced by this tradition including my brother Lester, a Unitarian Minister, Ethical Culture Leader, and Chairman of the Fellowship of Religious Humanists."[24] (Mr. Mondale is, or has been, a member of both the Council on Foreign Relations and the Trilateral Commission.)

Lester Mondale, Walter's older brother, is a signer of both The Humanist Manifesto I, the one written in 1933, and The Humanist Manifesto II, written in 1973.

The Humanist Manifesto II, published forty years after the first Manifesto, basically reiterated the beliefs of the first Manifesto, but this time the Humanists called for "... the building of a world community," based upon: "the development of a system of world law and a world order based upon transnational federal government."[24]

The world government would need a world religion, and the Humanists were volunteering.

Chapter 36
Education

Education is an important tool for training children in the knowledge of the past. The Bible, in Proverbs 22:6, tells why this is so: "Train up a child in the way he should go, and when he is old, he will not depart from it."

The Communist Party has also decided that education is important to the furthering of their philosophy. Education became one of their concerns in the United States when they adopted the following as a party slogan in 1919: "Give us one generation of small children to train to manhood and womanhood and we will set up the Bolshevist form of the Soviet Government."[1]

Even Hitler of the National Socialist Party in Germany sensed the importance of education. In a speech delivered in 1939, he proclaimed: "When an opponent declares: 'I will not come over to your side,' I calmly say, 'Your child belongs to us already. What are you? You will pass on. Your descendants, however, now stand in the new camp. In a short time they will know nothing else but this new community.' "[2]

Earlier, in 1937, he told the German people: "This New Reich will give its youth to no one, but will itself take youth and give to youth its own education and its own upbringing."[3]

This dedication to the training of the young in the ways of the collecti-
vist was confirmed in 1932 when William Z. Foster, then National Chairman
of the Communist Party, U.S.A., wrote a book entitled *Toward a Soviet
America* in which he observed: "Among the elementary measures the
American Soviet government will adopt to further the cultural revolution are
the following: the schools, colleges and universities will be coordinated and
grouped under a National Department of Education and its state and local
branches. The studies will be revolutionized, being cleansed of religious,
patriotic and other features of bourgeois ideology."[4]

Foster had aligned himself with the teachings of Karl Marx who wrote
this plank in the *Communist Manifesto* to assist the Communists in
communizing the "most advanced countries:"

10. Free education for all . . . .

Marx, like Hitler, Lenin, and the Communist Party, U.S.A., realized
that, if they could control the education of the young, they could control the
economic and social life the young would live under, and if all believed the
same things, there would be no opposition to the state.

This was confirmed by Bertrand Russell who wrote about an educator,
Johann Fichte, who, Russell claimed: "laid down that education should aim
at destroying free will so that after pupils are thus schooled they will be
incapable . . . of thinking or acting otherwise than as their school masters
would have wished."[5]

Russell went on to explain elsewhere: "Diet, injections, and injunctions
will combine from a very early age to produce the sort of character and the
sort of beliefs that the authorities consider desirable, and any serious criticism
of the powers that be will become psychologically impossible. Even if all are
miserable, all will believe themselves to be happy, because the government
will tell them that it is so."[6]

The new pattern of using the schools to mold the character the govern-
ment wants has been furthered by a national union of school teachers, the
National Education Association, (the NEA.) In one of their reports, entitled
"Education for the 70's," the NEA wrote:

> Schools will become clinics whose purpose is to provide
> individualized, psycho-social treatment for the student, and
> teachers must become psycho-social therapists.
>
> This will include biochemical and psychological mediation
> of learning, as drugs are introduced experimentally to improve in
> the learner such qualities as personality, concentration and
> memory.
>
> Children are to become the objects of experimentation.[7]

Such "experimentation" on children today includes the use of the drug

Ritalin to improve the behavior of certain of the students.

But it wasn't always this way.

The Americans did not turn their children over to the state to be educated by them in the beginning.

In fact, the original schools in America were private, basically Christian schools where the children were taught by the parents or by teachers hired by the parents. The original textbook was the Bible, and all expenses were paid for by the parents who wished their children to be taught as the parents wished.

Even America's founding fathers feared for the safety of their children by keeping the original government from the education of the young.

James Madison, for one, voiced his opposition to the use of government to teach children: "If Congress can employ money indefinitely to the general welfare... they may appoint teachers in every State.... The powers of Congress would subvert the very foundation, the very nature of the limited government established by the people of America."[8]

But even then there were forces at work designing state or national educational plans for the American people. The first law of such a nature was passed in 1642 by the Massachusetts legislature which required parents to teach their children to read the English language and to teach the principles of religion.[9]

This law was followed by another in 1647 requiring cities of over 50 householders in population to teach chilren to read and write. Those communities with over 100 families or householders had to set up a grammar school, the first public schools in the United States.[10]

Thomas Jefferson, certainly a man of mixed principles, submitted a bill to the Virginia legislature in 1779 that would have established a compulsory statewide public school system, but the Virginians were not accepting his proposal and refused to vote for the bill.

But the remainder of the states, with the exception of Massachusetts, continued allowing the parents to teach their children without laws and public schools.

There were those who persisted in their efforts to involve the federal (or state) government in the process of educating the children of the nation. One of these was the "father of modern socialism," Robert Owen.

Mr. Owen, a supporter of the voluntary method of proving that socialism would work, started a special school for the children of the mill workers at his socialist experiment known as New Lanark, Scotland. He started the education of these children at the age of one, but his attempts to teach socialism to the children of his workers failed when his socialist experiment failed.

Mr. Owen came to the United States and in 1825 started another socialist experiment, this time in New Harmony, Indiana. He called it "the focus of enlightened atheism."[11]

Owen, who believed that man's character had been "deformed by religious brainwashing," once again started his school for the children of the millworkers, and once again, in 1826, the experiment failed.

The great lesson learned by Owens and his followers was that education had to precede the creation of a socialist society. In other words, the American people were not yet ready to accept socialism, and from that moment on, they decided that they would promote national public education as the preliminary step to socialism.[12] The Owenites realized that the children had to be separated from their parents so that they could be taught the merits of the socialist system. The educational process started as soon as possible — age two was suggested — after they were removed from their parents. Owen realized that the parents were the primary force in teaching children the values of the society, and this practice had to cease if socialism was to succeed in the United States.

In 1829, one of Owens' supporters stated: "The great object was to get rid of Christianity and to convert our churches into halls of science. The plan was to establish... national schools from which all religion was to be excluded, in which nothing was to be taught but such knowledge as is verifiable by the senses, and to which all parents were to be compelled by law to send their children...."[13]

It was in 1829 that the "Owenites went underground and organized their activities nationwide in the form of a secret society in order to attain their goal of universal public education."[14]

Whether or not it was due to the efforts of the Owenite supporters or because of the efforts of others, the state of Massachusetts created the Board of Education and appointed Horace Mann as the first Secretary of the Board in 1837, only eight years later.

Mr. Mann toured the state, continuously preaching the need for public education. His efforts were successful, so successful that he became known as the "father of American public education."[15]

Mann wrote: "What the church has been for medieval man, the public school must become for democratic and rational man. God would be replaced by the concept of the public good."[16]

In March of 1840, a bill was introduced in the Massachusetts legislature to abolish the Board of Education. One of the supporters of the legislation told his fellow legislators: "The idea of the State controlling education-... seems ... a dangerous precedent [that] is greatly to be feared, that any attempt to force all of our schools and all our teachers upon one model would destroy all competition, all emulation, and even the spirit of improvement itself."[17]

The bill was defeated.

Today the critics of public education are saying things like: "The aim of education is no longer to impart facts and knowledge.... The aim... is to change the social values of the child away from values that have traditionally been considered fixed, permanent or absolute."[18]

John Dewey agreed with this assessment when he said that the schools: "Take an active part in determining the social order of the future as the teachers align themselves with the forces making for social control of economic forces."[19]

Dewey started his educational career in 1894 when he was hired at the University of Chicago. It was here that he started his "experimental or laboratory school." He worked here until 1904, when he resigned and moved to the Teacher's College at Columbia University. It was here that he was to have his greatest impact on the field of education.

Dewey apparently never taught the young student himself but concentrated on teaching the teachers. Today, twenty percent of all American school superintendents and forty percent of all teacher college heads have advanced degrees from Columbia where Dewey spent many years as the Department head.

Dewey had the pleasure of teaching four of the five Rockefeller brothers, including David and Nelson. David also went to the University of Chicago to obtain a doctorate degree.

Their grandfather, John D. Rockefeller, started the General Education Board, the forerunner to today's Rockefeller Foundation, as a means of introducing the world of education to the wealthy. The Board's chairman, Frederick T. Gates, wrote: "In our dreams, we have limitless resources and the people yield themselves with perfect docility to our molding hands. The present educational conventions fade from our minds and, unhampered by tradition, we work our good will upon a grateful and responsive rural folk...."[20]

Dewey's personal philosophy about atheism, socialism, and evolution had their effect upon the entire campus of Columbia, not just through the school of Education. One student at Columbia, Whittaker Chambers, who later became a member of the Communist Party, wrote this about his student days at the school: "When I entered, I was conservative in my view of life and politics, and I was undergoing a religious experience. By the time I left, entirely by my own choice, I was no longer a conservative and I had no religion."[21]

Dewey's committment to socialism and communism became more real when, in 1905, the British Fabian Society opened an American branch known as the Intercollegiate Socialist Society. John Dewey was one of its founders. In 1921, the Society changed its name to the League for Industrial

Democracy, and announced its purpose as "education for a new social order based on production for use and not for profit."[22]

Dewey later became the organization's president.

Later, in the late 1920's, Dewey went to Russia to help organize a Marxist educational system. But even the Russian Communist dictator Joseph Stalin couldn't tolerate Dewey's "progressive education," and Dewey had to return to the United States. Dewey's students in Russia were not so lucky, however, as Stalin banished all of them to Siberia.[23]

Dewey's ideas have been accepted by the American government, however, for in 1969, the Commission of Mental Health and Children issued a report which stated: "The school as the major socializing agency in the community must assume a direct responsibility for the attitudes and values of child development."[27]

In the United States, the family or the church has been the traditional agency for the teaching of the values to the child. It was apparent that the family unit and religious teaching had to be destroyed so that the school could become the new teacher of the values to the child. The Communist Party in 1968 stated the problem precisely: "In carrying the burden of tending for the children, individual mothers bear a responsibility that properly falls on society and government."[25]

The problem for the planners then became one of removing the mother from the home so that the child could be taught by the state. One of the greatest tools that the planners have is inflation, which causes the husband to ask his wife to join in the money-making endeavors of the family. This then poses the additional problem for the parents: how do they tend for the child who is now at home without the mother?

The government then steps forward with the solution to the problem that it created: it offers the struggling family a day care center for the child. And the child becomes the ward of the state at an even earlier age than before.

Others assist the destruction of the family by encouraging the mother to leave the home. The new move to "liberate" the wife from the tedious tasks of homemaking are intended to leave the young child at home without parental supervision. The "women's liberation" movement is sometimes even unwittingly supporting the intentional movement of the wife out of the home.

In addition, the planners also put pressure on those parents who decide to place their children in private schools which do not teach atheism, humanism or evolution. These parents cause the planners many problems, one of which was pointed out by former Harvard University President James B. Conant, who stated:

> I do believe, however, there is some reason to fear lest a dual system of secondary education may in some states, at least, come to

387

threaten the democratic unity provided by our public schools.

I refer to the desire of some people to increase the scope and number of private schools....

To my mind, our schools serve all creeds. The greater the portion of our youth who attend independent schools, the greater the threat to our democratic unity.[26]

Mr. Conant apparently didn't explain how the public schools could serve all creeds when in America's public schools today one party has the right to have the schools exclude something that they feel is in violation of their religious or non-religious beliefs. Take, for instance, the deletion of prayer in schools because it offended the atheist Madlyn Murray O'Hair.

The situation that allows someone to remove a teaching from the schools because it offends the values or a religious belief of either the family or an individual was written about by a minister named A.A. Hodge, in 1887:

It is capable of exact demonstration that, if every party in the state has the right of excluding from the public whatever he does not believe to be true, then he that believes most must give way to him that believes least, and then he that believes least must give way to him that believes absolutely nothing, no matter how small a minority the atheists or the agnostics may be.

It is self-evident that on this scheme, if it is consistently and persistently carried out in all parts of the country, the United States system of national popular education will be the most efficient and wide instrument for the propagation of Atheism which the world has ever seen.[27]

The government is assisting those who wish to eliminate the option that remains to the objecting parents: the private school. For instance, on May 20, 1979, the Supreme Court struck down legislation that gave parents a tax break should they opt to send their children to a private school, hence requiring those parents to pay for their children's education twice: once to the public schools and then again to the private school.

The next problem for the planners is to decide just when the education of the child should begin.

In 1974, N.E.A. President James Harris urged in an editorial that "money now spent... must be quadrupled in order... to provide for public education at the age of 3."[28]

The N.E.A.'s *Forecast for the 70's* indicated that the age that education should start should be moved to an earlier date. They stated: "As non-school, pre-school programs begin to operate, educators will assume a formal responsibility for children when they reach the age of two."[29]

Dr. Robert C. Wood, a member of the Council on Foreign Relations, and the President of the University of Massachusetts, urged that the age be moved even lower: "The state educational system [must] expand its teaching to children between the ages of one and five, because the family is failing to perform its function. Wood said that the family is continuing to fail in its responsibility to prepare children for schools and urged more early nursery schools and day care programs."[30]

Not wishing to be outdone, President Richard Nixon moved the date even further. He "declared the first five years of a child's life to be a period of special and specific federal concern."[31]

It could very well be that those who wish to get the children away from their parents will use the discoveries of an organization called the Educational Resource Services Center. They have concluded that children between the ages of four to six months can learn to read before they can talk or walk.[32]

Parents who believe that their children belong to them had best be concerned about this information before the educators decide that they should start teaching young children to read by taking them away from their parents at the age of four months.

The question of what happens to the parents who refuse to send their children to schools that teach values other than those that they want taught is the next logical question that must be asked.

In the fall of 1970, six children were removed from their parents and placed in a foster home because the parents refused to send them to a public school teaching "sex education" in conflict with their religious beliefs.[33]

In 1972, a father lost his daughter when he refused to allow her to be bussed into what he perceived was a high crime area. The judge fined the father.[34]

And recently, in August of 1981, a pastor's children were forced to go back to the school he had taken them out of because he felt the school was exposing his children to homosexuality and drugs in violation of his religions beliefs.[35]

These actions seem to be in accord with the position taken by German White, an official with the U.S. Office of Child Development who said: "Parents don't mean to be incompetent but they are, and the remedy is federal establishment of acceptable standards of child-raising."[36]

If the parents are thought to be incompenent they then are not capable of bringing up the children, and the state must replace them with state-approved parents.

These new parents are called teachers.

These state-approved parents also have two unions. They are called the National Education Association (the NEA) and the American Federation of Teachers (the AFT).

The NEA's Executive Secretary for almost twenty years, from 1935, was

Willard Givens who publicly stated: "We are convinced that we stand today at the verge of a great culture.... But to achieve these things, many drastic changes must be made. A dying laissez-faire [the free-enterprise system] must be completely destroyed, and all of us, including the owners, must be subjected to a large degree of social control."[37]

This union has taken many strong positions in the past, some of which are listed here:

1. Educate the youth for a global community;
2. Promote a stronger United Nations;
3. Promote the Declaration of Interdependence;
4. Oppose tuition tax credits;
5. Supports a National Health Plan (socialized medicine);
6. Opposes any legislation to benefit private schools;
7. The basics (3 r's, history, civics and geography) should not occupy more than ¼th of student's time;
8. Population control;
9. Secular Humanism;
10. Federal day-care centers; and
11. Increased federal aid and control of education.[38]

In addition to supporting controversial positions, the N.E.A. has opposed the following, amongst others:

1. Local control of public schools;
2. Local financing of public schools;
3. Parental supervision of textbooks;
4. Taxation programs that remove the obligation for payment of taxes from the homeowner; and
5. Tuition tax credits for parents who pay for both a public and private education.[39]

In addition, N.E.A. officials take positions that are made public through their various publications. A former N.E.A. president, Katherine Barrett, has said that "the teacher will be the conveyor of values, a philosopher. Teachers no longer will be victims of change; we will be agents of change."[40]

Lenin certainly agreed with this position when he said: "Only by radically remolding the teaching, organization and training of the youth shall we be able to ensure that the efforts of the younger generation will result in the creation of a society that will be unlike the old society, i.e., in the creation of a communist society."[41]

The N.E.A. has an answer for the teachers who figure this out and try to stay within the system to change things. This is the advice for these teachers:

"Teachers who conform to the mode are out of place. They might find fulfillment as tap-dance instructors . . . but they damage teaching, children, and themselves by staying in the classroom."[42]

The other teachers' union is called the American Federation of Teachers (the A.F.T.).

This organization received early support from the Communist Party of the United States in May, 1937: "It can be seen from this how important it is to build the American Federation of Teachers," and again: "The task of the Communist Party must be first and foremost to arouse the teachers to class-consciousness and to organize them into the American Federation of Teachers. . . . The American Federation of Teachers must concern itself primarily with the immediate problems of the teacher (salary, tenure, acadamic freedom, etc.). . . . The American Federation of Teachers is now launching a broad legislative campaign for federal aid to education [in 1937] . . . ."[43]

The total essence of education and its connection with Humanism was summarized by Charles Francis Potter in his book *Humanism, a New Religion*: "Education is thus a most powerful ally of Humanism, and every American public school is a school of Humanism. What can the theistic Sunday-schools, meeting for an hour once a week and teaching only a fraction of the children, do to stem the tide of a five-day program of humanistic teaching."[44]

But there is even a more sinister purpose behind education today. This was detailed by Dr. Medford Evans, who wrote that " . . . government schools make it a matter of policy to spend as much money as possible, and impart as little knowledge as possible since spending demonstrates power while keeping the scholars ignorant monopolizes power in the hands of the government insiders."[45]

Chapter 37
Victories

On November 16, 1956, Russian Communist Nikita Khrushchev spoke to the American people. He said: "Our firm conviction is that sooner or later Capitalism will give way to Socialism. Whether you like it or not, history is on our side. We will bury you."[1]

He later recanted and identified who the real "we" were who would do the burying of the American people. It was not going to be the Communists. "The United States will eventually fly the Communist Red flag.... The American people will hoist it themselves."[2]

When Whittaker Chambers, a member of the Communist Party, left the Communists in 1937, he made this rather prophetic statement: "We are leaving the winning world for the losing world."[3]

The question must be answered as to whether the Communist Conspiracy will be successful in having the American people raise the "Communist red flag" over America.

The conspiracy has suffered a series of very devastating defeats in their recent history in this nation. Each of these are probably not known as defeats to the American people, because it is doubtful that the majority of people even knew what the true purpose of the events were. But, nevertheless, they were losses to those out to collectivize the American nation, and true victories for those who cherish their freedoms.

These defeats were:

1.   The Soviet Negro Republic in America: The first attempt to establish a separate republic for the Negro in America within the borders of the United States came with the publication of a small pamphlet entitled *American Negro Problems* in 1928 by John Pepper, an alias for a Russian representative named Joseph Pogany. Stalin saw the possibilities of causing such a situation to exist where the United States government would have to deal with a separate nation inside its borders, and he sent Pogany to America to start the move towards a revolution to establish this republic.

A second pamphlet was published in 1935. It was called *The Negroes in a Soviet America* and was published by the Communist Party. It too called for the establishment of a Soviet Negro Republic, and a revolution to expropriate the lands of the capitalists. This Republic was to include major cities in Virginia, South Carolina, Georgia, Alabama, Louisiana, Arkansas, and Tennessee. After the Republic was created, it would then apply to the Russian government to recognize its right to self-determination.

One of the Negroes who saw through this revolution was Manning Johnson who had been a Communist for ten years before he resigned. He had risen to the highest position inside the Communist Party that a Negro could rise to, a position on the National Negro Commission of the Communist Party, U.S.A.

He became concerned that the Party was not interested in helping the black people but was attempting to involve them in a bloody revolution in which as many as five million blacks would die.

He wrote a book entitled *Color, Communism and Common Sense*, in 1958, as his way of warning the negroes of the danger of the plans the Party had for them. Mr. Johnson paid for his attempt to warn the American people with his life, as he died under rather questionable circumstances less than one year later.

Another Negro Communist, Leonard Patterson, testified on November 18, 1950, that he saw a bigger stake involved in the Party's attempts to establish a Soviet Negro Republic. He warned: "I left the Communist Party because I became convinced... that the Communist Party was only interested in promoting among the Negro people a national liberational movement that would aid the Communist Party in its efforts to create a proletarian revolution in the United States that would overthrow the government by force and violence through bloody full-time revolution, and substitute it with a Soviet form of government with a dictatorship of the proletariat."[4]

In any event, the Communists were not allowed to pull off their

393

revolution and the South still belongs to the United States.

2.   Civilian Police Review Boards: It was the intent of the conspiracy in this country to start a program to move the control of America's police departments to a central police force controlled by the national government. The vehicle to be used for this transfer of control was the charge of "police brutality" artificially created around the nation by the Communists and Communist sympathizers.

The plan was to encourage various cities around the nation to take control of the process whereby the police themselves investigate the charges against them and place that control in the hands of a group of government-appointed citizens. This then would ultimately transfer the investigation of these charges into the hands of the federal government, and they would ultimately control the local police forces around the nation.

These efforts to centralize the control of the local police forces were thwarted by a nationwide organization called the Support Your Local Police Committee, which organized small chapters all over the United States to promote the concept of keeping the local police forces independent. This organization created the bumper sticker "Support your local police and keep them independent" as a means of educating the American people.

3.   Martin Luther King: One of Martin Luther King's purposes was to foment civil strife in an attempt to divide the American people.

Dr. King's effectiveness in these efforts was severely damaged by the courageous efforts of a Negro woman named Julia Brown. She had spent more than nine years inside the Communist Party before she had surfaced to speak out about Dr. King's connections to the Communist movement in the United States.

Mrs. Brown was saying: "We [in the Communist Party] were also told to promote Martin Luther King to unite Negroes and whites behind him. . . . He was taking directions from Communists. I know for a fact the Communists would never have promoted him, financed him, and supported him if they couldn't trust him. I am certain as I can be that he knew what he was doing!"[5]

A nationwide organization of local committees was formed called the Truth About Civil Turmoil (TACT) and it promoted Mrs. Brown's speaking tours. In fact, her speeches in the South were arranged to precede those of Dr. King, and because of the charges she was making, Dr. King began cancelling his appearances all over the South whenever she was to speak before him.

4.   The American Indian Movement (AIM): The Senate Internal Security Security SubCommittee has concluded that AIM was a "frankly revolutionary organization which is committed to violence."

AIM's purpose was twofold. First, AIM was to create a separate Indian nation within the borders of the United States and then apply to the United Nations for membership as an independent nation. This would require the quartering of United Nations troops inside America to guarantee their status.

But the second purpose was revealed by their attorney William Kunstler who told AIM: "I promise you revolution by 1976. It is better to die in the streets than to go down with a whimper."[6]

Douglas Durham, a former Des Moines, Iowa, policeman who held top level positions in AIM while acting as an undercover operative for the FBI, surfaced and testified about the activities of this group. He charged that AIM was "a leader, and may even be the director, of the Communist scheme to disrupt our nation's bicentennial in 1976," (around July 4, 1976).[7]

The money for these activities comes from a variety of sources. Senator Jesse Helms identified this source in 1973: "At crucial stages in its development, AIM has been given material and moral assistance from the very federal government it is attacking."[8]

AIM had received at least $400,000 in grants from the Federal Office of Economic Opportunity.[9]

To explain just what AIM's purposes were, Mr. Durham went on a speaking tour of some sixty engagements in South Dakota and surrounding states.

AIM never disrupted the Bicentennial in 1976.

Mr. Durham told the people the truth about AIM, and AIM withered.

5.   Reies Lopez Tijerina: Mr. Tijerina, with a heavily armed revolutionary band, seized control of a town in Northern New Mexico in 1967. His purpose was to create an independent nation of Mexican Americans and Indians and then appeal to the United Nations. As in the case of the Negro Soviet Republic, the plan was to separate out a part of the United States and create an independent nation.

A speaking tour was arranged for the author Alan Stang for the area around Northern New Mexico, and about one million of his articles on the subject were distributed to the citizens of the area.

Once again, a courageous speaker exposed the truth about a program, and Mr. Tijerina's plans didn't materialize.

6.   Cesar Chavez: Cesar Chavez' purpose was to ". . . unite American agricultural workers in a single union under the control of revolutionary leaders — known Marxists and identified Communists. The goal, simply put, [was] control of America's food supply."[10]

Once control of the food supply was obtained, Cesar's union could strike during the picking season, forcing America to agree to nearly any terms or face the alternative of starvation.

The *Los Angeles Times* reported from whom Chavez was receiving his operating funds: "So far most of the Mexican-American civil rights activities have been funneled through War on Poverty [a program of the United States government] programs and through such organizations as the Ford Foundation."[11]

Chavez's union specifically received over $250,000 from the Federal Office of Economic Opportunity.[12] In fact, Chavez had received at least ten million dollars during his twelve years of organizing efforts.[13]

Someone thought his efforts were worth supporting.

Some of the others that supported Chavez were the "labor unions controlled by Walter Reuther, Black Nationalist coffers under the control of Stokely Carmichael, the Communist Party, the National Council of Churches... and the Federal Office of Economic Opportunity."[14]

The corollary purpose of Chavez's union was to spread the cause of revolution. His National Farm Workers Association (NFWA) had issued a *Worker's Manifesto*, which read, in part: "We shall strike. We shall pursue the revolution we have proposed. We are sons of the Mexican revolution, a revolution of the poor seeking bread and justice. Our revolution will not be armed, but we want a new social order.... We say that we are going to continue fighting until we die or we win. We shall overcome."[15]

In June, 1966, a speaker's tour was arranged for Mel O'Campo, one of Chavez's lieutenants who broke from the organization to expose Chavez' activities. And copies of an article by Gary Allen entitled "The Grapes — Communist Wrath in Delano" were distributed in large quantities wherever Mr. O'Campo spoke.

Mr. Chavez' efforts quickly became fruitless.

7.   Gun Registration or Confiscation: One of the major victories in the fight against the Conspiracy is the continuing success against those who wish to disarm the American public. There are many who believe that one of the reasons that John Kennedy, Robert Kennedy, Malcolm X, and Martin Luther King were assassinated by gunfire was to develop popular support for legislation to either register or confiscate the weapons of the American citizen. Each time, however, these efforts have failed, primarily because of the lobbying efforts of an organization called the National Rifle Association.

The reason that this organization has become the largest lobbying organization in the United States is primarily because these gun owners fear government, the only agency that can violate human rights. They take the position that the Second Amendment to the Constitution ("A well-regulated militia being necessary to the security of a free State, the right of the people to keep and bear arms shall not be infringed,") means exactly that: Congress shall pass *no* law confiscating the weapons of the citizens.

8.   The NRA was to become an "Ecology" organization: Because of the success of the NRA, efforts have been made to channel their lobbying efforts into some other area.

The effort to move the NRA into the ecology movement and out of the lobbying movement occurred in 1977. One of those who fought the change in directions said: "The organization was trying to dump anti-gun control activities in exchange for financial support from several foundations, including the Ford Foundation."[16]

One of the prime movers for this move into the area of support for ecology legislation was Robert O. Anderson, President of ARCO (Atlantic Richfield Company) and a Director of the Council on Foreign Relations.[17]

These efforts to move the NRA failed because enough members and other concerned citizens put pressure on the proper authorities in the organization to make certain that they did not change their direction.

9.   The Equal Rights Amendment: This Constituional Amendment, feared by some of its opponents as one of the greatest grabs of federal power in the history of the United States, is nearly through. It quickly sailed through the legislatures of twenty-two states the first year (three of which later rescinded their action by a vote of the state legislature) but since 1975 only one state has ratified.

The Amendment died when the time allotted to ratify it expired in June of 1982. It got into trouble when some of the women it was supposedly intended to help read the Amendment and discovered that it had some very serious defects in it. These women organized, became active in lobbying against it, and were successful in keeping their respective state legislatures from ratifying the Amendment.

There were some who voiced their opposition to the Amendment because they came to believe that its true purpose was to effectively shut down those American industries that traditionally hired more males than females, such as the mining industry.

This line of thinking contended that after the passage of the Amendment, the male dominated industries would have to hire the correct percentage of female workers: if fifty percent of the workers in the community were women, the mines would have to have the same percentage. If they had less, it would become prima facie evidence that the mines were guilty of past sexual discrimination, and they would have to shut down until they reached the correct percentage.

If the industry had difficulty in securing the additional female workers, it would not constitute reason enough to re-open. America's industry would have to find them.

This "quota system" would effectively shut down America's normally male dominated industries. It was feared that the government then could describe the situation, as the shortages of products became known to the American people, as a "national emergency," and then the government could offer the desired solution: government ownership or control of the industry, until the quotas were reached.

10.   The Occupational Safety and Health Administration (OSHA): This Federal agency, created by Congress in 1973, had the ability to enter the premises of any American business ostensibly to make a safety inspection to protect the working public.

Those who have studied the law that created OSHA claimed that the law not only violated at least three amendments of the Constitution, it also granted the agency, a part of the Executive branch of government, the ability to make and interpret law. This power violated the separation of powers doctrine of the founding fathers who granted only Congress the power to make laws and only the Judicial branch the power to interpret them.

It took the courageous effort of one American businessman, Bill Barlow of Pocatello, Idaho, to challenge OSHA's right to inspect his business place. Mr. Barlow contended that the Fourth Amendment to the Constitution ("The right of the people to be secure in their persons, houses, papers and effects, against unreasonable searches and seizures shall not be violated, and no warrants shall issue but upon probable cause, supported by oath or affirmation, and particularly describing the place to be searched and the persons or things to be seized,") required that OSHA must first secure a court-issued warrant before they could enter his premises.

Mr. Barlow took his case all the way to the Supreme Court and won! The Court correctly agreed with him.

OSHA had lost its bite!

11.   Miscellaneous Laws or Treaties Not Passed or Signed: Some of the laws and treaties that weren't passed or signed, but which were deemed to be important to the Conspiracy, were The Genocide Treaty, The Child Care Bill, Atlantic Union, Post Card Voter Registration, The Consumer Protection Agency, and The Common Situs Picketing Act.

The majority of these bills were defeated by a series of letter-writing campaigns to Congressman and Senators urging that they vote against the proposed legislation.

But the greatest victory of all has yet to be considered.

Chapter 38
The Greatest Victory

The greatest victory of all in the battle between the Conspiracy and those who love their freedoms was the failure of the Conspiracy to impose total government down on the American people on either May 1, 1976, (the two-hundredth anniversary of the founding of the Illuminati,) or on July 4, 1976, (the two-hundredth anniversary of the founding of the United States.)

The foundations for this revolutionary act were laid down in a plan made public in the February, 1946, issue of the *New World News*, a publication of the Moral Re-Armament of England.

It has been claimed that what has been called the "Dusseldorf Rules for Revolution" were first discovered in Dusseldorf, Germany, in the headquarters of a revolutionary organization by some Allied soldiers after World War I. However, these claims have never been verified, at least to the satisfaction of many historians.

In any event, these rules laid down an incredible plan to bring about the conditions that would lead to a revolution:

A.   Corrupt the young; get them away from religion. Get them interested in sex. Make them superficial; destroy their ruggedness.

B.   Get control of all means of publicity, thereby:

399

1. Get people's minds off their government by focusing their attention on athletics, sexy books and plays and other trivialities.
2. Divide the people into hostile groups by constantly harping on controversial matters of no importance.
3. Destroy the people's faith in their natural leaders by holding the latter up to contempt, ridicule and disgrace.
4. Always preach true democracy, but seize power as fast and ruthlessly as possible.
5. By encouraging government extravagence, destroy its credit, produce fear of inflation with rising prices and general discontent.
6. Incite unnecessary strikes in vital industries, encourage civil disorders and foster a lenient and soft attitude on the part of the government toward such disorders.

C. Cause the registration of all firearms on some pretext, with a view to confiscating them and leaving the population helpless.[1]

The Conspiracy apparently felt that these programs had succeeded in the main and that it was time to move towards their goal of total government.

One of the requirements for the plan to succeed, as envisioned by the planners, was a generation of young people, not only turned off by the establishment, but trained in guerilla warfare and the desire to rebel against the system. The major factor in creating this attitude amongst the young people of America was the Vietnamese War, created and controlled by the Conspiracy to create the conditions required for its plan to succeed: the war was to create first a drug culture in America and, secondly, a young society willing to rebel against the American government.

Jerry Rubin, one of the young rebels created by the establishment and the founder of a group called the Yippies, has written a book entitled *Do It!*, in which he details his interest and concerns about the rebellious age in which he lived.

He dedicated his book to: "Nancy, Dope, Color TV, and Violent Revolution" and admonished his readers to: "Read this book stoned [high on drugs]"[1]

Rubin admitted that the Vietnamese war was phony: "The Amerikans [sic] are fighting for nothing you can see, feel, touch or believe in. Their deaths are futile and wasted. 'Why die on Hamburger Hill?' asks the pot-smoking Amerikan [sic] soldier, as he points his gun at the head of the captain who ordered him to take a hill.... Vietnam is a symbol. The real Viet Kong [sic] are in San Diego."[2]

He realized that the real war was being fought, not in Vietnam, but in the cities and towns of America.

He commented about the real purpose of the drug called marijuana: "Marijuana is the Communist drug."

He wrote this about the new morality called Situation Ethics: "Yippies say if it's not fun, don't do it. We see sex, rock 'n roll and dope as part of a Communist plot to take over Amerika [sic]. The Yippie idea of fun is overthrowing the government. Yippies are Maoists." (supporters of the Chinese Communist Mao Tse Tung).

It is revealing that even though Jerry's book is in opposition to the establishment, it was published by a major publishing company that is part of the establishment: Ballantine Books, by arrangement with Simon & Schuster.

The beginning of the end of the Conspiracy's plans occurred during the 1968 Democratic Convention in Chicago. Viewers of that event will recall a small group of hippies-yippies turned to the streets, getting arrested for violating Chicago's laws. Jerry Rubin admitted that he was disappointed by the small turnout of these young people: "We once dreamed 500,000 people would come to Czechago [Jerry's spelling of Chicago]. We expected 50,000. Maybe 2,000 to 3,000 freaks . . . made it."

It is very revealing that Mr. Rubin used the figure of 500,000 as the number of protestors he hoped would respond to the call in Chicago. This was the exact number of people needed in two related incidents.

Colonel Edward Mandell House needed a 500,000 man army to enable Philip Dru to take over the Presidency and impose a dictatorship on the American people in his book *Philip Dru, Administrator.*

And 500,000 was the number of soldiers that Major General Smedley Butler was to command as he imposed a dictatorship on America in 1933.

Apparently those who believe that America should have a dictatorship instead of a Presidency feel it will take 500,000 protestors to convince the American people to accept the change at the top.

It is the theory of some that Chicago was a test to see how many people could be drawn to an event where there were going to be protests and in this case, the young people disappointed the Conspiracy: not enough of them came to Chicago. It is the theory of some that it was here that the Conspiracy started revising its plans.

Rubin admitted that the events at Chicago were planned: "We wanted disruption. We planned it. We were not innocent victims. We worked our plans for a year before we came here. We made our demands so outrageous because we wanted the city to deny us what we were asking. We did all of this with one purpose in mind—to make the city react as if it were a police state."[3]

The use of students for disruptive purposes was not new. The eleventh edition of the *Encyclopaedia Britannica,* published in 1911, described one attempt to use the young radicals for particular purposes, in Russia:

> Among the students of the universities and the higher techni-
> cal schools, Turgenev [a Russian writer] had noticed a new and
> strikingly original type—young men and women in slovenly
> attire, who called in question and ridiculed the generally received
> convictions and respectable conventionalities of social life and who
> talked of reorganizing society on strictly scientific principles.
>
> They reversed the traditional order of things in trivial matters
> of external appearance, the males allowing their hair to grow long
> and the female adepts cutting it short, and adding sometimes the
> additional badge of blue spectacles....
>
> Their appearance, manners, and conversation were apt to
> shock ordinary people, but to this they were profoundly indifferent,
> for they had raised themselves above the level of so-called public
> opinion, despised Philistine respectability and rather liked to
> scandalize people still under the influence of what they considered
> antiquated prejudices.
>
> For aesthetic culture, sentimentalism and refinement of every
> kind they had a profound and undisguised contempt.
>
> Among the antiquated institutions which had to be abolished
> as obstructions to real progress, were religion, family life, private
> property and centralized administration.
>
> Religion was to be replaced by exact sciences, family life by
> free love, private property by collectivism, and centralized adminis-
> tration by a federation of independent communes...."[4]

But even this example was not isolated. Economist Ludwig von Mises,
who was in Germany prior to World War I, wrote:

> In the decade preceding the First World War, Germany... wit-
> nessed the appearance of a phenomenon hitherto unheard of, the
> youth movement.
>
> Turbulent gangs of untidy boys and girls roamed the country,
> making much noise and shirking their school lessons....[5]

In other words, even the outlandish garb of the modern hippie or Jerry
Rubin's Yippies was something that was used to cause divisions among
populations in earlier times. These radicals, in pre-revolutionary Russia and
pre-World War I Germany, were being used by the establishment to condition the people to radical change. Such was the case in 1968, in the United
States.

Rubin admitted as much, that he knew the young people were being
used. He wrote: "Revolution is profitable. So the capitalists try to sell it."

And: "The hip capitalists have some allies within the revolutionary community: longhairs who work as intermediaries between the kids on the street and the millionaire businessmen."

Rubin also knew that there was another group who knew the young people were being used. He identified that group as well: "The hippies see us as politicos and the politicos see us as hippies. Only the right wing sees us for what we are."

One of the groups making up the "revolutionary community" was a group known as the Students for a Democratic Society. It was well known by the establishment that they were Communist in nature. In fact, an article in March 1969 reported: " 'Our primary task is to build a Marxist-Leninist revolutionary movement,' declared Michael Klonsky, executive secretary of the Students for a Democratic Society."[6]

The government through the House Internal Security Committee's Report on SDS' plans for America's High Schools, studied the SDS in great detail. The Chairman of the Committee, Congressman Richard Ichord, stated that: "The aims of the SDS were spelled out in an SDS position paper printed in June, 1969: 'The goal is the destruction of US imperialism and the achievement of a classless world: world communism.' "[7]

In 1980, an FBI agent said the group was bent on committing "arsons, bombings, assassinations—with the goal of overthrowing this country's democratic form of government, with the objective of establishing world Communism."[8]

Yet in spite of all of this evidence about the nature of the SDS, they continued to receive money from the establishment they were supposedly out to overthrow. In 1970, a group of Ohio legislators received a briefing on campus upheavals in which they heard: ". . . an Illinois commission report on that state's rioting said that $192,000 in Federal money and $85,000 in Carnegie Foundation funds were paid to [the] Students for a Democratic Society . . . during the fall of 1969."[9]

Another similar report came from a former undercover police intelligence operative who had participated in SDS demonstrations, David Gumaer, who reported that he had: "wondered where the money was coming from for all this activity, and soon discovered it came through radicals via the United Nations, from the Rockefeller Foundation, the Ford Foundation, United Auto Workers, as well as cigar boxes of American money from the Cuban embassy."[10]

Another student, James Kirk, confirmed Gumaer's report. Kirk, while a student at the University of Chicago, and on behalf of the FBI, became active in the SDS, the W.E.B. DuBois Club, the Black Panthers, and the Communist Party. In 1969, Mr. Kirk broke from the Party and the following year testified before the House and Senate Internal Security Committees. His testimony was as follows: "Young people . . . have no idea that they are playing into the hands of the Establishment they claim to hate. The radicals think they're fighting the forces of the super-rich, like Rockefeller and Ford, and don't realize that it is precisely such forces which are behind their own revolution, financing it, and using it for their own purposes."[11]

Still another student, James Simon Kunen, in his book entitled *The Strawberry Incident*, tells about a SDS strategy meeting he attended in which a student was giving a report on an SDS convention that he had recently attended. The student reported that ". . . men from Business International Roundtables, . . . tried to buy up a few radicals. These men are the world's industrialists and they convene to decide how our lives are going to go. They're the left wing of the ruling class. They offered to finance our demonstrations in Chicago. We were also offered ESSO [Rockefeller] money. They want us to make a lot of radical commotion so they can look more in the center as they move more to the left."[12]

Even the Black Panther leader Eldridge Cleaver started to figure it out, that the wealthy were buying themselves a revolution. In the introduction to Rubin's book *Do It!*, Mr. Cleaver wrote: "There is a danger to the healthy development of the American Revolution in the fact that often revolutionaries are manipulated by the ruling class to appear to be a bigger threat than they really are."[13]

Jerry Rubin further amplified Mr. Cleaver's thoughts about how the establishment made the revolution appear to be larger than it actually was. In chapter ten of his book, entitled *Every Revolutionary Needs a Color TV*, Rubin says: "Walter Cronkite is SDS's best organizer. Uncle Walter brings out the map of the U.S. with circles around the campuses that blew up today. The battle reports. Every kid out there is thinking, 'Wow, I wanna see my campus on that map.' TV is raising generations of kids who want to grow up and become demonstrators. Television proves the domino theory: one campus falls and they all fall. The media does not *report* 'news,' it *creates* it.' "

But even though it appeared that the Establishment would not be able to gather an army big enough to disrupt the Bicentennial, the plans continued.

In 1971, an organization was formed that later changed its name to the People's Bicentennial Commission (the PBC.) Jeremy Rifkin became its director.

Later, the Senate Internal Seurity Subcommittee investigated the PBC. They reported: "The *New York Times*, for example, on May 26, 1975, carried an article by Jeremy Rifkin on the subject of economic freedom. This article was basically a rewrite of the PBC's declaration of economic independence which calls for the elimination of the free-enterprise system or the 'corporate system' as they call it."[14]

Rifkin had made his views known to the public when he wrote the following in a radical newspaper in November, 1971: "A genuine understanding of the revolutionary ideals is what links Thomas Paine, Sam Adams, Benjamin Rush and the American people with Lenin, Mao [Tse Tung], and Che [Guevara], and the struggle of all oppressed people in the world."[15]

A further warning that the nation appeared to be preparing for trouble on July 4, 1976, was given by FBI director Clarence Kelley who reported on November 4, 1975, that: "terrorism will increase in connection with the nation's Bicentennial celebration."

The PBC continued, however, with its plans and issued an eight-page tabloid newspaper calling for 150,000 patriots to join with them in Washington D.C. on July 4, 1976, to "Declare your independence from big business." They advised the reader that the PBC was "planning a birthday party America will never forget."

Other individuals lined up in support of the PBC declaration. The tabloid reported that Rubin "Hurricane" Carter, Jane Fonda, Rev. Jesse Jackson, and Dr. Benjamin Spock, among others, would be speaking at the PBC rally on that day.

The costs of these activities were being met, at least in part, by the establishment once again, as, according to *Human Events* in its issue of October 11, 1975, the federally funded National Endowment for the Humanities had provided the PBC with nearly $400,000.

But the PBC did not make much of a ripple on July 4, 1976, as it was unable to draw nearly the number of people it would have taken to cause the incident that the establishment wanted.

In addition to the plans to disrupt the Bicentennial, there was a movement inside the United States to call a constitutional convention. One of those urging a re-write of the Constitution was Zbigniew Brzezinski, who wrote the following on page 258 of his book *Between Two Ages*: "The approaching two-hundredth anniversary of the Declaration could justify the call for a national constitutional convention to re-examine the nation's formal institutional framework. Either 1976 or 1989 could serve as a suitable target date...."

Confirmation that something was planned to happen was supported, in part, by the John Birch Society, which printed the following in the October, 1977, *Bulletin* to its members: "There came into our hands several months ago, through the kindness of some friend who evidently wanted to remain anonymous, one of [Clarence Douglas] Dillon's thin papers that apparently are quietly issued now and then to members of the echelons below him, who need such information and guidance as a basis of support."[16]

The Birch Society reasoned that whatever Mr. Dillon knew was important enough to be known to those who were trying to expose the Conspiracy. Mr. Dillon, they reasoned, was one of the those who should know the plans of the conspiracy, as he was the head of the international banking firm of Dillon, Read and Company, and Chairman of the Rockefeller Foundation. In addition, Mr. Dillon had served as Secretary of the Treasury, certainly one of the positions in the American government controlled by the Rockefeller interests, for a period of four years in the Kennedy and Johnson administrations, as well as being a member of the Council on Foreign Relations.

Mr. Dillon's letter, according to the Birch Society, revealed two very important facts: "One was that up until about 1970 many of the Insiders (although he did not call them that) had kept on hoping to make 1976 the successful target date for the ceremonial inauguration of their *new world order*. But, Mr. Dillon then proceeded to point out, by 1970 this schedule had been conceded by the top command to be impracticable. And he went on to lay down the new schedule, already in effect, which would require about fifteen years for completion."[17]

This meant that the Conspiracy was planning for something to occur on or about 1985, fifteen years, give or take a year or two, from the change in their plans in 1970.

The specific date of 1985 seemed to be in accord with the date being given by the Russian Communists. For instance, Soviet Communist Party chief Leonid Breshnev, in 1973, said this about the year 1985: "We Communists have got to string along with the capitalists for a while. We need their credits, their agriculture, and their technology. But we are going to continue massive military programs and by the *middle eighties* (1985?) we will be in a position to return to a much more aggressive foreign policy designed to gain the upper hand in our relationship with the West." Emphasis added.)[18]

He was more precise about the choice of years in a speech he made in Prague in 1973 to the Warsaw Pact leaders: "Trust us, comrades, for by 1985, as a consequence of what we are now achieving with detente, we will have achieved most of our objectives in Western Europe. We will have consolidated our position. We will have improved our economy. And a decisive shift in the correlation of forces will be such that, come 1985, we will be able to exert our will wherever we need to."[19]

Breshnev didn't say just how they were going to exert their will, but one version of what they might attempt came from Senator Barry Goldwater in August, 1971, according to the *Los Angeles Herald Examiner*, which headlined the article: "Goldwater Warns of Nuclear Blackmail by Russ." The article went on: "Senator Barry Goldwater said Saturday the world balance of power has shifted to the Soviet Union to such an extent that international nuclear blackmail is no longer impossible. 'The only conclusion is that the Soviet Union is out to establish a strategic military superiority so vast that it cannot be challenged and so that any policy the Soviet Union may decide upon can be backed with overwhelming strength.' ''[20]

So, according to the scenario just described, it would appear that the Russians, who have been slowly but steadily building the most potent military machine in the world and a nuclear superiority over the forces of the free West, (with the assistance of the United States,) could threaten the United States with a nuclear war This would force the American government into a position of having to decide whether they wished to go to war or accept some Russian ultimatum.

Other indications that 1985 might be the year for such a confrontation come from a variety of sources.

One is the book entitled *The Third World War, August, 1985*, by General Sir John Hackett and six of his colleagues, all retired NATO officers. This book was written in 1973, and contains the "dramatized game-plan for the next World War."[21]

The book details how the Soviet Union started the war on November 11, 1984, after "the initial workers' riots in Poland."[22]

The war develops and ultimately the Soviet Union is defeated, less than a month after it started.

There were warnings that the United States has been so strategically depleted to the point where it is in great danger. One such warning came in 1980 from fifty retired admirals and generals who warned that America was "in greater danger today than at any time since Pearl Harbor."

In fact, one individual, Henry Kissinger, is reportedly on record as saying that it probably was too late anyway, and that the United States should get the best deal it could in the struggle against the Soviet Union. In 1976, when Kissinger was Secretary of State, nationally syndicated columnist Ernest Cuneo wrote:

> Unimpeachable sources state that Dr. Henry Kissinger's model has shifted from 19th century Metternich to 20th century Spengler.
>
> What that means is that Kissinger has abandoned the Balance of Power policy to accept Spengler's position that the West is through and must accept a subordinate role because it is useless to resist the 'wave of the future.'
>
> The 'wave of the future' of course means Communist ascendancy.
>
> Kissinger's new position assumes that the American people do not have the courage or the strength to stand up to the Communists if it means war.
>
> Therefore, Kissinger is attempting to get the best terms possible as a competing world power.[23]

It seems to fit that the American government is being maneuvered into a position of not having the ability nor the means to resist Communist pressures so that, when the Russian government threatens America with nuclear war, the American people will demand that their government accept *any* solution other than a war. The American president will ask the Russians if there is any option they will accept other than nuclear war. Their response will be that the merging of the two countries into a world government will suffice, and the American people will breathe a sigh of relief when their offer is accepted by the American government.

An additional item would be needed to make the scenario and theory really work.

That would be a president that would not be afraid to stand up to the Russians, even though he knows that he does not have the military means to succeed. He would have to be a Republican who has long stood up against the Communists, one that would have sent military troops into a small island (Grenada) when he believed the nation was about to go Marxist. He couldn't be a member of the Democrat Party which has been consistently against any confrontation with the Communists on a face to face basis.

It appears that the Americans are playing two sides of the same coin: appearing to get tough with the Russians, and then not having the ability to withstand any offense put forward by the Russians.

Another piece of the puzzle that fits is the fact that America is being told that the government does not have the military or nuclear power to compete with the Russians in a military showdown. One evidence of this strategy was revealed in an interview with John Tower, Chairman of the Senate Armed Services Committee that reaffirmed the position of the retired admirals and generals who felt that America was in serious danger because of its reduced military strength. The headline to the article read: "U.S. Faces Nothing Less Than Military Inferiority."

The article was accompanied by graphs showing how dangerously behind the United States was in the numbers of bombers and missiles, warheads, and estimated megatonnage of warheads.

Two articles, about two months apart, revealed that the fear of a third world war concerns the American people, who feel that a nuclear war was possible within the next ten years.[24]

And all of the stories that are in the news about the ineptness of America's military forces (plane crashes because pilots are on drugs; fifty percent of all enlisted men are on drugs, etc.) are slowly convincing the public that, not only does America not have the military and nuclear power, but the military isn't ready to resist any aggressive act as well.

It is not difficult with this scenario, then, to understand why the American hostages in Iran were released shortly after the 1980 election (to unify the American people behind national patriotism) and why the military allowed the hostage rescue attempt to be so badly botched (one weekly newsletter mailed around the United States reported that friendly Arabian leaders are frightened and disillusioned about that bungled mission because they now see the United States as a weak ally.)

Another call to America's patriotism was the 1984 Olympics when, after Russia decided not to compete, America won an unprecedented number of medals. America's response to the medal winners was an unabashedly pro-American display of national patriotism (one flag manufacturer reported that his demand for flags was outpacing the supply). Americans have got to love their country enough not to have it blown apart by a nuclear war with Russia.

Another evidence that this scenario is correct is that President Reagan seems to be tarnish-proof (the press is calling him the "teflon president," nothing seems to stick to him). This is unusual because the conservative right has long stated that it never seems to get a good press, and that everything it does do is wrong in the eyes of the media. It is not too long ago that Americans should have forgotten the commercials and the media treatment of the conservative of the 1960's, Senator Barry Goldwater, when he ran for the presidency in 1964.

In November, 1981, two events occurred that were created to scare America's NATO allies against a nuclear war. One was President Reagan's then Secretary of State Haig's statement that NATO had contingency plans for firing a nuclear weapon for "demonstrative purposes" to demonstrate to the enemy that they were exceeding the limits of toleration in the conventional war. Presumably the bomb would be dropped in Europe, and this tended to frighten the citizens of America's allies.

The second event that served to alarm the NATO countries was the intrusion of a Soviet submarine into Swedish waters. The question of whether or not this submarine carried nuclear weapons was never made completely clear, but if the ship had the weapons aboard, the Swedish military did not know about the sub's presence until it was inside a restricted military zone. This activity tended to further frighten the NATO allies into fearing a nuclear war in Europe. Both activities, occurring so close to each other, were intended to convince the NATO allies that both sides could spring a nuclear attack easily without the Europeans knowing anything about it.

Another major block in the scenario wall was put into place on June 19, 1978, when President Jimmy Carter, by an unconstitutional Executive Order, created an organization known as the Federal Emergency Management Agency (FEMA). This organization is a civilian agency which has the capacity to administer a totalitarian government in the event of domestic or rinternational crisis.

FEMA has the authority to:

Relocate millions of workers, reorganize national industry and banking, and distribute all economic resources and transportation access;
Operate every level of government, through personnel currently in place throughout Washington and the rest of the country;
Institute total energy rationing; and
Order mass evacuation of residents in the perimeter of nuclear power plants.

It is an interesting coincidence that the Three Mile Island incident occurred just one day after FEMA became operational. FEMA arrived on the scene of the nuclear plant accident and according to *Fusion* magazine: "... fostered an atmosphere of panic, and lobbied for mass evacuations that would have given FEMA authority over all other federal, state and local governmental bodies, with the exception of the governor's office."[25]

There is some evidence that the nuclear event that occurred at Three Mile Island was an act of sabotage.

One bit of evidence is the fact that an anti-nuclear power article appeared in 1978 in a radical magazine called *Harrisburg* which envisioned an accident at the nearby Three Mile Island facility on March 28, 1979, the *exact* date on which the nuclear accident occurred.[26]

Another is the fact that the investigators who were studying the incident were unable to identify the individual who closed the valves of the backup cooling pumps which would have kept the reactor from overheating.[27]

In any event, the Three Mile nuclear incident was certainly a "non-event."

The charges that large amounts of radiation were released into the nearby environment were fraudulent.

Dr. Petr Beckmann, the distinguished editor of *Access to Energy*, and a professor of Electrical Engineering at the University of Colorado, set the matter into perspective:

The sum total of radioactivity released in the Harrisburg Grand Disaster was 80 millirems (official testimony by HEW Secretary.)
That is as much additional radiation as a certain person would receive by moving from Pennsylvania into the editorial offices of this newspaper (elevation 7,200 ft. in the ore-rich Rockies) for less than a year.
What kind of person?
The kind that stood naked near the plant 24 hours a day for the entire episode.[28]

In an attempt to quiet the furor about the immense danger to life from nuclear plants around the country, Dr. Edward Teller, a scientist who worked on the hydrogen bomb and on the safety of nuclear energy, placed a full-page advertisement in the *Wall Street Journal* on July 31, 1979. This advertisement carried answers to some of the main questions about Three Mile Island.

Some of those questions and answers were as follows:

Q. How dangerous is the release of low-level radiation from a nuclear power plant?

A. If you sat next to a nuclear power plant for a year, you would be exposed to less radiation than you would receive during a round-trip flight in a 747 from New York to Los Angeles.

Let me put it another way. The allowable radiation from a nuclear plant is five mrems (an appropriate unit used to make comparisons) per year. In Dallas, people get about 30 mrems per year from the natural background of buildings, rocks, etc. In Colorado, people get as much as 130 mrems per year from the natural background. Therefore, just by moving from Dallas to Boulder you would receive ten times more radiation per year than the person gets who lives next to a nuclear power plant.

Q. How much radiation were the people around Three Mile Island exposed to during the accident?

A. Let me put it this way. Your blood contains potassium 40, from which you get an internal dose of about 25 mrems of radiation per year. Among the people not working on the reactor, a handful may have gotten as much radiation as 25 mrems.

The timing of the creation of FEMA and the apparently sabotaged nuclear incident is indeed unusual. Is it possible that the Three Mile Island episode was created to test the incredible powers of FEMA?

FEMA's other crisis interventions include the relocation of the Cuban boat refugees in 1980. This episode allowed FEMA to test its ability to relocate thousands of people all over the United States. Is it possible that Cuba allowed the boat people to leave Cuba as a test of FEMA's ability to find new homes for these refugees?

Apparently President Ronald Reagan agreed that FEMA had done an excellent job. When he outlined his $3.4 billion, seven-year program to relocate the U.S. metropolitan population from potentially high risk areas after a nuclear war started, he designated FEMA as the agency to carry out the program.[29]

FEMA has an interesting history behind its creation. The 1979 Executive Order that created it was based on Presidential Review Memorandum 32, prepared by Samuel Huntington. The guiding assumption of PRM-32 was that constitutionally mandated institutions would not be able to deal with the scope of crises forseen for the 1970's and 1980's.

Three years earlier, Huntington had elaborated this assumption in his position paper for the Trilateral Commission, titled *The Crisis of Democracy*. Emergencies of the nature of Love Canal, the Cuban boatlift operation, and the Three Mile Island incident would require levels of austerity and social control impossible to achieve through democratic institutions, so Huntington recommended a series of national and supranational "crisis management" forms of government. These were put into effect by President Carter in June, 1978, after they were published in the Federal Register.[30]

One more evidence that the American people might permit their government to violate all of their Constitutional Rights because of some real or alleged emergency that was created by the government, occurred on October 16, 1970, in Canada.

This power grab occurred when Canadian Prime Minister Pierre-Elliott Trudeau, using the kidnapping of two officials by the Communist F.L.Q. "invoked the War Measures Act, suspended the Canadian Bill of Rights, and imposed a dictatorship on Canada. Trudeau now had the power of censorship, for instance, and could search without warrant and arrest without trial."[31]

It will be recalled that the Canadian people allowed these violations of their rights almost without a whimper, almost praising Trudeau for taking that action to stop the F.L.Q.

Two other indications that the Conspiracy plans on grabbing all of the power in the United States in 1985 come from two books, one written by Herman Kahn, the founder of the Hudson Institute, and possibly one of the principals in the writing of the *Report From Iron Mountain*, and the other by Allen Drury.

The book by Herman Kahn is called *Things to Come: Thinking About the 70's and the 80's*. Mr. Kahn, who calls himself "one of the 10 most famous obscure Americans," attempted to answer these questions by his book (co-authored with B. Bruce Briggs). They have written: "What are the chances of a nuclear confrontation in the next decade? How will the rising influence of Japan affect the world's balance of economic and political power? Is America's two-party system on the verge of collapse? These are some of the questions Herman Kahn and B. Bruce Briggs answer in this challenging new book, a discussion of what might happen from now until 1985."[32]

Notice that the scenario, even though the book is intended to examine the 70's and 80's (that means the period that should have been reviewed would have been until the end of 1989) the book ends with the year 1985. In fact, the year "1985" appears forty-one times in print, and the term "the decade 1975-1985" appears five times.

Are Mr. Kahn and Mr. Briggs trying to tell the American people something?

The second book is entitled *The Hill of Summer*, written as a novel by Allen Drury. It is about how: "Soviet leaders might make use of a 'window of opportunity' created by the U.S. disarmers, resulting in increasing Soviet brinkmanship and nuclear blackmail."

Mr. Drury has written about what Senator Goldwater warned the American people about back in 1971: nuclear blackmail by the Russian government.

It appears that 1985 is the year.

The author wishes to add a footnote about this last statement. There are several possibilities about the prediction that the planners will make their long-awaited move in 1985.

If the Conspiracy wants to discredit those who have exposed the Conspiracy, there wouldn't be a better way than to have all of the exposers point towards the year 1985. Then, if they wished to further conceal their efforts toward another year, they could postpone their plans for one more year, say, to 1986, so that those exposers would be made to look ridiculous.

The reader's attention is directed to the comment previously referred to by Zbigniew Brzezinski in his book *Between Two Ages* that discusses a re-writing of the Constitution in either 1976, a date obviously in the past, or in 1989, a date still in the future.

Maybe the date is 1989.

Perhaps it would be more accurate to say that something is planned for the period between 1985 and 1989.

The only thing for certain is that the Conspiracy wants total government and that the year they expect to achieve their goal is very near.

Those who love their freedoms had best be wary.

Chapter 39

Removal

On November 13, 1951, Richard Nixon denounced the Truman administration in a speech in Boston. His subject was corruption in high places:

> This Administration has proved that it is utterly incapable of cleaning out the corruption which has completely eroded it, and re-establishing the confidence and faith of the people in the morality and honesty of their government employees.
>
> The great tragedy, however, is not that corruption exists, but that it is defended and condoned by the President and other high Administration officials. We have had corruption defended by those in high places.
>
> If they don't recognize or admit that corruption exists, how can we expect them to clean it up?[1]

To understand the events of the Watergate episode, it becomes important to understand the plans of the Conspiracy and the counter-plans of the Nixon Administration.

In January, 1964, newsmen asked Nelson Rockefeller when he had first thought about being president of the United States. He replied: "Ever since

I was a kid. After all, when you think of what I had, what else was there to aspire to?"[2]

Nelson Rockefeller was committed to the aspirations of the Conspiracy about creating the New World Order. He is quoted as saying on July 26, 1968, according to the Associated Press, that as president "he would work toward international creation of 'a new world order' based on East-West cooperation instead of conflict."[3]

But even though Nelson Rockefeller was close to the inner circles of the Conspiracy, he was never inside those circles. It is the present author's contention that he was never scheduled to become the president of the United States, at least since the election of 1968.

That means that the Conspiracy promised Nelson the presidency but knew that it would not deliver it as promised. So there were four cross-currents at work in the years between 1964 and 1976. They were:

1. One was to make Richard Nixon the president of the United States;
2. The second was to remove Richard Nixon from office after his first election in 1968;
3. The third was to promise Nelson Rockefeller the presidency in 1976; and
4. The fourth was not to deliver what had been promised to Nelson.

The events at the Watergate building were intended to achieve three of these objectives after the first had succeeded.

But to understand Watergate, one must understand Richard Nixon and why the Conspiracy wanted him in office in 1968, only to want him out of office in 1973 and 1974.

Mr. Nixon has had an interesting career. It began in 1946 when he defeated incumbent Congressman Jerry Voorhis in California after World War II.

Congressman Voorhis was a champion of those who were fighting the Federal Reserve. He had written a book entitled *Out of Debt, Out of Danger*, in which he advocated the paying off of the national debt. Voorhis had also introduced legislation to repeal the Federal Reserve Act.

This behavior did not make the Congressman a favorite of the banking fraternity.

In a pamphlet he had written entitled *Dollars and Sense*, Congressman Voorhis stated that: "... the representatives of the American people in Congress should speedily proceed to transfer the ownership of the 12 central Federal Reserve banks from the private ownership of the member banks to the ownership of the nation itself."[4]

Suddenly out of nowhere, a candidate named Richard Nixon came forward to oppose him. It has been reported that the Eastern establishment had poured huge amounts of money into Nixon's campaign.

In any event, Richard Nixon defeated Congressman Jerry Voorhis and replaced him as the Congressman from that district.

The next step in Nixon's ascendancy to the presidency occurred in 1952, when Nixon assisted Dwight Eisenhower in stealing the Republican presidential nomination from "Mr. Republican," Robert Taft. It is commonly felt that Mr. Taft would be the Republican nominee for president, and that he would be able to defeat the Democratic candidate, whoever that nominee might be. Mr. Taft was a "conservative" and true anti-communist. He had to be defeated, and the man chosen to defeat him was Dwight David Eisenhower who had been held out of the election in 1948 for this purpose.

The control of the California delegation to the Republican National Convention was the key to the selection of the presidential candidate, and it appeared that Mr. Taft would carry California. Richard Nixon along with Earl Warren, then the governor of California, worked behind the scenes to secure the votes of the delegates from California for Eisenhower.

When Eisenhower was rewarded with the nomination, he rewarded those who had assisted him in securing it for him. He selected Nixon as his Vice-President, and later named Earl Warren to the Supreme Court.

Eisenhower later betrayed Nixon in 1960, when as president he told the American people that he couldn't think of a single thing that Nixon had done to assist him in the eight years of their administration. Nixon's chances in the 1960 election against John Kennedy were significantly damaged by that single comment.

It is conceivable that that statement was intended to keep Nixon away from the presidency in 1960, because it had been promised to him in 1968, and Nixon preferred that year over the year 1960 for reasons that will be discussed later.

In spite of Eisenhower's "non-support," there are those who felt that Nixon had actually won the 1960 election and was the duly elected president of the United States, but that vote fraud in Texas and Illinois gave the election to John Kennedy. Nixon had the opportunity to once and for all expose the nearly perpetual vote fraud suspected to exist in these two states, but he refused to contest the vote count and the election was won by Kennedy.

There are some who feel that the reason Nixon did not contest the election was that he had been offered the presidency in 1968. Nixon, it is felt, quickly reasoned that, even if he had won the election of 1960 and had been re-elected in 1964, his eight-year term in office would only get him to 1968, still short of the 1976 target date of the Conspiracy that he had understood and acknowledged. (Nixon was a member of the CFR). This would also explain why he decided not to run in 1964, leaving the Republican nomination to Barry Goldwater.

In 1962, Nixon returned to politics to run for governor of California. His basic intent was, not to defeat the incumbent Governor Pat Brown, but to defeat his fellow Republican, the conservative Joe Shell. It was also Nixon's desire to keep the California delegation to the 1964 Republican convention out of the control of the conservatives led by Mr. Shell.

It is well known that Nelson Rockefeller had wanted to win the 1964 Republican presidential nomination, and it was generally agreed that the California delegation was once again the key to his nomination, just as it had been in 1952.

So if Nixon defeated Shell in the primaries, he could assist the presiden tial aspirations of Nelson Rockefeller. Nixon did defeat Shell in the primary, thereby insuring at least temporarily that Shell would not control the 1964 California delegation. Nixon went on to lose to Pat Brown in the genera election, an election that Nixon did not care to win. Rockefeller's plans for the presidency had succeeded so far.

After he was defeated in 1962, Nixon told reporters that "you won t have me to kick around anymore," (or words to that effect), because he was leaving the political scene.

He went to New York and moved into the first floor of an expensive apartment building, (the rent was $100,000 a year), in New York. The occupant of the top floor of this building was Nelson Rockefeller, who also became his landlord, as Rockefeller owned the building. In addition, Nixon went to work for the law firm representing the Rockefeller interests and became a full partner at a salary of $200,000 a year.[5]

It was here that Nixon basically sat out the 1964 presidential election.

It is not known if Rockefeller completely understood the 1964 "Draft Goldwater" movement among the young people of the country, especially the young in California. But it is known that this movement was indeed a concern of the Conspiracy around Rockefeller. The California Young Republicans had swept control of their state organization away from the Rockefeller supporters and were booming Senator Goldwater for the presidency in 1964.

It appeared that Rockefeller would lose the key California delegation to the 1964 convention, and because of this loss, ultimately the nomination of the Republican Party.

And this is precisely what happened. The California Young Republicans assisted the Goldwater supporters to control the California delegation, and this key delegation led the remainder of the delegations in giving the nomination to Barry Goldwater.

Rockefeller had lost his best chance at the presidency.

The next step in the ascendancy of Richard Nixon occurred in 1968 when he won the presidency of the United States. He must have felt that the timing was opportune for the 1976 target date and that he would then be in a position to assume the presidency of the World. He must have known that this all-powerful position had been offered first to Woodrow Wilson and then to Franklin Roosevelt, and that both had been unable to assume this office because of the concerns of the American people.

Nixon "selected" Spiro Agnew as his vice president in 1968. By strange coincidence, Governor Agnew had been Nelson Rockefeller's 1968 campaign manager. It is hard to presume that those who selected him did not know about his "skeleton in the closet," allegations that Agnew had taken some money from certain contractors while he was governor of Maryland. (Agnew later wrote a book entitled *Go Quietly or Else*, in which he vehemently denied the allegations against him. That is interesting, because, if Agnew was innocent, then he was framed. He claims that he was forced out under veiled threats to his life made to him by Alexander Haig, a member of the CFR.) The door to this "closet" was later opened, and Agnew resigned.

That poses the question: was Agnew selected because they knew that they could remove him later, either with the truth about his alleged "kickbacks" or with their knowledge that the press would convince the American people that the false allegations were true?

If the previously detailed scenario is correct, that the Conspiracy altered its plans about the 1976 target date, and that the plans were changed in 1970, then the next quote that appeared in the *New York Times* makes sense. It appeared on May 21, 1971, and was written by James Reston, a member of the Council on Foreign Relations. It is presumed that it was a tip-off to the supporters of the Conspiracy around the nation who read the *New York Times*, owned and controlled by members of the CFR, that Nixon had been told of the change in the plans and that he was going through with plans of his own. The article read, in part: "Mr. Nixon would obviously like to preside over the creation of a new world order, and believes he sees an opportunity to do so in the last twenty months of his first term."[6] It was during the last twenty months of his first term that the details about the Watergate break-in were being formulated.

Robert Welch, founder of the John Birch Society, long an exposer of the Conspiracy, wrote the following in the October, 1971, *Bulletin* to all of the Society members: "The record seems to me to indicate quite clearly that, since at least 1960, Richard Nixon has had the all-pervading ambition, and the unshakable determination, to use the presidency of the United States as a stepping stone from which to become the first ruler of the world."[7]

Welch went on to reveal, in the same *Bulletin*, the precise date he anticipated that these plans would come into fruition: "And there are many reasons to believe it is their intention to achieve this goal, and have their regime sitting on top of a subdued and enslaved world, by the first of May,

1976."[8] (The first of May, 1976, would be the two-hundredth anniversary of the founding of the Illuminati.)

Unknown to the Society at that time, though, the Conspiracy had apparently revised its timetable, as was explained in the preceding chapter.

But, Nixon, sensing that he was to be removed from office, apparently decided that he could do this himself, and he surrounded himself with a group of individuals whom he felt he could trust, all non-members of the CFR. There were only two major exceptions, however, who were members of the CFR: Alexander Haig and Henry Kissinger. Both of these individuals had connections to the Rockefeller interests, and it is doubted that Nixon had any control over their selection for his Administration.

So on June 17, 1972, James W. McCord, (non-member of the CFR) and four Miami Cubans broke into the Watergate complex and were later arrested.

Watergate is an interesting building complex. A *Parade* magazine article revealed that the complex was owned by Generale Immobiliare, a giant construction company which was in turn owned by the Catholic Church. The same article further revealed that the Vatican had "major investments in such Banks as Chase Manhattan...and the various Rothschild banks in France."[9]

One thing is for certain, however. The break-in into the Watergate building has made this the most well-known office complex in Washington D.C. outside of the buildings occupied by the federal government.

The Watergate break-in was perhaps the most bungled break-in in the history of crime. One author, Victor Lasky, has written: "Rarely has there been a more inane caper. Everything went wrong—as if by design. It was almost as if they had been deliberately dropping clues."[10]

Those who have studied the break-in in any length have discovered incredible circumstances that surely indicate that the break-in was indeed intended to be discovered. Take, for instance, the following facts:

1. One of the burglars alerted a guard by replacing the tape over the door locks after the guard had discovered and removed the first one.
2. Even though their efforts had been discovered, the boss of the operation, G. Gordon Liddy, sent the burglars back to the Watergate.
3. The man posted as lookout saw the police enter the building but either failed to alert the men inside or his warning was ignored.[11]

The theory that Watergate was indeed intentionally bungled was offered in an article by Jim Hougan in *Harper's* magazine. The contents of that article were reviewed by Victor Lasky in *Human Events*. Mr. Lasky reports: "its basic finding is that the June, 1972, burglary...was not only bungled...but was most deliberately sabotaged.... What is alleged is that the Watergate caper was sabotaged by none other than James McCord, the FBI-trained employee of the U.S. Central Intelligence Agency who later blew the whistle on his fellow burglars. In other words, Jim Hougan argues that McCord was actually a double agent."[12]

That is not surprising, according to a book entitled *The Rockefeller File*, by Gary Allen, that claims: "The incredibly bungled Watergate break-in . . . was written and directed by Rockefeller front men."[13]

Allen identifies the "Rockefeller front men" as Alexander Haig and Henry Kissinger, the two members of the CFR who were Nixon's advisors.

It is also interesting that there was one individual who knew nothing about the Watergate break-in when it first occurred: "As it turned out, the one person who had absolutely no advance knowledge of the Watergate break-in was Richard M. Nixon."[14]

Another link in this incredible chain of events is an article that claims that "Deep Throat," the "mystery man" whose news leaks helped bring the Watergate scandals to a shattering climax, was identified in a new book as Richard Ober, a CIA counterintelligence agent.

It was the theory of Deborah Davis, in a book she authored, that Ober: "became a double agent in the White House for those who wanted the President of the United States to fall."

John Dean, a Nixon staff member involved with the Watergate affair, claimed that "Deep Throat" was Alexander Haig, a charge that General Haig quickly denied.

Another of the puzzling circumstances in the entire Watergate scenario was the tapes of the various conversations made between Nixon and his many advisors in the White House. These tapes were not under the control of Nixon himself as: "Voices automatically started the tape recorders spinning. Keep in mind that it was not Mr. Nixon who turned the recorders off and on."[15]

It is interesting how the tapes came to be in the White House in the first place. "While LBJ's (Lyndon Baines Johnson's) recording system had been installed by the Army Signal Corps, the Nixon monitors were installed by the Secret Service."

Newsweek magazine of September 23, 1974, added this revealing link in the chain: "While former White House chief of staff H.R. Haldeman awaits trial for his part in Watergate, the Secret Service chief he ousted from the White House last year has landed a plum job. Robert H. Taylor, 49, who tangled with Haldeman over Nixon security procedures, is now head of the private security forces of all of the far-flung Rockefeller family enterprises.'[16]

The main question never adequately answered by those covering the Watergate story was why President Nixon never destroyed the tapes that were in his sole possession that were so indicting of his Administration. One answer, perhaps the most plausible, is: "Either Nixon did not control the tapes, or he knew there was more than one set. In a word, he did not destroy them because he could not."[17]

Evidence for this conclusion seems persuasive. For instance, when the prosecuting judge John Sirica asked President Nixon to turn over the tapes he had in his possession, he asked for them in the following manner: "January 8, 1973 from 4:05 to 5:34 P.M. (E.O.B.) at approximately 10 minutes and 15 seconds into the conversation, a segment lasting 6 minutes and 31 seconds."[18]

The only way the judge could ask for certain tapes, specifying just when during the tape he wanted the conversations recorded therein, was if he knew exactly what was on the tapes beforehand. That was impossible unless the judge and the prosecution had a second copy of the tapes.

There are two more rather puzzling circumstances about those tapes.

One is that: ". . . no tapes contained his [Henry Kissinger's] advice, which is strange as he was Nixon's top advisor on national security."[19]

Apparently the public was being asked to believe that Kissinger never was in the Oval office so that he could be taped by the automatic taping machine talking to the president.

The second was the fact that it was: ". . . Alexander Haig who had control of the vault where the Watergate tapes were kept. Since it is perfectly clear that the subpoenas for the tapes were written by persons already possessing a detailed familiarity with their contents, it is painfully obvious that Haig had already provided them with copies of the pertinent excerpts."[20]

In summary, then, it was Kissinger and Haig that arranged for Nixon to be removed from office. And if Spiro Agnew is right, it was Alexander Haig that forced him to resign.

> The coup d' etat that knocked President Nixon out of the White House was carefully engineered by the two agents of the House of Rockefeller.
>
> It is now known that Henry Kissinger was responsible for creating the Plumbers squad the group that broke into Watergate) in the first place, while . . . Alexander Haig made sure that the most incriminating evidence on the tapes was given in advance to the men investigating (Nixon).
>
> Together, the two men forced . . . Nixon to resign, thus paving the way to get Rockefeller into the White House — without risking an election Rocky would surely lose.[21]

So Watergate had two purposes: One was to remove Nixon, and the other was to make Nelson Rockefeller the president of the United States.

At least these were the surface motives.

The next step became the removal of Spiro Agnew as vice president of the United States. This occurred on October 10, 1973, after the door to his "closet" was opened.

In Agnew's book, he explained that he had resigned from office following "veiled threats on his life relayed by Nixon's chief lieutenant, Alexander Haig." He claimed that Haig "desired not only to move me out, but in the course... to move Mr. Nixon out, too."

He concluded that Haig "knew enough about discrepancies in the Watergate tapes and that the truth about Nixon's involvement in the Watergate cover-up to be convinced that eventually the President himself must go. And Haig did not want me in line of succession."[22]

He added that "Haig might have him murdered if he hadn't [resigned]."

The possibility that Haig might have been able to have someone kill Agnew was confirmed in 1980 when G. Gordon Liddy, a Nixon aide, admitted that he had proposed the killing of columnist Jack Anderson to the White House in 1972 and that he had waited for White House approval which never came.

So there was at least one person on the Nixon staff who would have killed had he been asked to do so.

With Agnew out as vice president, Nixon now had to appoint a successor. There was widespread concern around the nation that Nixon was going to appoint Nelson Rockefeller. Now would have been the time to make certain that Rockefeller became president, if that was the promise of the Conspiracy. But Nixon did not select Rockefeller, he chose Gerald Ford instead.

This choice was amazing if the Conspiracy had promised Nelson the presidency. The only conclusion that fits is that they did not want him to become president, and therefore told Nixon to appoint Gerald Ford, who certainly had been groomed for such a task by the Conspiracy. (Gerald Ford, it will be recalled, had attended numerous Bilderberg meetings and personally knew Prince Bernhard, the organization's early leader. It is presumed that Mr. Ford knew that a centralized conspiracy existed.)

Nixon's choice of Ford is also startling when it is remembered that the basic intent of Watergate was to remove Nixon. That meant that the Conspiracy knew that the person whom Nixon chose would later become the president of the United States. If the Conspiracy had wanted Nelson Rockefeller, this would have been the time to make its move.

Once again, the only conclusion that fits is that Nelson Rockefeller was not to become the president of the United States as he had been promised.

However, to continue the illusion that Nelson would become president, Ford chose Nelson as his vice-president when he became president after Nixon resigned.

(One interesting sidelight to the resignation of President Nixon. It will be recalled that President Nixon was suffering from a swollen leg during the time he was preparing to resign. He made the statement that, if he had gone to Bethesda Naval Hospital to have it attended, he would "never come out alive." Is it possible that Nixon knew about Senator Joseph McCarthy and Secretary of Defense James Forrestal who both went to Bethesda Naval Hospital "never to come out alive?")

The next step came when two assassination attempts were made on President Ford's life, the first by Lynette "Squeaky" Fromme on September 5, 1975, who pointed a .45 caliber pistol at Ford, and the second on September 22, 1975, when Sara Jane Moore shot at Ford. Her attempt also failed.

One of the interesting facts about the Moore shooting is that she admitted that she had intended to make Nelson Rockefeller president of the United States. She said that she tried to shoot Ford to expose the nation's "phony system of government." She claimed that: "Ford is a nebbish.... It was the office of the presidency I was trying to attack. Killing Ford would have shaken a lot of people up. More importantly, it would have elevated Nelson Rockefeller to the presidency, and then people would see who the actual leaders of the country are."[23]

Miss Moore consented to an interview in the June, 1976, *Playboy* magazine wherein she hinted that there was a conspiracy involved in her attempt on President Ford's life. Excerpts from the interview reveal this point:

> Moore:
> I had done something very valuable for them (the FBI) in the fall of 1974. I will intrigue you a little with this: That was the point at which the seed of what finally happened on September 22, 1975, was planted. That was the one time when my political beliefs, what I wanted to have happen, coincided with something that the Bureau and the Secret Service wanted.
> Playboy:
> You have intrigued us. What was it?
> Moore:
> Maybe sometime I'll tell you about it. Not now.[24]

Later on in the interview, she partially amplified her remarks:

> Playboy:
> At what point did you decide, 'Aha, now I've got a gun, I'm going to use it on Ford?'
> Moore:
> That is the part that I don't think I can talk about. I just haven't figured out a way to talk about it and protect everyone. I'm

not saying that anyone helped me plan it. I'm not just saying that there are other things—which means there are other people, though not in terms of a conspiracy. There are areas I'm not willing to talk about for a lot of reasons.[25]

The writer of the introduction to the *Playboy* interview mentioned another strange circumstance about this case: "Adding to the air of mystery surrounding her case is the fact that U.S. District Judge Samuel Conti ... sealed all the trial evidence."[26]

Is it possible that there were rogue members of the Conspiracy that wanted Nelson Rockefeller to become the president of the United States and that they wanted Gerald Ford out of the line of succession?

So it appears that the Conspiracy accomplished its four goals:

1. Richard Nixon became the President of the United States;
2. Richard Nixon was removed from office;
3. Nelson Rockefeller was apparently promised the presidency; and
4. The Conspiracy didn't deliver the presidency as promised.

The overall goal of a dictatorship in the United States sometime between 1985 and 1989 still remains to be fulfilled.

Chapter 40
Assistance

The question of what the reader can do about this national crisis is perhaps the most important question posed by this study.

If this book has convinced the reader that there is indeed a giant conspiracy at work in the world, it is hoped that each will seek a solution to the problem.

The author is convinced that the only solution to this immoral Conspiracy that moral men and women can accept is a moral one, and the only moral solution to this enormous Conspiracy is education.

Education is not only part of the problem, it is also part of the solution.

Simply put, this means that all informed individuals must first continue to educate themselves to the point where they are convinced of the correctness of their position, and then secondly, they must be willing to do all within their moral power to inform other individuals of the menace this Conspiracy presents to the rights and freedoms of all free people.

There are really only two areas of activity for the concerned activist that the author has chosen to call:

    1. Non-Conspiratorial Assistance, and

    2. Conspiratorial Assistance.

These are organizations that will assist concerned individuals in their quest for additional information on the Conspiracy or for additional information about economics or politics from groups that do not teach the existence of a conspiracy.

1.   Non-Conspiratorial Assistance:
There are several excellent organizations that can assist the activist in acquiring the knowledge that it will take to enter the contest for the freedoms of the individual. These are:

A.   The National Center for Constitutional Studies:
This organization is a "non-profit, tax-exempt educational foundation dedicated to restoring constitutional principles in the tradition of the founding fathers."
It was founded by Cleon Skousen, an author of several books on the subject of the Conspiracy, most notably the book entitled *The Naked Capitalist*. He was in the FBI for sixteen years and served as the Police Chief of Salt Lake City for four years and as a teacher at Brigham Young University for seven years.
The Center publishes excellent books and treatises, including excellent tapes and lecture series, on the subject of the Constitution, the founding fathers, and the free-enterprise system.
They may be contacted at:
> The National Center for Constitutional Studies
> P.O. Box 31776
> Salt Lake City, Utah 84131

B.   The Foundation for Economic Education (FEE):
This organization is a "non-political, non-profit, educational champion of private property, the free market, the profit and loss system, and limited government."
They publish a monthly magazine which will be sent to those who request it without charge, explaining such economic subjects as inflation, money, tariffs, land use zoning, etc. The magazine is called *The Freeman*. (The Foundation does ask for donations to cover their costs, however.)
They also promote and sponsor seminars on these subjects.
The Foundation can be reached at:
> The Foundation for Economic Education
> Irvington-on-Hudson
> New York, 10533

C.   The Institute for Creation Research (the ICR):
The largest and best organized entity advancing the cause of creationism in the scientific world is the ICR. This organization is now actively debating the evolutionists on the college campuses around the United States and in foreign countries, and is having phenomenal success. They operate a large

publishing operation, making their books and publications available to all who desire them.

The Institute also publishes a monthly newsletter called *Acts and Facts*, which will be sent to those who request it at no charge to the reader, although they also request donations to help defray their costs.

They also put on a week-long seminar at various locations around the United States on the subject of the proofs of creationism that is well worth attending.

The ICR can be reached at: The Institute for Creation Research
2716 Madison Avenue
San Diego, California 92116

F. The Summit Ministries:

This organization's promotional material states that "The Summit is a Christian, summer youth retreat, located in Manitou Springs, Colorado. Today's teenagers are being pressured from every side to reject the Bible's teachings concerning God, His creation, and the role of the family. Through lectures and the finest films . . . Summit courses provide the needed antidote by emphasizing the Word of God and how Christianity affects every area of the believer's life. Students also study America's Christian heritage (freedom is a gift of God), the Marxist-Leninist threat to that freedom, and the Liberal-Humanist broadsides against Biblical Christianity. It is our purpose to arm Christian young people with facts and information concerning God, home, and country so that they will be able to hold fast to the true and the good in building their lives for the future."

They may be reached at: Summit Ministries
Postal Box 207
Manitou Springs, Colorado 80829

2. Conspiratorial Assistance:

There are two groups that know that an international Conspiracy exists: those that are members of the Conspiracy, and those that are trying to expose the Conspiracy.

The strategy of the conspiracy has always been: "Never try to refute the accusations, but always destroy the accuser."

J. Edgar Hoover, the late director of the Federal Bureau of Investigation, has been quoted as saying: "The best yardstick of the effectiveness of the fight against Communism is the fury of the smear attacks against the fighter."

Perhaps the greatest test of the effectiveness of the strongest exposer of the Conspiracy is that this group has survived the greatest onslaught of smear tactics in the history of the Conspiracy.

The charges that the John Birch Society was "anti-semitic, pro-communist, crazy, secret, hysterical or connected with the Ku Klux Klan" have all been proven false. But the ferocity of the attack against the Society shows that they were indeed correct in their assertions that the Conspiracy exists.

The Society was founded in 1958 by Robert Welch who sensed, quite correctly, that there was indeed a master conspiracy active in the major affairs of the United States and the world.

Mr. Welch was born in Chowan County, North Carolina in 1899. He graduated from the University of North Carolina in 1916 and attended the U.S. Naval Academy and Harvard Law School. He was an officer of a large company manufacturing candy from 1956 and was active in the campaign to elect Robert Taft as President in 1952. He served as a director of the National Association of Manufacturers during the years 1951-57 and was a vice-president of the Association from 1955 to 1957. He founded the monthly magazine *American Opinion* in 1956 and is the author of hundreds of published articles and essays.

Books written by Mr. Welch include *May God Forgive Us, The Life of John Birch, The Blue Book of the John Birch Society, The Politician, The New Americanism* and *The Romance of Education.*

Mr. Welch became an instant celebrity when his book entitled *The Politician* was made public in 1963. The book, about Dwight David Eisenhower, made the charge that President Eisenhower was a "dedicated, conscious agent of the Communist conspiracy." What Welch said in the book caused perhaps the greatest controversy of the early 1960's. Mr. Welch never intended for the book to be published, at least that early, but to protect himself and to make it clear just what he had said in the book, he published it in 1963. The book has had repeated reprintings, as the American people became first curious and then, after reading it, shocked by its contents.

Some, however, knew that Mr. Welch was correct in his views about the existence of the Master Conspiracy. One of these supporters came from an unlikely individual, Jerry Rubin, who wrote in his book *Do It!*: "The right wing is usually right too. . . . The John Birch Society understands the world we live in better than fools like Arthur Schlesinger Jr. and Max Lerner who don't know what . . . is happening."[1]

The Society has stated its position quite clearly: "The John Birch Society holds that the freedom, prosperity, moral character and very existence of the United States are threatened by a Conspiracy whose Insiders include men with power of decision not only in government but also, Big Business."[2]

They feared that the Conspiracy was a machination of evil people inside the American government, as Cicero felt of the Roman government. Cicero said: "You [the Roman Senate] have encouraged treason and have opened the gates to free the traitors. A nation can survive its fools, even the ambitious. But it cannot survive treason from within." And Petrach, a great Italian poet, who wrote: "Behold, the relics of Rome. Neither time nor the barbarian can boast the merit of this stupendous destruction; it was perpetrated by her own citizens, by the most illustrious of her sons."

In other words, Mr. Welch agreed with those observers of the past who feared an internal conspiracy more than the armies of a threatening conquerer.

So it was in 1958 that Mr. Welch met with eleven other American patriots in Indianapolis, Indiana, and formed the John Birch Society, as an educational organization to awaken tbe American people to the internal conspiracy sensed by others of the past.

Mr. Welch chose to name his new Society after the young John Birch, who was killed by the Chinese Communists on August 25, 1945. Mr. Welch felt that Captain Birch, who was in China in the American Army at the time and on a mission when he was killed, became the first casualty of the undeclared Third World War, the final war between capitalism and communism.

Mr. Welch, as he researched the buried story of John Birch, discovered that the American State Department had kept the circumstances of his death a secret, and he decided to break the true story to the American people. Mr. Welch found the circumstances of his death to be rather strange, as America was not at war with the Chinese Communists and could not imagine why his death had been covered up by the American government.

His story about John Birch became the book entitled *The Life of John Birch*. Mr. Welch also thought that the moral virtues and the values of Captain Birch also exemplified the traditional American values that were being eaten away by the new moral values of the "modern" American.

So, Mr. Welch was proud to name his newly created society after the American patriot, John Birch.

The Birch Society, in keeping with the high moral values that Birch himself embodied, offered the world a positive program: "We can never win unless both leadership and following have a positive dream which is more important as a hope than the negative nightmare is as a fear; unless the promise of what we can build supplies more motivation than the terror of what we must destroy, and unless this faith in the future is based on a deeper faith in eternal truths."[3]

Mr. Welch became aware that the truths that the organization supported were far more important than the distortions that had to be opposed, so he constructed an organization based on positive values. He wrote that these included:

1. A belief in a divine creator;
2. Belief in morality;
3. A belief in truth and honor and mercy and compassion;
4. In reverence and tradition as components of our spiritual environment;

5.   In the freedom and responsibility of every individual;
6.   In good will towards all men, and the application of the Golden Rule;
7.   In those loyalties to God and Country and Family;
8.   And in love and trust as primary motivations of our thoughts and of our actions in our relationships to God and Government and our fellow men.[4]

The basic belief, then, of the Birch Society was summed up in this short paragraph: "We have to be for something; we must know what that something is; and we must believe it is worth a fight to obtain. Reduced to its simplest and broadest terms, that something is:

Less Government, and More Responsibility, and
With God's Help, a Better World.[5]

Whom was Mr. Welch asking to join?

Merely being patriotic or anti-Communist is not sufficient qualifications for membership. We must have associated with us, now and in the future, only men and women of good will, good conscience, and religious ideals. For we are striving to set an example, by dedication, integrity, and purpose, in word and deed, which our children's children may follow without hesitation.[6]

Because Mr. Welch saw this as a world-wide battle: "the first in history, between light and darkness; between freedom and slavery; . . . for the souls and bodies of men,"[7] he was not optimistic unless freedom loving individuals had a greater vision: "We have no chance unless the specific battles are fought as part of a larger and more lasting movement to restore once again an upward reach in the heart of man."[8]

Mr. Welch not only was forming an organization but, in the *Blue Book of the John Birch Society*, which was a verbatim transcript of the speeches he delivered to the founding members of the Birch Society, he also made some rather prophetic statements. Here is what he wrote about Richard Nixon:

"[He is] an extremely smart man. He is one of the ablest, shrewdest, most disingenuous [not noble or honorable] and slipperiest politicians that ever showed up on the American scene."[9]

And this is what he said about the future Vietnamese War (once again, this was written in 1958:) "Others, like the very pretentious American Friends of Vietnam, in my opinion, form major parts of a whole plan and drive for gradually turning some country over to the Communists, while pretending to be leading the opposition."[10]

Because the Birch Society became successful at an early stage of its career, it became the subject of a vicious smear attack. In fact, Cleon Skousen, not a member of the Society, wrote that "A former member of the Communist Party National Committee personally told me: "The Communist leaders look upon the stamping out of the John Birch Society as a matter of life and death for the Party.""[11]

Mr. Welch was correct. There was a conspiracy, and the forces quickly aligned against him and the Society.

The smear tactics started on July 29, 1960, when the Communist Party in Moscow told the Party in America to "destroy anti-Communism."

This tactic was picked up and repeated by a manifesto of eighty-one Communist Parties in December, 1960, and they were also told to destroy "anti-communism."

And in January, 1961, the Communist Party of the United States singled out the Birch Society, as they were told to "render it ineffective." Later, on February 25, 1961, *People's World*, the official newspaper of the Communist Party, printed an article entitled: "Enter From Stage Right: The John Birch Society." In this article, the Birch Society was called "secret," and their members were called "fascists," and they met in "cells."

And within a matter of weeks, the news magazines of the United States picked up on these stories and they began their own smear jobs, in many cases using the same smear words as the *People's World* article.

On March 22, 1961, Mr. Welch sent Governor Pat Brown of California a telegram asking the California Senate Subcommittee on Un-American Activities to investigate the Birch Society openly to determine if these charges were correct. His request was granted, and after the open hearings were conducted, the Subcommittee issued its report in 1963. This is what it concluded about the Society:

> The John Birch Society to be a right, anti-communist fundamental organization. We have not found the Society to be either a secret or a Fascist organization.
>
> Nor have we found the great majority of its members in California to be mentally unstable, crackpots, or hysterical about the threat of Communist subversion.
>
> We believe that the reason the John Birch Society has attracted so many members is that it simply appeared to them to be the most effective, indeed the only, organization through which they could join in a national movement to learn the truth about the Communist menace, and then take some positive concerted action to prevent its spread.
>
> Our investigation and study was requested by the Society, which has been publicly charged with being a secret, Fascist, subversive, un-American, anti-Semitic organization.
>
> We have not found any of the accusations to be supported by the evidence.[12]

In other words, after fair and open deliberation by this Subcommittee, and after hearing both proponents and opponents, the only conclusion that could be drawn was that the vicious smear job was just that: a vicious smear job.

The Society approached the problem of the Conspiracy's existence in the only way a moral organization can counter lies and deception. They simply told the truth. The plan was to offer the American people the truth through a campaign of education. The Birch Society would have to become the largest university in the world to educate the American people on a one-to-one basis through a group of amateur professors.

The leadership of the Society realized that they would need their own book outlets so they quickly organized over 400 bookstores, the largest bookstore chain in the United States. They realized that they would have rather limited access to the public through the major media, so they organized a speaker's bureau (on the average, three times a night somewhere in the United States there is a paid speaker speaking on some aspect of the Conspiracy.)

It was the Birch Society that organized the speaking tours of Julia Brown, Mel O'Campo, David Gumaer, Sgt. Peter Stark, Douglas Durham, and the others who explained the nature of the Conspiracy to groups of willing listeners. It was the Birch Society that inspired authors, like Gary Allen, Alan Stang, G. Edward Griffin, Herman Dinsmore, and others, to write the books and pamphlets that were awakening the American people.

It was the Birch Society that printed the bumper stickers which reminded the American people to "Support Your Local Police and Keep Them Independent."

It was the Birch Society that helped expose the Council on Foreign Relations, the Trilateral Commission, and the Bilderberg group.

It was the Birch Society that formed the TRIM (Tax Reform Immediately) Committees to inform the American people of the intentional waste in Congress and to expose the voting records of their congressmen to the voting public. It was the Birch Society that, after the death of its national chairman, Congressman Larry McDonald aboard the Korean Airlines flight 007, formed the Larry McDonald Crusade to Stop Financing Communism, a national educational committee of citizens trying to stop the aid and trade that is keeping worldwide Communism alive. It was a member of the Birch Society, Bill Barlow, of Idaho, who took on the government in the issue of OSHA, and won. It is the Birch Society that has eighty paid Coordinators in various congressional districts or states to continue its educational efforts. It was the John Birch Society that circulated petitions among its fellow citizens to stop the aid and trade going on between the American and Russian governments. These petitions have been signed by over four million Americans.

The Birch Society, concerned about the influence of both the Communist Party and the Council on Foreign Relations in the magazines of America, publishes a weekly magazine, called *The Review of the News*, and a monthly magazine, called *American Opinion*, to continue their educational efforts and to present the other side of the various issues. (Those who wish to receive either or both of these well researched and topical magazines may subscribe to them through the John Birch Society, Belmont, Massachusetts, 02178.)

They have developed the largest publishing house of conspiratorial literature in the nation. It was the John Birch Society that published Anastosio Somoza's book, entitled *Nicaragua Betrayed*, that exposed President Carter's betrayal of that country. That book has been printed in both English and Spanish and is being widely circulated in Latin America to assist those countries in their fight against Communism.

Members of the Society meet twice a month and pay dues at the rate of $4.00 per month for men and $2.00 for women. They receive a monthly bulletin that explains the projects that all members work on together.

In summary, then, and in the words of the Society:

> It was the John Birch Society, taking the point on the hard issues and leading the way, that made possible the victories cited above.
>
> For more than two decades, the Society has labored assiduously to create an understanding among the American people of free market economics, of constitutional principles of government, and of dangers posed to the preservation of our Republic by the existence of a Master Conspiracy.
>
> We have taken matters of great import, little understood by our fellow citizens, and made them the overriding issues in an increasing number of political campaigns.
>
> We have helped many good citizens look beyond the surface gloss of media hype to question the basic principles underlying pieces of proposed legislation and to ask tough questions of political candidates to determine where they really stood on the issues....
>
> There is no other organization in the Americanist movement with the track record, the battle-tested membership, or the experience necessary to wage and win the critical campaigns ahead in the climactic fight for America.[14]

These words beg the final question:

> If the John Birch Society does not play the leading role in stopping the Communist Conspiracy, just who is there to do so?[15]

Chapter 41

*The man in the street does not notice the devil even when the
devil is holding him by the throat.*

Thus wrote Johann von Goethe.

The apathy of the American people, and for that matter, those around
the world as well, is legend.

General George Van Horne Moseley wrote: "Historians of the future
will marvel most of all at the non-resistance of those who had the most to
lose."

Edmund Burke posed a similar thought when he wrote: "Evil men
prosper when good men do nothing."

But it is not America's apathy that is the problem. The American people
can see that something is wrong in their nation. It is that most feel there is
nothing they can do about it. Because many feel that the problems are so
immense they conclude that they are powerless to change what is happening.

And this is exactly the thought that the Conspiracy wants the American
people to have.

Those who have taken the time to read this study are now aware of just
how serious the problem really is and they are the ones who must take up the
truth and disperse it to others.

This strategy was made clear by Robert Welch when he wrote in the
Blue Book of The John Birch Society:

We do not have to be too late, and we do not have to lose the fight.

Communism has its weaknesses, and the Communist Conspiracy had its vulnerable points.

We have many layers of strength not yet rotted by all of the infiltration or political sabotage to which we have been subjected.

Our danger is both immense and imminent; but it is not beyond the possibility of being overcome by the resistance that is still available.

All we must find and build and use, to win, is sufficient understanding. Let's create that understanding and build that resistance, with everything mortal men can put into the effort — while there is still time.[1]

There are those, of course, who will see this as an obligation. Someone once wrote:

> To be born a free man is an accident;
> to live a free man is a responsibility;
> to die a free man is an obligation.

In conclusion, those in Hungary who opposed the Russian slavemasters in October of 1956 understood the obligation of all free men to oppose slavery in every form. All they needed was the assistance of other freedom-loving people around the world and they, too, would have possessed the freedom that all men aspire to.

As one of the last acts of the uprising against the Russians, a group of freedom-fighters got control of a radio station and broadcast this message to the rest of the world:

> People of the world . . . help us!
> People of Europe, whom we once defended against the attacks of the Asiatic barbarians, listen now to the alarm bells ring.
> People of the civilized world, in the name of liberty and solidarity, we are asking for you to help.
> The light vanishes.
> The shadows grow darker hour by hour.
> Listen to our cry.
> God be with you and with us.

And with that the radio station went off the air. The Russians were the only ones listening, and they shut the station off the air.

They had succeeded in suppressing the uprising.

> No one came to the rescue.
> But the light does not need to vanish.

You now have the torch of truth.

How much light you spread is up to you.

CLASSES

The author has no idea where copies of this book might end up, so this information is for those interested in further study of the Conspiratorial View of History in the Southern Arizona area only.

The original research for this book was for a ten-week course I have been teaching since 1973, called a variety of things, from "Proofs of a Conspiracy," to "History Over-Easy," to "Who Rules America?"

If the reader wishes to become more acquainted with the machinations of the Conspiracy in a classroom setting, the author would like to cordially invite each reader to participate in these classes.

They are offered three times a year: winter (starting in September,) spring (starting in January,) and summer (starting in July,) and any time a small group of at least four people wish to make the commitment for either the ten-week, two hours a night, weekday-night class, or the five-week, four-hour Saturday-morning class. The class fees are nominal.

The author is also available for speaking engagements should the reader feel it would be appropriate, or for weekend seminars anywhere in the country.

QUESTION

I am frequently asked by students or friends who agree with me that the Conspiracy exists, why I believe I am allowed to continue teaching and writing about its existence. They cite the deaths of Abraham Lincoln, James Forrestal, Joseph McCarthy and Louis McFadden, among others, as evidence that those who expose the Conspiracy do so at their own risk.

I have no answer to that question.

I can only say that I am absolutely convinced that the Conspiracy exists and that they have a great deal to gain by the death of one who has figured it out.

I live in Arizona where a few years ago an investigative reporter had his car blow-up as he started it because he was reporting on corruption in that state. Why his enemies picked on him, and why mine have chosen not to pick on me, I do not know.

I will emphatically say this: if you hear about my car exploding because I rigged it so that it would explode, or that I suddenly "attempted to fly" from the top of a sixteen-story building, please accept my pre-death statement: I didn't do it!

If either of these circumstances occur, or any other mysterious thing happens to me, all I can ask is that you double your efforts in exposing this conspiracy . . . . in my memory,

the author

Footnotes

AN INTRODUCTION

1. James P. Warburg, *The West in Crisis*, (Garden City, New York: Doubleday & Company, Inc., 1959), p. 20.
2. Hedrick P. Smith, "Brzezinski Says Critics are Irked by his Accuracy," *The New York Times*, (January 18, 1981), p. L 3.
3. Carroll Quigley, *Tragedy and Hope*, (London: The Macmillan Company, 1966), p. 61.
4. Richard J. Whalen, *The Founding Father*, (New York, New York: The New American Library, 1964), p. 182.
5. Carroll Quigley, *Tragedy and Hope*, p. 950.
6. Gary Allen, *Ted Kennedy, In Over His Head*, (Atlanta, Los Angeles: '76 Press, 1980), p. 15.
7. Blair Coan, *The Red Web*, (Boston, Los Angeles: Western Islands, 1925), p. vi.
8. *Business Week*, (October 14, 1972), p. 80.
9. Donzella Cross Boyle, *Quest of a Hemisphere*, (Boston, Los Angeles: Western Islands, 1970), p. 167.
10. Joseph P. Lash, *Roosevelt and Churchill*, (New York: W.W. Norton & Company, Inc., 1976), p. 183.
11. Richard J. Whalen, *The Founding Father*, p. 461.

CHAPTER ONE: HISTORY DEFINED

1. Gary Allen, "They're Catching On (reprint)," *American Opinion*, (November, 1977), p. 1.
2. Norman Dodd, "Possible Power Center Behind the Foundations," Tax Exempt Foundations, *The Freemen Institute*, (June 1978) p. 76.
3. Gary Allen, "They're Catching On (reprint)," p. 20.
4. *International Covenants on Human Rights*, United Nations, (1967), p. 3.
5. *U.S. News & World Report*, (June 10, 1968), p. 100.

CHAPTER TWO: FREEDOM

1. Eugene Lyons, *Workers' Paradise Lost*, (New York: Twin Circle Publishing Co., 1961), p. 217.
2. "Revolution Down on the Farm," *Time*, (November 23, 1981), p. 51.
3. *Consumer Reports*, (February, 1979), p. 97.
4. *Consumer Reports*, (February, 1979), p. 97.
5. Howard E. Kershner, *God, Gold and Government*, (Englewood Cliffs, N.J.: Prentice-Hall, Inc.), p. 45.
6. The Duke of Northumberland, 1931; as quoted in: Harry M. Daugherty, *The Inside Story of The Harding Tragedy*, (Boston, Los Angeles: Western Islands, originally published in 1932), p. xx.
7. Robert Welch, "Republics and Democracies," *American Opinion*, (October, 1961), p. 9.
8. *Two Worlds*, (Bensenville, Illinois: Flick-Reedy Education Enterprises, 1966) p. 90.
9. Howard S. Katz, *The Warmongers*, (New York: Books in Focus, Inc., 1979) p. 281.
10. Frederic Bastiat, *The Law*, (Irvington-on-Hudson, New York: Foundation for Economic Education, Inc., 1979), p. 21.
11. Frederic Bastiat, *The Law*, p. 18.
12. Quoted in "The Price is Not Right," *The Freeman*, (1968), p. 271.
13. Robert V. Remini, *Andrew Jackson*, (New York: Harper & Row, 1966), p. 152.

CHAPTER THREE: FORMS OF GOVERNMENT

1. Robert Welch, *American Opinion*, (October, 1961), p. 27.
2. Robert Welch, *American Opinion*, (October, 1961), p. 27.
3. *The Freeman*, (October, 1981), p. 621.
4. *The Freeman*, (October, 1981), p. 621.
5. Jan Kozak, *And Not a Shot is Fired*, (New Canaan, Connecticut: The Long House, Inc., 1957), p. 16.
6. Nesta Webster, *World Revolution*, (London: Constable and Company, Ltd., 1921), p. 31.
7. "The Right Answers," *The Review of the News*, (October 3, 1973).
8. Martin Luther King Jr., *Saturday Review*, April 3, 1965), as quoted by G. Edward Griffin, *More Deadly Than War* (pamphlet), (Thousand Oaks, California: 1969), p. 27.
9. The Augusta Courier, (July 8, 1963), p. 4.
10. W.S. McBirnie, *The Truth About Martin Luther King*, (Glendale, California: Community Churches of America), p. 23.
11. Copy of sworn and notarized affidavit in possession of author, dated September 28, 1963.
12. Alan Stang, *It's Very Simple*, (Boston, Los Angeles: Western Islands, 1965), p. 153.

CHAPTER FOUR: ECONOMIC TERMS

1. "Soviet Use of Forced Labor Hit," *The Oregonian*, (June 21, 1974).
2. "The Right Answers," *The Review of the News*, (December 29, 1971).
3. Richard Vetterli and William E. Fort, Jr., *The Socialist Revolution*, (Los Angeles, Phoenix, New York: Clute International Corporation), p.71.
4. George Bernard Shaw, *Intelligent Woman's Guide to Socialism*, p. 470.
5. George Bernard Shaw, *Labour Monthly*, (October, 1921), quoted in Nesta Webster, *Surrender of an Empire*, (London, 1931), p. 95.
6. Stefan Possony, *Introduction to The Communist Manifesto*, (Belmont, Massachusetts: American Opinion, 1974); p. xxxii-xxxiii.
7. C.W. Guilleband, *The Social Policy of Nazi Germany*, (London: Cambridge University Press, 1941).
8. *Two Worlds*, p. 152.
9. Norman Thomas, *Democratic Socialism* (1953), quoted in W. Cleon Skousen, *The Naked Capitalist* (Salt Lake City: privately published by the reviewer, 1970), p. 130.
10. W. Cleon Skousen, *The Naked Capitalist*, p. 130.
11. Quoted in *The Dan Smoot Report*, (October 18, 1965), p. 335.
12. Rose Martin, *Fabian Freeway*, (Santa Monica, California: Fidelis Publishers, Inc., 1968), p. 340.
13. Marshall Josep Broz (Tito) quoted in *The Review of the News*, (December 1, 1971), p. 57.
14. Karl Marx, "The Socialist Program," quoted in *Contradictions of Communism*, 88th Congress, 2nd Session, (1964), p. 15.
15. *Contradictions of Communism*, p. 16.
16. Sam Brown, quoted in *The Review of the News*, (January 24, 1979).
17. Lyndon Baines Johnson, *Congressional Record*, (January 25, 1964).
18. William F. Buckley, Jr., quoted by John Chamberlain's review of Mr. Buckley's book entitled *Four Programs, A Program for the 70's*, in *The Freeman*, (March, 1974).
19. Pope Paul VI, *This is Progress*, (Chicago: Claretian Publications, 1974). p. 37.
20. "Administration Opens Battle on Socialism," *The Oregonian*, (January

26, 1975), p. A 11.

21. Leon Trotsky, quoted in Ludwig von Mises, *Planned Chaos*, (Irvington-on-Hudson, New York: The Foundation for Economic Education, Inc., 1947), p. 87.

22. "Civiletti Urges 'Card for all U.S. Workers' ", *The Arizona Daily Star*, (June 28, 1980), p. B-3.

23. *The Arizona Daily Star*, (March 25, 1981), p. C-2.

24. *The Arizona Daily Star*, (May 12, 1982), p. A-16.

25. "The Right Answers," *The Review of the News*, (August 23, 1972), p. 60.

26. Vo Nguyen Giap, quoted in "The Right Answers," *The Review of the News*, (March 21, 1973), p. 59.

27. Quoted in *The Review of the News*, (February 25, 1976), p. 30.

28. Quoted in *The Review of the News*, (May 13, 1981), p. 71.

CHAPTER FIVE: INFLATION

1. *The American Economic System . . . And Your Part In It*, (New York: The Advertising Council, Inc.), p. 13.

2. "Burns Says Inflation Can't Be Halted in '74," *The Oregonian*, (February 27, 1974), p. 7.

3. "Inflation, Recession a Cycle?," *Tucson Citizen*, (October 26, 1978).

4. Gary Allen, "By Freeing the Market," *American Opinion*, (December, 1981), p. 2.

5. "New Inflation Chief Calls Lifestyle Foe," *Tucson Citizen*, (October --, 1978).

6. "Smaller Piece of Pie Called Antidote For Inflation," *Arizona Daily Star*, (June 27, 1979).

7. *The Review of the News*, (July 5, 1979), p. 29.

8. *The Review of the News*, (April 18, 1979).

9. Gary Allen, "The Conspiracy," *American Opinion*, (May, 1968), p. 28.

10. James P. Warburg, *The West In Crisis*, p. 34.

11. *Consumer Reports*, February, 1979), p. 95.

CHAPTER SIX: MONEY AND GOLD

1. Stephen Birmingham, *Our Crowd*, (New York: Dell Publishing Co. Inc., 1967), p. 87.

2. Curtis B. Dall, *F.D.R., My Exploited Father-In-Law*, (Washington, D.C.: Action Associates, 1970), pp. 71-75.

3. Gary Allen, "Federal Reserve," *American Opinion*, (April, 1970), p. 69.

4. Werner Keller, *East Minus West Equals Zero*, (New York: G.P. Putnam's Sons, 19620, p. 194.

5. James P. Warburg, *The West in Crisis*, p. 35.

6. Carroll Quigley, *Tragedy and Hope*, p. 258.

7. Ludwig von Mises, quoted by Percy Greaves, *Understanding the Dollar Crisis*. (Boston, Los Angeles: Western Islands, 1973), p. xxi-xxii.

CHAPTER SEVEN: ADDITIONAL ECONOMIC TERMS

1. Antony Sutton, *Wall Street and the Bolshevik Revolution*, (New Rochelle, New York: Arlington House, 1974), p. 16.

2. William Hoffman, *David*, (New York: Lyle Stuart, Inc., 1971), p. 29.

3. Antony Sutton, *Wall Street and FDR*, (New Rochelle, New York: Arlington House, 1975), p. 72.

4. Antony Sutton, *Wall Street and the Bolshevik Revolution*, p. 100.

5. Carrol Quigley, *Tragedy and Hope*, p. 1058.

6. James P. Warburg, *The West in Crisis*, pp. 53-54.

CHAPTER EIGHT: THE SECRET SOCIETIES

1. Arthur Edward Waite, *The Real History of the Rosicrucians*, (Blauvelt,

New York: Steinerbooks, 1977), p. A.

2. Benjamin Disraeli, quoted in Nesta H. Webster, *Secret Societies and Subversive Movements*, (Christian Book Club of America), p. IV.

3. Robert Welch, *What is Communism* (pamphlet), (Belmont, San Marino: American Opinion, 1971), p. 20.

4. G. Edward Griffin, *The Capitalist Conspiracy*, (Thousand Oaks, California: American Media, 1971), p. 53.

5. Gary Allen, *Foundations* (pamphlet), (Belmont, Massachusetts: American Opinion), pp. 7-8.

6. Nesta Webster, *World Revolution*, p. 9.

7. Rene Fulop-Miller, *The Power and Secret of the Jesuits*, (Garden City, New York: Garden City Publishing Company, 1929), p. 376.

8. Rene Fulop-Miller, *The Power and Secret of the Jesuits*, p. 382.

9. Rene Fulop-Miller, *The Power and Secret of the Jesuits*, p. 387.

10. Rene Fulop-Miller, *The Power and Secret of the Jesuits*, p. 390.

11. Rene Fulop-Miller, *The Power and Secret of the Jesuits*, p. 390.

12. "John Paul tells Jesuits to avoid politics, abide by church rules," *The Arizona Daily Star*, (February 28, 1982), p. 6-A.

13. "Collision Course For Pope, Jesuits," *U.S. News & World Report*, (February 22, 1982), p. 60.

14. "World Jesuit Leaders Meet," *The Arizona Daily Star*, (February 24, 1982), p. A-7.

15. Nesta Webster, *Secret Societies and Subversive Movements*, p. 219.

16. Nesta Webster, *Secret Societies and Subversive Movements*, p. 215.

17. Nesta Webster, *Secret Societies and Subversive Movements*, p. 216.

18. Nesta Webster, *World Revolution*, p. 13.

19. Nesta Webster, *Secret Societies and Subversive Movements*, p. 214.

20. John Robison, *Proofs of a Conspiracy*, (Belmont, Massachusetts: Western Islands, 1967), p. 123.

21. John Robison, *Proofs of a Conspiracy*, p. 112.

22. Nesta Webster, *World Revolution*, p. 22.

23. *Seventeen Eighty Nine, An Unfinished Manuscript*, (Belmont, Massachusetts and San Marino, California: American Opinion, 1968), p. 78.

24. John Robison, *Proofs of a Conspiracy*, pp. 60-61.

25. Nesta Webster, *World Revolution*, p. 25.

26. Nesta Webster, *World Revolution*, p. 78.

27. *Seventeen Eighty Nine, an Unfinished Manuscript*, pp. 116-117.

28. John Robison, *Proofs of a Conspiracy* p. 7.

29. Albert Mackey, *An Encylopaedia of Freemasonry*, (Chicago, New York, London: The Masonic History Company, 1925), p. 628.

30. Albert Mackey, *An Encyclopaedia of Freemasonry*, p. 843.

31. Albert Mackey, *An Encyclopaedia of Freemasonry*, p. 347.

32. Albert Mackey, *An Encyclopaedia of Freemasonry*, p. 347.

33. "The Right Answers," *The Review of the News*, (July 19, 1972), p. 59.

34. "Thomas Jefferson," *Freemen Digest*, (Salt Lake City: The Freemen Institute, 1981), p. 83.

35. "Thomas Jefferson," *Freemen Digest*, p. 83.

36. "Revolution," *Life*, second part in a series of two, starting October 10, 1969), p. 68.

37. Nesta Webster, *The French Revolution*, (1919), p. 73.

38. Nesta Webster, *The French Revolution*, p. 79.

39. Nesta Webster, *The French Revolution*, p. 95.

40. Nesta Webster, *The French Revolution*, p. 40.

41. Nesta Webster, *The French Revolution*, p. 41.
42. Nesta Webster, *The French Revolution*, p. 95.
43. Nesta Webster, *The French Revolution*, p. IX.
44. Nesta Webster, *The French Revolution*, p. 17.
45. Nesta Webster, *The French Revolution*, p. 5.
46. Nesta Webster, *The French Revolution*, p. 5.
47. John Robison, *Proofs of a Conspiracy*, p. 7
48. *Seventeen Eighty Nine, an Unfinished Manuscript*, p. 33.
49. Rene Fulop-Miller, *The Power and Secret of the Jesuits*, p. 454.
50. A.N. Field, *The Evolution Hoax Exposed*, (Rockford, Illinois: Tan Books and Publishers, 1971), p. 12.

CHAPTER NINE: COMMUNISM

1. *The Review of the News*, (December 30, 1981), p. 56.
2. Richard Wurmbrand, *Was Karl Marx A Satanist?*, (Glendale, California: Diane Books Publishing Co., 1976), p. 7.
3. Richard Wurmbrand, *Was Karl Marx A Satanist?*, p. 20.
4. Richard Wurmbrand, *Was Karl Marx A Satanist?*, p. 19.
5. *The Review of the News*, (November 29, 1972), p. 60.
6. Richard Wurmbrand, *Was Karl Marx A Satanist?*, p. 4.
7. Nesta Webster, *World Revolution*, p. 173.
8. Karl Marx, *The Communist Manifesto*, (Brooklyn, New York: New York Labor News, 1948), p. 65.
9. Karl Marx, *The Communist Manifesto*, pp. 40-41.
10. Karl Marx, *The Communist Manifesto*, p. 42.
11. "Family Life Harmed by Government, Poll Says," *Arizona Republic*, (June 7, 1980), p. 1.
12. *Don Bell Reports*, (February 15, 1980), p. 1.
13. *The Review of the News*, (July 2, 1980), p. 30.
14. *Plain Truth Magazine*, (May, 1980), p. 16.
15. Gary North, *Poor Karl, the Myth of Marx's Poverty*, American Opinion, (April, 1971), p. 31.
16. Karl Marx, *The Communist Manifesto*, p. xi.
17. Karl Marx, *The Communist Manifesto*, p. xiii.
18. Karl Marx, *The Communist Manifesto*, p. 45.
19. Karl Marx, *The Communist Manifesto*, pp. 45-47.
20. Karl Marx, *The Communist Manifesto*, pp. 37-38.
21. "Demos back prostitution legalization," *The Oregonian*, (April 12, 1972), p. A-1.

CHAPTER TEN: THE RUSSIAN REVOLUTION

1. William Hoffman, *David*, p. 29.
2. Ferdinand Lundberg, *The Rockefeller Syndrome*, (Secaucus, New Jersey: Lyle Stuart, Inc.), p. 121.
3. Peter Collier and David Horowitz, *The Rockefellers: An American Dynasty*, (New York: Holt, Rinehart and Winston, 1976), p. 40.
4. Baron C. Wrangell-Rokassowsky, *Before the Storm*, (Ventimilia, Italy: Tipo-Litografia Ligure), p. 15.
5. Gary Allen, "Building Communism," *American Opinion*, (December, 1975), p. 38.
6. Zygmund Dobbs, "Sugar Keynes," *The Review of the News*, (June 23, 1971), p. 39.
7. Stephen Birmingham, *Our Crowd*, (New York: Dell Publishing Co. Inc., 1967), pp. 334-335.
8. *U.S. News & World Report*, (March 13, 1967), p. 67.

9. Antony Sutton, *Wall Street and the Bolshevik Revolution*, p. 21.
10. H.S. Kennan, *The Federal Reserve Bank*, p. 142.
11. Antony Sutton, *Wall Street and the Bolshevik Revolution*, p. 26.
12. Gary Null, *The Conspirator Who Saved the Romanovs*, (New York: Pinnacle Books, Inc., 1971), p. 17
13. Alan Stang, "The Tsar's Best Agent," *American Opinion*, March, 1976), p. 4.
14. Frank Capell, "The Kissinger Caper," *The Review of the News*, (March 20, 1974), p. 31.
15. Frank Capell, "The Kissinger Caper," p. 33.
16. "Documents Show U.S. Bid to Rescue Czar," *Detroit Free Press*, (December 16, 1970), p. 6-B.
17. "Documents Show U.S. Bid to Rescue Czar," p. 6-B.
18. Guy Richards, *The Hunt for the Czar*, (New York: Dell Publishing Co. Inc., 1970), p. 21.
19. Guy Richards, *The Hunt for the Czar*, p. 22.
20. Alan Stang, "The Tsar's Best Agent," p. 5.
21. Antony C. Sutton, *Wall Street and the Bolshevik Revolution*, pp. 103-104.
22. Michel Sturdza, *Betrayal by Rulers*, (Belmont, Nassachusetts: Western Islands, 1976), p. 115.
23. Michel Sturdza, *Betrayal by Rulers*, p. 11.
24. Donzella Cross Boyle, *Quest of a Hemisphere*, p. 558.
25. Donzella Cross Boyle, *Quest of a Hemisphere*, p. 553.
26. "Revolution," *Life*, (October 10, 1969), p. 112.
27. Michel Sturdza, *Betrayal by Rulers*, p. 76.
28. Rose Martin, *Fabian Freeway*, p. 33.
29. Michel Sturdza, *Betrayal by Rulers*, p. 11.
30. Antony Sutton, *Wall Street and the Bolshevik Revolution*, p. 83.
31. *U.S. News & World Report*, (March 13, 1967), p. 68.
32. "Correction Please," *The Review of the News*, (September 29, 1971), p. 43.
33. "New Books," *The Review of the News*, (May 21, 1975), p. 41.
34. Robert Goldstone, *The Russian Revolution*, (Greenwich, Connecticut: Fawcett Publications, 1966), p. 187.
35. Gary Allen, "The Conspiracy, Planning for Economic Collapse," *American Opinion*, (May, 1968), p. 33.
36. "The Right Answers," *The Review of the News*, (April 19, 1972), p. 59.
37. Edwin Ware Hullinger, *The Reforging of Russia*, (New York: E.P. Dutton & Co., 1925), pp. 247-248.
38. Antony Sutton, *Wall Street and the Bolshevik Revolution*, p. 60.
39. Antony Sutton, *Western Technology and Soviet Economic Development, 1945 to 1965*, (Stanford, California: Hoover Institution Press, 1973), p. 71.
40. George T. Eggleston, *Roosevelt, Churchill, and the World War II Opposition*, (Old Greenwich, Connecticut: The Devin-Adair Company, 1979), p. 129.
41. Eldorous L. Dayton, *Give 'em Hell, Harry*, (Old Greenwich, Connecticut: The Devin-Adair Company, 1956), p. 103.
42. "Revolution," *Life*, (October 10, 1969), p. 110.
43. Robert Goldstone, *The Russian Revolution*, p. 204.

CHAPTER ELEVEN: THE CUBAN REVOLUTION

1. M. Stanton Evans, *The Politics of Surrender*, (New York: The Devin-Adair Company, 1966), p. 129.
2. Fred Ward, *Inside Cuba Today*, condensed in Book Digest, May, 1979), p.

35.

3. Fred Ward, *Inside Cuba Today*, p. 39.
4. Fred Ward, *Inside Cuba Today*, p. 36.
5. Fred Ward, *Inside Cuba Today*, p. 41.
6. Fred Ward, *Inside Cuba Today*, p. 48.
7. "For War-Weary Cubans, Still More Sacrifices," *U.S. News & World Report*, (June 26, 1978), p. 39.
8. Fred Ward, *Inside Cuba Today*, p. 50.
9. *The Review of the News*, (April 30, 1980), p. 19.
10. Earle T. Smith's Letter to the Editor, *New York Times*, (September 26, 1979), p. A-24.
11. Alan Stang, *The Actor*, (Boston, Los Angeles: Western Islands, 1968), p. 313.
12. Frank Capell, *Henry Kissinger, Soviet Agent*, (Zarepath, New Jersey: The Herald of Freedom 1974), p. 19.
13. Nathaniel Weyl, *Red Star Over Cuba*, (New York: Hillman Books, 1961), p. 152.
14. Mario Lazo, *Dagger in the Heart, American Policy Failures in Cuba*, (New York: Twin Circles Publishing Co., 1968), p. 149.
15. Nathaniel Weyl, *Red Star Over Cuba*, p. 1g3.
16. Mario Lazo, *Dagger in the Heart, American Policy Failures in Cuba*, p. 176.
17. Nathaniel Weyl, *Red Star Over Cuba*, p. 95.
18. Herman Dinsmore, *All the News That Fits*, (New Rochelle, New York: Arlington House, 1969), p. 184.
19. Nathaniel Weyl, *Red Star Over Cuba*, p. 153.
20. Herman Dinsmore, *All the News That Fits*, p. 177.
21. Tad Szulc and Karl Meyer, *The Cuban Invasion, the Chronicle of a Disaster*, (New York: Ballantine Books, 1962), p. 103.
22. Tad Szulc and Karl Meyer, *The Cuban Invasion, the Chronicle of a Distaster*, p. 110.
23. Mario Lazo, *Dagger in the Heart, American Policy Failures in Cuba*, p. 268.
24. *New York Times*, (January 10, 1961), p. 1.
25. Robert F. Kennedy, *Thirteen Days, A Memoir of the Cuban Missile Crisis*, (New York: The New American Library, Inc., 1969), p. 24.
26. *New York Times*, (October 28, 1962).
27. *Life*, (November 23, 1962), pp. 38-39.
28. *U.S. News & World Report*, (March 25, 1982), p. 24.
29. Mario Lazo, *Dagger in the Heart, American Policy Failures in Cuba*, p. 94.
30. Mario Lazo, *Dagger in the Heart, American Policy Failures in Cuba*, p. 133 and p. 186.

CHAPTER TWELVE: THE AMERICAN REVOLUTION

1. Carroll Quigley, *Tragedy and Hope*, p. 325.
2. H.S. Kennan, *The Federal Reserve Bank*, (Los Angeles: The Noontide Press, 1966), p. 9.
3. Martin Larson, *The Federal Reserve and Our Manipulated Dollar*, (Old Greenwich, Connecticut: The Devin-Adair Company, 1975), p. 10.
4. Senator Robert L. Owen, *National Economy and the Banking System of the United States*, (Washington D.C.: United States Government Printing Office, 1939), p. 100.
5. Gary Allen, "The Bankers, Conspiratorial Origins of the Federal Reserve," *American Opinion*, (March, 1970), p. 1.

6. Donald Barr Chidsey, *Andrew Jackson, Hero*, (Nashville, New York: Thomas Nelson, Inc., 1976), p. 148.
7. Edwin H. Cady, editor, *Literature of the Early Republic*, (New York: Holt, Rinehart and Winston, 1950), p. 311.
8. Arthur Edward Waite, *The Real History of the Rosicrucians*, p. A.
9. Bernard Fay, *Revolution and Freemasonry*, (Boston: Little, Brown and Company, 1935), p. 307.
10. Bernard Fay, *Revolution and Freemasonry*, pp. 307-308.
11. Bernard Fay, *Revolution and Freemasonry*, p. 111.
12. Arthur Edward Waite, *A New Encylopaedia of Freemasonry*, (New York Weathervane Books, 1970), pp. 51-52.
13. Bernard Fay, *Revolution and Freemasonry*, pp. 230-231.
14. *The New Age*, (October, 1981), p. 46.
15. H.L. Haywood, *Freemasonry and the Bible*, (Great Britain: William Collins Sons and Co. Ltd., 1951), p. 24.
16. "Freemasonry dispute flares anew," *The Arizona Daily Star*, (March 21, 1981), p. 8-H.
17. Arthur Edward Waite, *A New Encyclopaedia of Freemasonry*, p. 32.
18. Arthur Edward Waite, *A New Encyclopaedia of Freemasonry*, p. xxxiv.
19. Arthur Edward Waite, *A New Encyclopaedia of Freemasonry*, p. xxxiv.
20. Neal Wilgus, *The Illuminoids*, (Albuquerque, New Nexico: Sun Publishing Company, 1978), p. 27.
21. H.S. Kennan, *The Federal Reserve*, p. 211.
22. H.S. Kennan, *The Federal Reserve*, p. 25.
23. H.S. Kennan, *The Federal Reserve*, p. 212.
24. Olga Suir, *Let Us Understand Russia* (New York: All-Slavic Publishing House Inc.), p. 10.
25. Bernard Fay, *Revolution and Freemasonry*, p. 243.
26. Bernard Fay, *Revolution and Freemasonry*, p. 250.
27. Bernard Fay, *Revolution and Freemasonry*, p. 251.
28. Bernard Fay, *Revolution and Freemasonry*, p. 246.
29. H.S. Kennan, *The Federal Reserve*, p. 247.
30. Arthur M. Schlesinger, Jr., *The Age of Jackson*, (New York: Mentor Books, 1945), pp. 6-7.
31. *The Works of Thomas Jefferson*, (Vol. 1), p. 130.
32. *Seventeen Eighty Nine, an Un-Finished Manuscript*, p. 116.
33. John Robison, *Proofs of a Conspiracy*, p. 239.
34. Robert V. Remini, *The Revolutionary Age of Andrew Jackson*, (New York: Avon Books, 1976), p. 117.
35. Martin Larson, *The Federal Reserve and Our Manipulated Dollar*.
36. Arthur M. Schlesinger, Jr., *The Age of Jackson*, p. 16.
37. Robert V. Remini, *The Revolutionary Age of Andrew Jackson*, p. 157.
38. Captain William Morgan, *Free Masonry Exposed*, p. III.
39. Robert V. Remini, *The Revolutionary Age of Andrew Jackson*, p. 133.
40. Captain William Morgan, *Free Masonry Exposed*, p. 19.
41. Arthur M. Schlesinger, Jr., *The Age of Jackson*, p. 18.
42. William P. Hoar, "Mainifest Destiny," *American Opinion*, (June, 1981), p. 43.
43. "Conventions Aren't What They Used to Be," *U.S. News & World Report*, (July 14, 1980), p. 34.
44. Albert G. Mackey, *An Encyclopaedia of Freemasonry*, p. 65.
45. David Brion Davis, *The Fear of Conspiracy*, (Ithaca and London: Cornell Paperbacks, 1971), p. 73.

46. Albert G. Mackey, *An Encyclopaedia of Freemasonry*, p. 15.
47. Robert Remini, *The Revolutionary Age of Andrew Jackson*, p. 123.
48. Robert Remini, *The Revolutionary Age of Andrew Jackson*, p. 123.
49. Robert Remini, *The Revolutionary Age of Andrew Jackson*, p. 125.
50. Robert Remini, *The Revolutionary Age of Andrew Jackson*, p. 128.
51. *Messages and Papers of the Presidents*, (Volume II), p. 1139.
52. Arthur M. Schlesinger Jr., *The Age of Jackson*, p. 44.
53. Robert V. Remini, *The Revolutionary Age of Andrew Jackson*, p. 148.
54. Arthur M. Schlesinger, Jr., *The Age of Jackson*, p. 44.
55. *The Occult Technology of Power*, (Dearborn, Michiqan: Alpine Enterprises, 1974), p. 22.
56. Arthur M. Schlesinger Jr., *The Age of Jackson*, p. 42.
57. Robert J. Donovan, *The Assassins*, (New York: Harper & Brothers, 1952), p. 83.
58. Robert V. Remini, *The Revolutionary Age of Andrew Jackson*, p. 154.
59. Robert V. Remini, *The Revolutionary Age of Andrew Jackson*, p. 155.
60. *Messages and Papers of the Presidents*, (Vol. II), p. 1511.

CHAPTER THIRTEEN: THE ROTHSCHILD FAMILY

1. Quoted in Gary Allen, "The Bankers, Conspiratorial Origins of the Federal Reserve," *American Opinion*, (March, 1970), p. 1.
2. Martin A. Larson, *The Federal Reserve*, p. 10.

CHAPTER FOURTEEN: THE MONROE DOCTRINE

1. Donzella Cross Boyle, *Quest of a Hemisphere*, p. 237.
2. Donzella Cross Boyle, *Quest of a Hemisphere*, p. 237.
3. *Congressional Record* - Senate, (April 25, 1916), p. 6781.
4. *Congressional Record* - Senate, (April 25, 1916), p. 6781.

CHAPTER FIFTEEN: THE CIVIL WAR

1. Otto Eisenshiml, *The Hidden Face of the Civil War*, (Indianapolis and New York: The Bobbs-Merrill Company, 1961). p. 5.
2. Otto Eisenshiml, *The Hidden Face of the Civil War*, p. 5.
3. Colonel Edward Mandell House, *Philip Dru, Administrator*, (New York: 1912), p. 119.
4. Stephen Birmingham, *Our Crowd*, p. 93.
5. Stephen Birmingham, *Our Crowd*, p. 93.
6. James D. Horan, *Confederate Agent, a Discovery in History*, (New York: Crown Publishers, 1954), p. 16.
7. William H. McIlhany II, *Klandestine*, (New Rochelle, New York: Arlington House, 1975), p. 12.
8. *Committee to Restore the Constitution*, (Fort Collins, Colorado), January, 1976 Bulletin.
9. James P. Morgan, *Abraham Lincoln, the Boy and the Man*, (Grosett & Dunlap. 1908), pp. 174-175.
10. Gene Smith, *High Crimes and Misdemeanors, The Impeachment and Trial of Andrew Johnson*, (New York: William Morrow and Company, Inc., 1977), p. 98.
11. James P. Morgan, *Abraham Lincoln, the Boy and the Man*, pp. 152-153.
12. Donzella Cross Boyle, *Quest of a Hemisphere*, p. 293.
13. Otto Eisenschiml, *The Hidden Face of the Civil War*, p. 22.
14. Bruce Catton, *Short History of the Civil War*, (New York: Dell Publishing Co., Inc., 1960), p. 27.
15. David Donald, editor, *Why the North Won the Civil War*, (London: Collier - Macmillan, 1962), p. 57.
16. David Donald, editor, *Why the North Won the Civil War*, p. 58.

17. James Morgan, *Abraham Lincoln, the Boy and the Man*, p. 207.
18. *American Opinion*, (February, 1980), p. 24.
19. Otto Eisenschiml, *The Hidden Face of the Civil War*, p. 25.
20. Jerry Voorhis, *Dollars and Sense*, (Washington: United States Government Printing Office, 1938), p. 2.
21. Otto Eisenschiml, *The Hidden Face of the Civil War*, pp. 18-19.
22. David Donald, *Why the North Won the Civil War*, p. 60.
23. Thomas R. Dye and L. Harmon Zeigler, *The Irony of Democracy, An Uncommon Introduction to American Politics*, (Belmont, California: Duxbury Press, 1972), p. 73.
24. H.S. Kennan, *The Federal Reserve Bank*, p. 9.
25. Senator Robert L. Owen, *National Economy and the Banking System of the United States*, pp. 99-100.
26. Bruce Catton, *Short History of the Civil War*, p. 110.
27. Baron C. Wrangell-Rokassowsky, *Before the Storm*.
28. Baron C. Wrangell-Rokassowsky, *Before the Storm*, p. 57.
29. Speech given at Springfield, Illinois, January 27, 1837.
30. John G. Nicoley and John Hay, *Abraham Lincoln: Complete Works*, (New York: New York Century Company, 1920), Vol. II, pp. 306, 354, 355.
31. Gene Smith, *High Crimes and Misdemeanors, The Impeachment and Trial of Andrew Johnson*, p. 61.
32. David Balsiger and Charles E. Sellier, Jr., *The Lincoln Conspiracy*, (Los Angeles: Shick Sunn Classic Books, 1977), caption under photograph between pages 160 and 161.
33. H.S. Kennan, *The Federal Reserve*, p. 246.
34. David Balsiger and Charles E. Sellier, Jr., *The Lincoln Conspiracy*, p. 294.
35. Gene Smith, *High Crimes and Misdemeanors, The Impeachment of Andrew Johnson*, p. 185.
36. Quoted in *Dan Smoot's Report*, (July 8, 1963), Volume 9, No. 27, p. 212.
37. Gene Smith, *High Crimes and Misdemeanors, The Impeachment of Andrew Johnson*, p. 157, 185.
39. Gene Smith, *High Crimes and Misdemeanors, The Impeachment of Andrew Johnson*, p. 194.
40. Del Schrader with Jesse James III, *Jesse James was One of His Names*, (Arcadia, California: Santa Anita Press, 1975), p. 187.

CHAPTER SIXTEEN: THE FEDERAL RESERVE
1. "Milestones," *Time*, (March 29, 1982), p. 73.
2. Gary Allen, "Tax of Trim," *American Opinion*, (January, 1975), p. 6.
3. William P. Hoar, "Lindbergh, Two Generations of Heroism," *American Opinion*, (May, 1977), p. 8.
4. *American Opinion*, May, 1976.
5. Colonel Edward Mandell House, *Philip Dru, Administrator*, p. 210.
6. Colonel Edward Mandell House, *Philip Dru, Administrator*, p. 70.
7. Colonel Edward Mandell House, *Philip Dru, Administrator*, p. 87.
8. Colonel Edward Mandell House, *Philip Dru, Administrator*, p. 221.
9. Colonel Edward Mandell House, *Philip Dru, Administrator*, p. 226.
10. Harry M. Daugherty, *The Inside Story of the Harding Tragedy*, (Boston, Los Angeles: Western Islands), p. xxvi.
11. William P. Hoar, "Andrew Carnegie," *American Opinion*, (December, 1975), p. 110.
12. Nesta Webster, *Surrender of an Empire*, (London, 1931), p. 59.
13. Gary Allen, "The CFR, Conspiracy to Rule the World," *American*

Opinion, (April, 1969), p. 11.

14. Frederick Lewis Allen, *Life*, (April 25, 1949).
15. H.S. Kennan, *The Federal Reserve*, p. 105.
16. "Footnote, Prelude to the Federal Reserve: The Currency Panic of 1907," *Dun's Review*, (December, 1977), p. 21.
17. Frank Vanderlip, "Farm Boy to Financier," *Saturday Evening Post*, (February 8, 1935).
18. H.S. Kennan, *The Federal Reserve*, p. 100.
19. Ferdinand Lundberg, *America's 60 Families*, (New York: The Vanguard Press, 1937), pp. 110, 112.
20. Board of Governors of the Federal Reserve System, *The Federal Reserve System*, (Board of Governors: Washington D.C., 1963), p. 1.
21. Gary Allen, "The Bankers, Conspiratorial Origins of the Federal Reserve," *American Opinion*, (March, 1978), p. 16.
22. Martin Larson, *The Federal Reserve*, p. 63.
23. Gary Allen, "The Bankers, Conspiratorial Origins of the Federal Reserve," p. 1.
24. Board of Governors, *The Federal Reserve System*, p. 75.
25. *The Review of the News*, (August 30, 1978).
26. *The Review of the News*, (December 5, 1979), p. 2.
27. *The Review of the News*, (February 27, 1980), p. 75.
28. Carroll Quigley, *Tragedy and Hope*, p. 49.
29. Gary Allen, "The Bankers, Conspiratorial Origins of the Federal Reserve," *American Opinion*, p. 24.
30. Gary Allen, "The Bankers, Conspiratorial Origins of the Federal Reserve," p. 24.
31. William P. Hoar, "Henry Ford," *American Opinion*, (April, 1978), pp. 20, 107.
32. Ferdinand Lundberg, *America's Sixty Families*, p. 221.
33. Gary Allen, "The Bankers, Conspiratorial Origins of the Federal Reserve," p. 27.
34. H.S. Kennan, *The Federal Reserve Bank*, p. 70.
35. John Kenneth Galbraith, *The Great Crash, 1929*, (New York: Time Incorporated, 1954), p. 102.
36. John Kenneth Galbraith, *The Great Crash, 1929*, p. 111.
37. Gary Allen, "Federal Reserve, the Anti-Economics of Boom and Bust," *American Opinion*, (April, 1970), p. 63.
38. Gary Allen, "Federal Reserve, the Anti-Economics of Boom and Bust," p. 63.
39. Gary Allen, "Federal Reserve, the Anti-Economics of Boom and Bust," p. 63.
40. "Crash of '29," *U.S, News & World Report*, (October 29, 1979), p. 34.
41. Louis McFadden, "Congressman on the Federal Reserve Corporation," *Congressional Record*, 1934, pp. 24, 26.
42. *Congressional Record*, Bound Volume, (May 23, 1933), pp. 4055-4058.
43. Martin Larson, *The Federal Reserve*, p. 99.
44. "Crash of '29," *U.S. News & World Report*, (October 29, 1979), p. 32.
45. John Kenneth Galbraith, *The Great Crash, 1929*, pp. 4, 174.
46. John Kenneth Galbraith, *The Great Crash, 1929*, p. 190.
47. Wright Patman's 1880th *Weekly Letter*, 1973.

CHAPTER SEVENTEEN: GRADUATED INCOME TAXES

1. Gary Allen, "Tax or Trim," *American Opinion*, (January, 1975), p. 75.
2. Gary Allen, "Tax or Trim," *American Opinion*, p. 66.

3. *Review of the News*, (March 20, 1974).
4. *Review of the News*, (December 10, 1980), p. 53.
5. *The Arizona Daily Star*, (September 13, 1980), p. 2-A.
6. *The Arizona Daily Star*, (March 13, 1980), p. 8-F.
7. *U.S. News & World Report*, (April 27, 1981), p. 25.
8. Susan L.M. Huck, "Giveaways," *American Opinion*, (July-August, 1972), p. 61.
9. *The Review of the News*, (February 20, 1980), p. 75.
10. *U.S. News & World Report*, (October 20, 1980), p. 67.
11. *The Oregonian*, (May 22, 1973.)

CHAPTER EIGHTEEN: NON-VIOLENT ORGANIZATIONS

1. Eudocio Ravises, *The Yenan Way*, (New York: Scribners, 1951), pp. 256-257.
2. Carroll Quigley, *Tragedy and Hope*, pp. 130-131.
3. Gary Allen, "The CFR, Conspiracy to Rule the World," *American Opinion*, (April, 1969), p. 4. (Pamphlet reprint.)
4. Gary Allen, "The CFR, Conspiracy to Rule the World," p. 6.
5. Rose Martin, *Fabian Freeway*, p. 99.
6. Rose Martin, *Fabian Freeway*, pp. 18-19.
7. Zygmund Dobbs, "Sugar Keynes," *American Opinion*, (January, 1970), p. 22
8. Zygmund Dobbs, *Keynes at Harvard*, (West Sayville, New York: Probe Research, Inc., 1960), p. 92.
9. John Kenneth Galbraith, *The Age of Uncertainty*, (Boston: Houghton Mifflin Company, 1977), p. 11.
10. *The Works of Thomas Jefferson*, (Volume 1, p. 130).
11. Gary Allen, "Who They Are, The Conspiracy to Destroy America," *American Opinion*, (October, 1972), p. 65.
12. *The Review of the News*, (April 9, 1980), pp. 37-38.
13. Gary Allen, "The CFR, Conspiracy to Rule the World," *American Opinion*, (April, 1969), p. 1.
14. Phoebe Courtney, *The CFR, Part II*, (Littleton, Colorado: The Independent American, 1975), p. 4.
15. Medford Evans, "Waking Up to the Conspiracy," *American Opinion*, (June, 1980), p. 38.
16. Gary Allen, "They Run America," *American Opinion*, (May, 1978), p. 71.
17. Gary Allen, *Jimmy Carter, Jimmy Carter*, (Seal Beach, California, '76 Press, 1976), p. 71.
18. Carroll Quigley, *Tragedy and Hope*, p. 73.
19. *The American Economic System . . . And Your Part in It*, p. 2.
20. *Congressional Record*, (February 9, 1917), (Volume 54), p. 2947.
21. Herman Dinsmore, *All the News That Fits*, (New Rochelle, New York: Arlington House, 1969), pp. 13, 167.
22. Whitaker Chambers, *Witness*, (New York: Random House, 1952), p. 475.
23. Gary Allen, "That Music," *American Opinion*, (February, 1969), p. 62.
24. *The Review of the News*, (November 5, 1969), p. 26.
25. Gary Allen, "That Music," p. 58.
26. *Tucson Citizen*, (April 30, 1982), p. 12A.
27. Gary Allen, "They're Catching On," *American Opinion*, (November, 1977), p. 87.
28. "Goodbye to Scandal," *Parade*, (March 23, 1980), p. 6.
29. "Bilderbergers," *American Opinion*, (November, 1964), p. 62.
30. Gary Allen, "Who They Are," *American Opinion*, (October, 1972), p. 69.

31. Gary Allen, "Little Brother," *American Opinion*, (April, 1975), p. 74.
32. *The Review of the News*, (March 15, ----), p. 60.
33. Gary Allen, "Foundations," *American Opinion*, (November, 1969), p. 3.
34. *Tax Exempt Foundations*, (Provo, Utah: The Freeman Digest, June, 1978) , p. 2.
35. *Tax Exempt Foundations*, p. 2.
36. Alan Stang, *The Actor*, (Boston, Los Angeles: Western Islands, 1968).
37. Alan Stang, "Foundations Pay the Way," *American Opinion*, (January, 1977). p. 5.
38. Gary Allen, *The Rockefeller File*, (Seal Beach, California: '76 Press, 1976), p. 49.
39. *The Review of the News*, (January 26, 1977), p. 15.
40. "Worth Repeating," *The Journal of Insurance*, (July, August, 1978), p. 7.
41. *The Arizona Daily Star*, (April 19, 1981), p. 2-D.
42. Francis X. Gannon, *Biographical Dictionary of the Left*, Volume I, (Boston, Los Angeles: Western Islands, 1969), pp. 116-117.
43. Francis X. Gannon, *Biographical Dictionary of the Left*, pp. 121, 123.
44. Robert Welch, *Again, May God Forgive Us*, (Belmont, Massachusetts: Belmont Publishing, 1952), p. 96.
45. *The Review of the News*, (November 12, 1975), p. 50.
46. *Tax Exempt Foundations*, (The Freeman Digest), p. 57.
47. Gary Allen, "Betraying China," *American Opinion*, (October, 1971), p. 1.
48. Gary Allen, "Betraying China," p. 1.
49. Gary Allen, "Betraying China," p. 2.
50. Robert Welch, *Again, May God Forgive Us*, pp. 156-157.
51. Gary Allen, "Betraying China," p. 12
52. Robert Welch, *Again, May God Forgive Us*, p. 158.
53. Gary Allen, "Betraying China," p. 12.
54. Robert Welch, *Again, May God Forgive Us*, p. 138.
55. Gary Allen, "Betraying China," p. 12.
56. Gary Allen, "Betraying China," p. 12.
57. Senator Joseph McCarthy, *America's Retreat From Victory*, (Belmont, Massachusetts: Western Islands, 1965), p. 90.
58. Senator Joseph McCarthy, *America's Retreat From Victory*, p. 90.
59. John T. Flynn, *While You Slept*, (Boston, Los Angeles: Western Islands, 1965), p. 14.
60. *The Review of the News*, (March 21, 1979), p. 25.
61. *The Review of the News*, (February 23, 1972), p. 30.
62. *The Review of the News*, (May 9, 1973), p. 29.
63. *The Review of the News*, (May 9, 1973), p. 30.
64. *The Review of the News*, (May 9, 1973), p. 29.
65. "From a China Traveler," David Rockefeller, *New York Times*, (August 10, 1973), p. L-31.
66. "Red China Chief Urges World to 'Defeat US,' " *The Oregon Journal*, (May 20, 1970).
67. "Weekly News Report," Congressman John Schmitz, (#71-30), released July 28, 1971.
68. "Weekly News Report," (#71-30).
69. Gary Allen, "Betraying China," *American Opinion*, (October, 1971), p. 23.
70. Gary Allen, "Betraying China," p. 23.
71. *The Review of the News*, (May 9, 1973), p. 30.
72. *The Review of the News*, (January 10, 1979), p. 7.

73. *The Arizona Daily Star*, (May 7, 1979), p. 5-B.
74. David Emerson Gumaer, "Apostasy, The National Council of Churches," *American Opinion*, (February, 1970), p. 50.
75. David Emerson Gumaer, "Apostasy, The National Council of Churches", p. 51.
76. David Emerson Gumaer, "Apostasy, The National Council of Churches," p. 55.
77. David Emerson Gumaer, "Apostasy, The National Council of Churches," p. 55.
78. David Emerson Gumaer, "Apostasy, The National Council of Churches," p. 57.
79. David Emerson Gumaer, "Apostasy, The National Council of Churches," p. 68.
80. Father Francis Fenton, "Deceiving Catholics About the Councils of Churches," *The Review of the News*, (November 1, 1972), p. 35.
81. *The Review of the News*, (May 21, 1975), p. 57.
82. Joseph A. Harriss, "Karl Marx or Jesus Christ?," Reader's Digest, August, 1982, p. 131.
83. *Oregon Journal*, (November 29, 1975), p. 6.
84. Joseph A. Harriss, "Karl Marx or Jesus Christ?," p. 132.
85. Joseph A. Harriss, "Karl Marx or Jesus Christ?," p. 132.
86. John Rees, "Avraham Shifrin," *The Review of the News*, (May 11, 1983), p. 33.
87. Nick F. Lucas, *Compare*, (Georgetown, South Carolina: Lighthouse Bookstore, 1980), p. 24.

CHAPTER NINETEEN: POPULATION CONTROL

1. Gary Allen, *American Opinion*, (May, 1970), p. 1.
2. *The Oregonian*, (February 24, 1973), p. 23.
3. Gary Allen, *American Opinion*, (May, 1970), pp. 12-13.
4. *Fusion* Magazine, (August, 1980), p. 8.
5. Zygmund Dobbs, *Keynes at Harvard*, p. 57.
6. *The Review of the News*, (September 29, 1976), p. 67.
7. *The Review of the News*, (October 19, 1977), p. 45.
8. *The Review of the News*, (May 31, 1978), p. 59.
9. *The Review of the News*, (September 4, 1974), p. 20.
10. *Fusion* magazine, (July, 1981), p. 52.
11. *Communist Persecution of Churches in Red China and North Korea*, House Committee on Un-American Activities, (March 26, 1959), p. 4.
12. Jack Nelson, *Population and Survival*, (Englewood Cliffs, New Jersey: Prentice Hall, 1972), p. 103.
13. *American Opinion*, (September, 1978), p. 96.
14. Alan Stang, "Zbig Brother," *American Opinion*, (February, 1978), p. 6.
15. *American Opinion*, (May, 1979), p. 17.
16. *American Opinion*, (May, 1979), p. 17.
17. *The Review of the News*, (September 19, 1979), p. 11.
18. "Subsidy predicted for childbearing," *Arizona Daily Star*, (April 12, 1981), p. A-11.
19. Gary Allen, "Ecology," *American Opinion*, (May, 1970), p. 2.
20. *The Oregonian*, (December 12, 1969).
21. *The Oregonian*, (February 23, 1970).
22. *The Arizona Daily Star*, (May 7, 1979).
23. *The Arizona Daily Star*, (October 18, 1981), p. 6-A.
24. Gary Allen, "Who They Are," *American Opinion*, (October, 1972), p. 65.

25. Pope Paul VI, *This Is Progress*, p. 57.

CHAPTER TWENTY: THE TRILATERAL COMMISSION

1. Robert L. Turner, *I'll Never Lie to You*, (New York: Ballantine Books, 1976), p. 48.
2. *The Review of the News*, (January 12, 1977), p. 29.
3. Robert W. Lee, "Confirming the Liberal Establishment," *American Opinion*, (March, 1981), p. 35.
4. Barry M. Goldwater, *With No Apologies*, (New York: Berkley Books, 1979), p. 299.
5. Barry M. Goldwater, *With No Apologies*, p. 299.
6. *The Rockefeller File*, p. 28, Gary Allen.
7. Ferdinand Lundberg, *The Rockefeller Syndrome*, p. 205.
8. *The Review of the News*, (July 3, 1974).
9. William Hoffman, *David*, (New York, Lyle Stuart, Inc., 1971), p. 20.
10. *The Review of the News*, (August 11, 1976), p. 13.
11. *New York Times*, (March 21, 1978), p. 16.
12. *New York Times*, (May 23, 1976), p. 50.
13. Jimmy Carter, *Why Not the Best?*, (Nashville, Tennessee: Broadman Press, 1975), p. 146.
14. Alan Stang, "Zbig Brother," *American Opinion*, (February, 1978), p. 6.
15. Zbigniew Brzezinski, *Between Two Ages*, (New York; Penguin Books, 1976), p. 300.
16. *American Opinion*, (July-August, 1980), p. 113.
17. *New York Times*, (January 18, 1981), p. L3.
18. *Washington Post*, (January 16, 1977).
19. *The Review of the News*, (July 21, 1976), p. 32.
20. *Arizona Daily Star*, (July 31, 1980), editorial page.
21. *American Opinion*, (September, 1980), p. 6
22. Barry Goldwater, *With No Apologies*, p. 297.
23. *The Review of the News*, (October 12, 1977), p. 45.
24. *American Opinion*, (July-August, 1977), p. 12.
25. Alan Stang, *The Actor*, p. 101.
26. *The Arizona Daily Star*, (December 6, 1978).
27. *The Review of the News*, (February 21, 1979), p. 32.
28. *The Review of the News*, (February 21, 1979), p. 33.
29. *The Review of the News*, (February 21, 1979), p. 33.
30. Antony Sutton, Patrick M. Wood, *Trilaterals Over Washington, II*, (Scottsdale, Arizona: The August Corporation, 1981), p. 173.
31. *The Arizona Daily Star*, (September 12, 1980), p. 10-A.
32. Norman Medvin, *The Energy Cartel*, (New York: Vintage Books, 1974), pp. 169-170.
33. *The Review of the News*, (December 12, 1979), p. 65.
34. *The Review of the News*, (April 19, 1978), p. 9.
35. *The Review of the News*, (December 28, 1977), p. 59.
36. *The Review of the News*, (December 7, 1977), p. 59.
37. *The Review of the News*, (January 25, 1978), p. 40.
38. Antony C. Sutton, Patrick M. Wood, *Trilaterals Over Washington, II*, p. 3.
39. *The Review of the News*, (April 12, 1978), p. 53.
40. *The Review of the News*, (December 10, 1980), p. 75.
41. *The Review of the News*, (October 1, 1980), p. 25.
42. Anastosio Somoza, *Nicaragua Betrayed*, (Boston, Los Angeles: Western Islands, 19805, p. 291.

43. Anastosio Somoza, *Nicaragua Betrayed*, p. 227.
44. Anastosio Somoza, *Nicaraqua Betrayed*, p. 402.
45. Anastosio Somoza, *Nicaragua Betrayed*, p. xi.
46. *The Review of the News*, (July 30, 1980), p. 32.
47. *The Review of the News*, (July 30, 1980), p. 38.
48. *The Review of the News*, (September 24, 1980), p. 21.
49. *The Plain Truth* magazine, (August, 1978).
50. *The Arizona Daily Star*, (August 1, 1980), p. 1.
51. *U.S. News & World Report*, (February 27, 1978).
52. *U.S. News & World Report*, (July 3, 1978).
53. *U.S. News & World Report*, (February 11, 1980).
54. *U.S. News & World Report*, (October 6, 1980).
55. "Ronald Reagan," *American Opinion*, (September, 1980), p. 99.
56. Antony Sutton and Patrick M. Wood, *Trilaterals Over Washington, II*.
57. Gary Allen, "Ronald Reagan," *American Opinion*, p. 90.

CHAPTER TWENTY-ONE: THE PURPOSE

1. Rose Martin, *Fabian Freeway*, p. 242.
2. *Two Worlds*, p. 152.
3. *Congressional Record*, (April 17, 1957), p. A-3080.
4. *American Opinion*, (April, 1982), p. 89.
5. *American Opinion*, (April, 1976), p. 9.
6. Gary Allen, "Richard Nixon," *American Opinion*, (January, 1971).
7. *The Review of the News*, (August 23, 1972 , p. 34.

CHAPTER TWENTY-TWO: IRON MOUNTAIN

1. *Report From Iron Mountain*, (New York: Dell Publishing Co., Inc., 1967).
2. Gary Allen, "Making Plans for a Dictatorship in America," April, 1971), *American Opinion*, p. 16.
3. William A. McWhirter, *Life*, (December 6, 1968).
4. William A. McWhirter, *Life*, (December 6, 1968).
5. William A. McWhirter, *Life*, (December 6, 1968).
6. Taylor Caldwell, *Ceremony of the Innocent*, (Greenwich, Connecticut: Fawcett Books, 1976), p. 289.

CHAPTER TWENTY-THREE: WORLD WAR I

1. *Bulletin*, The Committee to Restore the Constitution, (Fort Collins, Colorado; November, 1978), p. 1.
2. *Illustrated Sunday Herald*, February 8, 1920.
3. Arthur M. Schlesinger, Jr., *The Coming of the New Deal*, (Boston: Hougton Miffin, 1958).
4. Charles Callan Tansill, *America Goes to War*, (Boston: Little, Brown, 1938).
5. Colin Simpson, *The Lusitania*, (New York: Ballantine Books, 1972), p. 59.
6. Colin Simpson, *The Lusitania*, p. 89.
7. Colin Simpson, *The Lusitania*, p. 134.
8. Colin Simpson, *The Lusitania*, p. 6.
9. Gary Allen, "Deadly Lies," *American Opinion*, (May, 1976), p. 33.
10. Colin Simpson, *The Lusitania*, pp. 3-4.
11. Colin Simpson, *The Lusitania*, p. i.
12. Harry M. Daugherty, *The Harding Tragedy*, p. xxxvi.
13. Joseph Lash, *Roosevelt and Churchill*, p. 429.
14. William P. Hoar, "World War I," *American Opinion*, (January, 1976), p. 91.

15. Gary Allen, "Federal Reserve," *American Opinion*, (April, 1970), p. 53.
16. William P. Hoar, "The Treaty," *American Opinion*, (February, 1976), p. 35.
17. William P. Hoar, "The Treaty," p. 41.
18. Ferdinand Lundberg, *America's 60 Families*, p. 201.
19. William Hoffman, *David*, p. 51.
20. Nesta Webster, *Surrender of an Empire*, p. 59.

CHAPTER TWENTY-FOUR: WORLD WAR II

1. Jean-Michel Angebert, *The Occult and the Third Reich*, (New York: Macmillan Publishing Co., Inc., 1974), p. 4.
2. Trevor Ravenscroft, *The Spear of Destiny*, (New York: G.P. Putnam's Sons, 1973), p. 159.
3. Trevor Ravenscroft, *The Spear of Destiny*, p. 102.
4. Trevor Ravenscroft, *The Spear of Destiny*, p. 102.
5. Walter C. Langer, *The Mind of Adolf Hitler*, (New York, London: Basic Books, Inc.), pp. 100-102.
6. Walter C. Langer, *The Mind of Adolf Hitler*, p. 234.
7. Joseph Borkin, *The Crime and Punishment of I. G. Farben*, (New York: The Free Press, 1978), p. 1.
8. Antony C. Sutton, *Wall Street and the Rise of Hitler*, (Seal Beach, California: '76 Press, 1976), p. 33.
9. Carroll Quigley, *Tragedy and Hope*, p. 308.
10. Antony C. Sutton, *Wall Street and the Rise of Hitler*, p. 163.
11. Antony C. Sutton, *Wall Street and the Rise of Hitler*, p. 93.
12. Joseph Borkin, *The Crime and Punishment of I. G. Farben*, p. 49.
13. G. Edward Griffin, *World Without Cancer*, (Thousand Oaks, California: American Media, 1974), p. 254.
14. Joseph Borkin, *The Crime and Punishment of I. G. Farben*, p. 51.
15. *Daily Citizen*, (November 4, 1977).
16. *Daily Citizen*, (November 4, 1977).
17. *Wall Street and the Rise of Hitler*, p. 16.
18. William P. Hoar, "Reflections on the Great Depression," *American Opinion*, (June, 1979), p. 101.
19. Antony Sutton, *Wall Street and FDR*, (New Rochelle, New York: Arlington House, 1975), pp. 14, 15, 17.
20. Whitaker Chambers, *Witness*, p. 472.
21. Jules Archer, *The Plot to Seize the White House*, (New York: Hawthorn Books, Inc., 1973), p. ix.
22. Jules Archer, *The Plot to Seize the White House*, p. ix.
23. Jules Archer, *The Plot to Seize the White House*, p. 25.
24. Jules Archer, *The Plot to Seize the White House*, p. 130.
25. Jules Archer, *The Plot to Seize the White House*, p. 132.
26. Jules Archer, *The Plot to Seize the White House*, p. 168.
27. Jules Archer, *The Plot to Seize the White House*, p. 215.
28. "The Failure of the NRA," *The Review of the News*, (August 4, 1976).
29. James Farley, *Jim Farley's Story, The Roosevelt Years*, (New York, Toronto: McGraw-Hill Book Company, Inc. 1948), p. 39.
30. Harry Elmer Barnes, *Pearl Harbor After A Quarter of a Century*, (Torrance, California: Institute for Historical Review), p. 22.
31. Antony Sutton, *Wall Street and the Rise of Hitler*, pp. 15-16.
32. Antony Sutton, *Wall Street and the Rise of Hitler*, p. 79.
33. Antony Sutton, *Wall Street and the Rise of Hitler*, p. 110.
34. Antony Sutton, *Wall Street and the Rise of Hitler*, p. 35.

35. Antony Sutton, *Wall Street and the Rise of Hitler*, p. 31.
36. Antony Sutton, *Wall Street and the Rise of Hitler*, p. 31.
37. Antony Sutton, *Wall Street and the Rise of Hitler*, p. 63.
38. Antony Sutton, *Wall Street and the Rise of Hitler*, p. 65.
39. Antony Sutton, *Wall Street and the Rise of Hitler*, p. 23.
40. William Stevenson, *A Man Called Intrepid*, (New York: Ballantine Books, 1976), p. 385.
41. Joseph Borkin, *The Crime and Punishment of I. G. Farben*, p. 77.
42. Joseph Lash, *Roosevelt and Churchill*, p. 21.
43. Joseph Lash, *Roosevelt and Churchill*, pp. 32-33.
44. *Life*, (February 19, 1940), pp. 66-67.
45. Martin Larson, *The Federal Reserve*, p. 103.
46. Martin Larson, *The Federal Reserve*, p. 103.
47. Antony Sutton, *Wall Street and the Rise of Hitler*, p. 31.
48. Joseph Lash, *Roosevelt and Churchill*, p. 232.
49. Albert C. Wedemeyer, *Wedemeyer Reports*, (New York: Devin-Adair Company, 1958), p. 18.
50. John T. Flynn, *The Roosevelt Myth*, (New York: Devin Adair Company, 1948), p. 296.
51. Robert A. Theobold, *The Final Secret of Pearl Harbor*, (Old Greenwich, Connecticut: Devin-Adair Company, 1954), pp. 22-23.
52. Robert A. Theobold, *The Final Secret of Pearl Harbor*, p. 43.
53. Joseph Lash, *Roosevelt and Churchill*, p. 298.
54. Joseph Lash, *Roosevelt and Churchill*, p. 402.
55. Joseph Lash, *Roosevelt and Churchill*, p. 413.
56. *The Review of the News*, (April 10, 1974), p. 46.
57. Joseph Lash, *Roosevelt and Churchill*, p. 360.
58. *Dan Smoot Report*, November 15, 1965.
59. *American Opinion*, (April, 1964), p. 33.
60. *American Opinion*, (April, 1964), p. 33.
61. *American Opinion*, (April, 1964), p. 34.
62. Joseph Lash, *Roosevelt and Churchill*, p. 456.
63. Joseph Lash, *Roosevelt and Churchill*, p. 480.
64. "Pearl Harbor," *American Opinion*, (December, 1981), pp. 71-72.
65. Herman H. Dinsmore, *The Bleeding of America*, (Belmont, Massachusets: Western Islands, 1974), p. 132.
66. Robert A. Theobold, *The Final Secret of Pearl Harbor*, p. 76.
67. Robert A. Theobold, *The Final Secret of Pearl Harbor*, p. 53.
68. William Stevenson, *A Man Called Intrepid*, pp. 328-329.
69. Harry Elmer Barnes, *Pearl Harbor After a Quarter of a Century*, p. 84.
70. Curtis Dall, *FDR, My Exploited Father-In-Law*, p. 163.
71. Harry Elmer Barnes, *Pearl Harbor After a Quarter of a Century*, p. 52.
72. Harry Elmer Barnes, *Pearl Harbor After a Quarter of a Century*, p. 58.
73. Robert A. Theobold, *The Final Secret of Pearl Harbor*, p. v.
74. George T. Eggleston, *Roosevelt, Churchill and the World War II Opposition*, (Old Greenwich, Connecticut: The Devin-Adair Company, 1979), pp. xii-xiii.
75. *American Opinion*, (December, 1980), p. 33.
76. "Pearl Harbor," *American Opinion*, (December, 1981), p. 19.
77. *The Arizona Daily Star*, (December 6, 1981), p. C-1.
78. Robert A. Theobold, *The Final Secret of Pearl Harbor*, pp. 184-185.
79. Robert A. Theobold, *The Final Secret of Pearl Harbor*, pp. 184-185, 197.
80. "Walter Scott's Personality Parade," *Parade* magazine, (February 28,

1982), inside cover.

CHAPTER TWENTY-FIVE: COMMUNIST BETRAYALS

1. Robert W. Lee: *The United Nations Today* (pamphlet), (Belmont, Massachusetts: *American Opinion*, 1976), p. 5.
2. Phillip Knightley, *The First Casualty*, (New York, London: Harcourt Brace Jovanovich, 1975), p. 279.
3. Senator Joseph McCarthy, *America's Retreat From Victory*, p. 23.
4. Curtis Dall, *F.D.R. - My Exploited Father-In-Law*, pp. 146-147.
5. Albert C. Wedemeyer, *Wedemeyer Reports*, p. 418.
6. Curtis Dall, *F.D.R. - My Exploited Father-In-Law*, p. 152.
7. Curtis Dall, *F.D.R. - Ny Exploited Father-In-Law*, p. 154.
8. George Martin, *Madame Secretary, Frances Perkins*, (Boston: Houghton Mifflin Company, 1976), p. 456.
9. Frazier Hunt, *The Untold Story of Douglas MacArthur*, (New York: Manor Books, 1977), p. 380.
10. *The Review of the News*, (May 31, 1972), p. 60.
11. Eldorous L. Dayton, *Give 'em Hell, Harry*, (New York: The Devin-Adair Company, 1956), p. 139.
12. *The Oregonian*, (August 2, 1973).
13. *The Oregon Journal*, (December 28, 1970), p. 6.
14. Albert C. Wedemeyer, *Wedemeyer Reports*, p. 430.
15. "The Conspiracy Threatens America," *The Review of the News*, (August 5, 1970), p. 21.
16. *The Oregonian*, (January 17, 1974), p. 19.
17. William Manchester, *The Arms of Krupp*, (Boston: Little, Brown and Company, 1964), p. 720.
18. Robert Welch, *Again, May God Forgive Us*, pp. 68-69.
19. Alfred M. de Zayas, *Nemesis at Potsdam*, (London, Henley and Boston: Routledge & Kegan Paul, 1977), p. 68.
20. Alfred M. de Zayas, *Nemesis at Potsdam*, p. 66.
21. Alfred M. de Zoyas, *Nemesis at Potsdam*, p. 66.

CHAPTER TWENTY-SIX: THE ATOMIC BOMB

1. Frazier Hunt, *The Untold Story of Douglas MacArthur*, p. 390.
2. Frazier Hunt, *The Untold Story of Douglas MacArthur*, p. 375.
3. John Toland, "The Secret Attempts to Surrender," *Look*, (September 22, 1970), p. 33.
4. John Toland, "My God, What Have We Done?," *Look*, (October 6, 1970), p. 54.
5. John Toland, "My God, What Have We Done?," p. 53.
6. Senator Joseph McCarthy, *America's Retreat From Victory*, p. 48.
7. Rose Martin, *Selling of America*, (Santa Monica, California: Fidelis Publishers Inc., 1973), p. 46.
8. William Stevenson, *A Man Called Intrepid*, p. 491.
9. *Spotlight*, (October 15, 1979), p. 16.
10. Alfred de Zayas, *Nemesis at Potsdam*, p. xx.
11. Alfred de Zayas, *Nemesis at Potsdam*, p. xxii.
12. Aldred de Zayas, *Nemesis at Potsdam*, p. 203.
13. Alfred de Zayas, *Nemesis at Potsdam*, p. 115.
14. Alfred de Zayas, *Nemesis at Potsdam*, p. xix.
15. Carroll Quigley, *Tragedy and Hope*, p. 1310.
16. Albert C. Wedemeyer, *Wedemeyer Reports*, p. 92.
17. Prince Michel Sturdza, *The Suicide of Europe*, (Boston, Los Angeles: Western Islands, 1968), p. 68.

CHAPTER TWENTY-SEVEN: THE EXPOSERS

1. *American Opinion*, (February, 1971), p. 14.
2. Medford Evans, *The Assassination of Joe McCarthy*, (Boston, Los Angeles: Western Islands, 1970), p. 113.
3. *Congressional Record*, (December 6, 1950), p. 16179.
4. Charles L. Mee Jr., *Meeting At Potsdam*, (New York: Dell Publishing, 1975), p. 26.
5. Cornell Simpson, *The Death of James Forrestal*, (Boston, Los Angeles: Western Islands, 1966), p. 7.
6. Cornell Simpson, *The Death of James Forrestal*, p. 5.
7. Cornell Simpson, *The Death of James Forrestal*, p. 9.
8. Cornell Simpson, *The Death of James Forrestal*, p. 15.
9. *Congressional Record*, Senate, (December 6, 1950), p. 16181.
10. Cornell Simpson, *The Death of James Forrestal*, p. 41.
11. Cornell Simpson, *The Death of James Forrestal*, p. 82.
12. Cornell Simpson, *The Death of James Forrestal*, p. 84.
13. Walter Scott, "Personality Parade," *Parade* magazine, (May 24, 1981), inside cover.
14. Carrol Quigley, *Tragedy and Hope*, p. 913.
15. Cornell Simpson, *The Death of James Forrestal*, p. 147.
16. William F. Buckley, Jr., and L. Brent Bozell, *McCarthy and His Enemies*, (Chicago: Henry Regnery Company, 1954), p. 17.
17. Roy Cohn, *McCarthy, The Answer to Tail Gunner Joe*, (New York: Manor Books, Inc., 1977), p. 9.
18. Senator Joseph McCarthy, *America's Retreat From Victory*, pp. 8-9.
19. Senator Joseph McCarthy, *America's Retreat From Victory*, p. 37.
20. William F. Buckley, Jr., and L. Brent Bozell, *McCarthy and His Enemies*, p. 20.
21. Frank A. Capell, "McCarthyism," *American Opinion*, (January, 1973), p. 63.
22. James Drummey, "McCarthy," *American Opinion*, (May, 1964), p. 3.
23. Roy Cohn, *McCarthy: The Answer to Tail Gunner Joe*, p. 3.
24. Roy Cohn, *McCarthy: The Answer to Tail Gunner Joe*, p. 3.
25. James Drummey, "McCarthy," *American Opinion*, p. 3.
26. James Drummey, "McCarthy," *American Opinion*, p. 3.
27. *The Review of the News*, (March 28, 1979).
28. James Drummey, "McCarthy," *American Opinion*, back cover of pamphlet.
29. William F. Buckley, Jr., and L. Brent Bozell, *McCarthy and His Enemies*, p. 352.
30. William F. Buckley, Jr., and L. Brent Bozell, *McCarthy and His Enemies*, p. 352.
31. William F. Buckley, Jr., and L. Brent Bozell, *McCarthy and His Enemies*, p. 353.
32. William F. Buckley, Jr., and L. Brent Bozell, *McCarthy and His Enemies*, p. 388.
33. David Brion Davis, *The Fear of Conspiracy*, (Ithaca and London: Cornell Paperbacks, 1971), p. 4.
34. Frank A. Capell, "McCarthyism," *American Opinion*, p. 75.
35. Frank A. Capell, "McCarthyism," *American Opinion*, p. 69.
36. Frank A. Capell, "McCarthyism," *American Opinion*, p. 73.
37. Frank A. Capell, "McCarthyism," *American Opinion*, p. 73.
38. Richard J. Rovere, *Senator Joe McCarthy*, (New York: Harper & Row,

1959).

39. Roy Cohn, *McCarthy: The Answer to Tail Gunner Joe*, p. xv.
40. Dwight D. Eisenhower, "We Must Avoid the Perils of Extremism," *Reader's Digest*, (April, 1969), pp. 103-108.
41. James J. Drummey, "McCarthy," *American Opinion*, p. P.
42. Frank A. Capell, "McCarthyism," *American Opinion*, p. 77.
43. James J. Drummey, "McCarthy," *American Opinion*, p. 8.
44. Frank A. Capell, "McCarthyism," *American Opinion*, p. 75.
45. Senator Joseph McCarthy, *America's Retreat From Victory*, pp. 135-136.
46. Senator Joseph McCarthy, *America's Retreat From Victory*, p. 138.
47. Medford Evans, *The Assassination of Joe McCarthy*, p. 2.
48. Medford Evans, *The Assassination of Joe McCarthy*, p. 12.
49. Medford Evans, *The Assassination of Joe McCarthy*, p. 4.
50. Medford Evans, *The Assassination of Joe McCarthy*, p. 11.
51. Frank A. Capell, "McCarthyism," *American Opinion*, p. 78.
52. James J. Drummey, "McCarthy," *American Opinion*, p. 9.
53. Medford Evans, *The Assassination of Joe McCarthy*, p. 53.

CHAPTER TWENTY-EIGHT: THE KOREAN WAR

1. *American Opinion*, (December, 1980), p. 35.
2. Caroll Quigley, *Tragedy and Hope*, p. 972.
3. Frazier Hunt, *The Untold Story of Douglas MacArthur*, p. 447.
4. Douglas MacArthur, *Reminiscences*, (Greenwich, Connecticut:Fawcett Publications, 1964), pp. 373-374.
5. Reed Benson and Robert Lee, "What's Wrong With the United Nations," *The Review of the News*, (September 9, 1970), p. 9.
6. *American Opinion*, (December, 1980), p. 36.
7. G. Edward Griffin, *The Fearful Master*, (Boston, Los Angeles:Western Islands, 1964), p. 174.
8. Frazier Hunt, *The Untold Story of Douglas MacArthur*, p. 459.
9. Douglas MacArthur, *Reminiscences*, p. 408.
10. Frazier Hunt, *The Untold Story of Douglas MacArthur*, p. 459.
11. Frazier Hunt, *The Untold Story of Douglas MacArthur*, p. 459.
12. Douglas MacArthur, *Reminiscences*, p. 426.
13. G. Edward Griffin, *The Fearful Master*, p. 176.
14. G. Edward Griffin, *The Fearful Master*, p. 176.
15. G. Edward Griffin, *The Fearful Master*, p. 177.
16. G. Edward Griffin, *The Fearful Master*, p. 172.
17. Douglas MacArthur, *Reminiscences*, p. 419.
18. Douglas MacArthur, *Reminiscences*, p. 415.
19. Douglas MacArthur, *Reminiscences*, p. 426.
20. Douglas MacArthur, *Reminiscences*, p. 426.
21. Douglas MacArthur, *Reminiscences*, p. 423.
22. William P. Hoar, "The Forgotten War in Korea," *American Opinion*, (November, 1977), p. 18.
23. William P. Hoar, "The Forgotten War in Korea," p. 18.
24. Douglas MacArthur, *Reminiscences*, p. 440.
25. Eldorous L. Dayton, *Give 'em Hell, Harry*, p. 200.
26. Douglas MacArthur, *Reminiscences*, p. 447.
27. *American Opinion*, (July-August, 1980), p. 111.
28. *New York Times*, (June 10, 1953), pp. 1, 3.
29. Douglas MacArthur, *Reminiscences*, p. 464.
30. G. Edward Griffin, *The Fearful Master*, p. 178.

CHAPTER TWENTY-NINE: AID AND TRADE

1. *Report From Iron Mountain*, p. 47.
2. Antony Sutton, *National Suicide, Military Aid to the Soviet Union*, (New Rochelle, New York: Arlington House, 1973), p. 33.
3. Antony Sutton, *Wall Street and the Bolshevik Revolution*, (New Rochelle, New York: Arlington House, 1974), p. 17.
4. "Aid and Trade With the Enemy," *Congressional Record*, (August 17, 1972), p. E 7551, (Extension of Remarks.)
5. Antony Sutton, *National Suicide*, p. 16.
6. Rose B. Christensen, "Betraying Our Friends," *The Review of the News*, (June 2, 1971), p. 24.
7. *Dan Smoot Report*, (June 22, 1959).
8. *The Review of the News*, (May 11, 1977), p. 45.
9. Tom Anderson, *Utah Independent*, (June 7, 1979).
10. Antony C. Sutton, "The Sutton Testimony," *The Review of the News*, (May 15, 1974), p. 41.
11. Rose Martin, *Fabian Freeway*, p. 238.
12. *The Review of the News*, (May 20, 1970), pp. 29-30.
13. Antony C. Sutton, *National Suicide*, p. 17.
14. Hans Heymann, *We Can Do Business With the Soviet Union*, (New York, Chicago: Ziff Davis Publishing, 1945)
15. Gary Allen, "Building Communism," *American Opinion*, (December, 1975), p. 88.
16. Gary Allen, *The Rockefeller File*, (Seal Beach, California: '76 Press, 1976), p. 107.
17. Antony C. Sutton, *Western Technology and Soviet Economic Development*, 1945 to 1965, (Stanford, California: Hoover Institution Press, 1973), p. xxviii.
18. Antony C. Sutton, *Western Technology and Soviet Economic Development*, 1930 to 1945, Stanford, California: Hoover Institution Press, 1971), p. 274.
19. "Aid and Trade With The Enemy," *Congressional Record*, p. E7551.
20. Antony C. Sutton, "The Sutton Testimony," p. 33.
21. Antony C. Sutton, *Western Technology and Soviet Economic Development*, 1945 to 1965, p. 283.
22. Antony C. Sutton, *Western Technology and Soviet Economic Development*, 1945 to 1965, p. 49.
23. Antony C. Sutton, *National Suicide*, pp. 156-157.
24. George Racey Jordan, *From Major Jordan's Diaries*, (Boston, Los Angeles: Western Islands, 1965), pp. 72-106.
25. Joseph McCarthy, *America's Retreat From Victory*, pp. 33-34.
26. Antony C. Sutton, *Western Technology and Soviet Economic Development*, 1945 to 1965, p. 39.
27. Senator Joseph McCarthy, *America's Retreat From Victory*, p. 65.
28. *American Opinion*, (October, 1966), pp. 6-7.
29. George Racey Jordan, *From Major Jordan's Diaries*, p. 42.
30. George Racey Jordan, *From Major Jordan's Diaries*, p. 50.
31. James Roosevelt with Sam Toperoff, *A Family Matter*, (New York: Simon & Schuster Building, 1980).
32. *Wall Street Journal*, (April 25, 1975), p. 28.
33. Rose Martin, *Fabian Freeway*, p. 354.

CHAPTER THIRTY: TREASON

1. "Rocket pioneer von Braun dies," *Arizona Daily Star*, (June 18, 1977), pp. 1, 12, Section A.

2. Robert Goldston, *The Russian Revolution*, (Greenwich, Connecticut: Fawcett Publications, Inc., 1966), p. 206.

3. Leonid Vladimirov, *The Russian Space Bluff*, (New York: The Dial Press, 1973), p. 55.

4. Leonid Vladimirov, *The Russian Space Bluff*, p. 78.

5. Time, (April 7, 1980), pp. 76-77.

6. Leonid Vladimirov, *The Russian Space Bluff*, pp. 77-78.

7. Lloyd Mallan, *Russia and the Big Red Lie*, (Greenwich, Connecticut: Fawcett Publications, Inc., 1959), p. 14.

8. Lloyd Mallan, *Russia's Space Hoax*, (New York: Science and Mechanics Publishing Co., 1966), p. 27.

9. Lloyd Mallan, *Russia's Space Hoax*, p. 81.

10. Antony C. Sutton, *National Suicide*, p. 91.

11. *The Review of the News*, (March 26, 1975).

12. *The Review of the News*, (February 17, 1982), p. 67.

13. Antony Sutton, *National Suicide*, p. 100.

14. Antony Sutton, *National Suicide*, p. 42.

15. Antony Sutton, *National Suicide*, p. 46.

16. *Parade*, (March 18, 1973), p. 15.

17. *U.S. News & World Report*, (August 19, 1968), p. 79.

18. *U.S. News & World Report*, (November 18, 1968), p. 35.

19. *The Review of the News*, (September 3, 1969), p. 23.

20. *Export Control, 97th Quarterly Report*, (3rd Quarter, 1971), p. 11.

21. *Export Control, 97th Quarterly Report*, p. 13.

22. *American Opinion*, (July-August, 1972).

23. *Private Boycotts vs. The National Interest*, Department of State Publication 8117, pp. 18-19.

24. Quoted excerpts from the movie "No Substitute for Victory," p. 5.

25. *The Arizona Daily Star*, (May 9, 1972).

26. Quoted excerpts from the movie "No Substitute for Victory," p. 3.

27. *The Review of the News* (January 16, 1980), p. 7.

28. *The Review of the News*, (May 7, 1980), p. 76.

29. *The Review of the News*, (June 25, 1980), p. 2.

30. Gary Allen, "Federal Reserve," *American Opinion*, (April, 1980), p. 67.

31. *The Review of the News*, (March 19, 1975), p. 15.

32. Gary Allen, "Building Communism," *American Opinion*, (December, 1975), p. 95.

33. *Don Bell Reports, No. 32*, reprinted in The Utah Independent, August 24, 1978).

34. *Don Bell Reports, No. 32*.

35. Alan Stang, "Zbig Brother," *American Opinion*, (February, 1978), p. 6.

36. Zbigniew Brzezinski, *Between Two Ages*, pp. 56-57.

37. "Wells off China sought," *The Arizona Daily Star*, (July 20, 1978).

38. *The Review of the News*, (August 10, 1977), p. 57.

39. Congressman John G. Schmitz, "Peking's Narcotics Offensive," *The Review of the News*, (July 19, 1972), p. 34.

40. William E. Dunham, "Red China Pushes Drugs," *The Review of the News*, (August 11, 1971).

41. Congressman John G. Schmitz, "Peking's Narcotics Offensive," p. 34.

42. *The Oregonian*, (December 29, 1972).

43. *The Review of the News*, (January 25, 1978), p. 54.

44. *The Review of the News*, (June 13, 1979), p. 12.

45. *The Review of the News*, (November 29, 1972), p. 30.

46. *The New York Times,* (July 10, 1975), p. 27.
47. Quoted in *Imprimus,* Hillsdale College, 1975.

CHAPTER THIRTY-ONE: SCIENCE VERSUS REASON

1. *Time* magazine, (April 7, 1980), p. 65.
2. Publishers' Advertisement, *The Evolution of Man,* (Chicago: Charles H. Kerr & Company, 1905), p. 3.
3. Catalogue of Books, *The Evolution of Man,* pp. 9-10.
4. Sol Tax, Editor, *Issues In Evolution,* (University of Chicago Press, 1960), p. 45.
5. "Evolution... God's Method of Creating," *Plain Truth,* (June-July, 1974), p. 19.
6. W.L. Wilmhurst, *The Meaning of Masonry,* (New York: Bell Publishing Company, 1980), pp. 47, 94.
7. Henry M. Morris, "Evolution at the Smithsonian," *ICR Impact Series,* (December, 1979), p. i.
8. Henry N. Morris, *The Remarkable Birth of Planet Earth,* (Minneapolis, Minnesota: Dimension Books, 1972), p. 19.
9. Henry M. Morris, *The Remarkable Birth of Planet Earth,* p. 19.
10. Henry M. Morris, "Probability and Order Versus Evolution," *ICR Impact Series,* (July 1979), p. 1.
11. *The Arizona Daily Star,* (December 16, 1981), p. A-3.
12. "The Day the Dinosaurs Died," *Plain Truth,* (January, 191970), p. 70.
13. Jerry Bergman, "Does Academic Freedom Apply to Both Secular Humanists and Christians?," *ICR Impact,* (February, 1980).
14. Henry M. Morris, "Circular Reasoning in Evolutionary Geology," *ICR Impact Series,* (June, 1977), p. i.
15. John C. Whitcomb, Jr., and Henry M. Morris, *The Genesis Flood,* (Grand Rapids, Michigan: Baker Book House, 1961), p. 271.
16. Henry M. Morris, *The Remarkable Birth of Planet Earth,* p. 22.
17. Letter to the Editor From Duane T. Gish, The *News-Sentinel,* (March 4, 1975).
18. John C. Whitcomb, Jr., and Henry M. Morris, *The Genesis Flood,* p. 177.
19. Clifford Burdick, *Canyon of Canyons,* (Caldwell, Idaho: Bible-Science Association, Inc., 1974), pp. 42-43.
20. Gary E. Parker, "Creation, Selection & Variation," *ICR Impact,* (October, 1980), p. iii.
21. John C. Whitcomb, Jr. and Henry M . Morris, *The Genesis Flood,* p. 430.
22. *The Arizona Daily Star,* (April 4, 1982), p. 2-B.
23. Gary E. Parker, *Impact #101,* (November, 1981), p. ii.
24. Gary E. Parker, *Impact #101,* p. ii.
25. Henry M. Morris, *Impact #74,* (August, 1979), p. 11.
26. *Acts & Facts,* (August, 1976), (Volume 5, No. 8), p. 1.
27. T.G. Barnes, *Origin and Destiny of the Earth's Magnetic Field,* (San Diego: Institute for Creasion Research, 1973).
28. Max Blumer, "Submarine Seeps, Are They a Major Source of Open Ocean Oil Pollution," *Science,* (Volume 176), p. 1257.
29. *Impact,* (June, 1981), p. iii.
30. Henry M. Morris, "Evolution and the Population Problem," *Impact No. 21.*
31. Henry M. Morris, *The Remarkable Birth of Planet Earth,* p. 92.
32. Russell Akridge, "The Sun is Shrinking," *Impact #82,* (April, 1980).
33. Harold S. Slusher, *Age of the Cosmos,* (San Diego: Institute for Creation Research, 1980), pp. 41-42.

34. *Dake's Annotated Reference Bible*, p. 55.
35. Claire Chambers, *The Siecus Circle*, (Belmont, Massachusetts: Western Islands, 1977), p. 101.
36. *The Review of the News*, (July 16, 1975), p. 33.

CHAPTER THIRTY-TWO: ABORTION AND LAETRILE

1. G. Edward Griffin, *World Without Cancer*, Part II, p. 455.
2. G. Edward Griffin, *World Without Cancer*, Part II, p. 250.
3. G. Edward Griffin, *World Without Cancer*, Part II, pp. 250-251.
4. G. Edward Griffin, *World Without Cancer*, Part I, pp. 51-52.
5. G. Edward Griffin, *World Without Cancer*, Part I, p. 40.
6. *The Review of the News*, (February 1, 1978), p. 25.
7. "Laetrile," *American Opinion*, (February, 1974), p. 6.
8. *U.S. News & World Report*, (May 11, 1981), p. 18.
9. *The Review of the News*, (May 13, 1981), p. 21.
10. *The Review of the News*, (July 8, 1981), p. 16.
11. G. Edward Griffin, *World Without Cancer*, Part I, p. 19.

CHAPTER THIRTY-THREE: WORLD GOVERNMENT

1. *The Review of the News*, (May 2, 1973), p. 39.
2. James M. Warburg, *The West in Crisis*, p. 30.
3. *American Opinion*, (January, 1972), p. 69.
4. *The Review of the News*, (May 18, 1977), p. 60.
5. *The Utah Independent*, (September, 1977).
6. *American Opinion*, (February, 1977), p. 20.
7. *American Opinion*, (January, 1975), p. 25.
8. *The Review of the News*, (April 11, 1979), p. 15.
9. *American Opinion*, (April, 1977), p. 20.
10. *The Review of the News*, (April 7, 1976), p. 33
11. *Don Bell Reports*, (January 30, 1976), p. 2.
12. *Don Bell Reports*, (January 30, 1976), p. 1.

CHAPTER THIRTY-FOUR: PEACE

1. *The Report From Iron Mountain*, p. 47.
2. *The Report From Iron Mountain*, p. 58.
3. *The Review of the News*, (July 4, 1973), p. 28.
4. *The Oregon Journal*, (April 25, 1969), p. 5.

CHAPTER THIRTY-FIVE: HUMANISM

1. *Education USA*, (September 24, 1979), p. 29.
2. Gary Allan, "Foundations," *American Opinion*, (November, 1969), p. 11.
3. "Bulletin," Committee to Restore the Constitution, (November, 1978), p. 2.
4. Alan Stang, *The Actor*, p. 117.
5. *The Review of the News*, (October 24, 1973), p. 49.
6. Claire Chambers, *The Siecus Circle*, p. 104.
7. *The Review of the News*, (October 24, 1973), p. 49.
8. Henry M. Morris, "The Gospel of Creation and the Anti-Gospel of Evolution," *ICR Impact, No. 25*, p. iii.
9. *Humanist Manifesto I and II*, (Buffalo, New York: Prometheus Books, 1973), pp. 7-11.
10. "Education," *Saturday Review*, (August 10, 1974), p. 84.
11. G. Edward Griffin, *This is the John Birch Society*, (Thousand Oaks, California: American Media, 1972), p. 46.
12. *Two Worlds*, p. 107
13. W.L. Wilmhurst, *The Meaning of Masonry*, p. 96.
14. *The Review of the News*, (June 20, 1979), p. 29.

15. Gary Allen, "The Colleges," *American Opinion*, (May, 1973), p. 73.
16. *Boston Herald American*, (July 19, 1978).
17. "Parents Sue for 'Right,' 'Wrong,' in Sex Education," *Los Angeles Times*, (September 13, 1981), p. 3, Part I.
18. *The Review of the News*, (January 19, 1977), p. 45.
19. Claire Chambers, *The Siecus Circle*, p. 92.
20. Claire Chambers, *The Siecus Circle*, p. 93.
21. Barbara Morris, *Change Agents in the Schools*, (Upland, California: The Barbara M. Morris Report, 1979), p. 19.
22. Claire Chambers, *The Siecus Circle*, p. 77.
23. Claire Chambers, *The Siecus Circle*, p. 346.
24. *The Humanist Manifesto I and II*, p. 13-31.

CHAPTER THIRTY-SIX: EDUCATION

1. R.M. Whitney, *Reds in America*, (Boston, Los Angeles: Western Islands, 1970), p. 55.
2. William L. Shirer, *The Rise and Fall of the Third Reich*, (New York: Simon and Schuster, 1960), p. 249.
3. William L. Shirer, *The Rise and Fall of the Third Reich*, p. 249.
4. *The Review of the News*, (September 10, 1980), p. 37.
5. *New Education: Order or Chaos*, (Yorba Linda, California: Granger Graphics, Inc.).
6. John Steinbacker, *The Child Seducers*, (Educator Publications, 1970), p. 76.
7. Phyllis Schlafly Report, in the *Utah Independent*, (December 23, 1976).
8. W. Cleon Skousen in the *Utah Independent*, (June 14, 1979).
9. Samuel Blumenthal, *Is Public Education Necessary?*, (Old Greenwich, Connecticut: The Devin-Adair Company, 1981), p. 16.
10. Samuel Blumenthal, *Is Public Education Necessary?*, p. 17.
11. Samuel Blumenthal, *Is Public Education Necessary?*, p. 72.
12. Samuel Blumenthal, *Is Public Education Necessary?*, p. 79.
13. Samuel Blumenthal, *Is Public Education Necessary?*, pp. 95-96.
14. Samuel Blumenthal, *Is Public Education Necessary?*, p. 95
15. *Encyclopaedia Britannica*, 15th Edition, (Volume 11), p. 454.
16. Plyllis Schlafly Report, in the *Utah Independent*, (December 23, 1976).
17. Samuel Blumenthal, *Is Public Education Necessary?*, p. 227.
18. James C. Hefler, *Are Textbooks Harming Your Children?*, (Milford, Michigan,: Mott Media, 1979), p. 30.
19. Gary Allen, "New Education," *American Opinion*, (May, 1971), p. 4.
20. "Occasional Letter, No. 1," General Education Board, (1904).
21. Whitaker Chambers, *Witness*, (New York: Random House, 1952), p. 164.
22. Gary Allen, "New Education," *American Opinion*, p. 3.
23. Adam Ulam, *A History of Soviet Russia*, (New York: Draeger Publishers, 1976 , p. 102.
24. *The Review of the News*, (March 9, 1977), p. 45.
25. *New Program of the Communist Party, 2nd Draft*, (March, 1968), pp. 111-136.
26. *American Opinion*, (September, 1979), p. 53.
27. *American Opinion*, (November, 1981), p. 45.
28. "NEA, Education For a Global Community," *Freemen Digest*, p. 25.
29. *American Opinion*, (May 1971), p. 17.
30. *The Review of the News*, (June 15, 1979), p. 60.
31. *American Opinion*, (May, 1971), p. 17.
32. "Class Teaches Babies to Read," *The Arizona Daily Star*, (April 17, 1982),

p. 14-A.
33. *The Review of the News*, (May 24, 1972), p. 31.
34. *The Review of the News*, (May 24, 1972), p. 32.
35. *The Arizona Daily Star*, (August 19, 1981), p. A-7.
36. *The Review of the News*, (March 10, 1976), p. 47.
37. Gordon V. Drake, *Blackboard Power, NEA Threat to America*, (Tulsa, Oklahoma: Christian Crusade Publications, 1968), p. 14.
38. W. Cleon Skousen, in the *Utah Independent*, (June 14, 1979).
39. "N.E.A., Education for a Global Community," *Freemen Digest*, p. 1.
40. "N.E.A., Education for a Global Community," *Freemen Digest*, p. 29.
41. Gary Allen, "Red Teachers," *American Opinion*, (February, 1970), p. 1.
42. "Schools for the 70's and Beyond: A Call to Action," National Education Assocation (Washington, D.C., 1971), p. 76.
43. "The Schools and the People's Front," *The Communist*, (New York: The Communist Party of the U.S.A., May, 19375, pp. 439, 442, 444.
44. Quoted in inside cover, *New Education: Order or Chaos*.
45. Medford Evans, "The Schools," *American Opinion*, (May, 1973), p. 34.

CHAPTER THIRTY-SEVEN: VICTORIES
1. M. Stanton Evans, *The Politics of Surrender*, (New York: Devin-Adair, 1966), p. 26.
2. John Stormer, *None Dare Call It Treason*, (Florissane, Missouri: Liberty Bell Press, 1964), p. 9.
3. Whitaker Chambers, *Witness*, p. 25.
4. John Rousellot, "Civil Rights," *American Opinion*, (February, 1964), p. 7.
5. Julia Brown, "Please Don't Glorify Martin Luther King, (pamphlet,) (Belmont, Massachusetts: TACT Headquarters).
6. Alan Stang, "Red Indians," *American Opinion*, (September, 1975), p. 10.
7. Alan Stang, "Red Indians," *American Opinion*, p. 85.
8. *Congressional Record*, (April 2, 1973), p. 6280.
9. Susan L.M. Huck, "Renegades," *American Opinion*, (May, 1975), p. 1.
10. Rex T. Westerfield, "Sour Grapes," *American Opinion*, (December, 1968), p. 49.
11. *American Opinion*, (September, 1969), p. 3.
12. Rex T. Westerfield, "Sour Grapes," *American Opinion*, p. 56.
13. Susan L.M. Huck, "Little Cesar," (reprint), *The Review of the News*, (August 21, 1974), p. 13.
14. *American Opinion*, (September, 1969), p. 4.
15. Rex T. Westerfield, "Sour Grapes," *American Opinion*, p. 54.
16. "NRA Deputy Ousted in Dogma Coup," *Arizona Daily Star*, (May 23, 1977.)
17. R.D. Patrick Mahoney, "The NRA Backfire," *The Review of the News*, (April 13, 1977), p. 37.

CHAPTER THIRTY-EIGHT: THE GREATEST VICTORY
1. Medford Evans, "The Rules and the New York Times," *The Review of the News*, (October 21, 1970), p. 29.
2. Jerry Rubin, *"Do It!,"* (New York: Ballantine Books, 1970).
3. *The Review of the News*, (December 7, 1977).
4. Alan Stang, "The Great Con," *American Opinion*, (June, 1970), p. 57.
5. Alan Stang, "The Great Con," *American Opinion*, (June, 1970), p. 59.
6. "Students Rate Revolution As Primary Task," *The Oregonian*, (March 31, 1969), p. 12.
7. *American Opinion*, (February, 1972), p. 16.

8. *The Review of the News*, (October 8, 1980), p. 19.
9. *The Review of the News*, (August 5, 1970), p. 17.
10. "SDS Infiltrator Talks," *The Valley Times*, (February 25, 1971), p. 18.
11. G. Edward Griffin, *The Capitalist Conspiracy*, (Thousand Oaks: American Media, 1971), p. 42.
12. James Simon Kunen, *The Strawberry Statement*, (New York: Random House, 1968), p. 116.
13. Jerry Rubin, *"Do It!,"* introduction.
14. *The Review of the News*, (June 23, 1976), p. 33.
15. *The Review of the News*, (June 16, 1976), p. 33.
16. The John Birch Society *Bulletin*, (October, 1977), pp. 17-18.
17. The John Birch Society *Bulletin*, (October, 1977), pp. 17-18.
18. *American Opinion*, (March, 1977), pp. 7, 9,
19. *American Opinion*, (April, 1981), p. 31.
20. Los Angeles *Herald Examiner*, (August 15, 1971), p. A-2.
21. John Hackett et al, *The Third World War*, August, 1985, (New York: Berkeley Books, 1978).
22. John Hackett et al, *The Third World War*, August, 1985, p. 59.
23. *The Review of the News*, (November 19, 1980), p. 37.
24. "N-War possible in 10 years, poll says," *The Arizona Daily Star* p. 10-B; and "Moral Revulsion fuels disarmament drive, churches say," *The Arizona Daily Star*, (November 18, 1981) p. A-17.
25. "FEMA: Your Emergency Government in the Wings?," *Fusion* magazine, (August 1980), p. 13.
26. *The Review of the News*, (April 25, 1979), p. 57.
27. Paul Scott, "The Three Mile Island Mystery," *The Utah Independent*, (June 14, 1979), p. 4.
28. *The Review of the News*, (May 16, 1979), p. 60.
29. *The Review of the News*, (April 14, 1982), p. 19.
30. "FEMA: Your Emergency Government in the Wings?," *Fusion* magazine, p. 14.
31. "Canada, How the Communists Took Control," *American Opinion*, (April,1971), p. 61.
32. Herman Kahn and B. Bruce Briggs, *Things to Come: Thinking About the 70's and the 80's*, (New York: The MacMillan Company, 1972).
33. *The Review of the News*, (July 29, 1981).

CHAPTER THIRTY-NINE: REMOVAL

1. "History Repeats Itself," *Parade*, (January 20, 1974).
2. Michael Kramer and Sam Roberts, *"I Never Wanted to Be Vice-President of Anything!,"* (New York: Basic Books, Inc., 1976), p. 3.
3. *The Review of the News*, (March 6, 1974), p. 30.
4. Jerry Voorhis, *Dollars and Sense*, (a pamphlet,) (June 6, 1938), p. 21.
5. Frank Capell, *Henry Kissinger, Soviet Agent*, p. 110.
6. James Reston, "Cautious Nixon Strategy," *New York Times*, (May 21, 1979), p. 39.
7. Robert Welch, *A Timely Warning*, (a pamphlet,) p. 12.
8. Robert Welch, *A Timely Warning*, p. 5.
9. "Catholic Portfolio," *Parade*, (September 30, 1979) p. 15.
10. Victor Lasky, *It Didn't Start With Watergate*, (New York: Dell Publishing Co., Inc., 1977), p. 12.
11. Gary Allen, *The Rockefeller File*, (Seal Beach: '76 Press, 1976), p. 175.
12. Victor Lasky, "Was the Watergate Break-In Sabotaged?," *Human Events*, (February 2, 1980), p. 16.

13. Gary Allen, *The Rockefeller File*, p. 184.
14. Victor Lasky, *It Didn't Start with Watergate*, p. 275.
15. Gary Allen, *The Rockefeller File*, p. 177.
16. Gary Allen, *The Rockefeller File*, p. 180.
17. Gary Allen, *The Rockefeller File*, p. 179.
18. Gary Allen, *The Rockefeller File*, p. 179.
19. Frank Capell, *Henry Kissinger, Soviet Agent*, p. 10.
20. Gary Allen, *The Rockefeller File*, p. 182.
21. Gary Allen, *The Rockefeller File*, p. 168.
22. "Agnew sees himself as Nixon pawn in struggles," *Tucson Citizen*, (April 23, 1980), p. 1.
23. "Assailants stalked 8 other presidents," *The Arizona Daily Star*, (March 31, 1981), p. A-7.
24. "Playboy Interview: Sara Jane Moore," *Playboy*, (June, 1976), p. 84.
25. "Playboy Interview: Sara Jane Moore," p. 85.
26. "Playboy Interview: Sara Jane Moore," p. 69.

CHAPTER FORTY: ASSISTANCE

1. Jerry Rubin, *"Do It!,"* p. 148.
2. *American Opinion*, (February, 1974), p. 15.
3. *The Blue Book of the John Birch Society*, (Boston, Los Angeles: Western Islands, 1969), p. 114.
4. Robert Welch, "Which World Will It Be?," (Belmont, San Marino: *American Opinion*, 1970), p. 24.
5. *The Blue Book of the John Birch Society*, p. 129.
6. "The John Birch Society, A Report," a flyer inserted in the *Los Angeles Times*, 1963.
7. *The Blue Book of the John Birch Society*, p. 28.
8. *The Blue Book of the John Birch Society*, p. 115.
9. *The Blue Book of the John Birch Society*, p. 110.
10. *The Blue Book of the John Birch Society*, p. 148.
11. W. Cleon Skousen, "Target for Smear: The John Birch Society," Temple City, California: Publius & Associates).
12. "Twelth Report, Un-American Activities in California, 1963," the Senate Factfinding Sub-Committee on Un-American Activities, publisished by the Senate of the State of California, 1963), pp. 61-62.
13. Robert Welch, *More Stately Mansions*, (Belmont, Massachusetts: American Opinion, 1964), p. 28.
14. The John Birch Society *Bulletin*, (Belmont, Massachusetts: The John Birch Society, Inc.,) (January, 1982), p. 2.
15. Robert Welch, "What is the John Birch Society?," (Belmont, Massachusetts: American Opinion), p. 14.

CHAPTER FORTY-ONE: THE RESPONSIBILITY

1. Robert Welch, *The Blue Book of the John Birch Society*, p. 160.

Selected Bibliography

The following are some of the many books on this subject that can assist the student in better understanding the machinations of this Conspiracy. The author is aware that several of these books are no longer in print but urges serious readers to make every attempt to locate any book that interests them.

The author recommends the following source for books on this subject:

Any American Opinion Bookstore:

This nationwide bookstore chain is an excellent source of books of interest to the student of the Conspiracy. Should the student's hometown not have an American Opinion bookstore, or one nearby, it is recommended that the reader contact either:

American Opinion
Bookstore   For hard to locate books or
19 John Sims Parkway,
North   manuscripts, contact:
Valparaiso, Florida 32580
or:
American Opinion   Alan Davidson
Bookstore   American Opinion Bookstore
140 N.E. 28th Avenue   P.O. Box 391
Portland, Oregon 97232   Downey, California 90241

Both of these bookstores specialize in mail-order purchases and will be happy to place your name on a mailing list to keep you advised of current and past book titles.

AID AND TRADE

EAST MINUS WEST EQUALS ZERO, by Werner Keller

The Russian nation has been built by Western aid and trade since its founding in 862 A.D. Written by a German and translated into English.

NATIONAL SUICIDE, MILITARY AID TO THE SOVIET UNION, by Antony Sutton

This book documents the enormous aid that Russia has received from the Western nations. Includes the names of the companies that sell these goods to the Soviet Union.

WALL STREET AND THE BOLSHEVIK REVOLUTION, by Antony Sutton

Details how the Russian Revolutions of 1905 and 1917 were financed by European and American bankers.

FROM MAJOR JORDAN'S DIARIES, by George Racey Jordan

America supplied Russia with the strategic material it needed to wage a successful war against the Germans in World War II. This program was called Lend-Lease and it included the plans and materials to build the atomic bomb. This book is written by the American military officer who was charged with expediting the goods as they were being transshipped to Russia. The book includes copies of the bills of lading transferring uranium to the Russians.

CANCER AND LAETRILE

WORLD WITHOUT CANCER, by G. Edward Griffin

Presents the overwhelming evidence that vitamin therapy is effective in the treatment of cancer and the powerful forces at work to prevent this fact from becoming known to the public. Also introduces the reader into the chemical world of the holding company known as I.G. Farben, the oil world of Standard Oil, and the interlocking agreements between the two of them.

THE CIVIL WAR

THE LINCOLN CONSPIRACY, by David Balsiger and Charles Sellier Jr.

Presents shocking new evidence that indicts the Conspiracy behind the assassination of President Abraham Lincoln. Includes speculation that John Wilkes Booth was not killed in the barn after the assassination, but that he was in a conspiracy with Edwin Stanton, Lincoln's Secretary of War, who had the most to gain by the deaths of Lincoln and the other top officers in Lincoln's cabinet.

COMMUNISM

PHILIP DRU, ADMINISTRATOR, by Colonel Edward Mandell House

This novel, written in 1912 by President Woodrow Wilson's closest advisor, is about how it is possible to give an advanced country like the United States "Socialism as dreamt of by Karl Marx." The author wished for the Russian Revolution still 5 years away.

THE PLOT TO SEIZE THE WHITE HOUSE, by Jules Archer

A true account of the effort to bribe a well known America general named Smedley Butler into creating a dictatorship in the United States, just as outlined in Colonel House's book, *Philip Dru, Administrator*. Fortunately for the United States, General Butler was a patriot and he exposed the entire plan.

PROOFS OF A CONSPIRACY, by John Robison

This book, read by George Washington, exposes the secret group known as the Illuminati after it was revealed by the Bavarian government in 1786. It details the secret plans and goals of this organization and its founder, Adam Weishaupt.

SECRET SOCIETIES AND SUBVERSIVE MOVEMENTS by Nesta Webster

This book exposes the role of the Illuminati and the French Grand Orient Lodge of the Freemasons, among others, in the French Revolution of 1789. Written in 1920.

CONSPIRACY AGAINST GOD AND MAN, by Rev. Clarence Kelly

A study of the beginnings and early history of the Great Conspiracy (the Illuminati and the Grand Orient Lodge of Freemasonry, among others). Written by a Catholic priest.

THE NAKED CAPITALIST, by W. Cleon Skousen

A review of the book written by Dr. Carroll Quigley (*Tragedy and Hope*) that exposes the banking arm of the Conspiracy. This book covers the more important parts of Dr. Quigley's 1300 page book.

TRAGEDY AND HOPE, by Dr. Carroll Quigley

A 1300 page history of the banking arm of the Conspiracy by one who claims to have been made privy to its secret papers. Dr. Quigley states that "he has no aversion to its aims," and was attempting to force the Conspiracy out of its secret meeting rooms. A must reading for those who want proof that the Conspiracy exists, from one who is a well known supporter.

THE COUNCIL ON FOREIGN RELATIONS

THE INVISIBLE GOVERNMENT, by Dan Smoot

When this book was first published in 1962, almost no one but its members had heard of the Council on Foreign Relations, but today it is discussed by both the liberals and conservatives. The book includes recent membership lists to show the connection between the business world and the communist world.

THE CFR - PART II, by Phoebe Courtney
An excellent book that exposes the CFR. Written in 1975.

ECONOMICS
ECONOMICS IN ONE LESSON, by Henry Hazlitt
A short and sure way to understand basic economics, in simple and understandable terms, by a brilliant and lucid free-market economist.

WHAT YOU SHOULD KNOW ABOUT INFLATION, by Henry Hazlitt
This book explains the elements of inflation in simple terms: what it is, what is its cause, and what can be done about it.

UNDERSTANDING THE DOLLAR CRISIS, by Percy L.Greaves, Jr.
Exanmines the monetary problems of inflation and credit expansion, as well as the causes and cures of recessions and depressions. Written by a student of the dean of the Austrian (free market) economists, Ludwig von Mises. Includes an examination of the 1929 stock market crash.

EDUCATION
ARE TEXTBOOKS HARMING YOUR CHILDREN, by James C. Hefley
Today's textbooks have substituted opinion shaping for teaching, personality molding for basic skills, and ideological propaganda for factual content.

CHANGE AGENTS IN THE SCHOOLS, by Barbara M. Morris
Discusses humanism, sex education, drug education (to promote drug use?), the "one world" mentality, and the desire to get "back to basics."

THE FEDERAL RESERVE
THE FEDERAL RESERVE AND OUR MANIPULATED DOLLAR, by Dr. Martin Larson
Examines the nature of money, its function in an industrial society, and how it has been manipulated by powerful international forces which constitute an invisible empire. Details the early history of the Federal Reserve Law passed in 1913, the Civil War, etc.

THE FEDERAL RESERVE, THE MOST FANTASTIC AND UNBELIEV-ABLE FRAUD IN HISTORY, by H.S. Kennan
Starting in 1912 with the election of President Woodrow Wilson, this book examines the greatest money grab in the history of America. Includes a discussion of the confiscation of America's gold supply in 1933.

FREEMASONRY
REVOLUTION AND FREEMASONRY, by Bernard Fay
The early history of the Freemasons, including their roles in the French Revolution of 1789 and the American Revolution of 1776.

GOVERNMENT
THE LAW, by Frederick Bastiat
This is perhaps the most brilliant book ever written on the subject of the government. First published in 1850. It was written by Bastiat, a French economist, statesman and author.

HUMANISM
HUMANIST MANIFESTO I AND II
The complete texts of these two Manifestos, the first being printed in 1933, the second in 1973.

SECULAR HUMANISM, by Homer Duncan
A brief history of humanism, called by the author the "most dangerous religion in America."

THE JOHN BIRCH SOCIETY
THE BLUE BOOK OF THE JOHN BIRCH SOCIETY, by Robert Welch

Records the speeches that Mr. Welch made at the founding meetings of the Birch Society in 1958. Presents the vision of the conspiratorialists: "the upward reach in the hearts of man."

THIS IS THE JOHN BIRCH SOCIETY, by G. Edward Griffin

An introduction to the John Birch Society, its ideological principles, program of action, and long-range objectives. This is an invitation to membership. Written by a long-time member of the Society.

PERSONALITIES

THE POLITICIAN, by Robert Welch

Mr. Welch called President Dwight Eisenhower (the subject of this book) a "conscious, dedicated agent of the Communist Conspiracy." The American people were told by the media that Mr. Welch had called him a "Communist," but hundreds of thousands of the book were still purchased so that the readers could read the well documented facts that led Welch to that conclusion. The book became a best seller in the early beginnings of the "anti-conspiracy" movement.

THE ROCKEFELLER FILE, by Gary Allen

Starts with John D. ("Competition is a sin"); includes a discussion on David; ends with the story about Nelson (the man who desperately wanted to be president.) Includes a discussion on Cyrus Eaton, a prime promotor of US-USSR trade, and the Council on Foreign Relations and Trilateral Commission. Some believe that this book kept Nelson out of the presidency after the artificially contrived Watergate affair was created for that purpose.

KISSINGER, by Gary Allen

The connection of Kissinger to the mightiest combine of power, finance and influence: the Rockefeller family. Includes the claims of the Communist agent who charged that Kissinger was a KGB agent (he claimed that Kissinger's code name was Bor).

HENRY KISSINGER, SOVIET AGENT, by Frank Capell

Details the incredible charge that the former Secretary of State was a Soviet agent before he went to Harvard University after World War II.

WAS KARL MARX A SATANIST?, by Richard Wumbrand

The author examines the circumstantial evidence that Marx was a Satan worshiper.

RED CHINA

AMERICA'S RETREAT FROM VICTORY, by Senator Joseph McCarthy

How Secretary of State George Marshall assisted in the betrayal of Free China into the hands of the Communists. This book probably prompted the destruction of the Senator.

WHILE YOU SLEPT, OUR TRAGEDY IN ASIA AND WHO MADE IT, by John Flynn

How American was deliberately propagandized that Chaing Kai Shek was "evil," and that Mao Tse Tung was "good," (not a Communist). Implicates the Rockefeller-supported Institute of Pacific Relations.

WEDEMEYER REPORTS, by General Albert C. Wedemeyer

How Russia won World War II with American assistance; how America assisted the Communization of China; how Pearl Harbor was planned by the American government; and how this great American general, who was at many of the meetings that shaped these events, was ostracized by the media for trying to prevent them from occurring.

RUSSIA

CZARISM AND REVOLUTION, by Arsene de Goulevitch

The truth about Russia under the reign of the Czar of Russia, written by a Russian. Russia was the most rapidly industrializing nation in the world before the Revolution of 1917. Includes statements about the funding of the revolution by wealthy "capitalists."

BEFORE THE STORM, by Baron C. Wrangell-Rokassowsky

The story of Russia since about 1850 (including the sending of the Russian fleet into American waters during the Civil War). Discusses the evidence that Russia was indeed developing a middle class and an industrial base prior to the Russian Revolution of 1917.

THE RESCUE OF THE ROMONAVS, by Guy Richards

There are two versions of what happened to the Czar of Russia and his family: the official version, and the truth! The truth is that they survived (the Czar lived to 1952). Possibly their safety was guaranteed by an agreement between the Communists and the German government (the Kaiser of Germany was a relative of the Czar's).

IMPERIAL AGENT, THE GOLONIEWSKI - ROMANOV CASE, by Guy Richards

The son of the Czar (the child with the hemophilia) survived the revolution of 1917 and became a Colonel in the Polish Secret Police. He named a series of Communist spies in various western governments when he defected, each of which was found guilty in courts of law. The American government, under the direction of the CIA, kept him hidden, even though they knew his claims to be the son of the Czar were true, and then attempted to discredit him when he charged that Henry Kissinger was a KGB agent.

THE CONSPIRATOR WHO SAVED THE ROMANOVS, by Gary Null

Further evidence that the Czar and his family were not massacred.

THE HUNT FOR THE CZAR, by Guy Richards

Another version of the rescue of the Romanovs.

THE FILE ON THE TSAR, by Anthony Summers

Another explanation of how the Czar and his family survived the Bolshevik Revolution and the purported "massacre."

THE SECOND BANK OF THE UNITED STATES

THE REVOLUTIONARY AGE OF ANDREW JACKSON, by Robert V. Remini

Details the battle between President Andrew Jackson and the Second Bank of the United States. Jackson nearly paid with his life.

SOCIALISM

THE FABIAN FREEWAY, by Rose Martin

Details the history of the Fabian Society of England, whose goals have always been to capture the English speaking world (including the United States) for the forces of socialism. Details the "non-violent" forces of Marxism, and how they frequently cooperate with the "violent" arm.

KEYNES AT HARVARD, by Zygmund Dobbs

How the leftists-socialists have infiltrated Harvard University. Discusses the economically deceptive ideas of John Maynard Keynes, the Bolshevik advisor to President Franklin Roosevelt. Includes the quote from George Bernard Shaw ("You might be executed in a kindly manner").

SPACE

THE RUSSIAN SPACE BLUFF, by Leonid Vladimirov

This book, written by a Russian space writer who defected to the free world (England), exposes the Russian space effort as a giant hoax. For instance, the author reports that Russia bunches its rockets on a single column because it does not have the technology to develop a single-stage rocket; and that they learn their technological information from American trade publications. He asks the question as to why the free world doesn't know the truth: "Are they all fools in the West?"

RUSSIA'S SPACE HOAX, by Lloyd Mallan

Over 14 months of research uncovers evidence that Russia faked the "walk in space," the "moon probe," the "manned probes," etc.

THE TRILATERAL COMMISSION

TRILATERALS OVER WASHINGTON, Volumes I and II, by Antony Sutton and Patrick M. Wood

Excellent sources of information about the Trilateral Commission. Written in 1978 and 1981.

THE UNITED NATIONS

THE FEARFUL MASTER, A SECOND LOOK AT THE UNITED NATIONS, by G. Edward Griffin

This book sets forth the double standard which guides the UN along its devious and treacherous path toward world domination through a world government. Included is a discussion of the UN war against Katanga, (the UN "peace-keeping" forces murdered, pillaged, and raped many women in that country). Probably the most honest and authoritative book written about the United Nations.

WARS

THE FINAL SECRET OF PEARL HARBOR, by Admiral Robert Theobold

How President Roosevelt planned the attack on Pearl Harbor by forcing the Japanese into that position. Roosevelt's plans required that no word be sent to alert the Pacific fleet in Pearl Harbor.

THE LUSITANIA, by Colin Simpson

How the British government, with the assistance of the American government, planned the sinking of this passenger ship, carrying munitions being sent from America to England (by J.P. Morgan) in order to lure America into World War I. The book indicts Morgan, Winston Churchill, Colonel Edward Mandell House, and Franklin Roosevelt in the planning of America's entry into the War.

THE OCCULT AND THE THIRD REICH, by Jean-Michel Angebert

The story about how Hitler became involved with an occult society, the Thule Society, that believed that "good" was Aryan and "bad" was Jewish. Includes the connection of the "music with the theme of the master Aryan race" of the composer Richard Wagner, and Adolf Hitler's anti-semitism.

REPORT FROM IRON MOUNTAIN ON THE POSSIBILITY AND DESIRABILITY OF PEACE, no author indicated

The incredible document that calmly explains why wars are desirable; why drafts of young people are instituted; why governments are obligated to be wasteful; and why the government feels compelled to control the size of population.

WALL STREET AND THE RISE OF HITLER, by Antony Sutton

The book that makes every previous book on World War II obsolete. The incredible story of the American financiers who provided some of the capital and material that Hitler needed to launch and fight World War II.

THE CRIME AND PUNISHMENT OF I.G. FARBEN, by Joseph Borkin

The startling account of the unholy alliance of Adolf Hitler and Germany's huge chemical combine, the I.G. Farben Company. Details the connection between the Standard Oil Company of the Rockefellers and Farben. The author points out how certain of the board of directors of I.G. Farben, the German members, were tried as war criminals at the Nuremberg Trials after the war, and certain others, the American members, were not.

PEARL HARBOR AFTER A QUARTER OF A CENTURY, by Harry Elmer Barnes

An explanation of how America planned the attack at Pearl Harbor to start World War II.

THE SPEAR OF DESTINY, by Trevor Ravenscroft

"Since it pierced the side of Christ nearly two thousand years ago, it is said that whoever claims the Spear of Longinus (the Roman soldier who possessed the spear that was used against Christ) (currently in Vienna, Austria), and understands the Occult Powers it serves, holds the destiny of the world in his hands. This is the story of the power-crazed leaders from Herod the Great to Hitler, who sought to dominate the world with the Spear's remarkable force for Good or Evil." Includes a discussion of the Thule Society.

Glossary

The Accidental Theory of History: Historical events occur by accident, for no apparent reason. Govermental rulers are powerless to prevent the event from happening.

Capital Good: Goods utilized for producing or acquiring consumption goods.

The Conspiratorial View of History: Historical events occur by design, for reasons that are not made known to the people.

Cartel: A few sellers in a market place set the price of a good or service sold.

Conspiracy: A combination of people, working in secret, for an evil or unlawful purpose.

Consumption Good: Goods acquired for consumption purposes.

Capitalism: Any economic system that utilizes capital goods in acquiring or producing consumption goods.

Creationism: The theory that all basic animal and plant types were brought into existence by acts of God using special processes which are not operative today.

Demagogue: A speaker who seeks to make capital of social discontent and gain political influence.

Economic Systems:
Free Enterprise System: Where the capital goods are owned and controlled by the individual.

Fascism: Where the capital goods are owned by the individual and controlled by the state.

Socialism: Where the capital goods are owned and controlled by the state.

Communism: Where the capital goods are owned and controlled by coercive monopolies.

Fiat Money: Paper money of government issue which is legal tender by fiat or law, does not represent nor is it based upon gold and contains no promise of redemption.

Governmental Types:

Anarchy:	Rule by no one
Democracy:	Rule by the majority
Dictatorship:	Rule by one man
Oligarchy:	Rule by a few, or the minority
Republic:	Rule by law
Theocracy:	Rule by God

Humanism: The religious belief that man shapes his own destiny. It is a constructive philosophy, a non-theistic religion, a way of life.

Inflation: A relatively sharp and sudden increase in the quantity of money, or credit, or both, relative to the amount of exchange business. Inflation always produces a rise in the price level.

Liberty: Rights with responsibilities.

License: No rights with no responsibilities.

Money: Anything that people will accept in exchange for goods or services in a belief that they may in turn exchange it for other goods and services.

Monopoly: One seller of a particular good, or a provider of a particular service, in a given market place.

Natural Monopoly: Created freely by the personal preferences of the people in the marketplace.

Coercive Monopoly: Created by the government, where force is used to restrict the access of others to the marketplace.

Monopsony: One seller in a marketplace.

Organic Evolution: The theory that all living things have arisen by a materialistic evolutionary process from a single source which itself arose from a dead, inanimate world.

Privilege: A freedom to act morally but only after permission has been granted by some governmental entity.

Repudiation: The refusal of a national or state government to pay real or alleged pecuniary obligations.

Right: A freedom to act morally without asking permission.

Symbiosis: The intimate living together of two dissimilar organisms in a mutually beneficial relationship.

Treason: "Treason against the United States shall consist in levying war against them, or in adhering to their enemies, giving them aid and comfort." (Article 3, Section 3, U.S. Constitution).

INDEX

Rifkin, Jeremy: 404-405
Rigby, Dr.: 86-87
Right, definition: 14
Ritalin: 384
Robison, John: 83-84, 132, 197
Rockefeller, David: 196, 207-208, 210, 217, 228, 232-234, 240, 245, 386, 403
Rockefeller Family: 178, 210, 262, 327, 420
Rockefeller File, The: 420
Rockefeller Foundation: 195, 207, 209-211, 228, 365, 369, 376, 386, 406
Rockefeller, John D.: 73, 99, 386
Rockefeller, John D. Jr.: 221
Rockefeller, Laurence: 228
Rockefeller, Nelson: 198, 386, 414-415, 417-418, 422-424
Rockefeller, Rodman: 344
Rockefeller Syndrome, The: 233
Rogers, William: 312
Rolls-Royce: 332, 339
Roosevelt, Franklin D.: 7, 47, 65-66, 73, 112, 127, 168, 182, 188, 214, 250, 257, 260, 269-271, 275-282, 284-289, 291, 300, 304, 311, 317, 328, 330-331, 333, 344, 418
Roosevelt, James: 330-331
Roosevelt, Theodore: 127, 166, 171-173, 260
Root, Elihu: 260
Rosenbaum, Ron: 205-206
Rosenburg, Ethel and Julius: 330
Rostow, Walt Whitman: 193
Rothbard, Murray N.: 55
Rothschild Bank (London): 157
Rothschild Bank (Paris): 102, 419
Rothschild, Carl: 139
Rothschild, Edmond de: 207
Rothschild Family: 100, 152, 155, 160, 168, 193, 265
Rothschild-Freres: 258
Rothschild, James: 139
Rothschild, Meyer: 139-140
Rothschild, Nathan: 139-141
Rothschild, N.M. Co.: 66, 165, 344
Rothschild, Solomon: 139
Rothschilds, the Financial Rulers of Nations, The: 152
Rovere, Richard H.: 312-313
Royal Dutch Shell: 74, 327
Rubin, Jerry: 400-402, 404, 428
Rubottom, Roy: 116
Rudd, Eldon: 216
Rusk, Dean: 118, 193, 238, 253
Russell, Bertrand: 383

Russia, 1917: 101
Russian Revolution, The: 112
Russian Space Bluff, The: 335
S.
Salinger, Nicole: 22-23
Sandinistas: 245
Santa Ana Register: 336
Satanist Church: 91
Satterfield, John C.: 41
Saturday Review: 40, 378
Saturday Review of Literature: 215
Schickelgruber, Maria Anna: 265-266
Schiff, Jacob: 102, 197
Schlesinger, Arthur Jr.: 47, 118, 428
Schmidt, , Helmut: 207
Schmitz, John: 9, 346
Science of Evolution: 354
Scientific American: 338
Scopes Trial: 362
Scott, Walter: 284, 308
Seal of the United States: 127
Secretary of Defense: 198
Secretary of State: 198
Secretary of the Treasury: 198
Secular Humanism: 376
Select Committee to Investigate Foundations and Comparable Organizations: 208
Senate Internal Security Subcommittee: 403-404
Senator Joe McCarthy: 312-313
Sequence (science): 357-358
Sevareid, Eric: 196
Seward, William: 135, 156, 159, 161
Seymour, Charles: 168
Shah of Iran: 240-242
Sharp, U.S. Grant: 342
Shaw, George Bernard: 46, 194
Shearer, Lloyd: 340
Sheehy, Monsignor Maurice: 306-308
Shell, Joe: 417
Shell Oil: 210, 242, 252
Sherman, William Tecumseh: 151
Shifrin, Avraham: 222
Shiite Moslem Sect: 242
Short, Walter C.: 284
Simon & Schuster: 401
Simpson, Colin: 259
Sinclair, Harry: 263
Sinclair Oil: 263
Singer Sewing Machine: 269
Sirica, John: 421
Situation Ethics: 379, 401
Skousen, Cleon: 426, 430

White, Harry Dexter: 214, 216
Whitehall Laboratories: 364
Why Not The Best?: 235
Wickramisinghe, Chandra 352
Wieland, William: 116, 122
Wiener, Alexander: 106
Willard, Joseph: 133
William, Maurice: 212
Williamson, Hugh: 29
Wilmhurst, W.L.: 377
Wilson, Woodrow: 103, 105, 108-
    109, 158, 168-169, 171-173, 198,
    257-262, 271-272, 325, 418
Wiseman, William: 105
With No Apologies: 232, 239
Witness: 202
Wood, Leonard: 241, 260, 262
Wood, Robert C.: 388
Worker's Manifesto: 396
World Affairs Council: 370-371
World Council of Churches: 222
World Health Organization: 368
World Revolution: 37
*World Without Cancer, Parts I and
    II*: 365
Wormser, Rene: 375
Wright, Edmund 160
Wright, Loyd: 41
Wright-Patterson Air Force Base:
    333
World Population Conference: 229

Y.
Yale University: 206
Yalta Conference: 287-288, 311, 317,
    328
Yarroll, William: 204
Yerkes Regional Primate Research
    Center: 359
Young, Arthur: 213

Z.
Zappa, Frank: 203
Zinchenko, Constantine: 319
Zinjanthropus Man: 359
Zyklon B Gas: 267, 280